501 JAPANESE VERBS

FULLY DESCRIBED
IN ALL INFLECTIONS,
MOODS, ASPECTS AND
FORMALITY LEVELS

by

Roland A. Lange, Ph.D.

Formerly Associate Professor of Japanese
Language and Linguistics
Columbia University, New York

BARRON'S EDUCATIONAL SERIES, Inc.
New York ● London ● Sydney ● Toronto

All inquiries should be addressed to:

Barron's Educational Series, Inc.
250 Wireless Boulevard
Hauppauge, New York 11788

Library of Congress Catalog Card No. 87-33105

International Standard Book No. 0-8120-3991-2

Library of Congress Cataloging-in-Publication Data
Lange, Roland A.
    501 Japanese verbs : fully described in all inflection moods,
aspects, and formality levels / by Roland A. Lange.
        p.   cm.
    Previous ed. published as: 201 Japanese verbs. 1971.
    Includes indexes.
    ISBN 0-8120-3991-2
    1. Japanese language–Verb.   I. Lange, Roland A.   201 Japanese
verbs.   II. Title.   III. Title: Five hundred one Japanese verbs.
PL585.L3 1988
495.6'82421–dc19   87-33105
                                                                    CIP

PRINTED IN THE UNITED STATES OF AMERICA

0   800   987654

CONTENTS

INTRODUCTION

IN ORDER TO LEARN A FOREIGN LANGUAGE efficiently students must follow a series of organized, graded lessons which cover the essential points of grammar, pronunciation, vocabulary, and usage. They must not only *study* such material to learn new words and grammatical constructions, but also *practice* what they have already learned in drill sessions with native speakers of the language. There are a number of textbooks designed to give that sort of well-rounded introduction to Japanese. (One which explains grammar and usage particularly well is Eleanor H. Jorden's *Beginning Japanese*.)

This handbook of Japanese verbs is not designed to provide students with a complete course in Japanese. Rather, it is a reference work which gives a concise, easy-to-understand description of Japanese verbal inflection and derivation, together with tables showing all the necessary forms of 501 important and widely used Japanese verbs.

501 Japanese Verbs should be of help to both beginning and advanced students. For beginners, it constitutes a valuable aid in learning basic verbal inflection. Most textbooks only provide students with a few examples to illustrate the principles of inflection. This means that students are hampered because there is no way to check a given form of an unfamiliar verb. With *501 Japanese Verbs* students will be able to quickly verify the form in which they are interested. By presenting the full array of verbal inflection and derivation in tables, this book also enables beginning students to see the language as a system, rather than as a haphazard collection of stems and endings.

More advanced students will also profit from this systematic view of the language, because it will help them to organize the many verb forms they have learned into a systematic body of data. Such formalization is especially necessary for anyone who plans to teach the language some day.

PRONUNCIATION

A detailed treatment of the Japanese sound system is beyond the scope of this work, but it is necessary to give some explanation of the value of the letters used in our romanization (which is similar to that employed in Jorden's *Beginning Japanese*). In the following explanation, italics represent our romanization while English sounds and words used as examples are enclosed in single quotation marks. (A more extensive description of Japanese pronunciation, which includes a section on pitch accent, is available on pages xxi to xlv of part 1 of *Beginning Japanese*.)

I VOWELS

Symbol	Nearest American English Equivalent
a	'o' in 'cot'
i	'ee' in 'steep'
u	'u' in 'put'
e	'e' in 'pet'
o	'o' in 'post'

NOTE: All *Japanese vowels* are short and tense in comparison with their *English equivalents*. In Japanese the lips are not rounded and the vowels do not glide off into dipthongs. When occurring between voiceless consonants, *i* and *u* are whispered.

II CONSONANTS

Symbol		Nearest American English Equivalent			Special Remarks
k	before *k*	'ck'	in	'sick-call'	held for full beat*
	before vowels	'k'	in	'kangaroo'	
g	as word initial	'g'	in	'goat'	
	elsewhere	'g'	in	'goat' or	
		'ng'	in	'singer'	
s	before *s*	'ss'	in	'grass-skirt'	full beat*
	before *i*	'sh'	in	'sheep'	further forward in mouth than
	before *a, e, o, u*	's'	in	'sip'	English sound

*See description of the Japanese 'syllable' below

v

z	before *i*	'j'	in	'jest'	further forward
	before *a, e, o, u*	'z'	in	'zest'	further forward
t	before *t*	't-'	in	'hot-toddy'	full beat*
	before *i*	'ch'	in	'cheat'	tongue touches
	before *u*	'ts'	in	'tsetse fly'	teeth
	elsewhere	't'	in	'teen'	tongue touches
d		'd'	in	'deep'	teeth
n		'n'	in	'cone'	tongue touches teeth
n̄	before *k, g*	'n'	in	'angle'	full beat*
	before *p, b, m*	'm'	in	'mine'	full beat*
	before *z, t, d, n, r*	'n'	in	'pun'	full beat*
	elsewhere	no English equivalent			made by raising tongue toward, but not touching, roof of mouth and humming through nose. Before *o*, sounds like $\bar{n} + w + o$; before *e*, sounds like $\bar{n} + y + e$
h	before *i*	'h'	in	'heap'	with more friction
	before *u*	'wh'	in	'whom'	made by puffing air between lips
	before *a, e, o*	'h'	in	'holly'	
p	before *p*	'p-'	in	'hip-pocket'	full beat*
	elsewhere	'p'	in	'compare'	
b		'b'	in	'combine'	
m		'm'	in	'mince'	
w		'w'	in	'went'	
y		'y'	in	'yacht'	
r		no American equivalent, but similar to the 'r' of 'very' in clipped British pronunciation			made by single flip of tongue tip against ridge behind teeth

*See description of the Japanese 'syllable' below

III CONSONANT CLUSTERS

Symbol	Nearest American English Equivalent		
ky	'c'	in	'curious'
gy	'g'	in	'angular'
sy	'sh'	in	'sheep'
zy	'j'	in	'jest'
ty	'ch'	in	'cheer'
ny	'n'	in	'menu'
hy	'H'	in	'Hubert'
			(in those American dialects in which the 'H' is not silent)
py	'p'	in	'pure'
by	'b'	in	'bureau'
my	'm'	in	'amuse'
ry	flapped 'r' followed by palatalization.		

The Japanese equivalent of the English syllable is not really a syllable but a mora, a unit of relative meter like a beat in music. People may speak quickly or slowly, but within a given stream of speech each mora will occupy the same length of time. This is true regardless of the type or number of sounds which make up each mora. For instance, the five words

sa.ku.ra	'cherry'
a.o.i.	'blue'
hi.ñ.i	'quality'
ki.p.pu	'ticket'
ryo.ka.ñ	'inn'

each consist of three mora (with the division indicated by dots) and each takes the same length of time to say. These examples serve to illustrate all the possible mora types in Japanese: a single vowel, a vowel preceded by a single consonant, a vowel preceded by a cluster of consonant plus *y*, and a single consonant. Only five consonants occur as independent mora: *k* (only before *k*), *s* (only before *s*), *t* (only before *t*), *p* (only before *p*), and *ñ* (in all occurrences).

The system of syllable division in Japanese can be summed up in two simple rules:

1. *THERE IS NEVER MORE THAN ONE VOWEL IN A SYL-LABLE.* This holds true whether the vowels are of the same type or of different types. A word like *oi* 'nephew' is pronounced as *o + i*, not as the 'oy' in the English word 'boy.' A word like *yooi* 'preparation' is pronounced as *yo + o + i*. In some romanization systems two *o*, *a*, or *u* which occur in juxtaposition are treated as a single 'long vowel' and are written as *ō*, *ā*, and *ū*, respectively. In this book, however, they are written as *oo*, *aa*, and *uu*.

2. *EXCEPT FOR THOSE CONSONANTS WHICH OCCUR AS INDEPENDENT MORA* (*ñ* in all occurrences and *k*, *s*, *t*, and *p* before themselves) *CONSONANTS ARE ALWAYS PRONOUNCED WITH THE VOWELS WHICH FOLLOW THEM.* Thus the words *beñkyoo* 'study', *haññoo* 'reaction', and *hakkiri* 'clearly' are pronounced as *be.ñ.kyo.o*, *ha.ñ.no.o*, and *ha.k.ki.ri*.

Japanese does not have a stress accent like that of English in which some syllables of a word are given special prominence by being pronounced louder than others. Instead, Japanese has a pitch accent system. This means that syllables are all pronounced with about the same force (sometimes giving a rather monotonous impression to the stress-accent oriented American) but some are pronounced on a higher pitch than others.

There is considerable variation in pitch accent depending upon regional dialect, but in the Tokyo accent, which is the standard for education and public discourse throughout Japan, there are three possible patterns, each of which is illustrated in one of the following words. (The solid line above the words indicates relative pitch.)

koomori 'bat' a high-pitched syllable followed by low-pitched syllable(s)

tomodati 'friend' a low-pitched syllable followed by high-pitched syllable(s)

mizuumi 'lake' high-pitched syllable(s) preceded by a single low-pitched syllable and followed by low-pitched syllable(s)

As seen above, there is always a change in pitch between the first and second mora of a word. (This example also illustrates why the romanization used in this book uses *oo* rather than *ō*. If *ō* were used it would be impossible to show the change in pitch between the first two mora of *koomori*.)

What is most perceptible to the human ear is the contrast between a high-pitched mora and an immediately following low-pitched mora. Therefore, words such as *tomodati* which do not have this contrast sound flat, and are said to be unaccented or to have a "flat accent." There are also words such as *imooto* 'younger sister' which have what might be called a latent accent in their final syllable. When spoken by themselves they sound as flat as *tomodati*, but their accent is revealed when they become part of a longer pause group. For instance, when the particle *ga* is added to *tomodati* the resulting *tomodati ga* remains flat, but when this same particle is added to *imooto* it produces *imooto ga*, revealing the latent accent by providing a following low-pitched syllable.

When indicating pitch accent in this book we shall use the mark ' above a vowel to indicate a high-pitched syllable immediately before a low-pitched syllable. Thus the above examples would be rendered: *kóomori*, *tomodati* (unaccented, so no mark), *mizuúmi*, and *imootó*.

It should be mentioned that Japanese pitch accent patterns operate for pause groups, each of which will have one of the three patterns described above. When a word is uttered in isolation it forms a pause group of its own, so its intrinsic accent pattern will be apparent. But when it is incorporated into a larger pause group the accent may shift. For example, the copula *désu* has what might be called a recessive accent. It appears in isolation or when preceded by an inaccented word, but it is lost when following a word with its own accent. The following examples show this clearly.

	kore + désu ka gives *Kore désu ka.*	'Is it this?'
but	*dóko + désu ka* gives *Dóko desu ka.*	'Where is it?'

SPEECH LEVELS

Languages are arbitrary systems used for communication within the societies which develop them. Since societies differ in their view of the world, one can expect that languages will differ not only in vocabulary and pronunciation, but also in their fundamental grammatical categories. When native speakers of English confront the Japanese verb this expectation is fully borne out. Instead of the familiar (to them) distinctions involving number and person, they find distinctions between levels of formality and deference which serve to indicate the speaker's relationship to the person spoken to or about.

Proper use of these grammatical categories requires keen judgment as to the relative social status of speaker, listener, and referent, the complexities of overlapping in-group/out-group status, and whether an occasion or relationship is formal or informal. These judgments must be in line with *JAPANESE* social views, so students' success or failure will depend upon their knowledge of Japanese social customs and attitudes. Within the scope of this book we can only give some explanations regarding the working of these categories as a linguistic system.

FORMALITY

The two sentences *Otya o noñda.* and *Otya o nomimasita.* both mean 'I (you, he, she, it, we, or they) drank tea,' but the second is more formal (and polite) than the first. While the formal sentence with *nomimasita* could be used under any circumstances without giving offence, an adult Japanese would use the sentence with *noñda* only on informal occasions when speaking to persons of lower social status or to persons of the same status with whom he or she was on close terms, such as members of one's immediate family or close friends at school or at work. While formal and informal sentences are used by both men and women, in general, women's speech tends to be more formal and polite than that of men. (Women also tend to make greater use of the honorific and humble deference levels which are discussed below.)

The style of speech is usually kept uniform throughout a conversation, and is determined by the form of the final verb, adjective, or copula in a sentence. It is this which expresses the general tone of the occasion and of *the relationship between the speaker and the person spoken to.* Since it is the final verb (adjective or copula) which sets the style, other verbs (adjectives or copula) which may occur earlier in the sentence are usually of the shorter, informal type, even in formal speech. For example, the sentence *Kare ga otya o noñda kara, watakushi mo nomimasita.* 'He drank tea, so I drank tea too.' is in the formal style even though it contains the informal *noñda. Students must be familiar with both forms of the verb, but should use only the formal sentence style* until they have learned to whom and under what circumstances they may use the informal style without offending the person spoken to or appearing ludicrous.

DEFERENCE

While the formality style expresses the speaker's attitude toward *the person he is speaking to,* the deference level expresses the speaker's attitude toward *the person he is speaking about.* As far as verbs are concerned, the deference level shows the speaker's attitude toward the subject of the verb (even though the subject of the verb may not be mentioned explicitly in the sentence). There are three basic levels: honorific, plain or neutral, and humble when the subject is a person, and another 'neutral-polite' category wnen the subject is inanimate. The plain level is the most common, with the honorific and humble levels being used when the speaker wishes to express special deference or respect toward someone. The categories of formality and deference operate independently of each other so that each verb form can be classified according to both systems as in the following table, which shows a partial paradigm of the verb *kak.u* 'write.'

	INFORMAL	FORMAL
Honorific	okaki ni naru	okaki ni narimasu
Neutral	kaku	kakimasu
Humble	okaki suru	okaki simasu
	okaki itasu	okaki itasimasu

In addition to indicating respect, the use of the humble or honorific level serves to vaguely identify the subject because one never uses the honorific to refer to oneself, nor the humble to refer to the person one is speaking to.* So while *kakimasu* could mean 'I (you, he, she, it, we, or they) write.' *okaki ni narimasu* could not mean 'I (or we) write.' nor could *okaki simasu* mean 'You write.' In the absence of other context the honorific level will refer to an action of the listener, and the humble level will refer to an action of the speaker.

As with the category of formality, the best guide to proper use of deference levels is a thorough knowledge of Japanese social custom. Until the student gains this he can follow the general principle that honorifics are used most often in reference to actions performed by the listener or members of his family, and humble forms are used most often in referring to actions performed by the speaker.

INFLECTION AND DERIVATION OF JAPANESE VERBS

Japanese has two main classes of verbs: those with stems ending in *i* or *e* and those whose stems end in consonants. We shall call them Class I and II respectively. The following is a list of basic inflectional endings (informal) using *ake.ru* 'open' and *ka + .u* 'win' as examples. Here the dot shows the division between stem and ending, but it will also be used

---

*An exception to this is the humble presumptive in which the person spoken to is sometimes covered in an inclusive 'we.' For example, *Takusii de mairimasyoo ka* may mean 'Shall we (you and I) go by taxi?'

at times to mark the division between the infinitive of a verb and an infinitive-based ending.

	Class I	Class II
Infinitive	ake	kat.i
Indicative	ake.ru	kat.u
Imperative I*	ake.ro	kat.e
Presumptive	ake.yoo	kat.oo
Provisional	ake.reba	kat.eba
Gerund	ake.te	kat.te
Past Indicative	ake.ta	kat.ta
Past Presumptive	ake.taroo	kat.taroo
Conditional	ake.tara	kat.tara
Alternative	ake.tari	kat.tari

*This form is used only by male speakers when speaking harshly. Otherwise it is replaced by more polite informal imperative expressions. Two common ones which we will label informal imperatives II and III are infinitive + *nasai* (imperative of *nasar.u* 'to do') and gerund + kudasai (imperative of *kudasar.u* 'give to me'). Of these the second is the more polite and is the one preferred for general use in making requests.

Comparing the endings for the two verb classes we find that in the last five categories they are the same (*-te, -ta, -taroo, -tara,* and *-tari*) but in the first five categories they differ as follows:

	Class I	Class II
Infinitive	-zero	-i
Indicative	-ru	-u
Imperative	-ro	-e
Presumptive	-yoo	-oo
Provisional	-reba	-eba

Except for the discrepancy between the vowels in the two imperative endings, the differences between the endings can be accounted for by a rule to the effect that the initial vowel of a suffix is lost when the stem ends in a vowel (Class I), and the initial consonant of a suffix is lost when the stem ends in a consonant (Class II). For example, *kat- + -i = kat.i,* but *ake- + -i = ake*; while *ake- + -ru = ake.ru,* but *kat- + -ru = kat.u.*

Turning now to the verb stems we find that both Class I *ake-* and Class II *kat-* remain constant throughout the ten categories. This behaviour is typical of Class I verb stems, but not of Class II verb stems. *All Class II verb stems which do not end in -t- undergo a change when attached directly to one of the five suffixes which begin with -t- (-te, -ta, -taroo, -tara, and -tari).*

These changes differ according to the final consonant of the stem, but all Class II stems which end in the same consonant undergo the same change. All of the possible changes are illustrated in the following list of examples. (-te is used as an example, but the change would be the same before any of the other four -t- endings.)

kas- + -te	becomes kasi.te	(kas.u 'lend')
kak- + -te	becomes kai.te	(kak.u 'write')
kag- + -te	becomes kai.de	(kag.u 'sniff')
yob- + -te	becomes yoñ.de	(yob.u 'call')
yom- + -te	becomes yoñ.de	(yom.u 'read')
sin- + -te	becomes siñ.de	(sin.u 'die')
kar- + -te	becomes kat.te	(kar.u 'cut')
kaw- + -te	becomes kat.te	(ka(w).u 'buy')*

*Since in Japanese w only occurs before a, Class II verbs whose stems end in this sound do not show it in all forms of the verb, but only when the suffix begins with a.

This concludes our outline of inflection, but Japanese verbs have many more forms which are the result of derivation or the addition of various auxiliary endings. Up until now we have considered only informal affirmative forms. Our next step is to cover the formal affirmative which in both verb classes is derived by attaching the auxilary verb -mas.u to the infinitive of the original verb. -mas-u occurs only as an ending for other verbs and has no substantive meaning of its own, serving only to raise the level of formality of the verb to which it is attached.

In general -mas.u behaves like a Class II verb, but it lacks an infinitive, has dual forms in the provisional, and has a Class I-type ending -yoo in the presumptive.

Indicative	-mas.u
Imperative	-mas.e
Presumptive	-mas.yoo
Provisional	-mas.eba / -mas.ureba
Gerund	-masi.te
Past Indicative	-masi.ta
Past Presumptive	-masi.taroo
Conditional	-masi.tara
Alternative	-masi.tari

All of these forms except the presumptive and the past and non-past indicative indicate a higher than normal level of formality or politeness. As a rule the imperative -*mas.e* is only used with honorific verbs such as *nasar,u* 'to do,' and *kudasar.u* 'give to me.' In the past presumptive the infinitive + *masi.taroo* is usually replaced by a combination of the informal past indicative + *des.yoo* (the formal presumptive form of the copula). A similar construction using *des.yoo* is also used in the non-past presumptive category. This differs from the -*mas.yoo* form not in degree of formality, but in the identity of the subject and other modal content. Consequently the -*mas.yoo* form and the informal indicative + *des.yoo* form will be labeled presumptive I and II respectively. The two forms using *des.yoo* are paralleled by informal ones using *dar.oo* the informal presumptive form of the copula.

We are now ready to move to the informal negative category. Here we find that, except for the imperative and presumptive, the "verb" is really an adjective derived by adding the adjectival ending -*ana.i* 'negative' to the stem of the verb. The resulting negative adjective then inflects like any other adjective. It will be noted that our earlier juncture rule works for -*ana.i* too because the initial vowel -*a*- is lost when it is joined to a Class I stem ending in a vowel.

		Class I	Class II
Indicative		ake.nai	kat.anai
Imperative	I	ake.ru na	kat.u na
	II	ake.nasaru na	kati.nasaru na
	III	ake.nai de kudasai	kat.anai de kudasai
Presumptive	*I	ake.mai	kat.umai
	II	ake.nai daroo	kat.anai daroo
Provisional		ake.nakereba	kat.anakereba
Gerund	I	ake.nai de	kat.anai de
	**II	ake.nakute	kat.anakute

*In the Class I presumptive I there is optional variation between *ake.mai*, in which *mai* follows the stem directly, and *ake.ru.mai* in which it follows the affirmative non-past indicative as it does with Class II verbs. We shall use the shorter form in our tables.
**While gerund I has the same range of uses as the affirmative gerund, the negative gerund II is more limited. It is not used with auxiliary 'giving' verbs to form polite request or polite command constructions such as negative inperative III.

Past Indicative	ake.nakatta	kat.anakatta
Past Presumptive	ake.nakattaroo	kat.anakattaroo
	ake.nakatta daroo	kat.anakatta daroo
Conditional	ake.nakattara	kat.anakattara
Alternative	ake.nakattari	kat.anakattari

Here we find three informal imperative constructions corresponding to those mentioned in connection with the informal affirmative imperative. The '*na*' used to form the negative imperative **I** is a negative command particle.

In the formal negative category we find the -*mas.u* ending again as well as various compounds using the copula.

		Class I	Class II
Indicative		ake.maseñ	kati.maseñ
Imperative		oake nasaimasu na	okati nasaimasu na
Presumptive	I	ake.masumai	kati.masumai
	II	ake.nai desyoo	kat.anai desyoo
Provisional*		ake-maseñ nara(ba)	kati.maseñ nara(ba)
Gerund		ake.maseñ de	kati.maseñ de
Past Indicative		ake.maseñ desita	kati.maseñ desita
Past Presumptive		ake.maseñ desitaroo	kati.maseñ desitaroo
		ake.nakatta desyoo	kat.anakatta desyoo
Conditional		ake.maseñ desitara	kati.maseñ desitara
Alternative		ake.maseñ desitari	kati.maseñ desitari

The semantic difference between the presumptive I and II is the same as that between the two forms of the affirmative formal presumptive. The imperative, gerund, and alternative forms given here occur only in conjunction with honorifics or when using a very formal style.

Up till now we have dealt with derivational endings such as -*mas.u* and -*ana.i* which have a range of inflection only within a given category such as 'formal' or 'informal negative.' *The remaining derivations are different in that they result in new verbs which can themselves take the entire range of inflectional and derivational endings which we have described up to this point.* (See pages 411 and 482 for examples.)

First we will consider the derivation of the passive, potential, causative,

*Of the two possible provisional forms of the copula: *nara* and *naraba*, the shorter version is used more often in colloquial conversation and is the one we shall use hereinafter in our tables.

and causative passive forms. Since the inflectional endings for these newly derived verbs will be the same as those we have already given for Class I verbs we will show only their informal affirmative indicative (citation) form in the tables which follow.

	(Original) Class I	(Original) Class II
Passive	ake.rareru	kat.areru
Potential	ake.rareru	kat.eru
Causative	ake.saseru	kat.aseru
Causative Passive	ake.saserareru	kat.aserareru

Since the newly formed verbs belong to Class I, the division between stem and ending of the passive would be *akerare.ru, katare.ru,* and so forth. It will be noted that the chief difference between the derivation in original Class I and Class II verbs is that original Class II verbs end up with a separate form for the passive and potential while original Class I verbs use the same derived form for both of these categories. In addition to the causative passive endings shown above (*-saserareru* and *-aserareru*) there are non standard shorter endings *-sasareru* and *-asareru* which have the same meaning. We will not include these in the tables in the main body of the text, but they would be used with any verb which takes the longer forms.

The last two categories are the honorific and humble. Two forms are given for each, the second being that which shows the higher level of deference on the part of the speaker. Here, once again, we are dealing with completely new verbs so we present only their citation forms.

		Class I	Class II
Honorific	I	oake ni naru	okati ni naru
	II	oake nasaru	okati nasaru
Humble	I	oake suru	okati suru
	II	oake itasu	okati itasu

This table shows the typical derivation of honorific and humble forms wherein the infinitive of the original verb becomes a noun by the addition of the prefix *o-* and the inflectional endings are provided by the verbs *nar.u* ('to become'), *nasar.u, su.ru,* and *itas.u* (all 'to do'). Of these *nar.u* and *itas.u* are Class II verbs but *su.ru* and *nasar.u* are irregular. The student should consult the appropriate tables in the main body of the text to find out the inflectional forms of these two verbs as well as those of the seven other irregular verbs *ar.u, gozar.u, ik.u, irassyar.u, kudasar.u, ku.ru,* and *ossyar.u.*

In the honorific and humble categories a number of common verbs do not follow the typical pattern, but instead use suppletive forms which are not derived from the original verb. For instance, the verbs *nasar.u* and *itas.u* encountered above are, respectively, honorific and humble equivalents of the verb *su.ru*. Normally in such a case there will be only one form each for the honorific and humble categories.

Next we will present tables for the verbs *ake.ru* and *kat.u* showing all the inflectional and derivational categories which we have discussed. The form of these tables is the same as that which will be used throughout the main body of our text. (There is no standard arrangement or list of categories in use for teaching Japanese. The names for the ten basic inflectional categories have been taken from Bloch's study on inflection, but the content and arrangement of the tables in this book represent the author's opinion as to the most important forms of the Japanese verb and the most convenient arrangement for their presentation.) In order to assist the student in learning the distinctions between these verb forms the Japanese tables are followed by a chart containing English translations of each form of *ake.ru*. But before proceeding to these tables, three forms of the verb—the infinitive, the informal indicative, and the informal gerund—demand some additional comment.

THE INFINITIVE

The infinitive is the form of the verb which is used in making compound words. We have already seen how the additional of the prefix *o-* 'deference' changes an infinitive into a noun. There are, in addition, a number of nouns which are added to the end of infinitives to form compound nouns. For instance, *kata* 'method' and *te* 'hand, doer,' when added to the infinitive of *tuka.u* 'to use' give *tukaikata* 'way of using,' and *tukaite* 'one who uses.' Indeed, there are many infinitives which function as nouns without the addition of other elements. For example:

Infinite/Noun	Meaning	Verb	Meaning
kañgae	'idea'	kañgae.ru	'to think, consider'
warai	'laughter'	wara.u	'to laugh'
yorokobi	'joy'	yorokob.u	'to be happy'
nagusame	'consolation'	nagusame.ru	'to console, comfort'
utagai	'doubt, suspicion'	utaga.u	'to doubt, suspect'

To form an adjective from the infinitive, one simply adds one of a number of adjectival endings. We have already seen this happen when the negative ending *-anai* was added to the infinitive of verbs to form the informal nonpast negative indicative as in *ake.nai*. Other important endings of this type are *-ta.i* 'desiderative,' *-yasu.i* 'easy,' and *-nikui* 'difficult.' By attaching these endings to *kaki* one gets *kakitai*, *kakiyasui*, *and kakinikui* which mean respectively 'want to write,' 'easy to write,' and 'difficult to write.'

There are also many verbs which are attached to the infinitives of other verbs to make compound verbs. We have already encountered *-mas.u* which is by far the most common. Three other important ones are *-tagar.u* 'non-first-person desiderative' (which, like *-mas.u*, occurs only as an ending in compound verbs), *-hazimeru* 'to begin,' and *-naosu* 'to repair or fix.' If we add these to *kaki* we get three new verbs: *kakitagaru* 'to wish to write,' *kakihazimeru* 'to begin to write,' and *kakinaosu* 'to rewrite.' Verbs indicating direction are very productive in combination with verbs of motion. For example, when the infinitive of the verb *tob.u* 'to jump, fly' is attached to *agar.u* 'rise,' *ori.ru* 'to descend,' *kos.u* 'to cross over,' and *mawar.u* 'revolve,' one gets the new verbs *tobiagar.u* 'to jump up,' *tobiori.ru* 'to jump down,' *tobikos.u* 'to jump over,' and *tobimawar.u* 'to jump around.'

THE INDICATIVE

It is important to remember that all indicative verb forms can function as complete one-word sentences requiring neither subjects nor objects. Thus, regardless of whether they be formal or informal, past or non-past, affirmative or negative,

Akeru.	or Akemasu.	'(Someone) opens/will open (it).'
Aketa.	or Akemasita.	'(Someone) opened (it).'
Akenai.	or Akemaseñ.	'(Someone) does not/will not open (it).'
Akenakatta. or Akemaseñ desita.		'(Someone) did not open (it).

are all sentences.

When we add more information such as subject, object, time, and location, the indicative becomes the last word in a longer sentence as in:

Mado o akeru. or Mado o akemasu.	'(Someone) opens/will open the window.'
Ano hito ga aketa. or Ano hito ga akemasita.	'That person opened (it).'
Kyoo wa akenai. or Kyoo wa akemaseñ.	'(Someone) will not open (it) today.'

The informal indicative plays a very important role in Japanese modification because it is the form which is used to modify nouns. In Japanese the modifier, be it verb, adjective, or noun, always precedes the noun which it modifies. Since the indicative is a sentence or ends a sentence, one is, in effect, modifying nouns with sentences. For example, the sentence *Mado o aketa.* '(Someone) opened the window,' can be used as a modifier in such phrases as:

mado o aketa hito	'the person who opened the window'
mado o aketa toki	'the time when (someone) opened the window'
mado o aketa syooko	'the proof that (someone) opened the window'
mado o aketa riyuu	'the reason why (someone) opened the window'
mado o aketa kekka	'the result of (someone) having opened the window'

THE INFORMAL GERUND

When ending a sentence (with or without following particles), the informal gerund indicates an informal request as in:

	Tyotto matte (yo).	'Wait a minute.'
	Soo ossyaranai de.	'Don't say that.'
and	Hayaku kite (yo).	'Come quickly.'

Gerunds have many functions when occurring within a sentence. When a sentence simply lists a number of actions without contrasting them or citing one as the cause of the other, all but the last action are often expressed by gerunds. For example, the two sentences *A-san wa zyuusu o nomimasita.* 'Mr. A drank juice.' and *B-san wa koohii o nomimasita.* 'Mr. B drank coffee.' can be combined in one sentence as *A-san wa zyuusu o nonde, B-san was koohii o nomimasita.* 'Mr. A drank juice, and Mr. B drank coffee.' If one wished to give strong contrast to these two actions, one would abandon the gerund in favor of an independent clause ending with the indicative: *A-san wa zyuusu o nonda ga, B-san wa koohii o nomimasita.* 'Mr. A drank juice, but Mr. B drank coffee.' Similarly, one would use the indicative if a cause-and-effect relationship is to be expressed as in *A-san ga koohii o nonda kara, B-san mo koohii o nomimasita.* 'Mr. A drank coffee, so Mr. B drank coffee too.'

A sentence in which the subject of all actions is the same, and which uses a gerund for all but the last verb in the sentence, indicates that the actions were performed in chronological order. For instance: *Kao o aratte, gohan o tabete, gakkoo e ikimasita.* means 'I (you, he, they etc.)

washed my face, ate, and went to school.' But *Kao o aratte, gakkoo e itte, gohañ o tabemasita.* would mean 'I (you, he, they etc.) washed my face, went to school, and ate.'

The gerund has no tense, mode or aspect of its own, so all such information is expressed by the final verb in the sentence. Therefore, if we change the above sentence to *Kao o aratte, gohañ o tabete, gakkoo e ikimasyoo.* its meaning becomes 'Let's wash our faces, eat, and go to school.'

Gerunds within sentences are also used to express manner as in *Eki made aruite ikimasita.* 'I, (he, they etc.) went to the station on foot.' and *Nani mo iwanai de dete ikimasita.* 'I (he, she etc.) left without saying anything.'

We have already seen that in the informal imperative III the gerund combines with the imperative of *kudasar.u* to make a polite request as in *Akete kudasai.* 'Please open it.' and *Akenai de kudasai.* 'Please don't open it.' While the gerund may combine with any other verb if the combination makes sense, certain combinations which occur frequently have taken on special fixed meanings. Perhaps the most important of these is the combination of the informal affirmative gerund plus *i.ru* 'to exist.' Generally speaking, when the gerund of a transitive verb is used with *i.ru* the combination shows continuing action as in the English progressive, but when the gerund of an intransitive verb is used the combination shows the existence of a continuing state. A good example of this contrast is seen in comparing combinations using the gerunds of two verbs which mean 'to open.' *Ake.ru* is transitive and would be used to convey such information as 'I opened the door,' while *ak.u* is transitive and is used to convey such information as 'The door opened.' The transitive gerund *akete* plus *i.ru* means 'I (or someone else) am opening it.' On the other hand, *aite iru* from *ak.u* means 'It is (in the state of being) open,' *NOT* 'it is opening.'

Other productive gerund-verb combinations are those in which the gerund precedes *sima.u* 'to finish,' *oku* 'to put or place,' and the various verbs for giving and receiving. That with *sima.u* means 'to do something completely, to finish doing something,' or 'to end up by doing something.' That with *ok.u* means 'to do something in advance or with reference to the future,' while those with verbs for giving and receiving mean 'to perform an action for the benefit of another, to have another perform an action for one's own benefit,' or simply 'to benefit from the action of another.' The informal imperative III, which used the gerund plus the appropriate form of *kudasar.u* 'give to me,' falls into this last group. Verbs of giving and receiving will be discussed at greater length following the main verb tables.

We should also mention the use of the gerund in combination with the particles *mo* and *wa* to express permission and prohibition. In asking for permission one uses the gerund plus *mo* as in *Mite mo ii desu ka.* 'May I look (at it)?' To answer that question in the affirmative one might say *Hai (mite mo) ii desu.* 'Yes, you may (look at it).' To refuse permission one might use the gerund plus *wa* as in *Iie (mite wa) ikemaseñ.* 'No, you must not (look at it).'

We are now ready for our sample verb tables and tables of English equivalents.

		AFFIRMATIVE	NEGATIVE
Indicative	**INFORMAl**	akeru	akenai
	FORMAL	akemasu	akemaseñ
Imperativ	**INFORMAL I**	akero	akeru na
	II	akenasai	akenasaru na
	III	akete kudasai	akenai de kudasai
	FORMAL	oake nasaimase	oake nasaimasu na
Presumptive	**INFORMAL I**	akeyoo	akemai
	II	akeru daroo	akenai daroo
	FORMAL I	akemasyoo	akemasumai
	II	akeru desyoo	akenai desyoo
Provisional	**INFORMAL**	akereba	akenakereba
	FORMAL	akemaseba	akemaseñ narā
		akemasureba	
Gerund	**INFORMAL I**	akete	akenai de
	II		akenakute
	FORMAL	akemasite	akemaseñ de
Past Ind.	**INFORMAL**	aketa	akenakatta
	FORMAL	akemasita	akemaseñ desita
Past Presump.	**INFORMAL**	aketaroo	akenakattaroo
		aketa daroo	akenakatta daroo
	FORMAL	akemasitaroo	akemaseñ desitaroo
		aketa desyoo	akenakatta desyoo
Conditional	**INFORMAL**	aketara	akenakattara
	FORMAL	akemasitara	akemaseñ desitara
Alternative	**INFORMAL**	aketari	akenakattari
	FORMAL	akemasitari	akemaseñ desitari

		INFORMAL AFFIRMATIVE INDICATIVE
Passive		akerareru
Potential		akerareru
Causative		akesaseru
Causative Pass.		akesaserareru
Honorific	**I**	oake ni naru
	II	oake nasaru
Humble	**I**	oake suru
	II	oake itasu

		AFFIRMATIVE	NEGATIVE
Indicative	**INFORMAL**	katu	katanai
	FORMAL	katimasu	katimaseñ
Imperative	**INFORMAL I**	kate	katu na
	II	katinasai	katinasaru na
	III	katte kudasai	katanai de kudasai
	FORMAL	okati nasaimase	okati nasaimasu na
Presumptive	**INFORMAL I**	katoo	katumai
	II	katu daroo	katanai daroo
	FORMAL I	katimasyoo	katimasumai
	II	katu desyoo	katanai desyoo
Provisional	**INFORMAL**	kateba	katanakereba
	FORMAL	katimaseba	katimaseñ nara
		katimasureba	
Gerund	**INFORMAL I**	katte	katanai de
	II		katanakute
	FORMAL	katimasite	katimaseñ de
Past Ind.	**INFORMAL**	katta	katanakatta
	FORMAL	katimasita	katimaseñ desita
Past Presump.	**INFORMAL**	kattaroo	katanakattaroo
		katta daroo	katanakatta daroo
	FORMAL	katimasitaroo	katimaseñ desitaroo
		katta desyoo	katanakatta desyoo
Conditional	**INFORMAL**	kattara	katanakattara
	FORMAL	katimasitara	katimaseñ desitara
Alternative	**INFORMAL**	kattari	katanakattari
	FORMAL	katimasitari	katimaseñ desitari

INFORMAL AFFIRMATIVE INDICATIVE

Passive		katareru
Potential		kateru
Causative		kataseru
Causative Pass.		kataserareru

Honorific	**I**	okati ni naru
	II	okati nasaru
Humble	**I**	
	II	

In the following table of English equivalents two conventions have been adopted in order to avoid undue redundancy.

1.   The same English translation is used to represent both the formal and informal verb forms, with the understanding that the formal will be more polite in tone.

2.   Only affirmative translations are given because except where noted the student can easily deduce the meaning of the corresponding negative form.

Needless to say the translations offered here cannot hope to cover all possible cases because meaning is influenced by context. Nevertheless, they should serve to delineate the main semantic boundaries between the various forms.

Infinitive		opening (This form is non-commital as to level of formality, tense, aspect, affirmative or negative. It merely serves as a base for many endings, and sometimes to end a phrase.)
Indicative		I open (it), you open (it), he (she, it) opens (it), we (you, they) open (it)
	or:	I (you, he, she, it, we, you, they) will open (it)
Imperative		open (it)! (The Informal Imperative III and the Formal Imperative are closer to 'please open it.')
Presumptive	**I:**	I am going to open (it), we are going to open (it) or: Let's open (it) * (There is no negative form which corresponds to this second meaning of presumptive I.)
	II:	I (you, he, she, it, we, they) probably open (it) or: I am probably going to open (it), you are probably going to open (it), he (she, it) is probably going to open (it), we (you, they) are probably going to open (it)
Provisional		if I (you, she, he, it, we, they) open (it)
Gerund		opening (it) (Non-commital as to tense and aspect which are established by the final verb in a clause or sentence.)

*NOTE: In this book and in Japanese dictionaries the informal affirmative indicative is used as the citation form for verbs.

Past Indicative	I (you, he, she, it, we, they) opened (it)
or:	I (you, he, she, it, we, they) have opened (it)
or:	I (you, he, she, it, we, they) had opened (it) (*Indicates completed action.*)
Past Presumptive	I (you, he, she, it, we, they) probably opened (it)
or:	I (you, he, she, it, we, they) probably have opened (it)
or:	I (you, he, she, it, we, they) probably had opened (it)
Conditional	if I (you, he, she, it, we, they) should open (it)
or:	if I (you, he, she, it, we, they) were to open (it)
or:	when I (you, he, she, it, we, they) open (it)
or:	when I (you, he, she, it, we, they) opened (it)
Alternative	opening (it) and — (Non-commital as to tense and aspect. It merely indicates that two or more actions were, are, or will be performed alternately.)
Passive	is opened (by someone or something)
or·	will be opened (by someone or something)
or:	is opened (by someone) with bad result (for someone else)
or:	will be opened (by someone) with bad result (for someone else) (*This form is sometimes also used as a sort of honorific to show deference for the person who performs the action.*)
Potential	can be opened
or:	can open (it)
Causative	I make (someone) open (it), you make (someone) open (it), he (she, it) makes (someone) open (it), we (you, they) make (someone) open (it)
or:	I (you, he, she, it, we, they) will make (someone) open (it)
or:	I allow (someone) to open (it), you allow (someone) to open (it), he (she, it) allows (someone) to open (it), we (you, they) allow (someone) to open (it)
or:	I (you, he, she, it, we, they) will allow (someone) to open (it)
Causative Pass.	I am made to open (it), you are made to open (it), he (she, it) is made to open (it), we (you, they) are made to open (it)
or:	I (you, he, she, it, we, they) will be made to open (it)

Honorific		you open (it), he (she) opens (it) they open (it)
	or:	you (he, she, they) will open (it) (all showing deference to the subject of the verb.)
Humble		I (we, or a member of my 'in group') open (it)
	or:	I (we, or a member of my 'in group') will open (it) *(The speaker shows deference by lowering his own position.)*

ACCENT TABLES

We shall now present tables giving the basic accent patterns for verbs. Since the patterns for Class I and Class II verbs are different, four tables will be given, one for an accented verb and one for an unaccented verb in each class. The accent mark indicates a high-pitched mora directly preceding a low-pitched mora. Thus *akéru* indicates ‾akeru‾. The absence of an accent mark indicates a word in which all but the first mora have a high pitch as in ‾osieru‾.

Since the accent pattern is the same for all verbs of a given type in the same class, verb tables in the main part of the book will only show the accent for the citation form. Since *wakár.u* is a Class II verb and is marked as accented, it will be clear that the accent of its gerund is *wakátte*, that of its non-past negative indicative is *wakaránai*, and so on. (The accent for other Japanese verbs can be found in *Kenkyusha's Japanese-English Dictionary*.)

It should be kept in mind that the accent shown in these tables is for the verb form in isolation and may change when the verb becomes part of a larger pause group.

tábe

tabé.ru

TRANSITIVE   *to eat*

		AFFIRMATIVE	NEGATIVE
Indicative	**INFORMAL**	tabéru	tabénai
	FORMAL	tabemásu	tabemaséñ
Imperative	**INFORMAL I**	tabéro	tabéru na
	II	tabenasái	tabenasáru na
	III	tábete kudasai	tabénai de kudasai
	FORMAL	mesiagarimáse	mesiagarimásu na
Presumptive	**INFORMAL I**	tabeyóo	tabemái
	II	tabéru daroo	tabénai daroo
	FORMAL I	tabemasyóo	tabemasumái
	II	tabéru desyoo	tabénai desyoo
Provisional	**INFORMAL**	tabéreba	tabénakereba
	FORMAL	tabemáseba	tabemaséñ nara
		tabemasúreba	
Gerund	**INFORMAL I**	tábete	tabénai de
	II		tabénakute
	FORMAL	tabemásite	tabemaséñ de
Past Ind.	**INFORMAL**	tábeta	tabénakatta
	FORMAL	tabemásita	tabemaséñ desita
Past Presump.	**INFORMAL**	tábetaroo	tabénakattaroo
		tábeta daroo	tabénakatta daroo
	FORMAL	tabemásitaroo	tabemaséñ desitaroo
		tábeta desyoo	tabénakatta desyoo
Conditional	**INFORMAL**	tábetara	tabénakattara
	FORMAL	tabemásitara	tabemaséñ desitara
Alternative	**INFORMAL**	tábetari	tabénakattari
	FORMAL	tabemásitari	tabemaséñ desitari

		INFORMAL AFFIRMATIVE INDICATIVE
Passive		taberaréru
Potential		taberaréru
Causative		tabesaséru
Causative Pass.		tabesaseraréru
Honorific	**I**	mesiagaru
	II	
Humble	**I**	itadaku
	II	

hará.ʉ   **harái**
to pay   TRANSITIVE

		AFFIRMATIVE	NEGATIVE
Indicative	INFORMAL	haráu	harawánai
	FORMAL	haraimásu	haraimaséñ
Imperative	INFORMAL I	haráe	haráu na
	II	harainasái	harainasáru na
	III	harátte kudasai	harawánai de kudasai
	FORMAL	oharai nasaimáse	oharai nasaimásu na
Presumptive	INFORMAL I	haraóo	haraumái
	II	haráu daroo	harawánai daroo
	FORMAL I	haraimasyóo	haraimasumái
	II	haráu desyoo	harawánai desyoo
Provisional	INFORMAL	haráeba	harawánakereba
	FORMAL	haraimáseba	haraimaséñ nara
		haraimasúreba	
Gerund	INFORMAL I	harátte	harawánai de
	II		harawánakute
	FORMAL	haraimásite	haraimaséñ de
Past Ind.	INFORMAL	harátta	harawánakatta
	FORMAL	haraimásita	haraimaséñ desita
Past Presump.	INFORMAL	haráttaroo	harawánakattaroo
		harátta daroo	harawánakatta daroo
	FORMAL	haraimásitaroo	haraimaséñ desitaroo
		harátta desyoo	harawánakatta desyoo
Conditional	INFORMAL	haráttara	harawánakattara
	FORMAL	haraimásitara	haraimaséñ desitara
Alternative	INFORMAL	haráttari	harawánakattari
	FORMAL	haraimásitari	haraimaséñ desitari

		INFORMAL AFFIRMATIVE INDICATIVE
Passive		harawaréru
Potential		haraéru
Causative		harawaséru
Causative Pass.		harawaseraréru
Honorific	I	oharai ni náru
	II	oharai nasáru
Humble	I	oharai suru
	II	oharai itasu

osie

osie.ru

TRANSITIVE *to teach, to inform*

		AFFIRMATIVE	NEGATIVE
Indicative	**INFORMAL**	osieru	osienai
	FORMAL	osiemásu	osiemaséñ
Imperative	**INFORMAL I**	osieró	osierú na
	II	osienasái	osienasarú na
	III	osiete kudasái	osienai de kudasái
	FORMAL	oosie nasaimáse	oosie nasaimásu na
Presumptive	**INFORMAL I**	*osieyóo	osiemái
	II	osieru daróo	osienai daróo
	FORMAL I	osiemasyóo	osiemasumái
	II	osieru desyóo	osienai desyóo
Provisional	**INFORMAL**	osieréba	osienákereba
	FORMAL	osiemáseba	osiemaséñ nara
		osiemasúreba	
Gerund	**INFORMAL I**	osiete	osienai de
	II		osienákute
	FORMAL	osiemásite	osiemaséñ de
Past Ind.	**INFORMAL**	osieta	osienákatta
	FORMAL	osiemásita	osiemaséñ desita
Past Presump.	**INFORMAL**	*osietaróo	osienákattaroo
		osieta daróo	osienákatta daroo
	FORMAL	osiemásitaroo	osiemaséñ desitaroo
		osieta desyóo	osienákatta desyoo
Conditional	**INFORMAL**	osietára	osienákattara
	FORMAL	osiemásitara	osiemaséñ desitara
Alternative	**INFORMAL**	osietári	osienákattari
	FORMAL	osiemásitari	osiemaséñ desitari

		INFORMAL AFFIRMATIVE INDICATIVE
Passive		osierareru
Potential		osierareru
Causative		osiesaseru
Causative Pass.		osiesaserareru
Honorific	**I**	oosie ni náru
	II	oosie nasáru
Humble	**I**	oosie suru
	II	oosie itasu

*There are alternate unaccented forms *osieyoo* and *osietaroo*.

ara.u
to wash TRANSITIVE

		AFFIRMATIVE	NEGATIVE
Indicative	INFORMAL	arau	arawanai
	FORMAL	araimásu	araimaséñ
Imperative	INFORMAL I	araé	araú na
	II	arainasái	arainasáru na
	III	aratte kudasái	arawanai de kudasái
	FORMAL	oarai nasaimáse	oarai nasaimásu na
Presumptive	INFORMAL I*	araóo	araumái
	II	arau daróo	arawanai daróo
	FORMAL I	araimasyóo	araimasumái
	II	arau desyóo	arawanai desyóo
Provisional	INFORMAL	araéba	arawanákereba
	FORMAL	araimáseba	araimaséñ nara
		araimasúreba	
Gerund	INFORMAL I	aratte	arawanai de
	II		arawanákute
	FORMAL	araimásite	araimaséñ de
Past Ind.	INFORMAL	aratta	arawanákatta
	FORMAL	araimásita	araimaséñ desita
Past Presump.	INFORMAL*	arattaróo	arawanákattaroo
		aratta daróo	arawanákatta daroo
	FORMAL	araimásitaroo	araimaséñ desitaroo
		aratta desyóo	arawanákatta desyoo
Conditional	INFORMAL	arattára	arawanákattara
	FORMAL	araimásitara	araimaséñ desitara
Alternative	INFORMAL	arattári	arawanákattari
	FORMAL	araimásitari	araimaséñ desitari

		INFORMAL AFFIRMATIVE INDICATIVE
Passive		arawareru
Potential		araeru
Causative		arawaseru
Causative Pass.		arawaserareru
Honorific	I	oarai ni náru
	II	oarai nasáru
Humble	I	oarai suru
	II	oarai itasu

xxx

*There are alternate unaccented forms *araoo* and *arattaroo*.

VARIATION IN THE ACCENT OF 'UNACCENTED VERBS' DEPENDING ON ENVIRONMENT**

1. The informal affirmative non-past and past indicative forms of unaccented verbs acquire an accent peak on their final mora when they occur immediately before the particles *ga*, *ka*, *kara*, *keredo*, *si*, and **yori*, the sentence particles *ka*, *kai*, *sa*, and *wa*, the noun-substitute *no*, and some forms of the copula.

Examples: *agarú kara*, *akerú keredo*, *hatarakú yori*, *hazimetá desyoo* (alternates with *hazimeta desyóo*) and *kaetá no*.

2. The informal affirmative gerund of unaccented verbs acquires an accent on its final syllable when it occurs immediately before the particles *mo* and *wa* and the sentence particle *yo*.
Examples: *kiité mo*, *kesité wa*, and *kimeté yo*.

LOANWORD + *SURU* VERBS

All of the verbs with which we have dealt thus far have been composed of native Japanese elements. Japanese also contains a vast number of verbs which are derived from foreign loanwords (often nouns) by the addition of the native Japanese verb *suru* 'to do.' Thus

siñpai	'worry'	+ suru gives siñpai suru 'to worry'
kekkoñ	'marriage'	+ suru gives kekkoñ suru 'to marry'
and hakkeñ	'discovery'	+ suru gives hakkeñ suru 'to discover'

Up to the mid nineteenth century the vast majority of such verbs were derived from vocabulary borrowed from Chinese. But from the Meiji period onward an increasing amount of vocabulary has been borrowed from European languages, and from English, French, and German, in particular. These loanwords, which have now reached flood proportions, are assimilated to Japanese in the same manner as the Chinese borrowings. Therefore, one finds in common use today such 'Japanese verbs' as *kopii suru* 'to copy,' *anauñsu suru* 'to announce,' and *saiñ suru* 'to sign.'

If they wish to communicate effectively in Japanese, English-speaking students must keep three points firmly in mind when dealing with Japanese verbs based on borrowings from English.

---

*In the case of *yori*, this alternates with the pattern of unaccented verb plus accented *yóri* as in *hataraku yóri*.
**The author is indebted to Professor Eleanor H. Jorden for her excellent treatment of these variations in the appendix to *Beginning Japanese*.

1) The words must be pronounced as they are by Japanese, not as they are in the original English. Remember, they are Japanese verbs.

2) Their meanings may differ as much from the original English as does their pronunciation.

3) They cannot be coined at random by combining any English word with *suru*. Use ones which you have observed Japanese using, and consult a native speaker if in doubt as to whether a particular combination is in use.

We shall now present one table for verbs of this type derived from Chinese nouns and one for those derived from English nouns. It will be noted that these verbs lack type I honorific and humble forms, that SOME Chinese-derived verbs are prefixed by *go-* rather than *o-* in the formal imperative and honorific forms, and that English-derived verbs are usually not prefixed by either.

		AFFIRMATIVE	NEGATIVE
Indicative	**INFORMAL**	beñkyoo suru	beñkyoo sinai
	FORMAL	beñkyoo simasu	beñkyoo simaseñ
Imperative	**INFORMAL I**	beñkyoo siro	beñkyoo suru na
	II	beñkyoo sinasai	beñkyoo sinasaru na
	III	beñkyoo site kudasai	beñkyoo sinai de kudasai
	FORMAL	gobeñkyoo nasaimase	gobeñkyoo nasaimasu na
Presumptive	**INFORMAL I**	beñkyoo siyoo	beñkyoo surumai
	II	beñkyoo suru daroo	beñkyoo sinai daroo
	FORMAL I	beñkyoo simasyoo	beñkyoo simasumai
	II	beñkyoo suru desyoo	beñkyoo sinai desyoo
Provisional	**INFORMAL**	beñkyoo sureba	beñkyoo sinakereba
	FORMAL	beñkyoo simaseba	beñkyoo simaseñ nara
		beñkyoo simasureba	
Gerund	**INFORMAL I**	beñkyoo site	beñkyoo sinai de
	II		beñkyoo sinakute
	FORMAL	beñkyoo simasite	beñkyoo simaseñ de
Past Ind.	**INFORMAL**	beñkyoo sita	beñkyoo sinakatta
	FORMAL	beñkyoo simasita	beñkyoo simaseñ desita
Past Presump.	**INFORMAL**	beñkyoo sitaroo	beñkyoo sinakattaroo
		beñkyoo sita daroo	beñkyoo sinakatta daroo
	FORMAL	beñkyoo simasitaroo	beñkyoo simaseñ desitaroo
		beñkyoo sita desyoo	beñkyoo sinakatta desyoo
Conditional	**INFORMAL**	beñkyoo sitara	beñkyoo sinakattara
	FORMAL	beñkyoo simasitara	beñkyoo simaseñ desitara
Alternative	**INFORMAL**	beñkyoo sitari	beñkyoo sinakattari
	FORMAL	beñkyoo simasitari	beñkyoo simaseñ desitari

		INFORMAL AFFIRMATIVE INDICATIVE
Passive		beñkyoo sareru
Potential		beñkyoo dekiru
Causative		beñkyoo saseru
Causative Pass.		beñkyoo saserareru
Honorific	**I**	
	II	gobeñkyoo nasaru
Humble	**I**	
	II	beñkyoo itasu

		AFFIRMATIVE	NEGATIVE
Indicative	**INFORMAL**	kopii suru	kopii sinai
	FORMAL	kopii simasu	kopii simaseñ
Imperative	**INFORMAL I**	kopii siro	kopii suru na
	II	kopii sinasai	kopii sinasara na
	III	kopii site kudasai	kopii sinai de kudasai
	FORMAL	kopii nasaimase	kopii nasaimasu na
Presumptive	**INFORMAL I**	kopii siyoo	kopii surumai
	II	kopii suru daroo	kopii sinai daroo
	FORMAL I	kopii simasyoo	kopii simasumai
	II	kopii suru desyoo	kopii sinai desyoo
Provisional	**INFORMAL**	kopii sureba	kopii sinakereba
	FORMAL	kopii simaseba	kopii simaseñ nara
		kopii simasureba	
Gerund	**INFORMAL I**	kopii site	kopii sinai de
	II		kopii sinakute
	FORMAL	kopii simasite	kopii simaseñ de
Past Ind.	**INFORMAL**	kopii sita	kopii sinakatta
	FORMAL	kopii simasita	kopii simaseñ desita
Past Presump.	**INFORMAL**	kopii sitaroo	kopii sinakattaroo
		kopii sita daroo	kopii sinakatta daroo
	FORMAL	kopii simasitaroo	kopii simaseñ desitaroo
		kopii sita desyoo	kopii sinakatta desyoo
Conditional	**INFORMAL**	kopii sitara	kopii sinakattara
	FORMAL	kopii simasitara	kopii simaseñ desitara
Alternative	**INFORMAL**	kopii sitari	kopii sinakattari
	FORMAL	kopii simasitari	kopii simaseñ desitari

INFORMAL AFFIRMATIVE INDICATIVE

Passive	kopii sareru
Potential	kopii dekiru
Causative	kopii saseru
Causative Pass.	kopii saserareru

Honorific	**I**	
	II	kopii nasaru
Humble	**I**	
	II	kopii itasu

ROMANIZATION

The first system of romanization for Japanese was devised by Portuguese missionaries in the sixteenth century, at which time it was used in a number of remarkable books, including a Japanese-Portuguese dictionary which is today used by Japanese scholars as the principal source for data on Japanese pronunciation of that period.

With the reopening of Japan to contact with Europe in the mid nineteenth century romanizations were developed based on the spelling in various European languages: a French-type romanization, a German-type romanization, and so on. Among them was an English-type romanization which came to be called "Hepburn romanization" because it first appeared in a Japanese-English dictionary published by James Curtis Hepburn, an American Medical missionary. It is this system, with some variation, which is commonly used in the U.S. press today.

Within Japan the debate on which romanization system is best has been long, and at times bitter, with competing factions each publishing materials written in their own system. The Japanese government has sought to bring scholars to a consensus on the matter, but even the designation of an official system in 1954 failed to end the debate.

The two main differences between the Hepburn romanization and the one used in this book are their treatment of two identical vowels which occur in juxtaposition and their treatment of certain consonants when they occur before the vowels *i* and *u*. We have already discussed the advantages of *oo* versus *o* in the section on pitch accent, so we will confine our discussion here to the second difference.

Whereas the Hepburn system has: our system has:

sa	shi	su	se	so		sa	si	su	se	so
za	ji	zu	ze	zo		za	zi	zu	ze	zo
ta	chi	tsu	te	to		ta	ti	tu	te	to
ha	hi	fu	he	ho		ha	hi	hu	he	ho

The Hepburn system uses *shi*, *ji*, *chi*, *tsu*, and *fu* because to the ear of a native speaker of English the consonants in the syllables thus represented sound closer to ENGLISH sh, j, ch, ts, and f than they do to ENGLISH s, z, t, and h. Thus it is based upon the perception of speakers of English and on distinctions which are valid in English. Our romanization is based upon the perception of speakers of Japanese and upon distinctions which are valid in Japanese. Analysis of the sound system of Japanese shows that although the pronunciation of JAPANESE *s*, *z*, *t*, and *h* is influenced by a following *i* or *u* it is perceived by Japanese as the same sound as when it occurs before other vowels.

Any system of romanization which represents all the sounds of Japanese in a consistent manner can be used in teaching Japanese IF THE ACTUAL JAPANESE PRONUNCIATION REPRESENTED BY THE LETTERS IS CLEARLY AND FULLY EXPLAINED AND DEMONSTRATED.

But the ideal romanization for Japanese is one which is based, not upon the sound systems of French, German, or English, but upon the sound system of Japanese. It is one in which each Japanese phoneme (minimum significant unit of sound) is consistently represented by its own symbol or combination of symbols. This is particularly true in a book like this, in which we are trying to give the clearest possible picture of Japanese inflection and derivation. Our romanization happens to be similar to the official Japanese romanization, and to that used in *Beginning Japanese*, but the main reason for our choice is that this romanization represents the Japanese sound system accurately, and hence, represents Japanese inflected forms accurately.

For example, when one uses the Hepburn system the infinitive, indicative, and imperative I of the verb *kat.u* become *kach.i*, *kats.u*, and *kat.e*, giving the impression that the stem ends in three different consonants. Similarly, these same forms for the verb *kas.u* 'to lend' would be rendered as *kash.i*, *kas.u*, and *kas.e* giving the false impression that the stem ends in two different consonants. Thus, an attempt to conform to English spelling would result in a distortion of Japanese inflection.

TABLES OF 501 JAPANESE VERBS

We are now ready to enter the main body of the text, which consists of tables of 501 common Japanese verbs showing all of the forms which were presented in our sample tables. The verbs are intransitive unless designated as transitive.

It is likely that students will approach this book looking for two basic types of information. Some will be seeking the inflection and derivation of a Japanese verb whose citation form they already know, while others will be trying to find a Japanese verb which fits a particular meaning in English. To provide for the first case, our verb tables are arranged alphabetically according to the citation form of the verb. Thus students who want to find out a particular form of the verb *taberu* can find it easily on page 419 between *suwaru* and *tadoru*. For the convenience of students who are seeking a verb with a given meaning in English, an English to Japanese index of all 501 verbs is provided beginning on page 505. Here students can look up 'begin' and find listed the intransitive verb *hazimaru* and the transitive verb *hazimeru* on pages 70 and 71 respectively. Thus, within the narrow limits of 501 verbs, this text also serves as a sort of Japanese-English, English-Japanese dictionary.

		AFFIRMATIVE	NEGATIVE
Indicative	INFORMAL	agaru	agaranai
	FORMAL	agarimasu	agarimaseñ
Imperative	INFORMAL I	agare	agaru na
	II	agarinasai	agarinasaru na
	III	agatte kudasai	agaranai de kudasai
	FORMAL	oagari nasaimase	oagari nasaimasu na
Presumptive	INFORMAL I	agaroo	agarumai
	II	agaru daroo	agaranai daroo
	FORMAL I	agarimasyoo	agarimasumai
	II	agaru desyoo	agaranai desyoo
Provisional	INFORMAL	agareba	agaranakereba
	FORMAL	agarimaseba	agarimaseñ nara
		agarimasureba	
Gerund	INFORMAL I	agatte	agaranai de
	II		agaranakute
	FORMAL	agarimasite	agarimaseñ de
Past Ind.	INFORMAL	agatta	agaranakatta
	FORMAL	agarimasita	agarimaseñ desita
Past Presump.	INFORMAL	agattaroo	agaranakattaroo
		agatta daroo	agaranakatta daroo
	FORMAL	agarimasitaroo	agarimaseñ desitaroo
		agatta desyoo	agaranakatta desyoo
Conditional	INFORMAL	agattara	agaranakattara
	FORMAL	agarimasitara	agarimaseñ desitara
Alternative	INFORMAL	agattari	agaranakattari
	FORMAL	agarimasitari	agarimaseñ desitari

		INFORMAL AFFIRMATIVE INDICATIVE
Passive		agarareru
Potential		agareru
Causative		agaraseru
Causative Pass.		agaraserareru

Honorific	I	oagari ni naru
	II	oagari nasaru
Humble	I	
	II	

		AFFIRMATIVE	NEGATIVE
Indicative	INFORMAL	ageru	agenai
	FORMAL	agemasu	agemaseñ
Imperative	INFORMAL I	agero	ageru na
	II	agenasai	agenasaru na
	III	agete kudasai	agenai de kudasai
	FORMAL	oage nasaimase	oage nasaimasu na
Presumptive	INFORMAL I	ageyoo	agemai
	II	ageru daroo	agenai daroo
	FORMAL I	agemasyoo	agemasumai
	II	ageru desyoo	agenai desyoo
Provisional	INFORMAL	agereba	agenakereba
	FORMAL	agemaseba	agemaseñ nara
		agemasureba	
Gerund	INFORMAL I	agete	agenai de
	II		agenakute
	FORMAL	agemasite	agemaseñ de
Past Ind.	INFORMAL	ageta	agenakatta
	FORMAL	agemasita	agemaseñ desita
Past Presump.	INFORMAL	agetaroo	agenakattaroo
		ageta daroo	agenakatta daroo
	FORMAL	agemasitaroo	agemaseñ desitaroo
		ageta desyoo	agenakatta desyoo
Conditional	INFORMAL	agetara	agenakattara
	FORMAL	agemasitara	agemaseñ desitara
Alternative	INFORMAL	agetari	agenakattari
	FORMAL	agemasitari	agemaseñ desitari

	INFORMAL AFFIRMATIVE INDICATIVE
Passive	agerareru
Potential	agerareru
Causative	agesaseru
Causative Pass.	agesaserareru

Honorific	I	oage ni naru
	II	oage nasaru
Humble	I	sasiageru
	II	

TRANSITIVE   *to reveal, disclose*

		AFFIRMATIVE	NEGATIVE
Indicative	**INFORMAL**	akasu	akasanai
	FORMAL	akasimasu	akasimaseñ
Imperative	**INFORMAL I**	akase	akasu na
	II	akasinasai	akasinasaru na
	III	akasite kudasai	akasanai de kudasai
	FORMAL	oakasi nasaimase	oakasi nasaimasu na
Presumptive	**INFORMAL I**	akasoo	akasumai
	II	akasu daroo	akasanai daroo
	FORMAL I	akasimasyoo	akasimasumai
	II	akasu desyoo	akasanai desyoo
Provisional	**INFORMAL**	akaseba	akasanakereba
	FORMAL	akasimaseba	akasimaseñ nara
		akasimasureba	
Gerund	**INFORMAL I**	akasite	akasanaide
	II		akasanakute
	FORMAL	akasimasite	akasimaseñ de
Past Ind.	**INFORMAL**	akasita	akasanakatta
	FORMAL	akasimasita	akasimaseñ desita
Past Presump.	**INFORMAL**	akasitaroo	akasanakattaroo
		akasita daroo	akasanakatta daroo
	FORMAL	akasimasitaroo	akasimaseñ desitaroo
		akasita desyoo	akasanakatta desyoo
Conditional	**INFORMAL**	akasitara	akasanakattara
	FORMAL	akasimasitara	akasimaseñ desitara
Alternative	**INFORMAL**	akasitari	akasanakattari
	FORMAL	akasimasitari	akasimaseñ desitari

INFORMAL AFFIRMATIVE INDICATIVE

Passive		akasareru
Potential		akaseru
Causative		akasaseru
Causative Pass.		akasaserareru

Honorific	**I**	oakasi ni naru
	II	oakasi nasaru
Humble	**I**	oakasi suru
	II	oakasi itasu

		AFFIRMATIVE	NEGATIVE
Indicative	INFORMAL	akeru	akenai
	FORMAL	akemasu	akemaseñ
Imperative	INFORMAL I	akero	akeru na
	II	akenasai	akenasaru na
	III	akete kudasai	akenai de kudasai
	FORMAL	oake nasaimase	oake nasaimasu na
Presumptive	INFORMAL I	akeyoo	akemai
	II	akeru daroo	akenai daroo
	FORMAL I	akemasyoo	akemasumai
	II	akeru desyoo	akenai desyoo
Provisional	INFORMAL	akereba	akenakereba
	FORMAL	akemaseba	akemaseñ nara
		akemasureba	
Gerund	INFORMAL I	akete	akenai de
	II		akenakute
	FORMAL	akemasite	akemaseñ de
Past Ind.	INFORMAL	aketa	akenakatta
	FORMAL	akemasita	akemaseñ desita
Past Presump.	INFORMAL	aketaroo	akenakattaroo
		aketa daroo	akenakatta daroo
	FORMAL	akemasitaroo	akemaseñ desitaroo
		aketa desyoo	akenakatta desyoo
Conditional	INFORMAL	aketara	akenakattara
	FORMAL	akemasitara	akemaseñ desitara
Alternative	INFORMAL	aketari	akenakattari
	FORMAL	akemasitari	akemaseñ desitari

		INFORMAL AFFIRMATIVE INDICATIVE
Passive		akerareru
Potential		akerareru
Causative		akesaseru
Causative Pass.		akesaserareru
Honorific	I	oake ni naru
	II	oake nasaru
Humble	I	oake suru
	II	oake itasu

TRANSITIVE   *to abandon* (an idea), *to resign oneself* (to)

		AFFIRMATIVE	NEGATIVE
Indicative	**INFORMAL**	akirameru	akiramenai
	FORMAL	akiramemasu	akiramemaseñ
Imperative	**INFORMAL I**	akiramero	akirameru na
	II	akiramenasai	akiramenasaru na
	III	akiramete kudasai	akiramenai de kudasai
	FORMAL	oakirame nasaimase	oakirame nasaimasu na
Presumptive	**INFORMAL I**	akirameyoo	akiramemai
	II	akirameru daroo	akiramenai daroo
	FORMAL I	akiramemasyoo	akiramemasumai
	II	akirameru desyoo	akiramenai desyoo
Provisional	**INFORMAL**	akiramereba	akiramenakereba
	FORMAL	akiramemaseba	akiramemaseñ nara
		akiramemasureba	
Gerund	**INFORMAL I**	akiramete	akiramenai de
	II		akiramenakute
	FORMAL	akiramemasite	akiramemaseñ de
Past Ind.	**INFORMAL**	akirameta	akiramenakatta
	FORMAL	akiramemasita	akiramemaseñ desita
Past Presump.	**INFORMAL**	akirametaroo	akiramenakattaroo
		akirameta daroo	akiramenakatta daroo
	FORMAL	akiramemasitaroo	akiramemaseñ desitaroo
		akirameta desyoo	akiramenakatta desyoo
Conditional	**INFORMAL**	akirametara	akiramenakattara
	FORMAL	akiramemasitara	akiramemaseñ desitara
Alternative	**INFORMAL**	akirametari	akiramenakattari
	FORMAL	akiramemasitari	akiramemaseñ desitari

		INFORMAL AFFIRMATIVE INDICATIVE
Passive		akiramerareru
Potential		akiramerareru
Causative		akiramesaseru
Causative Pass.		akiramesaserareru
Honorific	**I**	oakirame ni naru
	II	oakirame nasaru
Humble	**I**	oakirame suru
	II	oakirame itasu

to grow tired of, lose interest in

		AFFIRMATIVE	NEGATIVE
Indicative	**INFORMAL**	akiru	akinai
	FORMAL	akımasu	akimaseñ
Imperative	**INFORMAL I**		akiru na
	II		akinasaru na
	III		akinai de kudasai
	FORMAL		oaki nasimasu na
Presumptive	**INFORMAL I**	akiyoo	akimai
	II	akiru daroo	akinai daroo
	FORMAL I	akimasyoo	akimasumai
	II	akiru desyoo	akinai desyoo
Provisional	**INFORMAL**	akireba	akinakereba
	FORMAL	akimaseba	akimaseñ nara
		akimasureba	
Gerund	**INFORMAL I**	akite	akinai de
	II		akinakute
	FORMAL	akimasite	akimaseñ de
Past Ind.	**INFORMAL**	akita	akinakatta
	FORMAL	akimasita	akimaseñ desita
Past Presump.	**INFORMAL**	akitaroo	akinakattaroo
		akita daroo	akinakatta daroo
	FORMAL	akimasitaroo	akimaseñ desitaroo
		akita desyoo	akinakatta desyoo
Conditional	**INFORMAL**	akitara	akinakattara
	FORMAL	akimasitara	akimaseñ desitara
Alternative	**INFORMAL**	akitari	akinakattari
	FORMAL	akimasitari	akimaseñ desitari

		INFORMAL AFFIRMATIVE INDICATIVE
Passive		akirareru
Potential		akirareru
Causative		akısaseru
Causative Pass.		akisaserareru
Honorific	**I**	oaki ni naru
	II	oaki nasaru
Humble	**I**	
	II	

		AFFIRMATIVE	NEGATIVE
Indicative	**INFORMAL**	aku	akanai
	FORMAL	akimasu	akimaseñ
Imperative	**INFORMAL I**		
	II		
	III		
	FORMAL		
Presumptive	**INFORMAL I**	akoo	akumai
	II	aku daroo	akanai daroo
	FORMAL I	akimasyoo	akimasumai
	II	aku desyoo	akanai desyoo
Provisional	**INFORMAL**	akeba	akanakereba
	FORMAL	akimaseba	akimaseñ nara
		akimasureba	
Gerund	**INFORMAL I**	aite	akanai de
	II		akanakute
	FORMAL	akimasite	akimaseñ de
Past Ind.	**INFORMAL**	aita	akanakatta
	FORMAL	akimasita	akimaseñ desita
Past Presump.	**INFORMAL**	aitaroo	akanakattaroo
		aita daroo	akanakatta daroo
	FORMAL	akimasitaroo	akimaseñ desitaroo
		aita desyoo	akanakatta desyoo
Conditional	**INFORMAL**	aitara	akanakattara
	FORMAL	akimasitara	akimaseñ desitara
Alternative	**INFORMAL**	aitari	akanakattari
	FORMAL	akimasitari	akimaseñ desitari

INFORMAL AFFIRMATIVE INDICATIVE

Passive		
Potential		
Causative		
Causative Pass.		

Honorific	I	
	II	
Humble	I	
	II	

7

		AFFIRMATIVE	NEGATIVE
Indicative	**INFORMAL**	anadoru	anadoranai
	FORMAL	anadorimasu	anadorimaseñ
Imperative	**INFORMAL I**	anadore	anadoru na
	II	anadorinasai	anadorinasaru na
	III	anadotte kudasai	anadoranai de kudasai
	FORMAL		oanadori nasaimasu na
Presumptive	**INFORMAL I**	anadoroo	anadorumai
	II	anadoru daroo	anadoranai daroo
	FORMAL I	anadorimasyoo	anadorimasumai
	II	anadoru desyoo	anadoranai desyoo
Provisional	**INFORMAL**	anadoreba	anadoranakereba
	FORMAL	anadorimaseba	anadorimaseñ nara
		anadorimasureba	
Gerund	**INFORMAL I**	anadotte	anadoranai de
	II		anadoranakute
	FORMAL	anadorimasite	anadorimaseñ de
Past Ind.	**INFORMAL**	anadotta	anadoranakatta
	FORMAL	anadorimasita	anadorimaseñ desita
Past Presump.	**INFORMAL**	anadottaroo	anadoranakattaroo
		anadotta daroo	anadoranakatta daroo
	FORMAL	anadorimasitaroo	anadorimaseñ desitaroo
		anadotta desyoo	anadoranakatta desyoo
Conditional	**INFORMAL**	anadottara	anadoranakattara
	FORMAL	anadorimasitara	anadorimaseñ desitara
Alternative	**INFORMAL**	anadottari	anadoranakattari
	FORMAL	anadorimasitari	anadorimaseñ desitari

		INFORMAL AFFIRMATIVE INDICATIVE
Passive		anadorareru
Potential		anadoreru
Causative		anadoraseru
Causative Pass.		anadoraserareru
Honorific	**I**	oanadori ni naru
	II	oanadori nasaru
Humble	**I**	
	II	

		AFFIRMATIVE	NEGATIVE
Indicative	**INFORMAL**	añnai suru	añnai sinai
	FORMAL	añnai simasu	añnai simaseñ
Imperative	**INFORMAL I**	añnai siro	añnai suru na
	II	añnai sinasai	añnai sinasaru na
	III	añnai site kudasai	añnai sinai de kudasai
	FORMAL	añnai nasaimase	añnai nasaimasu na
Presumptive	**INFORMAL I**	añnai siyoo	añnai surumai
	II	añnai suru daroo	añnai sinai daroo
	FORMAL I	añnai simasyoo	añnai simasumai
	II	añnai suru desyoo	añnai sinai desyoo
Provisional	**INFORMAL**	añnai sureba	añnai sinakereba
	FORMAL	añnai simaseba	añnai simaseñ nara
		añnai simasureba	
Gerund	**INFORMAL I**	añnai site	añnai sinai de
	II		añnai sinakute
	FORMAL	añnai simasite	añnai simaseñ de
Past Ind.	**INFORMAL**	añnai sita	añnai sinakatta
	FORMAL	añnai simasita	añnai simaseñ desita
Past Presump.	**INFORMAL**	añnai sitaroo	añnai sinakattaroo
		añnai sita daroo	añnai sinakatta daroo
	FORMAL	añnai simasitaroo	añnai simaseñ desitaroo
		añnai sita desyoo	añnai sinakatta desyoo
Conditional	**INFORMAL**	añnai sitara	añnai sinakattara
	FORMAL	añnai simasitara	añnai simaseñ desitara
Alternative	**INFORMAL**	añnai sitari	añnai sinakattari
	FORMAL	añnai simasitari	añnai simaseñ desitari

INFORMAL AFFIRMATIVE INDICATIVE

Passive	añnai sareru
Potential	añnai dekiru
Causative	añnai saseru
Causative Pass.	añnai saserareru

Honorific	**I**	
	II	añnai nasaru
Humble	**I**	
	II	añnai itasu

9

to put one's mind at ease, to be relieved

		AFFIRMATIVE	NEGATIVE
Indicative	**INFORMAL**	añsiñ suru	añsiñ sinai
	FORMAL	añsiñ simasu	añsiñ simaseñ
Imperative	**INFORMAL I**	añsiñ siro	añsiñ suru na
	II	añsiñ sinasai	añsiñ sinasaru na
	III	añsiñ site kudasai	añsiñ sinai de kudasai
	FORMAL	añsiñ nasaimase	añsiñ nasaimasu na
Presumptive	**INFORMAL I**	añsiñ siyoo	añsiñ surumai
	II	añsiñ suru daroo	añsiñ sinai daroo
	FORMAL I	añsiñ simasyoo	añsiñ simasumai
	II	añsiñ suru desyoo	añsiñ sinai desyoo
Provisional	**INFORMAL**	añsiñ sureba	añsiñ sinakereba
	FORMAL	añsiñ simaseba	añsiñ simaseñ nara
		añsiñ simasureba	
Gerund	**INFORMAL I**	añsiñ site	añsiñ sinai de
	II		añsiñ sinakute
	FORMAL	añsiñ simasite	añsiñ simaseñ de
Past Ina.	**INFORMAL**	añsiñ sita	añsiñ sinakatta
	FORMAL	añsiñ simasita	añsiñ simaseñ desita
Past Presump.	**INFORMAL**	añsiñ sitaroo	añsiñ sinakattaroo
		añsiñ sita daroo	añsiñ sinakatta daroo
	FORMAL	añsiñ simasitaroo	añsiñ simaseñ desitaroo
		añsiñ sita desyoo	añsiñ sinakatta desyoo
Conditional	**INFORMAL**	añsiñ sitara	añsiñ sinakattara
	FORMAL	añsiñ simasitara	añsiñ simaseñ desitara
Alternative	**INFORMAL**	añsiñ sitari	añsiñ sinakattari
	FORMAL	añsiñ simasitari	añsiñ simaseñ desitari

		INFORMAL AFFIRMATIVE INDICATIVE
Passive		añsiñ sareru
Potential		añsiñ dekiru
Causative		añsiñ saseru
Causative Pass.		añsiñ saserareru

Honorific	**I**	
	II	añsiñ nasaru
Humble	**I**	
	II	añsiñ itasu

		AFFIRMATIVE	NEGATIVE
Indicative	**INFORMAL**	arasou	arasowanai
	FORMAL	arasoimasu	arasoimaseñ
Imperative	**INFORMAL I**	arasoe	arasou na
	II	arasoinasai	arasoinasaru na
	III	arasotte kudasai	arasowanai de kudasai
	FORMAL	oarasoi nasaimase	oarasoi nasaimasu na
Presumptive	**INFORMAL I**	arasooo	arasoumai
	II	arasou daroo	arasowanai daroo
	FORMAL I	arasoimasyoo	arasoimasumai
	II	arasou desyoo	arasowanai desyoo
Provisional	**INFORMAL**	arasoeba	arasowanakereba
	FORMAL	arasoimaseba	arasoimaseñ nara
		arasoimasureba	
Gerund	**INFORMAL I**	arasotte	arasowanai de
	II		arasowanakute
	FORMAL	arasoimasite	arasoimaseñ de
Past Ind.	**INFORMAL**	arasotta	arasowanakatta
	FORMAL	arasoimasita	arasoimaseñ desita
Past Presump.	**INFORMAL**	arasottaroo	arasowanakattaroo
		arasotta daroo	arasowanakatta daroo
	FORMAL	arasoimasitaroo	arasoimaseñ desitaroo
		arasotta desyoo	arasowanakatta desyoo
Conditional	**INFORMAL**	arasottara	arasowanakattara
	FORMAL	arasoimasitara	arasoimaseñ desitara
Alternative	**INFORMAL**	arasottari	arasowanakattari
	FORMAL	arasoimasitari	arasoimaseñ desitari

		INFORMAL AFFIRMATIVE INDICATIVE
Passive		arasowareru
Potential		arasoeru
Causative		arasowaseru
Causative Pass.		arasowaserareru
Honorific	**I**	oarasoi ni naru
	II	oarasoi nasaru
Humble	**I**	oarasoi suru
	II	oarasoi itasu

to devastate, to lay waste   TRANSITIVE

		AFFIRMATIVE	NEGATIVE
Indicative	**INFORMAL**	arasu	arasanai
	FORMAL	arasimasu	arasimaseñ
Imperative	**INFORMAL I**	arase	arasu na
	II	arasinasai	arasinasaru na
	III	arasite kudasai	arasanai de kudasai
	FORMAL	oarasi nasaimase	oarasi nasaimasu na
Presumptive	**INFORMAL I**	arasoo	arasumai
	II	arasu daroo	arasanai daroo
	FORMAL I	arasimasyoo	arasimasumai
	II	arasu desyoo	arasanai desyoo
Provisional	**INFORMAL**	araseba	arasanakereba
	FORMAL	arasimaseba	arasimaseñ nara
		arasimasureba	
Gerund	**INFORMAL I**	arasite	arasanai de
	II		arasanakute
	FORMAL	arasimasite	arasimaseñ de
Past Ind.	**INFORMAL**	arasita	arasanakatta
	FORMAL	arasimasıta	arasimaseñ desita
Past Presump.	**INFORMAL**	arasitaroo	arasanakattaroo
		arasita daroo	arasanakatta daroo
	FORMAL	arasimasitaroo	arasimaseñ desitaroo
		arasita desyoo	arasanakatta desyoo
Conditional	**INFORMAL**	arasitara	arasanakattara
	FORMAL	arasimasitara	arasimaseñ desitara
Alternative	**INFORMAL**	arasıta	arasanakattari
	FORMAL	arasimasitari	arasimaseñ desitari

INFORMAL AFFIRMATIVE INDICATIVE

Passive		arasareru
Potential		araseru
Causative		arasaseru
Causative Pass.		arasaserareru
Honorific	**I**	oarasi ni naru
	II	oarasi nasaru
Humble	**I**	oarasi suru
	II	oarasi itasu

		AFFIRMATIVE	NEGATIVE
Indicative	**INFORMAL**	aratamaru	aratamaranai
	FORMAL	aratamarimasu	aratamarimaseñ
Imperative	**INFORMAL I**	aratamare	aratamaru na
	II	aratamarinasai	aratamarinasaru na
	III	aratamatte kudasai	aratamaranai de kudasai
	FORMAL	oaratamari nasaimase	oaratamari nasaimasu na
Presumptive	**INFORMAL I**	aratamaroo	aratamarumai
	II	aratamaru daroo	aratamaranai daroo
	FORMAL I	aratamarimasyoo	aratamarimasumai
	II	aratamaru desyoo	aratamaranai desyoo
Provisional	**INFORMAL**	aratamareba	aratamaranakereba
	FORMAL	aratamarimaseba	aratamarimaseñ nara
		aratamarimasureba	
Gerund	**INFORMAL I**	aratamatte	aratamaranai de
	II		aratamaranakute
	FORMAL	aratamarimasite	aratamarimaseñ de
Past Ind.	**INFORMAL**	aratamatta	aratamaranakatta
	FORMAL	aratamarimasita	aratamarimaseñ desita
Past Presump.	**INFORMAL**	aratamattaroo	aratamaranakattaroo
		aratamatta daroo	aratamaranakatta daroo
	FORMAL	aratamarimasitaroo	aratamarimaseñ desitaroo
		aratamatta desyoo	aratamaranakatta desyoo
Conditional	**INFORMAL**	aratamattara	aratamaranakattara
	FORMAL	aratamarimasitara	aratamarimaseñ desitara
Alternative	**INFORMAL**	aratamattari	aratamaranakattari
	FORMAL	aratamarimasitari	aratamarimaseñ desitari

		INFORMAL AFFIRMATIVE INDICATIVE
Passive		aratamarareru
Potential		aratamareru
Causative		aratamaraseru
Causative Pass.		aratamaraserareru

Honorific	**I**	oaratamari ni naru
	II	oaratamari nasaru
Humble	**I**	
	II	

13

			AFFIRMATIVE	NEGATIVE
Indicative	**INFORMAL**		aratameru	aratamenai
	FORMAL		aratamemasu	aratamemaseñ
Imperative	**INFORMAL**	**I**	aratamero	aratameru na
		II	aratamenasai	aratamenasaru na
		III	aratamete kudasai	aratamenai de kudasai
	FORMAL		oaratame nasaimase	oaratame nasaimasu na
Presumptive	**INFORMAL**	**I**	aratameyoo	aratamemai
		II	aratameru daroo	aratamenai daroo
	FORMAL	**I**	aratamemasyoo	aratamemasumai
		II	aratameru desyoo	aratamenai desyoo
Provisional	**INFORMAL**		aratamereba	aratamenakereba
	FORMAL		aratamemaseba	aratamemaseñ nara
			aratamemasureba	
Gerund	**INFORMAL**	**I**	aratamete	aratamenai de
		II		aratamenakute
	FORMAL		aratamemasite	aratamemaseñ de
Past Ind.	**INFORMAL**		aratameta	aratamenakatta
	FORMAL		aratamemasita	aratamemaseñ desita
Past Presump.	**INFORMAL**		aratametaroo	aratamenakattaroo
			aratameta daroo	aretamenakatta daroo
	FORMAL		aratamemasitaroo	aratamemaseñ desitaroo
			aratameta desyoo	aratamenakatta desyoo
Conditional	**INFORMAL**		aratametara	aratamenakattara
	FORMAL		aratamemasitara	aratamemeseñ desitara
Alternative	**INFORMAL**		aratametari	aratamenakattari
	FORMAL		aratamemasitari	aratamemaseñ desitari

INFORMAL AFFIRMATIVE INDICATIVE

Passive		aratamerareru
Potential		aratamerareru
Causative		aratamesaseru
Causative Pass.		aratamesaserareru

Honorific	**I**	oaratame ni naru
	II	oaratame nasaru
Humble	**I**	oaratame suru
	II	oaratame itasu

		AFFIRMATIVE	NEGATIVE
Indicative	INFORMAL	arau	arawanai
	FORMAL	araimasu	araimaseñ
Imperative	INFORMAL I	arae	arau na
	II	arainasai	arainasaru na
	III	aratte kudasai	arawanai de kudasai
	FORMAL	oarai nasaimase	oarai nasaimasu na
Presumptive	INFORMAL I	araoo	araumai
	II	arau daroo	arawanai daroo
	FORMAL I	araimasyoo	araimasumai
	II	arau desyoo	arawanai desyoo
Provisional	INFORMAL	araeba	arawanakereba
	FORMAL	araimaseba	araimaseñ nara
		araimasureba	
Gerund	INFORMAL I	aratte	arawanai de
	II		arawanakute
	FORMAL	araimasite	araimaseñ de
Past Ind.	INFORMAL	aratta	arawanakatta
	FORMAL	araimasita	araimaseñ desita
Past Presump.	INFORMAL	arattaroo	arawanakattaroo
		aratta daroo	arawanakatta daroo
	FORMAL	araimasitaroo	araimaseñ desitaroo
		aratta desyoo	arawanakatta desyoo
Conditional	INFORMAL	arattara	arawanakattara
	FORMAL	araimasitara	araimaseñ desitara
Alternative	INFORMAL	arattari	arawanakattari
	FORMAL	araimasitari	araimaseñ desitari

		INFORMAL AFFIRMATIVE INDICATIVE
Passive		arawareru
Potential		araeru
Causative		arawaseru
Causative Pass.		arawaserareru

Honorific	I	oarai ni naru
	II	oarai nasaru
Humble	I	oarai suru
	II	oarai itasu

		AFFIRMATIVE	NEGATIVE
Indicative	INFORMAL	arawareru	arawarenai
	FORMAL	arawaremasu	arawaremaseñ
Imperative	INFORMAL I	arawarero	arawareru na
	II	arawarenasai	arawarenasaru na
	III	arawarete kudasai	arawarenai de kudasai
	FORMAL		
Presumptive	INFORMAL I	arawareyoo	arawaremai
	II	arawareru daroo	arawarenai daroo
	FORMAL I	arawaremasyoo	arawaremasumai
	II	arawareru desyoo	arawarenai desyoo
Provisional	INFORMAL	arawarereba	arawarenakereba
	FORMAL	arawaremaseba	arawaremaseñ nara
		arawaremasureba	
Gerund	INFORMAL I	arawarete	arawarenai de
	II		arawarenakute
	FORMAL	arawaremasite	arawaremaseñ de
Past Ind.	INFORMAL	arawareta	arawarenakatta
	FORMAL	arawaremasita	arawaremaseñ desita
Past Presump.	INFORMAL	arawaretaroo	arawarenakattaroo
		arawareta daroo	arawarenakatta daroo
	FORMAL	arawaremasitaroo	arawaremaseñ desitaroo
		arawareta desyoo	arawarenakatta desyoo
Conditional	INFORMAL	arawaretara	arawarenakattara
	FORMAL	arawaremasitara	arawaremaseñ desitara
Alternative	INFORMAL	arawaretari	arawarenakattari
	FORMAL	arawaremasitari	arawaremaseñ desitari

INFORMAL AFFIRMATIVE INDICATIVE

Passive	
Potential	arawarerareru
Causative	arawaresaseru
Causative Pass.	arawaresaserareru

Honorific	I
	II
Humble	I
	II

		AFFIRMATIVE	NEGATIVE
Indicative	**INFORMAL**	arawasu	arawasanai
	FORMAL	arawasimasu	arawasimaseñ
Imperative	**INFORMAL I**	arawase	arawasu na
	II	arawasinasai	arawasinasaru na
	III	arawasite kudasai	arawasanai de kudasai
	FORMAL	oarawasi nasaimase	oarawasi nasaimasu na
Presumptive	**INFORMAL I**	arawasoo	arawasumai
	II	arawasu daroo	arawasanai daroo
	FORMAL I	arawasimasyoo	arawasimasumai
	II	arawasu desyoo	arawasanai desyoo
Provisional	**INFORMAL**	arawaseba	arawasanakereba
	FORMAL	arawasimaseba	arawasimaseñ nara
		arawasimasureba	
Gerund	**INFORMAL I**	arawasite	arawasanai de
	II		arawasanakute
	FORMAL	arawasimasite	arawasimaseñ de
Past Ind.	**INFORMAL**	arawasita	arawasanakatta
	FORMAL	arawasimasita	arawasimaseñ desita
Past Presump.	**INFORMAL**	arawasitaroo	arawasanakattaroo
		arawasita daroo	arawasanakatta daroo
	FORMAL	arawasimasitaroo	arawasimaseñ desitaroo
		arawasita desyoo	arawasanakatta desyoo
Conditional	**INFORMAL**	arawasitara	arawasanakattara
	FORMAL	arawasimasitara	arawasimaseñ desitara
Alternative	**INFORMAL**	arawasitari	arawasanakattari
	FORMAL	arawasimasitari	arawasimaseñ desitari

	INFORMAL AFFIRMATIVE INDICATIVE
Passive	arawasareru
Potential	arawaseru
Causative	arawasaseru
Causative Pass.	arawasaserareru

Honorific	**I**	oarawasi ni naru
	II	oarawasi nasaru
Humble	**I**	
	II	

		AFFIRMATIVE	NEGATIVE
Indicative	**INFORMAL**	aru	nai
	FORMAL	arimasu	arimaseñ
Imperative	**INFORMAL I**		
	II		
	III		
	FORMAL		
Presumptive	**INFORMAL I**	aroo	arumai
	II	aru daroo	nai daroo
	FORMAL I	arimasyoo	arimasumai
	II	aru desyoo	nai desyoo
Provisional	**INFORMAL**	areba	nakereba
	FORMAL	arimaseba	arimaseñ nara
		arimasureba	
Gerund	**INFORMAL I**	atte	
	II		nakute
	FORMAL	arimasite	arimaseñ de
Past Ind.	**INFORMAL**	atta	nakatta
	FORMAL	arimasita	arimaseñ desita
Past Presump.	**INFORMAL**	attaroo	nakattaroo
		atta daroo	nakatta daroo
	FORMAL	arimasitaroo	arimaseñ desitaroo
		atta desyoo	nakatta desyoo
Conditional	**INFORMAL**	attara	nakattara
	FORMAL	arimasitara	arimaseñ desitara
Alternative	**INFORMAL**	attari	nakattari
	FORMAL	arimasitari	arimaseñ desitari

INFORMAL AFFIRMATIVE INDICATIVE

Passive

Potential

Causative

Causative Pass.

Polite*   gozaru

*This is neither honorific nor humble (because the subject is inanimate), but rather neutral polite.

		AFFIRMATIVE	NEGATIVE
Indicative	**INFORMAL**	aruku	arukanai
	FORMAL	arukimasu	arukimaseñ
Imperative	**INFORMAL I**	aruke	aruku na
	II	arukinasai	arukinasaru na
	III	aruite kudasai	arukanai de kudasai
	FORMAL	oaruki nasaimase	oaruki nasaimasu na
Presumptive	**INFORMAL I**	arukoo	arukumai
	II	aruku daroo	arukanai daroo
	FORMAL I	arukimasyoo	arukimasumai
	II	aruku desyoo	arukanai desyoo
Provisional	**INFORMAL**	arukeba	arukanakereba
	FORMAL	arukimaseba	arukimaseñ nara
		arukimasureba	
Gerund	**INFORMAL I**	aruite	arukanai de
	II		arukanakute
	FORMAL	arukimasite	arukimaseñ de
Past Ind.	**INFORMAL**	aruita	arukanakatta
	FORMAL	arukimasita	arukimaseñ desita
Past Presump.	**INFORMAL**	aruitaroo	arukanattaroo
		aruita daroo	arukanakatta daroo
	FORMAL	arukimasitaroo	arukimaseñ desitaroo
		aruita desyoo	arukanakatta desyoo
Conditional	**INFORMAL**	aruitara	arukanakattara
	FORMAL	arukimasitara	arukimaseñ desitara
Alternative	**INFORMAL**	aruitari	arukanakattari
	FORMAL	arukimasitari	arukimaseñ desitari

	INFORMAL AFFIRMATIVE INDICATIVE	
Passive	arukareru	
Potential	arukeru	
Causative	arukaseru	
Causative Pass.	arukaserareru	

Honorific	**I**	oaruki ni naru
	II	oaruki nasaru
Humble	**I**	
	II	

			AFFIRMATIVE	NEGATIVE
Indicative	**INFORMAL**		asobu	asobanai
	FORMAL		asobimasu	asobimaseñ
Imperative	**INFORMAL**	**I**	asobe	asobu na
		II	asobinasai	asobinasaru na
		III	asoñde kudasai	asobanai de kudasai
	FORMAL		oasobi nasaimase	oasobi nasimasu na
Presumptive	**INFORMAL**	**I**	asoboo	asobumai
		II	asobu daroo	asobanai daroo
	FORMAL	**I**	asobimasyoo	asobimasumai
		II	asobu desyoo	asobanai desyoo
Provisional	**INFORMAL**		asobeba	asobanakereba
	FORMAL		asobimaseba	asobimaseñ nara
			asobimasureba	
Gerund	**INFORMAL**	**I**	asoñde	asobanai de
		II		asobanakute
	FORMAL		asobimasite	asobimaseñ de
Past Ind.	**INFORMAL**		asoñda	asobanakatta
	FORMAL		asobimasita	asobimaseñ desita
Past Presump.	**INFORMAL**		asoñdaroo	asobanakattaroo
			asoñda daroo	asobanakatta daroo
	FORMAL		asobimasitaroo	asobimaseñ desitaroo
			asoñda desyoo	asobanakatta desyoo
Conditional	**INFORMAL**		asoñdara	asobanakattara
	FORMAL		asobimasitara	asobimaseñ desitara
Alternative	**INFORMAL**		asoñdari	asobanakattari
	FORMAL		asobimasitari	asobimaseñ desitari

		INFORMAL AFFIRMATIVE INDICATIVE
Passive		asobareru
Potential		asoberu
Causative		asobaseru
Causative Pass.		asobaserareru
Honorific	**I**	oasobi ni naru
	II	oasobi nasaru
Humble	**I**	
	II	

to strike (against), *to apply to*

			AFFIRMATIVE	NEGATIVE
Indicative	**INFORMAL**		ataru	ataranai
	FORMAL		atarimasu	atarimaseñ
Imperative	**INFORMAL**	**I**	atare	ataru na
		II	atarinasai	atarinasaru na
		III	atatte kudasai	ataranai de kudasai
	FORMAL		oatari nasaimase	oatari nasaimasu na
Presumptive	**INFORMAL**	**I**	ataroo	atarumai
		II	ataru daroo	ataranai daroo
	FORMAL	**I**	atarimasyoo	atarimasumai
		II	ataru desyoo	ataranai desyoo
Provisional	**INFORMAL**		atareba	ataranakereba
	FORMAL		atarimaseba	atarimaseñ nara
			atarimasureba	
Gerund	**INFORMAL**	**I**	atatte	ataranai de
		II		ataranakute
	FORMAL		atarimasite	atarimaseñ de
Past Ind.	**INFORMAL**		atatta	ataranakatta
	FORMAL		atarimasita	atarimaseñ desita
Past Presump.	**INFORMAL**		atattaroo	ataranakattaroo
			atatta daroo	ataranakatta daroo
	FORMAL		atarimasitaroo	atarimaseñ desitaroo
			atatta desyoo	ataranakatta desyoo
Conditional	**INFORMAL**		atattara	ataranakattara
	FORMAL		atarimasitara	atarimaseñ desitara
Alternative	**INFORMAL**		atattari	ataranakattari
	FORMAL		atarimasitari	atarimaseñ desitari

		INFORMAL AFFIRMATIVE INDICATIVE
Passive		atarareru
Potential		atareru
Causative		ataraseru
Causative Pass.		ataraserareru
Honorific	**I**	oatari ni naru
	II	oatari nasaru
Humble	**I**	
	II	

		AFFIRMATIVE	NEGATIVE
Indicative	INFORMAL	atatamaru	atatamaranai
	FORMAL	atatamarimasu	atatamarimaseñ
Imperative	INFORMAL I	atatamare	atatamaru na
	II	atatamarinasai	atatamarinasaru na
	III	atatamatte kudasai	atatamaranai de kudasai
	FORMAL	oatatamari nasaimase	oatatamari nasaimasu na
Presumptive	INFORMAL I	atatamaroo	atatamarumai
	II	atatamaru daroo	atatamaranai daroo
	FORMAL I	atatamarimasyoo	atatamarimasumai
	II	atatamaru desyoo	atatamaranai desyoo
Provisional	INFORMAL	atatamareba	atatamaranakereba
	FORMAL	atatamarimaseba	atatamarimaseñ nara
		atatamarimasureba	
Gerund	INFORMAL I	atatamatte	atatamaranai de
	II		atatamaranakute
	FORMAL	atatamarimasite	atatamarimaseñ de
Past Ind.	INFORMAL	atatamatta	atatamaranakatta
	FORMAL	atatamarimasita	atatamarimaseñ desita
Past Presump.	INFORMAL	atatamattaroo	atatamaranakattaroo
		atatamatta daroo	atatamaranakatta daroo
	FORMAL	atatamarimasitaroo	atatamarimaseñ desitaroo
		atatamatta desyoo	atatamaranakatta desyoo
Conditional	INFORMAL	atatamattara	atatamaranakattara
	FORMAL	atatamarimasitara	atatamarimaseñ desitara
Alternative	INFORMAL	atatamattari	atatamaranakattari
	FORMAL	atatamarimasitari	atatamarimaseñ desitari

		INFORMAL AFFIRMATIVE INDICATIVE
Passive		atatamarareru
Potential		atatamareru
Causative		atatamaraseru
Causative Pass.		atatamaraserareru

Honorific	I	oatatamari ni naru
	II	oatatamari nasaru
Humble	I	
	II	

		AFFIRMATIVE	NEGATIVE
Indicative	**INFORMAL**	atatameru	atatamenai
	FORMAL	atatamemasu	atatamemaseñ
Imperative	**INFORMAL I**	atatamero	atatameru na
	II	atatamenasai	atatamenasaru na
	III	atatamete kudasai	atatamenai de kudasai
	FORMAL	oatatame nasaimase	oatatame nasaimasu na
Presumptive	**INFORMAL I**	atatameyoo	atatamemai
	II	atatameru daroo	atatamenai daroo
	FORMAL I	atatamemasyoo	atatamemasumai
	II	atatameru desyoo	atatamenai desyoo
Provisional	**INFORMAL**	atatamereba	atatamenakereba
	FORMAL	atatamemaseba	atatamemaseñ nara
		atatamemasureba	
Gerund	**INFORMAL I**	atatamete	atatamenai de
	II		atatamenakute
	FORMAL	atatamemasite	atatamemaseñ de
Past Ind.	**INFORMAL**	atatameta	atatamenakatta
	FORMAL	atatamemasita	atatamemaseñ desita
Past Presump.	**INFORMAL**	atatametaroo	atatamenakattaroo
		atatameta daroo	atatamenakatta daroo
	FORMAL	atatamemasitaroo	atatamemaseñ desitaroo
		atatameta desyoo	atatamenakatta desyoo
Conditional	**INFORMAL**	atatametara	atatamenakattara
	FORMAL	atatamemasitara	atatamemaseñ desitara
Alternative	**INFORMAL**	atatametari	atatamenakattari
	FORMAL	atatamemasitari	atatamemaseñ desitari

INFORMAL AFFIRMATIVE INDICATIVE

Passive		atatamerareru
Potential		atatamerareru
Causative		atatamesaseru
Causative Pass.		atatamesaserareru

Honorific	**I**	oatatame ni naru
	II	oatatame nasaru
Humble	**I**	oatatame suru
	II	oatatame itasu

		AFFIRMATIVE	NEGATIVE
Indicative	INFORMAL	atumaru	atumaranai
	FORMAL	atumarimasu	atumarimaseñ
Imperative	INFORMAL I	atumare	atumaru na
	II	atumarinasai	atumarinasaru na
	III	atumatte kudasai	atumaranai de kudasai
	FORMAL	oatumari nasaimase	oatumari nasaimasu na
Presumptive	INFORMAL I	atumaroo	atumarumai
	II	atumaru daroo	atumaranai daroo
	FORMAL I	atumarimasyoo	atumarimasumai
	II	atumaru desyoo	atumaranai desyoo
Provisional	INFORMAL	atumareba	atumaranakereba
	FORMAL	atumarimaseba	atumarimaseñ nara
		atumarimasureba	
Gerund	INFORMAL I	atumatte	atumaranai de
	II		atumaranakute
	FORMAL	atumarimasite	atumarimaseñ de
Past Ind.	INFORMAL	atumatta	atumaranakatta
	FORMAL	atumarimasita	atumarimaseñ desita
Past Presump.	INFORMAL	atumattaroo	atumaranakattaroo
		atumatta daroo	atumaranakatta daroo
	FORMAL	atumarimasitaroo	atumarimaseñ desitaroo
		atumatta desyoo	atumaranakatta desyoo
Conditional	INFORMAL	atumattara	atumaranakattara
	FORMAL	atumarimasitara	atumarimaseñ desitara
Alternative	INFORMAL	atumattari	atumaranakattari
	FORMAL	atumarimasitari	atumarimaseñ desitari

INFORMAL AFFIRMATIVE INDICATIVE

Passive		atumarareru
Potential		atumareru
Causative		atumaraseru
Causative Pass.		atumaraserareru
Honorific	I	oatumari ni naru
	II	oatumari nasaru
Humble	I	oatumari suru
	II	oatumari itasu

			AFFIRMATIVE	NEGATIVE
Indicative	INFORMAL		atumeru	atumenai
	FORMAL		atumemasu	atumemaseñ
Imperative	INFORMAL	I	atumero	atumeru na
		II	atumenasai	atumenasaru na
		III	atumete kudasai	atumenai de kudasai
	FORMAL		oatume nasaimase	oatume nasaimasu na
Presumptive	INFORMAL	I	atumeyoo	atumemai
		II	atumeru daroo	atumenai daroo
	FORMAL	I	atumemasyoo	atumemasumai
		II	atumeru desyoo	atumenai desyoo
Provisional	INFORMAL		atumereba	atumenakereba
	FORMAL		atumemaseba	atumemaseñ nara
			atumemasureba	
Gerund	INFORMAL	I	atumete	atumenai de
		II		atumenakute
	FORMAL		atumemasite	atumemaseñ de
Past Ind.	INFORMAL		atumeta	atumenakatta
	FORMAL		atumemasita	atumemaseñ desita
Past Presump.	INFORMAL		atumetaroo	atumenakattaroo
			atumeta daroo	atumenakatta daroo
	FORMAL		atumemesitaroo	atumemaseñ desitaroo
			atumeta desyoo	atumenakatta desyoo
Conditional	INFORMAL		atumetara	atumenakattara
	FORMAL		atumemasitara	atumemaseñ desitara
Alternative	INFORMAL		atumetari	atumenakattari
	FORMAL		atumemasitari	atumemaseñ desitari

		INFORMAL AFFIRMATIVE INDICATIVE
Passive		atumerareru
Potential		atumerareru
Causative		atumesaseru
Causative Pass.		atumesaserareru
Honorific	I	oatume ni naru
	II	oatume nasaru
Humble	I	oatume suru
	II	oatume itasu

		AFFIRMATIVE	NEGATIVE
Indicative	**INFORMAL**	au	awanai
	FORMAL	aimasu	aimaseñ
Imperative	**INFORMAL I**	ae	au na
	II	ainasai	ainasaru na
	III	atte kudasai	awanai de kudasai
	FORMAL	oai nasaimase	oai nasaimasu na
Presumptive	**INFORMAL I**	aoo	aumai
	II	au daroo	awanai daroo
	FORMAL I	aimasyoo	aimasumai
	II	au desyoo	awanai desyoo
Provisional	**INFORMAL**	aeba	awanakereba
	FORMAL	aimaseba	aimaseñ nara
		aimasureba	
Gerund	**INFORMAL I**	atte	awanai de
	II		awanakute
	FORMAL	aimasite	aimaseñ de
Past Ind.	**INFORMAL**	atta	awanakatta
	FORMAL	aimasita	aimaseñ desita
Past Presump.	**INFORMAL**	attaroo	awanakattaroo
		atta daroo	awanakatta daroo
	FORMAL	aimasitaroo	aimaseñ desitaroo
		atta desyoo	awanakatta desyoo
Conditional	**INFORMAL**	attara	awanakattara
	FORMAL	aimasitara	aimaseñ desitara
Alternative	**INFORMAL**	attari	awanakattari
	FORMAL	aimasitari	aimaseñ desitari

		INFORMAL AFFIRMATIVE INDICATIVE
Passive		awareru
Potential		aeru
Causative		awaseru
Causative Pass.		awaserareru
Honorific	**I**	oai ni naru
	II	oai nasaru
Humble	**I**	ome ni kakaru
	II	

to lose one's composure

		AFFIRMATIVE	NEGATIVE
Indicative	**INFORMAL**	awateru	awatenai
	FORMAL	awatemasu	awatemaseñ
Imperative	**INFORMAL I**	awatero	awateru na
	II	awatenasai	awatenasaru na
	III	awatete kudasai	awatenai de kudasai
	FORMAL	oawate nasaimase	oawate nasaimasu na
Presumptive	**INFORMAL I**	awateyoo	awatemai
	II	awateru daroo	awatenai daroo
	FORMAL I	awatemasyoo	awatemasumai
	II	awateru desyoo	awatenai desyoo
Provisional	**INFORMAL**	awatereba	awatenakereba
	FORMAL	awatemaseba	awatemaseñ nara
		awatemasureba	
Gerund	**INFORMAL I**	awatete	awatenai de
	II		awatenakute
	FORMAL	awatemasite	awatemaseñ de
Past Ind.	**INFORMAL**	awateta	awatenakatta
	FORMAL	awatemasita	awatemaseñ desita
Past Presump.	**INFORMAL**	awatetaroo	awatenakattaroo
		awateta daroo	awatenakatta daroo
	FORMAL	awatemasitaroo	awatemaseñ desitaroo
		awateta desyoo	awatenakatta desyoo
Conditional	**INFORMAL**	awatetara	awatenakattara
	FORMAL	awatemasitara	awatemaseñ desitara
Alternative	**INFORMAL**	awatetari	awatenakattari
	FORMAL	awatemasitari	awatemaseñ desitari

INFORMAL AFFIRMATIVE INDICATIVE

Passive		awaterareru
Potential		awaterareru
Causative		awatesaseru
Causative Pass.		awatesaserareru

Honorific	**I**	oawate ni naru
	II	oawate nasaru
Humble	**I**	
	II	

		AFFIRMATIVE	NEGATIVE
Indicative	**INFORMAL**	ayamaru	ayamaranai
	FORMAL	ayamarimasu	ayamarimaseñ
Imperative	**INFORMAL I**	ayamare	ayamaru na
	II	ayamarinasai	ayamarinasaru na
	III	ayamatte kudasai	ayamaranai de kudasai
	FORMAL	oayamari nasaimase	oayamari nasaimasu na
Presumptive	**INFORMAL I**	ayamaroo	ayamarumai
	II	ayamaru daroo	ayamaranai daroo
	FORMAL I	ayamarimasyoo	ayamarimasumai
	II	ayamaru desyoo	ayamaranai desyoo
Provisional	**INFORMAL**	ayamareba	ayamaranakereba
	FORMAL	ayamarimaseba	ayamarimaseñ nara
		ayamarimasureba	
Gerund	**INFORMAL I**	ayamatte	ayamaranai de
	II		ayamaranakute
	FORMAL	ayamarimasite	ayamarimaseñ de
Past Ind.	**INFORMAL**	ayamatta	ayamaranakatta
	FORMAL	ayamarimasita	ayamarimaseñ desita
Past Presump.	**INFORMAL**	ayamattaroo	ayamaranakattaroo
		ayamatta daroo	ayamaranakatta daroo
	FORMAL	ayamarimasitaroo	ayamarimaseñ desitaroo
		ayamatta desyoo	ayamaranakatta desyoo
Conditional	**INFORMAL**	ayamattara	ayamaranakattara
	FORMAL	ayamarimasitara	ayamarimaseñ desitara
Alternative	**INFORMAL**	ayamattari	ayamaranakattari
	FORMAL	ayamarimasitari	ayamarimaseñ desitari

INFORMAL AFFIRMATIVE INDICATIVE

Passive		ayamarareru
Potential		ayamareru
Causative		ayamaraseru
Causative Pass.		ayamaraserareru

Honorific	**I**	oayamari ni naru
	II	oayamari nasaru
Humble	**I**	oayamari suru
	II	oayamari itasu

		AFFIRMATIVE	**NEGATIVE**
Indicative	**INFORMAL**	ayasimu	ayasimanai
	FORMAL	ayasimimasu	ayasimimaseñ
Imperative	**INFORMAL I**	ayasime	ayasimu na
	II	ayasiminasai	ayasiminasaru na
	III	ayasiñde kudasai	ayasimanai de kudasai
	FORMAL	oayasimi nasaimase	oayasimi nasaimasu na
Presumptive	**INFORMAL I**	ayasimoo	ayasimumai
	II	ayasimu daroo	ayasimanai daroo
	FORMAL I	ayasimimasyoo	ayasimimasumai
	II	ayasimu desyoo	ayasimanai desyoo
Provisional	**INFORMAL**	ayasimeba	ayasimanakereba
	FORMAL	ayasimimaseba	ayasimimaseñ nara
		ayasimimasureba	
Gerund	**INFORMAL I**	ayasiñde	ayasimanai de
	II		ayasimanakute
	FORMAL	ayasimimasite	ayasimimaseñ de
Past Ind.	**INFORMAL**	ayasiñda	ayasimanakatta
	FORMAL	ayasimimasita	ayasimimaseñ dcsita
Past Presump.	**INFORMAL**	ayasiñdaroo	ayasimanakattaroo
		ayasiñda daroo	ayasimanakatta daroo
	FORMAL	ayasimimasitaroo	ayasimimaseñ desitaroo
		ayasiñda desyoo	ayasimanakatta desyoo
Conditional	**INFORMAL**	ayasiñdara	ayasimanakattara
	FORMAL	ayasimimasitara	ayasimimaseñ desitara
Alternative	**INFORMAL**	ayasiñdari	ayasimanakattari
	FORMAL	ayasimimasitari	ayasimimaseñ desitari

		INFORMAL AFFIRMATIVE INDICATIVE
Passive		ayasimareru
Potential		ayasimeru
Causative		ayasimaseru
Causative Pass.		ayasimaserareru
Honorific	**I**	oayasimi ni naru
	II	oayasimi nasaru
Humble	**I**	oayasimi suru
	II	oayasimi itasu

		AFFIRMATIVE	NEGATIVE
Indicative	**INFORMAL**	ayaturu	ayaturanai
	FORMAL	ayaturimasu	ayaturimaseñ
Imperative	**INFORMAL I**	ayature	ayaturu na
	II	ayaturinasai	ayaturinasaru na
	III	ayatutte kudasaı	ayaturanai de kudasai
	FORMAL	oayaturi nasaimase	oayaturi nasaimasu na
Presumptive	**INFORMAL I**	ayaturoo	ayaturumai
	II	ayaturu daroo	ayaturanai daroo
	FORMAL I	ayaturimasyoo	ayaturimasumai
	II	ayaturu desyoo	ayaturanai desyoo
Provisional	**INFORMAL**	ayatureba	ayaturanakereba
	FORMAL	ayaturimaseba	ayaturimaseñ nara
		ayaturimasureba	
Gerund	**INFORMAL I**	ayatutte	ayaturanai de
	II		ayaturanakute
	FORMAL	ayaturimasite	ayaturimaseñ de
Past Ind.	**INFORMAL**	ayatutta	ayaturanakatta
	FORMAL	ayaturimasita	ayaturimaseñ desita
Past Presump.	**INFORMAL**	ayatuttaroo	ayaturanakattaroo
		ayatutta daroo	ayaturanakatta daroo
	FORMAL	ayaturimasitaroo	ayaturimaseñ desitaroo
		ayatutta desyoo	ayaturanakatta desyoo
Conditional	**INFORMAL**	ayatuttara	ayaturanakattara
	FORMAL	ayaturimasitara	ayaturimaseñ desitara
Alternative	**INFORMAL**	ayatuttari	ayaturanakattari
	FORMAL	ayaturimasitari	ayaturimaseñ desitari

INFORMAL AFFIRMATIVE INDICATIVE

Passive		ayaturareru
Potential		ayatureru
Causative		ayaturaseru
Causative Pass.		ayaturaserareru

Honorific	**I**	oayaturi ni naru
	II	oayaturi nasaru
Humble	**I**	oayaturi suru
	II	oayaturi itasu

		AFFIRMATIVE	NEGATIVE
Indicative	INFORMAL	azukaru	azukaranai
	FORMAL	azukarimasu	azukarimaseñ
Imperative	INFORMAL I	azukare	azukaru na
	II	azukarinasai	azukarinasaru na
	III	azukatte kudasai	azukaranai de kudasai
	FORMAL	oazukari nasaimase	oazukari nasaimasu na
Presumptive	INFORMAL I	azukaroo	azukarumai
	II	azukaru daroo	azukaranai daroo
	FORMAL I	azukarimasyoo	azukarimasumai
	II	azukaru desyoo	azukaranai desyoo
Provisional	INFORMAL	azukareba	azukaranakereba
	FORMAL	azukarimaseba	azukarimaseñ nara
		azukarimasureba	
Gerund	INFORMAL I	azukatte	azukaranai de
	II		azukaranakute
	FORMAL	azukarimasite	azukarimaseñ de
Past Ind.	INFORMAL	azukatta	azukaranakatta
	FORMAL	azukarimasita	azukarimaseñ desita
Past Presump.	INFORMAL	azukattaroo	azukaranakattaroo
		azukatta daroo	azukaranakatta daroo
	FORMAL	azukarimasitaroo	azukarimaseñ desitaroo
		azukatta desyoo	azukaranakatta desyoo
Conditional	INFORMAL	azukattara	azukaranakattara
	FORMAL	azukarimasitara	azukarimaseñ desitara
Alternative	INFORMAL	azukattari	azukaranakattari
	FORMAL	azukarimasitari	azukarimaseñ desitari

INFORMAL AFFIRMATIVE INDICATIVE

Passive	azukarareru
Potential	azukareru
Causative	azukaraseru
Causative Pass.	azukaraserareru

Honorific	I	oazukari ni naru
	II	oazukari nasaru
Humble	I	oazukari suru
	II	oazukari itasu

			AFFIRMATIVE	NEGATIVE
Indicative	**INFORMAL**		azukeru	azukenai
	FORMAL		azukemasu	azukemaseñ
Imperative	**INFORMAL**	**I**	azukero	azukeru na
		II	azukenasai	azukenasaru na
		III	azukete kudasai	azukenai de kudasai
	FORMAL		oazuke nasaimase	oazuke nasaimasu na
Presumptive	**INFORMAL**	**I**	azukeyoo	azukemai
		II	azukeru daroo	azukenai daroo
	FORMAL	**I**	azukemasyoo	azukemasumai
		II	azukeru desyoo	azukenai desyoo
Provisional	**INFORMAL**		azukereba	azukenakereba
	FORMAL		azukemaseba	azukemaseñ nara
			azukemasureba	
Gerund	**INFORMAL**	**I**	azukete	azukenai de
		II		azukenakute
	FORMAL		azukemasite	azukemaseñ de
Past Ind.	**INFORMAL**		azuketa	azukenakatta
	FORMAL		azukemasita	azukemaseñ desita
Past Presump.	**INFORMAL**		azuketaroo	azukenakattaroo
			azuketa daroo	azukenakatta daroo
	FORMAL		azukemasitaroo	azukemaseñ desitaroo
			azuketa desyoo	azukenakatta desyoo
Conditional	**INFORMAL**		azuketara	azukenakattara
	FORMAL		azukemasitara	azukemaseñ desitara
Alternative	**INFORMAL**		azuketari	azukenakattari
	FORMAL		azukemasitari	azukemaseñ desitari

		INFORMAL AFFIRMATIVE INDICATIVE
Passive		azukerareru
Potential		azukerareru
Causative		azukesaseru
Causative Pass.		azukesaserareru
Honorific	**I**	oazuke ni naru
	II	oazuke nasaru
Humble	**I**	oazuke suru
	II	oazuke itasu

		AFFIRMATIVE	NEGATIVE
Indicative	**INFORMAL**	beñkyoo suru	beñkyoo sinai
	FORMAL	beñkyoo simasu	beñkyoo simaseñ
Imperative	**INFORMAL I**	beñkyoo siro	beñkyoo suru na
	II	beñkyoo sinasai	beñkyoo sinasaru na
	III	beñkyoo site kudasai	beñkyoo sinai de kudasai
	FORMAL	gobeñkyoo nasaimase	gobeñkyoo nasaimasu na
Presumptive	**INFORMAL I**	beñkyoo siyoo	beñkyoo surumai
	II	beñkyoo suru daroo	beñkyoo sinai daroo
	FORMAL I	beñkyoo simasyoo	beñkyoo simasumai
	II	beñkyoo suru desyoo	beñkyoo sinai desyoo
Provisional	**INFORMAL**	beñkyoo sureba	beñkyoo sinakereba
	FORMAL	beñkyoo simaseba	beñkyoo simaseñ nara
		beñkyoo simasureba	
Gerund	**INFORMAL I**	beñkyoo site	beñkyoo sinai de
	II		beñkyoo sinakute
	FORMAL	beñkyoo simasite	beñkyoo simaseñ de
Past Ind.	**INFORMAL**	beñkyoo sita	beñkyoo sinakatta
	FORMAL	beñkyoo simasita	beñkyoo simaseñ desita
Past Presump.	**INFORMAL**	beñkyoo sitaroo	beñkyoo sinakattaroo
		beñkyoo sita daroo	beñkyoo sinakatta daroo
	FORMAL	beñkyoo simasitaroo	beñkyoo simaseñ desitaroo
		beñkyoo sita desyoo	beñkyoo sinakatta desyoo
Conditional	**INFORMAL**	beñkyoo sitara	beñkyoo sinakattara
	FORMAL	beñkyoo simasitara	beñkyoo simaseñ desitara
Alternative	**INFORMAL**	beñkyoo sitari	beñkyoo sinakattari
	FORMAL	beñkyoo simasitari	beñkyoo simaseñ desitari

INFORMAL AFFIRMATIVE INDICATIVE

Passive		beñkyoo sareru
Potential		beñkyoo dekiru
Causative		beñkyoo saseru
Causative Pass.		beñkyoo saserareru

Honorific	**I**	
	II	gobeñkyoo nasaru
Humble	**I**	
	II	beñkyoo itasu

to be startled, to be surprised　　　TRANSITIVE

		AFFIRMATIVE	NEGATIVE
Indicative	**INFORMAL**	bikkuri suru	bikkuri sinai
	FORMAL	bikkuri simasu	bikkuri simaseñ
Imperative	**INFORMAL I**	bikkuri siro	bikkuri suru na
	II	bikkuri sinasai	bikkuri sinasaru na
	III	bikkuri site kudasai	bikkuri sinai de kudasai
	FORMAL	bikkuri nasaimase	bikkuri nasaimasu na
Presumptive	**INFORMAL I**	bikkuri siyoo	bikkuri surumai
	II	bikkuri suru daroo	bikkuri sinai daroo
	FORMAL I	bikkuri simasyoo	bikkuri simasumai
	II	bikkuri suru desyoo	bikkuri sinai desyoo
Provisional	**INFORMAL**	bikkuri sureba	bikkuri sinakereba
	FORMAL	bikkuri simaseba	bikkuri simaseñ nara
		bikkuri simasureba	
Gerund	**INFORMAL I**	bikkuri site	bikkuri sinai de
	II		bikkuri sinakute
	FORMAL	bikkuri simasite	bikkuri simaseñ de
Past Ind.	**INFORMAL**	bikkuri sita	bikkuri sinakatta
	FORMAL	bikkuri simasita	bikkuri simaseñ desita
Past Presump.	**INFORMAL**	bikkuri sitaroo	bikkuri sinakattaroo
		bikkuri sita daroo	bikkuri sinakatta daroo
	FORMAL	bikkuri simasitaroo	bikkuri simaseñ desitaroo
		bikkuri sita desyoo	bikkuri sinakatta desyoo
Conditional	**INFORMAL**	bikkuri sitara	bikkuri sinakattara
	FORMAL	bikkuri simasitara	bikkuri simaseñ desitara
Alternative	**INFORMAL**	bikkuri sitari	bikkuri sinakattari
	FORMAL	bikkuri simasitari	bikkuri simaseñ desitari

	INFORMAL AFFIRMATIVE INDICATIVE
Passive	bikkuri sareru
Potential	bikkuri dekiru
Causative	bikkuri saseru
Causative Pass.	bikkuri saserareru

Honorific	**I**	
	II	bikkuri nasaru
Humble	**I**	
	II	bikkuri itasu

		AFFIRMATIVE	NEGATIVE
Indicative	**INFORMAL**	butukaru	butukaranai
	FORMAL	butukarimasu	butukarimaseñ
Imperative	**INFORMAL I**	butukare	butukaru na
	II	butukarinasai	butukarinasaru na
	III	butukatte kudasai	butukaranai de kudasai
	FORMAL	obutukari nasaimase	obutukari nasaimasu na
Presumptive	**INFORMAL I**	butukaroo	butukarumai
	II	butukaru daroo	butukaranai daroo
	FORMAL I	butukarimasyoo	butukarimasumai
	II	butukaru desyoo	butukaranai desyoo
Provisional	**INFORMAL**	butukareba	butukaranakereba
	FORMAL	butukarimaseba	butukarimaseñ nara
		butukarimasureba	
Gerund	**INFORMAL I**	butukatte	butukaranai de
	II		butukaranakute
	FORMAL	butukarimasite	butukarimaseñ de
Past Ind.	**INFORMAL**	butukatta	butukaranakatta
	FORMAL	butukarimasita	butukarimaseñ desita
Past Presump.	**INFORMAL**	butukattaroo	butukaranakattaroo
		butukatta daroo	butukaranakatta daroo
	FORMAL	butukarimasitaroo	butukarimaseñ desitaroo
		butukatta desyoo	butukaranakatta desyoo
Conditional	**INFORMAL**	butukattara	butukaranakattara
	FORMAL	butukarimasitara	butukarimaseñ desitara
Alternative	**INFORMAL**	butukattari	butukaranakattari
	FORMAL	butukarimasitari	butukarimaseñ desitari

		INFORMAL AFFIRMATIVE INDICATIVE
Passive		butukarareru
Potential		butukareru
Causative		butukaraseru
Causative Pass.		butukaraserareru

Honorific	**I**	obutukari ni naru
	II	obutukari nasaru
Humble	**I**	obutukari suru
	II	obutukari itasu

to throw at, to hurl against   TRANSITIVE

			AFFIRMATIVE	NEGATIVE
Indicative	**INFORMAL**		butukeru	butukenai
	FORMAL		butukemasu	butukemaseñ
Imperative	**INFORMAL I**		butukero	butukeru na
		II	butukenasai	butukenasaru na
		III	butukete kudasai	butukenai de kudasai
	FORMAL		obutuke nasaimase	obutuke nasaimasu na
Presumptive	**INFORMAL I**		butukeyoo	butukemai
		II	butukeru daroo	butukenai daroo
	FORMAL	**I**	butukemasyoo	butukemasumai
		II	butukeru desyoo	butukenai desyoo
Provisional	**INFORMAL**		butukereba	butukenakereba
	FORMAL		butukemaseba	butukemaseñ nara
			butukemasureba	
Gerund	**INFORMAL I**		butukete	butukenai de
		II		butukenakute
	FORMAL		butukemasite	butukemaseñ de
Past Ind.	**INFORMAL**		butuketa	butukenakatta
	FORMAL		butukemasita	butukemaseñ desita
Past Presump.	**INFORMAL**		butuketaroo	butukenakattaroo
			butuketa daroo	butukenakatta daroo
	FORMAL		butukemasitaroo	butukemaseñ desitaroo
			butuketa desyoo	butukenakatta desyoo
Conditional	**INFORMAL**		butuketara	butukenakattara
	FORMAL		butukemasitara	butukemaseñ desitara
Alternative	**INFORMAL**		butuketari	butukenakattari
	FORMAL		butukemasitari	butukemaseñ desitari

INFORMAL AFFIRMATIVE INDICATIVE

Passive		butukerareru
Potential		butukerareru
Causative		butukesaseru
Causative Pass.		butukesaserareru

Honorific	**I**	obutuke ni naru
	II	obutuke nasaru
Humble	**I**	obutuke suru
	II	obutuke itasu

TRANSITIVE   *to represent* (a group etc.)

		AFFIRMATIVE	NEGATIVE
Indicative	INFORMAL	daihyoo suru	daihyoo sinai
	FORMAL	daihyoo simasu	daihyoo simaseñ
Imperative	INFORMAL I	daihyoo siro	daihyoo suru na
	II	daihyoo sinasai	daihyoo sinasaru na
	III	daihyoo site kudasai	daihyoo sinai de kudasai
	FORMAL	daihyoo nasaimase	daihyoo nasaimasu na
Presumptive	INFORMAL I	daihyoo siyoo	daihyoo surumai
	II	daihyoo suru daroo	daihyoo sinai daroo
	FORMAL I	daihyoo simasyoo	daihyoo simasumai
	II	daihyoo suru desyoo	daihyoo sinai desyoo
Provisional	INFORMAL	daihyoo sureba	daihyoo sinakereba
	FORMAL	daihyoo simaseba	daihyoo simaseñ nara
		daihyoo simasureba	
Gerund	INFORMAL I	daihyoo site	daihyoo sinai de
	II		daihyoo sinakute
	FORMAL	daihyoo simasite	daihyoo simaseñ de
Past Ind.	INFORMAL	daihyoo sita	daihyoo sinakatta
	FORMAL	daihyoo simasita	daihyoo simaseñ desita
Past Presump.	INFORMAL	daihyoo sitaroo	daihyoo sinakattaroo
		daihyoo sita daroo	daihyoo sinakatta daroo
	FORMAL	daihyoo simasitaroo	daihyoo simaseñ desitaroo
		daihyoo sita desyoo	daihyoo sinakatta desyoo
Conditional	INFORMAL	daihyoo sitara	daihyoo sinakattara
	FORMAL	daihyoo simasitara	daihyoo simaseñ desitara
Alternative	INFORMAL	daihyoo sitari	daihyoo sinakattari
	FORMAL	daihyoo simasitari	daihyoo simaseñ desitari

		INFORMAL AFFIRMATIVE INDICATIVE
Passive		daihyoo sareru
Potential		daihyoo dekiru
Causative		daihyoo saseru
Causative Pass.		daihyoo saserareru
Honorific	I	
	II	daihyoo nasaru
Humble	I	
	II	daihyoo itasu

		AFFIRMATIVE	NEGATIVE
Indicative	**INFORMAL**	daku	dakanai
	FORMAL	dakimasu	dakimaseñ
Imperative	**INFORMAL I**	dake	daku na
	II	dakinasai	dakinasaru na
	III	daite kudasai	dakanai de kudasai
	FORMAL	odaki nasaimase	odaki nasaimasu na
Presumptive	**INFORMAL I**	dakoo	dakumai
	II	daku daroo	dakanai daroo
	FORMAL I	dakimasyoo	dakimasumai
	II	daku desyoo	dakanai desyoo
Provisional	**INFORMAL**	dakeba	dakanakereba
	FORMAL	dakimaseba	dakimaseñ nara
		dakimasureba	
Gerund	**INFORMAL I**	daite	dakanai de
	II		dakanakute
	FORMAL	dakimasite	dakimaseñ de
Past Ind.	**INFORMAL**	daita	dakanakatta
	FORMAL	dakimasita	dakimaseñ desita
Past Presump.	**INFORMAL**	daitaroo	dakanakattaroo
		daita daroo	dakanakatta daroo
	FORMAL	dakimasitaroo	dakimaseñ desitaroo
		daita desyoo	dakanakatta desyoo
Conditional	**INFORMAL**	daitara	dakanakattara
	FORMAL	dakimasitara	dakimaseñ desitara
Alternative	**INFORMAL**	daitari	dakanakattari
	FORMAL	dakimasitari	dakimaseñ desitari

		INFORMAL AFFIRMATIVE INDICATIVE
Passive		dakareru
Potential		dakeru
Causative		dakaseru
Causative Pass.		dakaserareru
Honorific	**I**	odaki ni naru
	II	odaki nasaru
Humble	**I**	odaki suru
	II	odaki itasu

		AFFIRMATIVE	NEGATIVE
Indicative	INFORMAL	damaru	damaranai
	FORMAL	damarimasu	damarimaseñ
Imperative	INFORMAL I	damare	damaru na
	II	damarinasai	damarinasaru na
	III	damatte kudasai	damaranai de kudasai
	FORMAL	odamari nasaimase	odamari nasaimasu na
Presumptive	INFORMAL I	damaroo	damarumai
	II	damaru daroo	damaranai daroo
	FORMAL I	damarimasyoo	damarimasumai
	II	damaru desyoo	damaranai desyoo
Provisional	INFORMAL	damareba	damaranakereba
	FORMAL	damarimaseba	damarimaseñ nara
		damarimasureba	
Gerund	INFORMAL I	damatte	damaranai de
	II		damaranakute
	FORMAL	damarimasite	damarimaseñ de
Past Ind.	INFORMAL	damatta	damaranakatta
	FORMAL	damarimasita	damarimaseñ desita
Past Presump.	INFORMAL	damattaroo	damaranakattaroo
		damatta daroo	damaranakatta daroo
	FORMAL	damarimasitaroo	damarimaseñ desitaroo
		damatta desyoo	damaranakatta desyoo
Conditional	INFORMAL	damattara	damaranakattara
	FORMAL	damarimasitara	damarimaseñ desitara
Alternative	INFORMAL	damattari	damaranakattari
	FORMAL	damarimasitari	damarimaseñ desitari

		INFORMAL AFFIRMATIVE INDICATIVE
Passive		damarareru
Potential		damareru
Causative		damaraseru
Causative Pass.		damaraserareru

Honorific	I	odamari ni naru
	II	odamari nasaru
Humble	I	
	II	

to trick   TRANSITIVE

			AFFIRMATIVE	NEGATIVE
Indicative	**INFORMAL**		damasu	damasanai
	FORMAL		damasimasu	damasimaseñ
Imperative	**INFORMAL I**		damase	damasu na
		II	damasinasai	damasinasaru na
		III	damasite kudasai	damasanai de kudasai
	FORMAL		odamasi nasaimase	odamasi nasaimasu na
Presumptive	**INFORMAL I**		damasoo	damasumai
		II	damasu daroo	damasanai daroo
	FORMAL	**I**	damasimasyoo	damasimasumai
		II	damasu desyoo	damasanai desyoo
Provisional	**INFORMAL**		damaseba	damasanakereba
	FORMAL		damasimaseba	damasimaseñ nara
			damasimasureba	
Gerund	**INFORMAL I**		damasite	damasanai de
		II		damasanakute
	FORMAL		damasimasite	damasimaseñ de
Past Ind.	**INFORMAL**		damasita	damasanakatta
	FORMAL		damasimasita	damasimaseñ desita
Past Presump.	**INFORMAL**		damasitaroo	damasanakattaroo
			damasita daroo	damasanakatta daroo
	FORMAL		damasimasitaroo	damasimaseñ desitaroo
			damasita desyoo	damasanakatta desyoo
Conditional	**INFORMAL**		damasitara	damasanakattara
	FORMAL		damasimasitara	damasimaseñ desitara
Alternative	**INFORMAL**		damasitari	damasanakattari
	FORMAL		damasimasitari	damasimaseñ desitari

		INFORMAL AFFIRMATIVE INDICATIVE
Passive		damasareru
Potential		damaseru
Causative		damasaseru
Causative Pass.		damasaserareru
Honorific	**I**	odamasi ni naru
	II	odamasi nasaru
Humble	**I**	
	II	

		AFFIRMATIVE	NEGATIVE
Indicative	**INFORMAL**	dasu	dasanai
	FORMAL	dasimasu	dasimaseñ
Imperative	**INFORMAL I**	dase	dasu na
	II	dasinasai	dasinasaru na
	III	dasite kudasai	dasanai de kudasai
	FORMAL	odasi nasaimase	odasi nasaimasu na
Presumptive	**INFORMAL I**	dasoo	dasumai
	II	dasu daroo	dasanai daroo
	FORMAL I	dasimasyoo	dasimasumai
	II	dasu desyoo	dasanai desyoo
Provisional	**INFORMAL**	daseba	dasanakereba
	FORMAL	dasimaseba	dasimaseñ nara
		dasimasureba	
Gerund	**INFORMAL I**	dasite	dasanai de
	II		dasanakute
	FORMAL	dasimasite	dasimaseñ de
Past Ind.	**INFORMAL**	dasita	dasanakatta
	FORMAL	dasimasita	dasimaseñ desita
Past Presump.	**INFORMAL**	dasitaroo	dasanakattaroo
		dasita daroo	dasanakatta daroo
	FORMAL	dasimasitaroo	dasimaseñ desitaroo
		dasita desyoo	dasanakatta desyoo
Conditional	**INFORMAL**	dasitara	dasanakattara
	FORMAL	dasimasitara	dasimaseñ desitara
Alternative	**INFORMAL**	dasitari	dasanakattari
	FORMAL	dasimasitari	dasimaseñ desitari

		INFORMAL AFFIRMATIVE INDICATIVE
Passive		dasareru
Potential		daseru
Causative		dasaseru
Causative Pass.		dasaserareru

Honorific	**I**	odasi ni naru
	II	odasi nasaru
Humble	**I**	odasi suru
	II	odasi itasu

		AFFIRMATIVE	NEGATIVE
Indicative	**INFORMAL**	deau	deawanai
	FORMAL	deaimasu	deaimaseñ
Imperative	**INFORMAL I**		
	II		
	III		
	FORMAL		
Presumptive	**INFORMAL I**	deaoo	deaumai
	II	deau daroo	deawanai daroo
	FORMAL I	deaimasyoo	deaimasumai
	II	deau desyoo	deawanai desyoo
Provisional	**INFORMAL**	deaeba	deawanakereba
	FORMAL	deaimaseba	deaimaseñ nara
		deaimasureba	
Gerund	**INFORMAL I**	deatte	deawanai de
	II		deawanakute
	FORMAL	deaimasite	deaimaseñ de
Past Ind.	**INFORMAL**	deatta	deawanakatta
	FORMAL	deaimasita	deaimaseñ desita
Past Presump.	**INFORMAL**	deattaroo	deawanakattaroo
		deatta daroo	deawanakatta daroo
	FORMAL	deaimasitaroo	deaimaseñ desitaroo
		deatta desyoo	deawanakatta desyoo
Conditional	**INFORMAL**	deattara	deawanakattara
	FORMAL	deaimasitara	deaimaseñ desitara
Alternative	**INFORMAL**	deattari	deawanakattari
	FORMAL	deaimasitari	deaimaseñ desitari

		INFORMAL AFFIRMATIVE INDICATIVE
Passive		deawareru
Potential		deaeru
Causative		deawaseru
Causative Pass.		deawaserareru
Honorific	**I**	odeai ni naru
	II	odeai nasaru
Humble	**I**	odeai suru
	II	odeai itasu

		AFFIRMATIVE	**NEGATIVE**
Indicative	**INFORMAL**	dekiru	dekinai
	FORMAL	dekimasu	dekimaseñ
Imperative	**INFORMAL I**	dekiro	dekiru na
	II	dekinasai	dekinasaru na
	III		
	FORMAL		
Presumptive	**INFORMAL I**	dekiyoo	dekimai
	II	dekiru daroo	dekinai daroo
	FORMAL I	dekimasyoo	dekimasumai
	II	dekiru desyoo	dekinai desyoo
Provisional	**INFORMAL**	dekireba	dekinakereba
	FORMAL	dekimaseba	dekimaseñ nara
		dekimasureba	
Gerund	**INFORMAL I**	dekite	dekinai de
	II		dekinakute
	FORMAL	dekimasite	dekimaseñ de
Past Ind.	**INFORMAL**	dekita	dekinakatta
	FORMAL	dekimasita	dekimaseñ desita
Past Presump.	**INFORMAL**	dekitaroo	dekinakattaroo
		dekita daroo	dekinakatta daroo
	FORMAL	dekimasitaroo	dekimaseñ desitaroo
		dekita desyoo	dekinakatta desyoo
Conditional	**INFORMAL**	dekitara	dekinakattara
	FORMAL	dekimasitara	dekimaseñ desitara
Alternative	**INFORMAL**	dekitari	dekinakattari
	FORMAL	dekimasitari	dekimaseñ desitari

INFORMAL AFFIRMATIVE INDICATIVE

Passive		
Potential		
Causative		
Causative Pass.		

Honorific	I	odeki ni naru
	II	odeki nasaru
Humble	I	
	II	

		AFFIRMATIVE	NEGATIVE
Indicative	**INFORMAL**	deru	denai
	FORMAL	demasu	demaseñ
Imperative	**INFORMAL I**	dero	deru na
	II	denasai	denasaru na
	III	dete kudasai	denai de kudasai
	FORMAL	ode nasaimase	ode nasaimasu na
Presumptive	**INFORMAL I**	deyoo	demai
	II	deru daroo	denai daroo
	FORMAL I	demasyoo	demasumai
	II	deru desyoo	denai desyoo
Provisional	**INFORMAL**	dereba	denakereba
	FORMAL	demaseba	demaseñ nara
		demasureba	
Gerund	**INFORMAL I**	dete	denai de
	II		denakute
	FORMAL	demasite	demaseñ de
Past Ind.	**INFORMAL**	deta	denakatta
	FORMAL	demasita	demaseñ desita
Past Presump.	**INFORMAL**	detaroo	denakattaroo
		deta daroo	denakatta daroo
	FORMAL	demasitaroo	demaseñ desitaroo
		deta desyoo	denakatta desyoo
Conditional	**INFORMAL**	detara	denakattara
	FORMAL	demasitara	demaseñ desitara
Alternative	**INFORMAL**	detari	denakattari
	FORMAL	demasitari	demaseñ desitari

		INFORMAL AFFIRMATIVE INDICATIVE
Passive		derareru
Potential		derareru
Causative		desaseru
Causative Pass.		desaserareru

Honorific	**I**	ode ni naru
	II	ode nasaru
Humble	**I**	
	II	

TRANSITIVE   *to restrain oneself in deference to others*

		AFFIRMATIVE	**NEGATIVE**
Indicative	**INFORMAL**	eñryo suru	eñryo sinai
	FORMAL	eñryo simasu	eñryo simaseñ
Imperative	**INFORMAL I**	eñryo siro	eñryo suru na
	II	eñryo sinasai	eñryo sinasaru na
	III	eñryo site kudasai	eñryo sinai de kudasai
	FORMAL	goeñryo nasaimase	goeñryo nasaimasu na
Presumptive	**INFORMAL I**	eñryo siyoo	eñryo surumai
	II	eñryo suru daroo	eñryo sinai daroo
	FORMAL I	eñryo simasyoo	eñryo simasumai
	II	eñryo suru desyoo	eñryo sinai desyoo
Provisional	**INFORMAL**	eñryo sureba	eñryo sinakereba
	FORMAL	eñryo simaseba	eñryo simaseñ nara
		eñryo simasureba	
Gerund	**INFORMAL I**	eñryo site	eñryo sinai de
	II		eñryo sinakute
	FORMAL	eñryo simasite	eñryo simaseñ de
Past Ind.	**INFORMAL**	eñryo sita	eñryo sinakatta
	FORMAL	eñryo simasita	eñryo simaseñ desita
Past Presump.	**INFORMAL**	eñryo sitaroo	eñryo sinakattaroo
		eñryo sita daroo	eñryo sinakatta daroo
	FORMAL	eñryo simasitaroo	eñryo simaseñ desitaroo
		eñryo sita desyoo	eñryo sinakatta desyoo
Conditional	**INFORMAL**	eñryo sitara	eñryo sinakattara
	FORMAL	eñryo simasitara	eñryo simaseñ desitara
Alternative	**INFORMAL**	eñryo sitari	eñryo sinakattari
	FORMAL	eñryo simasitari	eñryo simaseñ desitari

		INFORMAL AFFIRMATIVE INDICATIVE
Passive		eñryo sareru
Potential		eñryo dekiru
Causative		eñryo saseru
Causative Pass.		eñryo saserareru
Honorific	**I**	
	II	goeñryo nasaru
Humble	**I**	goeñryo suru
	II	goeñryo itasu

		AFFIRMATIVE	NEGATIVE
Indicative	**INFORMAL**	erabu	erabanai
	FORMAL	erabimasu	erabimaseñ
Imperative	**INFORMAL I**	erabe	erabu na
	II	erabinasai	erabinasaru na
	III	erañde kudasai	erabanai de kudasai
	FORMAL	oerabi nasaimase	oerabi nasaimasu na
Presumptive	**INFORMAL I**	eraboo	erabumai
	II	erabu daroo	erabanai daroo
	FORMAL I	erabimasyoo	erabimasumai
	II	erabu desyoo	erabanai desyoo
Provisional	**INFORMAL**	erabeba	erabanakereba
	FORMAL	erabimaseba	erabimaseñ nara
		erabimasureba	
Gerund	**INFORMAL I**	erañde	erabanai de
	II		erabanakute
	FORMAL	erabimasite	erabimaseñ de
Past Ind.	**INFORMAL**	erañda	erabanakatta
	FORMAL	erabimasita	erabimaseñ desita
Past Presump.	**INFORMAL**	erañdaroo	erabanakattaroo
		erañda daroo	erabanakatta daroo
	FORMAL	erabimasitaroo	erabimaseñ desitaroo
		erañda desyoo	erabanakatta desyoo
Conditional	**INFORMAL**	erañdara	erabanakattara
	FORMAL	erabimasitara	erabimaseñ desitara
Alternative	**INFORMAL**	erañdari	erabanakattari
	FORMAL	erabimasitari	erabimaseñ desitari

		INFORMAL AFFIRMATIVE INDICATIVE
Passive		erabareru
Potential		eraberu
Causative		erabaseru
Causative Pass.		erabaserareru

Honorific	**I**	oerabi ni naru
	II	oerabi nasaru
Humble	**I**	oerabi suru
	II	oerabi itasu

		AFFIRMATIVE	**NEGATIVE**
Indicative	**INFORMAL**	eru	enai
	FORMAL	emasu	emaseñ
Imperative	**INFORMAL I**	ero	eru na
	II	enasai	enasaru na
	III	ete kudasai	enai de kudasai
	FORMAL		
Presumptive	**INFORMAL I**	eyoo	emai
	II	eru daroo	enai daroo
	FORMAL I	emasyoo	emasumai
	II	eru desyoo	enai desyoo
Provisional	**INFORMAL**	ereba	enakereba
	FORMAL	emaseba	emaseñ nara
		emasureba	
Gerund	**INFORMAL I**	ete	enai de
	II		enakute
	FORMAL	emasite	emaseñ de
Past Ind.	**INFORMAL**	eta	enakatta
	FORMAL	emasita	emaseñ desita
Past Presump.	**INFORMAL**	etaroo	enakattaroo
		eta daroo	enakatta daroo
	FORMAL	emasitaroo	emaseñ desitaroo
		eta desyoo	enakatta desyoo
Conditional	**INFORMAL**	etara	enakattara
	FORMAL	emasitara	emaseñ desitara
Alternative	**INFORMAL**	etari	enakattari
	FORMAL	emasitari	emaseñ desitari

	INFORMAL AFFIRMATIVE INDICATIVE
Passive	erareru
Potential	erareru
Causative	esaseru
Causative Pass.	esaserareru

Honorific	**I**	
	II	
Humble	**I**	
	II	

		AFFIRMATIVE	NEGATIVE
Indicative	**INFORMAL**	gakkari suru	gakkari sinai
	FORMAL	gakkari simasu	gakkari simaseñ
Imperative	**INFORMAL I**	gakkari siro	gakkari suru na
	II	gakkari sinasai	gakkari sinasaru na
	III	gakkari site kudasai	gakkari sinai de kudasai
	FORMAL	gakkari nasaimase	gakkari nasaimasu na
Presumptive	**INFORMAL I**	gakkari siyoo	gakkari surumai
	II	gakkari suru daroo	gakkari sinai daroo
	FORMAL I	gakkari simasyoo	gakkari simasumai
	II	gakkari suru desyoo	gakkari sinai desyoo
Provisional	**INFORMAL**	gakkari sureba	gakkari sinakereba
	FORMAL	gakkari simaseba	gakkari simaseñ nara
		gakkari simasureba	
Gerund	**INFORMAL I**	gakkari site	gakkari sinai de
	II		gakkari sinakute
	FORMAL	gakkari simasite	gakkari simaseñ de
Past Ind.	**INFORMAL**	gakkari sita	gakkari sinakatta
	FORMAL	gakkari simasita	gakkari simaseñ desita
Past Presump.	**INFORMAL**	gakkari sitaroo	gakkari sinakattaroo
		gakkari sita daroo	gakkari sinakatta daroo
	FORMAL	gakkari simasitaroo	gakkari simaseñ desitaroo
		gakkari sita desyoo	gakkari sinakatta desyoo
Conditional	**INFORMAL**	gakkari sitara	gakkari sinakattara
	FORMAL	gakkari simasitara	gakkari simaseñ desitara
Alternative	**INFORMAL**	gakkari sitari	gakkari sinakattari
	FORMAL	gakkari simasitari	gakkari simaseñ desitari

	INFORMAL AFFIRMATIVE INDICATIVE
Passive	gakkari sareru
Potential	gakkari dekiru
Causative	gakkari saseru
Causative Pass.	gakkari saserareru

Honorific	**I**	
	II	gakkari nasaru
Humble	**I**	
	II	gakkari itasu

gañbár.u

TRANSITIVE   *to stand firm, to exert oneself*

		AFFIRMATIVE	NEGATIVE
Indicative	**INFORMAL**	gañbaru	gañbaranai
	FORMAL	gañbarimasu	gañbarimaseñ
Imperative	**INFORMAL I**	gañbare	gañbaru na
	II	gañbarinasai	gañbarinasaru na
	III	gañbatte kudasai	gañbaranai de kudasai
	FORMAL	ogañbari nasaimase	ogañbari nasaimasu na
Presumptive	**INFORMAL I**	gañbaroo	gañbarumai
	II	gañbaru daroo	gañbaranai daroo
	FORMAL I	gañbarimasyoo	gañbarimasumai
	II	gañbaru desyoo	gañbaranai desyoo
Provisional	**INFORMAL**	gañbareba	gañbaranakereba
	FORMAL	gañbarimaseba	gañbarimaseñ nara
		gañbarimasureba	
Gerund	**INFORMAL I**	gañbatte	gañbaranai de
	II		gañbaranakute
	FORMAL	gañbarimasite	gañbarimaseñ de
Past Ind.	**INFORMAL**	gañbatta	gañbaranakatta
	FORMAL	gañbarimasita	gañbarimaseñ desita
Past Presump.	**INFORMAL**	gañbattaroo	gañbaranakattaroo
		gañbatta daroo	gañbaranakatta daroo
	FORMAL	gañbarimasitaroo	gañbarimaseñ desitaroo
		gañbatta desyoo	gañbaranakatta desyoo
Conditional	**INFORMAL**	gañbattara	gañbaranakattara
	FORMAL	gañbarimasitara	gañbarimaseñ desitara
Alternative	**INFORMAL**	gañbattari	gañbaranakattari
	FORMAL	gañbarimasitari	gañbarimaseñ desitari

		INFORMAL AFFIRMATIVE INDICATIVE
Passive		gañbarareru
Potential		gañbareru
Causative		gañbaraseru
Causative Pass.		gañbaraserareru
Honorific	**I**	ogañbari ni naru
	II	ogañbari nasaru
Humble	**I**	
	II	

to exist (inanimate neutral polite)*

		AFFIRMATIVE	NEGATIVE
Indicative	**INFORMAL**	gozaru	
	FORMAL	gozaimasu	gozaimaseñ
Imperative	**INFORMAL I**		
	II		
	III		
	FORMAL		
Presumptive	**INFORMAL I**	gozaroo	gozarumai
	II		
	FORMAL I	gozaimasyoo	gozaimasumai
	II		
Provisional	**INFORMAL**		
	FORMAL	gozaimaseba	gozaimaseñ nara
		gozaimasureba	
Gerund	**INFORMAL I**		
	II		
	FORMAL	gozaimasite	gozaimaseñ de
Past Ind.	**INFORMAL**		
	FORMAL	gozaimasita	gozaimaseñ desita
Past Presump.	**INFORMAL**		
	FORMAL	gozaimasitaroo	gozaimaseñ desitaroo
Conditional	**INFORMAL**		
	FORMAL	gozaimasitara	gozaimaseñ desitara
Alternative	**INFORMAL**		
	FORMAL	gozaimasitari	gozaimaseñ desitari

	INFORMAL AFFIRMATIVE INDICATIVE
Passive	
Potential	
Causative	
Causative Pass.	

Honorific	I	
	II	
Humble	I	
	II	

*The forms *gozaru*, *gozaroo*, and *gozarumai* are rarely used in standard conversation, being replaced by their formal equivalents.

		AFFIRMATIVE	NEGATIVE
Indicative	INFORMAL	hagemasu	hagemasanai
	FORMAL	hagemasimasu	hagemasimaseñ
Imperative	INFORMAL I	hagemase	hagemasu na
	II	hagemasinasai	hagemasinasaru na
	III	hagemasite kudasai	hagemasanai de kudasai
	FORMAL	ohagemasi nasaimase	ohagemasi nasaimasu na
Presumptive	INFORMAL I	hagemasoo	hagemasumai
	II	hagemasu daroo	hagemasanai daroo
	FORMAL I	hagemasimasyoo	hagemasimasumai
	II	hagemasu desyoo	hagemasanai desyoo
Provisional	INFORMAL	hagemaseba	hagemasanakereba
	FORMAL	hagemasimaseba	hagemasimaseñ nara
		hagemasimasureba	
Gerund	INFORMAL I	hagemasite	hagemasanai de
	II		hagemasanakute
	FORMAL	hagemasimasite	hagemasimaseñ de
Past Ind.	INFORMAL	hagemasita	hagemasanakatta
	FORMAL	hagemasimasita	hagemasimaseñ desita
Past Presump.	INFORMAL	hagemasitaroo	hagemasanakattaroo
		hagemasita daroo	hagemasanakatta daroo
	FORMAL	hagemasimasitaroo	hagemasimaseñ desitaroo
		hagemasita desyoo	hagemasanakatta desyoo
Conditional	INFORMAL	hagemasitara	hagemasanakattara
	FORMAL	hagemasimasitara	hagemasimaseñ desitara
Alternative	INFORMAL	hagemasitari	hagemasanakattari
	FORMAL	hagemasimasitari	hagemasimaseñ desitari

	INFORMAL AFFIRMATIVE INDICATIVE
Passive	hagemasareru
Potential	hagemaseru
Causative	hagemasaseru
Causative Pass.	hagemasaserareru

Honorific	I	ohagemasi ni naru
	II	ohagemasi nasaru
Humble	I	ohagemasi suru
	II	ohagemasi itasu

		AFFIRMATIVE	NEGATIVE
Indicative	INFORMAL	hagemu	hagemanai
	FORMAL	hagemimasu	hagemimaseñ
Imperative	INFORMAL I	hageme	hagemu na
	II	hageminasai	hageminasaru na
	III	hageñde kudasai	hagemanai de kudasai
	FORMAL	ohagemi nasaimase	ohagemi nasaimasu na
Presumptive	INFORMAL I	hagemoo	hagemumai
	II	hagemu daroo	hagemanai daroo
	FORMAL I	hagemimasyoo	hagemimasumai
	II	hagemu desyoo	hagemanai desyoo
Provisional	INFORMAL	hagemeba	hagemanakereba
	FORMAL	hagemimaseba	hagemimaseñ nara
		hagemimasureba	
Gerund	INFORMAL I	hageñde	hagemanai de
	II		hagemanakute
	FORMAL	hagemimasite	hagemimaseñ de
Past Ind.	INFORMAL	hageñda	hagemanakatta
	FORMAL	hagemimasita	hagemimaseñ desita
Past Presump.	INFORMAL	hageñdaroo	hagemanakattaroo
		hageñda daroo	hagemanakatta daroo
	FORMAL	hagemimasitaroo	hagemimaseñ desitaroo
		hageñda desyoo	hagemanakatta desyoo
Conditional	INFORMAL	hageñdara	hagemanakattara
	FORMAL	hagemimasitara	hagemimaseñ desitara
Alternative	INFORMAL	hageñdari	hagemanakattari
	FORMAL	hagemimasitari	hagemimaseñ desitari

		INFORMAL AFFIRMATIVE INDICATIVE
Passive		hagemareru
Potential		hagemeru
Causative		hagemaseru
Causative Pass.		hagemaserareru
Honorific	I	ohagemi ni naru
	II	ohagemi nasaru
Humble	I	
	II	

		AFFIRMATIVE	NEGATIVE
Indicative	**INFORMAL**	hairu	hairanai
	FORMAL	hairimasu	hairimaseñ
Imperative	**INFORMAL I**	haire	hairu na
	II	hairinasai	hairinasaru na
	III	haitte kudasai	hairanai de kudasai
	FORMAL	ohairi nasaimase	ohairi nasaimasu na
Presumptive	**INFORMAL I**	hairoo	hairumai
	II	hairu daroo	hairanai daroo
	FORMAL I	hairimasyoo	hairimasumai
	II	hairu desyoo	hairanai desyoo
Provisional	**INFORMAL**	haireba	hairanakereba
	FORMAL	hairimaseba	hairimaseñ nara
		hairimasureba	
Gerund	**INFORMAL I**	haitte	hairanai de
	II		hairanakute
	FORMAL	hairimasite	hairimaseñ de
Past Ind.	**INFORMAL**	haitta	hairanakatta
	FORMAL	hairimasita	hairimaseñ desita
Past Presump.	**INFORMAL**	haittaroo	hairanakattaroo
		haitta daroo	hairanakatta daroo
	FORMAL	hairimasitaroo	hairimaseñ desitaroo
		haitta desyoo	hairanakatta desyoo
Conditional	**INFORMAL**	haittara	hairanakattara
	FORMAL	hairimasitara	hairimaseñ desitara
Alternative	**INFORMAL**	haittari	hairanakattari
	FORMAL	hairimasitari	hairimasen desitari

INFORMAL AFFIRMATIVE INDICATIVE

Passive		hairareru
Potential		haireru
Causative		hairaseru
Causative Pass.		hairaserareru
Honorific	**I**	ohairi ni naru
	II	ohairi nasaru
Humble	**I**	
	II	

		AFFIRMATIVE	NEGATIVE
Indicative	**INFORMAL**	hakaru	hakaranai
	FORMAL	hakarimasu	hakarimaseñ
Imperative	**INFORMAL I**	hakare	hakaru na
	II	hakarinasai	hakarinasaru na
	III	hakatte kudasai	hakaranai de kudasai
	FORMAL	ohakari nasaimase	ohakari nasaimasu na
Presumptive	**INFORMAL I**	hakaroo	hakarumai
	II	hakaru daroo	hakaranai daroo
	FORMAL I	hakarimasyoo	hakarimasumai
	II	hakaru desyoo	hakaranai desyoo
Provisional	**INFORMAL**	hakareba	hakaranakereba
	FORMAL	hakarimaseba	hakarimaseñ nara
		hakarimasureba	
Gerund	**INFORMAL I**	hakatte	hakaranai de
	II		hakaranakute
	FORMAL	hakarimasite	hakarimaseñ de
Past Ind.	**INFORMAL**	hakatta	hakaranakatta
	FORMAL	hakarimasita	hakarimaseñ desita
Past Presump.	**INFORMAL**	hakattaroo	hakaranakattaroo
		hakatta daroo	hakaranakatta daroo
	FORMAL	hakarimasitaroo	hakarimaseñ desitaroo
		hakatta desyoo	hakaranakatta desyoo
Conditional	**INFORMAL**	hakattara	hakaranakattara
	FORMAL	hakarimasitara	hakarimaseñ desitara
Alternative	**INFORMAL**	hakattari	hakaranakattari
	FORMAL	hakarimasitari	hakarimaseñ desitari

		INFORMAL AFFIRMATIVE INDICATIVE
Passive		hakarareru
Potential		hakareru
Causative		hakaraseru
Causative Pass.		hakaraserareru

Honorific	**I**	ohakari ni naru
	II	ohakari nasaru
Humble	**I**	ohakari suru
	II	ohakari itasu

		AFFIRMATIVE	NEGATIVE
Indicative	**INFORMAL**	hakaru	hakaranai
	FORMAL	hakarimasu	hakarimaseñ
Imperative	**INFORMAL I**	hakare	hakaru na
	II	hakarinasai	hakarinasaru na
	III	hakatte kudasai	hakaranai de kudasai
	FORMAL	ohakari nasaimase	ohakari nasaimasu na
Presumptive	**INFORMAL I**	hakaroo	hakarumai
	II	hakaru daroo	hakaranai daroo
	FORMAL I	hakarimasyoo	hakarimasumai
	II	hakaru desyoo	hakaranai desyoo
Provisional	**INFORMAL**	hakareba	hakaranakereba
	FORMAL	hakarimaseba	hakarimaseñ nara
		hakarimasureba	
Gerund	**INFORMAL I**	hakatte	hakaranai de
	II		hakaranakute
	FORMAL	hakarimasite	hakarimaseñ de
Past Ind.	**INFORMAL**	hakatta	hakaranakatta
	FORMAL	hakarimasita	hakarimaseñ desita
Past Presump.	**INFORMAL**	hakattaroo	hakaranakattaroo
		hakatta daroo	hakaranakatta daroo
	FORMAL	hakarimasitaroo	hakarimaseñ desitaroo
		hakatta desyoo	hakaranakatta desyoo
Conditional	**INFORMAL**	hakattara	hakaranakattara
	FORMAL	hakarimasitara	hakarimaseñ desitara
Alternative	**INFORMAL**	hakattari	hakaranakattari
	FORMAL	hakarimasitari	hakarimaseñ desitari

INFORMAL AFFIRMATIVE INDICATIVE

Passive		hakarareru
Potential		hakareru
Causative		hakaraseru
Causative Pass.		hakaraserareru

Honorific	**I**	ohakari ni naru
	II	ohakari nasaru
Humble	**I**	ohakari suru
	II	ohakari itasu

to discover   TRANSITIVE

		AFFIRMATIVE	**NEGATIVE**
Indicative	**INFORMAL**	hakkeñ suru	hakkeñ sinai
	FORMAL	hakkeñ simasu	hakkeñ simaseñ
Imperative	**INFORMAL I**	hakkeñ siro	hakkeñ suru na
	II	hakkeñ sinasai	hakkeñ sinasaru na
	III	hakkeñ site kudasai	hakkeñ sinai de kudasai
	FORMAL	gohakkeñ nasaimase	gohakkeñ nasaimasu na
Presumptive	**INFORMAL I**	hakkeñ siyoo	hakkeñ surumai
	II	hakkeñ suru daroo	hakkeñ sinai daroo
	FORMAL I	hakkeñ simasyoo	hakkeñ simasumai
	II	hakkeñ suru desyoo	hakkeñ sinai desyoo
Provisional	**INFORMAL**	hakkeñ sureba	hakkeñ sinakereba
	FORMAL	hakkeñ simaseba	hakkeñ simaseñ nara
		hakkeñ simasureba	
Gerund	**INFORMAL I**	hakkeñ site	hakkeñ sinai de
	II		hakkeñ sinakute
	FORMAL	hakkeñ simasite	hakkeñ simaseñ de
Past Ind.	**INFORMAL**	hakkeñ sita	hakkeñ sinakatta
	FORMAL	hakkeñ simasita	hakkeñ simaseñ desita
Past Presump.	**INFORMAL**	hakkeñ sitaroo	hakkeñ sinakattaroo
		hakkeñ sita daroo	hakkeñ sinakatta daroo
	FORMAL	hakkeñ simasitaroo	hakkeñ simaseñ desitaroo
		hakkeñ sita desyoo	hakkeñ sinakatta desyoo
Conditional	**INFORMAL**	hakkeñ sitara	hakkeñ sinakattara
	FORMAL	hakkeñ simasitara	hakkeñ simaseñ desitara
Alternative	**INFORMAL**	hakkeñ sitari	hakkeñ sinakattari
	FORMAL	hakkeñ simasitari	hakkeñ simaseñ desitari

		INFORMAL AFFIRMATIVE INDICATIVE
Passive		hakkeñ sareru
Potential		hakkeñ dekiru
Causative		hakkeñ saseru
Causative Pass.		hakkeñ saserareru
Honorific	**I**	
	II	hakkeñ nasaru
Humble	**I**	
	II	hakkeñ itasu

TRANSITIVE   *to put on or wear on the feet or legs* (as with shoes, trousers, etc.)

		AFFIRMATIVE	**NEGATIVE**
Indicative	**INFORMAL**	haku	hakanai
	FORMAL	hakimasu	hakimaseñ
Imperative	**INFORMAL I**	hake	haku na
	II	hakinasai	hakinasaru na
	III	haite kudasai	hakanai de kudasai
	FORMAL	ohaki nasaimase	ohaki nasimasu na
Presumptive	**INFORMAL I**	hakoo	hakumaı
	II	haku daroo	hakanai daroo
	FORMAL I	hakimasyoo	hakimasumai
	II	haku desyoo	hakanai desyoo
Provisional	**INFORMAL**	hakeba	hakanakereba
	FORMAL	hakimaseba	hakimaseñ nara
		hakimasureba	
Gerund	**INFORMAL I**	haite	hakanai de
	II		hakanakute
	FORMAL	hakimasite	hakimaseñ de
Past Ind.	**INFORMAL**	haita	hakanakatta
	FORMAL	hakimasita	hakimaseñ desita
Past Presump.	**INFORMAL**	haitaroo	hakanakattaroo
		haita daroo	hakanakatta daroo
	FORMAL	hakimasitaroo	hakimaseñ desitaroo
		haita desyoo	hakanakatta desyoo
Conditional	**INFORMAL**	haitara	hakanakattara
	FORMAL	hakimasitara	hakimaseñ desitara
Alternative	**INFORMAL**	haitari	hakanakattari
	FORMAL	hakimasitari	hakimaseñ desitari

		INFORMAL AFFIRMATIVE INDICATIVE
Passive		hakareru
Potential		hakeru
Causative		hakaseru
Causative Pass.		hakaserareru
Honorific	**I**	ohaki ni naru
	II	ohaki nasaru
Humble	**I**	
	II	

		AFFIRMATIVE	NEGATIVE
Indicative	**INFORMAL**	hanareru	hanarenai
	FORMAL	hanaremasu	hanaremaseñ
Imperative	**INFORMAL I**	hanarero	hanareru na
	II	hanarenasai	hanarenasaru na
	III	hanarete kudasai	hanarenai de kudasai
	FORMAL	ohanare nasaimase	ohanare nasaimasu na
Presumptive	**INFORMAL I**	hanareyoo	hanaremai
	II	hanareru daroo	hanarenai daroo
	FORMAL I	hanaremasyoo	hanaremasumai
	II	hanareru desyoo	hanarenai desyoo
Provisional	**INFORMAL**	hanarereba	hanarenakereba
	FORMAL	hanaremaseba	hanaremaseñ nara
		hanaremasureba	
Gerund	**INFORMAL I**	hanarete	hanarenai de
	II		hanarenakute
	FORMAL	hanaremasite	hanaremaseñ de
Past Ind.	**INFORMAL**	hanareta	hanarenakatta
	FORMAL	hanaremasita	hanaremaseñ desita
Past Presump.	**INFORMAL**	hanaretaroo	hanarenakattaroo
		hanareta daroo	hanarenakatta daroo
	FORMAL	hanaremasitaroo	hanaremaseñ desitaroo
		hanareta desyoo	hanarenakatta desyoo
Conditional	**INFORMAL**	hanaretara	hanarenakattara
	FORMAL	hanaremasitara	hanaremaseñ desitara
Alternative	**INFORMAL**	hanaretari	hanarenakattari
	FORMAL	hanaremasitari	hanaremaseñ desitari

INFORMAL AFFIRMATIVE INDICATIVE

Passive		hanarerareru
Potential		hanarerareru
Causative		hanaresaseru
Causative Pass.		hanaresaserareru

Honorific	**I**	ohanare ni naru
	II	ohanare nasaru
Humble	**I**	ohanare suru
	II	ohanare itasu

		AFFIRMATIVE	NEGATIVE
Indicative	INFORMAL	hanasu	hanasanai
	FORMAL	hanasimasu	hanasimaseñ
Imperative	INFORMAL I	hanase	hanasu na
	II	hanasinasai	hanasinasaru na
	III	hanasite kudasai	hanasanai de kudasai
	FORMAL	ohanasi nasaimase	ohanasi nasaimasu na
Presumptive	INFORMAL I	hanasoo	hanasumai
	II	hanasu daroo	hanasanai daroo
	FORMAL I	hanasimasyoo	hanasimasumai
	II	hanasu desyoo	hanasanai desyoo
Provisional	INFORMAL	hanaseba	hanasanakereba
	FORMAL	hanasimaseba	hanasimaseñ nara
		hanasimasureba	
Gerund	INFORMAL I	hanasite	hanasanai de
	II		hanasanakute
	FORMAL	hanasimasite	hanasimaseñ de
Past Ind.	INFORMAL	hanasita	hanasanakatta
	FORMAL	hanasimasita	hanasimaseñ desita
Past Presump.	INFORMAL	hanasitaroo	hanasanakattaroo
		hanasita daroo	hanasanakatta daroo
	FORMAL	hanasimasitaroo	hanasimaseñ desitaroo
		hanasita desyoo	hanasanakatta desyoo
Conditional	INFORMAL	hanasitara	hanasanakattara
	FORMAL	hanasimasitara	hanasimaseñ desitara
Alternative	INFORMAL	hanasitari	hanasanakattari
	FORMAL	hanasimasitari	hanasimaseñ desitari

		INFORMAL AFFIRMATIVE INDICATIVE
Passive		hanasareru
Potential		hanaseru
Causative		hanasaseru
Causative Pass.		hanasaserareru
Honorific	I	ohanasi ni naru
	II	ohanasi nasaru
Humble	I	ohanasi suru
	II	ohanasi itasu

		AFFIRMATIVE	NEGATIVE
Indicative	**INFORMAL**	hanasu	hanasanai
	FORMAL	hanasimasu	hanasimaseñ
Imperative	**INFORMAL I**	hanase	hanasu na
	II	hanasinasai	hanasinasaru na
	III	hanasite kudasai	hanasanai de kudasai
	FORMAL	ohanasi nasaimase	ohanasi nasaimasu na
Presumptive	**INFORMAL I**	hanasoo	hanasumai
	II	hanasu daroo	hanasanai daroo
	FORMAL I	hanasimasyoo	hanasimasumai
	II	hanasu desyoo	hanasanai desyoo
Provisional	**INFORMAL**	hanaseba	hanasanakereba
	FORMAL	hanasimaseba	hanasimaseñ nara
		hanasimasureba	
Gerund	**INFORMAL I**	hanasite	hanasanai de
	II		hanasanakute
	FORMAL	hanasimasite	hanasimaseñ de
Past Ind.	**INFORMAL**	hanasita	hanasanakatta
	FORMAL	hanasimasita	hanasimaseñ desita
Past Presump.	**INFORMAL**	hanasitaroo	hanasanakattaroo
		hanasita daroo	hanasanakatta daroo
	FORMAL	hanasimasitaroo	hanasimaseñ desitaroo
		hanasita desyoo	hanasanakatta desyoo
Conditional	**INFORMAL**	hanasitara	hanasanakattara
	FORMAL	hanasimasitara	hanasimaseñ desitara
Alternative	**INFORMAL**	hanasitari	hanasanakattari
	FORMAL	hanasimasitari	hanasimaseñ desitari

INFORMAL AFFIRMATIVE INDICATIVE

Passive		hanasareru
Potential		hanaseru
Causative		hanasaseru
Causative Pass.		hanasaserareru

Honorific	**I**	ohanasi ni naru
	II	ohanasi nasaru
Humble	**I**	ohanasi suru
	II	ohanasi itasu

		AFFIRMATIVE	NEGATIVE
Indicative	**INFORMAL**	haneru	hanenai
	FORMAL	hanemasu	hanemaseñ
Imperative	**INFORMAL I**	hanero	haneru na
	II	hanenasai	hanenasaru na
	III	hanete kudasai	hanenai de kudasai
	FORMAL	ohane nasaimase	ohane nasaimasu na
Presumptive	**INFORMAL I**	haneyoo	hanemai
	II	haneru daroo	hanenai daroo
	FORMAL I	hanemasyoo	hanemasumai
	II	haneru desyoo	hanenai desyoo
Provisional	**INFORMAL**	hanereba	hanenakereba
	FORMAL	hanemaseba	hanemaseñ nara
		hanemasureba	
Gerund	**INFORMAL I**	hanete	hanenai de
	II		hanenakute
	FORMAL	hanemasite	hanemaseñ de
Past Ind.	**INFORMAL**	haneta	hanenakatta
	FORMAL	hanemasita	hanemaseñ desita
Past Presump.	**INFORMAL**	hanetaroo	hanenakattaroo
		haneta daroo	hanenakatta daroo
	FORMAL	hanemasitaroo	hanemaseñ desitaroo
		haneta desyoo	hanenakatta desyoo
Conditional	**INFORMAL**	hanetara	hanenakattara
	FORMAL	hanemasitara	hanemaseñ desitara
Alternative	**INFORMAL**	hanetari	hanenakattari
	FORMAL	hanemasitari	hanemaseñ desitari

INFORMAL AFFIRMATIVE INDICATIVE

Passive		hanerareru
Potential		hanerareru
Causative		hanesaseru
Causative Pass.		hanesaserareru

Honorific	**I**	ohane ni naru
	II	ohane nasaru
Humble	**I**	
	II	

			AFFIRMATIVE	NEGATIVE
Indicative	**INFORMAL**		hañtai suru	hañtai sinai
	FORMAL		hañtai simasu	hañtai simaseñ
Imperative	**INFORMAL**	**I**	hañtai siro	hañtai suru na
		II	hañtai sinasai	hañtai sinasaru na
		III	hañtai site kudasai	hañtai sinai de kudasai
	FORMAL			
Presumptive	**INFORMAL**	**I**	hañtai siyoo	hañtai surumai
		II	hañtai suru daroo	hañtai sinai daroo
	FORMAL	**I**	hañtai simasyoo	hañtai simasumai
		II	hañtai suru desyoo	hañtai sinai desyoo
Provisional	**INFORMAL**		hañtai sureba	hañtai sinakereba
	FORMAL		hañtai simaseba	hañtai simaseñ nara
			hañtai simasureba	
Gerund	**INFORMAL**	**I**	hañtai site	hañtai sinai de
		II		hañtai sinakute
	FORMAL		hañtai simasite	hañtai simaseñ de
Past Ind.	**INFORMAL**		hañtai sita	hañtai sinakatta
	FORMAL		hañtai simasita	hañtai simaseñ desita
Past Presump.	**INFORMAL**		hañtai sitaroo	hañtai sinakattaroo
			hañtai sita daroo	hañtai sinakatta daroo
	FORMAL		hañtai simasitaroo	hañtai simaseñ desitaroo
			hañtai sita desyoo	hañtai sinakatta desyoo
Conditional	**INFORMAL**		hañtai sitara	hañtai sinakattara
	FORMAL		hañtai simasitara	hañtai simaseñ desitara
Alternative	**INFORMAL**		hañtai sitari	hañtai sinakattari
	FORMAL		hañtai simasitari	hañtai simaseñ desitari

		INFORMAL AFFIRMATIVE INDICATIVE
Passive		hañtai sareru
Potential		hañtai dekiru
Causative		hañtai saseru
Causative Pass.		hañtai saserareru
Honorific	**I**	
	II	hañtai nasaru
Humble	**I**	
	II	hañtai itasu

		AFFIRMATIVE	NEGATIVE
Indicative	**INFORMAL**	harau	harawanai
	FORMAL	haraimasu	haraimaseñ
Imperative	**INFORMAL I**	harae	harau na
	II	harainasai	harainasaru na
	III	haratte kudasai	harawanai de kudasai
	FORMAL	oharai nasaimase	oharai nasaimasu na
Presumptive	**INFORMAL I**	haraoo	haraumai
	II	harau daroo	harawanai daroo
	FORMAL I	haraimasyoo	haraimasumai
	II	harau desyoo	harawanai desyoo
Provisional	**INFORMAL**	haraeba	harawanakereba
	FORMAL	haraimaseba	haraimaseñ nara
		haraimasureba	
Gerund	**INFORMAL I**	haratte	harawanai de
	II		harawanakute
	FORMAL	haraimasite	haraimaseñ de
Past Ind.	**INFORMAL**	haratta	harawanakatta
	FORMAL	haraimasita	haraimaseñ desita
Past Presump.	**INFORMAL**	harattaroo	harawanakattaroo
		haratta daroo	harawanakatta daroo
	FORMAL	haraimasitaroo	haraimaseñ desitaroo
		haratta desyoo	harawanakatta desyoo
Conditional	**INFORMAL**	harattara	harawanakattara
	FORMAL	haraimasitara	haraimaseñ desitara
Alternative	**INFORMAL**	harattari	harawanakattari
	FORMAL	haraimasitari	haraimaseñ desitari

INFORMAL AFFIRMATIVE INDICATIVE

Passive		harawareru
Potential		haraeru
Causative		harawaseru
Causative Pass.		harawaserareru
Honorific	**I**	oharai ni naru
	II	oharai nasaru
Humble	**I**	oharai suru
	II	oharai itasu

			AFFIRMATIVE	NEGATIVE
Indicative	**INFORMAL**		hareru	harenai
	FORMAL		haremasu	haremaseñ
Imperative	**INFORMAL I**		harero	hareru na
	II		harenasai	harenasaru na
	III			
	FORMAL			
Presumptive	**INFORMAL I**		hareyoo	haremai
	II		hareru daroo	harenai daroo
	FORMAL I		haremasyoo	haremasumai
	II		hareru desyoo	harenai desyoo
Provisional	**INFORMAL**		harereba	harenakereba
	FORMAL		haremaseba	haremaseñ nara
			haremasureba	
Gerund	**INFORMAL I**		harete	harenai de
	II			harenakute
	FORMAL		haremasite	haremaseñ de
Past Ind.	**INFORMAL**		hareta	harenakatta
	FORMAL		haremasita	haremaseñ desita
Past Presump.	**INFORMAL**		haretaroo	harenakattaroo
			hareta daroo	harenakatta daroo
	FORMAL		haremasitaroo	haremaseñ desitaroo
			hareta desyoo	harenakatta desyoo
Conditional	**INFORMAL**		haretara	harenakattara
	FORMAL		haremasitara	haremaseñ desitara
Alternative	**INFORMAL**		haretari	harenakattari
	FORMAL		haremasitari	haremaseñ desitari

INFORMAL AFFIRMATIVE INDICATIVE

Passive		
Potential		harerareru
Causative		haresaseru
Causative Pass.		
Honorific	**I**	
	II	
Humble	**I**	
	II	

TRANSITIVE   *to catch or hold between two things*

		AFFIRMATIVE	NEGATIVE
Indicative	**INFORMAL**	hasamu	hasamanai
	FORMAL	hasamimasu	hasamimaseñ
Imperative	**INFORMAL I**	hasame	hasamu na
	II	hasaminasai	hasaminasaru na
	III	hasañde kudasai	hasamanai de kudasai
	FORMAL	ohasami nasaimase	ohasami nasaimasu na
Presumptive	**INFORMAL I**	hasamoo	hasamumai
	II	hasamu daroo	hasamanai daroo
	FORMAL I	hasamimasyoo	hasamimasumai
	II	hasamu desyoo	hasamanai desyoo
Provisional	**INFORMAL**	hasameba	hasamanakereba
	FORMAL	hasamimaseba	hasamimaseñ nara
		hasamimasureba	
Gerund	**INFORMAL I**	hasañde	hasamanai de
	II		hasamanakute
	FORMAL	hasamimasite	hasamimaseñ de
Past Ind.	**INFORMAL**	hasañda	hasamanakatta
	FORMAL	hasamimasita	hasamimaseñ desita
Past Presump.	**INFORMAL**	hasañdaroo	hasamanakattaroo
		hasañda daroo	hasamanakatta daroo
	FORMAL	hasamimasitaroo	hasamimaseñ desitaroo
		hasañda desyoo	hasamanakatta desyoo
Conditional	**INFORMAL**	hasañdara	hasamanakattara
	FORMAL	hasamimasitara	hasamimaseñ desitara
Alternative	**INFORMAL**	hasañdari	hasamanakattari
	FORMAL	hasamimasitari	hasamimaseñ desitari

	INFORMAL AFFIRMATIVE INDICATIVE
Passive	hasamareru
Potential	hasameru
Causative	hasamaseru
Causative Pass.	hasamaserareru

Honorific	**I**	ohasami ni naru
	II	ohasami nasaru
Humble	**I**	ohasami suru
	II	ohasami itasu

		AFFIRMATIVE	NEGATIVE
Indicative	INFORMAL	hasiru	hasiranai
	FORMAL	hasirimasu	hasirimaseñ
Imperative	INFORMAL I	hasire	hasiru na
	II	hasirinasai	hasirinasaru na
	III	hasitte kudasai	hasiranai de kudasai
	FORMAL	ohasiri nasaimase	ohasiri nasaimasu na
Presumptive	INFORMAL I	hasiroo	hasirumai
	II	hasiru daroo	hasiranai daroo
	FORMAL I	hasirimasyoo	hasirimasumai
	II	hasiru desyoo	hasiranai desyoo
Provisional	INFORMAL	hasireba	hasiranakereba
	FORMAL	hasirimaseba	hasirimaseñ nara
		hasirimasureba	
Gerund	INFORMAL I	hasitte	hasiranai de
	II		hasiranakute
	FORMAL	hasirimasite	hasirimaseñ de
Past Ind.	INFORMAL	hasitta	hasiranakatta
	FORMAL	hasirimasita	hasirimaseñ desita
Past Presump.	INFORMAL	hasittaroo	hasiranakattaroo
		hasitta daroo	hasiranakatta daroo
	FORMAL	hasirimasitaroo	hasirimaseñ desitaroo
		hasitta desyoo	hasiranakatta desyoo
Conditional	INFORMAL	hasittara	hasiranakattara
	FORMAL	hasirimasitara	hasirimaseñ desitara
Alternative	INFORMAL	hasittari	hasiranakattari
	FORMAL	hasirimasitari	hasirimaseñ desitari

INFORMAL AFFIRMATIVE INDICATIVE

Passive		hasirareru
Potential		hasireru
Causative		hasiraseru
Causative Pass.		hasiraserareru

Honorific	I	ohasiri ni naru
	II	ohasiri nasaru
Humble	I	ohasiri suru
	II	ohasiri itasu

		AFFIRMATIVE	NEGATIVE
Indicative	INFORMAL	hataraku	hatarakanai
	FORMAL	hatarakimasu	hatarakimaseñ
Imperative	INFORMAL I	hatarake	hataraku na
	II	hatarakinasai	hatarakinasaru na
	III	hataraite kudasai	hatarakanai de kudasai
	FORMAL	ohataraki nasaimase	ohataraki nasaimasu na
Presumptive	INFORMAL I	hatarakoo	hatarakumai
	II	hataraku daroo	hatarakanai daroo
	FORMAL I	hatarakimasyoo	hatarakimasumai
	II	hataraku desyoo	hatarakanai desyoo
Provisional	INFORMAL	hatarakeba	hatarakanakereba
	FORMAL	hatarakimaseba	hatarakimaseñ nara
		hatarakimasureba	
Gerund	INFORMAL I	hataraite	hatarakanai de
	II		hatarakanakute
	FORMAL	hatarakimasite	hatarakimaseñ de
Past Ind.	INFORMAL	hataraita	hatarakanakatta
	FORMAL	hatarakimasita	hatarakimaseñ desita
Past Presump.	INFORMAL	hataraitaroo	hatarakanakattaroo
		hataraita daroo	hatarakanakatta daroo
	FORMAL	hatarakimasitaroo	hatarakimaseñ desitaroo
		hataraita desyoo	hatarakanakatta desyoo
Conditional	INFORMAL	hataraitara	hatarakanakattara
	FORMAL	hatarakimasitara	hatarakimaseñ desitara
Alternative	INFORMAL	hataraitari	hatarakanakattari
	FORMAL	hatarakimasitari	hatarakimaseñ desitari

INFORMAL AFFIRMATIVE INDICATIVE

Passive		
Potential		hatarakeru
Causative		hatarakaseru
Causative Pass.		hatarakaserareru
Honorific	I	ohataraki ni naru
	II	ohataraki nasaru
Humble	I	
	II	

		AFFIRMATIVE	NEGATIVE
Indicative	**INFORMAL**	hatumei suru	hatumei sinai
	FORMAL	hatumei simasu	hatumei simaseñ
Imperative	**INFORMAL I**	hatumei siro	hatumei suru na
	II	hatumei sinasai	hatumei sinasaru na
	III	hatumei site kudasai	hatumei sinai de kudasai
	FORMAL		
Presumptive	**INFORMAL I**	hatumei siyoo	hatumei surumai
	II	hatumei suru daroo	hatumei sinai daroo
	FORMAL I	hatumei simasyoo	hatumei simasumai
	II	hatumei suru desyoo	hatumei sinai desyoo
Provisional	**INFORMAL**	hatumei sureba	hatumei sinakereba
	FORMAL	hatumei simaseba	hatumei simaseñ nara
		hatumei simasureba	
Gerund	**INFORMAL I**	hatumei site	hatumei sinai de
	II		hatumei sinakute
	FORMAL	hatumei simasite	hatumei simaseñ de
Past Ind.	**INFORMAL**	hatumei sita	hatumei sinakatta
	FORMAL	hatumei simasita	hatumei simaseñ desita
Past Presump.	**INFORMAL**	hatumei sitaroo	hatumei sinakattaroo
		hatumei sita daroo	hatumei sinakatta daroo
	FORMAL	hatumei simasitaroo	hatumei simaseñ desitaroo
		hatumei sita desyoo	hatumei sinakatta desyoo
Conditional	**INFORMAL**	hatumei sitara	hatumei sinakattara
	FORMAL	hatumei simasitara	hatumei simaseñ desitara
Alternative	**INFORMAL**	hatumei sitari	hatumei sinakattari
	FORMAL	hatumei simasitari	hatumei simaseñ desitari

	INFORMAL AFFIRMATIVE INDICATIVE
Passive	hatumei sareru
Potential	hatumei dekiru
Causative	hatumei saseru
Causative Pass.	hatumei saserareru

Honorific	**I**	
	II	hatumei nasaru
Humble	**I**	
	II	hatumei itasu

		AFFIRMATIVE	NEGATIVE
Indicative	**INFORMAL**	hayaru	hayaranai
	FORMAL	hayarimasu	hayarimaseñ
Imperative	**INFORMAL I**	hayare	hayaru na
	II		
	III		
	FORMAL		
Presumptive	**INFORMAL I**	hayaroo	hayarumai
	II	hayaru daroo	hayaranai daroo
	FORMAL I	hayarimasyoo	hayarimasumai
	II	hayaru desyoo	hayaranai desyoo
Provisional	**INFORMAL**	hayareba	hayaranakereba
	FORMAL	hayarimaseba	hayarimaseñ nara
		hayarimasureba	
Gerund	**INFORMAL I**	hayatte	hayaranai de
	II		hayaranakute
	FORMAL	hayarimasite	hayarimaseñ de
Past Ind.	**INFORMAL**	hayatta	hayaranakatta
	FORMAL	hayarimasita	hayarimaseñ desita
Past Presump.	**INFORMAL**	hayattaroo	hayaranakattaroo
		hayatta daroo	hayaranakatta daroo
	FORMAL	hayarimasitaroo	hayarimaseñ desitaroo
		hayatta desyoo	hayaranakatta desyoo
Conditional	**INFORMAL**	hayattara	hayaranakattara
	FORMAL	hayarimasitara	hayarimaseñ desitara
Alternative	**INFORMAL**	hayattari	hayaranakattari
	FORMAL	hayarimasitari	hayarimaseñ desitari

INFORMAL AFFIRMATIVE INDICATIVE

Passive		
Potential		
Causative		hayaraseru
Causative Pass.		hayaraserareru
Honorific	**I**	
	II	
Humble	**I**	
	II	

		AFFIRMATIVE	NEGATIVE
Indicative	**INFORMAL**	hazimaru	hazimaranai
	FORMAL	hazimarimasu	hazimarimaseñ
Imperative	**INFORMAL I**	hazimare	hazimaru na
	II		
	III		
	FORMAL		
Presumptive	**INFORMAL I**	hazimaroo	hazimarumai
	II	hazimaru daroo	hazimaranai daroo
	FORMAL I	hazimarimasyoo	hazimarimasumai
	II	hazimaru desyoo	hazimaranai desyoo
Provisional	**INFORMAL**	hazimareba	hazimaranakereba
	FORMAL	hazimarimaseba	hazimarimaseñ nara
		hazimarimasureba	
Gerund	**INFORMAL I**	hazimatte	hazimaranai de
	II		hazimaranakute
	FORMAL	hazimarimasite	hazimarimaseñ de
Past Ind.	**INFORMAL**	hazimatta	hazimaranakatta
	FORMAL	hazimarimasita	hazimarimaseñ desita
Past Presump.	**INFORMAL**	hazimattaroo	hazimaranakattaroo
		hazimatta daroo	hazimaranakatta daroo
	FORMAL	hazimarimasitaroo	hazimarimaseñ desitaroo
		hazimatta desyoo	hazimaranakatta desyoo
Conditional	**INFORMAL**	hazimattara	hazimaranakattara
	FORMAL	hazimarimasitara	hazimarimaseñ desitara
Alternative	**INFORMAL**	hazimattari	hazimaranakattari
	FORMAL	hazimarimasitari	hazimarimaseñ desitari

INFORMAL AFFIRMATIVE INDICATIVE

Passive		
Potential		
Causative	hazimaraseru	
Causative Pass.		
Honorific	**I**	
	II	
Humble	**I**	
	II	

		AFFIRMATIVE	**NEGATIVE**
Indicative	**INFORMAL**	hazimeru	hazimenai
	FORMAL	hazimemasu	hazimemaseñ
Imperative	**INFORMAL I**	hazimero	hazimeru na
	II	hazimenasai	hazimenasaru na
	III	hazimete kudasai	hazimenai de kudasai
	FORMAL	ohazime nasaimase	ohazime nasaimasu na
Presumptive	**INFORMAL I**	hazimeyoo	hazimemai
	II	hazimeru daroo	hazimenai daroo
	FORMAL I	hazimemasyoo	hazimemasumai
	II	hazimeru desyoo	hazimenai desyoo
Provisional	**INFORMAL**	hazimereba	hazimenakereba
	FORMAL	hazimemaseba	hazimemaseñ nara
		hazimemasureba	
Gerund	**INFORMAL I**	hazimete	hazimenai de
	II		hazimenakute
	FORMAL	hazimemasite	hazimemaseñ de
Past Ind.	**INFORMAL**	hazimeta	hazimenakatta
	FORMAL	hazimemasita	hazimemaseñ desita
Past Presump.	**INFORMAL**	hazimetaroo	hazimenakattaroo
		hazimeta daroo	hazimenakatta daroo
	FORMAL	hazimemasitaroo	hazimemaseñ desitaroo
		hazimeta desyoo	hazimenakatta desyoo
Conditional	**INFORMAL**	hazimetara	hazimenakattara
	FORMAL	hazimemasitara	hazimemaseñ desitara
Alternative	**INFORMAL**	hazimetari	hazimenakattari
	FORMAL	hazimemasitari	hazimemaseñ desitari

INFORMAL AFFIRMATIVE INDICATIVE

Passive		hazimerareru
Potential		hazimerareru
Causative		hazimesaseru
Causative Pass.		hazimesaserareru
Honorific	**I**	ohazime ni naru
	II	ohazime nasaru
Humble	**I**	
	II	

to become disconnected, to go wide of the mark   TRANSITIVE

		AFFIRMATIVE	NEGATIVE
Indicative	**INFORMAL**	hazureru	hazurenai
	FORMAL	hazuremasu	hazuremaseñ
Imperative	**INFORMAL I**	hazurero	hazureru na
	II	hazurenasai	hazurenasaru na
	III	hazurete kudasai	hazurenai de kudasai
	FORMAL	ohazure nasaimase	ohazure nasaimasu na
Presumptive	**INFORMAL I**	hazureyoo	hazuremai
	II	hazureru daroo	hazurenai daroo
	FORMAL I	hazuremasyoo	hazuremasumai
	II	hazureru desyoo	hazurenai desyoo
Provisional	**INFORMAL**	hazurereba	hazurenakereba
	FORMAL	hazuremaseba	hazuremaseñ nara
		hazuremasureba	
Gerund	**INFORMAL I**	hazurete	hazurenai de
	II		hazurenakute
	FORMAL	hazuremasite	hazuremaseñ de
Past Ind.	**INFORMAL**	hazureta	hazurenakatta
	FORMAL	hazuremasita	hazuremaseñ desita
Past Presump.	**INFORMAL**	hazuretaroo	hazurenakattaroo
		hazureta daroo	hazurenakatta daroo
	FORMAL	hazuremasitaroo	hazuremaseñ desitaroo
		hazureta desyoo	hazurenakatta desyoo
Conditional	**INFORMAL**	hazuretara	hazurenakattara
	FORMAL	hazuremasitara	hazuremaseñ desitara
Alternative	**INFORMAL**	hazuretari	hazurenakattari
	FORMAL	hazuremasitari	hazuremaseñ desitari

INFORMAL AFFIRMATIVE INDICATIVE

Passive	hazurerareru
Potential	hazurerareru
Causative	hazuresaseru
Causative Pass.	hazuresaserareru

Honorific	**I**	ohazure ni naru
	II	ohazure nasaru
Humble	**I**	
	II	

		AFFIRMATIVE	NEGATIVE
Indicative	**INFORMAL**	hazusu	hazusanai
	FORMAL	hazusimasu	hazusimaseñ
Imperative	**INFORMAL I**	hazuse	hazusu na
	II	hazusinasai	hazusinasaru na
	III	hazusite kudasai	hazusanai de kudasai
	FORMAL	ohazusi nasaimase	ohazusi nasaimasu na
Presumptive	**INFORMAL I**	hazusoo	hazusumai
	II	hazusu daroo	hazusanai daroo
	FORMAL I	hazusimasyoo	hazusimasumai
	II	hazusu desyoo	hazusanai desyoo
Provisional	**INFORMAL**	hazuseba	hazusanakereba
	FORMAL	hazusimaseba	hazusimaseñ nara
		hazusimasureba	
Gerund	**INFORMAL I**	hazusite	hazusanai de
	II		hazusanakute
	FORMAL	hazusimasite	hazusimaseñ de
Past Ind.	**INFORMAL**	hazusita	hazusanakatta
	FORMAL	hazusimasita	hazusimaseñ desita
Past Presump.	**INFORMAL**	hazusitaroo	hazusanakattaroo
		hazusita daroo	hazusanakatta daroo
	FORMAL	hazusimasitaroo	hazusimaseñ desitaroo
		hazusita desyoo	hazusanakatta desyoo
Conditional	**INFORMAL**	hazusitara	hazusanakattara
	FORMAL	hazusimasitara	hazusimaseñ desitara
Alternative	**INFORMAL**	hazusitari	hazusanakattari
	FORMAL	hazusimasitari	hazusimaseñ desitari

INFORMAL AFFIRMATIVE INDICATIVE

Passive	hazusareru
Potential	hazuseru
Causative	hazusaseru
Causative Pass.	hazusaserareru

Honorific	**I**	ohazusi ni naru
	II	ohazusi nasaru
Humble	**I**	ohazusi suru
	II	ohazusi itasu

			AFFIRMATIVE	NEGATIVE
Indicative	INFORMAL		heru	heranai
	FORMAL		herimasu	herimaseñ
Imperative	INFORMAL	I	here	heru na
		II	herinasai	herinasaru na
		III	hette kudasai	heranai de kudasai
	FORMAL		oheri nasaimase	oheri nasaimasu na
Presumptive	INFORMAL	I	heroo	herumai
		II	heru daroo	heranai daroo
	FORMAL	I	herimasyoo	herimasumai
		II	heru desyoo	heranai desyoo
Provisional	INFORMAL		hereba	heranakereba
	FORMAL		herimaseba	herimaseñ nara
			herimasureba	
Gerund	INFORMAL	I	hette	heranai de
		II		heranakute
	FORMAL		herimasite	herimaseñ de
Past Ind.	INFORMAL		hetta	heranakatta
	FORMAL		herimasita	herimaseñ desita
Past Presump.	INFORMAL		hettaroo	heranakattaroo
			hetta daroo	heranakatta daroo
	FORMAL		herimasitaroo	herimaseñ desitaroo
			hetta desyoo	heranakatta desyoo
Conditional	INFORMAL		hettara	heranakattara
	FORMAL		herimasitara	herimaseñ desitara
Alternative	INFORMAL		hettari	heranakattari
	FORMAL		herimasitari	herimaseñ desitari

		INFORMAL AFFIRMATIVE INDICATIVE
Passive		herareru
Potential		hereru
Causative		heraseru
Causative Pass.		heraserareru
Honorific	I	oheri ni naru
	II	oheri nasaru
Humble	I	
	II	

TRANSITIVE   *to pass through*

		AFFIRMATIVE	NEGATIVE
Indicative	**INFORMAL**	heru	henai
	FORMAL	hemasu	hemaseñ
Imperative	**INFORMAL I**	hero	heru na
	II	henasai	henasaru na
	III	hete kudasai	henai de kudasai
	FORMAL	ohe nasaimase	ohe nasaimasu na
Presumptive	**INFORMAL I**	heyoo	hemai
	II	heru daroo	henai daroo
	FORMAL I	hemasyoo	hemasumai
	II	heru desyoo	henai desyoo
Provisional	**INFORMAL**	hereba	henakereba
	FORMAL	hemaseba	hemaseñ nara
		hemasureba	
Gerund	**INFORMAL I**	hete	henai de
	II		henakute
	FORMAL	hemasite	hemaseñ de
Past Ind.	**INFORMAL**	heta	henakatta
	FORMAL	hemasita	hemaseñ desita
Past Presump.	**INFORMAL**	hetaroo	henakattaroo
		heta daroo	henakatta daroo
	FORMAL	hemasitaroo	hemaseñ desitaroo
		heta desyoo	henakatta desyoo
Conditional	**INFORMAL**	hetara	henakattara
	FORMAL	hemasitara	hemaseñ desitara
Alternative	**INFORMAL**	hetari	henakattari
	FORMAL	hemasitari	hemaseñ desitari

INFORMAL AFFIRMATIVE INDICATIVE

Passive		herareru
Potential		herareru
Causative		hesaseru
Causative Pass		hesaserareru
Honorific	**I**	ohe ni naru
	II	ohe nasaru
Humble	**I**	
	II	

		AFFIRMATIVE	NEGATIVE
Indicative	**INFORMAL**	heturau	heturawanai
	FORMAL	heturaimasu	heturaimaseñ
Imperative	**INFORMAL I**	heturae	heturau na
	II	heturainasai	heturainasaru na
	III	heturatte kudasai	heturawanai de kudasai
	FORMAL	oheturai nasaimase	oheturai nasaimasu na
Presumptive	**INFORMAL I**	heturaoo	heturaumai
	II	heturau daroo	heturawanai daroo
	FORMAL I	heturaimasyoo	heturaimasumai
	II	heturau desyoo	heturawanai desyoo
Provisional	**INFORMAL**	heturaeba	heturawanakereba
	FORMAL	heturaimaseba	heturaimaseñ nara
		heturaimasureba	
Gerund	**INFORMAL I**	heturatte	heturawanai de
	II		heturawanakute
	FORMAL	heturaimasite	heturaimaseñ de
Past Ind.	**INFORMAL**	heturatta	heturawanakatta
	FORMAL	heturaimasita	heturaimaseñ desita
Past Presump.	**INFORMAL**	heturattaroo	heturawanakattaroo
		heturatta daroo	heturawanakatta daroo
	FORMAL	heturaimasitaroo	heturaimaseñ desitaroo
		heturatta desyoo	heturawanakatta desyoo
Conditional	**INFORMAL**	heturattara	heturawanakattara
	FORMAL	heturaimasitara	heturaimaseñ desitara
Alternative	**INFORMAL**	heturattari	heturawanakattari
	FORMAL	heturaimasitari	heturaimaseñ desitari

	INFORMAL AFFIRMATIVE INDICATIVE
Passive	heturawareru
Potential	heturaeru
Causative	heturawaseru
Causative Pass.	heturawaserareru

Honorific	**I**	oheturai ni naru
	II	oheturai nasaru
Humble	**I**	oheturai suru
	II	oheturai itasu

		AFFIRMATIVE	NEGATIVE
Indicative	**INFORMAL**	hikaru	hikaranai
	FORMAL	hikarimasu	hikarimaseñ
Imperative	**INFORMAL I**	hikare	hikaru na
	II	hikarinasai	hikarinasaru na
	III	hikatte kudasai	hikaranai de kudasai
	FORMAL	ohikari nasaimase	ohikari nasaimasu na
Presumptive	**INFORMAI I**	hikaroo	hikarumai
	II	hikaru daroo	hikaranai daroo
	FORMAL I	hikarimasyoo	hikarimasumai
	II	hikaru desyoo	hikaranai desyoo
Provisional	**INFORMAL**	hikareba	hikaranakereba
	FORMAL	hikarimaseba	hikarimaseñ nara
		hikarimasureba	
Gerund	**INFORMAL I**	hikatte	hikaranai de
	II		hikaranakute
	FORMAL	hikarimasite	hikarimaseñ de
Past Ind.	**INFORMAL**	hikatta	hikaranakatta
	FORMAL	hikarimasita	hikarimaseñ desita
Past Presump.	**INFORMAL**	hikattaroo	hikaranakattaroo
		hikatta daroo	hikaranakatta daroo
	FORMAL	hikarimasitaroo	hikarimaseñ desitaroo
		hikatta desyoo	hikaranakatta desyoo
Conditional	**INFORMAL**	hikattara	hikaranakattara
	FORMAL	hikarimasitara	hikarimaseñ desitara
Alternative	**INFORMAL**	hikattari	hikaranakattari
	FORMAL	hikarimasitari	hikarimaseñ desitari

		INFORMAL AFFIRMATIVE INDICATIVE
Passive		hikarareru
Potential		hikareru
Causative		hikaraseru
Causative Pass.		hikaraserareru
Honorific	**I**	ohikari ni naru
	II	ohikari nasaru
Humble	**I**	
	II	

77

		AFFIRMATIVE	NEGATIVE
Indicative	**INFORMAL**	hikiukeru	hikiukenai
	FORMAL	hikiukemasu	hikiukemaseñ
Imperative	**INFORMAL I**	hikiukero	hikiukeru na
	II	hikiukenasai	hikiukenasaru na
	III	hikiukete kudasai	hikiukenai de kudasai
	FORMAL	ohikiuke nasaimase	ohikiuke nasaimasu na
Presumptive	**INFORMAL I**	hikiukeyoo	hikiukemai
	II	hikiukeru daroo	hikiukenai daroo
	FORMAL I	hikiukemasyoo	hikiukemasumai
	II	hikiukeru desyoo	hikiukenai desyoo
Provisional	**INFORMAL**	hikiukereba	hikiukenakereba
	FORMAL	hikiukemaseba	hikiukemaseñ nara
		hikiukemasureba	
Gerund	**INFORMAL I**	hikiukete	hikiukenai de
	II		hikiukenakute
	FORMAL	hikiukemasite	hikiukemaseñ de
Past Ind.	**INFORMAL**	hikiuketa	hikiukenakatta
	FORMAL	hikiukemasita	hikiukemaseñ desita
Past Presump.	**INFORMAL**	hikiuketaroo	hikiukenakattaroo
		hikiuketa daroo	hikiukenakatta daroo
	FORMAL	hikiukemasitaroo	hikiukemaseñ desitaroo
		hikiuketa desyoo	hikiukenakatta desyoo
Conditional	**INFORMAL**	hikiuketara	hikiukenakattara
	FORMAL	hikiukemasitara	hikiukemaseñ desitara
Alternative	**INFORMAL**	hikiuketari	hikiukenakattari
	FORMAL	hikiukemasitari	hikiukemaseñ desitari

INFORMAL AFFIRMATIVE INDICATIVE

Passive		hikiukerareru
Potential		hikiukerareru
Causative		hikiukesaseru
Causative Pass.		hikiukesaserareru

Honorific	**I**	ohikiuke ni naru
	II	ohikiuke nasaru
Humble	**I**	ohikiuke suru
	II	ohikiuke itasu

		AFFIRMATIVE	NEGATIVE
Indicative	**INFORMAL**	hiku	hikanai
	FORMAL	hikimasu	hikimaseñ
Imperative	**INFORMAL I**	hike	hiku na
	II	hikinasai	hikinasaru na
	III	hiite kudasai	hikanai de kudasai
	FORMAL	ohiki nasaimase	ohiki nasaimasu na
Presumptive	**INFORMAL I**	hikoo	hikumai
	II	hiku daroo	hikanai daroo
	FORMAL I	hikimasyoo	hikimasumai
	II	hiku desyoo	hikanai desyoo
Provisional	**INFORMAL**	hikeba	hikanakereḇa
	FORMAL	hikimaseba	hikimaseñ nara
		hikimasureba	
Gerund	**INFORMAL I**	hiite	hikanai de
	II		hikanakute
	FORMAL	hikimasite	hikimaseñ de
Past Ind.	**INFORMAL**	hiita	hikanakatta
	FORMAL	hikimasita	hikimaseñ desita
Past Presump.	**INFORMAL**	hiitaroo	hikanakattaroo
		hiita daroo	hikanakatta daroo
	FORMAL	hikimasitaroo	hikimaseñ desitaroo
		hiita desyoo	hikanakatta desyoo
Conditional	**INFORMAL**	hittara	hikanakattara
	FORMAL	hikimasitara	hikimaseñ desitara
Alternative	**INFORMAL**	hiitari	hikanakattari
	FORMAL	hikimasitari	hikimaseñ desitari

INFORMAL AFFIRMATIVE INDICATIVE

Passive		hikareru
Potential		hikeru
Causative		hikaseru
Causative Pass.		hikaserareru

Honorific	**I**	ohiki ni naru
	II	ohiki nasaru
Humble	**I**	ohiki suru
	II	ohiki itasu

		AFFIRMATIVE	NEGATIVE
Indicative	**INFORMAL**	hineru	hineranai
	FORMAL	hinerimasu	hinerimaseñ
Imperative	**INFORMAL I**	hinere	hineru na
	II	hinerinasai	hinerinasaru na
	III	hinette kudasai	hineranai de kudasai
	FORMAL	ohineri nasaimase	ohineri nasaimasu na
Presumptive	**INFORMAL I**	hineroo	hinerumai
	II	hineru daroo	hineranai daroo
	FORMAL I	hinerimasyoo	hinerimasumai
	II	hineru desyoo	hineranai desyoo
Provisional	**INFORMAL**	hinereba	hineranakereba
	FORMAL	hinerimaseba	hinerimaseñ nara
		hinerimasureba	
Gerund	**INFORMAL I**	hinette	hineranai de
	II		hineranakute
	FORMAL	hinerimasite	hinerimaseñ de
Past Ind.	**INFORMAL**	hinetta	hineranakatta
	FORMAL	hinerimasita	hinerimaseñ desita
Past Presump.	**INFORMAL**	hinettaroo	hineranakattaroo
		hinetta daroo	hineranakatta daroo
	FORMAL	hinerimasitaroo	hinerimaseñ desitaroo
		hinetta desyoo	hineranakatta desyoo
Conditional	**INFORMAL**	hinettara	hineranakattara
	FORMAL	hinerimasitara	hinerimaseñ desitara
Alternative	**INFORMAL**	hinettari	hineranakattari
	FORMAL	hinerimasitari	hinerimaseñ desitari

	INFORMAL AFFIRMATIVE INDICATIVE
Passive	hinerareru
Potential	hinereru
Causative	hineraseru
Causative Pass.	hineraserareru

Honorific	**I**	ohineri ni naru
	II	ohineri nasaru
Humble	**I**	ohineri suru
	II	ohineri itasu

		AFFIRMATIVE	NEGATIVE
Indicative	INFORMAL	hiraku	hirakanai
	FORMAL	hirakimasu	hirakimaseñ
Imperative	INFORMAL I	hirake	hiraku na
	II	hirakinasai	hirakinasaru na
	III	hiraite kudasai	hirakanai de kudasai
	FORMAL	ohiraki nasaimase	ohiraki nasaimasu na
Presumptive	INFORMAL I	hirakoo	hirakumai
	II	hiraku daroo	hirakanai daroo
	FORMAL I	hirakimasyoo	hirakimasumai
	II	hiraku desyoo	hirakanai desyoo
Provisional	INFORMAL	hirakeba	hirakanakereba
	FORMAL	hirakimaseba	hirakimaseñ nara
		hirakimasureba	
Gerund	INFORMAL I	hiraite	hirakanai de
	II		hirakanakute
	FORMAL	hirakimasite	hirakimaseñ de
Past Ind.	INFORMAL	hiraita	hirakanakatta
	FORMAL	hirakimasita	hirakimaseñ desita
Past Presump.	INFORMAL	hiraitaroo	hirakanakattaroo
		hiraita daroo	hirakanakatta daroo
	FORMAL	hirakimasitaroo	hirakimaseñ desitaroo
		hiraita desyoo	hirakanakatta desyoo
Conditional	INFORMAL	hiraitara	hirakanakattara
	FORMAL	hirakimasitara	hirakimaseñ desitara
Alternative	INFORMAL	hiraitari	hirakanakattari
	FORMAL	hirakimasitari	hirakimaseñ desitari

INFORMAL AFFIRMATIVE INDICATIVE

Passive		hirakareru
Potential		hirakeru
Causative		hirakaseru
Causative Pass.		hirakaserareru
Honorific	I	ohiraki ni naru
	II	ohiraki nasaru
Humble	I	ohiraki suru
	II	ohiraki itasu

		AFFIRMATIVE	NEGATIVE
Indicative	**INFORMAL**	hiromaru	hiromaranai
	FORMAL	hiromarimasu	hiromarimaseñ
Imperative	**INFORMAL I**	hiromare	hiromaru na
	II	hiromarinasai	hiromarinasaru na
	III	hiromatte kudasai	hiromaranai de kudasai
	FORMAL	ohiromari nasaimase	ohiromari nasaimasu na
Presumptive	**INFORMAL I**	hiromaroo	hiromarumai
	II	hiromaru daroo	hiromaranai daroo
	FORMAL I	hiromarimasyoo	hiromarimasumai
	II	hiromaru desyoo	hiromaranai desyoo
Provisional	**INFORMAL**	hiromareba	hiromaranakereba
	FORMAL	hiromarimaseba	hiromarimaseñ nara
		hiromarimasureba	
Gerund	**INFORMAL I**	hiromatte	hiromaranai de
	II		hiromaranakute
	FORMAL	hiromarimasite	hiromarimaseñ de
Past Ind.	**INFORMAL**	hiromatta	hiromaranakatta
	FORMAL	hiromarimasita	hiromarimaseñ desita
Past Presump.	**INFORMAL**	hiromattaroo	hiromaranakattaroo
		hiromatta daroo	hiromaranakatta daroo
	FORMAL	hiromarimasitaroo	hiromarimaseñ desitaroo
		hiromatta desyoo	hiromaranakatta desyoo
Conditional	**INFORMAL**	hiromattara	hiromaranakattara
	FORMAL	hiromarimasitara	hiromarimaseñ desitara
Alternative	**INFORMAL**	hiromattari	hiromaranakattari
	FORMAL	hiromarimasitari	hiromarimaseñ desitari

INFORMAL AFFIRMATIVE INDICATIVE

Passive	hiromarareru
Potential	hiromareru
Causative	hiromaraseru
Causative Pass.	hiromaraserareru

Honorific	**I**	
	II	
Humble	**I**	
	II	

TRANSITIVE   *to spread, to make popular*

		AFFIRMATIVE	NEGATIVE
Indicative	**INFORMAL**	hiromeru	hiromenai
	FORMAL	hiromemasu	hiromemaseñ
Imperative	**INFORMAL I**	hiromero	hiromeru na
	II	hiromenasai	hiromenasaru na
	III	hiromete kudasai	hiromenai de kudasai
	FORMAL	ohirome nasaimase	ohirome nasaimasu na
Presumptive	**INFORMAL I**	hiromeyoo	hiromemai
	II	hiromeru daroo	hiromenai daroo
	FORMAL I	hiromemasyoo	hiromemasumai
	II	hiromeru desyoo	hiromenai desyoo
Provisional	**INFORMAL**	hiromereba	hiromenakereba
	FORMAL	hiromemaseba	hiromemaseñ nara
		hiromemasureba	
Gerund	**INFORMAL I**	hiromete	hiromenai de
	II		hiromenakute
	FORMAL	hiromemasite	hiromemaseñ de
Past Ind.	**INFORMAL**	hirometa	hiromenakatta
	FORMAL	hiromemasita	hiromemaseñ desita
Past Presump.	**INFORMAL**	hirometaroo	hiromenakattaroo
		hirometa daroo	hiromenakatta daroo
	FORMAL	hiromemasitaroo	hiromemaseñ desitaroo
		hirometa desyoo	hiromenakatta desyoo
Conditional	**INFORMAL**	hirometara	hiromenakattara
	FORMAL	hiromemasitara	hiromemaseñ desitara
Alternative	**INFORMAL**	hirometari	hiromenakattari
	FORMAL	hiromemasitari	hiromemaseñ desitari

		INFORMAL AFFIRMATIVE INDICATIVE
Passive		hiromerareru
Potential		hiromerareru
Causative		hiromesaseru
Causative Pass.		hiromesaserareru
Honorific	**I**	ohirome ni naru
	II	ohirome nasaru
Humble	**I**	ohirome suru
	II	ohirome itasu

to pick up (from ground etc.) *to find* (by accident)   TRANSITIVE

		AFFIRMATIVE	NEGATIVE
Indicative	**INFORMAL**	hirou	hirowanai
	FORMAL	hiroimasu	hiroimaseñ
Imperative	**INFORMAL I**	hiroe	hirou na
	II	hiroinasai	hiroinasaru na
	III	hirotte kudasai	hirowanai de kudasai
	FORMAL	ohiroi nasaimase	ohiroi nasaimasu na
Presumptive	**INFORMAL I**	hirooo	hiroumai
	II	hirou daroo	hirowanai daroo
	FORMAL I	hiroimasyoo	hiroimasumai
	II	hirou desyoo	hirowanai desyoo
Provisional	**INFORMAL**	hiroeba	hirowanakereba
	FORMAL	hiroimaseba	hiroimaseñ nara
		hiroimasureba	
Gerund	**INFORMAL I**	hirotte	hirowanai de
	II		hirowanakute
	FORMAL	hiroimasite	hiroimaseñ de
Past Ind.	**INFORMAL**	hirotta	hirowanakatta
	FORMAL	hiroimasita	hiroimaseñ desita
Past Presump.	**INFORMAL**	hirottaroo	hirowanakattaroo
		hirotta daroo	hirowanakatta daroo
	FORMAL	hiroimasitaroo	hiroimaseñ desitaroo
		hirotta desyoo	hirowanakatta desyoo
Conditional	**INFORMAL**	hirottara	hirowanakattara
	FORMAL	hiroimasitara	hiroimaseñ desitara
Alternative	**INFORMAL**	hirottari	hirowanakattari
	FORMAL	hiroimasitari	hiroimaseñ desitari

		INFORMAL AFFIRMATIVE INDICATIVE
Passive		hirowareru
Potential		hiroeru
Causative		hirowaseru
Causative Pass.		hirowaserareru
Honorific	**I**	ohiroi ni naru
	II	ohiroi nasaru
Humble	**I**	ohiroi suru
	II	ohiroi itasu

TRANSITIVE   *to conceal, to lower one's voice*

		AFFIRMATIVE	NEGATIVE
Indicative	**INFORMAL**	hisomeru	hisomenai
	FORMAL	hisomemasu	hisomemaseñ
Imperative	**INFORMAL I**	hisomero	hisomeru na
	II	hisomenasai	hisomenasaru na
	III	hisomete kudasai	hisomenai de kudasai
	FORMAL	ohisome nasaimase	ohisome nasaimasu na
Presumptive	**INFORMAL I**	hisomeyoo	hisomemai
	II	hisomeru daroo	hisomenai daroo
	FORMAL I	hisomemasyoo	hisomemasumai
	II	hisomeru desyoo	hisomenai desyoo
Provisional	**INFORMAL**	hisomereba	hisomenakereba
	FORMAL	hisomemaseba	hisomemaseñ nara
		hisomemasureba	
Gerund	**INFORMAL I**	hisomete	hisomenai de
	II		hisomenakute
	FORMAL	hisomemasite	hisomemaseñ de
Past Ind.	**INFORMAL**	hisometa	hisomenakatta
	FORMAL	hisomemasita	hisomemaseñ desita
Past Presump.	**INFORMAL**	hisometaroo	hisomenakattaroo
		hisometa daroo	hisomenakatta daroo
	FORMAL	hisomemasitaroo	hisomemaseñ desitaroo
		hisometa desyoo	hisomenakatta desyoo
Conditional	**INFORMAL**	hisometara	hisomenakattara
	FORMAL	hisomemasitara	hisomemaseñ desitara
Alternative	**INFORMAL**	hisometari	hisomenakattari
	FORMAL	hisomemasitari	hisomemaseñ desitari

		INFORMAL AFFIRMATIVE INDICATIVE
Passive		hisomerareru
Potential		hisomerareru
Causative		hisomesaseru
Causative Pass.		hisomesaserareru
Honorific	**I**	ohisome ni naru
	II	ohisome nasaru
Humble	**I**	ohisome suru
	II	ohisome itasu

		AFFIRMATIVE	NEGATIVE
Indicative	**INFORMAL**	hisomu	hisomanai
	FORMAL	hisomimasu	hisomimaseñ
Imperative	**INFORMAL I**	hisome	hisomu na
	II	hisominasai	hisominasaru na
	III	hisoñde kudasai	hisomanai de kudasai
	FORMAL	ohisomi nasaimase	ohisomi nasaimasu na
Presumptive	**INFORMAL I**	hisomoo	hisomumai
	II	hisomu daroo	hisomanai daroo
	FORMAL I	hisomimasyoo	hisomimasumai
	II	hisumu desyoo	hisomanai desyoo
Provisional	**INFORMAL**	hisomeba	hisomanakereba
	FORMAL	hisomimaseba	hisomimaseñ nara
		hisomimasureba	
Gerund	**INFORMAL I**	hisoñde	hisomanai de
	II		hisomanakute
	FORMAL	hisomimasite	hisomimaseñ de
Past Ind.	**INFORMAL**	hisoñda	hisomanakatta
	FORMAL	hisomimasita	hisomimaseñ desita
Past Presump.	**INFORMAL**	hisoñdaroo	hisomanakattaroo
		hisoñda daroo	hisomanakatta daroo
	FORMAL	hisomimasitaroo	hisomimaseñ desitaroo
		hisoñda desyoo	hisomanakatta desyoo
Conditional	**INFORMAL**	hisoñdara	hisomanakattara
	FORMAL	hisomimasitara	hisomimaseñ desitara
Alternative	**INFORMAL**	hisoñdari	hisomanakattari
	FORMAL	hisomimasitari	hisomimaseñ desitari

		INFORMAL AFFIRMATIVE INDICATIVE
Passive		hisomareru
Potential		hisomeru
Causative		hisomaseru
Causative Pass.		hisomaserareru

Honorific	**I**	ohisomi ni naru
	II	ohisomi nasaru
Humble	**I**	
	II	

TRANSITIVE   *to make fun of, to tease*

		AFFIRMATIVE	NEGATIVE
Indicative	INFORMAL	hiyakasu	hiyakasanai
	FORMAL	hiyakasimasu	hiyakasimaseñ
Imperative	INFORMAL I	hiyakase	hiyakasu na
	II	hiyakasinasai	hiyakasinasaru na
	III	hiyakasite kudasai	hiyakasanai de kudasai
	FORMAL	ohiyakasi nasaimase	ohiyakasi nasaimasu na
Presumptive	INFORMAL I	hiyakasoo	hiyakasumai
	II	hiyakasu daroo	hiyakasanai daroo
	FORMAL I	hiyakasimasyoo	hiyakasimasumai
	II	hiyakasu desyoo	hiyakasanai desyoo
Provisional	INFORMAL	hiyakaseba	hiyakasanakereba
	FORMAL	hiyakasimaseba	hiyakasimaseñ nara
		hiyakasimasureba	
Gerund	INFORMAL I	hiyakasite	hiyakasanai de
	II		hiyakasanakute
	FORMAL	hiyakasimasite	hiyakasimaseñ de
Past Ind.	INFORMAL	hiyakasita	hiyakasanakatta
	FORMAL	hiyakasimasita	hiyakasimaseñ desita
Past Presump.	INFORMAL	hiyakasitaroo	hiyakasanakattaroo
		hiyakasita daroo	hiyakasanakatta daroo
	FORMAL	hiyakasimasitaroo	hiyakasimaseñ desitaroo
		hiyakasita desyoo	hiyakasanakatta desyoo
Conditional	INFORMAL	hiyakasitara	hiyakasanakattara
	FORMAL	hiyakasimasitara	hiyakasimaseñ desitara
Alternative	INFORMAL	hiyakasitari	hiyakasanakattari
	FORMAL	hiyakasimasitari	hiyakasimaseñ desitari

INFORMAL AFFIRMATIVE INDICATIVE

Passive		hiyakasareru
Potential		hiyakaseru
Causative		hiyakasaseru
Causative Pass.		hiyakasaserareru
Honorific	I	ohiyakasi ni naru
	II	ohiyakasi nasaru
Humble	I	ohiyakasi suru
	II	ohiyakasi itasu

		AFFIRMATIVE	NEGATIVE
Indicative	**INFORMAL**	hiyasu	hiyasanai
	FORMAL	hiyasimasu	hiyasimaseñ
Imperative	**INFORMAL I**	hiyase	hiyasu na
	II	hiyasinasai	hiyasinasaru na
	III	hiyasite kudasai	hiyasanai de kudasai
	FORMAL	ohiyasi nasaimase	ohiyasi nasaimasu na
Presumptive	**INFORMAL I**	hiyasoo	hiyasumai
	II	hiyasu daroo	hiyasanai daroo
	FORMAL I	hiyasimasyoo	hiyasimasumai
	II	hiyasu desyoo	hiyasanai desyoo
Provisional	**INFORMAL**	hiyaseba	hiyasanakereba
	FORMAL	hiyasimaseba	hiyasimaseñ nara
		hiyasimasureba	
Gerund	**INFORMAL I**	hiyasite	hiyasanai de
	II		hiyasanakute
	FORMAL	hiyasimasite	hiyasimaseñ de
Past Ind.	**INFORMAL**	hiyasita	hiyasanakatta
	FORMAL	hiyasimasita	hiyasimaseñ desita
Past Presump.	**INFORMAL**	hiyasitaroo	hiyasanakattaroo
		hiyasita daroo	hiyasanakatta daroo
	FORMAL	hiyasimasitaroo	hiyasimaseñ desitaroo
		hiyasita desyoo	hiyasanakatta desyoo
Conditional	**INFORMAL**	hiyasitara	hiyasanakattara
	FORMAL	hiyasimasitara	hiyasimaseñ desitara
Alternative	**INFORMAL**	hiyasitari	hiyasanakattari
	FORMAL	hiyasimasitari	hiyasimaseñ desitari

		INFORMAL AFFIRMATIVE INDICATIVE
Passive		hiyasareru
Potential		hiyaseru
Causative		hiyasaseru
Causative Pass.		hiyasaserareru
Honorific	**I**	ohiyasi ni naru
	II	ohiyasi nasaru
Humble	**I**	ohiyasi suru
	II	ohiyasi itasu

		AFFIRMATIVE	NEGATIVE
Indicative	**INFORMAL**	hizamazuku	hizamazukanai
	FORMAL	hizamazukimasu	hizamazukimaseñ
Imperative	**INFORMAL I**	hizamazuke	hizamazuku na
	II	hizamazukinasai	hizamazukinasaru na
	III	hizamazuite kudasai	hizamazukanai de kudasai
	FORMAL	ohizamazuki nasaimase	ohizamazuki nasaimasu na
Presumptive	**INFORMAL I**	hizamazukoo	hizamazukumai
	II	hizamazuku daroo	hizamazukanai daroo
	FORMAL I	hizamazukimasyoo	hizamazukimasumai
	II	hizamazuku desyoo	hizamazukanai desyoo
Provisional	**INFORMAL**	hizamazukeba	hizamazukanakereba
	FORMAL	hizamazukimaseba	hizamazukimaseñ nara
		hizamazukimasureba	
Gerund	**INFORMAL I**	hizamazuite	hizamazukanai de
	II		hizamazukanakute
	FORMAL	hizamazukimasite	hizamazukimaseñ de
Past Ind.	**INFORMAL**	hizamazuita	hizamazukanakatta
	FORMAL	hizamazukimasita	hizamazukimaseñ desita
Past Presump.	**INFORMAL**	hizamazuitaroo	hizamazukanakattaroo
		hizamazuita daroo	hizamazukanakatta daroo
	FORMAL	hizamazukimasitaroo	hizamazukimaseñ desitaroo
		hizamazuita desyoo	hizamazukanakatta desyoo
Conditional	**INFORMAL**	hizamazuitara	hizamazukanakattara
	FORMAL	hizamazukimasitara	hizamazukimaseñ desitara
Alternative	**INFORMAL**	hizamazuitari	hizamazukanakattari
	FORMAL	hizamazukimasitari	hizamazukimaseñ desitari

		INFORMAL AFFIRMATIVE INDICATIVE
Passive		hizamazukareru
Potential		hizamazukeru
Causative		hizamazukaseru
Causative Pass.		hizamazukaserareru

Honorific	**I**	ohizamazuki ni naru
	II	ohizamazuki nasaru
Humble	**I**	ohizamazuki suru
	II	ohizamazuki itasu

		AFFIRMATIVE	NEGATIVE
Indicative	INFORMAL	hodokeru	hodokenai
	FORMAL	hodokemasu	hodokemaseñ
Imperative	INFORMAL I	hodokero	hodokeru na
	II		
	III		
	FORMAL		
Presumptive	INFORMAL I	hodokeyoo	hodokemai
	II	hodokeru daroo	hodokenai daroo
	FORMAL I	hodokemasyoo	hodokemasumai
	II	hodokeru desyoo	hodokenai desyoo
Provisional	INFORMAL	hodokereba	hodokenakereba
	FORMAL	hodokemaseba	hodokemaseñ nara
		hodokemasureba	
Gerund	INFORMAL I	hodokete	hodokenai de
	II		hodokenakute
	FORMAL	hodokemasite	hodokemaseñ de
Past Ind.	INFORMAL	hodoketa	hodokenakatta
	FORMAL	hodokemasita	hodokemaseñ desita
Past Presump.	INFORMAL	hodoketaroo	hodokenakattaroo
		hodoketa daroo	hodokenakatta daroo
	FORMAL	hodokemasitaroo	hodokemaseñ desitaroo
		hodoketa desyoo	hodokenakatta desyoo
Conditional	INFORMAL	hodoketara	hodokenattara
	FORMAL	hodokemasitara	hodokemaseñ desitara
Alternative	INFORMAL	hodoketari	hodokenakattari
	FORMAL	hodokemasitari	hodokemaseñ desitari

		INFORMAL AFFIRMATIVE INDICATIVE
Passive		hodokerareru
Potential		hodokerareru
Causative		hodokesaseru
Causative Pass.		hodokesaserareru

Honorific	I	ohodoke ni naru
	II	ohodoke nasaru
Humble	I	
	II	

		AFFIRMATIVE	NEGATIVE
Indicative	**INFORMAL**	hodoku	hodokanai
	FORMAL	hodokimasu	hodokimaseñ
Imperative	**INFORMAL I**	hodoke	hodoku na
	II	hodokinasai	hodokinasaru na
	III	hodoite kudasai	hodokanai de kudasai
	FORMAL	ohodoki nasaimase	ohodoki nasaimasu na
Presumptive	**INFORMAL I**	hodokoo	hodokumai
	II	hodoku daroo	hodokanai daroo
	FORMAL I	hodokimasyoo	hodokimasumai
	II	hodoku desyoo	hodokanai desyoo
Provisional	**INFORMAL**	hodokeba	hodokanakereba
	FORMAL	hodokimaseba	hodokimaseñ nara
		hodokimasureba	
Gerund	**INFORMAL I**	hodoite	hodokanai de
	II		hodokanakute
	FORMAL	hodokimasite	hodokimaseñ de
Past Ind.	**INFORMAL**	hodoita	hodokanakatta
	FORMAL	hodokimasita	hodokimaseñ desita
Past Presump.	**INFORMAL**	hodoitaroo	hodokanakattaroo
		hodoita daroo	hodokanakatta daroo
	FORMAL	hodokimasitaroo	hodokimaseñ desitaroo
		hodoita desyoo	hodokanakatta desyoo
Conditional	**INFORMAL**	hodoitara	hodokanakattara
	FORMAL	hodokimasitara	hodokimaseñ desitara
Alternative	**INFORMAL**	hodoitari	hodokanakattari
	FORMAL	hodokimasitari	hodokimaseñ desitari

INFORMAL AFFIRMATIVE INDICATIVE

Passive		hodokareru
Potential		hodokeru
Causative		hodokaseru
Causative Pass.		hodokaserareru

Honorific	**I**	ohodoki ni naru
	II	ohodoki nasaru
Humble	**I**	ohodoki suru
	II	ohodoki itasu

		AFFIRMATIVE	NEGATIVE
Indicative	**INFORMAL**	homeru	homenai
	FORMAL	homemasu	homemaseñ
Imperative	**INFORMAL I**	homero	homeru na
	II	homenasai	homenasaru na
	III	homete kudasai	homenai de kudasai
	FORMAL	ohome nasaimase	ohome nasaimasu na
Presumptive	**INFORMAL I**	homeyoo	homemai
	II	homeru daroo	homenai daroo
	FORMAL I	homemasyoo	homemasumai
	II	homeru desyoo	homenai desyoo
Provisional	**INFORMAL**	homereba	homenakereba
	FORMAL	homemaseba	homemaseñ nara
		homemasureba	
Gerund	**INFORMAL I**	homete	homenai de
	II		homenakute
	FORMAL	homemasite	homemaseñ de
Past Ind.	**INFORMAL**	hometa	homenakatta
	FORMAL	homemasita	homemaseñ desita
Past Presump.	**INFORMAL**	hometaroo	homenakattaroo
		hometa daroo	homenakatta daroo
	FORMAL	homemasitaroo	homemaseñ desitaroo
		hometa desyoo	homenakatta desyoo
Conditional	**INFORMAL**	hometara	homenakattara
	FORMAL	homemasitara	homemaseñ desitara
Alternative	**INFORMAL**	hometari	homenakattari
	FORMAL	homemasitari	homemaseñ desitari

		INFORMAL AFFIRMATIVE INDICATIVE
Passive		homerareru
Potential		homerareru
Causative		homesaseru
Causative Pass.		homesaserareru
Honorific	**I**	ohome ni naru
	II	ohome nasaru
Humble	**I**	ohome suru
	II	ohome itasu

		AFFIRMATIVE	NEGATIVE
Indicative	**INFORMAL**	honomekasu	honomekasanai
	FORMAL	honomekasimasu	honomekasimaseñ
Imperative	**INFORMAL I**	honomekase	honomekasu na
	II	honomekasinasai	honomekasinasaru na
	III	honomekasite kudasai	honomekasanai de kudasai
	FORMAL	ohonomekasi nasaimase	ohonomekasi nasaimasu na
Presumptive	**INFORMAL I**	honomekasoo	honomekasumai
	II	honomekasu daroo	honomekasanai daroo
	FORMAL I	honomekasimasyoo	honomekasimasumai
	II	honomekasu desyoo	honomekasanai desyoo
Provisional	**INFORMAL**	honomekaseba	honomekasanakereba
	FORMAL	honomekasimaseba	honomekasimaseñ nara
		honomekasimasureba	
Gerund	**INFORMAL I**	honomekasite	honomekasanai de
	II		honomekasanakute
	FORMAL	honomekasimasite	honomekasimaseñ de
Past Ind.	**INFORMAL**	honomekasita	honomekasanakatta
	FORMAL	honomckasimasita	honomekasimaseñ desita
Past Presump.	**INFORMAL**	honomekasitaroo	honomekasanakattaroo
		honomekasita daroo	honomekasanakatta daroo
	FORMAL	honomekasimasitaroo	honomekasimaseñ desitaroo
		honomekasita desyoo	honomekasanakatta desyoo
Conditional	**INFORMAL**	honomekasitara	honomekasanakattara
	FORMAL	honomekasimasitara	honomekasimaseñ desitara
Alternative	**INFORMAL**	honomekasitari	honomekasanakattari
	FORMAL	honomekasimasitari	honomekasimaseñ desitari

	INFORMAL AFFIRMATIVE INDICATIVE
Passive	honomekasareru
Potential	honomekaseru
Causative	honomekasaseru
Causative Pass.	honomekasaserareru
Honorific **I**	ohonomekasi ni naru
II	ohonomekasi nasaru
Humble **I**	ohonomekasi suru
II	ohonomekasi itasu

to bury (a person)   TRANSITIVE

		AFFIRMATIVE	NEGATIVE
Indicative	**INFORMAL**	hoomuru	hoomuranai
	FORMAL	hoomurimasu	hoomurimaseñ
Imperative	**INFORMAL I**	hoomure	hoomuru na
	II	hoomurinasai	hoomurinasaru na
	III	hoomutte kudasai	hoomuranai de kudasai
	FORMAL	ohoomuri nasaimase	ohoomuri nasaimasu na
Presumptive	**INFORMAL I**	hoomuroo	hoomurumai
	II	hoomuru daroo	hoomuranai daroo
	FORMAL I	hoomurimasyoo	hoomurimasumai
	II	hoomuru desyoo	hoomuranai desyoo
Provisional	**INFORMAL**	hoomureba	hoomuranakereba
	FORMAL	hoomurimaseba	hoomurimaseñ nara
		hoomurimasureba	
Gerund	**INFORMAL I**	hoomutte	hoomuranai de
	II		hoomuranakute
	FORMAL	hoomurimasite	hoomurimaseñ de
Past Ind.	**INFORMAL**	hoomutta	hoomuranakatta
	FORMAL	hoomurimasita	hoomurimaseñ desita
Past Presump.	**INFORMAL**	hoomuttaroo	hoomuranakattaroo
		hoomutta daroo	hoomuranakatta daroo
	FORMAL	hoomurimasitaroo	hoomurimaseñ desitaroo
		hoomutta desyoo	hoomuranakatta desyoo
Conditional	**INFORMAL**	hoomuttara	hoomuranakattara
	FORMAL	hoomurimasitara	hoomurimaseñ desitara
Alternative	**INFORMAL**	hoomuttari	hoomuranakattari
	FORMAL	hoomurimasitari	hoomurimaseñ desitari

	INFORMAL AFFIRMATIVE INDICATIVE
Passive	hoomurareru
Potential	hoomureru
Causative	hoomuraseru
Causative Pass.	hoomuraserareru

Honorific	**I**	ohoomuri ni naru
	II	ohoomuri nasaru
Humble	**I**	
	II	

		AFFIRMATIVE	NEGATIVE
Indicative	**INFORMAL**	horeru	horenai
	FORMAL	horemasu	horemaseñ
Imperative	**INFORMAL I**	horero	horeru na
	II	horenasai	horenasaru na
	III	horete kudasai	horenai de kudasai
	FORMAL	ohore nasaimase	ohore nasaimasu na
Presumptive	**INFORMAL I**	horeyoo	horemai
	II	horeru daroo	horenai daroo
	FORMAL I	horemasyoo	horemasumai
	II	horeru desyoo	horenai desyoo
Provisional	**INFORMAL**	horereba	horenakereba
	FORMAL	horemaseba	horemaseñ nara
		horemasureba	
Gerund	**INFORMAL I**	horete	horenai de
	II		horenakute
	FORMAL	horemasite	horemaseñ de
Past Ind.	**INFORMAL**	horeta	horenakatta
	FORMAL	horemasita	horemaseñ desita
Past Presump.	**INFORMAL**	horetaroo	horenakattaroo
		horeta daroo	horenakatta daroo
	FORMAL	horemasitaroo	horemaseñ desitaroo
		horeta desyoo	horenakatta desyoo
Conditional	**INFORMAL**	horetara	horenakattara
	FORMAL	horemasitara	horemaseñ desitara
Alternative	**INFORMAL**	horetari	horenakattari
	FORMAL	horemasitari	horemaseñ desitari

		INFORMAL AFFIRMATIVE INDICATIVE
Passive		horerareru
Potential		horerareru
Causative		horesaseru
Causative Pass.		horesaserareru
Honorific	**I**	ohore ni naru
	II	ohore nasaru
Humble	**I**	ohore suru
	II	ohore itasu

to fall into ruin, to be overthrown

		AFFIRMATIVE	NEGATIVE
Indicative	INFORMAL	horobiru	horobinai
	FORMAL	horobimasu	horobimaseñ
Imperative	INFORMAL I	horobiro	horobiru na
	II	horobinasai	horobinasaru na
	III	horobite kudasai	horobinai de kudasai
	FORMAL	ohorobi nasaimase	ohorobi nasaimasu na
Presumptive	INFORMAL I	horobiyoo	horobimai
	II	horobiru daroo	horobinai daroo
	FORMAL I	horobimasyoo	horobimasumai
	II	horobiru desyoo	horobinai desyoo
Provisional	INFORMAL	horobireba	horobinakereba
	FORMAL	horobimaseba	horobimaseñ nara
		horobimasureba	
Gerund	INFORMAL I	horobite	horobinai de
	II		horobinakute
	FORMAL	horobimasite	horobimaseñ de
Past Ind.	INFORMAL	horobita	horobinakatta
	FORMAL	horobimasita	horobimaseñ desita
Past Presump.	INFORMAL	horobitaroo	horobinakattaroo
		horobita daroo	horobinakatta daroo
	FORMAL	horobimasitaroo	horobimaseñ desitaroo
		horobita desyoo	horobinakatta desyoo
Conditional	INFORMAL	horobitara	horobinakattara
	FORMAL	horobimasitara	horobimaseñ desitara
Alternative	INFORMAL	horobitari	horobinakattari
	FORMAL	horobimasitari	horobimaseñ desitari

		INFORMAL AFFIRMATIVE INDICATIVE
Passive		horobirareru
Potential		horobirareru
Causative		horobisaseru
Causative Pass.		horobisaserareru
Honorific	I	ohorobi ni naru
	II	ohorobi nasaru
Humble	I	
	II	

TRANSITIVE   *to ruin, to overthrow*

		AFFIRMATIVE	**NEGATIVE**
Indicative	**INFORMAL**	horobosu	horobosanai
	FORMAL	horobosimasu	horobosimaseñ
Imperative	**INFORMAL I**	horobose	horobosu na
	II	horobosinasai	horobosinasaru na
	III	horobosite kudasai	horobosanai de kudasai
	FORMAL	ohorobosi nasaimase	ohorobosi nasaimasu na
Presumptive	**INFORMAL I**	horobosoo	horobosumai
	II	horobosu daroo	horobosanai daroo
	FORMAL I	horobosimasyoo	horobosimasumai
	II	horobosu desyoo	horobosanai desyoo
Provisional	**INFORMAL**	horoboseba	horobosanakereba
	FORMAL	horobosimaseba	horobosimaseñ nara
		horobosimasureba	
Gerund	**INFORMAL I**	horobosite	horobosanai de
	II		horobosanakute
	FORMAL	horobosimasite	horobosimaseñ de
Past Ind.	**INFORMAL**	horobosita	horobosanakatta
	FORMAL	horobosimasita	horobosimaseñ desita
Past Presump.	**INFORMAL**	horobositaroo	horobosanakattaroo
		horobosita daroo	horobosanakatta daroo
	FORMAL	horobosimasitaroo	horobosimaseñ desitaroo
		horobosita desyoo	horobosanakatta desyoo
Conditional	**INFORMAL**	horobositara	horobosanakattara
	FORMAL	horobosimasitara	horobosimaseñ desitara
Alternative	**INFORMAL**	horobositari	horobosanakattari
	FORMAL	horobosimasitari	horobosimaseñ desitari

		INFORMAL AFFIRMATIVE INDICATIVE
Passive		horobosareru
Potential		horoboseru
Causative		horobosaseru
Causative Pass.		horobosaserareru

Honorific	**I**	ohorobosi ni naru
	II	ohorobosi nasaru
Humble	**I**	ohorobosi suru
	II	ohorobosi itasu

		AFFIRMATIVE	NEGATIVE
Indicative	**INFORMAL**	horu	horanai
	FORMAL	horimasu	horimaseñ
Imperative	**INFORMAL I**	hore	horu na
	II	horinasai	horinasaru na
	III	hotte kudasai	horanai de kudasai
	FORMAL	ohori nasaimase	ohori nasaimasu na
Presumptive	**INFORMAL I**	horoo	horumai
	II	horu daroo	horanai daroo
	FORMAL I	horimasyoo	horimasumai
	II	horu desyoo	horanai desyoo
Provisional	**INFORMAL**	horeba	horanakereba
	FORMAL	horimaseba	horimaseñ nara
		horimasureba	
Gerund	**INFORMAL I**	hotte	horanai de
	II		horanakute
	FORMAL	horimasite	horimaseñ de
Past Ind.	**INFORMAL**	hotta	horanakatta
	FORMAL	horimasita	horimaseñ desita
Past Presump.	**INFORMAL**	hottaroo	horanakattaroo
		hotta daroo	horanakatta daroo
	FORMAL	horimasitaroo	horimaseñ desitaroo
		hotta desyoo	horanakatta desyoo
Conditional	**INFORMAL**	hottara	horanakattara
	FORMAL	horimasitara	horimaseñ desitara
Alternative	**INFORMAL**	hottari	horanakattari
	FORMAL	horimasitari	horimaseñ desitari

		INFORMAL AFFIRMATIVE INDICATIVE
Passive		horareru
Potential		horeru
Causative		horaseru
Causative Pass.		horaserareru
Honorific	**I**	ohori ni naru
	II	ohori nasaru
Humble	**I**	ohori suru
	II	ohori itasu

		AFFIRMATIVE	NEGATIVE
Indicative	INFORMAL	hosigaru	hosigaranai
	FORMAL	hosigarimasu	hosigarimaseñ
Imperative	INFORMAL I	hosigare	hosigaru na
	II	hosigarinasai	hosigarinasaru na
	III	hosigatte kudasai	hosigaranai de kudasai
	FORMAL	ohosigari nasaimase	ohosigari nasaimasu na
Presumptive	INFORMAL I	hosigaroo	hosigarumai
	II	hosigaru daroo	hosigaranai daroo
	FORMAL I	hosigarimasyoo	hosigarimasumai
	II	hosigaru desyoo	hosigaranai desyoo
Provisional	INFORMAL	hosigareba	hosigaranakereba
	FORMAL	hosigarimaseba	hosigarimaseñ nara
		hosigarimasureba	
Gerund	INFORMAL I	hosigatte	hosigaranai de
	II		hosigaranakute
	FORMAL	hosigarimasite	hosigarimaseñ de
Past Ind.	INFORMAL	hosigatta	hosigaranakatta
	FORMAL	hosigarimasita	hosigarimaseñ desita
Past Presump.	INFORMAL	hosigattaroo	hosigaranakattaroo
		hosigatta daroo	hosigaranakatta daroo
	FORMAL	hosigarimasitaroo	hosigarimaseñ desitaroo
		hosigatta desyoo	hosigaranakatta desyoo
Conditional	INFORMAL	hosigattara	hosigaranakattara
	FORMAL	hosigarimasitara	hosigarimaseñ desitara
Alternative	INFORMAL	hosigattari	hosigaranakattari
	FORMAL	hosigarimasitari	hosigarimaseñ desitari

		INFORMAL AFFIRMATIVE INDICATIVE
Passive		hosigarareru
Potential		hosigareru
Causative		hosigaraseru
Causative Pass.		hosigaraserareru
Honorific	I	ohosigari ni naru
	II	ohosigari nasaru
Humble	I	
	II	

		AFFIRMATIVE	NEGATIVE
Indicative	**INFORMAL**	hosu	hosanai
	FORMAL	hosimasu	hosimaseñ
Imperative	**INFORMAL I**	hose	hosu na
	II	hosinasai	hosinasaru na
	III	hosite kudasai	hosanai de kudasai
	FORMAL	ohosi nasaimase	ohosi nasaimasu na
Presumptive	**INFORMAL I**	hosoo	hosumai
	II	hosu daroo	hosanai daroo
	FORMAL I	hosimasyoo	hosimasumai
	II	hosu desyoo	hosanai desyoo
Provisional	**INFORMAL**	hoseba	hosanakereba
	FORMAL	hosimaseba	hosimaseñ nara
		hosimasureba	
Gerund	**INFORMAL I**	hosite	hosanai de
	II		hosanakute
	FORMAL	hosimasite	hosimaseñ de
Past Ind.	**INFORMAL**	hosita	hosanakatta
	FORMAL	hosimasita	hosimaseñ desita
Past Presump.	**INFORMAL**	hositaroo	hosanakattaroo
		hosita daroo	hosanakatta daroo
	FORMAL	hosimasitaroo	hosimaseñ desitaroo
		hosita desyoo	hosanakatta desyoo
Conditional	**INFORMAL**	hositara	hosanakattara
	FORMAL	hosimasitara	hosimaseñ desitara
Alternative	**INFORMAL**	hositari	hosanakattari
	FORMAL	hosimasitari	hosimaseñ desitari

INFORMAL AFFIRMATIVE INDICATIVE

Passive		hosareru
Potential		hoseru
Causative		hosaseru
Causative Pass.		hosaserareru
Honorific	**I**	ohosi ni naru
	II	ohosi nasaru
Humble	**I**	ohosi suru
	II	ohosi itasu

		AFFIRMATIVE	NEGATIVE
Indicative	**INFORMAL**	hueru	huenai
	FORMAL	huemasu	huemaseñ
Imperative	**INFORMAL I**	huero	hueru na
	II	huenasai	huenasaru na
	III	huete kudasai	huenai de kudasai
	FORMAL	ohue nasaimase	ohue nasaimasu na
Presumptive	**INFORMAL I**	hueyoo	huemai
	II	hueru daroo	huenai daroo
	FORMAL I	huemasyoo	huemasumai
	II	hueru desyoo	huenai desyoo
Provisional	**INFORMAL**	huereba	huenakereba
	FORMAL	huemaseba	huemaseñ nara
		huemasureba	
Gerund	**INFORMAL I**	huete	huenai de
	II		huenakute
	FORMAL	huemasite	huemaseñ de
Past Ind.	**INFORMAL**	hueta	huenakatta
	FORMAL	huemasita	huemaseñ desita
Past Presump.	**INFORMAL**	huetaroo	huenakattaroo
		hueta daroo	huenakatta daroo
	FORMAL	huemasitaroo	huemaseñ desitaroo
		hueta desyoo	huenakatta desyoo
Conditional	**INFORMAL**	huetara	huenakattara
	FORMAL	huemasitara	huemaseñ desitara
Alternative	**INFORMAL**	huetari	huenakattari
	FORMAL	huemasitari	huemaseñ desitari

		INFORMAL AFFIRMATIVE INDICATIVE
Passive		huerareru
Potential		huerareru
Causative		huesaseru
Causative Pass.		huesaserareru
Honorific	**I**	ohue ni naru
	II	ohue nasaru
Humble	**I**	
	II	

		AFFIRMATIVE	NEGATIVE
Indicative	**INFORMAL**	hukamaru	hukamaranai
	FORMAL	hukamarimasu	hukamarimaseñ
Imperative	**INFORMAL I**	hukamare	hukamaru na
	II	hukamarinasai	hukamarinasaru na
	III	hukamatte kudasai	hukamaranai de kudasai
	FORMAL	ohukamari nasaimase	ohukamari nasaimasu na
Presumptive	**INFORMAL I**	hukamaroo	hukamarumai
	II	hukamaru daroo	hukamaranai daroo
	FORMAL I	hukamarimasyoo	hukamarimasumai
	II	hukamaru desyoo	hukamaranai desyoo
Provisional	**INFORMAL**	hukamareba	hukamaranakereba
	FORMAL	hukamarimaseba	hukamarimaseñ nara
		hukamarimasureba	
Gerund	**INFORMAL I**	hukamatte	hukamaranai de
	II		hukamaranakute
	FORMAL	hukamarimasite	hukamarimaseñ de
Past Ind.	**INFORMAL**	hukamatta	hukamaranakatta
	FORMAL	hukamarimasita	hukamarimaseñ desita
Past Presump.	**INFORMAL**	hukamattaroo	hukamaranakattaroo
		hukamatta daroo	hukamaranakatta daroo
	FORMAL	hukamarimasitaroo	hukamarimaseñ desitaroo
		hukamatta desyoo	hukamaranakatta desyoo
Conditional	**INFORMAL**	hukamattara	hukamaranakattara
	FORMAL	hukamarimasitara	hukamarimaseñ desitara
Alternative	**INFORMAL**	hukamattari	hukamaranakattari
	FORMAL	hukamarimasitari	hukamarimaseñ desitari

		INFORMAL AFFIRMATIVE INDICATIVE
Passive		hukamarareru
Potential		hukamareru
Causative		hukamaraseru
Causative Pass.		hukamaraserareru
Honorific	**I**	ohukamari ni naru
	II	ohukamari nasaru
Humble	**I**	
	II	

		AFFIRMATIVE	NEGATIVE
Indicative	**INFORMAL**	hukameru	hukamenai
	FORMAL	hukamemasu	hukamemaseñ
Imperative	**INFORMAL I**	hukamero	hukameru na
	II	hukamenasai	hukamenasaru na
	III	hukamete kudasai	hukamenai de kudasai
	FORMAL	ohukame nasaimase	ohukame nasaimasu na
Presumptive	**INFORMAL I**	hukameyoo	hukamemai
	II	hukameru daroo	hukamenai daroo
	FORMAL I	hukamemasyoo	hukamemasumai
	II	hukameru desyoo	hukamenai desyoo
Provisional	**INFORMAL**	hukamereba	hukamenakereba
	FORMAL	hukamemaseba	hukamemaseñ nara
		hukamemasureba	
Gerund	**INFORMAL I**	hukamete	hukamenai de
	II		hukamenakute
	FORMAL	hukamemasite	hukamemaseñ de
Past Ind.	**INFORMAL**	hukameta	hukamenakatta
	FORMAL	hukamemasita	hukamemaseñ desita
Past Presump.	**INFORMAL**	hukametaroo	hukamenakattaroo
		hukameta daroo	hukamenakatta daroo
	FORMAL	hukamemasitaroo	hukamemaseñ desitaroo
		hukameta desyoo	hukamenakatta desyoo
Conditional	**INFORMAL**	hukametara	hukamenakattara
	FORMAL	hukamemasitara	hukamemaseñ desitara
Alternative	**INFORMAL**	hukametari	hukamenakattari
	FORMAL	hukamemasitari	hukamemaseñ desitari

INFORMAL AFFIRMATIVE INDICATIVE

Passive		hukamerareru
Potential		hukamerareru
Causative		hukamesaseru
Causative Pass.		hukamesaserareru

Honorific	**I**	ohukame ni naru
	II	ohukame nasaru
Humble	**I**	ohukame suru
	II	ohukame itasu

			AFFIRMATIVE	NEGATIVE
Indicative	**INFORMAL**		huku	hukanai
	FORMAL		hukimasu	hukimaseñ
Imperative	**INFORMAL**	**I**	huke	huku na
		II	hukinasai	hukinasaru na
		III	huite kudasai	hukanai de kudasai
	FORMAL		ohuki nasaimase	ohuki nasaimasu na
Presumptive	**INFORMAL**	**I**	hukoo	hukumai
		II	huku daroo	hukanai daroo
	FORMAL	**I**	hukimasyoo	hukimasumai
		II	huku desyoo	hukanai desyoo
Provisional	**INFORMAL**		hukeba	hukanakereba
	FORMAL		hukimaseba	hukimaseñ nara
			hukimasureba	
Gerund	**INFORMAL**	**I**	huite	hukanai de
		II		hukanakute
	FORMAL		hukimasite	hukimaseñ de
Past Ind.	**INFORMAL**		huita	hukanakatta
	FORMAL		hukimasita	hukimaseñ desita
Past Presump.	**INFORMAL**		huitaroo	hukanakattaroo
			huita daroo	hukanakatta daroo
	FORMAL		hukimasitaroo	hukimaseñ desitaroo
			huita desyoo	hukanakatta desyoo
Conditional	**INFORMAL**		huitara	hukanakattara
	FORMAL		hukimasitara	hukimaseñ desitara
Alternative	**INFORMAL**		huitari	hukanakattari
	FORMAL		hukimasitari	hukimaseñ desitari

		INFORMAL AFFIRMATIVE INDICATIVE
Passive		hukareru
Potential		hukeru
Causative		hukaseru
Causative Pass.		hukaserareru
Honorific	**I**	ohuki ni naru
	II	ohuki nasaru
Humble	**I**	ohuki suru
	II	ohuki itasu

			AFFIRMATIVE	NEGATIVE
Indicative	**INFORMAL**		huku	hukanai
	FORMAL		hukimasu	hukimaseñ
Imperative	**INFORMAL**	**I**	huke	huku na
		II	hukinasai	hukinasaru na
		III	huite kudasai	hukanai de kudasai
	FORMAL		ohuki nasaimase	ohuki nasaimasu na
Presumptive	**INFORMAL**	**I**	hukoo	hukumai
		II	huku daroo	hukanai daroo
	FORMAL	**I**	hukimasyoo	hukimasumai
		II	huku desyoo	hukanai desyoo
Provisional	**INFORMAL**		hukeba	hukanakereba
	FORMAL		hukimaseba	hukimaseñ nara
			hukimasureba	
Gerund	**INFORMAL**	**I**	huite	hukanai de
		II		hukanakute
	FORMAL		hukimasite	hukimaseñ de
Past Ind.	**INFORMAL**		huita	hukanakatta
	FORMAL		hukimasita	hukimaseñ desita
Past Presump.	**INFORMAL**		huitaroo	hukanakattaroo
			huita daroo	hukanakatta daroo
	FORMAL		hukimasitaroo	hukimaseñ desitaroo
			huita desyoo	hukanakatta desyoo
Conditional	**INFORMAL**		huitara	hukanakattara
	FORMAL		hukimasitara	hukimaseñ desitara
Alternative	**INFORMAL**		huitari	hukanakattari
	FORMAL		hukimasitari	hukimaseñ desitari

			INFORMAL AFFIRMATIVE INDICATIVE
Passive			hukareru
Potential			hukeru
Causative			hukaseru
Causative Pass.			hukaserareru
Honorific		**I**	ohuki ni naru
		II	ohuki nasaru
Humble		**I**	ohuki suru
		II	ohuki itasu

		AFFIRMATIVE	NEGATIVE
Indicative	**INFORMAL**	hukumeru	hukumenai
	FORMAL	hukumemasu	hukumemaseñ
Imperative	**INFORMAL I**	hukumero	hukumeru na
	II	hukumenasai	hukumenasaru na
	III	hukumete kudasai	hukumenai de kudasai
	FORMAL	ohukume nasaimase	ohukume nasaimasu na
Presumptive	**INFORMAL I**	hukumeyoo	hukumemai
	II	hukumeru daroo	hukumenai daroo
	FORMAL I	hukumemasyoo	hukumemasumai
	II	hukumeru desyoo	hukumenai desyoo
Provisional	**INFORMAL**	hukumereba	hukumenakereba
	FORMAL	hukumemaseba	hukumemaseñ nara
		hukumemasureba	
Gerund	**INFORMAL I**	hukumete	hukumenai de
	II		hukumenakute
	FORMAL	hukumemasite	hukumemaseñ de
Past Ind.	**INFORMAL**	hukumeta	hukumenakatta
	FORMAL	hukumemasita	hukumemaseñ desita
Past Presump.	**INFORMAL**	hukumetaroo	hukumenakattaroo
		hukumeta daroo	hukumenakatta daroo
	FORMAL	hukumemasitaroo	hukumemaseñ desitaroo
		hukumeta desyoo	hukumenakatta desyoo
Conditional	**INFORMAL**	hukumetara	hukumenakattara
	FORMAL	hukumemasitara	hukumemaseñ desitara
Alternative	**INFORMAL**	hukumetari	hukumenakattari
	FORMAL	hukumemasitari	hukumemaseñ desitari

		INFORMAL AFFIRMATIVE INDICATIVE
Passive		hukumerareru
Potential		hukumerareru
Causative		hukumesaseru
Causative Pass.		hukumesaserareru
Honorific	**I**	ohukume ni naru
	II	ohukume nasaru
Humble	**I**	ohukume suru
	II	ohukume itasu

		AFFIRMATIVE	**NEGATIVE**
Indicative	**INFORMAL**	humu	humanai
	FORMAL	humimasu	humimaseñ
Imperative	**INFORMAL I**	hume	humu na
	II	huminasai	huminasaru na
	III	huñde kudasai	humanai de kudasai
	FORMAL	ohumi nasaimase	ohumi nasaimasu na
Presumptive	**INFORMAL I**	humoo	humumai
	II	humu daroo	humanai daroo
	FORMAL I	humimasyoo	humimasumai
	II	humu desyoo	humanai desyoo
Provisional	**INFORMAL**	humeba	humanakereba
	FORMAL	humimaseba	humimaseñ nara
		humimasureba	
Gerund	**INFORMAL I**	huñde	humanai de
	II		humanakute
	FORMAL	humimasite	humimaseñ de
Past Ind.	**INFORMAL**	huñda	humanakatta
	FORMAL	humimasita	humimaseñ desita
Past Presump.	**INFORMAL**	huñdaroo	humanakattaroo
		huñda daroo	humanakatta daroo
	FORMAL	humimasitaroo	humimaseñ desitaroo
		huñda desyoo	humanakatta desyoo
Conditional	**INFORMAL**	huñdara	humanakattara
	FORMAL	humimasitara	humimaseñ desitara
Alternative	**INFORMAL**	huñdari	humanakattari
	FORMAL	humimasitari	humimaseñ desitari

INFORMAL AFFIRMATIVE INDICATIVE

Passive		humareru
Potential		humeru
Causative		humaseru
Causative Pass.		humaserareru
Honorific	**I**	ohumi ni naru
	II	ohumi nasaru
Humble	**I**	ohumi suru
	II	ohumi itasu

		AFFIRMATIVE	NEGATIVE
Indicative	**INFORMAL**	hureru	hurenai
	FORMAL	huremasu	huremaseñ
Imperative	**INFORMAL I**	hurero	hureru na
	II	hurenasai	hurenasaru na
	III	hurete kudasai	hurenai de kudasai
	FORMAL	ohure nasaimase	ohure nasaimasu na
Presumptive	**INFORMAL I**	hureyoo	huremai
	II	hureru daroo	hurenai daroo
	FORMAL I	huremasyoo	huremasumai
	II	hureru desyoo	hurenai desyoo
Provisional	**INFORMAL**	hurereba	hurenakereba
	FORMAL	huremaseba	huremaseñ nara
		huremasureba	
Gerund	**INFORMAL I**	hurete	hurenai de
	II		hurenakute
	FORMAL	huremasite	huremaseñ de
Past Ind.	**INFORMAL**	hureta	hurenakatta
	FORMAL	huremasita	huremaseñ desita
Past Presump.	**INFORMAL**	huretaroo	hurenakattaroo
		hureta daroo	hurenakatta daroo
	FORMAL	huremasitaroo	huremaseñ desitaroo
		hureta desyoo	hurenakatta desyoo
Conditional	**INFORMAL**	huretara	hurenakattara
	FORMAL	huremasitara	huremaseñ desitara
Alternative	**INFORMAL**	huretari	hurenakattari
	FORMAL	huremasitari	huremaseñ desitari

INFORMAL AFFIRMATIVE INDICATIVE

Passive		hurerareru
Potential		hurerareru
Causative		huresaseru
Causative Pass.		huresaserareru

Honorific	**I**	ohure ni naru
	II	ohure nasaru
Humble	**I**	ohure suru
	II	ohure itasu

TRANSITIVE   *to look back, to think back*

		AFFIRMATIVE	NEGATIVE
Indicative	INFORMAL	hurikaeru	hurikaeranai
	FORMAL	hurikaerimasu	hurikaerimaseñ
Imperative	INFORMAL I	hurikaere	hurikaeru na
	II	hurikaerinasai	hurikaerinasaru na
	III	hurikaette kudasai	hurikaeranai de kudasai
	FORMAL	ohurikaeri nasaimase	ohurikaeri nasaimasu na
Presumptive	INFORMAL I	hurikaeroo	hurikaerumai
	II	hurikaeru daroo	hurikaeranai daroo
	FORMAL I	hurikaerimasyoo	hurikaerimasumai
	II	hurikaeru desyoo	hurikaeranai desyoo
Provisional	INFORMAL	hurikaereba	hurikaeranakereba
	FORMAL	hurikaerimaseba	hurikaerimaseñ nara
		hurikaerimasureba	
Gerund	INFORMAL I	hurikaette	hurikaeranai de
	II		hurikaeranakute
	FORMAL	hurikaerimasite	hurikaerimaseñ de
Past Ind.	INFORMAL	hurikaetta	hurikaeranakatta
	FORMAL	hurikaerimasita	hurikaerimaseñ desita
Past Presump.	INFORMAL	hurikaettaroo	hurikaeranakattaroo
		hurikaetta daroo	hurikaeranakatta daroo
	FORMAL	hurikaerimasitaroo	hurikaerimaseñ desitaroo
		hurikaetta desyoo	hurikaeranakatta desyoo
Conditional	INFORMAL	hurikaettara	hurikaeranakattara
	FORMAL	hurikaerimasitara	hurikaerimaseñ desitara
Alternative	INFORMAL	hurikaettari	hurikaeranakattari
	FORMAL	hurikaerimasitari	hurikaerimaseñ desitari

		INFORMAL AFFIRMATIVE INDICATIVE
Passive		hurikaerareru
Potential		hurikaereru
Causative		hurikaeraseru
Causative Pass.		hurikaeraserareru

Honorific	I	ohurikaeri ni naru
	II	ohurikaeri nasaru
Humble	I	
	II	

		AFFIRMATIVE	NEGATIVE
Indicative	INFORMAL	hurimawasu	hurimawasanai
	FORMAL	hurimawasimasu	hurimawasimaseñ
Imperative	INFORMAL I	hurimawase	hurimawasu na
	II	hurimawasinasai	hurimawasinasaru na
	III	hurimawasite kudasai	hurimawasanai de kudasai
	FORMAL	ohurimawasi nasaimase	ohurimawasi nasaimasu na
Presumptive	INFORMAL I	hurimawasoo	hurimawasumai
	II	hurimawasu daroo	hurimawasanai daroo
	FORMAL I	hurimawasimasyoo	hurimawasimasumai
	II	hurimawasu desyoo	hurimawasanai desyoo
Provisional	INFORMAL	hurimawaseba	hurimawasanakereba
	FORMAL	hurimawasimaseba	hurimawasimaseñ nara
		hurimawasimasureba	
Gerund	INFORMAL I	hurimawasite	hurimawasanai de
	II		hurimawasanakute
	FORMAL	hurimawasimasite	hurimawasimaseñ de
Past Ind.	INFORMAL	hurimawasita	hurimawasanakatta
	FORMAL	hurimawasimasita	hurimawasimaseñ desita
Past Presump.	INFORMAL	hurimawasitaroo	hurimawasanakattaroo
		hurimawasita daroo	hurimawasanakatta daroo
	FORMAL	hurimawasimasitaroo	hurimawasimaseñ desitaroo
		hurimawasita desyoo	hurimawasanakatta desyoo
Conditional	INFORMAL	hurimawasitara	hurimawasanakattara
	FORMAL	hurimawasimasitara	hurimawasimaseñ desitara
Alternative	INFORMAL	hurimawasitari	hurimawasanakattari
	FORMAL	hurimawasimasitari	hurimawasimaseñ desitari

INFORMAL AFFIRMATIVE INDICATIVE

Passive		hurimawasareru
Potential		hurimawaseru
Causative		hurimawasaseru
Causative Pass.		hurimawasaserareru
Honorific	I	ohurimawasi ni naru
	II	ohurimawasi nasaru
Humble	I	ohurimawasi suru
	II	ohurimawasi itasu

110

		AFFIRMATIVE	NEGATIVE
Indicative	**INFORMAL**	huru	huranai
	FORMAL	hurimasu	hurimaseñ
Imperative	**INFORMAL I**	hure	huru na
	II	hurinasai	hurinasaru na
	III	hutte kudasai	huranai de kudasai
	FORMAL		
Presumptive	**INFORMAL I**	huroo	hurumai
	II	huru daroo	huranai daroo
	FORMAL I	hurimasyoo	hurimasumai
	II	huru desyoo	huranai desyoo
Provisional	**INFORMAL**	hureba	huranakereba
	FORMAL	hurimaseba	hurimaseñ nara
		hurimasureba	
Gerund	**INFORMAL I**	hutte	huranai de
	II		huranakute
	FORMAL	hurimasite	hurimaseñ de
Past Ind.	**INFORMAL**	hutta	huranakatta
	FORMAL	hurimasita	hurimaseñ desita
Past Presump.	**INFORMAL**	huttaroo	huranakattaroo
		hutta daroo	huranakatta daroo
	FORMAL	hurimasitaroo	hurimaseñ desitaroo
		hutta desyoo	huranakatta desyoo
Conditional	**INFORMAL**	huttara	huranakattara
	FORMAL	hurimasitara	hurimaseñ desitara
Alternative	**INFORMAL**	huttari	huranakattari
	FORMAL	hurimasitari	hurimaseñ desitari

	INFORMAL AFFIRMATIVE INDICATIVE
Passive	hurareru
Potential	hureru
Causative	huraseru
Causative Pass.	huraserareru

Honorific	**I**	
	II	
Humble	**I**	
	II	

		AFFIRMATIVE	NEGATIVE
Indicative	**INFORMAL**	hurueru	huruenai
	FORMAL	huruemasu	huruemaseñ
Imperative	**INFORMAL I**	huruero	hurueru na
	II	huruenasai	huruenasaru na
	III	huruete kudasai	huruenai de kudasai
	FORMAL	ohurue nasaimase	ohurue nasaimasu na
Presumptive	**INFORMAL I**	hurueyoo	huruemai
	II	hurueru daroo	huruenai daroo
	FORMAL I	huruemasyoo	huruemasumai
	II	hurueru desyoo	huruenai desyoo
Provisional	**INFORMAL**	huruereba	huruenakereba
	FORMAL	huruemaseba	huruemaseñ nara
		huruemasureba	
Gerund	**INFORMAL I**	huruete	huruenai de
	II		huruenakute
	FORMAL	huruemasite	huruemaseñ de
Past Ind.	**INFORMAL**	hurueta	huruenakatta
	FORMAL	huruemasita	huruemaseñ desita
Past Presump.	**INFORMAL**	huruetaroo	huruenakattaroo
		hurueta daroo	huruenakatta daroo
	FORMAL	huruemasitaroo	huruemaseñ desitaroo
		hurueta desyoo	huruenakatta desyoo
Conditional	**INFORMAL**	huruetara	huruenakattara
	FORMAL	huruemasitara	huruemaseñ desitara
Alternative	**INFORMAL**	huruetari	huruenakattari
	FORMAL	huruemasitari	huruemaseñ desitari

INFORMAL AFFIRMATIVE INDICATIVE

Passive		huruerareru
Potential		huruerareru
Causative		huruesaseru
Causative Pass.		huruesaserareru
Honorific	**I**	ohurue ni naru
	II	ohurue nasaru
Humble	**I**	
	II	

		AFFIRMATIVE	NEGATIVE
Indicative	**INFORMAL**	husagaru	husagaranai
	FORMAL	husagarimasu	husagarimaseñ
Imperative	**INFORMAL I**	husagare	husagaru na
	II	husagarinasai	husagarinasaru na
	III		
	FORMAL		
Presumptive	**INFORMAL I**	husagaroo	husagarumai
	II	husagaru daroo	husagaranai daroo
	FORMAL I	husagarimasyoo	husagarimasumai
	II	husagaru desyoo	husagaranai desyoo
Provisional	**INFORMAL**	husagareba	husagaranakereba
	FORMAL	husagarimaseba	husagarimaseñ nara
		husagarimasureba	
Gerund	**INFORMAL I**	husagatte	husagaranai de
	II		husagaranakute
	FORMAL	husagarimasite	husagarimaseñ de
Past Ind.	**INFORMAL**	husagatta	husagaranakatta
	FORMAL	husagarimasita	husagarimaseñ desita
Past Presump.	**INFORMAL**	husagattaroo	husagaranakattaroo
		husagatta daroo	husagaranakatta daroo
	FORMAL	husagarimasitaroo	husagarimaseñ desitaroo
		husagatta desyoo	husagaranakatta desyoo
Conditional	**INFORMAL**	husagattara	husagaranakattara
	FORMAL	husagarimasitara	husagarimaseñ desitara
Alternative	**INFORMAL**	husagattari	husagaranakattari
	FORMAL	husagarimasitari	husagarimaseñ desitari

		INFORMAL AFFIRMATIVE INDICATIVE
Passive		husagarareru
Potential		husagareru
Causative		husagaraseru
Causative Pass.		husagaraserareru
Honorific	**I**	ohusagari ni naru
	II	ohusagari nasaru
Humble	**I**	
	II	

		AFFIRMATIVE	NEGATIVE
Indicative	**INFORMAL**	husagu	husaganai
	FORMAL	husagimasu	husagimaseñ
Imperative	**INFORMAL I**	husage	husagu na
	II	husaginasai	husaginasaru na
	III	husaide kudasai	husaganai de kudasai
	FORMAL	ohusagi nasaimase	ohusagi nasaimasu na
Presumptive	**INFORMAL I**	husagoo	husagumai
	II	husagu daroo	husaganai daroo
	FORMAL I	husagimasyoo	husagimasumai
	II	husagu desyoo	husaganai desyoo
Provisional	**INFORMAL**	husageba	husaganakereba
	FORMAL	husagimaseba	husagimaseñ nara
		husagimasureba	
Gerund	**INFORMAL I**	husaide	husaganai de
	II		husaganakute
	FORMAL	husagimasite	husagimaseñ de
Past Ind.	**INFORMAL**	husaida	husaganakatta
	FORMAL	husagimasita	husagimaseñ desita
Past Presump.	**INFORMAL**	husaidaroo	husaganakattaroo
		husaida daroo	husaganakatta daroo
	FORMAL	husagimasitaroo	husagimaseñ desitaroo
		husaida desyoo	husaganakatta desyoo
Conditional	**INFORMAL**	husaidara	husaganakattara
	FORMAL	husagimasitara	husagimaseñ desitara
Alternative	**INFORMAL**	husaidari	husaganakattari
	FORMAL	husagimasitari	husagimaseñ desitari

INFORMAL AFFIRMATIVE INDICATIVE

Passive		husagareru
Potential		husageru
Causative		husagaseru
Causative Pass.		husagaserareru

Honorific	**I**	ohusagi ni naru
	II	ohusagi nasaru
Humble	**I**	ohusagi suru
	II	ohusagi itasu

		AFFIRMATIVE	NEGATIVE
Indicative	**INFORMAL**	husagu	husaganai
	FORMAL	husagimasu	husagimaseñ
Imperative	**INFORMAL I**	husage	husagu na
	II	husaginasai	husaginasaru na
	III	husaide kudasai	husaganai de kudasai
	FORMAL	ohusagi nasaimase	ohusagi nasaimasu na
Presumptive	**INFORMAL I**	husagoo	husagumai
	II	husagu daroo	husaganai daroo
	FORMAL I	husagimasyoo	husagimasumai
	II	husagu desyoo	husaganai desyoo
Provisional	**INFORMAL**	husageba	husaganakereba
	FORMAL	husagimaseba	husagimaseñ nara
		husagimasureba	
Gerund	**INFORMAL I**	husaide	husaganai de
	II		husaganakute
	FORMAL	husagimasite	husagimaseñ de
Past Ind.	**INFORMAL**	husaida	husaganakatta
	FORMAL	husagimasita	husagimaseñ desita
Past Presump.	**INFORMAL**	husaidaroo	husaganakattaroo
		husaida daroo	husaganakatta daroo
	FORMAL	husagimasitaroo	husagimaseñ desitaroo
		husaida desyoo	husaganakatta desyoo
Conditional	**INFORMAL**	husaidara	husaganakattara
	FORMAL	husagimasitara	husagimaseñ desitara
Alternative	**INFORMAL**	husaidari	husaganakattari
	FORMAL	husagimasitari	husagimaseñ desitari

		INFORMAL AFFIRMATIVE INDICATIVE
Passive		husagareru
Potential		husageru
Causative		husagaseru
Causative Pass.		husagaserareru
Honorific	**I**	ohusagi ni naru
	II	ohusagi nasaru
Humble	**I**	ohusagi suru
	II	ohusagi itasu

		AFFIRMATIVE	NEGATIVE
Indicative	**INFORMAL**	husegu	huseganai
	FORMAL	husegimasu	husegimaseñ
Imperative	**INFORMAL I**	husege	husegu na
	II	huseginasai	huseginasaru na
	III	huseide kudasai	huseganai de kudasai
	FORMAL	ohusegi nasaimase	ohusegi nasaimasu na
Presumptive	**INFORMAL I**	husegoo	husegumai
	II	husegu daroo	huseganai daroo
	FORMAL I	husegimasyoo	husegimasumai
	II	husegu desyoo	huseganai desyoo
Provisional	**INFORMAL**	husegeba	huseganakereba
	FORMAL	husegimaseba	husegimaseñ nara
		husegimasureba	
Gerund	**INFORMAL I**	huseide	huseganai de
	II		huseganakute
	FORMAL	husegimasite	husegimaseñ de
Past Ind.	**INFORMAL**	huseida	huseganakatta
	FORMAL	husegimasita	husegimaseñ desita
Past Presump.	**INFORMAL**	huseidaroo	huseganakattaroo
		huseida daroo	huseganakatta daroo
	FORMAL	husegimasitaroo	husegimaseñ desitaroo
		huseida desyoo	huseganakatta desyoo
Conditional	**INFORMAL**	huseidara	huseganakattara
	FORMAL	husegimasitara	husegimaseñ desitara
Alternative	**INFORMAL**	huseidari	huseganakattari
	FORMAL	husegimasitari	husegimaseñ desitari

		INFORMAL AFFIRMATIVE INDICATIVE
Passive		husegareru
Potential		husegeru
Causative		husegaseru
Causative Pass.		husegaserareru
Honorific	**I**	ohusegi ni naru
	II	ohusegi nasaru
Humble	**I**	ohusegi suru
	II	ohusegi itasu

		AFFIRMATIVE	NEGATIVE
Indicative	**INFORMAL**	huseru	huseranai
	FORMAL	huserimasu	huserimaseñ
Imperative	**INFORMAL I**		huseru na
	II	huserinasai	huserinasaru na
	III	husette kudasai	huseranai de kudasai
	FORMAL	ohuseri nasaimase	ohuseri nasaimasu na
Presumptive	**INFORMAL I**	huseroo	huserumai
	II	huseru daroo	huseranai daroo
	FORMAL I	huserimasyoo	huserimasumai
	II	huseru desyoo	huseranai desyoo
Provisional	**INFORMAL**	husereba	huseranakereba
	FORMAL	huserimaseba	huserimaseñ nara
		huserimasureba	
Gerund	**INFORMAL I**	husette	huseranai de
	II		huseranakute
	FORMAL	huserimasite	huserimaseñ de
Past Ind.	**INFORMAL**	husetta	huseranakatta
	FORMAL	huserimasita	huserimaseñ desita
Past Presump.	**INFORMAL**	husettaroo	huseranakattaroo
		husetta daroo	huseranakatta daroo
	FORMAL	huserimasitaroo	huserimaseñ desitaroo
		husetta desyoo	huseranakatta desyoo
Conditional	**INFORMAL**	husettara	huseranakattara
	FORMAL	huserimasitara	huserimaseñ desitara
Alternative	**INFORMAL**	husettari	huseranakattari
	FORMAL	huserimasitari	huserimaseñ desitari

INFORMAL AFFIRMATIVE INDICATIVE

Passive	huserareru
Potential	husereru
Causative	huseraseru
Causative Pass.	huseraserareru

Honorific	**I**	ohuseri ni naru
	II	ohuseri nasaru
Humble	**I**	
	II	

to lay (something) *face down*   TRANSITIVE

			AFFIRMATIVE	NEGATIVE
Indicative	**INFORMAL**		huseru	husenai
	FORMAL		husemasu	husemaseñ
Imperative	**INFORMAL**	**I**	husero	huseru na
		II	husenasai	husenasaru na
		III	husete kudasai	husenai de kudasai
	FORMAL		ohuse nasaimase	ohuse nasaimasu na
Presumptive	**INFORMAL**	**I**	huseyoo	husemai
		II	huseru daroo	husenai daroo
	FORMAL	**I**	husemasyoo	husemasumai
		II	huseru desyoo	husenai desyoo
Provisional	**INFORMAL**		husereba	husenakereba
	FORMAL		husemaseba	husemaseñ nara
			husemasureba	
Gerund	**INFORMAL**	**I**	husete	husenai de
		II		husenakute
	FORMAL		husemasite	husemaseñ de
Past Ind.	**INFORMAL**		huseta	husenakatta
	FORMAL		husemasita	husemaseñ desita
Past Presump.	**INFORMAL**		husetaroo	husenakattaroo
			huseta daroo	husenakatta daroo
	FORMAL		husemasitaroo	husemaseñ desitaroo
			huseta desyoo	husenakatta desyoo
Conditional	**INFORMAL**		husetara	husenakattara
	FORMAL		husemasitara	husemaseñ desitara
Alternative	**INFORMAL**		husetari	husenakattari
	FORMAL		husemasitari	husemaseñ desitari

		INFORMAL AFFIRMATIVE INDICATIVE
Passive		huserareru
Potential		huserareru
Causative		husesaseru
Causative Pass.		husesaserareru
Honorific	**I**	ohuse ni naru
	II	ohuse nasaru
Humble	**I**	ohuse suru
	II	ohuse itasu

		AFFIRMATIVE	NEGATIVE
Indicative	**INFORMAL**	hutoru	hutoranai
	FORMAL	hutorimasu	hutorimaseñ
Imperative	**INFORMAL I**	hutore	hutoru na
	II	hutorinasai	hutorinasaru na
	III	hutotte kudasai	hutoranai de kudasai
	FORMAL	ohutori nasaimase	ohutori nasaimasu na
Presumptive	**INFORMAL I**	hutoroo	hutorumai
	II	hutoru daroo	hutoranai daroo
	FORMAL I	hutorimasyoo	hutorimasumai
	II	hutoru desyoo	hutoranai desyoo
Provisional	**INFORMAL**	hutoreba	hutoranakereba
	FORMAL	hutorimaseba	hutorimaseñ nara
		hutorimasureba	
Gerund	**INFORMAL I**	hutotte	hutoranai de
	II		hutoranakute
	FORMAL	hutorimasite	hutorimaseñ de
Past Ind.	**INFORMAL**	hutotta	hutoranakatta
	FORMAL	hutorimasita	hutorimaseñ desita
Past Presump.	**INFORMAL**	hutottaroo	hutoranakattaroo
		hutotta daroo	hutoranakatta daroo
	FORMAL	hutorimasitaroo	hutorimaseñ desitaroo
		hutotta desyoo	hutoranakatta desyoo
Conditional	**INFORMAL**	hutottara	hutoranakattara
	FORMAL	hutorimasitara	hutorimaseñ desitara
Alternative	**INFORMAL**	hutottari	hutoranakattari
	FORMAL	hutorimasitari	hutorimaseñ desitari

		INFORMAL AFFIRMATIVE INDICATIVE
Passive		hutorareru
Potential		hutoreru
Causative		hutoraseru
Causative Pass.		hutoraserareru
Honorific	**I**	ohutori ni naru
	II	ohutori nasaru
Humble	**I**	
	II	

		AFFIRMATIVE	NEGATIVE
Indicative	**INFORMAL**	huyasu	huyasanai
	FORMAL	huyasimasu	huyasimaseñ
Imperative	**INFORMAL I**	huyase	huyasu na
	II	huyasinasai	huyasinasaru na
	III	huyasite kudasai	huyasanai de kudasai
	FORMAL	ohuyasi nasaimase	ohuyasi nasaimasu na
Presumptive	**INFORMAL I**	huyasoo	huyasumai
	II	huyasu daroo	huyasanai daroo
	FORMAL I	huyasimasyoo	huyasimasumai
	II	huyasu desyoo	huyasanai desyoo
Provisional	**INFORMAL**	huyaseba	huyasanakereba
	FORMAL	huyasimaseba	huyasimaseñ nara
		huyasimasureba	
Gerund	**INFORMAL I**	huyasite	huyasanai de
	II		huyasanakute
	FORMAL	huyasimasite	huyasimaseñ de
Past Ind.	**INFORMAL**	huyasita	huyasanakatta
	FORMAL	huyasimasita	huyasimaseñ desita
Past Presump.	**INFORMAL**	huyasitaroo	huyasanakattaroo
		huyasita daroo	huyasanakatta daroo
	FORMAL	huyasimasitaroo	huyasimaseñ desitaroo
		huyasita desyoo	huyasanakatta desyoo
Conditional	**INFORMAL**	huyasitara	huyasanakattara
	FORMAL	huyasimasitara	huyasimaseñ desitara
Alternative	**INFORMAL**	huyasitari	huyasanakattari
	FORMAL	huyasimasitari	huyasimaseñ desitari

INFORMAL AFFIRMATIVE INDICATIVE

Passive		huyasareru
Potential		huyaseru
Causative		huyasaseru
Causative Pass.		huyasaserareru
Honorific	**I**	ohuyasi ni naru
	II	ohuyasi nasaru
Humble	**I**	ohuyasi suru
	II	ohuyasi itasu

120

		AFFIRMATIVE	NEGATIVE
Indicative	**INFORMAL**	huzakeru	huzakenai
	FORMAL	huzakemasu	huzakemaseñ
Imperative	**INFORMAL I**	huzakero	huzakeru na
	II	huzakenasai	huzakenasaru na
	III	huzakete kudasai	huzakenai de kudasai
	FORMAL	ohuzake nasaimase	ohuzake nasaimasu na
Presumptive	**INFORMAL I**	huzakeyoo	huzakemai
	II	huzakeru daroo	huzakenai daroo
	FORMAL I	huzakemasyoo	huzakemasumai
	II	huzakeru desyoo	huzakenai desyoo
Provisional	**INFORMAL**	huzakereba	huzakenakereba
	FORMAL	huzakemaseba	huzakemaseñ nara
		huzakemasureba	
Gerund	**INFORMAL I**	huzakete	huzakenai de
	II		huzakenakute
	FORMAL	huzakemasite	huzakemaseñ de
Past Ind.	**INFORMAL**	huzaketa	huzakenakatta
	FORMAL	huzakemasita	huzakemaseñ desita
Past Presump.	**INFORMAL**	huzaketaroo	huzakenakattaroo
		huzaketa daroo	huzakenakatta daroo
	FORMAL	huzakemasitaroo	huzakemaseñ desitaroo
		huzaketa desyoo	huzakenakatta desyoo
Conditional	**INFORMAL**	huzaketara	huzakenakattara
	FORMAL	huzakemasitara	huzakemaseñ desitara
Alternative	**INFORMAL**	huzaketari	huzakenakattari
	FORMAL	huzakemasitari	huzakemaseñ desitari

INFORMAL AFFIRMATIVE INDICATIVE

Passive		huzakerareru
Potential		huzakerareru
Causative		huzakesaseru
Causative Pass.		huzakesaserareru

Honorific	**I**	ohuzake ni naru
	II	ohuzake nasaru
Humble	**I**	ohuzake suru
	II	ohuzake itasu

to boast, to put on airs   TRANSITIVE

		AFFIRMATIVE	NEGATIVE
Indicative	**INFORMAL**	ibaru	ibaranai
	FORMAL	ibarimasu	ibarimaseñ
Imperative	**INFORMAL I**	ibare	ibaru na
	II	ibarinasai	ibarinasaru na
	III	ibatte kudasai	ibaranai de kudasai
	FORMAL	oibari nasaimase	oibari nasaimasu na
Presumptive	**INFORMAL I**	ibaroo	ibarumai
	II	ibaru daroo	ibaranai daroo
	FORMAL I	ibarimasyoo	ibarimasumai
	II	ibaru desyoo	ibaranai desyoo
Provisional	**INFORMAL**	ibareba	ibaranakereba
	FORMAL	ibarimaseba	ibarimaseñ nara
		ibarimasureba	
Gerund	**INFORMAL I**	ibatte	ibaranai de
	II		ibaranakute
	FORMAL	ibarimasite	ibarimaseñ de
Past Ind.	**INFORMAL**	ibatta	ibaranakatta
	FORMAL	ibarimasita	ibarimaseñ desita
Past Presump.	**INFORMAL**	ibattaroo	ibaranakattaroo
		ibatta daroo	ibaranakatta daroo
	FORMAL	ibarimasitaroo	ibarimaseñ desitaroo
		ibatta desyoo	ibaranakatta desyoo
Conditional	**INFORMAL**	ibattara	ibaranakattara
	FORMAL	ibarimasitara	ibarimaseñ desitara
Alternative	**INFORMAL**	ibattari	ibaranakattari
	FORMAL	ibarimasitari	ibarimaseñ desitari

		INFORMAL AFFIRMATIVE INDICATIVE
Passive		ibarareru
Potential		ibareru
Causative		ibaraseru
Causative Pass.		ibaraserareru
Honorific	**I**	oibari ni naru
	II	oibari nasaru
Humble	**I**	
	II	

		AFFIRMATIVE	NEGATIVE
Indicative	**INFORMAL**	idomu	idomanai
	FORMAL	idomimasu	idomimaseñ
Imperative	**INFORMAL I**	idome	idomu na
	II	idominasai	idominasaru na
	III	idoñde kudasai	idomanai de kudasai
	FORMAL	oidomi nasaimase	oidomi nasaimasu na
Presumptive	**INFORMAL I**	idomoo	idomumai
	II	idomu daroo	idomanai daroo
	FORMAL I	idomimasyoo	idomimasumai
	II	idomu desyoo	idomanai desyoo
Provisional	**INFORMAL**	idomeba	idomanakereba
	FORMAL	idomimaseba	idomimaseñ nara
		idomimasureba	
Gerund	**INFORMAL I**	idoñde	idomanai de
	II		idomanakute
	FORMAL	idomimasite	idomimaseñ de
Past Ind.	**INFORMAL**	idoñda	idomanakatta
	FORMAL	idomimasita	idomimaseñ desita
Past Presump.	**INFORMAL**	idoñdaroo	idomanakattaroo
		idoñda daroo	idomanakatta daroo
	FORMAL	idomimasitaroo	idomimaseñ desitaroo
		idoñda desyoo	idomanakatta desyoo
Conditional	**INFORMAL**	idoñdara	idomanakattara
	FORMAL	idomimasitara	idomimaseñ desitara
Alternative	**INFORMAL**	idoñdari	idomanakattari
	FORMAL	idomimasitari	idomimaseñ desitari

INFORMAL AFFIRMATIVE INDICATIVE

Passive		idomareru
Potential		idomeru
Causative		idomaseru
Causative Pass.		idomaserareru
Honorific	**I**	oidomi ni naru
	II	oidomi nasaru
Humble	**I**	oidomi suru
	II	oidomi itasu

to express in words   TRANSITIVE

		AFFIRMATIVE	NEGATIVE
Indicative	**INFORMAL**	iiarawasu	iiarawasanai
	FORMAL	iiarawasimasu	iiarawasimaseñ
Imperative	**INFORMAL I**	iiarawase	iiarawasu na
	II	iiarawasinasai	iiarawasinasaru na
	III	iiarawasite kudasai	iiarawasanai de kudasai
	FORMAL	oiiarawasi nasaimase	oiiarawasi nasaimasu na
Presumptive	**INFORMAL I**	iiarawasoo	iiarawasumai
	II	iiarawasu daroo	iiarawasanai daroo
	FORMAL I	iiarawasimasyoo	iiarawasimasumai
	II	iiarawasu desyoo	iiarawasanai desyoo
Provisional	**INFORMAL**	iiarawaseba	iiarawasanakereba
	FORMAL	iiarawasimaseba	iiarawasimaseñ nara
		iiarawasimasureba	
Gerund	**INFORMAL I**	iiarawasite	iiarawasanai de
	II		iiarawasanakute
	FORMAL	iiarawasimasite	iiarawasimaseñ de
Past Ind.	**INFORMAL**	iiarawasita	iiarawasanakatta
	FORMAL	iiarawasimasita	iiarawasimaseñ desita
Past Presump.	**INFORMAL**	iiarawasitaroo	iiarawasanakattaroo
		iiarawasita daroo	iiarawasanakatta daroo
	FORMAL	iiarawasimasitaroo	iiarawasimaseñ desitaroo
		iiarawasita desyoo	iiarawasanakatta desyoo
Conditional	**INFORMAL**	iiarawasitara	iiarawasanakattara
	FORMAL	iiarawasimasitara	iiarawasimaseñ desitara
Alternative	**INFORMAL**	iiarawasitari	iiarawasanakattari
	FORMAL	iiarawasimasitari	iiarawasimaseñ desitari

INFORMAL AFFIRMATIVE INDICATIVE

Passive		iiarawasareru
Potential		iiarawaseru
Causative		iiarawasaseru
Causative Pass.		iiarawasaserareru

Honorific	**I**	oiiarawasi ni naru
	II	oiiarawasi nasaru
Humble	**I**	
	II	

TRANSITIVE   *to arrange beforehand*

		AFFIRMATIVE	NEGATIVE
Indicative	**INFORMAL**	iiawaseru	iiawasenai
	FORMAL	iiawasemasu	iiawasemaseñ
Imperative	**INFORMAL I**	iiawasero	iiawaseru na
	II	iiawasenasai	iiawasenasaru na
	III	iiawasete kudasai	iiawasenai de kudasai
	FORMAL	oiiawase nasaimase	oiiawase nasaimasu na
Presumptive	**INFORMAL I**	iiawaseyoo	iiawasemai
	II	iiawaseru daroo	iiawasenai daroo
	FORMAL I	iiawasemasyoo	iiawasemasumai
	II	iiawaseru desyoo	iiawasenai desyoo
Provisional	**INFORMAL**	iiawasereba	iiawasenakereba
	FORMAL	iiawasemaseba	iiawasemaseñ nara
		iiawasemasureba	
Gerund	**INFORMAL I**	iiawasete	iiawasenai de
	II		iiawasenakute
	FORMAL	iiawasemasite	iiawasemaseñ de
Past Ind.	**INFORMAL**	iiawaseta	iiawasenakatta
	FORMAL	iiawasemasita	iiawasemaseñ desita
Past Presump.	**INFORMAL**	iiawasetaroo	iiawasenakattaroo
		iiawaseta daroo	iiawasenakatta daroo
	FORMAL	iiawasemasitaroo	iiawasemaseñ desitaroo
		iiawaseta desyoo	iiawasenakatta desyoo
Conditional	**INFORMAL**	iiawasetara	iiawasenakattara
	FORMAL	iiawasemasitara	iiawasemaseñ desitara
Alternative	**INFORMAL**	iiawasetari	iiawasenakattari
	FORMAL	iiawasemasitari	iiawasemaseñ desitari

		INFORMAL AFFIRMATIVE INDICATIVE
Passive		iiawaserareru
Potential		iiawaserareru
Causative		iiawasesaseru
Causative Pass.		iiawasesaserareru
Honorific	**I**	oiiawase ni naru
	II	oiiawase nasaru
Humble	**I**	oiiawase suru
	II	oiiawase itasu

		AFFIRMATIVE	**NEGATIVE**
Indicative	**INFORMAL**	iidasu	iidasanai
	FORMAL	iidasimasu	iidasimaseñ
Imperative	**INFORMAL I**	iidase	iidasu na
	II	iidasinasai	iidasinasaru na
	III	iidasite kudasai	iidasanai de kudasai
	FORMAL	oiidasi nasaimase	oiidasi nasaimasu na
Presumptive	**INFORMAL I**	iidasoo	iidasumai
	II	iidasu daroo	iidasanai daroo
	FORMAL I	iidasimasyoo	iidasimasumai
	II	iidasu desyoo	iidasanai desyoo
Provisional	**INFORMAL**	iidaseba	iidasanakereba
	FORMAL	iidasimaseba	iidasimaseñ nara
		iidasimasureba	
Gerund	**INFORMAL I**	iidasite	iidasanai de
	II		iidasanakute
	FORMAL	iidasimasite	iidasimaseñ de
Past Ind.	**INFORMAL**	iidasita	iidasanakatta
	FORMAL	iidasimasita	iidasimaseñ desita
Past Presump.	**INFORMAL**	iidasitaroo	iidasanakattaroo
		iidasita daroo	iidasanakatta daroo
	FORMAL	iidasimasitaroo	iidasimaseñ desitaroo
		iidasita desyoo	iidasanakatta desyoo
Conditional	**INFORMAL**	iidasitara	iidasanakattara
	FORMAL	iidasimasitara	iidasimaseñ desitara
Alternative	**INFORMAL**	iidasitari	iidasanakattari
	FORMAL	iidasimasitari	iidasimaseñ desitari

INFORMAL AFFIRMATIVE INDICATIVE

Passive	iidasareru
Potential	iidaseru
Causative	iidasaseru
Causative Pass.	iidasaserareru

Honorific	**I**	oiidasi ni naru
	II	oiidasi nasaru
Humble	**I**	
	II	

TRANSITIVE   *to circulate* (a rumor)

		AFFIRMATIVE	NEGATIVE
Indicative	**INFORMAL**	iihurasu	iihurasanai
	FORMAL	iihurasimasu	iihurasimaseñ
Imperative	**INFORMAL I**	iihurase	iihurasu na
	II	iihurasinasai	iihurasinasaru na
	III	iihurasite kudasai	iihurasanai de kudasai
	FORMAL	oiihurasi nasaimase	oiihurasi nasaimasu na
Presumptive	**INFORMAL I**	iihurasoo	iihurasumai
	II	iihurasu daroo	iihurasanai daroo
	FORMAL I	iihurasimasyoo	iihurasimasumai
	II	iihurasu desyoo	iihurasanai desyoo
Provisional	**INFORMAL**	iihuraseba	iihurasanakereba
	FORMAL	iihurasimaseba	iihurasimaseñ nara
Gerund	**INFORMAL I**	iihurasite	iihurasanai de
	II		iihurasanakute
	FORMAL	iihurasimasite	iihurasimaseñ de
Past Ind.	**INFORMAL**	iihurasita	iihurasanakatta
	FORMAL	iihurasimasita	iihurasimaseñ desita
Past Presump.	**INFORMAL**	iihurasitaroo	iihurasanakattaroo
		iihurasita daroo	iihurasanakatta daroo
	FORMAL	iihurasimasitaroo	iihurasimaseñ desitaroo
		iihurasita desyoo	iihurasanakatta desyoo
Conditional	**INFORMAL**	iihurasitara	iihurasanakattara
	FORMAL	iihurasimasitara	iihurasimaseñ desitara
Alternative	**INFORMAL**	iihurasitari	iihurasanakattari
	FORMAL	iihurasimasitari	iihurasimaseñ desitari

INFORMAL AFFIRMATIVE INDICATIVE

Passive		iihurasareru
Potential		iihuraseru
Causative		iihurasaseru
Causative Pass.		iihurasaserareru

Honorific	**I**	oiihurasi ni naru
	II	oiihurasi nasaru
Humble	**I**	
	II	

		AFFIRMATIVE	NEGATIVE
Indicative	**INFORMAL**	iikaesu	iikaesanai
	FORMAL	iikaesimasu	iikaesimaseñ
Imperative	**INFORMAL I**	iikaese	iikaesu na
	II	iikaesinasai	iikaesinasaru na
	III	iikaesite kudasai	iikaesanai de kudasai
	FORMAL	oiikaesi nasaimase	oiikaesi nasaimasu na
Presumptive	**INFORMAL I**	iikaesoo	iikaesumai
	II	iikaesu daroo	iikaesanai daroo
	FORMAL I	iikaesimasyoo	iikaesimasumai
	II	iikaesu desyoo	iikaesanai desyoo
Provisional	**INFORMAL**	iikaeseba	iikaesanakereba
	FORMAL	iikaesimaseba	iikaesimaseñ nara
		iikaesimasureba	
Gerund	**INFORMAL I**	iikaesite	iikaesanai de
	II		iikaesanakute
	FORMAL	iikaesimasite	iikaesimaseñ de
Past Ind.	**INFORMAL**	iikaesita	iikaesanakatta
	FORMAL	iikaesimasita	iikaesimaseñ desita
Past Presump.	**INFORMAL**	iikaesitaroo	iikaesanakattaroo
		iikaesita daroo	iikaesakatta daroo
	FORMAL	iikaesimasitaroo	iikaesimaseñ desitaroo
		iikaesita desyoo	iikaesanakatta desyoo
Conditional	**INFORMAL**	iikaesitara	iikaesanakattara
	FORMAL	iikaesimasitara	iikaesimaseñ desitara
Alternative	**INFORMAL**	iikaesitari	iikaesanakattari
	FORMAL	iikaesimasitari	iikaesimaseñ desitari

INFORMAL AFFIRMATIVE INDICATIVE

Passive		iikaesareru
Potential		iikaeseru
Causative		iikaesaseru
Causative Pass.		iikaesaserareru
Honorific	**I**	oiikaesi ni naru
	II	oiikaesi nasaru
Humble	**I**	oiikaesi suru
	II	oiikaesi itasu

TRANSITIVE   *to rephrase, to correct oneself*

		AFFIRMATIVE	NEGATIVE
Indicative	**INFORMAL**	iinaosu	iinaosanai
	FORMAL	iinaosimasu	iinaosimaseñ
Imperative	**INFORMAL I**	iinaose	iinaosu na
	II	iinaosinasai	iinaosinasaru na
	III	iinaosite kudasai	iinosanai de kudasai
	FORMAL	oiinaosi nasaimase	oiinaosi nasaimasu na
Presumptive	**INFORMAL I**	iinaosoo	iinaosumai
	II	iinaosu daroo	iinaosanai daroo
	FORMAL I	iinaosimasyoo	iinaosimasumai
	II	iinaosu desyoo	iinaosanai desyoo
Provisional	**INFORMAL**	iinaoseba	iinaosanakereba
	FORMAL	iinaosimaseba	iinaosimaseñ nara
		iinaosimasureba	
Gerund	**INFORMAL I**	iinaosite	iinaosanai de
	II		iinaosanakute
	FORMAL	iinaosimasite	iinaosimaseñ de
Past Ind.	**INFORMAL**	iinaosita	iinaosanakatta
	FORMAL	iinaosimasita	iinaosimaseñ desita
Past Presump.	**INFORMAL**	iinaositaroo	iinaosanakattaroo
		iinaosita daroo	iinaosanakatta daroo
	FORMAL	iinaosimasitaroo	iinaosimaseñ desitaroo
		iinaosita desyoo	iinaosanakatta desyoo
Conditional	**INFORMAL**	iinaositara	iinaosanakattara
	FORMAL	iinaosimasitara	iinasimaseñ desitara
Alternative	**INFORMAL**	iinaositari	iinaosanakattari
	FORMAL	iinaosimasitari	iinaosimaseñ desitari

		INFORMAL AFFIRMATIVE INDICATIVE
Passive		iinaosareru
Potential		iinaoseru
Causative		iinaosaseru
Causative Pass.		iinaosaserareru
Honorific	**I**	oiinaosi ni naru
	II	oiinaosi nasaru
Humble	**I**	
	II	

to give an evasive answer, to talk oneself out of difficulty

		AFFIRMATIVE	NEGATIVE
Indicative	**INFORMAL**	iinukeru	iinukenai
	FORMAL	iinukemasu	iinukemaseñ
Imperative	**INFORMAL I**	iinukero	iinukeru na
	II	iinukenasai	iinukenasaru na
	III	iinukete kudasai	iinukenai de kudasai
	FORMAL	oiinuke nasaimase	oiinuke nasaimasu na
Presumptive	**INFORMAL I**	iinukeyoo	iinukemai
	II	iinukeru daroo	iinukenai daroo
	FORMAL I	iinukemasyoo	iinukemasumai
	II	iinukeru desyoo	iinukenai desyoo
Provisional	**INFORMAL**	iinukereba	iinukenakereba
	FORMAL	iinukemaseba	iinukemaseñ nara
		iinukemasureba	
Gerund	**INFORMAL I**	iinukete	iinukenai de
	II		iinukenakute
	FORMAL	iinukemasite	iinukemaseñ de
Past Ind.	**INFORMAL**	iinuketa	iinukenakatta
	FORMAL	iinukemasita	iinukemaseñ desita
Past Presump.	**INFORMAL**	iinuketaroo	iinukenakattaroo
		iinuketa daroo	iinukenakatta daroo
	FORMAL	iinukemasitaroo	iinukemaseñ desitaroo
		iinuketa desyoo	iinukenakatta desyoo
Conditional	**INFORMAL**	iinuketara	iinukenakattara
	FORMAL	iinukemasitara	iinukemaseñ desitara
Alternative	**INFORMAL**	iinuketari	iinukenakattari
	FORMAL	iinukemasitari	iinukemaseñ desitari

		INFORMAL AFFIRMATIVE INDICATIVE
Passive		iinukerareru
Potential		iinukerareru
Causative		iinukesaseru
Causative Pass.		iinukesaserareru
Honorific	**I**	oiinuke ni naru
	II	oiinuke nasaru
Humble	**I**	
	II	

TRANSITIVE   *to exaggerate, to say too much*

			AFFIRMATIVE	NEGATIVE
Indicative	**INFORMAL**		iisugiru	iisuginai
	FORMAL		iisugimasu	iisugimaseñ
Imperative	**INFORMAL**	**I**	iisugiro	iisugiru na
		II	iisuginasai	iisuginasaru na
		III	iisugite kudasai	iisuginai de kudasai
	FORMAL		oiisugi nasaimase	oiisugi nasaimasu na
Presumptive	**INFORMAL**	**I**	iisugiyoo	iisugimai
		II	iisugiru daroo	iisuginai daroo
	FORMAL	**I**	iisugimasyoo	iisugimasumai
		II	iisugiru desyoo	iisuginai desyoo
Provisional	**INFORMAL**		iisugireba	iisuginakereba
	FORMAL		iisugimaseba	iisugimaseñ nara
			iisugimasureba	
Gerund	**INFORMAL**	**I**	iisugite	iisuginai de
		II		iisuginakute
	FORMAL		iisugimasite	iisugimaseñ de
Past Ind.	**INFORMAL**		iisugita	iisuginakatta
	FORMAL		iisugimasita	iisugimaseñ desita
Past Presump.	**INFORMAL**		iisugitaroo	iisuginakattaroo
			iisugita daroo	iisuginakatta daroo
	FORMAL		iisugimasitaroo	iisugimaseñ desitaroo
			iisugita desyoo	iisuginakatta desyoo
Conditional	**INFORMAL**		iisugitara	iisuginakattara
	FORMAL		iisugimasitara	iisugimaseñ desitara
Alternative	**INFORMAL**		iisugitari	iisuginakattari
	FORMAL		iisugimasitari	iisugimaseñ desitari

		INFORMAL AFFIRMATIVE INDICATIVE
Passive		iisugirareru
Potential		iisugirareru
Causative		iisugisaseru
Causative Pass.		iisugisaserareru
Honorific	**I**	oiisugi ni naru
	II	oiisugi nasaru
Humble	**I**	
	II	

to tell (a person to do something)   TRANSITIVE

		AFFIRMATIVE	NEGATIVE
Indicative	**INFORMAL**	iitukeru	iitukenai
	FORMAL	iitukemasu	iitukemaseñ
Imperative	**INFORMAL I**	iitukero	iitukeru na
	II	iitukenasai	iitukenasaru na
	III	iitukete kudasai	iitukenai de kudasai
	FORMAL	oiituke nasaimase	oiituke nasaimasu na
Presumptive	**INFORMAL I**	iitukeyoo	iitukemai
	II	iitukeru daroo	iitukenai daroo
	FORMAL I	iitukemasyoo	iitukemasumai
	II	iitukeru desyoo	iitukenai desyoo
Provisional	**INFORMAL**	iitukereba	iitukenakereba
	FORMAL	iitukemaseba	iitukemaseñ nara
		iitukemasureba	
Gerund	**INFORMAL I**	iitukete	iitukenai de
	II		iitukenakute
	FORMAL	iitukemasite	iitukemaseñ de
Past Ind.	**INFORMAL**	iituketa	iitukenakatta
	FORMAL	iitukemasita	iitukemaseñ desita
Past Presump.	**INFORMAL**	iituketaroo	iitukenakattaroo
		iituketa daroo	iitukenakatta daroo
	FORMAL	iitukemasitaroo	iitukemaseñ desitaroo
		iituketa desyoo	iitukenakatta desyoo
Conditional	**INFORMAL**	iituketara	iitukenakattara
	FORMAL	iitukemasitara	iitukemaseñ desitara
Alternative	**INFORMAL**	iituketari	iitukenakattari
	FORMAL	iitukemasitari	iitukemaseñ desitari

	INFORMAL AFFIRMATIVE INDICATIVE
Passive	iitukerareru
Potential	iitukerareru
Causative	iitukesaseru
Causative Pass.	iitukesaserareru

Honorific	**I**	oiituke ni naru
	II	oiituke nasaru
Humble	**I**	
	II	

TRANSITIVE   *to make excuses* (for one's error)

		AFFIRMATIVE	NEGATIVE
Indicative	INFORMAL	iitukurou	iitukurowanai
	FORMAL	iitukuroimasu	iitukuroimaseñ
Imperative	INFORMAL I	iitukuroe	iitukurou na
	II	iitukuroinasai	iitukuroinasaru na
	III	iitukurotte kudasai	iitukurowanai de kudasai
	FORMAL	oiitukuroi nasaimase	oiitukuroi nasaimasu na
Presumptive	INFORMAL I	iitukurooo	iitukuroumai
	II	iitukurou daroo	iitukurowanai daroo
	FORMAL I	iitukuroimasyoo	iitukuroimasumai
	II	iitukurou desyoo	iitukurowanai daroo
Provisional	INFORMAL	iitukuroeba	iitukurowanakereba
	FORMAL	iitukuroimaseba	iitukuroimaseñ nara
		iitukuroimasureba	
Gerund	INFORMAL I	iitukurotte	iitukurowanai de
	II		iitukurowanakute
	FORMAL	iitukuroimasite	iitukuroimaseñ de
Past Ind.	INFORMAL	iitukurotta	iitukurowanakatta
	FORMAL	iitukuroimasita	iitukuroimaseñ desita
Past Presump.	INFORMAL	iitukurottaroo	iitukurowanakattaroo
		iitukurotta daroo	iitukurowanakatta daroo
	FORMAL	iitukuroimasitaroo	iitukuroimaseñ desitaroo
		iitukurotta desyoo	iitukurowanakatta desyoo
Conditional	INFORMAL	iitukurottara	iitukurowanakattara
	FORMAL	iitukuroimasitara	iitukuroimaseñ desitara
Alternative	INFORMAL	iitukurottari	iitukurowanakattari
	FORMAL	iitukuroimasitari	iitukuroimaseñ desitari

		INFORMAL AFFIRMATIVE INDICATIVE
Passive		iitukurowareru
Potential		iitukuroeru
Causative		iitukurowaseru
Causative Pass.		iitukurowaserareru
Honorific	I	oiitukuroi ni naru
	II	oiitukuroi nasaru
Humble	I	oiitukuroi suru
	II	oiitukuroi itasu

to tell everything, to exhaust (a subject)   TRANSITIVE

		AFFIRMATIVE	NEGATIVE
Indicative	**INFORMAL**	iitukusu	iitukusanai
	FORMAL	iitukusimasu	iitukusimaseñ
Imperative	**INFORMAL I**	iitukuse	iitukusu na
	II	iitukusinasai	iitukusinasaru na
	III	iitukusite kudasai	iitukusanai de kudasai
	FORMAL	oiitukusi nasaimase	oiitukusi nasaimasu na
Presumptive	**INFORMAL I**	iitukusoo	iitukusumai
	II	iitukusu daroo	iitukusanai daroo
	FORMAL I	iitukusimasyoo	iitukusimasumai
	II	iitukusu desyoo	iitukusanai desyoo
Provisional	**INFORMAL**	iitukuseba	iitukusanakereba
	FORMAL	iitukusimaseba	iitukusimaseñ nara
		iitukusimasureba	
Gerund	**INFORMAL I**	iitukusite	iitukusanai de
	II		iitukusanakute
	FORMAL	iitukusimasite	iitukusimaseñ de
Past Ind.	**INFORMAL**	iitukusita	iitukusanakatta
	FORMAL	iitukusimasita	iitukusimaseñ desita
Past Presump.	**INFORMAL**	iitukusitaroo	iitukusanakattaroo
		iitukusita daroo	iitukusanakatta daroo
	FORMAL	iitukusimasitaroo	iitukusimaseñ desitaroo
		iitukusita desyoo	iitukusanakatta desyoo
Conditional	**INFORMAL**	iitukusitara	iitukusanakattara
	FORMAL	iitukusimasitara	iitukusimaseñ desitara
Alternative	**INFORMAL**	iitukusitari	iitukusanakattari
	FORMAL	iitukusimasitari	iitukusimaseñ desitari

		INFORMAL AFFIRMATIVE INDICATIVE
Passive		iitukusareru
Potential		iitukuseru
Causative		iitukusaseru
Causative Pass.		iitukusaserareru
Honorific	I	oiitukusi ni naru
	II	oiitukusi nasaru
Humble	I	
	II	

TRANSITIVE   *to court, to make advances to*

		AFFIRMATIVE	NEGATIVE
Indicative	**INFORMAL**	iiyoru	iiyoranai
	FORMAL	iiyorimasu	iiyorimaseñ
Imperative	**INFORMAL I**	iiyore	iiyoru na
	II	iiyorinasai	iiyorinasaru na
	III	iiyotte kudasai	iiyoranai de kudasai
	FORMAL	oiiyori nasaimase	oiiyori nasaimasu na
Presumptive	**INFORMAL I**	iiyoroo	iiyorumai
	II	iiyoru daroo	iiyoranai daroo
	FORMAL I	iiyorimasyoo	iiyorimasumai
	II	iiyoru desyoo	iiyoranai desyoo
Provisional	**INFORMAL**	iiyoreba	iiyoranakereba
	FORMAL	iiyorimaseba	iiyorimaseñ nara
		iiyorimasureba	
Gerund	**INFORMAL I**	iiyotte	iiyoranai de
	II		iiyoranakute
	FORMAL	iiyorimasite	iiyorimaseñ de
Past Ind.	**INFORMAL**	iiyotta	iiyoranakatta
	FORMAL	iiyorimasita	iiyorimaseñ desita
Past Presump.	**INFORMAL**	iiyottaroo	iiyoranakattaroo
		iiyotta daroo	iiyoranakatta daroo
	FORMAL	iiyorimasitaroo	iiyorimaseñ desitaroo
		iiyotta desyoo	iiyoranakatta desyoo
Conditional	**INFORMAL**	iiyottara	iiyoranakattara
	FORMAL	iiyorimasitara	iiyorimaseñ desitara
Alternative	**INFORMAL**	iiyottari	iiyoranakattari
	FORMAL	iiyorimasitari	iiyorimaseñ desitari

		INFORMAL AFFIRMATIVE INDICATIVE
Passive		iiyorareru
Potential		iiyoreru
Causative		iiyoraseru
Causative Pass.		iiyoraserareru

Honorific	**I**	oiiyori ni naru
	II	oiiyori nasaru
Humble	**I**	oiiyori suru
	II	oiiyori itasu

		AFFIRMATIVE	NEGATIVE
Indicative	**INFORMAL**	ikiru	ikinai
	FORMAL	ikimasu	ikimaseñ
Imperative	**INFORMAL I**	ikiro	ikiru na
	II	ikinasai	ikinasaru na
	III	ikite kudasai	ikinai de kudasai
	FORMAL	oiki nasaimase	oiki nasaimasu na
Presumptive	**INFORMAL I**	ikiyoo	ikimai
	II	ikiru daroo	ikinai daroo
	FORMAL I	ikimasyoo	ikimasumai
	II	ikiru desyoo	ikinai desyoo
Provisional	**INFORMAL**	ikireba	ikinakereba
	FORMAL	ikimaseba	ikimaseñ nara
		ikimasureba	
Gerund	**INFORMAL I**	ikite	ikinai de
	II		ikinakute
	FORMAL	ikimasite	ikimaseñ de
Past Ind.	**INFORMAL**	ikita	ikinakatta
	FORMAL	ikimasita	ikimaseñ desita
Past Presump.	**INFORMAL**	ikitaroo	ikinakattaroo
		ikita daroo	ikinakatta daroo
	FORMAL	ikimasitaroo	ikimaseñ desitaroo
		ikita desyoo	ikinakatta desyoo
Conditional	**INFORMAL**	ikitara	ikinakattara
	FORMAL	ikimasitara	ikimaseñ desitara
Alternative	**INFORMAL**	ikitari	ikinakattari
	FORMAL	ikimasitari	ikimaseñ desitari

		INFORMAL AFFIRMATIVE INDICATIVE
Passive		ikirareru
Potential		ikirareru
Causative		ikisaseru
Causative Pass.		ikisaserareru
Honorific	**I**	oiki ni naru
	II	oiki nasaru
Humble	**I**	
	II	

		AFFIRMATIVE	NEGATIVE
Indicative	**INFORMAL**	iku	ikanai
	FORMAL	ikimasu	ikimaseñ
Imperative	**INFORMAL I**	ike	iku na
	II	ikinasai	ikinasaru na
	III	itte kudasai	ikanai de kudasai
	FORMAL	oide nasaimase	oide nasaimasu na
Presumptive	**INFORMAL I**	ikoo	ikumai
	II	iku daroo	ikanai daroo
	FORMAL I	ikimasyoo	ikimasumai
	II	iku desyoo	ikanai desyoo
Provisional	**INFORMAL**	ikeba	ikanakereba
	FORMAL	ikimaseba	ikimaseñ nara
		ikimasureba	
Gerund	**INFORMAL I**	itte	ikanai de
	II		ikanakute
	FORMAL	ikimasite	ikimaseñ de
Past Ind.	**INFORMAL**	itta	ikanakatta
	FORMAL	ikimasita	ikimaseñ desita
Past Presump.	**INFORMAL**	ittaroo	ikanakattaroo
		itta daroo	ikanakatta daroo
	FORMAL	ikimasitaroo	ikimaseñ desitaroo
		itta desyoo	ikanakatta desyoo
Conditional	**INFORMAL**	ittara	ikanakattara
	FORMAL	ikimasitara	ikimaseñ desitara
Alternative	**INFORMAL**	ittari	ikanakattari
	FORMAL	ikimasitari	ikimaseñ desitari

	INFORMAL AFFIRMATIVE INDICATIVE	
Passive	ikareru	
Potential	ikareru	ikeru
Causative	ikaseru	
Causative Pass.	ikaserareru	
Honorific	irassyaru	{ oide ni naru (I) { oide nasaru (II)
Humble		
	mairu	

		AFFIRMATIVE	NEGATIVE
Indicative	**INFORMAL**	imasimeru	imasimenai
	FORMAL	imasimemasu	imasimemaseñ
Imperative	**INFORMAL I**	imasimero	imasimeru na
	II	imasimenasai	imasimenasaru na
	III	imasimete kudasai	imasimenai de kudasai
	FORMAL	oimasime nasaimase	oimasime nasaimasu na
Presumptive	**INFORMAL I**	imasimeyoo	imasimenai
	II	imasimeru daroo	imasimenai daroo
	FORMAL I	imasimemasyoo	imasimemasumai
	II	imasimeru desyoo	imasimenai desyoo
Provisional	**INFORMAL**	imasimereba	imasimenakereba
	FORMAL	imasimemaseba	imasimemaseñ nara
		imasimemasureba	
Gerund	**INFORMAL I**	imasimete	imasimenai de
	II		imasimenakute
	FORMAL	imasimemasite	imasimemaseñ de
Past Ind.	**INFORMAL**	imasimeta	imasimenakatta
	FORMAL	imasimemasita	imasimemaseñ desita
Past Presump.	**INFORMAL**	imasimetaroo	imasimenakattaroo
		imasimeta daroo	imasimenakatta daroo
	FORMAL	imasimemasitaroo	imasimemaseñ desitaroo
		imasimeta desyoo	imasimenakatta desyoo
Conditional	**INFORMAL**	imasimetara	imasimenakattara
	FORMAL	imasimemasitara	imasimemaseñ desitara
Alternative	**INFORMAL**	imasimetari	imasimenakattari
	FORMAL	imasimemasitari	imasimemaseñ desitari

		INFORMAL AFFIRMATIVE INDICATIVE
Passive		imasimerareru
Potential		imasimerareru
Causative		imasimesaseru
Causative Pass.		imasimesaserareru

Honorific	**I**	oimasime ni naru
	II	oimasime nasaru
Humble	**I**	oimasime suru
	II	oimasime itasu

to assume a threatening attitude

		AFFIRMATIVE	NEGATIVE
Indicative	**INFORMAL**	inaoru	inaoranai
	FORMAL	inaorimasu	inaorimaseñ
Imperative	**INFORMAL I**	inaore	inaoru na
	II	inaorinasai	inaorinasaru na
	III	inaotte kudasai	inaoranai de kudasai
	FORMAL	oinaori nasaimase	oinaori nasaimasu na
Presumptive	**INFORMAL I**	inaoroo	inaorumai
	II	inaoru daroo	inaoranai daroo
	FORMAL I	inaorimasyoo	inaorimasumai
	II	inaoru desyoo	inaoranai desyoo
Provisional	**INFORMAL**	inaoreba	inaoranakereba
	FORMAL	inaorimaseba	inaorimaseñ nara
		inaorimasureba	
Gerund	**INFORMAL I**	inaotte	inaoranai de
	II		inaoranakute
	FORMAL	inaorimasite	inaorimaseñ de
Past Ind.	**INFORMAL**	inaotta	inaoranakatta
	FORMAL	inaorimasita	inaorimaseñ desita
Past Presump.	**INFORMAL**	inaottaroo	inaoranakattaroo
		inaotta daroo	inaoranakatta daroo
	FORMAL	inaorimasitaroo	inaorimaseñ desitaroo
		inaotta desyoo	inaoranakatta desyoo
Conditional	**INFORMAL**	inaottara	inaoranakattara
	FORMAL	inaorimasitara	inaorimaseñ desitara
Alternative	**INFORMAL**	inaottari	inaoranakattari
	FORMAL	inaorimasitari	inaorimaseñ desitari

		INFORMAL AFFIRMATIVE INDICATIVE
Passive		inaorareru
Potential		inaoreru
Causative		inaoraseru
Causative Pass.		inaoraserareru
Honorific	**I**	oinaori ni naru
	II	oinaori nasaru
Humble	**I**	
	II	

to pray, to wish for   TRANSITIVE

		AFFIRMATIVE	NEGATIVE
Indicative	INFORMAL	inoru	inoranai
	FORMAL	inorimasu	inorimaseñ
Imperative	INFORMAL I	inore	inoru na
	II	inorinasai	inorinasaru na
	III	inotte kudasai	inoranai de kudasai
	FORMAL	oinori nasaimase	oinori nasaimasu na
Presumptive	INFORMAL I	inoroo	inorumai
	II	inoru daroo	inoranai daroo
	FORMAL I	inorimasyoo	inorimasumai
	II	inoru desyoo	inoranai desyoo
Provisional	INFORMAL	inoreba	inoranakereba
	FORMAL	inorimaseba	inorimaseñ nara
		inorimasureba	
Gerund	INFORMAL I	inotte	inoranai de
	II		inoranakute
	FORMAL	inorimasite	inorimaseñ de
Past Ind.	INFORMAL	inotta	inoranakatta
	FORMAL	inorimasita	inorimaseñ desita
Past Presump.	INFORMAL	inottaroo	inoranakattaroo
		inotta daroo	inoranakatta daroo
	FORMAL	inorimasitaroo	inorimaseñ desitaroo
		inotta desyoo	inoranakatta desyoo
Conditional	INFORMAL	inottara	inoranakattara
	FORMAL	inorimasitara	inorimaseñ desitara
Alternative	INFORMAL	inottari	inoranakattari
	FORMAL	inorimasitari	inorimaseñ desitari

INFORMAL AFFIRMATIVE INDICATIVE

Passive		inorareru
Potential		inoreru
Causative		inoraseru
Causative Pass.		inoraserareru

Honorific	I	oinori ni naru
	II	oinori nasaru
Humble	I	oinori suru
	II	oinori itasu

to come, to go, to exist (animate honorific)

		AFFIRMATIVE	NEGATIVE
Indicative	**INFORMAL**	irassyaru	irassyaranai
	FORMAL	irassyaimasu	irassyaimaseñ
Imperative	**INFORMAL I**	irassyai	irassyaru na
	II		
	III	irassyatte kudasai	irassyaranai de kudasai
	FORMAL	irassyaimase	irassyaimasu na
Presumptive	**INFORMAL I**	irassyaroo	irassyarumai
	II	irassyaru daroo	irassyaranai daroo
	FORMAL I	irassyaimasyoo	irassyaimasumai
	II	irassyaru desyoo	irassyaranai desyoo
Provisional	**INFORMAL**	irassyareba	irassyaranakereba
	FORMAL	irassyaimaseba	irassyaimaseñ nara
		irassyaimasureba	
Gerund	**INFORMAL I**	irassyatte*	irassyaranai de
	II		irassyaranakute
	FORMAL	irassyaimasite	irassyaimaseñ de
Past Ind.	**INFORMAL**	irassyatta*	irassyaranakatta
	FORMAL	irassyaimasita	irassyaimaseñ desita
Past Presump.	**INFORMAL**	irassyattaroo*	irassyaranakattaroo
		irassyatta daroo	irassyaranakatta daroo
	FORMAL	irassyaimasitaroo	irassyaimaseñ desitaroo
		irassyatta desyoo	irassyaranakatta desyoo
Conditional	**INFORMAL**	irassyattara*	irassyaranakattara
	FORMAL	irassyaimasitara	irassyaimaseñ desitara
Alternative	**INFORMAL**	irassyattari*	irassyaranakattari
	FORMAL	irassyaimasitari	irassyaimaseñ desitari

INFORMAL AFFIRMATIVE INDICATIVE

Passive	
Potential	
Causative	
Causative Pass.	

Honorific	I
	II
Humble	I
	II

*Shorter forms: *irasite, irasita, irasitaroo, irasitara,* and *irasitari* also occur in the same environments as the longer forms given above.

to insert   TRANSITIVE

		AFFIRMATIVE	NEGATIVE
Indicative	**INFORMAL**	ireru	irenai
	FORMAL	iremasu	iremaseñ
Imperative	**INFORMAL I**	irero	ireru na
	II	irenasai	irenasaru na
	III	irete kudasai	irenai de kudasai
	FORMAL	oire nasaimase	oire nasaimasu na
Presumptive	**INFORMAL I**	ireyoo	iremai
	II	ireru daroo	irenai daroo
	FORMAL I	iremasyoo	iremasumai
	II	ireru desyoo	irenai desyoo
Provisional	**INFORMAL**	irereba	irenakereba
	FORMAL	iremaseba	iremaseñ nara
		iremasureba	
Gerund	**INFORMAL I**	irete	irenai de
	II		irenakute
	FORMAL	iremasite	iremaseñ de
Past Ind.	**INFORMAL**	ireta	irenakatta
	FORMAL	iremasita	iremaseñ desita
Past Presump.	**INFORMAL**	iretaroo	irenakattaroo
		ireta daroo	irenakatta daroo
	FORMAL	iremasitaroo	iremaseñ desitaroo
		ireta desyoo	irenakatta desyoo
Conditional	**INFORMAL**	iretara	irenakattara
	FORMAL	iremasitara	iremaseñ desitara
Alternative	**INFORMAL**	iretari	irenakattari
	FORMAL	iremasitari	iremaseñ desitari

		INFORMAL AFFIRMATIVE INDICATIVE
Passive		irerareru
Potential		irerareru
Causative		iresaseru
Causative Pass.		iresaserareru
Honorific	**I**	oire ni naru
	II	oire nasaru
Humble	**I**	oire suru
	II	oire itasu

o exıst (of animate subjects)

		AFFIRMATIVE	NEGATIVE
Indicative	**INFORMAL**	iru	inai
	FORMAL	imasu	imaseñ
Imperative	**INFORMAL I**	iro	iru na
	II	inasai	inasaru na
	III	ite kudasai	inai de kudasai
	FORMAL	oide nasaimase	oide nasaimasu na
Presumptive	**INFORMAL I**	iyoo	imai
	II	iru daroo	inai daroo
	FORMAL I	imasyoo	imasumai
	II	iru desyoo	inai desyoo
Provisional	**INFORMAL**	ireba	inakereba
	FORMAL	imaseba	imaseñ nara
		imasureba	
Gerund	**INFORMAL I**	ite	inai de
	II		inakute
	FORMAL	imasite	imaseñ de
Past Ind.	**INFORMAL**	ita	inakatta
	FORMAL	imasita	imaseñ desita
Past Presump.	**INFORMAL**	itaroo	inakattaroo
		ita daroo	inakatta daroo
	FORMAL	imasitaroo	imaseñ desitaroo
		ita desyoo	inakatta desyoo
Conditional	**INFORMAL**	itara	inakattara
	FORMAL	imasitara	imaseñ desitara
Alternative	**INFORMAL**	itari	inakattari
	FORMAL	imasitari	imaseñ desitari

		INFORMAL AFFIRMATIVE INDICATIVE	
Passive		irareru	
Potential		irareru	
Causative		isaseru	
Causative Pass.		isaserareru	
Honorific		irassyaru	oide ni naru
Humble		oru	

		AFFIRMATIVE	NEGATIVE
Indicative	**INFORMAL**	iru	iranai
	FORMAL	irimasu	irimaseñ
Imperative	**INFORMAL I**		
	II		
	III		
	FORMAL		
Presumptive	**INFORMAL I**	iroo	irumai
	II	iru daroo	iranai daroo
	FORMAL I	irimasyoo	irimasumai
	II	iru desyoo	iranai desyoo
Provisional	**INFORMAL**	ireba	iranakereba
	FORMAL	irimaseba	irimaseñ nara
		irimasureba	
Gerund	**INFORMAL I**	itte	iranai de
	II		iranakute
	FORMAL	irimasite	irimaseñ de
Past Ind.	**INFORMAL**	itta	iranakatta
	FORMAL	irimasita	irimaseñ desita
Past Presump.	**INFORMAL**	ittaroo	iranakattaroo
		itta daroo	iranakatta daroo
	FORMAL	irimasitaroo	irimaseñ desitaroo
		itta desyoo	iranakatta desyoo
Conditional	**INFORMAL**	ittara	iranakattara
	FORMAL	irimasitara	irimaseñ desitara
Alternative	**INFORMAL**	ittari	iranakattari
	FORMAL	irimasitari	irimaseñ desitari

INFORMAL AFFIRMATIVE INDICATIVE

Passive	
Potential	
Causative	
Causative Pass.	

Honorific	I
	II
Humble	I
	II

		AFFIRMATIVE	NEGATIVE
Indicative	**INFORMAL**	isogu	isoganai
	FORMAL	isogimasu	isogimaseñ
Imperative	**INFORMAL I**	isoge	isogu na
	II	isoginasai	isoginasaru na
	III	isoide kudasai	isoganai de kudasai
	FORMAL	oisogi nasaimase	oisogi nasaimasu na
Presumptive	**INFORMAL I**	isogoo	isogumai
	II	isogu daroo	isoganai daroo
	FORMAL I	isogimasyoo	isogimasumai
	II	isogu desyoo	isoganai desyoo
Provisional	**INFORMAL**	isogeba	isoganakereba
	FORMAL	isogimaseba	isogimaseñ nara
		isogimasureba	
Gerund	**INFORMAL I**	isoide	isoganai de
	II		isoganakute
	FORMAL	isogimasite	isogimaseñ de
Past Ind.	**INFORMAL**	isoida	isoganakatta
	FORMAL	isogimasita	isogimaseñ desita
Past Presump.	**INFORMAL**	isoidaroo	isoganakattaroo
		isoida daroo	isoganakatta daroo
	FORMAL	isogimasitaroo	isogimaseñ desitaroo
		isoida desyoo	isoganakatta desyoo
Conditional	**INFORMAL**	isoidara	isoganakattara
	FORMAL	isogimasitara	isogimaseñ desitara
Alternative	**INFORMAL**	isoidari	isoganakattari
	FORMAL	isogimasitari	isogimaseñ desitari

INFORMAL AFFIRMATIVE INDICATIVE

Passive	isogareru
Potential	isogeru
Causative	isogaseru
Causative Pass.	isogaserareru

Honorific	**I**	oisogi ni naru
	II	oisogi nasaru
Humble	**I**	
	II	

to receive, to take food or drink (humble)   TRANSITIVE

		AFFIRMATIVE	NEGATIVE
Indicative	**INFORMAL**	itadaku	itadakanai
	FORMAL	itadakimasu	itadakimaseñ
Imperative	**INFORMAL I**		
	II		
	III		
	FORMAL		
Presumptive	**INFORMAL I**	itadakoo	itadakumai
	II	itadaku daroo	itadakanai daroo
	FORMAL I	itadakimasyoo	itadakimasumai
	II	itadaku desyoo	itadakanai desyoo
Provisional	**INFORMAL**	itadakeba	itadakanakereba
	FORMAL	itadakimaseba	itadakimaseñ nara
		itadakimasureba	
Gerund	**INFORMAL I**	itadaite	itadakanai de
	II		itadakanakute
	FORMAL	itadakimasite	itadakimaseñ de
Past Ind.	**INFORMAL**	itadaita	itadakanakatta
	FORMAL	itadakimasita	itadakimaseñ desita
Past Presump.	**INFORMAL**	itadaitaroo	itadakanakattaroo
		itadaita daroo	itadakanakatta daroo
	FORMAL	itadakimasitaroo	itadakimaseñ desitaroo
		itadaita desyoo	itadakanakatta desyoo
Conditional	**INFORMAL**	itadaitara	itadakanakattara
	FORMAL	itadakimasitara	itadakimaseñ desitara
Alternative	**INFORMAL**	itadaitari	itadakanakattari
	FORMAL	itadakimasitari	itadakimaseñ desitari

INFORMAL AFFIRMATIVE INDICATIVE

Passive		
Potential	itadakeru	
Causative	itadakaseru	
Causative Pass.	itadakaserareru	

Honorific	**I**	
	II	
Humble	**I**	
	II	

		AFFIRMATIVE	NEGATIVE
Indicative	INFORMAL	itamu	itamanai
	FORMAL	itamimasu	itamimaseñ
Imperative	INFORMAL I		
	II		
	III		
	FORMAL		
Presumptive	INFORMAL I	itamoo	itamumai
	II	itamu daroo	itamanai daroo
	FORMAL I	itamimasyoo	itamimasumai
	II	itamu desyoo	itamanai desyoo
Provisional	INFORMAL	itameba	itamanakereba
	FORMAL	itamimaseba	itamimaseñ nara
		itamimasureba	
Gerund	INFORMAL I	itañde	itamanai de
	II		itamanakute
	FORMAL	itamimasite	itamimaseñ de
Past Ind.	INFORMAL	itañda	itamanakatta
	FORMAL	itamimasita	itamimaseñ desita
Past Presump.	INFORMAL	itañdaroo	itamanakattaroo
		itañda daroo	itamanakatta daroo
	FORMAL	itamimasitaroo	itamimaseñ desitaroo
		itañda desyoo	itamanakatta desyoo
Conditional	INFORMAL	itañdara	itamanakattara
	FORMAL	itamimasitara	itamimaseñ desitara
Alternative	INFORMAL	itañdari	itamanakattari
	FORMAL	itamimasitari	itamimaseñ desitari

		INFORMAL AFFIRMATIVE INDICATIVE
Passive		itamareru
Potential		itameru
Causative		itamaseru
Causative Pass.		itamaserareru
Honorific	I	oitami ni naru
	II	oitami nasaru
Humble	I	
	II	

		AFFIRMATIVE	NEGATIVE
Indicative	**INFORMAL**	itasu	itasanai
	FORMAL	itasimasu	itasimaseñ
Imperative	**INFORMAL I**	itase	itasu na
	II		
	III		
	FORMAL		
Presumptive	**INFORMAL I**	itasoo	itasumai
	II	itasu daroo	itasanai daroo
	FORMAL I	itasimasyoo	itasimasumai
	II	itasu desyoo	itasanai desyoo
Provisional	**INFORMAL**	itaseba	itasanakereba
	FORMAL	itasimaseba	itasimaseñ nara
		itasimasureba	
Gerund	**INFORMAL I**	itasite	itasanai de
	II		itasanakute
	FORMAL	itasimasite	itasimaseñ de
Past Ind.	**INFORMAL**	itasita	itasanakatta
	FORMAL	itasimasita	itasimaseñ desita
Past Presump.	**INFORMAL**	itasitaroo	itasanakattaroo
		itasita daroo	itasanakatta daroo
	FORMAL	itasimasitaroo	itasimaseñ desitaroo
		itasita desyoo	itasanakatta desyoo
Conditional	**INFORMAL**	itasitara	itasanakattara
	FORMAL	itasimasitara	itasimaseñ desitara
Alternative	**INFORMAL**	itasitari	itasanakattari
	FORMAL	itasimasitari	itasimaseñ desitari

INFORMAL AFFIRMATIVE INDICATIVE

Passive		
Potential		
Causative		
Causative Pass.		
Honorific	I	
	II	
Humble	I	
	II	

		AFFIRMATIVE	NEGATIVE
Indicative	**INFORMAL**	ituwaru	ituwaranai
	FORMAL	ituwarimasu	ituwarimaseñ
Imperative	**INFORMAL I**	ituware	ituwaru na
	II	ituwarinasai	ituwarinasaru na
	III	ituwatte kudasai	ituwaranai de kudasai
	FORMAL	oituwari nasaimase	oituwari nasaimasu na
Presumptive	**INFORMAL I**	ituwaroo	ituwarumai
	II	ituwaru daroo	ituwaranai daroo
	FORMAL I	ituwarimasyoo	ituwarimasumai
	II	ituwaru desyoo	ituwaranai desyoo
Provisional	**INFORMAL**	ituwareba	ituwaranakereba
	FORMAL	ituwarimaseba	ituwarimaseñ nara
		ituwarimasureba	
Gerund	**INFORMAL I**	ituwatte	ituwaranai de
	II		ituwaranakute
	FORMAL	ituwarimasite	ituwarimaseñ de
Past Ind.	**INFORMAL**	ituwatta	ituwaranakatta
	FORMAL	ituwarimasita	ituwarimaseñ desita
Past Presump.	**INFORMAL**	ituwattaroo	ituwaranakattaroo
		ituwatta daroo	ituwaranakatta daroo
	FORMAL	ituwarimasitaroo	ituwarimaseñ desitaroo
		ituwatta desyoo	ituwaranakatta desyoo
Conditional	**INFORMAL**	ituwattara	ituwaranakattara
	FORMAL	ituwarimasitara	ituwarimaseñ desitara
Alternative	**INFORMAL**	ituwattari	ituwaranakattari
	FORMAL	ituwarimasitari	ituwarimaseñ desitari

		INFORMAL AFFIRMATIVE INDICATIVE
Passive		ituwarareru
Potential		ituwareru
Causative		ituwaraseru
Causative Pass.		ituwaraserareru
Honorific	**I**	oituwari ni naru
	II	oituwari nasaru
Humble	**I**	oituwari suru
	II	oituwari itasu

to say, to tell   TRANSITIVE

		AFFIRMATIVE	NEGATIVE
Indicative	**INFORMAL**	iu	iwanai
	FORMAL	iimasu	iimaseñ
Imperative	**INFORMAL I**	ie	iu na
	II	iinasai	iinasaru na
	III	itte kudasai	iwanai de kudasai
	FORMAL	ossyaimase	ossyaimasu na
Presumptive	**INFORMAL I**	ioo	iumai
	II	iu daroo	iwanai daroo
	FORMAL I	iimasyoo	iimasumai
	II	iu desyoo	iwanai desyoo
Provisional	**INFORMAL**	ieba	iwanakereba
	FORMAL	iimaseba	iimaseñ nara
		iimasureba	
Gerund	**INFORMAL I**	itte	iwanai de
	II		iwanakute
	FORMAL	iimasite	iimaseñ de
Past Ind.	**INFORMAL**	itta	iwanakatta
	FORMAL	iimasita	iimaseñ desita
Past Presump.	**INFORMAL**	ittaroo	iwanakattaroo
		itta daroo	iwanakatta daroo
	FORMAL	iimasitaroo	iimaseñ desitaroo
		itta desyoo	iwanakatta desyoo
Conditional	**INFORMAL**	ittara	iwanakattara
	FORMAL	iimasitara	iimaseñ desitara
Alternative	**INFORMAL**	ittari	iwanakattari
	FORMAL	iimasitari	iimaseñ desitari

	INFORMAL AFFIRMATIVE INDICATIVE
Passive	iwareru
Potential	ieru
Causative	iwaseru
Causative Pass.	iwaserareru
Honorific	ossyaru
Humble	moosu

		AFFIRMATIVE	NEGATIVE
Indicative	**INFORMAL**	iwau	iwawanai
	FORMAL	iwaimasu	iwaimaseñ
Imperative	**INFORMAL I**	iwae	iwau na
	II	iwainasai	iwainasaru na
	III	iwatte kudasai	iwawanai de kudasai
	FORMAL	oiwai nasaimase	oiwai nasaimasu na
Presumptive	**INFORMAL I**	iwaoo	iwaumai
	II	iwau daroo	iwawanai daroo
	FORMAL I	iwaimasyoo	iwaimasumai
	II	iwau desyoo	iwawanai desyoo
Provisional	**INFORMAL**	iwaeba	iwawanakereba
	FORMAL	iwaimaseba	iwaimaseñ nara
		iwaimasureba	
Gerund	**INFORMAL I**	iwatte	iwawanai de
	II		iwawanakute
	FORMAL	iwaimasite	iwaimaseñ de
Past Ind.	**INFORMAL**	iwatta	iwawanakatta
	FORMAL	iwaimasita	iwaimaseñ desita
Past Presump.	**INFORMAL**	iwattaroo	iwawanakattaroo
		iwatta daroo	iwawanakatta daroo
	FORMAL	iwaimasitaroo	iwaimaseñ desitaroo
		iwatta desyoo	iwawanakatta desyoo
Conditional	**INFORMAL**	iwattara	iwawanakattara
	FORMAL	iwaimasitara	iwaimaseñ desitara
Alternative	**INFORMAL**	iwattari	iwawanakattari
	FORMAL	iwaimasitari	iwaimaseñ desitari

INFORMAL AFFIRMATIVE INDICATIVE

Passive		iwawareru
Potential		iwaeru
Causative		iwawaseru
Causative Pass.		iwawaserareru
Honorific	**I**	oiwai ni naru
	II	oiwai nasaru
Humble	**I**	oiwai suru
	II	oiwai itasu

to dislike, to hate   TRANSITIVE

		AFFIRMATIVE	**NEGATIVE**
Indicative	**INFORMAL**	iyagaru	iyagaranai
	FORMAL	iyagarimasu	iyagarimaseñ
Imperative	**INFORMAL I**	iyagare	iyagaru na
	II	iyagarinasai	iyagarinasaru na
	III	iyagatte kudasai	iyagaranai de kudasai
	FORMAL	oiyagari nasaimase	oiyagari nasaimasu na
Presumptive	**INFORMAL I**	iyagaroo	iyagarumai
	II	iyagaru daroo	iyagaranai daroo
	FORMAL I	iyagarimasyoo	iyagarimasumai
	II	iyagaru desyoo	iyagaranai desyoo
Provisional	**INFORMAL**	iyagareba	iyagaranakereba
	FORMAL	iyagarimaseba	iyagarimaseñ nara
		iyagarimasureba	
Gerund	**INFORMAL I**	iyagatte	iyagaranai de
	II		iyagaranakute
	FORMAL	iyagarimasite	iyagarimaseñ de
Past Ind.	**INFORMAL**	iyagatta	iyagaranakatta
	FORMAL	iyagarimasita	iyagarimaseñ desita
Past Presump.	**INFORMAL**	iyagattaroo	iyagaranakattaroo
		iyagatta daroo	iyagaranakatta daroo
	FORMAL	iyagarimasitaroo	iyagarimaseñ desitaroo
		iyagatta desyoo	iyagaranakatta desyoo
Conditional	**INFORMAL**	iyagattara	iyagaranakattara
	FORMAL	iyagarimasitara	iyagarimaseñ desitara
Alternative	**INFORMAL**	iyagattari	iyagaranakattari
	FORMAL	iyagarimasitari	iyagarimaseñ desitari

		INFORMAL AFFIRMATIVE INDICATIVE
Passive		iyagarareru
Potential		
Causative		iyagaraseru
Causative Pass.		iyagaraserareru
Honorific	**I**	oiyagari ni naru
	II	oiyagari nasaru
Humble	**I**	
	II	

TRANSITIVE   *to despise, to hold in contempt*

		AFFIRMATIVE	NEGATIVE
Indicative	**INFORMAL**	iyasimu	iyasimanai
	FORMAL	iyasimimasu	iyasimimaseñ
Imperative	**INFORMAL I**	iyasime	iyasimu na
	II	iyasiminasai	iyasiminasaru na
	III	iyasiñde kudasai	iyasimanai de kudasai
	FORMAL	oiyasimi nasaimase	oiyasimi nasaimasu na
Presumptive	**INFORMAL I**	iyasimoo	iyasimumai
	II	iyasimu daroo	iyasimanai daroo
	FORMAL I	iyasimimasyoo	iyasimimasumai
	II	iyasimu desyoo	iyasimanai desyoo
Provisional	**INFORMAL**	iyasimeba	iyasimanakereba
	FORMAL	iyasimimaseba	iyasimimaseñ nara
		iyasimimasureba	
Gerund	**INFORMAL I**	iyasiñde	iyasimanai de
	II		iyasimanakute
	FORMAL	iyasimimasite	iyasimimaseñ de
Past Ind.	**INFORMAL**	iyasiñda	iyasimanakatta
	FORMAL	iyasimimasita	iyasimimaseñ desita
Past Presump.	**INFORMAL**	iyasiñdaroo	iyasimanakattaroo
		iyasiñda daroo	iyasimanakatta daroo
	FORMAL	iyasimimasitaroo	iyasimimaseñ desitaroo
		iyasiñda desyoo	iyasimanakatta desyoo
Conditional	**INFORMAL**	iyasiñdara	iyasimanakattara
	FORMAL	iyasimimasitara	iyasimimaseñ desitara
Alternative	**INFORMAL**	iyasiñdari	iyasimanakattari
	FORMAL	iyasimimasitari	iyasimimaseñ desitari

		INFORMAL AFFIRMATIVE INDICATIVE
Passive		iyasimareru
Potential		iyasimeru
Causative		iyasimaseru
Causative Pass.		iyasimaserareru
Honorific	**I**	oiyasimi ni naru
	II	oiyasimi nasaru
Humble	**I**	oiyasimi suru
	II	oiyasimi itasu

		AFFIRMATIVE	NEGATIVE
Indicative	**INFORMAL**	izimeru	izimenai
	FORMAL	izimemasu	izimemaseñ
Imperative	**INFORMAL I**	izimero	izimeru na
	II	izimenasai	izimenasaru na
	III	izimete kudasai	izimenai de kudasai
	FORMAL	oizime nasaimase	oizime nasaimasu na
Presumptive	**INFORMAL I**	izimeyoo	izimemai
	II	izimeru daroo	izimenai daroo
	FORMAL I	izimemasyoo	izimemasumai
	II	izimeru desyoo	izimenai desyoo
Provisional	**INFORMAL**	izimereba	izimenakereba
	FORMAL	izimemaseba	izimemaseñ nara
		izimemasureba	
Gerund	**INFORMAL I**	izimete	izimenai de
	II		izimenakute
	FORMAL	izimemasite	izimemaseñ de
Past Ind.	**INFORMAL**	izimeta	izimenakatta
	FORMAL	izimemasita	izimemaseñ desita
Past Presump.	**INFORMAL**	izimetaroo	izimenakattaroo
		izimeta daroo	izimenakatta daroo
	FORMAL	izimemasitaroo	izimemaseñ desitaroo
		izimeta desyoo	izimenakatta desyoo
Conditional	**INFORMAL**	izimetara	izimenakattara
	FORMAL	izimemasitara	izimemaseñ desitara
Alternative	**INFORMAL**	izimetari	izimenakattari
	FORMAL	izimemasitari	izimemaseñ desitari

		INFORMAL AFFIRMATIVE INDICATIVE
Passive		izimerareru
Potential		izimerareru
Causative		izimesaseru
Causative Pass.		izimesaserareru

Honorific	**I**	oizime ni naru
	II	oizime nasaru
Humble	**I**	oizime suru
	II	oizime itasu

		AFFIRMATIVE	NEGATIVE
Indicative	**INFORMAL**	iziru	iziranai
	FORMAL	izirimasu	izirimaseñ
Imperative	**INFORMAL I**	izire	iziru na
	II	izirinasai	izirinasaru na
	III	izitte kudasai	iziranai de kudasai
	FORMAL	oiziri nasaimase	oiziri nasaimasu na
Presumptive	**INFORMAL I**	iziroo	izirumai
	II	iziru daroo	iziranai daroo
	FORMAL I	izirimasyoo	izirimasumai
	II	iziru desyoo	iziranai desyoo
Provisional	**INFORMAL**	izireba	iziranakereba
	FORMAL	izirimaseba	izirimaseñ nara
		izirimasureba	
Gerund	**INFORMAL I**	izitte	iziranai de
	II		iziranakute
	FORMAL	izirimasite	izirimaseñ de
Past Ind.	**INFORMAL**	izitta	iziranakatta
	FORMAL	izirimasita	izirimaseñ desita
Past Presump.	**INFORMAL**	izittaroo	iziranakattaroo
		izitta daroo	iziranakatta daroo
	FORMAL	izirimasitaroo	izirimaseñ desitaroo
		izitta desyoo	iziranakatta desyoo
Conditional	**INFORMAL**	izittara	iziranakattara
	FORMAL	izirimasitara	izirimaseñ desitara
Alternative	**INFORMAL**	izittari	iziranakattari
	FORMAL	izirimasitari	izirimaseñ desitari

	INFORMAL AFFIRMATIVE INDICATIVE	
Passive		izirareru
Potential		izireru
Causative		iziraseru
Causative Pass.		iziraserareru

Honorific	**I**	oiziri ni naru
	II	oiziri nasaru
Humble	**I**	oiziri suru
	II	oiziri itasu

to protect, to take a person under one's wing   TRANSITIVE

		AFFIRMATIVE	NEGATIVE
Indicative	**INFORMAL**	kabau	kabawanai
	FORMAL	kabaimasu	kabaimaseñ
Imperative	**INFORMAL I**	kabae	kabau na
	II	kabainasai	kabainasaru na
	III	kabatte kudasai	kabawanai de kudasai
	FORMAL	okabai nasaimase	okabai nasaimasu na
Presumptive	**INFORMAL I**	kabaoo	kabaumai
	II	kabau daroo	kabawanai daroo
	FORMAL I	kabaimasyoo	kabaimasumai
	II	kabau desyoo	kabawanai desyoo
Provisional	**INFORMAL**	kabaeba	kabawanakereba
	FORMAL	kabaimaseba	kabaimaseñ nara
		kabaimasureba	
Gerund	**INFORMAL I**	kabatte	kabawanai de
	II		kabawanakute
	FORMAL	kabaimasite	kabaimaseñ de
Past Ind.	**INFORMAL**	kabatta	kabawanakatta
	FORMAL	kabaimasita	kabaimaseñ desita
Past Presump.	**INFORMAL**	kabattaroo	kabawanakattaroo
		kabatta daroo	kabawanakatta daroo
	FORMAL	kabaimasitaroo	kabaimaseñ desitaroo
		kabatta desyoo	kabawanakatta desyoo
Conditional	**INFORMAL**	kabattara	kabawanakattara
	FORMAL	kabaimasitara	kabaimaseñ desitara
Alternative	**INFORMAL**	kabattari	kabawanakattari
	FORMAL	kabaimasitari	kabaimaseñ desitari

INFORMAL AFFIRMATIVE INDICATIVE

Passive		kabawareru
Potential		kabaeru
Causative		kabawaseru
Causative Pass.		kabawaserareru

Honorific	**I**	okabai ni naru
	II	okabai nasaru
Humble	**I**	okabai suru
	II	okabai itasu

		AFFIRMATIVE	NEGATIVE
Indicative	**INFORMAL**	kaburu	kaburanai
	FORMAL	kaburimasu	kaburimaseñ
Imperative	**INFORMAL I**	kabure	kaburu na
	II	kaburinasaı	kaburinasaru na
	III	kabutte kudasai	kaburanai de kudasai
	FORMAL	okaburi nasaimase	okaburi nasaimasu na
Presumptive	**INFORMAL I**	kaburoo	kaburumai
	II	kaburu daroo	kaburanai daroo
	FORMAL I	kaburimasyoo	kaburimasumai
	II	kaburu desyoo	kaburanai desyoo
Provisional	**INFORMAL**	kabureba	kaburanakereba
	FORMAL	kaburimaseba	kaburimaseñ nara
		kaburimasureba	
Gerund	**INFORMAL I**	kabutte	kaburanai de
	II		kaburanakute
	FORMAL	kaburimasite	kaburimaseñ de
Past Ind.	**INFORMAL**	kabutta	kaburanakatta
	FORMAL	kaburimasita	kaburimaseñ desita
Past Presump.	**INFORMAL**	kabuttaroo	kaburanakattaroo
		kabutta daroo	kaburanakatta daroo
	FORMAL	kaburimasitaroo	kaburimaseñ desitaroo
		kabutta desyoo	kaburanakatta desyoo
Conditional	**INFORMAL**	kabuttara	kaburanakattara
	FORMAL	kaburimasitara	kaburimaseñ desitara
Alternative	**INFORMAL**	kabuttari	kaburanakattari
	FORMAL	kaburimasitari	kaburimaseñ desitari

	INFORMAL AFFIRMATIVE INDICATIVE
Passive	kaburareru
Potential	kabureru
Causative	kaburaseru
Causative Pass.	kaburaserareru

Honorific	**I**	okaburi ni naru
	II	okaburi nasaru
Humble	**I**	okaburi suru
	II	okaburi itasu

		AFFIRMATIVE	**NEGATIVE**
Indicative	**INFORMAL**	kaeru	kaenai
	FORMAL	kaemasu	kaemaseñ
Imperative	**INFORMAL I**	kaero	kaeru na
	II	kaenasai	kaenasaru na
	III	kaete kudasai	kaenai de kudasai
	FORMAL	okae nasaimase	okae nasaimasu na
Presumptive	**INFORMAL I**	kaeyoo	kaemai
	II	kaeru daroo	kaenai daroo
	FORMAL I	kaemasyoo	kaemasumai
	II	kaeru desyoo	kaenai desyoo
Provisional	**INFORMAL**	kaereba	kaenakereba
	FORMAL	kaemaseba	kaemaseñ nara
		kaemasureba	
Gerund	**INFORMAL I**	kaete	kaenai de
	II		kaenakute
	FORMAL	kaemasite	kaemaseñ de
Past Ind.	**INFORMAL**	kaeta	kaenakatta
	FORMAL	kaemasita	kaemaseñ desita
Past Presump.	**INFORMAL**	kaetaroo	kaenakattaroo
		kaeta daroo	kaenakatta daroo
	FORMAL	kaemasitaroo	kaemaseñ desitaroo
		kaeta desyoo	kaenakatta desyoo
Conditional	**INFORMAL**	kaetara	kaenakattara
	FORMAL	kaemasitara	kaemaseñ desitara
Alternative	**INFORMAL**	kaetari	kaenakattari
	FORMAL	kaemasitari	kaemaseñ desitari

		INFORMAL AFFIRMATIVE INDICATIVE
Passive		kaerareru
Potential		kaerareru
Causative		kaesaseru
Causative Pass.		kaesaserareru

Honorific	**I**	okae ni naru
	II	okae nasaru
Humble	**I**	okae suru
	II	okae itasu

		AFFIRMATIVE	NEGATIVE
Indicative	**INFORMAL**	kaeru	kaeranai
	FORMAL	kaerimasu	kaerimaseñ
Imperative	**INFORMAL I**	kaere	kaeru na
	II	kaerinasai	kaerinasaru na
	III	kaette kudasai	kaeranai de kudasai
	FORMAL	okaeri nasaimase	okaeri nasaimasu na
Presumptive	**INFORMAL I**	kaeroo	kaerumai
	II	kaeru daroo	kaeranai daroo
	FORMAL I	kaerimasyoo	kaerimasumai
	II	kaeru desyoo	kaeranai desyoo
Provisional	**INFORMAL**	kaereba	kaeranakereba
	FORMAL	kaerimaseba	kaerimaseñ nara
		kaerimasureba	
Gerund	**INFORMAL I**	kaette	kaeranai de
	II		kaeranakute
	FORMAL	kaerimasite	kaerimaseñ de
Past Ind.	**INFORMAL**	kaetta	kaeranakatta
	FORMAL	kaerimasita	kaerimaseñ desita
Past Presump.	**INFORMAL**	kaettaroo	kaeranakattaroo
		kaetta daroo	kaeranakatta daroo
	FORMAL	kaerimasitaroo	kaerimaseñ desitaroo
		kaetta desyoo	kaeranakatta desyoo
Conditional	**INFORMAL**	kaettara	kaeranakattara
	FORMAL	kaerimasitara	kaerimaseñ desitara
Alternative	**INFORMAL**	kaettari	kaeranakattari
	FORMAL	kaerimasitari	kaerimaseñ desitari

INFORMAL AFFIRMATIVE INDICATIVE

Passive		kaerareru
Potential		kaereru
Causative		kaeraseru
Causative Pass.		kaeraserareru
Honorific	**I**	okaeri ni naru
	II	okaeri nasaru
Humble	**I**	
	II	

to return (something to someone)   TRANSITIVE

		AFFIRMATIVE	NEGATIVE
Indicative	**INFORMAL**	kaesu	kaesanai
	FORMAL	kaesimasu	kaesimaseñ
Imperative	**INFORMAL I**	kaese	kaesu na
	II	kaesinasai	kaesinasaru na
	III	kaesite kudasai	kaesanai de kudasai
	FORMAL	okaesi nasaimase	okaesi nasaimasu na
Presumptive	**INFORMAL I**	kaesoo	kaesumai
	II	kaesu daroo	kaesanai daroo
	FORMAL I	kaesimasyoo	kaesimasumai
	II	kaesu desyoo	kaesanai desyoo
Provisional	**INFORMAL**	kaeseba	kaesanakereba
	FORMAL	kaesimaseba	kaesimaseñ nara
		kaesimasureba	
Gerund	**INFORMAL I**	kaesite	kaesanai de
	II		kaesanakute
	FORMAL	kaesimasite	kaesimaseñ de
Past Ind.	**INFORMAL**	kaesita	kaesanakatta
	FORMAL	kaesimasita	kaesimaseñ desita
Past Presump.	**INFORMAL**	kaesitaroo	kaesanakattaroo
		kaesita daroo	kaesanakatta daroo
	FORMAL	kaesimasitaroo	kaesimaseñ desitaroo
		kaesita desyoo	kaesanakatta desyoo
Conditional	**INFORMAL**	kaesitara	kaesanakattara
	FORMAL	kaesimasitara	kaesimaseñ desitara
Alternative	**INFORMAL**	kaesitari	kaesanakattari
	FORMAL	kaesimasitari	kaesimaseñ desitari

		INFORMAL AFFIRMATIVE INDICATIVE
Passive		kaesareru
Potential		kaeseru
Causative		kaesaseru
Causative Pass.		kaesaserareru
Honorific	**I**	okaesi ni naru
	II	okaesi nasaru
Humble	**I**	okaesi suru
	II	okaesi itasu

kagayák.u
to shine, to sparkle

		AFFIRMATIVE	NEGATIVE
Indicative	INFORMAL	kagayaku	kagayakanai
	FORMAL	kagayakimasu	kagayakimaseñ
Imperative	INFORMAL I	kagayake	kagayaku na
	II	kagayakinasai	kagayakinasaru na
	III	kagayaite kudasai	kagayakanai de kudasai
	FORMAL	okagayaki nasaimase	okagayaki nasaimasu na
Presumptive	INFORMAL I	kagayakoo	kagayakumai
	II	kagayaku daroo	kagayakanai daroo
	FORMAL I	kagayakimasyoo	kagayakimasumai
	II	kagayaku desyoo	kagayakanai desyoo
Provisional	INFORMAL	kagayakeba	kagayakanakereba
	FORMAL	kagayakimaseba	kagayakimaseñ nara
		kagayakimasureba	
Gerund	INFORMAL I	kagayaite	kagayakanai de
	II		kagayakanakute
	FORMAL	kagayakimasite	kagayakimaseñ de
Past Ind.	INFORMAL	kagayaita	kagayakanakatta
	FORMAL	kagayakimasita	kagayakimaseñ desita
Past Presump.	INFORMAL	kagayaitaroo	kagayakanakattaroo
		kagayaita daroo	kagayakanakatta daroo
	FORMAL	kagayakimasitaroo	kagayakimaseñ desitaroo
		kagayaita desyoo	kagayakanakatta desyoo
Conditional	INFORMAL	kagayaitara	kagayakanakattara
	FORMAL	kagayakimasitara	kagayakimaseñ desitara
Alternative	INFORMAL	kagayaitari	kagayakanakattari
	FORMAL	kagayakimasitari	kagayakimaseñ desitari

		INFORMAL AFFIRMATIVE INDICATIVE
Passive		kagayakareru
Potential		kagayakeru
Causative		kagayakaseru
Causative Pass.		kagayakaserareru
Honorific	I	okagayaki ni naru
	II	okagayaki nasaru
Humble	I	
	II	

		AFFIRMATIVE	NEGATIVE
Indicative	**INFORMAL**	kagiru	kagiranai
	FORMAL	kagirimasu	kagirimaseñ
Imperative	**INFORMAL I**	kagire	kagiru na
	II	kagirinasai	kagirinasaru na
	III	kagitte kudasai	kagiranai de kudasai
	FORMAL	okagiri nasaimase	okagiri nasaimasu na
Presumptive	**INFORMAL I**	kagiroo	kagirumai
	II	kagiru daroo	kagiranai daroo
	FORMAL I	kagirimasyoo	kagirimasumai
	II	kagiru desyoo	kagiranai desyoo
Provisional	**INFORMAL**	kagireba	kagiranakereba
	FORMAL	kagirimaseba	kagirimaseñ nara
		kagirimasureba	
Gerund	**INFORMAL I**	kagitte	kagiranai de
	II		kagiranakute
	FORMAL	kagirimasite	kagirimaseñ de
Past Ind.	**INFORMAL**	kagitta	kagiranakatta
	FORMAL	kagirimasita	kagirimaseñ desita
Past Presump.	**INFORMAL**	kagittaroo	kagiranakattaroo
		kagitta daroo	kagiranakatta daroo
	FORMAL	kagirimasitaroo	kagirimaseñ desitaroo
		kagitta desyoo	kagiranakatta desyoo
Conditional	**INFORMAL**	kagittara	kagiranakattara
	FORMAL	kagirimasitara	kagirimaseñ desitara
Alternative	**INFORMAL**	kagittari	kagiranakattari
	FORMAL	kagirimasitari	kagirimaseñ desitari

		INFORMAL AFFIRMATIVE INDICATIVE
Passive		kagirareru
Potential		kagireru
Causative		kagiraseru
Causative Pass.		kagiraserareru

Honorific	**I**	okagiri ni naru
	II	okagiri nasaru
Humble	**I**	okagiri suru
	II	okagiri itasu

TRANSITIVE   *to hold in one's arms, to employ*

		AFFIRMATIVE	NEGATIVE
Indicative	**INFORMAL**	kakaeru	kakaenai
	FORMAL	kakaemasu	kakaemaseñ
Imperative	**INFORMAL I**	kakaero	kakaeru na
	II	kakaenasai	kakaenasaru na
	III	kakaete kudasai	kakaenai de kudasai
	FORMAL	okakae nasaimase	okakae nasaimasu na
Presumptive	**INFORMAL I**	kakaeyoo	kakaemai
	II	kakaeru daroo	kakaenai daroo
	FORMAL I	kakaemasyoo	kakaemasumai
	II	kakaeru desyoo	kakaenai desyoo
Provisional	**INFORMAL**	kakaereba	kakaenakereba
	FORMAL	kakaemaseba	kakaemaseñ nara
		kakaemasureba	
Gerund	**INFORMAL I**	kakaete	kakaenai de
	II		kakaenakute
	FORMAL	kakaemasite	kakaemaseñ de
Past Ind.	**INFORMAL**	kakaeta	kakaenakatta
	FORMAL	kakaemasita	kakaemaseñ desita
Past Presump.	**INFORMAL**	kakaetaroo	kakaenakattaroo
		kakaeta daroo	kakaenakatta daroo
	FORMAL	kakaemasitaroo	kakaemaseñ desitaroo
		kakaeta desyoo	kakaenakatta desyoo
Conditional	**INFORMAL**	kakaetara	kakaenakattara
	FORMAL	kakaemasitara	kakaemaseñ desitara
Alternative	**INFORMAL**	kakaetari	kakaenakattari
	FORMAL	kakaemasitari	kakaemaseñ desitari

	INFORMAL AFFIRMATIVE INDICATIVE
Passive	kakaerareru
Potential	kakaerareru
Causative	kakaesaseru
Causative Pass.	kakaesaserareru

Honorific	**I**	okakae ni naru
	II	okakae nasaru
Humble	**I**	okakae suru
	II	okakae itasu

		AFFIRMATIVE	NEGATIVE
Indicative	**INFORMAL**	kakageru	kakagenai
	FORMAL	kakagemasu	kakagemaseñ
Imperative	**INFORMAL I**	kakagero	kakageru na
	II	kakagenasai	kakagenasaru na
	III	kakagete kudasai	kakagenai de kudasai
	FORMAL	okakage nasaimase	okakage nasaimasu na
Presumptive	**INFORMAL I**	kakageyoo	kakagemai
	II	kakageru daroo	kakagenai daroo
	FORMAL I	kakagemasyoo	kakagemasumai
	II	kakageru desyoo	kakagenai desyoo
Provisional	**INFORMAL**	kakagereba	kakagenakereba
	FORMAL	kakagemaseba	kakagemaseñ nara
		kakagemasureba	
Gerund	**INFORMAL I**	kakagete	kakagenai de
	II		kakagenakute
	FORMAL	kakagemasite	kakagemaseñ de
Past Ind.	**INFORMAL**	kakageta	kakagenakatta
	FORMAL	kakagemasita	kakagemaseñ desita
Past Presump.	**INFORMAL**	kakagetaroo	kakagenakattaroo
		kakageta daroo	kakagenakatta daroo
	FORMAL	kakagemasitaroo	kakagemaseñ desitaroo
		kakageta desyoo	kakagenakatta desyoo
Conditional	**INFORMAL**	kakagetara	kakagenakattara
	FORMAL	kakagemasitara	kakagemaseñ desitara
Alternative	**INFORMAL**	kakagetari	kakagenakattari
	FORMAL	kakagemasitari	kakagemaseñ desitari

		INFORMAL AFFIRMATIVE INDICATIVE
Passive		kakagerareru
Potential		kakagerareru
Causative		kakagesaseru
Causative Pass.		kakagesaserareru
Honorific	**I**	okakage ni naru
	II	okakage nasaru
Humble	**I**	okakage suru
	II	okakage itasu

to begin, to be hanging (from), *to require* (time, money etc.)

		AFFIRMATIVE	NEGATIVE
Indicative	INFORMAL	kakaru	kakaranai
	FORMAL	kakarimasu	kakarimaseñ
Imperative	INFORMAL I	kakare	kakaru na
	II	kakarinasai	kakarinasaru na
	III	kakatte kudasai	kakaranai de kudasai
	FORMAL	okakari nasaimase	okakari nasaimasu na
Presumptive	INFORMAL I	kakaroo	kakarumai
	II	kakaru daroo	kakaranai daroo
	FORMAL I	kakarimasyoo	kakarimasumai
	II	kakaru desyoo	kakaranai desyoo
Provisional	INFORMAL	kakareba	kakaranakereba
	FORMAL	kakarimaseba	kakarimaseñ nara
		kakarimasureba	
Gerund	INFORMAL I	kakatte	kakaranai de
	II		kakaranakute
	FORMAL	kakarimasite	kakarimaseñ de
Past Ind.	INFORMAL	kakatta	kakaranakatta
	FORMAL	kakarimasita	kakarimaseñ desita
Past Presump.	INFORMAL	kakattaroo	kakaranakattaroo
		kakatta daroo	kakaranakatta daroo
	FORMAL	kakarimasitaroo	kakarimaseñ desitaroo
		kakatta desyoo	kakaranakatta desyoo
Conditional	INFORMAL	kakattara	kakaranakattara
	FORMAL	kakarimasitara	kakarimaseñ desitara
Alternative	INFORMAL	kakattari	kakaranakattari
	FORMAL	kakarimasitari	kakarimaseñ desitari

		INFORMAL AFFIRMATIVE INDICATIVE
Passive		kakarareru
Potential		kakareru
Causative		kakaraseru
Causative Pass.		kakaraserareru
Honorific	I	okakari ni naru
	II	okakari nasaru
Humble	I	okakari suru
	II	okakari itasu

kakawár.u

to affect, to concern

kakawarı

		AFFIRMATIVE	NEGATIVE
Indicative	INFORMAL	kakawaru	kakawaranai
	FORMAL	kakawarimasu	kakawarimaseñ
Imperative	INFORMAL I	kakaware	kakawaru na
	II	kakawarinasai	kakawarinasaru na
	III	kakawatte kudasai	kakawaranai de kudasai
	FORMAL	okakawari nasaimase	okakawari nasaimasu na
Presumptive	INFORMAL I	kakawaroo	kakawarumai
	II	kakawaru daroo	kakawaranai daroo
	FORMAL I	kakawarimasyoo	kakawarimasumai
	II	kakawaru desyoo	kakawaranai desyoo
Provisional	INFORMAL	kakawareba	kakawaranakereba
	FORMAL	kakawarimaseba	kakawarimaseñ nara
		kakawarimasureba	
Gerund	INFORMAL I	kakawatte	kakawaranai de
	II		kakawaranakute
	FORMAL	kakawarimasite	kakawarimaseñ de
Past Ind.	INFORMAL	kakawatta	kakawaranakatta
	FORMAL	kakawarimasita	kakawarimaseñ desita
Past Presump.	INFORMAL	kakawattaroo	kakawaranakattaroo
		kakawatta daroo	kakawaranakatta daroo
	FORMAL	kakawarimasitaroo	kakawarimaseñ desitaroo
		kakawatta desyoo	kakawaranakatta desyoo
Conditional	INFORMAL	kakawattara	kakawaranakattara
	FORMAL	kakawarimasitara	kakawarimaseñ desitara
Alternative	INFORMAL	kakawattari	kakawaranakattari
	FORMAL	kakawarimasitari	kakawarimaseñ desitari

		INFORMAL AFFIRMATIVE INDICATIVE
Passive		kakawarareru
Potential		kakawareru
Causative		kakawaraseru
Causative Pass.		kakawaraserareru
Honorific	I	okakawari ni naru
	II	okakawari nasaru
Humble	I	
	II	

		AFFIRMATIVE	**NEGATIVE**
Indicative	**INFORMAL**	kakeru	kakenai
	FORMAL	kakemasu	kakemaseñ
Imperative	**INFORMAL I**	kakero	kakeru na
	II	kakenasai	kakenasaru na
	III	kakete kudasai	kakenai de kudasai
	FORMAL	okake nasaimase	okake nasaimasu na
Presumptive	**INFORMAL I**	kakeyoo	kakemai
	II	kakeru daroo	kakenai daroo
	FORMAL I	kakemasyoo	kakemasumai
	II	kakeru desyoo	kakenai desyoo
Provisional	**INFORMAL**	kakereba	kakenakereba
	FORMAL	kakemaseba	kakemaseñ nara
		kakemasureba	
Gerund	**INFORMAL I**	kakete	kakenai de
	II		kakenakute
	FORMAL	kakemasite	kakemaseñ de
Past Ind.	**INFORMAL**	kaketa	kakenakatta
	FORMAL	kakemasita	kakemaseñ desita
Past Presump.	**INFORMAL**	kaketaroo	kakenakattaroo
		kaketa daroo	kakenakatta daroo
	FORMAL	kakemasitaroo	kakemaseñ desitaroo
		kaketa desyoo	kakenakatta desyoo
Conditional	**INFORMAL**	kaketara	kakenakattara
	FORMAL	kakemasitara	kakemaseñ desitara
Alternative	**INFORMAL**	kaketari	kakenakattari
	FORMAL	kakemasitari	kakemaseñ desitari

		INFORMAL AFFIRMATIVE INDICATIVE
Passive		kakerareru
Potential		kakerareru
Causative		kakesaseru
Causative Pass.		kakesaserareru
Honorific	**I**	okake ni naru
	II	okake nasaru
Humble	**I**	okake suru
	II	okake itasu

to wager, to risk   TRANSITIVE

		AFFIRMATIVE	NEGATIVE
Indicative	**INFORMAL**	kakeru	kakenai
	FORMAL	kakemasu	kakemaseñ
Imperative	**INFORMAL I**	kakero	kakeru na
	II	kakenasai	kakenasaru na
	III	kakete kudasai	kakenai de kudasai
	FORMAL	okake nasaimase	okake nasaimasu na
Presumptive	**INFORMAL I**	kakeyoo	kakemai
	II	kakeru daroo	kakenai daroo
	FORMAL I	kakemasyoo	kakemasumai
	II	kakeru desyoo	kakenai desyoo
Provisional	**INFORMAL**	kakereba	kakenakereba
	FORMAL	kakemaseba	kakemaseñ nara
		kakemasureba	
Gerund	**INFORMAL I**	kakete	kakenai de
	II		kakenakute
	FORMAL	kakemasite	kakemaseñ de
Past Ind.	**INFORMAL**	kaketa	kakenakatta
	FORMAL	kakemasita	kakemaseñ desita
Past Presump.	**INFORMAL**	kaketaroo	kakenakattaroo
		kaketa daroo	kakenakatta daroo
	FORMAL	kakemasitaroo	kakemaseñ desitaroo
		kaketa desyoo	kakenakatta desyoo
Conditional	**INFORMAL**	kaketara	kakenakattara
	FORMAL	kakemasitara	kakemaseñ desitara
Alternative	**INFORMAL**	kaketari	kakenakattari
	FORMAL	kakemasitari	kakemaseñ desitari

INFORMAL AFFIRMATIVE INDICATIVE

Passive		kakerareru
Potential		kakerareru
Causative		kakesaseru
Causative Pass.		kakesaserareru
Honorific	**I**	okake ni naru
	II	okake nasaru
Humble	**I**	okake suru
	II	okake itasu

		AFFIRMATIVE	NEGATIVE
Indicative	**INFORMAL**	kakomu	kakomanai
	FORMAL	kakomimasu	kakomimaseñ
Imperative	**INFORMAL I**	kakome	kakomu na
	II	kakominasai	kakominasaru na
	III	kakoñde kudasai	kakomanai de kudasai
	FORMAL	okakomi nasaimase	okakomi nasaimasu na
Presumptive	**INFORMAL I**	kakomoo	kakomumai
	II	kakomu daroo	kakomanai daroo
	FORMAL I	kakomimasyoo	kakomimasumai
	II	kakomu desyoo	kakomanai desyoo
Provisional	**INFORMAL**	kakomeba	kakomanakereba
	FORMAL	kakomimaseba	kakomimaseñ nara
		kakomimasureba	
Gerund	**INFORMAL I**	kakoñde	kakomanai de
	II		kakomanakute
	FORMAL	kakomimasite	kakomimaseñ de
Past Ind.	**INFORMAL**	kakoñda	kakomanakatta
	FORMAL	kakomimasita	kakomimaseñ desita
Past Presump.	**INFORMAL**	kakoñdaroo	kakomanakattaroo
		kakoñda daroo	kakomanakatta daroo
	FORMAL	kakomimasitaroo	kakomimaseñ desitaroo
		kakoñda desyoo	kakomanakatta desyoo
Conditional	**INFORMAL**	kakoñdara	kakomanakattara
	FORMAL	kakomimasitara	kakomimaseñ desitara
Alternative	**INFORMAL**	kakoñdari	kakomanakattari
	FORMAL	kakomimasitari	kakomimaseñ desitari

		INFORMAL AFFIRMATIVE INDICATIVE
Passive		kakomareru
Potential		kakomeru
Causative		kakomaseru
Causative Pass.		kakomaserareru

Honorific	**I**	okakomi ni naru
	II	okakomi nasaru
Humble	**I**	okakomi suru
	II	okakomi itasu

		AFFIRMATIVE	NEGATIVE
Indicative	**INFORMAL**	kaku	kakanai
	FORMAL	kakimasu	kakimaseñ
Imperative	**INFORMAL I**	kake	kaku na
	II	kakinasai	kakinasaru na
	III	kaite kudasai	kakanai de kudasai
	FORMAL	okaki nasaimase	okaki nasaimasu na
Presumptive	**INFORMAL I**	kakoo	kakumai
	II	kaku daroo	kakanai daroo
	FORMAL　I	kakimasyoo	kakimasumai
	II	kaku desyoo	kakanai desyoo
Provisional	**INFORMAL**	kakeba	kakanakereba
	FORMAL	kakimaseba	kakimaseñ nara
		kakimasureba	
Gerund	**INFORMAL I**	kaite	kakanai de
	II		kakanakute
	FORMAL	kakimasite	kakimaseñ de
Past Ind.	**INFORMAL**	kaita	kakanakatta
	FORMAL	kakimasita	kakimaseñ desita
Past Presump.	**INFORMAL**	kaitaroo	kakanakattaroo
		kaita daroo	kakanakatta daroo
	FORMAL	kakimasitaroo	kakimaseñ desitaroo
		kaita desyoo	kakanakatta desyoo
Conditional	**INFORMAL**	kaitara	kakanakattara
	FORMAL	kakimasitara	kakimaseñ desitara
Alternative	**INFORMAL**	kaitari	kakanakattari
	FORMAL	kakimasitari	kakimaseñ desitari

		INFORMAL AFFIRMATIVE INDICATIVE
Passive		kakareru
Potential		kakeru
Causative		kakaseru
Causative Pass.		kakaserareru
Honorific	**I**	okaki ni naru
	II	okaki nasaru
Humble	**I**	okaki suru
	II	okaki itasu

TRANSITIVE   *to lack, to be wanting, to chip*

		AFFIRMATIVE	NEGATIVE
Indicative	**INFORMAL**	kaku	kakanai
	FORMAL	kakimasu	kakimaseñ
Imperative	**INFORMAL I**	kake	kaku na
	II	kakinasai	kakinasaru na
	III	kaite kudasai	kakanai de kudasai
	FORMAL	okaki nasaimase	okaki nasaimasu na
Presumptive	**INFORMAL I**	kakoo	kakumai
	II	kaku daroo	kakanai daroo
	FORMAL I	kakimasyoo	kakimasumai
	II	kaku desyoo	kakanai desyoo
Provisional	**INFORMAL**	kakeba	kakanakereba
	FORMAL	kakimaseba	kakimaseñ nara
		kakimasureba	
Gerund	**INFORMAL I**	kaite	kakanai de
	II		kakanakute
	FORMAL	kakimasite	kakimaseñ de
Past Ind.	**INFORMAL**	kaita	kakanakatta
	FORMAL	kakimasita	kakimaseñ desita
Past Presump.	**INFORMAL**	kaitaroo	kakanakattaroo
		kaita daroo	kakanakatta daroo
	FORMAL	kakimasitaroo	kakimaseñ desitaroo
		kaita desyoo	kakanakatta desyoo
Conditional	**INFORMAL**	kaitara	kakanakattara
	FORMAL	kakimasitara	kakimaseñ desitara
Alternative	**INFORMAL**	kaitari	kakanakattari
	FORMAL	kakimasitari	kakimaseñ desitari

		INFORMAL AFFIRMATIVE INDICATIVE
Passive		kakareru
Potential		kakeru
Causative		kakaseru
Causative Pass.		kakaserareru
Honorific	**I**	okaki ni naru
	II	okaki nasaru
Humble	**I**	okaki suru
	II	okaki itasu

to hide (oneself)

		AFFIRMATIVE	NEGATIVE
Indicative	**INFORMAL**	kakureru	kakurenai
	FORMAL	kakuremasu	kakuremaseñ
Imperative	**INFORMAL I**	kakurero	kakureru na
	II	kakurenasai	kakurenasaru na
	III	kakurete kudasai	kakurenai de kudasai
	FORMAL	okakure nasaimase	okakure nasaimasu na
Presumptive	**INFORMAL I**	kakureyoo	kakuremai
	II	kakureru daroo	kakurenai daroo
	FORMAL I	kakuremasyoo	kakuremasumai
	II	kakureru desyoo	kakurenai desyoo
Provisional	**INFORMAL**	kakurereba	kakurenakereba
	FORMAL	kakuremaseba	kakuremaseñ nara
		kakuremasureba	
Gerund	**INFORMAL I**	kakurete	kakurenai de
	II		kakurenakute
	FORMAL	kakuremasite	kakuremaseñ de
Past Ind.	**INFORMAL**	kakureta	kakurenakatta
	FORMAL	kakuremasita	kakuremaseñ desita
Past Presump.	**INFORMAL**	kakuretaroo	kakurenakattaroo
		kakureta daroo	kakurenakatta daroo
	FORMAL	kakuremasitaroo	kakuremaseñ desitaroo
		kakureta desyoo	kakurenakatta desyoo
Conditional	**INFORMAL**	kakuretara	kakurenakattara
	FORMAL	kakuremasitara	kakuremaseñ desitara
Alternative	**INFORMAL**	kakuretari	kakurenakattari
	FORMAL	kakuremasitari	kakuremaseñ desitari

		INFORMAL AFFIRMATIVE INDICATIVE
Passive		kakurerareru
Potential		kakurerareru
Causative		kakuresaseru
Causative Pass.		kakuresaserareru
Honorific	**I**	okakure ni naru
	II	okakure nasaru
Humble	**I**	
	II	

TRANSITIVE   *to hide* (something)

		AFFIRMATIVE	NEGATIVE
Indicative	**INFORMAL**	kakusu	kakusanai
	FORMAL	kakusimasu	kakusimaseñ
Imperative	**INFORMAL I**	kakuse	kakusu na
	II	kakusinasai	kakusinasaru na
	III	kakusite kudasai	kakusanai de kudasai
	FORMAL	okakusi nasaimase	okakusi nasaimasu na
Presumptive	**INFORMAL I**	kakusoo	kakusumai
	II	kakusu daroo	kakusanai daroo
	FORMAL I	kakusimasyoo	kakusimasumai
	II	kakusu desyoo	kakusanai desyoo
Provisional	**INFORMAL**	kakuseba	kakusanakereba
	FORMAL	kakusimaseba	kakusimaseñ nara
		kakusimasureba	
Gerund	**INFORMAL I**	kakusite	kakusanai de
	II		kakusanakute
	FORMAL	kakusimasite	kakusimaseñ de
Past Ind.	**INFORMAL**	kakusita	kakusanakatta
	FORMAL	kakusimasita	kakusimaseñ desita
Past Presump.	**INFORMAL**	kakusitaroo	kakusanakattaroo
		kakusita daroo	kakusanakatta daroo
	FORMAL	kakusimasitaroo	kakusimaseñ desitaroo
		kakusita desyoo	kakusanakatta desyoo
Conditional	**INFORMAL**	kakusitara	kakusanakattara
	FORMAL	kakusimasitara	kakusimaseñ desitara
Alternative	**INFORMAL**	kakusitari	kakusanakattari
	FORMAL	kakusimasitari	kakusimaseñ desitari

		INFORMAL AFFIRMATIVE INDICATIVE
Passive		kakusareru
Potential		kakuseru
Causative		kakusaseru
Causative Pass.		kakusaserareru
Honorific	**I**	okakusi ni naru
	II	okakusi nasaru
Humble	**I**	okakusi suru
	II	okakusi itasu

173

to assume a defensive posture, to stand prepared   TRANSITIVE

		AFFIRMATIVE	NEGATIVE
Indicative	**INFORMAL**	kamaeru	kamaenai
	FORMAL	kamaemasu	kamaemaseñ
Imperative	**INFORMAL I**	kamaero	kamaeru na
	II	kamaenasai	kamaenasaru na
	III	kamaete kudasai	kamaenai de kudasai
	FORMAL	okamae nasaimase	okamae nasaimasu na
Presumptive	**INFORMAL I**	kamaeyoo	kamaemai
	II	kamaeru daroo	kamaenai daroo
	FORMAL I	kamaemasyoo	kamaemasumai
	II	kamaeru desyoo	kamaenai desyoo
Provisional	**INFORMAL**	kamaereba	kamaenakereba
	FORMAL	kamaemaseba	kamaemaseñ nara
		kamaemasureba	
Gerund	**INFORMAL I**	kamaete	kamaenai de
	II		kamaenakute
	FORMAL	kamaemasite	kamaemaseñ de
Past Ind.	**INFORMAL**	kamaeta	kamaenakatta
	FORMAL	kamaemasita	kamaemaseñ desita
Past Presump.	**INFORMAL**	kamaetaroo	kamaenakattaroo
		kamaeta daroo	kamaenakatta daroo
	FORMAL	kamaemasitaroo	kamaemaseñ desitaroo
		kamaeta desyoo	kamaenakatta desyoo
Conditional	**INFORMAL**	kamaetara	kamaenakattara
	FORMAL	kamaemasitara	kamaemaseñ desitara
Alternative	**INFORMAL**	kamaetari	kamaenakattari
	FORMAL	kamaemasitari	kamaemaseñ desitari

		INFORMAL AFFIRMATIVE INDICATIVE
Passive		kamaerareru
Potential		kamaerareru
Causative		kamaesaseru
Causative Pass.		kamaesaserareru
Honorific	**I**	okamae ni naru
	II	okamae nasaru
Humble	**I**	
	II	

TRANSITIVE　　*to mind, to care about*

		AFFIRMATIVE	NEGATIVE
Indicative	INFORMAL	kamau	kamawanai
	FORMAL	kamaimasu	kamaimaseñ
Imperative	INFORMAL I	kamae	kamau na
	II	kamainasai	kamainasaru na
	III	kamatte kudasai	kamawanai de kudasai
	FORMAL	okamai nasaimase	okamai nasaimasu na
Presumptive	INFORMAL I	kamaoo	kamaumai
	II	kamau daroo	kamawanai daroo
	FORMAL I	kamaimasyoo	kamaimasumai
	II	kamau desyoo	kamawanai desyoo
Provisional	INFORMAL	kamaeba	kamawanakereba
	FORMAL	kamaimaseba	kamaimaseñ nara
		kamaimasureba	
Gerund	INFORMAL I	kamatte	kamawanai de
	II		kamawanakute
	FORMAL	kamaimasite	kamaimaseñ de
Past Ind.	INFORMAL	kamatta	kamawanakatta
	FORMAL	kamaimasita	kamaimaseñ desita
Past Presump.	INFORMAL	kamattaroo	kamawanakattaroo
		kamatta daroo	kamawanakatta daroo
	FORMAL	kamaimasitaroo	kamaimaseñ desitaroo
		kamatta desyoo	kamawanakatta desyoo
Conditional	INFORMAL	kamattara	kamawanakattara
	FORMAL	kamaimasitara	kamaimaseñ desitara
Alternative	INFORMAL	kamattari	kamawanakattari
	FORMAL	kamaimasitari	kamaimaseñ desitari

INFORMAL AFFIRMATIVE INDICATIVE

Passive		
Potential		kamaeru
Causative		kamawaseru
Causative Pass.		kamawaserareru

Honorific	I	okamai ni naru
	II	okamai nasaru
Humble	I	okamai suru
	II	okamai itasu

		AFFIRMATIVE	NEGATIVE
Indicative	**INFORMAL**	kamu	kamanai
	FORMAL	kamimasu	kamimaseñ
Imperative	**INFORMAL I**	kame	kamu na
	II	kaminasai	kaminasaru na
	III	kañde kudasai	kamanai de kudasai
	FORMAL	okami nasaimase	okami nasaimasu na
Presumptive	**INFORMAL I**	kamoo	kamumai
	II	kamu daroo	kamanai daroo
	FORMAL I	kamimasyoo	kamimasumai
	II	kamu desyoo	kamanai desyoo
Provisional	**INFORMAL**	kameba	kamanakereba
	FORMAL	kamimaseba	kamimaseñ nara
		kamimasureba	
Gerund	**INFORMAL I**	kañde	kamanai de
	II		kamanakute
	FORMAL	kamimasite	kamimaseñ de
Past Ind.	**INFORMAL**	kañda	kamanakatta
	FORMAL	kamimasita	kamimaseñ desita
Past Presump.	**INFORMAL**	kañdaroo	kamanakattaroo
		kañda daroo	kamanakatta daroo
	FORMAL	kamimasitaroo	kamimaseñ desitaroo
		kañda desyoo	kamanakatta desyoo
Conditional	**INFORMAL**	kañdara	kamanakattara
	FORMAL	kamimasitara	kamimaseñ desitara
Alternative	**INFORMAL**	kañdari	kamanakattari
	FORMAL	kamimasitari	kamimaseñ desitari

INFORMAL AFFIRMATIVE INDICATIVE

Passive		kamareru
Potential		kameru
Causative		kamaseru
Causative Pass.		kamaserareru

Honorific	**I**	okami ni naru
	II	okami nasaru
Humble	**I**	okami suru
	II	okami itasu

TRANSITIVE　　*to grant a request, hear a prayer*

		AFFIRMATIVE	NEGATIVE
Indicative	**INFORMAL**	kanaeru	kanaenai
	FORMAL	kanaemasu	kanaemaseñ
Imperative	**INFORMAL I**	kanaero	kanaeru na
	II	kanaenasai	kanaenasaru na
	III	kanaete kudasai	kanaenai de kudasai
	FORMAL	okanae nasaimase	okanae nasimasu na
Presumptive	**INFORMAL I**	kanaeyoo	kanaemai
	II	kanaeru daroo	kanaenai daroo
	FORMAL I	kanaemasyoo	kanaemasumai
	II	kanaeru desyoo	kanaenai desyoo
Provisional	**INFORMAL**	kanaereba	kanaenakereba
	FORMAL	kanaemaseba	kanaemaseñ nara
		kanaemasureba	
Gerund	**INFORMAL I**	kanaete	kanaenai de
	II		kanaenakute
	FORMAL	kanaemasite	kanaemaseñ de
Past Ind.	**INFORMAL**	kanaeta	kanaenakatta
	FORMAL	kanaemasita	kanaemaseñ desita
Past Presump.	**INFORMAL**	kanaetaroo	kanaenakattaroo
		kanaeta daroo	kanaenakatta daroo
	FORMAL	kanaemasitaroo	kanaemaseñ desitaroo
		kanaeta desyoo	kanaenakatta desyoo
Conditional	**INFORMAL**	kanaetara	kanaenakattara
	FORMAL	kanaemasitara	kanaemaseñ desitara
Alternative	**INFORMAL**	kanaetari	kanaenakattari
	FORMAL	kanaemasitari	kanaemaseñ desitari

		INFORMAL AFFIRMATIVE INDICATIVE
Passive		kanaerareru
Potential		kanaerareru
Causative		kanaesaseru
Causative Pass.		kanaesaserareru
Honorific	**I**	okanae ni naru
	II	okanae nasaru
Humble	**I**	okanae suru
	II	okanae itasu

		AFFIRMATIVE	NEGATIVE
Indicative	**INFORMAL**	kanasimu	kanasimanai
	FORMAL	kanasimimasu	kanasimimaseñ
Imperative	**INFORMAL I**	kanasime	kanasimu na
	II	kanasiminasai	kanasiminasaru na
	III	kanasiñde kudasai	kanasimanai de kudasai
	FORMAL	okanasimi nasaimase	okanasimi nasaimasu na
Presumptive	**INFORMAL I**	kanasimoo	kanasimumai
	II	kanasimu daroo	kanasimanai daroo
	FORMAL I	kanasimimasyoo	kanasimimasumai
	II	kanasimu desyoo	kanasimanai desyoo
Provisional	**INFORMAL**	kanasimeba	kanasimanakereba
	FORMAL	kanasimimaseba	kanasimimaseñ nara
		kanasimimasureba	
Gerund	**INFORMAL I**	kanasiñde	kanasimanai de
	II		kanasimanakute
	FORMAL	kanasimimasite	kanasimimaseñ de
Past Ind.	**INFORMAL**	kanasiñda	kanasimanakatta
	FORMAL	kanasimimasita	kanasimimaseñ desita
Past Presump.	**INFORMAL**	kanasiñdaroo	kanasimanakattaroo
		kanasiñda daroo	kanasimanakatta daroo
	FORMAL	kanasimimasitaroo	kanasimimaseñ desitaroo
		kanasiñda desyoo	kanasimanakatta desyoo
Conditional	**INFORMAL**	kanasiñdara	kanasimanakattara
	FORMAL	kanasimimasitara	kanasimimaseñ desitara
Alternative	**INFORMAL**	kanasiñdari	kanasimanakattari
	FORMAL	kanasimimasitari	kanasimimaseñ desitari

INFORMAL AFFIRMATIVE INDICATIVE

Passive		kanasimareru
Potential		kanasimeru
Causative		kanasimaseru
Causative Pass.		kanasimaserareru

Honorific	**I**	okanasimi ni naru
	II	okanasimi nasaru
Humble	**I**	
	II	

		AFFIRMATIVE	NEGATIVE
Indicative	**INFORMAL**	kanau	kanawanai
	FORMAL	kanaimasu	kanaimaseñ
Imperative	**INFORMAL I**		
	II		
	III		
	FORMAL		
Presumptive	**INFORMAL I**	kanaoo	kanaumai
	II	kanau daroo	kanawanai daroo
	FORMAL I	kanaimasyoo	kanaimasumai
	II	kanau desyoo	kanawanai desyoo
Provisional	**INFORMAL**	kanaeba	kanawanakereba
	FORMAL	kanaimaseba	kanaimaseñ nara
		kanaimasureba	
Gerund	**INFORMAL I**	kanatte	kanawanai de
	II		kanawanakute
	FORMAL	kanaimasite	kanaimaseñ de
Past Ind.	**INFORMAL**	kanatta	kanawanakatta
	FORMAL	kanaimasita	kanaimaseñ desita
Past Presump.	**INFORMAL**	kanattaroo	kanawanakattaroo
		kanatta daroo	kanawanakatta daroo
	FORMAL	kanaimasitaroo	kanaimaseñ desitaroo
		kanatta desyoo	kanawanakatta desyoo
Conditional	**INFORMAL**	kanattara	kanawanakattara
	FORMAL	kanaimsitara	kanaimaseñ desitara
Alternative	**INFORMAL**	kanattari	kanawanakattari
	FORMAL	kanaimasitari	kanaimaseñ desitari

		INFORMAL AFFIRMATIVE INDICATIVE
Passive		kanawareru
Potential		kanaeru
Causative		kanawaseru
Causative Pass.		kanawaserareru
Honorific	**I**	
	II	
Humble	**I**	
	II	

		AFFIRMATIVE	NEGATIVE
Indicative	INFORMAL	kañgaeru	kañgaenai
	FORMAL	kañgaemasu	kañgaemaseñ
Imperative	INFORMAL I	kañgaero	kañgaeru na
	II	kañgaenasai	kañgaenasaru na
	III	kañgaete kudasai	kañgaenai de kudasai
	FORMAL	okañgae nasaimase	okañgae nasaimasu na
Presumptive	INFORMAL I	kañgaeyoo	kañgaemai
	II	kañgaeru daroo	kañgaenai daroo
	FORMAL I	kañgaemasyoo	kañgaemasumai
	II	kañgaeru desyoo	kañgaenai desyoo
Provisional	INFORMAL	kañgaereba	kañgaenakereba
	FORMAL	kañgaemaseba	kañgaemaseñ nara
		kañgaemasureba	
Gerund	INFORMAL I	kañgaete	kañgaenai de
	II		kañgaenakute
	FORMAL	kañgaemasite	kañgaemaseñ de
Past Ind.	INFORMAL	kañgaeta	kañgaenakatta
	FORMAL	kañgaemasita	kañgaemaseñ desita
Past Presump.	INFORMAL	kañgaetaroo	kañgaenakattaroo
		kañgaeta daroo	kañgaenakatta daroo
	FORMAL	kañgaemasitaroo	kañgaemaseñ desitaroo
		kañgaeta desyoo	kañgaenakatta desyoo
Conditional	INFORMAL	kañgaetara	kañgaenakattara
	FORMAL	kañgaemasitara	kañgaemaseñ desitara
Alternative	INFORMAL	kañgaetari	kañgaenakattari
	FORMAL	kañgaemasitari	kañgaemaseñ desitari

INFORMAL AFFIRMATIVE INDICATIVE

Passive	kañgaerareru
Potential	kañgaerareru
Causative	kañgaesaseru
Causative Pass.	kañgaesaserareru

Honorific	I	okañgae ni naru
	II	okañgae nasaru
Humble	I	
	II	

TRANSITIVE   *to feel, to sense*

		AFFIRMATIVE	NEGATIVE
Indicative	**INFORMAL**	kañziru	kañzinai
	FORMAL	kañzimasu	kañzimaseñ
Imperative	**INFORMAL I**	kañziro	kañziru na
	II	kañzinasai	kañzinasaru na
	III	kañzite kudasai	kañzinai de kudasai
	FORMAL	okañzi nasaimase	okañzi nasaimasu na
Presumptive	**INFORMAL I**	kañziyoo	kañzimai
	II	kañziru daroo	kañzinai daroo
	FORMAL I	kañzimasyoo	kañzimasumai
	II	kañziru desyoo	kañzinai desyoo
Provisional	**INFORMAL**	kañzireba	kañzinakereba
	FORMAL	kañzimaseba	kañzimaseñ nara
		kañzimasureba	
Gerund	**INFORMAL I**	kañzite	kañzinai de
	II		kañzinakute
	FORMAL	kañzimasite	kañzimaseñ de
Past Ind.	**INFORMAL**	kañzita	kañzinakatta
	FORMAL	kañzimasita	kañzimaseñ desita
Past Presump.	**INFORMAL**	kañzitaroo	kañzinakattaroo
		kañzita daroo	kañzinakatta daroo
	FORMAL	kañzimasitaroo	kañzimaseñ desitaroo
		kañzita desyoo	kañzinakatta desyoo
Conditional	**INFORMAL**	kañzitara	kañzinakattara
	FORMAL	kañzimasitara	kañzimaseñ desitara
Alternative	**INFORMAL**	kañzitari	kañzinakattari
	FORMAL	kañzimasitari	kañzimaseñ desitari

INFORMAL AFFIRMATIVE INDICATIVE

Passive		kañzirareru
Potential		kañzirareru
Causative		kañzisaseru
Causative Pass.		kañzisaserareru
Honorific	**I**	okañzi ni naru
	II	okañzi nasaru
Humble	**I**	
	II	

		AFFIRMATIVE	NEGATIVE
Indicative	**INFORMAL**	karakau	karakawanai
	FORMAL	karakaimasu	karakaimaseñ
Imperative	**INFORMAL I**	karakae	karakau na
	II	karakainasai	karakainasaru na
	III	karakatte kudasai	karakawanai de kudasai
	FORMAL	okarakai nasaimase	okarakai nasaimasu na
Presumptive	**INFORMAL I**	karakaoo	karakaumai
	II	karakau daroo	karakawanai daroo
	FORMAL I	karakaimasyoo	karakaimasumai
	II	karakau desyoo	karakawanai desyoo
Provisional	**INFORMAL**	karakaeba	karakawanakereba
	FORMAL	karakaimaseba	karakaimaseñ nara
		karakaimasureba	
Gerund	**INFORMAL I**	karakatte	karakawanai de
	II		karakawanakute
	FORMAL	karakaimasite	karakaimaseñ de
Past Ind.	**INFORMAL**	karakatta	karakawanakatta
	FORMAL	karakaimasita	karakaimaseñ desita
Past Presump.	**INFORMAL**	karakattaroo	karakawanakattaroo
		karakatta daroo	karakawanakatta daroo
	FORMAL	karakaimasitaroo	karakaimaseñ desitaroo
		karakatta desyoo	karakawanakatta desyoo
Conditional	**INFORMAL**	karakattara	karakawanakattara
	FORMAL	karakaimasitara	karakaimaseñ desitara
Alternative	**INFORMAL**	karakattari	karakawanakattari
	FORMAL	karakaimasitari	karakaimaseñ desitari

		INFORMAL AFFIRMATIVE INDICATIVE
Passive		karakawareru
Potential		karakaeru
Causative		karakawaseru
Causative Pass.		karakawaserareru
Honorific	**I**	okarakai ni naru
	II	okarakai nasaru
Humble	**I**	okarakai suru
	II	okarakai itasu

to wither, to die (of a plant)

		AFFIRMATIVE	NEGATIVE
Indicative	**INFORMAL**	kareru	karenai
	FORMAL	karemasu	karemaseñ
Imperative	**INFORMAL I**	karero	kareru na
	II		
	III		
	FORMAL		
Presumptive	**INFORMAL I**	kareyoo	karemai
	II	kareru daroo	karenai daroo
	FORMAL I	karemasyoo	karemasumai
	II	kareru desyoo	karenai desyoo
Provisional	**INFORMAL**	karereba	karenakereba
	FORMAL	karemaseba	karemaseñ nara
		karemasureba	
Gerund	**INFORMAL I**	karete	karenai de
	II		karenakute
	FORMAL	karemasite	karemaseñ de
Past Ind.	**INFORMAL**	kareta	karenakatta
	FORMAL	karemasita	karemaseñ desita
Past Presump.	**INFORMAL**	karetaroo	karenakattaroo
		kareta daroo	karenakatta daroo
	FORMAL	karemasitaroo	karemaseñ desitaroo
		kareta desyoo	karenakatta desyoo
Conditional	**INFORMAL**	karetara	karenakattara
	FORMAL	karemasitara	karemaseñ desitara
Alternative	**INFORMAL**	karetari	karenakattari
	FORMAL	karemasitari	karemaseñ desitari

		INFORMAL AFFIRMATIVE INDICATIVE
Passive		karerareru
Potential		karerareru
Causative		karesaseru
Causative Pass.		karesaserareru
Honorific	**I**	okare ni naru
	II	okare nasaru
Humble	**I**	
	II	

		AFFIRMATIVE	**NEGATIVE**
Indicative	**INFORMAL**	kariru	karinai
	FORMAL	karimasu	karimaseñ
Imperative	**INFORMAL I**	kariro	kariru na
	II	karinasai	karinasaru na
	III	karite kudasai	karinai de kudasai
	FORMAL	okari nasaimase	okari nasaimasu na
Presumptive	**INFORMAL I**	kariyoo	karimai
	II	kariru daroo	karinai daroo
	FORMAL I	karimasyoo	karimasumai
	II	kariru desyoo	karinai desyoo
Provisional	**INFORMAL**	karireba	karinakereba
	FORMAL	karimaseba	karimaseñ nara
		karimasureba	
Gerund	**INFORMAL I**	karite	karinai de
	II		karinakute
	FORMAL	karimasite	karimaseñ de
Past Ind.	**INFORMAL**	karita	karinakatta
	FORMAL	karimasita	karimaseñ desita
Past Presump.	**INFORMAL**	karitaroo	karinakattaroo
		karita daroo	karinakatta daroo
	FORMAL	karimasitaroo	karimaseñ desitaroo
		karita desyoo	karinakatta desyoo
Conditional	**INFORMAL**	karitara	karinakattara
	FORMAL	karimasitara	karimaseñ desitara
Alternative	**INFORMAL**	karitari	karinakattari
	FORMAL	karimasitari	karimaseñ desitari

INFORMAL AFFIRMATIVE INDICATIVE

Passive		karirareru
Potential		karirareru
Causative		karisaseru
Causative Pass.		karisaserareru

Honorific	**I**	okari ni naru
	II	okari nasaru
Humble	**I**	okari suru
	II	okari itasu

		AFFIRMATIVE	NEGATIVE
Indicative	**INFORMAL**	kasanaru	kasanaranai
	FORMAL	kasanarimasu	kasanarimaseñ
Imperative	**INFORMAL I**	kasanare	kasanaru na
	II	kasanarinasai	kasanarinasaru na
	III	kasanatte kudasai	kasanaranai de kudasai
	FORMAL	okasanari nasaimase	okasanari nasaimasu na
Presumptive	**INFORMAL I**	kasanaroo	kasanarumai
	II	kasanaru daroo	kasanaranai daroo
	FORMAL I	kasanarimasyoo	kasanarimasumai
	II	kasanaru desyoo	kasanaranai desyoo
Provisional	**INFORMAL**	kasanareba	kasanaranakereba
	FORMAL	kasanarimaseba	kasanarimaseñ nara
		kasanarimasureba	
Gerund	**INFORMAL I**	kasanatte	kasanaranai de
	II		kasanaranakute
	FORMAL	kasanarimasite	kasanarimaseñ de
Past Ind.	**INFORMAL**	kasanatta	kasanaranakatta
	FORMAL	kasanarimasita	kasanarimaseñ desita
Past Presump.	**INFORMAL**	kasanattaroo	kasanaranakattaroo
		kasanatta daroo	kasanaranakatta daroo
	FORMAL	kasanarimasitaroo	kasanarimaseñ desitaroo
		kasanatta desyoo	kasanaranakatta desyoo
Conditional	**INFORMAL**	kasanattara	kasanaranakattara
	FORMAL	kasanarimasitara	kasanarimaseñ desitara
Alternative	**INFORMAL**	kasanattari	kasanaranakattari
	FORMAL	kasanarimasitari	kasanarimaseñ desitari

		INFORMAL AFFIRMATIVE INDICATIVE
Passive		kasanarareru
Potential		kasanareru
Causative		kasanaraseru
Causative Pass.		kasanaraserareru
Honorific	**I**	okasanari ni naru
	II	okasanari nasaru
Humble	**I**	
	II	

		AFFIRMATIVE	NEGATIVE
Indicative	**INFORMAL**	kasaneru	kasanenai
	FORMAL	kasanemasu	kasanemaseñ
Imperative	**INFORMAL I**	kasanero	kasaneru na
	II	kasanenasai	kasanenasaru na
	III	kasanete kudasai	kasanenai de kudasai
	FORMAL	okasane nasaimase	okasane nasaimasu na
Presumptive	**INFORMAL I**	kasaneyoo	kasanemai
	II	kasaneru daroo	kasanenai daroo
	FORMAL I	kasanemasyoo	kasanemasumai
	II	kasaneru desyoo	kasanenai desyoo
Provisional	**INFORMAL**	kasanereba	kasanenakereba
	FORMAL	kasanemaseba	kasanemaseñ nara
		kasanemasureba	
Gerund	**INFORMAL I**	kasanete	kasanenai de
	II		kasanenakute
	FORMAL	kasanemasite	kasanemaseñ de
Past Ind.	**INFORMAL**	kasaneta	kasanenakatta
	FORMAL	kasanemasita	kasanemaseñ desita
Past Presump.	**INFORMAL**	kasanetaroo	kasanenakattaroo
		kasaneta daroo	kasanenakatta daroo
	FORMAL	kasanemasitaroo	kasanemaseñ desitaroo
		kasaneta desyoo	kasanenakatta desyoo
Conditional	**INFORMAL**	kasanetara	kasanenakattara
	FORMAL	kasanemasitara	kasanemaseñ desitara
Alternative	**INFORMAL**	kasanetari	kasanenakattari
	FORMAL	kasanemasitari	kasanemaseñ desitari

		INFORMAL AFFIRMATIVE INDICATIVE
Passive		kasanerareru
Potential		kasanerareru
Causative		kasanesaseru
Causative Pass.		kasanesaserareru
Honorific	**I**	okasane ni naru
	II	okasane nasaru
Humble	**I**	okasane suru
	II	okasane itasu

kaség.u

TRANSITIVE   *to earn one's living*

		AFFIRMATIVE	NEGATIVE
Indicative	**INFORMAL**	kasegu	kaseganai
	FORMAL	kasegimasu	kasegimaseñ
Imperative	**INFORMAL I**	kasege	kasegu na
	II	kaseginasai	kaseginasaru na
	III	kaseide kudasai	kaseganai de kudasai
	FORMAL	okasegi nasaimase	okasegi nasaimasu na
Presumptive	**INFORMAL I**	kasegoo	kasegumai
	II	kasegu daroo	kaseganai daroo
	FORMAL I	kasegimasyoo	kasegimasumai
	II	kasegu desyoo	kaseganai desyoo
Provisional	**INFORMAL**	kasegeba	kaseganakereba
	FORMAL	kasegimaseba	kasegimaseñ nara
		kasegimasureba	
Gerund	**INFORMAL I**	kaseide	kaseganai de
	II		kaseganakute
	FORMAL	kasegimasite	kasegimaseñ de
Past Ind.	**INFORMAL**	kaseida	kaseganakatta
	FORMAL	kasegimasita	kasegimaseñ desita
Past Presump.	**INFORMAL**	kaseidaroo	kaseganakattaroo
		kaseida daroo	kaseganakatta daroo
	FORMAL	kasegimasitaroo	kasegimaseñ desitaroo
		kaseida desyoo	kaseganakatta desyoo
Conditional	**INFORMAL**	kaseidara	kaseganakattara
	FORMAL	kasegimasitara	kasegimaseñ desitara
Alternative	**INFORMAL**	kaseidari	kaseganakattari
	FORMAL	kasegimasitari	kasegimaseñ desitari

		INFORMAL AFFIRMATIVE INDICATIVE
Passive		kasegareru
Potential		kasegeru
Causative		kasegaseru
Causative Pass.		kasegaserareru
Honorific	**I**	okasegi ni naru
	II	okasegi nasaru
Humble	**I**	okasegi suru
	II	okasegi itasu

187

			AFFIRMATIVE	NEGATIVE
Indicative	INFORMAL		kasu	kasanai
	FORMAL		kasimasu	kasimaseñ
Imperative	INFORMAL	I	kase	kasu na
		II	kasinasai	kasinasaru na
		III	kasite kudasai	kasanai de kudasai
	FORMAL		okasi nasaimase	okasi nasaimasu na
Presumptive	INFORMAL	I	kasoo	kasumai
		II	kasu daroo	kasanai daroo
	FORMAL	I	kasimasyoo	kasimasumai
		II	kasu desyoo	kasanai desyoo
Provisional	INFORMAL		kaseba	kasanakereba
	FORMAL		kasimaseba	kasimaseñ nara
			kasimasureba	
Gerund	INFORMAL	I	kasite	kasanai de
		II		kasanakute
	FORMAL		kasimasite	kasimaseñ de
Past Ind.	INFORMAL		kasita	kasanakatta
	FORMAL		kasimasita	kasimaseñ desita
Past Presump.	INFORMAL		kasitaroo	kasanakattaroo
			kasita daroo	kasanakatta daroo
	FORMAL		kasimasitaroo	kasimaseñ desitaroo
			kasita desyoo	kasanakatta desyoo
Conditional	INFORMAL		kasitara	kasanakattara
	FORMAL		kasimasitara	kasimaseñ desitara
Alternative	INFORMAL		kasitari	kasanakattari
	FORMAL		kasimasitari	kasimaseñ desitari

		INFORMAL AFFIRMATIVE INDICATIVE
Passive		kasareru
Potential		kaseru
Causative		kasaseru
Causative Pass.		kasaserareru

Honorific	I	okasi ni naru
	II	okasi nasaru
Humble	I	okasi suru
	II	okasi itasu

		AFFIRMATIVE	NEGATIVE
Indicative	INFORMAL	kasumu	kasumanai
	FORMAL	kasumimasu	kasumimaseñ
Imperative	INFORMAL I	kasume	kasumu na
	II	kasuminasai	kasuminasaru na
	III	kasuñde kudasai	kasumanai de kudasai
	FORMAL	okasumi nasaimase	okasumi nasaimasu na
Presumptive	INFORMAL I	kasumoo	kasumumai
	II	kasumu daroo	kasumanai daroo
	FORMAL I	kasumimasyoo	kasumimasumai
	II	kasumu desyoo	kasumanai desyoo
Provisional	INFORMAL	kasumeba	kasumanakereba
	FORMAL	kasumimaseba	kasumimaseñ nara
		kasumimasureba	
Gerund	INFORMAL I	kasuñde	kasumanai de
	II		kasumanakute
	FORMAL	kasumimasite	kasumimaseñ de
Past Ind.	INFORMAL	kasuñda	kasumanakatta
	FORMAL	kasumimasita	kasumimaseñ desita
Past Presump.	INFORMAL	kasuñdaroo	kasumanakattaroo
		kasuñda daroo	kasumanakatta daroo
	FORMAL	kasumimasitaroo	kasumimaseñ desitaroo
		kasuñda desyoo	kasumanakatta desyoo
Conditional	INFORMAL	kasuñdara	kasumanakattara
	FORMAL	kasumimasitara	kasumimaseñ desitara
Alternative	INFORMAL	kasuñdari	kasumanakattari
	FORMAL	kasumimasitari	kasumimaseñ desitari

		INFORMAL AFFIRMATIVE INDICATIVE
Passive		kasumareru
Potential		kasumeru
Causative		kasumaseru
Causative Pass.		kasumaserareru
Honorific	I	
	II	
Humble	I	
	II	

		AFFIRMATIVE	NEGATIVE
Indicative	**INFORMAL**	katamaru	katamaranai
	FORMAL	katamarimasu	katamarimaseñ
Imperative	**INFORMAL I**	katamare	katamaru na
	II	katamarinasai	katamarinasaru na
	III	katamatte kudasai	katamaranai de kudasai
	FORMAL	okatamari nasaimase	okatamari nasimasu na
Presumptive	**INFORMAL I**	katamaroo	katamarumai
	II	katamaru daroo	katamaranai daroo
	FORMAL I	katamarimasyoo	katamarimasumai
	II	katamaru desyoo	katamaranai desyoo
Provisional	**INFORMAL**	katamareba	katamaranakereba
	FORMAL	katamarimaseba	katamarimaseñ nara
		katamarimasureba	
Gerund	**INFORMAL I**	katamatte	katamaranai de
	II		katamaranakute
	FORMAL	katamarimasite	katamarimaseñ de
Past Ind.	**INFORMAL**	katamatta	katamaranakatta
	FORMAL	katamarimasita	katamarimaseñ desita
Past Presump.	**INFORMAL**	katamattaroo	katamaranakattaroo
		katamatta daroo	katamaranakatta daroo
	FORMAL	katamarimasitaroo	katamarimaseñ desitaroo
		katamatta desyoo	katamaranakatta desyoo
Conditional	**INFORMAL**	katamattara	katamaranakattara
	FORMAL	katamarimasitara	katamarimaseñ desitara
Alternative	**INFORMAL**	katamattari	katamaranakattari
	FORMAL	katamarimasitari	katamarimaseñ desitari

		INFORMAL AFFIRMATIVE INDICATIVE
Passive		katamarareru
Potential		katamareru
Causative		katamaraseru
Causative Pass.		katamaraserareru
Honorific	**I**	okatamari ni naru
	II	okatamari nasaru
Humble	**I**	
	II	

			AFFIRMATIVE	NEGATIVE
Indicative	**INFORMAL**		katameru	katamenai
	FORMAL		katamemasu	katamemaseñ
Imperative	**INFORMAL**	**I**	katamero	katameru na
		II	katamenasai	katamenasaru na
		III	katamete kudasai	katamenai de kudasai
	FORMAL		okatame nasaimase	okatame nasaimasu na
Presumptive	**INFORMAL**	**I**	katameyoo	katamemai
		II	katameru daroo	katamenai daroo
	FORMAL	**I**	katamemasyoo	katamemasumai
		II	katameru desyoo	katamenai desyoo
Provisional	**INFORMAL**		katamereba	katamenakereba
	FORMAL		katamemaseba	katamemaseñ nara
			katamemasureba	
Gerund	**INFORMAL**	**I**	katamete	katamenai de
		II		katamenakute
	FORMAL		katamemasite	katamemaseñ de
Past Ind.	**INFORMAL**		katameta	katamenakatta
	FORMAL		katamemasita	katamemaseñ desita
Past Presump.	**INFORMAL**		katametaroo	katamenakattaroo
			katameta daroo	katamenakatta daroo
	FORMAL		katamemasitaroo	katamemaseñ desitaroo
			katameta desyoo	katamenakatta desyoo
Conditional	**INFORMAL**		katametara	katamenakattara
	FORMAL		katamemasitara	katamemaseñ desitara
Alternative	**INFORMAL**		katametari	katamenakattari
	FORMAL		katamemasitari	katamemaseñ desitari

		INFORMAL AFFIRMATIVE INDICATIVE
Passive		katamerareru
Potential		katamerareru
Causative		katamesaseru
Causative Pass.		katamesaserareru
Honorific	**I**	okatame ni naru
	II	okatame nasaru
Humble	**I**	okatame suru
	II	okatame itasu

katamúk.u
to lean (toward), *to be slanted*

		AFFIRMATIVE	NEGATIVE
Indicative	**INFORMAL**	katamuku	katamukanai
	FORMAL	katamukimasu	katamukimaseñ
Imperative	**INFORMAL I**	katamuke	katamuku na
	II	katamukinasai	katamukinasaru na
	III	katamuite kudasai	katamukanai de kudasai
	FORMAL	okatamuki nasaimase	okatamuki nasaimasu na
Presumptive	**INFORMAL I**	katamukoo	katamukumai
	II	katamuku daroo	katamukanai daroo
	FORMAL I	katamukimasyoo	katamukimasumai
	II	katamuku desyoo	katamukanai desyoo
Provisional	**INFORMAL**	katamukeba	katamukanakereba
	FORMAL	katamukimaseba	katamukimaseñ nara
		katamukimasureba	
Gerund	**INFORMAL I**	katamuite	katamukanai de
	II		katamukanakute
	FORMAL	katamukimasite	katamukimaseñ de
Past Ind.	**INFORMAL**	katamuita	katamukanakatta
	FORMAL	katamukimasita	katamukimaseñ desita
Past Presump.	**INFORMAL**	katamuitaroo	katamukanakattaroo
		katamuita daroo	katamukanakatta daroo
	FORMAL	katamukimasitaroo	katamukimaseñ desitaroo
		katamuita desyoo	katamukanakatta desyoo
Conditional	**INFORMAL**	katamuitara	katamukanakattara
	FORMAL	katamukimasitara	katamukimaseñ desitara
Alternative	**INFORMAL**	katamuitari	katamukanakattari
	FORMAL	katamukimasitari	katamukimaseñ desitari

		INFORMAL AFFIRMATIVE INDICATIVE
Passive		katamukareru
Potential		katamukeru
Causative		katamukaseru
Causative Pass.		katamukaserareru
Honorific	**I**	okatamuki ni naru
	II	okatamuki nasaru
Humble	**I**	
	II	

192

		AFFIRMATIVE	NEGATIVE
Indicative	**INFORMAL**	katazukeru	katazukenai
	FORMAL	katazukemasu	katazukemaseñ
Imperative	**INFORMAL I**	katazukero	katazukeru na
	II	katazukenasai	katazukenasaru na
	III	katazukete kudasai	katazukenai de kudasai
	FORMAL	okatazuke nasaimase	okatazuke nasaimasu na
Presumptive	**INFORMAL I**	katazukeyoo	katazukemai
	II	katazukeru daroo	katazukenai daroo
	FORMAL I	katazukemasyoo	katazukemasumai
	II	katazukeru desyoo	katazukenai desyoo
Provisional	**INFORMAL**	katazukereba	katazukenakereba
	FORMAL	katazukemaseba	katazukemaseñ nara
		katazukemasureba	
Gerund	**INFORMAL I**	katazukete	katazukenai de
	II		katazukenakute
	FORMAL	katazukemasite	katazukemaseñ de
Past Ind.	**INFORMAL**	katazuketa	katazukenakatta
	FORMAL	katazukemasita	katazukemaseñ desita
Past Presump.	**INFORMAL**	katazuketaroo	katazukenakattaroo
		katazuketa daroo	katazukenakatta daroo
	FORMAL	katazukemasitaroo	katazukemaseñ desitaroo
		katazuketa desyoo	katazukenakatta desyoo
Conditional	**INFORMAL**	katazuketara	katazukenakattara
	FORMAL	katazukemasitara	katazukemaseñ desitara
Alternative	**INFORMAL**	katazuketari	katazukenakattari
	FORMAL	katazukemasitari	katazukemaseñ desitari

INFORMAL AFFIRMATIVE INDICATIVE

Passive		katazukerareru
Potential		katazukerareru
Causative		katazukesaseru
Causative Pass.		katazukesaserareru
Honorific	**I**	okatazuke ni naru
	II	okatazuke nasaru
Humble	**I**	okatazuke suru
	II	okatazuke itasu

		AFFIRMATIVE	NEGATIVE
Indicative	**INFORMAL**	katu	katanai
	FORMAL	katimasu	katimaseñ
Imperative	**INFORMAL I**	kate	katu na
	II	katinasai	katinasaru na
	III	katte kudasai	katanai de kudasai
	FORMAL	okati nasaimase	okati nasaimasu na
Presumptive	**INFORMAL I**	katoo	katumai
	II	katu daroo	katanai daroo
	FORMAL I	katimasyoo	katimasumai
	II	katu desyoo	katanai desyoo
Provisional	**INFORMAL**	kateba	katanakereba
	FORMAL	katimaseba	katimaseñ nara
		katimasureba	
Gerund	**INFORMAL I**	katte	katanai de
	II		katanakute
	FORMAL	katimasite	katimaseñ de
Past Ind.	**INFORMAL**	katta	katanakatta
	FORMAL	katimasita	katimaseñ desita
Past Presump.	**INFORMAL**	kattaroo	katanakattaroo
		katta daroo	katanakatta daroo
	FORMAL	katimasitaroo	katimaseñ desitaroo
		katta desyoo	katanakatta desyoo
Conditional	**INFORMAL**	kattara	katanakattara
	FORMAL	katimasitara	katimaseñ desitara
Alternative	**INFORMAL**	kattari	katanakattari
	FORMAL	katimasitari	katimaseñ desitari

INFORMAL AFFIRMATIVE INDICATIVE

Passive		katareru
Potential		kateru
Causative		kataseru
Causative Pass.		kataserareru

Honorific	**I**	okati ni naru
	II	okati nasaru
Humble	**I**	
	II	

		AFFIRMATIVE	**NEGATIVE**
Indicative	**INFORMAL**	katugu	katuganai
	FORMAL	katugimasu	katugimaseñ
Imperative	**INFORMAL I**	katuge	katugu na
	II	katuginasai	katuginasaru na
	III	katuide kudasai	katuganai de kudasai
	FORMAL	okatugi nasaimase	okatugi nasaimasu na
Presumptive	**INFORMAL I**	katugoo	katugumai
	II	katugu daroo	katuganai daroo
	FORMAL I	katugimasyoo	katugimasumai
	II	katugu desyoo	katuganai desyoo
Provisional	**INFORMAL**	katugeba	katuganakereba
	FORMAL	katugimaseba	katugimaseñ nara
		katugimasureba	
Gerund	**INFORMAL I**	katuide	katuganai de
	II		katuganakute
	FORMAL	katugimasite	katugimaseñ de
Past Ind.	**INFORMAL**	katuida	katuganakatta
	FORMAL	katugimasita	katugimaseñ desita
Past Presump.	**INFORMAL**	katuidaroo	katuganakattaroo
		katuida daroo	katuganakatta daroo
	FORMAL	katugimasitaroo	katugimaseñ desitaroo
		katuida desyoo	katuganakatta desyoo
Conditional	**INFORMAL**	katuidara	katuganakattara
	FORMAL	katugimasitara	katugimaseñ desitara
Alternative	**INFORMAL**	katuidari	katuganakattari
	FORMAL	katugimasitari	katugimaseñ desitari

INFORMAL AFFIRMATIVE INDICATIVE

Passive		katugareru
Potential		katugeru
Causative		katugaseru
Causative Pass.		katugaserareru

Honorific	**I**	okatugi ni naru
	II	okatugi nasaru
Humble	**I**	okatugi suru
	II	okatugi itasu

		AFFIRMATIVE	NEGATIVE
Indicative	**INFORMAL**	kau	kawanai
	FORMAL	kaimasu	kaimaseñ
Imperative	**INFORMAL I**	kae	kau na
	II	kainasai	kainasaru na
	III	katte kudasai	kawanai de kudasai
	FORMAL	okai nasaimase	okai nasaimasu na
Presumptive	**INFORMAL I**	kaoo	kaumai
	II	kau daroo	kawanai daroo
	FORMAL I	kaimasyoo	kaimasumai
	II	kau desyoo	kawanai desyoo
Provisional	**INFORMAL**	kaeba	kawanakereba
	FORMAL	kaimaseba	kaimaseñ nara
		kaimasureba	
Gerund	**INFORMAL I**	katte	kawanai de
	II		kawanakute
	FORMAL	kaimasite	kaimaseñ de
Past Ind.	**INFORMAL**	katta	kawanakatta
	FORMAL	kaimasita	kaimaseñ desita
Past Presump.	**INFORMAL**	kattaroo	kawanakattaroo
		katta daroo	kawanakatta daroo
	FORMAL	kaimasitaroo	kaimaseñ desitaroo
		katta desyoo	kawanakatta desyoo
Conditional	**INFORMAL**	kattara	kawanakattara
	FORMAL	kaimasitara	kaimaseñ desitara
Alternative	**INFORMAL**	kattari	kawanakattari
	FORMAL	kaimasitari	kaimaseñ desitari

INFORMAL AFFIRMATIVE INDICATIVE

Passive		kawareru
Potential		kaeru
Causative		kawaseru
Causative Pass.		kawaserareru
Honorific	**I**	okai ni naru
	II	okai nasaru
Humble	**I**	okai suru
	II	okai itasu

196

TRANSITIVE   *to keep* (an animal)

		AFFIRMATIVE	NEGATIVE
Indicative	**INFORMAL**	kau	kawanai
	FORMAL	kaimasu	kaimaseñ
Imperative	**INFORMAL I**	kae	kau na
	II	kainasai	kainasaru na
	III	katte kudasai	kawanai de kudasai
	FORMAL	okai nasaimase	okai nasaimasu na
Presumptive	**INFORMAL I**	kaoo	kaumai
	II	kau daroo	kawanai daroo
	FORMAL I	kaimasyoo	kaimasumai
	II	kau desyoo	kawanai desyoo
Provisional	**INFORMAL**	kaeba	kawanakereba
	FORMAL	kaimaseba	kaimaseñ nara
		kaimasureba	
Gerund	**INFORMAL I**	katte	kawanai de
	II		kawanakute
	FORMAL	kaimasite	kaimaseñ de
Past Ind.	**INFORMAL**	katta	kawanakatta
	FORMAL	kaimasita	kaimaseñ desita
Past Presump.	**INFORMAL**	kattaroo	kawanakattaroo
		katta daroo	kawanakatta daroo
	FORMAL	kaimasitaroo	kaimaseñ desitaroo
		katta desyoo	kawanakatta desyoo
Conditional	**INFORMAL**	kattara	kawanakattara
	FORMAL	kaimasitara	kaimaseñ desitara
Alternative	**INFORMAL**	kattari	kawanakattari
	FORMAL	kaimasitari	kaimaseñ desitari

		INFORMAL AFFIRMATIVE INDICATIVE
Passive		kawareru
Potential		kaeru
Causative		kawaseru
Causative Pass.		kawaserareru
Honorific	**I**	okai ni naru
	II	okai nasaru
Humble	**I**	okai suru
	II	okai itasu

to love or treat with affection (someone or something weaker than oneself)   TRANSITIVE

		AFFIRMATIVE	NEGATIVE
Indicative	**INFORMAL**	kawaigaru	kawaigaranai
	FORMAL	kawaigarimasu	kawaigarimaseñ
Imperative	**INFORMAL I**	kawaigare	kawaigaru na
	II	kawaigarinasai	kawaigarinasaru na
	III	kawaigatte kudasai	kawaigaranai de kudasai
	FORMAL	okawaigari nasaimase	okawaigari nasaimasu na
Presumptive	**INFORMAL I**	kawaigaroo	kawaigarumai
	II	kawaigaru daroo	kawaigaranai daroo
	FORMAL I	kawaigarimasyoo	kawaigarimasumai
	II	kawaigaru desyoo	kawaigaranai desyoo
Provisional	**INFORMAL**	kawaigareba	kawaigaranakereba
	FORMAL	kawaigarimaseba	kawaigarimaseñ nara
		kawaigarimasureba	
Gerund	**INFORMAL I**	kawaigatte	kawaigaranai de
	II		kawaigaranakute
	FORMAL	kawaigarimasite	kawaigarimaseñ de
Past Ind.	**INFORMAL**	kawaigatta	kawaigaranakatta
	FORMAL	kawaigarimasita	kawaigarimaseñ desita
Past Presump.	**INFORMAL**	kawaigattaroo	kawaigaranakattaroo
		kawaigatta daroo	kawaigaranakatta daroo
	FORMAL	kawaigarimasitaroo	kawaigarimaseñ desitaroo
		kawaigatta desyoo	kawaigaranakatta desyoo
Conditional	**INFORMAL**	kawaigattara	kawaigaranakattara
	FORMAL	kawaigarimasitara	kawaigarimaseñ desitara
Alternative	**INFORMAL**	kawaigattari	kawaigaranakattari
	FORMAL	kawaigarimasitari	kawaigarimaseñ desitari

		INFORMAL AFFIRMATIVE INDICATIVE
Passive		kawaigarareru
Potential		kawaigareru
Causative		kawaigaraseru
Causative Pass.		kawaigaraserareru
Honorific	**I**	okawaigari ni naru
	II	okawaigari nasaru
Humble	**I**	
	II	

			AFFIRMATIVE	NEGATIVE
Indicative	**INFORMAL**		kawakasu	kawakasanai
	FORMAL		kawakasimasu	kawakasimaseñ
Imperative	**INFORMAL I**		kawakase	kawakasu na
		II	kawakasinasai	kawakasinasaru na
		III	kawakasite kudasai	kawakasanai de kudasai
	FORMAL		okawakasi nasaimase	okawakasi nasaimasu na
Presumptive	**INFORMAL I**		kawakasoo	kawakasumai
		II	kawakasu daroo	kawakasanai daroo
	FORMAL	**I**	kawakasimasyoo	kawakasimasumai
		II	kawakasu desyoo	kawakasanai desyoo
Provisional	**INFORMAL**		kawakaseba	kawakasanakereba
	FORMAL		kawakasimaseba	kawakasimaseñ nara
			kawakasimasureba	
Gerund	**INFORMAL I**		kawakasite	kawakasanai de
		II		kawakasanakute
	FORMAL		kawakasimasite	kawakasimaseñ de
Past Ind.	**INFORMAL**		kawakasita	kawakasanakatta
	FORMAL		kawakasimasita	kawakasimaseñ desita
Past Presump.	**INFORMAL**		kawakasitaroo	kawakasanakattaroo
			kawakasita daroo	kawakasanakatta daroo
	FORMAL		kawakasimasitaroo	kawakasimaseñ desitaroo
			kawakasita desyoo	kawakasanakatta desyoo
Conditional	**INFORMAL**		kawakasitara	kawakasanakattara
	FORMAL		kawakasimasitara	kawakasimaseñ desitara
Alternative	**INFORMAL**		kawakasitari	kawakasanakattari
	FORMAL		kawakasimasitari	kawakasimaseñ desitari

		INFORMAL AFFIRMATIVE INDICATIVE
Passive		kawakasareru
Potential		kawakaseru
Causative		kawakasaseru
Causative Pass.		kawakasaserareru

Honorific	**I**	okawakasi ni naru
	II	okawakasi nasaru
Humble	**I**	okawakasi suru
	II	okawakasi itasu

		AFFIRMATIVE	NEGATIVE
Indicative	**INFORMAL**	kawaku	kawakanai
	FORMAL	kawakimasu	kawakimaseñ
Imperative	**INFORMAL I**	kawake	kawaku na
	II		
	III		
	FORMAL		
Presumptive	**INFORMAL I**	kawakoo	kawakumai
	II	kawaku daroo	kawakanai daroo
	FORMAL I	kawakimasyoo	kawakimasumai
	II	kawaku desyoo	kawakanai desyoo
Provisional	**INFORMAL**	kawakeba	kawakanakereba
	FORMAL	kawakimaseba	kawakimaseñ nara
		kawakimasureba	
Gerund	**INFORMAL I**	kawaite	kawakanai de
	II		kawakanakute
	FORMAL	kawakimasite	kawakimaseñ de
Past Ind.	**INFORMAL**	kawaita	kawakanakatta
	FORMAL	kawakimasita	kawakimaseñ desita
Past Presump.	**INFORMAL**	kawaitaroo	kawakanakattaroo
		kawaita daroo	kawakanakatta daroo
	FORMAL	kawakimasitaroo	kawakimaseñ desitaroo
		kawaita desyoo	kawakanakatta desyoo
Conditional	**INFORMAL**	kawaitara	kawakanakattara
	FORMAL	kawakimasitara	kawakimaseñ desitara
Alternative	**INFORMAL**	kawaitari	kawakanakattari
	FORMAL	kawakimasitari	kawakimaseñ desitari

INFORMAL AFFIRMATIVE INDICATIVE

Passive	
Potential	
Causative	
Causative Pass.	

Honorific	I
	II
Humble	I
	II

200

		AFFIRMATIVE	NEGATIVE
Indicative	**INFORMAL**	kawaru	kawaranai
	FORMAL	kawarimasu	kawarimaseñ
Imperative	**INFORMAL I**	kaware	kawaru na
	II	kawarinasai	kawarinasaru na
	III	kawatte kudasai	kawaranai de kudasai
	FORMAL	okawari nasaimase	okawari nasaimasu na
Presumptive	**INFORMAL I**	kawaroo	kawarumai
	II	kawaru daroo	kawaranai daroo
	FORMAL I	kawarimasyoo	kawarimasumai
	II	kawaru desyoo	kawaranai desyoo
Provisional	**INFORMAL**	kawareba	kawaranakereba
	FORMAL	kawarimaseba	kawarimaseñ nara
		kawarimasureba	
Gerund	**INFORMAL I**	kawatte	kawaranai de
	II		kawaranakute
	FORMAL	kawarimasite	kawarimaseñ de
Past Ind.	**INFORMAL**	kawatta	kawaranakatta
	FORMAL	kawarimasita	kawarimaseñ desita
Past Presump.	**INFORMAL**	kawattaroo	kawaranakattaroo
		kawatta daroo	kawaranakatta daroo
	FORMAL	kawarimasitaroo	kawarimaseñ desitaroo
		kawatta desyoo	kawaranakatta desyoo
Conditional	**INFORMAL**	kawattara	kawaranakattara
	FORMAL	kawarimasitara	kawarimaseñ desitara
Alternative	**INFORMAL**	kawattari	kawaranakattari
	FORMAL	kawarimasitari	kawarimaseñ desitari

		INFORMAL AFFIRMATIVE INDICATIVE
Passive		kawarareru
Potential		kawareru
Causative		kawaraseru
Causative Pass.		kawaraserareru
Honorific	**I**	okawari ni naru
	II	okawari nasaru
Humble	**I**	
	II	

		AFFIRMATIVE	NEGATIVE
Indicative	**INFORMAL**	kayou	kayowanai
	FORMAL	kayoimasu	kayoimaseñ
Imperative	**INFORMAL I**	kayoe	kayou na
	II	kayoinasai	kayoinasaru na
	III	kayotte kudasai	kayowanai de kudasai
	FORMAL	okayoi nasaimase	okayoi nasaimasu na
Presumptive	**INFORMAL I**	kayooo	kayoumai
	II	kayou daroo	kayowanai daroo
	FORMAL I	kayoimasyoo	kayoimasumai
	II	kayou desyoo	kayowanai desyoo
Provisional	**INFORMAL**	kayoeba	kayowanakereba
	FORMAL	kayoimaseba	kayoimaseñ nara
		kayoimasureba	
Gerund	**INFORMAL I**	kayotte	kayowanai de
	II		kayowanakute
	FORMAL	kayoimasite	kayoimaseñ de
Past Ind.	**INFORMAL**	kayotta	kayowanakatta
	FORMAL	kayoimasita	kayoimaseñ desita
Past Presump.	**INFORMAL**	kayottaroo	kayowanakattaroo
		kayotta daroo	kayowanakatta daroo
	FORMAL	kayoimasitaroo	kayoimaseñ desitaroo
		kayotta desyoo	kayowanakatta desyoo
Conditional	**INFORMAL**	kayottara	kayowanakattara
	FORMAL	kayoimasitara	kayoimaseñ desitara
Alternative	**INFORMAL**	kayottari	kayowanakattari
	FORMAL	kayoimasitari	kayoimaseñ desitari

		INFORMAL AFFIRMATIVE INDICATIVE
Passive		kayowareru
Potential		kayoeru
Causative		kayowaseru
Causative Pass.		kayowaserareru
Honorific	**I**	okayoi ni naru
	II	okayoi nasaru
Humble	**I**	
	II	

TRANSITIVE   *to ornament, to decorate*

		AFFIRMATIVE	NEGATIVE
Indicative	INFORMAL	kazaru	kazaranai
	FORMAL	kazarimasu	kazarimaseñ
Imperative	INFORMAL I	kazare	kazaru na
	II	kazarinasai	kazarinasaru na
	III	kazatte kudasai	kazaranai de kudasai
	FORMAL	okazari nasaimase	okazari nasaimasu na
Presumptive	INFORMAL I	kazaroo	kazarumai
	II	kazaru daroo	kazaranai daroo
	FORMAL I	kazarimasyoo	kazarimasumai
	II	kazaru desyoo	kazaranai desyoo
Provisional	INFORMAL	kazareba	kazaranakereba
	FORMAL	kazarimaseba	kazarimaseñ nara
		kazarimasureba	
Gerund	INFORMAL I	kazatte	kazaranai de
	II		kazaranakute
	FORMAL	kazarimasite	kazarimaseñ de
Past Ind.	INFORMAL	kazatta	kazaranakatta
	FORMAL	kazarimasita	kazarimaseñ desita
Past Presump.	INFORMAL	kazattaroo	kazaranakattaroo
		kazatta daroo	kazaranakatta daroo
	FORMAL	kazarimasitaroo	kazarimaseñ desitaroo
		kazatta desyoo	kazaranakatta desyoo
Conditional	INFORMAL	kazattara	kazaranakattara
	FORMAL	kazarimasitara	kazarimaseñ desitara
Alternative	INFORMAL	kazattari	kazaranakattari
	FORMAL	kazarimasitari	kazarimaseñ desitari

INFORMAL AFFIRMATIVE INDICATIVE

Passive		kazarareru
Potential		kazareru
Causative		kazaraseru
Causative Pass.		kazaraserareru
Honorific	I	okazari ni naru
	II	okazari nasaru
Humble	I	okazari suru
	II	okazari itasu

		AFFIRMATIVE	NEGATIVE
Indicative	**INFORMAL**	kaziru	kaziranai
	FORMAL	kazirimasu	kazirimaseñ
Imperative	**INFORMAL I**	kazire	kaziru na
	II	kazirinasai	kazirinasaru na
	III	kazitte kudasai	kaziranai de kudasai
	FORMAL	okaziri nasaimase	okaziri nasaimasu na
Presumptive	**INFORMAL I**	kaziroo	kazirumai
	II	kaziru daroo	kaziranai daroo
	FORMAL I	kazirimasyoo	kazirimasumai
	II	kaziru desyoo	kaziranai desyoo
Provisional	**INFORMAL**	kazireba	kaziranakereba
	FORMAL	kazirimaseba	kazirimaseñ nara
		kazirimasureba	
Gerund	**INFORMAL I**	kazitte	kaziranai de
	II		kaziranakute
	FORMAL	kazirimasite	kazirimaseñ de
Past Ind.	**INFORMAL**	kazitta	kaziranakatta
	FORMAL	kazirimasita	kazirimaseñ desita
Past Presump.	**INFORMAL**	kazittaroo	kaziranakattaroo
		kazitta daroo	kaziranakatta daroo
	FORMAL	kazirimasitaroo	kazirimaseñ desitaroo
		kazitta desyoo	kaziranakatta desyoo
Conditional	**INFORMAL**	kazittara	kaziranakattara
	FORMAL	kazirimasitara	kazirimaseñ desitara
Alternative	**INFORMAL**	kazittari	kaziranakattari
	FORMAL	kazirimasitari	kazirimaseñ desitari

	INFORMAL AFFIRMATIVE INDICATIVE
Passive	kazirareru
Potential	kazireru
Causative	kaziraseru
Causative Pass.	kaziraserareru
Honorific	okaziri ni naru
	okaziri nasaru
Humble	

		AFFIRMATIVE	NEGATIVE
Indicative	**INFORMAL**	kazoeru	kazoenai
	FORMAL	kazoemasu	kazoemaseñ
Imperative	**INFORMAL I**	kazoero	kazoeru na
	II	kazoenasai	kazoenasaru na
	III	kazoete kudasai	kazoenai de kudasai
	FORMAL	okazoe nasaimase	okazoe nasaimasu na
Presumptive	**INFORMAL I**	kazoeyoo	kazoemai
	II	kazoeru daroo	kazoenai daroo
	FORMAL I	kazoemasyoo	kazoemasumai
	II	kazoeru desyoo	kazoenai desyoo
Provisional	**INFORMAL**	kazoereba	kazoenakereba
	FORMAL	kazoemaseba	kazoemaseñ nara
		kazoemasureba	
Gerund	**INFORMAL I**	kazoete	kazoenai de
	II		kazoenakute
	FORMAL	kazoemasite	kazoemaseñ de
Past Ind.	**INFORMAL**	kazoeta	kazoenakatta
	FORMAL	kazoemasita	kazoemaseñ desita
Past Presump.	**INFORMAL**	kazoetaroo	kazoenakattaroo
		kazoeta daroo	kazoenakatta daroo
	FORMAL	kazoemasitaroo	kazoemaseñ desitaroo
		kazoeta desyoo	kazoenakatta desyoo
Conditional	**INFORMAL**	kazoetara	kazoenakattara
	FORMAL	kazoemasitara	kazoemaseñ desitara
Alternative	**INFORMAL**	kazoetari	kazoenakattari
	FORMAL	kazoemasitari	kazoemaseñ desitari

INFORMAL AFFIRMATIVE INDICATIVE

Passive		kazoerareru
Potential		kazoerareru
Causative		kazoesaseru
Causative Pass.		kazoesaserareru

Honorific	**I**	okazoe ni naru
	II	okazoe nasaru
Humble	**I**	okazoe suru
	II	okazoe itasu

		AFFIRMATIVE	NEGATIVE
Indicative	**INFORMAL**	kegasu	kegasanai
	FORMAL	kegasimasu	kegasimaseñ
Imperative	**INFORMAL I**	kegase	kegasu na
	II	kegasinasai	kegasinasaru na
	III	kegasite kudasai	kegasanai de kudasai
	FORMAL	okegasi nasaimase	okegasi nasaimasu na
Presumptive	**INFORMAL I**	kegasoo	kegasumai
	II	kegasu daroo	kegasanai daroo
	FORMAL I	kegasimasyoo	kegasimasumai
	II	kegasu desyoo	kegasanai desyoo
Provisional	**INFORMAL**	kegaseba	kegasanakereba
	FORMAL	kegasimaseba	kegasimaseñ nara
		kegasimasureba	
Gerund	**INFORMAL I**	kegasite	kegasanai de
	II		kegasanakute
	FORMAL	kegasimasite	kegasimaseñ de
Past Ind.	**INFORMAL**	kegasita	kegasanakatta
	FORMAL	kegasimasita	kegasimaseñ desita
Past Presump.	**INFORMAL**	kegasitaroo	kegasanakattaroo
		kegasita daroo	kegasanakatta daroo
	FORMAL	kegasimasitaroo	kegasimaseñ desitaroo
		kegasita desyoo	kegasanakatta desyoo
Conditional	**INFORMAL**	kegasitara	kegasanakattara
	FORMAL	kegasimasitara	kegasimaseñ desitara
Alternative	**INFORMAL**	kegasitari	kegasanakattari
	FORMAL	kegasimasitari	kegasimaseñ desitari

		INFORMAL AFFIRMATIVE INDICATIVE
Passive		kegasareru
Potential		kegaseru
Causative		kegasaseru
Causative Pass.		kegasaserareru
Honorific	**I**	okegasi ni naru
	II	okegasi nasaru
Humble	**I**	
	II	

TRANSITIVE   *to erase, to extinguish*

		AFFIRMATIVE	NEGATIVE
Indicative	**INFORMAL**	kesu	kesanai
	FORMAL	kesimasu	kesimaseñ
Imperative	**INFORMAL I**	kese	kesu na
	II	kesinasai	kesinasaru na
	III	kesite kudasai	kesanai de kudasai
	FORMAL	okesi nasaimase	okesi nasaimasu na
Presumptive	**INFORMAL I**	kesoo	kesumai
	II	kesu daroo	kesanai daroo
	FORMAL I	kesimasyoo	kesimasumai
	II	kesu desyoo	kesanai desyoo
Provisional	**INFORMAL**	keseba	kesanakereba
	FORMAL	kesimaseba	kesimaseñ nara
		kesimasureba	
Gerund	**INFORMAL I**	kesite	kesanai de
	II		kesanakute
	FORMAL	kesimasite	kesimaseñ de
Past Ind.	**INFORMAL**	kesita	kesanakatta
	FORMAL	kesimasita	kesimaseñ desita
Past Presump.	**INFORMAL**	kesitaroo	kesanakattaroo
		kesita daroo	kesanakatta daroo
	FORMAL	kesimasitaroo	kesimaseñ desitaroo
		kesita desyoo	kesanakatta desyoo
Conditional	**INFORMAL**	kesitara	kesanakattara
	FORMAL	kesimasitara	kesimaseñ desitara
Alternative	**INFORMAL**	kesitari	kesanakattari
	FORMAL	kesimasitari	kesimaseñ desitari

		INFORMAL AFFIRMATIVE INDICATIVE
Passive		kesareru
Potential		keseru
Causative		kesaseru
Causative Pass.		kesaserareru
Honorific	**I**	okesi ni naru
	II	okesi nasaru
Humble	**I**	okesi suru
	II	okesi itasu

to give oneself airs, to be affected

		AFFIRMATIVE	NEGATIVE
Indicative	**INFORMAL**	kidoru	kidoranai
	FORMAL	kidorimasu	kidorimaseñ
Imperative	**INFORMAL I**	kidore	kidoru na
	II	kidorinasai	kidorinasaru na
	III	kidotte kudasai	kidoranai de kudasai
	FORMAL	okidori nasaimase	okidori nasaimasu na
Presumptive	**INFORMAL I**	kidoroo	kidorumai
	II	kidoru daroo	kidoranai daroo
	FORMAL I	kidorimasyoo	kidorimasumai
	II	kidoru desyoo	kidoranai desyoo
Provisional	**INFORMAL**	kidoreba	kidoranakereba
	FORMAL	kidorimaseba	kidorimaseñ nara
		kidorimasureba	
Gerund	**INFORMAL I**	kidotte	kidoranai de
	II		kidoranakute
	FORMAL	kidorimasite	kidorimaseñ de
Past Ind.	**INFORMAL**	kidotta	kidoranakatta
	FORMAL	kidorimasita	kidorimaseñ desita
Past Presump.	**INFORMAL**	kidottaroo	kidoranakattaroo
		kidotta daroo	kidoranakatta daroo
	FORMAL	kidorimasitaroo	kidorimaseñ desitaroo
		kidotta desyoo	kidoranakatta desyoo
Conditional	**INFORMAL**	kidottara	kidoranakattara
	FORMAL	kidorimasitara	kidorimaseñ desitara
Alternative	**INFORMAL**	kidottari	kidoranakattari
	FORMAL	kidorimasitari	kidorimaseñ desitari

		INFORMAL AFFIRMATIVE INDICATIVE
Passive		kidorareru
Potential		kidoreru
Causative		kidoraseru
Causative Pass.		kidoraserareru
Honorific	**I**	okidori ni naru
	II	okidori nasaru
Humble	**I**	
	II	

		AFFIRMATIVE	NEGATIVE
Indicative	**INFORMAL**	kieru	kienai
	FORMAL	kiemasu	kiemaseñ
Imperative	**INFORMAL I**	kiero	kieru na
	II		
	III		
	FORMAL		
Presumptive	**INFORMAL I**	kieyoo	kiemai
	II	kieru daroo	kienai daroo
	FORMAL I	kiemasyoo	kiemasumai
	II	kieru desyoo	kienai desyoo
Provisional	**INFORMAL**	kiereba	kienakereba
	FORMAL	kiemaseba	kiemaseñ nara
		kiemasureba	
Gerund	**INFORMAL I**	kiete	kienai de
	II		kienakute
	FORMAL	kiemasite	kiemaseñ de
Past Ind.	**INFORMAL**	kieta	kienakatta
	FORMAL	kiemasita	kiemaseñ desita
Past Presump.	**INFORMAL**	kietaroo	kienakattaroo
		kieta daroo	kienakatta daroo
	FORMAL	kiemasitaroo	kiemaseñ desitaroo
		kieta desyoo	kienakatta desyoo
Conditional	**INFORMAL**	kietara	kienakattara
	FORMAL	kiemasitara	kiemaseñ desitara
Alternative	**INFORMAL**	kietari	kienakattari
	FORMAL	kiemasitari	kiemaseñ desitari

		INFORMAL AFFIRMATIVE INDICATIVE
Passive		kierareru
Potential		kierareru
Causative		kiesaseru
Causative Pass.		kiesaserareru
Honorific	**I**	
	II	
Humble	**I**	
	II	

		AFFIRMATIVE	NEGATIVE
Indicative	**INFORMAL**	kikaeru	kikaenai
	FORMAL	kikaemasu	kikaemaseñ
Imperative	**INFORMAL I**	kikaero	kikaeru na
	II	kikaenasai	kikaenasaru na
	III	kikaete kudasai	kikaenai de kudasai
	FORMAL	okikae nasaimase	okikae nasaimasu na
Presumptive	**INFORMAL I**	kikaeyoo	kikaemai
	II	kikaeru daroo	kikaenai daroo
	FORMAL I	kikaemasyoo	kikaemasumai
	II	kikaeru desyoo	kikaenai desyoo
Provisional	**INFORMAL**	kikaereba	kikaenakereba
	FORMAL	kikaemaseba	kikaemaseñ nara
		kikaemasureba	
Gerund	**INFORMAL I**	kikaete	kikaenai de
	II		kikaenakute
	FORMAL	kikaemasite	kikaemaseñ de
Past Ind.	**INFORMAL**	kikaeta	kikaenakatta
	FORMAL	kikaemasita	kikaemaseñ desita
Past Presump.	**INFORMAL**	kikaetaroo	kikaenakattaroo
		kikaeta daroo	kikaenakatta daroo
	FORMAL	kikaemasitaroo	kikaemaseñ desitaroo
		kikaeta desyoo	kikaenakatta desyoo
Conditional	**INFORMAL**	kikaetara	kikaenakattara
	FORMAL	kikaemasitara	kikaemaseñ desitara
Alternative	**INFORMAL**	kikaetari	kikaenakattari
	FORMAL	kikaemasitari	kikaemaseñ desitari

INFORMAL AFFIRMATIVE INDICATIVE

Passive		kikaerareru
Potential		kikaerareru
Causative		kikaesaseru
Causative Pass.		kikaesaserareru

Honorific	**I**	okikae ni naru
	II	okikae nasaru
Humble	**I**	
	II	

		AFFIRMATIVE	NEGATIVE
Indicative	**INFORMAL**	kikoeru	kikoenai
	FORMAL	kikoemasu	kikoemaseñ
Imperative	**INFORMAL I**		
	II		
	III		
	FORMAL		
Presumptive	**INFORMAL I**	kikoeyoo	kikoemai
	II	kikoeru daroo	kikoenai daroo
	FORMAL I	kikoemasyoo	kikoemasumai
	II	kikoeru desyoo	kikoenai desyoo
Provisional	**INFORMAL**	kikoereba	kikoenakereba
	FORMAL	kikoemaseba	kikoemaseñ nara
		kikoemasureba	
Gerund	**INFORMAL I**	kikoete	kikoenai de
	II		kikoenakute
	FORMAL	kikoemasite	kikoemaseñ de
Past Ind.	**INFORMAL**	kikoeta	kikoenakatta
	FORMAL	kikoemasita	kikoemaseñ desita
Past Presump.	**INFORMAL**	kikoetaroo	kikoenakattaroo
		kikoeta daroo	kikoenakatta daroo
	FORMAL	kikoemasitaroo	kikoemaseñ desitaroo
		kikoeta desyoo	kikoenakatta desyoo
Conditional	**INFORMAL**	kikoetara	kikoenakattara
	FORMAL	kikoemasitara	kikoemaseñ desitara
Alternative	**INFORMAL**	kikoetari	kikoenakattari
	FORMAL	kikoemasitari	kikoemaseñ desitari

INFORMAL AFFIRMATIVE INDICATIVE

Passive		
Potential		
Causative		
Causative Pass.		
Honorific	**I**	
	II	
Humble	**I**	
	II	

to ask, to listen, to hear   TRANSITIVE

		AFFIRMATIVE	NEGATIVE
Indicative	**INFORMAL**	kiku	kikanai
	FORMAL	kikimasu	kikimaseñ
Imperative	**INFORMAL I**	kike	kiku na
	II	kikinasai	kikinasaru na
	III	kiite kudasai	kikanai de kudasai
	FORMAL	okiki nasaimase	okiki nasaimasu na
Presumptive	**INFORMAL I**	kikoo	kikumai
	II	kiku daroo	kikanai daroo
	FORMAL I	kikimasyoo	kikimasumai
	II	kiku desyoo	kikanai desyoo
Provisional	**INFORMAL**	kikeba	kikanakereba
	FORMAL	kikimaseba	kikimaseñ nara
		kikimasureba	
Gerund	**INFORMAL I**	kiite	kikanai de
	II		kikanakute
	FORMAL	kikimasite	kikimaseñ de
Past Ind.	**INFORMAL**	kiita	kikanakatta
	FORMAL	kikimasita	kikimaseñ desita
Past Presump.	**INFORMAL**	kiitaroo	kikanakattaroo
		kiita daroo	kikanakatta daroo
	FORMAL	kikimasitaroo	kikimaseñ desitaroo
		kiita desyoo	kikanakatta desyoo
Conditional	**INFORMAL**	kiitara	kikanakattara
	FORMAL	kikimasitara	kikimaseñ desitara
Alternative	**INFORMAL**	kiitari .	kikanakattari
	FORMAL	kikimasitari	kikimaseñ desitari

		INFORMAL AFFIRMATIVE INDICATIVE	
Passive		kikareru	
Potential		kikeru*	
Causative		kikaseru	
Causative Pass.		kikaserareru	

Honorific	**I**	okiki ni naru	
	II	okiki nasaru	
*Humble**		ukagau	uketamawaru

*Only in the sense of 'can ask or listen,' 'to be audible' is a separate verb *kikoeru*.
**Ukagau* means 'to ask,' while *uketamawaru* means 'to hear or listen.'

		AFFIRMATIVE	NEGATIVE
Indicative	**INFORMAL**	kiku	kikanai
	FORMAL	kikimasu	kikimaseñ
Imperative	**INFORMAL I**	kike	kiku na
	II		
	III		
	FORMAL		
Presumptive	**INFORMAL I**	kikoo	kikumai
	II	kiku daroo	kikanai daroo
	FORMAL I	kikimasyoo	kikimasumai
	II	kiku desyoo	kikanai desyoo
Provisional	**INFORMAL**	kikeba	kikanakereba
	FORMAL	kikimaseba	kikimaseñ nara
		kikimasureba	
Gerund	**INFORMAL I**	kiite	kikanai de
	II		kikanakute
	FORMAL	kikimasite	kikimaseñ de
Past Ind.	**INFORMAL**	kiita	kikanakatta
	FORMAL	kikimasita	kikimaseñ desita
Past Presump.	**INFORMAL**	kiitaroo	kikanakattaroo
		kiita daroo	kikanakatta daroo
	FORMAL	kikimasitaroo	kikimaseñ desitaroo
		kiita desyoo	kikanakatta desyoo
Conditional	**INFORMAL**	kiitara	kikanakattara
	FORMAL	kikimasitara	kikimaseñ desitara
Alternative	**INFORMAL**	kiitari	kikanakattari
	FORMAL	kikimasitari	kikimaseñ desitari

		INFORMAL AFFIRMATIVE INDICATIVE
Passive		kikareru
Potential		
Causative		kikaseru
Causative Pass.		kikaserareru
Honorific	**I**	
	II	
Humble	**I**	
	II	

		AFFIRMATIVE	NEGATIVE
Indicative	**INFORMAL**	kimaru	kimaranai
	FORMAL	kimarimasu	kimarimaseñ
Imperative	**INFORMAL I**		
	II		
	III		
	FORMAL		
Presumptive	**INFORMAL I**	kimaroo	kimarumai
	II	kimaru daroo	kimaranai daroo
	FORMAL I	kimarimasyoo	kimarimasumai
	II	kimaru desyoo	kimaranai desyoo
Provisional	**INFORMAL**	kimareba	kimaranakereba
	FORMAL	kimarimaseba	kimarimaseñ nara
		kimarimasureba	
Gerund	**INFORMAL I**	kimatte	kimaranai de
	II		kimaranakute
	FORMAL	kimarimasite	kimarimaseñ de
Past Ind.	**INFORMAL**	kimatta	kimaranakatta
	FORMAL	kimarimasita	kimarimaseñ desita
Past Presump.	**INFORMAL**	kimattaroo	kimaranakattaroo
		kimatta daroo	kimaranakatta daroo
	FORMAL	kimarimasitaroo	kimarimaseñ desitaroo
		kimatta desyoo	kimaranakatta desyoo
Conditional	**INFORMAL**	kimattara	kimaranakattara
	FORMAL	kimarimasitara	kimarimaseñ desitara
Alternative	**INFORMAL**	kimattari	kimaranakattari
	FORMAL	kimarimasitari	kimarimaseñ desitari

INFORMAL AFFIRMATIVE INDICATIVE

Passive	kimarareru
Potential	kimareru
Causative	kimaraseru
Causative Pass.	kimaraserareru

Honorific	**I**
	II
Humble	**I**
	II

		AFFIRMATIVE	NEGATIVE
Indicative	**INFORMAL**	kimeru	kimenai
	FORMAL	kimemasu	kimemaseñ
Imperative	**INFORMAL I**	kimero	kimeru na
	II	kimenasai	kimenasaru na
	III	kimete kudasai	kimenai de kudasai
	FORMAL	okime nasaimase	okime nasaimasu na
Presumptive	**INFORMAL I**	kimeyoo	kimemai
	II	kimeru daroo	kimenai daroo
	FORMAL **I**	kimemasyoo	kimemasumai
	II	kimeru desyoo	kimenai desyoo
Provisional	**INFORMAL**	kimereba	kimenakereba
	FORMAL	kimemaseba	kimemaseñ nara
		kimemasureba	
Gerund	**INFORMAL I**	kimete	kimenai de
	II		kimenakute
	FORMAL	kimemasite	kimemaseñ de
Past Ind.	**INFORMAL**	kimeta	kimenakatta
	FORMAL	kimemasita	kimemaseñ desita
Past Presump.	**INFORMAL**	kimetaroo	kimenakattaroo
		kimeta daroo	kimenakatta daroo
	FORMAL	kimemasitaroo	kimemaseñ desitaroo
		kimeta desyoo	kimenakatta desyoo
Conditional	**INFORMAL**	kimetara	kimenakattara
	FORMAL	kimemasitara	kimemaseñ desitara
Alternative	**INFORMAL**	kimetari	kimenakattari
	FORMAL	kimemasitari	kimemaseñ desitari

		INFORMAL AFFIRMATIVE INDICATIVE
Passive		kimerareru
Potential		kimerareru
Causative		kimesaseru
Causative Pass.		kimesaserareru
Honorific	**I**	okime ni naru
	II	okime nasaru
Humble	**I**	okime suru
	II	okime itasu

			AFFIRMATIVE	NEGATIVE
Indicative	**INFORMAL**		kiñziru	kiñzinai
	FORMAL		kiñzimasu	kiñzimaseñ
Imperative	**INFORMAL**	**I**	kiñziro	kiñziru na
		II	kiñzinasai	kiñzinasaru na
		III	kiñzite kudasai	kiñzinai de kudasai
	FORMAL		okiñzi nasaimase	okiñzi nasaimasu na
Presumptive	**INFORMAL**	**I**	kiñziyoo	kiñzimai
		II	kiñziru daroo	kiñzinai daroo
	FORMAL	**I**	kiñzimasyoo	kiñzimasumai
		II	kiñziru desyoo	kiñzinai desyoo
Provisional	**INFORMAL**		kiñzireba	kiñzinakereba
	FORMAL		kiñzimaseba	kiñzimaseñ nara
			kiñzimasureba	
Gerund	**INFORMAL**	**I**	kiñzite	kiñzinai de
		II		kiñzinakute
	FORMAL		kiñzimasite	kiñzimaseñ de
Past Ind.	**INFORMAL**		kiñzita	kiñzinakatta
	FORMAL		kiñzimasita	kiñzimaseñ desita
Past Presump.	**INFORMAL**		kiñzitaroo	kiñzinakattaroo
			kiñzita daroo	kiñzinakatta daroo
	FORMAL		kiñzimasitaroo	kiñzimaseñ desitaroo
			kiñzita desyoo	kiñzinakatta desyoo
Conditional	**INFORMAL**		kiñzitara	kiñzinakattara
	FORMAL		kiñzimasitara	kiñzimaseñ desitara
Alternative	**INFORMAL**		kiñzitari	kiñzinakattari
	FORMAL		kiñzimasitari	kiñzimaseñ desitari

INFORMAL AFFIRMATIVE INDICATIVE

Passive		kiñzirareru
Potential		kiñzirareru
Causative		kiñzisaseru
Causative Pass.		kiñzisaserareru
Honorific	**I**	okiñzi ni naru
	II	okiñzi nasaru
Humble	**I**	okiñzi suru
	II	okiñzi itasu

		AFFIRMATIVE	NEGATIVE
Indicative	**INFORMAL**	kiru	kiranai
	FORMAL	kirimasu	kirimaseñ
Imperative	**INFORMAL I**	kire	kiru na
	II	kirinasai	kirinasaru na
	III	kitte kudasai	kiranai de kudasai
	FORMAL	okiri nasaimase	okiri nasaimasu na
Presumptive	**INFORMAL I**	kiroo	kirumai
	II	kiru daroo	kiranai daroo
	FORMAL I	kirimasyoo	kirimasumai
	II	kiru desyoo	kiranai desyoo
Provisional	**INFORMAL**	kireba	kiranakereba
	FORMAL	kirimaseba	kirimaseñ nara
		kirimasureba	
Gerund	**INFORMAL I**	kitte	kiranai de
	II		kiranakute
	FORMAL	kirimasite	kirimaseñ de
Past Ind.	**INFORMAL**	kitta	kiranakatta
	FORMAL	kirimasita	kirimaseñ desita
Past Presump.	**INFORMAL**	kittaroo	kiranakattaroo
		kitta daroo	kiranakatta daroo
	FORMAL	kirimasitaroo	kirimaseñ desitaroo
		kitta desyoo	kiranakatta desyoo
Conditional	**INFORMAL**	kittara	kiranakattara
	FORMAL	kirimasitara	kirimaseñ desitara
Alternative	**INFORMAL**	kittari	kiranakattari
	FORMAL	kirimasitari	kirimaseñ desitari

INFORMAL AFFIRMATIVE INDICATIVE

Passive		kirareru
Potential		kireru
Causative		kiraseru
Causative Pass.		kiraserareru

Honorific	**I**	okiri ni naru
	II	okiri nasaru
Humble	**I**	okiri suru
	II	okiri itasu

to put on, *to wear* (on the body as with a coat, suit, or dress)   TRANSITIVE

			AFFIRMATIVE	NEGATIVE
Indicative	**INFORMAL**		kiru	kinai
	FORMAL		kimasu	kimaseñ
Imperative	**INFORMAL I**		kiro	kiru na
		II	kinasai	kinasaru na
		III	kite kudasai	kinai de kudasai
	FORMAL		omesi nasaimase	omesi nasaimasu na
Presumptive	**INFORMAL I**		kiyoo	kimai
		II	kiru daroo	kinai daroo
	FORMAL	**I**	kimasyoo	kimasumai
		II	kiru desyoo	kinai desyoo
Provisional	**INFORMAL**		kireba	kinakereba
	FORMAL		kimaseba	kimaseñ nara
			kimasureba	
Gerund	**INFORMAL I**		kite	kinai de
		II		kinakute
	FORMAL		kimasite	kimaseñ de
Past Ind.	**INFORMAL**		kita	kinakatta
	FORMAL		kimasita	kimaseñ desita
Past Presump.	**INFORMAL**		kitaroo	kinakattaroo
			kita daroo	kinakatta daroo
	FORMAL		kimasitaroo	kimaseñ desitaroo
			kita desyoo	kinakatta desyoo
Conditional	**INFORMAL**		kitara	kinakattara
	FORMAL		kimasitara	kimaseñ desitara
Alternative	**INFORMAL**		kitari	kinakattari
	FORMAL		kimasitari	kimaseñ desitari

		INFORMAL AFFIRMATIVE INDICATIVE
Passive		kirareru
Potential		kirareru
Causative		kisaseru
Causative Pass.		kisaserareru
Honorific	**I**	omesi ni naru
	II	omesi nasaru
Humble	**I**	
	II	

		AFFIRMATIVE	NEGATIVE
Indicative	**INFORMAL**	kisou	kisowanai
	FORMAL	kisoimasu	kisoimaseñ
Imperative	**INFORMAL I**	kisoe	kisou na
	II	kisoinasai	kisoinasaru na
	III	kisotte kudasai	kisowanai de kudasai
	FORMAL	okisoi nasaimase	okisoi nasaimasu na
Presumptive	**INFORMAL I**	kisooo	kisoumai
	II	kisou daroo	kisowanai daroo
	FORMAL I	kisoimasyoo	kisoimasumai
	II	kisou desyoo	kisowanai desyoo
Provisional	**INFORMAL**	kisoeba	kisowanakereba
	FORMAL	kisoimaseba	kisoimaseñ nara
		kisoimasureba	
Gerund	**INFORMAL I**	kisotte	kisowanai de
	II		kisowanakute
	FORMAL	kisoimasite	kisoimaseñ de
Past Ind.	**INFORMAL**	kisotta	kisowanakatta
	FORMAL	kisoimasita	kisoimaseñ desita
Past Presump.	**INFORMAL**	kisottaroo	kisowanakattaroo
		kisotta daroo	kisowanakatta daroo
	FORMAL	kisoimasitaroo	kisoimaseñ desitaroo
		kisotta desyoo	kisowanakatta desyoo
Conditional	**INFORMAL**	kisottara	kisowanakattara
	FORMAL	kisoimasitara	kisoimaseñ desitara
Alternative	**INFORMAL**	kisottari	kisowanakattari
	FORMAL	kisoimasitari	kisoimaseñ desitari

		INFORMAL AFFIRMATIVE INDICATIVE
Passive		kisowareru
Potential		kisoeru
Causative		kisowaseru
Causative Pass.		kisowaserareru
Honorific	**I**	okisoi ni naru
	II	okisoi nasaru
Humble	**I**	okisoi suru
	II	okisoi itasu

		AFFIRMATIVE	NEGATIVE
Indicative	**INFORMAL**	kiwamaru	kiwamaranai
	FORMAL	kiwamarimasu	kiwamarimaseñ
Imperative	**INFORMAL I**		
	II		
	III		
	FORMAL		
Presumptive	**INFORMAL I**	kiwamaroo	kiwamarumai
	II	kiwamaru daroo	kiwamaranai daroo
	FORMAL I	kiwamarimasyoo	kiwamarimasumai
	II	kiwamaru desyoo	kiwamaranai desyoo
Provisional	**INFORMAL**	kiwamareba	kiwamaranakereba
	FORMAL	kiwamarimaseba	kiwamarimaseñ nara
		kiwamarimasureba	
Gerund	**INFORMAL I**	kiwamatte	kiwamaranai de
	II		kiwamaranakute
	FORMAL	kiwamarimasite	kiwamarimaseñ de
Past Ind.	**INFORMAL**	kiwamatta	kiwamaranakatta
	FORMAL	kiwamarimasita	kiwamarimaseñ desita
Past Presump.	**INFORMAL**	kiwamattaroo	kiwamaranakattaroo
		kiwamatta daroo	kiwamaranakatta daroo
	FORMAL	kiwamarimasitaroo	kiwamarimaseñ desitaroo
		kiwamatta desyoo	kiwamaranakatta desyoo
Conditional	**INFORMAL**	kiwamattara	kiwamaranakattara
	FORMAL	kiwamarimasitara	kiwamarimaseñ desitara
Alternative	**INFORMAL**	kiwamattari	kiwamaranakattari
	FORMAL	kiwamarimasitari	kiwamarimaseñ desitari

INFORMAL AFFIRMATIVE INDICATIVE

Passive	
Potential	
Causative	kiwamaraseru
Causative Pass.	kiwamaraserareru

Honorific	**I**	
	II	
Humble	**I**	
	II	

		AFFIRMATIVE	NEGATIVE
Indicative	**INFORMAL**	kizukau	kizukawanai
	FORMAL	kizukaimasu	kizukaimaseñ
Imperative	**INFORMAL I**	kizukae	kizukau na
	II	kizukainasai	kizukainasaru na
	III	kizukatte kudasai	kizukawanai de kudasai
	FORMAL	okizukai nasaimase	okizukai nasaimasu na
Presumptive	**INFORMAL I**	kizukaoo	kizukaumai
	II	kizukau daroo	kizukawanai daroo
	FORMAL I	kizukaimasyoo	kizukaimasumai
	II	kizukau desyoo	kizukawanai desyoo
Provisional	**INFORMAL**	kizukaeba	kizukawanakereba
	FORMAL	kizukaimaseba	kizukaimaseñ nara
		kizukaimasureba	
Gerund	**INFORMAL I**	kizukatte	kizukawanai de
	II		kizukawanakute
	FORMAL	kizukaimasite	kizukaimaseñ de
Past Ind.	**INFORMAL**	kizukatta	kizukawanakatta
	FORMAL	kizukaimasita	kizukaimaseñ desita
Past Presump.	**INFORMAL**	kizukattaroo	kizukawanakattaroo
		kizukatta daroo	kizukawanakatta daroo
	FORMAL	kizukaimasitaroo	kizukaimaseñ desitaroo
		kizukatta desyoo	kizukawanakatta desyoo
Conditional	**INFORMAL**	kizukattara	kizukawanakattara
	FORMAL	kizukaimasitara	kizukaimaseñ desitara
Alternative	**INFORMAL**	kizukattari	kizukawanakattari
	FORMAL	kizukaimasitari	kizukaimaseñ desitari

		INFORMAL AFFIRMATIVE INDICATIVE
Passive		kizukawareru
Potential		kizukaeru
Causative		kizukawaseru
Causative Pass.		kizukawaserareru
Honorific	**I**	okizukai ni naru
	II	okizukai nasaru
Humble	**I**	okizukai suru
	II	okizukai itasu

		AFFIRMATIVE	NEGATIVE
Indicative	**INFORMAL**	kizuku	kizukanai
	FORMAL	kizukimasu	kizukimaseñ
Imperative	**INFORMAL I**	kizuke	kizuku na
	II	kizukinasai	kizukinasaru na
	III	kizuite kudasai	kizukanai de kudasai
	FORMAL	okizuki nasaimase	okizuki nasaimasu na
Presumptive	**INFORMAL I**	kizukoo	kizukumai
	II	kizuku daroo	kizukanai daroo
	FORMAL I	kizukimasyoo	kizukimasumai
	II	kizuku desyoo	kizukanai desyoo
Provisional	**INFORMAL**	kizukeba	kizukanakereba
	FORMAL	kizukimaseba	kizukimaseñ nara
		kizukimasureba	
Gerund	**INFORMAL I**	kizuite	kizukanai de
	II		kizukanakute
	FORMAL	kizukimasite	kizukimaseñ de
Past Ind.	**INFORMAL**	kizuita	kizukanakatta
	FORMAL	kizukimasita	kizukimaseñ desita
Past Presump.	**INFORMAL**	kizuitaroo	kizukanakattaroo
		kizuita daroo	kizukanakatta daroo
	FORMAL	kizukimasitaroo	kizukimaseñ desitaroo
		kizuita desyoo	kizukanakatta desyoo
Conditional	**INFORMAL**	kizuitara	kizukanakattara
	FORMAL	kizukimasitara	kizukimaseñ desitara
Alternative	**INFORMAL**	kizuitari	kizukanakattari
	FORMAL	kizukimasitari	kizukimaseñ desitari

INFORMAL AFFIRMATIVE INDICATIVE

Passive		kizukareru
Potential		kizukeru
Causative		kizukaseru
Causative Pass.		kizukaserareru

Honorific	**I**	okizuki ni naru
	II	okizuki nasaru
Humble	**I**	
	II	

		AFFIRMATIVE	NEGATIVE
Indicative	INFORMAL	kizutukeru	kizutukenai
	FORMAL	kizutukemasu	kizutukemaseñ
Imperative	INFORMAL I	kizutukero	kizutukeru na
	II	kizutukenasai	kizutukenasaru na
	III	kizutukete kudasai	kizutukenai de kudasai
	FORMAL	okizutuke nasaimase	okizutuke nasaimasu na
Presumptive	INFORMAL I	kizutukeyoo	kizutukemai
	II	kizutukeru daroo	kizutukenai daroo
	FORMAL I	kizutukemasyoo	kizutukemasumai
	II	kizutukeru desyoo	kizutukenai desyoo
Provisional	INFORMAL	kizutukereba	kizutukenakereba
	FORMAL	kizutukemaseba	kizutukemaseñ nara
		kizutukemasureba	
Gerund	INFORMAL I	kizutukete	kizukenai de
	II		kizutukenakute
	FORMAL	kizutukemasite	kizutukemaseñ de
Past Ind.	INFORMAL	kizutuketa	kizutukenakatta
	FORMAL	kizutukemasita	kizutukemaseñ desita
Past Presump.	INFORMAL	kizutuketaroo	kizutukenakattaroo
		kizutuketa daroo	kizutukenakatta daroo
	FORMAL	kizutukemasitaroo	kizutukemaseñ desitaroo
		kizutuketa desyoo	kizutukenakatta desyoo
Conditional	INFORMAL	kizutukettara	kizutukenakattara
	FORMAL	kizutukemasitara	kizutukemaseñ desitara
Alternative	INFORMAL	kizutuketari	kizutukenakattari
	FORMAL	kizutukemasitari	kizutukemaseñ desitari

INFORMAL AFFIRMATIVE INDICATIVE

Passive	kizutukerareru
Potential	kizutukerareru
Causative	kizutukesaseru
Causative Pass.	kizutukesaserareru

Honorific	I	okizutuke ni naru
	II	okizutuke nasaru
Humble	I	okizutuke suru
	II	okizutuke itasu

		AFFIRMATIVE	NEGATIVE
Indicative	**INFORMAL**	kobamu	kobamanai
	FORMAL	kobamimasu	kobamimaseñ
Imperative	**INFORMAL I**	kobame	kobamu na
	II	kobaminasai	kobaminasaru na
	III	kobañde kudasai	kobamanai de kudasai
	FORMAL	okobami nasaimase	okobami nasaimasu na
Presumptive	**INFORMAL I**	kobamoo	kobamumai
	II	kobamu daroo	kobamanai daroo
	FORMAL I	kobamimasyoo	kobamimasumai
	II	kobamu desyoo	kobamanai desyoo
Provisional	**INFORMAL**	kobameba	kobamanakereba
	FORMAL	kobamimaseba	kobamimaseñ nara
		kobamimasureba	
Gerund	**INFORMAL I**	kobañde	kobamanai de
	II		kobamanakute
	FORMAL	kobamimasite	kobamimaseñ de
Past Ind.	**INFORMAL**	kobañda	kobamanakatta
	FORMAL	kobamimasita	kobamimaseñ desita
Past Presump.	**INFORMAL**	kobañdaroo	kobamanakattaroo
		kobañda daroo	kobamanakatta daroo
	FORMAL	kobamimasitaroo	kobamimaseñ desitaroo
		kobañda desyoo	kobamanakatta desyoo
Conditional	**INFORMAL**	kobañdara	kobamanakattara
	FORMAL	kobamimasitara	kobamimaseñ desitara
Alternative	**INFORMAL**	kobañdari	kobamanakattari
	FORMAL	kobamimasitari	kobamimaseñ desitari

		INFORMAL AFFIRMATIVE INDICATIVE
Passive		kobamareru
Potential		kobameru
Causative		kobamaseru
Causative Pass.		kobamaserareru
Honorific	**I**	okobami ni naru
	II	okobami nasaru
Humble	**I**	okobami suru
	II	okobami itasu

		AFFIRMATIVE	NEGATIVE
Indicative	**INFORMAL**	koboreru	koborenai
	FORMAL	koboremasu	koboremaseñ
Imperative	**INFORMAL I**	koborero	koboreru na
	II		
	III		
	FORMAL		
Presumptive	**INFORMAL I**	koboreyoo	koboremai
	II	koboreru daroo	koborenai daroo
	FORMAL I	koboremasyoo	koboremasumai
	II	koboreru desyoo	koborenai desyoo
Provisional	**INFORMAL**	koborereba	koborenakereba
	FORMAL	koboremaseba	koboremaseñ nara
		koboremasureba	
Gerund	**INFORMAL I**	koborete	koborenai de
	II		koborenakute
	FORMAL	koboremasite	koboremaseñ de
Past Ind.	**INFORMAL**	koboreta	koborenakatta
	FORMAL	koboremasita	koboremaseñ desita
Past Presump.	**INFORMAL**	koboretaroo	koborenakattaroo
		koboreta daroo	koborenakatta daroo
	FORMAL	koboremasitaroo	koboremaseñ desitaroo
		koboreta desyoo	koborenakatta desyoo
Conditional	**INFORMAL**	koboretara	koborenakattara
	FORMAL	koboremasitara	koboremaseñ desitara
Alternative	**INFORMAL**	koboretari	koborenakattari
	FORMAL	koboremasitari	koboremaseñ desitari

		INFORMAL AFFIRMATIVE INDICATIVE
Passive		koborerareru
Potential		koborerareru
Causative		koboresaseru
Causative Pass.		
Honorific	**I**	
	II	
Humble	**I**	
	II	

		AFFIRMATIVE	NEGATIVE
Indicative	**INFORMAL**	kobosu	kobosanai
	FORMAL	kobosimasu	kobosimaseñ
Imperative	**INFORMAL I**	kobose	kobosu na
	II	kobosinasai	kobosinasaru na
	III	kobosite kudasai	kobosanai de kudasai
	FORMAL	okobosi nasaimase	okobosi nasaimasu na
Presumptive	**INFORMAL I**	kobosoo	kobosumai
	II	kobosu daroo	kobosanai daroo
	FORMAL I	kobosimasyoo	kobosimasumai
	II	kobosu desyoo	kobosanai desyoo
Provisional	**INFORMAL**	koboseba	kobosanakereba
	FORMAL	kobosimaseba	kobosimaseñ nara
		kobosimasureba	
Gerund	**INFORMAL I**	kobosite	kobosanai de
	II		kobosanakute
	FORMAL	kobosimasite	kobosimaseñ de
Past Ind.	**INFORMAL**	kobosita	kobosanakatta
	FORMAL	kobosimasita	kobosimaseñ desita
Past Presump.	**INFORMAL**	kobositaroo	kobosanakattaroo
		kobosita daroo	kobosanakatta daroo
	FORMAL	kobosimasitaroo	kobosimaseñ desitaroo
		kobosita desyoo	kobosanakatta desyoo
Conditional	**INFORMAL**	kobositara	kobosanakattara
	FORMAL	kobosimasitara	kobosimaseñ desitara
Alternative	**INFORMAL**	kobositari	kobosanakattari
	FORMAL	kobosimasitari	kobosimaseñ desitari

		INFORMAL AFFIRMATIVE INDICATIVE
Passive		kobosareru
Potential		koboseru
Causative		kobosaseru
Causative Pass.		kobosaserareru

Honorific	**I**	okobosi ni naru
	II	okobosi nasaru
Humble	**I**	okobosi suru
	II	okobosi itasu

		AFFIRMATIVE	NEGATIVE
Indicative	**INFORMAL**	kodawaru	kodawaranai
	FORMAL	kodawarimasu	kodawarimaseñ
Imperative	**INFORMAL I**	kodaware	kodawaru na
	II	kodawarinasai	kodawarinasaru na
	III	kodawatte kudasai	kodawaranai de kudasai
	FORMAL	okodawari nasaimase	okodawari nasaimasu na
Presumptive	**INFORMAL I**	kodawaroo	kodawarumai
	II	kodawaru daroo	kodawaranai daroo
	FORMAL I	kodawarimasyoo	kodawarimasumai
	II	kodawaru desyoo	kodawaranai desyoo
Provisional	**INFORMAL**	kodawareba	kodawaranakereba
	FORMAL	kodawarimaseba	kodawarimaseñ nara
		kodawarimasureba	
Gerund	**INFORMAL I**	kodawatte	kodawaranai de
	II		kodawaranakute
	FORMAL	kodawarimasite	kodawarimaseñ de
Past Ind.	**INFORMAL**	kodawatta	kodawaranakatta
	FORMAL	kodawarimasita	kodawarimaseñ desita
Past Presump.	**INFORMAL**	kodawattaroo	kodawaranakattaroo
		kodawatta daroo	kodawaranakatta daroo
	FORMAL	kodawarimasitaroo	kodawarimaseñ desitaroo
		kodawatta desyoo	kodawaranakatta desyoo
Conditional	**INFORMAL**	kodawattara	kodawaranakattara
	FORMAL	kodawarimasitara	kodawarimaseñ desitara
Alternative	**INFORMAL**	kodawattari	kodawaranakattari
	FORMAL	kodawarimasitari	kodawarimaseñ desitari

		INFORMAL AFFIRMATIVE INDICATIVE
Passive		kodawarareru
Potential		kodawareru
Causative		kodawaraseru
Causative Pass.		kodawaraserareru
Honorific	**I**	okodawari ni naru
	II	okodawari nasaru
Humble	**I**	
	II	

to grow stout, to grow fertile (of land)

		AFFIRMATIVE	NEGATIVE
Indicative	**INFORMAL**	koeru	koenai
	FORMAL	koemasu	koemaseñ
Imperative	**INFORMAL I**	koero	koeru na
	II	koenasai	koenasaru na
	III	koete kudasai	koenai de kudasai
	FORMAL	okoe nasaimase	okoe nasaimasu na
Presumptive	**INFORMAL I**	koeyoo	koemai
	II	koeru daroo	koenai daroo
	FORMAL I	koemasyoo	koemasumai
	II	koeru desyoo	koenai desyoo
Provisional	**INFORMAL**	koereba	koenakereba
	FORMAL	koemaseba	koemaseñ nara
		koemasureba	
Gerund	**INFORMAL I**	koete	koenai de
	II		koenakute
	FORMAL	koemasite	koemaseñ de
Past Ind.	**INFORMAL**	koeta	koenakatta
	FORMAL	koemasita	koemaseñ desita
Past Presump.	**INFORMAL**	koetaroo	koenakattaroo
		koeta daroo	koenakatta daroo
	FORMAL	koemasitaroo	koemaseñ desitaroo
		koeta desyoo	koenakatta desyoo
Conditional	**INFORMAL**	koetara	koenakattara
	FORMAL	koemasitara	koemaseñ desitara
Alternative	**INFORMAL**	koetari	koenakattari
	FORMAL	koemasitari	koemaseñ desitari

		INFORMAL AFFIRMATIVE INDICATIVE
Passive		koerareru
Potential		koerareru
Causative		koesaseru
Causative Pass.		koesaserareru
Honorific	**I**	okoe ni naru
	II	okoe nasaru
Humble	**I**	
	II	

		AFFIRMATIVE	NEGATIVE
Indicative	**INFORMAL**	koeru	koenai
	FORMAL	koemasu	koemaseñ
Imperative	**INFORMAL I**	koero	koeru na
	II	koenasai	koenasaru na
	III	koete kudasai	koenai de kudasai
	FORMAL	okoe nasaimase	okoe nasaimasu na
Presumptive	**INFORMAL I**	koeyoo	koemai
	II	koeru daroo	koenai daroo
	FORMAL I	koemasyoo	koemasumai
	II	koeru desyoo	koenai desyoo
Provisional	**INFORMAL**	koereba	koenakereba
	FORMAL	koemaseba	koemaseñ nara
		koemasureba	
Gerund	**INFORMAL I**	koete	koenai de
	II		koenakute
	FORMAL	koemasite	koemaseñ de
Past Ind.	**INFORMAL**	koeta	koenakatta
	FORMAL	koemasita	koemaseñ desita
Past Presump.	**INFORMAL**	koetaroo	koenakattaroo
		koeta daroo	koenakatta daroo
	FORMAL	koemasitaroo	koemaseñ desitaroo
		koeta desyoo	koenakatta desyoo
Conditional	**INFORMAL**	koetara	koenakattara
	FORMAL	koemasitara	koemaseñ desitara
Alternative	**INFORMAL**	koetari	koenakattari
	FORMAL	koemasitari	koemaseñ desitari

INFORMAL AFFIRMATIVE INDICATIVE

Passive		koerareru
Potential		koerareru
Causative		koesaseru
Causative Pass.		koesaserareru

Honorific	**I**	okoe ni naru
	II	okoe nasaru
Humble	**I**	okoe suru
	II	okoe itasu

		AFFIRMATIVE	NEGATIVE
Indicative	**INFORMAL**	kogeru	kogenai
	FORMAL	kogemasu	kogemaseñ
Imperative	**INFORMAL I**	kogero	kogeru na
	II	kogenasai	kogenasaru na
	III	kogete kudasai	kogenai de kudasai
	FORMAL	okoge nasaimase	okoge nasaimasu na
Presumptive	**INFORMAL I**	kogeyoo	kogemai
	II	kogeru daroo	kogenai daroo
	FORMAL I	kogemasyoo	kogemasumai
	II	kogeru desyoo	kogenai desyoo
Provisional	**INFORMAL**	kogereba	kogenakereba
	FORMAL	kogemaseba	kogemaseñ nara
		kogemasureba	
Gerund	**INFORMAL I**	kogete	kogenai de
	II		kogenakute
	FORMAL	kogemasite	kogemaseñ de
Past Ind.	**INFORMAL**	kogeta	kogenakatta
	FORMAL	kogemasita	kogemaseñ desita
Past Presump.	**INFORMAL**	kogetaroo	kogenakattaroo
		kogeta daroo	kogenakatta daroo
	FORMAL	kogemasitaroo	kogemaseñ desitaroo
		kogeta desyoo	kogenakatta desyoo
Conditional	**INFORMAL**	kogetara	kogenakattara
	FORMAL	kogemasitara	kogemaseñ desitara
Alternative	**INFORMAL**	kogetari	kogenakattari
	FORMAL	kogemasitari	kogemaseñ desitari

		INFORMAL AFFIRMATIVE INDICATIVE
Passive		kogerareru
Potential		kogerareru
Causative		kogesaseru
Causative Pass.		kogesaserareru
Honorific	**I**	okoge ni naru
	II	okoge nasaru
Humble	**I**	
	II	

		AFFIRMATIVE	NEGATIVE
Indicative	**INFORMAL**	kogu	koganai
	FORMAL	kogimasu	kogimaseñ
Imperative	**INFORMAL I**	koge	kogu na
	II	koginasai	koginasaru na
	III	koide kudasai	koganai de kudasai
	FORMAL	okogi nasaimase	okogi nasaimasu na
Presumptive	**INFORMAL I**	kogoo	kogumai
	II	kogu daroo	koganai daroo
	FORMAL I	kogimasyoo	kogimasumai
	II	kogu desyoo	koganai desyoo
Provisional	**INFORMAL**	kogeba	koganakereba
	FORMAL	kogimaseba	kogimaseñ nara
		kogimasureba	
Gerund	**INFORMAL I**	koide	koganai de
	II		koganakute
	FORMAL	kogimasite	kogimaseñ de
Past Ind.	**INFORMAL**	koida	koganakatta
	FORMAL	kogimasita	kogimaseñ desita
Past Presump.	**INFORMAL**	koidaroo	koganakattaroo
		koida daroo	koganakatta daroo
	FORMAL	kogimasitaroo	kogimaseñ desitaroo
		koida desyoo	koganakatta desyoo
Conditional	**INFORMAL**	koidara	koganakattara
	FORMAL	kogimasitara	kogimaseñ desitara
Alternative	**INFORMAL**	koidari	koganakattari
	FORMAL	kogimasitari	kogimaseñ desitari

		INFORMAL AFFIRMATIVE INDICATIVE
Passive		kogareru
Potential		kogeru
Causative		kogaseru
Causative Pass.		kogaserareru
Honorific	**I**	okogi ni naru
	II	okogi nasaru
Humble	**I**	okogi suru
	II	okogi itasu

231

to work someone hard   TRANSITIVE

		AFFIRMATIVE	NEGATIVE
Indicative	**INFORMAL**	kokitukau	kokitukawanai
	FORMAL	kokitukaimasu	kokitukaimaseñ
Imperative	**INFORMAL I**	kokitukae	kokitukau na
	II	kokitukainasai	kokitukainasaru na
	III	kokitukatte kudasai	kokitukawanai de kudasai
	FORMAL		
Presumptive	**INFORMAL I**	kokitukaoo	kokitukaumai
	II	kokitukau daroo	kokitukawanai daroo
	FORMAL I	kokitukaimasyoo	kokitukaimasumai
	II	kokitukau desyoo	kokitukawanai desyoo
Provisional	**INFORMAL**	kokitukaeba	kokitukawanakereba
	FORMAL	kokitukaimaseba	kokitukaimaseñ nara
		kokitukaimasureba	
Gerund	**INFORMAL I**	kokitukatte	kokitukawanai de
	II		kokitukawanakute
	FORMAL	kokitukaimasite	kokitukaimaseñ de
Past Ind.	**INFORMAL**	kokitukatta	kokitukawanakatta
	FORMAL	kokitukaimasita	kokitukaimaseñ desita
Past Presump.	**INFORMAL**	kokitukattaroo	kokitukawanakattaroo
		kokitukatta daroo	kokitukawanakatta daroo
	FORMAL	kokitukaimasitaroo	kokitukaimaseñ desitaroo
		kokitukatta desyoo	kokitukawanakatta desyoo
Conditional	**INFORMAL**	kokitukattara	kokitukawanakattara
	FORMAL	kokitukaimasitara	kokitukaimaseñ desitara
Alternative	**INFORMAL**	kokitukattari	kokitukawanakattari
	FORMAL	kokitukaimasitari	kokitukaimaseñ desitari

	INFORMAL AFFIRMATIVE INDICATIVE
Passive	kokitukawareru
Potential	kokitukaeru
Causative	kokitukawaseru
Causative Pass.	kokitukawaserareru

Honorific	**I**	
	II	
Humble	**I**	
	II	

		AFFIRMATIVE	NEGATIVE
Indicative	**INFORMAL**	kokoroeru	kokoroenai
	FORMAL	kokoroemasu	kokoroemaseñ
Imperative	**INFORMAL I**	kokoroero	kokoroeru na
	II		
	III		
	FORMAL		
Presumptive	**INFORMAL I**	kokoroeyo·	kokoroemai
	II	kokoroeru aaro·	kokoroenai daroo
	FORMAL I	kokoroemasyoo	kokoroemasumai
	II	kokoroeru desyoo	kokoroenai desyoo
Provisional	**INFORMAL**	kokoroereba	kokoroenakereba
	FORMAL	kokoroemaseba	kokoroemaseñ nara
		kokoroemasureba	
Gerund	**INFORMAL I**	kokoroete	kokoroenai de
	II		kokoroenakute
	FORMAL	kokoroemasite	kokoroemaseñ de
Past Ind.	**INFORMAL**	kokoroeta	kokoroenakatta
	FORMAL	kokoroemasita	kokoroemaseñ desita
Past Presump.	**INFORMAL**	kokoroetaroo	kokoroenakattaroo
		kokoroeta daroo	kokoroenakatta daroo
	FORMAL	kokoroemasitaroo	kokoroemaseñ desitaroo
		kokoroeta desyoo	kokoroenakatta desyoo
Conditional	**INFORMAL**	kokoroetara	kokoroenakattara
	FORMAL	kokoroemasitara	kokoroemaseñ desitara
Alternative	**INFORMAL**	kokoroetari	kokoroenakattari
	FORMAL	kokoroemasitari	kokoroemaseñ desitari

		INFORMAL AFFIRMATIVE INDICATIVE
Passive		kokoroerareru
Potential		kokoroerareru
Causative		kokoroesaseru
Causative Pass.		kokoroesaserareru
Honorific	**I**	okokoroe ni naru
	II	okokoroe nasaru
Humble	**I**	
	II	

		AFFIRMATIVE	NEGATIVE
Indicative	**INFORMAL**	kokoromiru	kokorominai
	FORMAL	kokoromimasu	kokoromimaseñ
Imperative	**INFORMAL I**	kokoromiro	kokoromiru na
	II	kokorominasai	kokorominasaru na
	III	kokoromite kudasai	kokorominai de kudasai
	FORMAL	okokoromi nasaimase	okokoromi nasaimasu na
Presumptive	**INFORMAL I**	kokoromiyoo	kokoromimai
	II	kokoromiru daroo	kokorominai daroo
	FORMAL I	kokoromimasyoo	kokoromimasumai
	II	kokoromiru desyoo	kokorominai desyoo
Provisional	**INFORMAL**	kokoromireba	kokorominakereba
	FORMAL	kokoromimaseba	kokoromimaseñ nara
		kokoromimasureba	
Gerund	**INFORMAL I**	kokoromite	kokorominai de
	II		kokorominakute
	FORMAL	kokoromimasite	kokoromimaseñ de
Past Ind.	**INFORMAL**	kokoromita	kokorominakatta
	FORMAL	kokoromimasita	kokoromimaseñ desita
Past Presump.	**INFORMAL**	kokoromitaroo	kokorominakattaroo
		kokoromita daroo	kokorominakatta daroo
	FORMAL	kokoromimasitaroo	kokoromimaseñ desitaroo
		kokoromita desyoo	kokorominakatta desyoo
Conditional	**INFORMAL**	kokoromitara	kokorominakattara
	FORMAL	kokoromimasitara	kokoromimaseñ desitara
Alternative	**INFORMAL**	kokoromitari	kokorominakattari
	FORMAL	kokoromimasitari	kokoromimaseñ desitari

INFORMAL AFFIRMATIVE INDICATIVE

Passive	kokoromirareru
Potential	kokoromirareru
Causative	kokoromisaseru
Causative Pass.	kokoromisaserareru

Honorific	**I**	okokoromi ni naru
	II	okokoromi nasaru
Humble	**I**	okokoromi suru
	II	okokoromi itasu

		AFFIRMATIVE	NEGATIVE
Indicative	**INFORMAL**	kokorozasu	kokorozasanai
	FORMAL	kokorozasimasu	kokorozasimaseñ
Imperative	**INFORMAL I**	kokorozase	kokorozasu na
	II	kokorozasinasai	kokorozasinasaru na
	III	kokorozasite kudasai	kokorozasanai de kudasai
	FORMAL	okokorozasi nasaimase	okokorozasi nasaimasu na
Presumptive	**INFORMAL I**	kokorozasoo	kokorozasumai
	II	kokorozasu daroo	kokorozasanai daroo
	FORMAL I	kokorozasimasyoo	kokorozasimasumai
	II	kokorozasu desyoo	kokorozasanai desyoo
Provisional	**INFORMAL**	kokorozaseba	kokorozasanakereba
	FORMAL	kokorozasimaseba	kokorozasimaseñ nara
		kokorozasimasureba	
Gerund	**INFORMAL I**	kokorozasite	kokorozasanai de
	II		kokorozasanakute
	FORMAL	kokorozasimasite	kokorozasimaseñ de
Past Ind.	**INFORMAL**	kokorozasita	kokorozasanakatta
	FORMAL	kokorozasimasita	kokorozasimaseñ desita
Past Presump.	**INFORMAL**	kokorozasitaroo	kokorozasanakattaroo
		kokorozasita daroo	kokorozasanakatta daroo
	FORMAL	kokorozasimasitaroo	kokorozasimaseñ desitaroo
		kokorozasita desyoo	kokorozasanakatta desyoo
Conditional	**INFORMAL**	kokorozasitara	kokorozasanakattara
	FORMAL	kokorozasimasitara	kokorozasimaseñ desitara
Alternative	**INFORMAL**	kokorozasitari	kokorozasanakattari
	FORMAL	kokorozasimasitari	kokorozasimaseñ desitari

		INFORMAL AFFIRMATIVE INDICATIVE
Passive		kokorozasareru
Potential		kokorozaseru
Causative		kokorozasaseru
Causative Pass.		kokorozasaserareru
Honorific	**I**	okokorozasi ni naru
	II	okokorozasi nasaru
Humble	**I**	
	II	

		AFFIRMATIVE	NEGATIVE
Indicative	**INFORMAL**	komaru	komaranai
	FORMAL	komarimasu	komarimaseñ
Imperative	**INFORMAL I**	komare	komaru na
	II		
	III		
	FORMAL		
Presumptive	**INFORMAL I**	komaroo	komarumai
	II	komaru daroo	komaranai daroo
	FORMAL I	komarimasyoo	komarimasumai
	II	komaru desyoo	komaranai desyoo
Provisional	**INFORMAL**	komareba	komaranakereba
	FORMAL	komarimaseba	komarimaseñ nara
		komarimasureba	
Gerund	**INFORMAL I**	komatte	komaranai de
	II		komaranakute
	FORMAL	komarimasite	komarimaseñ de
Past Ind.	**INFORMAL**	komatta	komaranakatta
	FORMAL	komarimasita	komarimaseñ desita
Past Presump.	**INFORMAL**	komattaroo	komaranakattaroo
		komatta daroo	komaranakatta daroo
	FORMAL	komarimasitaroo	komarimaseñ desitaroo
		komatta desyoo	komaranakatta desyoo
Conditional	**INFORMAL**	komattara	komaranakattara
	FORMAL	komarimasitara	komarimaseñ desitara
Alternative	**INFORMAL**	komattari	komaranakattari
	FORMAL	komarimasitari	komarimaseñ desitari

		INFORMAL AFFIRMATIVE INDICATIVE
Passive		komarareru
Potential		
Causative		komaraseru
Causative Pass.		komaraserareru

Honorific	**I**	okomari ni naru
	II	okomari nasaru
Humble	**I**	
	II	

		AFFIRMATIVE	NEGATIVE
Indicative	**INFORMAL**	komu	komanai
	FORMAL	komimasu	komimaseñ
Imperative	**INFORMAL I**		
	II		
	III		
	FORMAL		
Presumptive	**INFORMAL I**	komoo	komumai
	II	komu daroo	komanai daroo
	FORMAL I	komimasyoo	komimasumai
	II	komu desyoo	komanai desyoo
Provisional	**INFORMAL**	komeba	komanakereba
	FORMAL	komimaseba	komimaseñ nara
		komimasureba	
Gerund	**INFORMAL I**	koñde	komanai de
	II		komanakute
	FORMAL	komimasite	komimaseñ de
Past Ind.	**INFORMAL**	koñda	komanakatta
	FORMAL	komimasita	komimaseñ desita
Past Presump.	**INFORMAL**	koñdaroo	komanakattaroo
		koñda daroo	komanakatta daroo
	FORMAL	komimasitaroo	komimaseñ desitaroo
		koñda desyoo	komanakatta desyoo
Conditional	**INFORMAL**	koñdara	komanakattara
	FORMAL	komimasitara	komimaseñ desitara
Alternative	**INFORMAL**	koñdari	komanakattari
	FORMAL	komimasitari	komimaseñ desitari

INFORMAL AFFIRMATIVE INDICATIVE

Passive	
Potential	
Causative	
Causative Pass.	
Honorific	**I**
	II
Humble	**I**
	II

		AFFIRMATIVE	NEGATIVE
Indicative	**INFORMAL**	konomu	konomanai
	FORMAL	konomimasu	konomimaseñ
Imperative	**INFORMAL I**	konome	konomu na
	II	konominasai	konominasaru na
	III	konoñde kudasai	konomanai de kudasai
	FORMAL	okonomi nasaimase	okonomi nasaimasu na
Presumptive	**INFORMAL I**	konomoo	konomumai
	II	konomu daroo	konomanai daroo
	FORMAL I	konomimasyoo	konomimasumai
	II	konomu desyoo	konomanai desyoo
Provisional	**INFORMAL**	konomeba	konomanakereba
	FORMAL	konomimaseba	konomimaseñ nara
		konomimasureba	
Gerund	**INFORMAL I**	konoñde	konomanai de
	II		konomanakute
	FORMAL	konomimasite	konomimaseñ de
Past Ind.	**INFORMAL**	konoñda	konomanakatta
	FORMAL	konomimasita	konomimaseñ desita
Past Presump.	**INFORMAL**	konoñdaroo	konomanakattaroo
		konoñda daroo	konomanakatta daroo
	FORMAL	konomimasitaroo	konomimaseñ desitaroo
		konoñda desyoo	konomanakatta desyoo
Conditional	**INFORMAL**	konoñdara	konomanakattara
	FORMAL	konomimasitara	konomimaseñ desitara
Alternative	**INFORMAL**	konoñdari	konomanakattari
	FORMAL	konomimasitari	konomimaseñ desitari

INFORMAL AFFIRMATIVE INDICATIVE

Passive		konomareru
Potential		konomeru
Causative		konomaseru
Causative Pass.		konomaserareru

Honorific	**I**	okonomi ni naru
	II	okonomi nasaru
Humble	**I**	
	II	

		AFFIRMATIVE	NEGATIVE
Indicative	**INFORMAL**	kooru	kooranai
	FORMAL	koorimasu	koorimaseñ
Imperative	**INFORMAL I**	koore	kooru na
	II		
	III		
	FORMAL		
Presumptive	**INFORMAL I**	kooroo	koorumai
	II	kooru daroo	kooranai daroo
	FORMAL I	koorimasyoo	koorimasumai
	II	kooru desyoo	kooranai desyoo
Provisional	**INFORMAL**	kooreba	kooranakereba
	FORMAL	koorimaseba	koorimaseñ nara
		koorimasureba	
Gerund	**INFORMAL I**	kootte	kooranai de
	II		kooranakute
	FORMAL	koorimasite	koorimaseñ de
Past Ind.	**INFORMAL**	kootta	kooranakatta
	FORMAL	koorimasita	koorimaseñ desita
Past Presump.	**INFORMAL**	koottaroo	kooranakattaroo
		kootta daroo	kooranakatta daroo
	FORMAL	koorimasitaroo	koorimaseñ desitaroo
		kootta desyoo	kooranakatta desyoo
Conditional	**INFORMAL**	koottara	kooranakattara
	FORMAL	koorimasitara	koorimaseñ desitara
Alternative	**INFORMAL**	koottari	kooranakattari
	FORMAL	koorimasitari	koorimaseñ desitari

INFORMAL AFFIRMATIVE INDICATIVE

Passive	koorareru
Potential	kooreru
Causative	kooraseru
Causative Pass.	kooraserareru

Honorific	**I**	
	II	
Humble	**I**	
	II	

239

		AFFIRMATIVE	NEGATIVE
Indicative	**INFORMAL**	koraeru	koraenai
	FORMAL	koraemasu	koraemaseñ
Imperative	**INFORMAL I**	koraero	koraeru na
	II	koraenasai	koraenasaru na
	III	koraete kudasai	koraenai de kudasai
	FORMAL	okorae nasaimase	okorae nasaimasu na
Presumptive	**INFORMAL I**	koraeyoo	koraemai
	II	koraeru daroo	koraenai daroo
	FORMAL I	koraemasyoo	koraemasumai
	II	koraeru desyoo	koraenai desyoo
Provisional	**INFORMAL**	koraereba	koraenakereba
	FORMAL	koraemaseba	koraemaseñ nara
		koraemasureba	
Gerund	**INFORMAL I**	koraete	koraenai de
	II		koraenakute
	FORMAL	koraemasite	koraemaseñ de
Past Ind.	**INFORMAL**	koraeta	koraenakatta
	FORMAL	koraemasita	koraemaseñ desita
Past Presump.	**INFORMAL**	koraetaroo	koraenakattaroo
		koraeta daroo	koraenakatta daroo
	FORMAL	koraemasitaroo	koraemaseñ desitaroo
		koraeta desyoo	koraenakatta desyoo
Conditional	**INFORMAL**	koraetara	koraenakattara
	FORMAL	koraemasitara	koraemaseñ desitara
Alternative	**INFORMAL**	koraetari	koraenakattari
	FORMAL	koraemasitari	koraemaseñ desitari

INFORMAL AFFIRMATIVE INDICATIVE

Passive	koraerareru
Potential	koraerareru
Causative	koraesaseru
Causative Pass.	koraesaserareru

Honorific	**I**	okorae ni naru
	II	okorae nasaru
Humble	**I**	okorae suru
	II	okorae itasu

		AFFIRMATIVE	**NEGATIVE**
Indicative	**INFORMAL**	korasimeru	korasimenai
	FORMAL	korasimemasu	korasimemaseñ
Imperative	**INFORMAL I**	korasimero	korasimeru na
	II	korasimenasai	korasimenasaru na
	III	korasimete kudasai	korasimenai de kudasai
	FORMAL	okorasime nasaimase	okorasime nasaimasu na
Presumptive	**INFORMAL I**	korasimeyoo	korasimemai
	II	korasimeru daroo	korasimenai daroo
	FORMAL I	korasimemasyoo	korasimemasumai
	II	korasimeru desyoo	korasimenai desyoo
Provisional	**INFORMAL**	korasimereba	korasimenakereba
	FORMAL	korasimemaseba	korasimemaseñ nara
		korasimemasureba	
Gerund	**INFORMAL I**	korasimete	korasimenai de
	II		korasimenakute
	FORMAL	korasimemasite	korasimemaseñ de
Past Ind.	**INFORMAL**	korasimeta	korasimenakatta
	FORMAL	korasimemasita	korasimemaseñ desita
Past Presump.	**INFORMAL**	korasimetaroo	korasimenakattaroo
		korasimeta daroo	korasimenakatta daroo
	FORMAL	korasimemasitaroo	korasimemaseñ desitaroo
		korasimeta desyoo	korasimenakatta desyoo
Conditional	**INFORMAL**	korasimetara	korasimenakattara
	FORMAL	korasimemasitara	korasimemaseñ desitara
Alternative	**INFORMAL**	korasimetari	korasimenakattari
	FORMAL	korasimemasitari	korasimemaseñ desitari

INFORMAL AFFIRMATIVE INDICATIVE

Passive		korasimerareru
Potential		korasimerareru
Causative		korasimesaseru
Causative Pass.		korasimesaserareru

Honorific	**I**	okorasime ni naru
	II	okorasime nasaru
Humble	**I**	okorasime suru
	II	okorasime itasu

to concentrate (one's attention), *to devote oneself to*   TRANSITIVE

		AFFIRMATIVE	NEGATIVE
Indicative	INFORMAL	korasu	korasanai
	FORMAL	korasimasu	korasimaseñ
Imperative	INFORMAL I	korase	korasu na
	II	korasinasai	korasinasaru na
	III	korasite kudasai	korasanai de kudasai
	FORMAL	okorasi nasaimase	okorasi nasaimasu na
Presumptive	INFORMAL I	korasoo	korasumai
	II	korasu daroo	korasanai daroo
	FORMAL I	korasimasyoo	korasimasumai
	II	korasu desyoo	korasanai desyoo
Provisional	INFORMAL	koraseba	korasanakereba
	FORMAL	korasimaseba	korasimaseñ nara
		korasimasureba	
Gerund	INFORMAL I	korasite	korasanai de
	II		korasanakute
	FORMAL	korasimasite	korasimaseñ de
Past Ind.	INFORMAL	korasita	korasanakatta
	FORMAL	korasimasita	korasimaseñ desita
Past Presump.	INFORMAL	korasitaroo	korasanakattaroo
		korasita daroo	korasanakatta daroo
	FORMAL	korasimasitaroo	korasimaseñ desitaroo
		korasita desyoo	korasanakatta desyoo
Conditional	INFORMAL	korasitara	korasanakattara
	FORMAL	korasimasitara	korasimaseñ desitara
Alternative	INFORMAL	korasitari	korasanakattari
	FORMAL	korasimasitari	korasimaseñ desitari

INFORMAL AFFIRMATIVE INDICATIVE

Passive		korasareru
Potential		koraseru
Causative		korasaseru
Causative Pass.		korasaserareru
Honorific	I	okorasi ni naru
	II	okorasi nasaru
Humble	I	okorasi suru
	II	okorasi itasu

			AFFIRMATIVE	NEGATIVE
Indicative	**INFORMAL**		korobu	korobanai
	FORMAL		korobimasu	korobimaseñ
Imperative	**INFORMAL**	**I**	korobe	korobu na
		II	korobinasai	korobinasaru na
		III	koroñde kudasai	korobanai de kudasai
	FORMAL		okorobi nasaimase	okorobi nasaimasu na
Presumptive	**INFORMAL**	**I**	koroboo	korobumai
		II	korobu daroo	korobanai daroo
	FORMAL	**I**	korobimasyoo	korobimasumai
		II	korobu desyoo	korobanai desyoo
Provisional	**INFORMAL**		korobeba	korobanakereba
	FORMAL		korobimaseba	korobimaseñ nara
			korobimasureba	
Gerund	**INFORMAL**	**I**	koroñde	korobanai de
		II		korobanakute
	FORMAL		korobimasite	korobimaseñ de
Past Ind.	**INFORMAL**		koroñda	korobanakatta
	FORMAL		korobimasita	korobimaseñ desita
Past Presump.	**INFORMAL**		koroñdaroo	korobanakattaroo
			koroñda daroo	korobanakatta daroo
	FORMAL		korobimasitaroo	korobimaseñ desitaroo
			koroñda desyoo	korobanakatta desyoo
Conditional	**INFORMAL**		koroñdara	korobanakattara
	FORMAL		korobimasitara	korobimaseñ desitara
Alternative	**INFORMAL**		koroñdari	korobanakattari
	FORMAL		korobimasitari	korobimaseñ desitari

INFORMAL AFFIRMATIVE INDICATIVE

Passive		korobareru
Potential		koroberu
Causative		korobaseru
Causative Pass.		korobaserareru
Honorific	**I**	okorobi ni naru
	II	okorobi nasaru
Humble	**I**	
	II	

		AFFIRMATIVE	NEGATIVE
Indicative	**INFORMAL**	korosu	korosanai
	FORMAL	korosimasu	korosimaseñ
Imperative	**INFORMAL I**	korose	korosu na
	II	korosinasai	korosinasaru na
	III	korosite kudasai	korosanai de kudasai
	FORMAL	okorosi nasaimase	okorosi nasaimasu na
Presumptive	**INFORMAL I**	korosoo	korosumai
	II	korosu daroo	korosanai daroo
	FORMAL I	korosimasyoo	korosimasumai
	II	korosu desyoo	korosanai desyoo
Provisional	**INFORMAL**	koroseba	korosanakereba
	FORMAL	korosimaseba	korosimaseñ nara
		korosimasureba	
Gerund	**INFORMAL I**	korosite	korosanai de
	II		korosanakute
	FORMAL	korosimasite	korosimaseñ de
Past Ind.	**INFORMAL**	korosita	korosanakatta
	FORMAL	korosimasita	korosimaseñ desita
Past Presump.	**INFORMAL**	korositaroo	korosanakattaroo
		korosita daroo	korosanakatta daroo
	FORMAL	korosimasitaroo	korosimaseñ desitaroo
		korosita desyoo	korosanakatta desyoo
Conditional	**INFORMAL**	korositara	korosanakattara
	FORMAL	korosimasitara	korosimaseñ desitara
Alternative	**INFORMAL**	korositari	korosanakattari
	FORMAL	korosimasitari	korosimaseñ desitari

		INFORMAL AFFIRMATIVE INDICATIVE
Passive		korosareru
Potential		koroseru
Causative		korosaseru
Causative Pass.		korosaserareru

Honorific	**I**	okorosi ni naru
	II	okorosi nasaru
Humble	**I**	okorosi suru
	II	okorosi itasu

		AFFIRMATIVE	NEGATIVE
Indicative	**INFORMAL**	kosikakeru	kosikakenai
	FORMAL	kosikakemasu	kosikakemaseñ
Imperative	**INFORMAL I**	kosikakero	kosikakeru na
	II	kosikakenasai	kosikakenasaru na
	III	kosikakete kudasai	kosikakenai de kudasai
	FORMAL	okosikake nasaimase	okosikake nasaimasu na
Presumptive	**INFORMAL I**	kosikakeyoo	kosikakemai
	II	kosikakeru daroo	kosikakenai daroo
	FORMAL I	kosikakemasyoo	kosikakemasumai
	II	kosikakeru desyoo	kosikakenai desyoo
Provisional	**INFORMAL**	kosikakereba	kosikakenakereba
	FORMAL	kosikakemaseba	kosikakemaseñ nara
		kosikakemasureba	
Gerund	**INFORMAL I**	kosikakete	kosikakenai de
	II		kosikakenakute
	FORMAL	kosikakemasite	kosikakemaseñ de
Past Ind.	**INFORMAL**	kosikaketa	kosikakenakatta
	FORMAL	kosikakemasita	kosikakemaseñ desita
Past Presump.	**INFORMAL**	kosikaketaroo	kosikakenakattaroo
		kosikaketa daroo	kosikakenakatta daroo
	FORMAL	kosikakemasitaroo	kosikakemaseñ desitaroo
		kosikaketa desyoo	kosikakenakatta desyoo
Conditional	**INFORMAL**	kosikaketara	kosikakenakattara
	FORMAL	kosikakemasitara	kosikakemaseñ desitara
Alternative	**INFORMAL**	kosikaketari	kosikakenakattari
	FORMAL	kosikakemasitari	kosikakemaseñ desitari

		INFORMAL AFFIRMATIVE INDICATIVE
Passive		kosikakerareru
Potential		kosikakerareru
Causative		kosikakesaseru
Causative Pass.		kosikakesaserareru
Honorific	**I**	okosikake ni naru
	II	okosikake nasaru
Humble	**I**	
	II	

to make, to manufacture   TRANSITIVE

		AFFIRMATIVE	NEGATIVE
Indicative	**INFORMAL**	kosiraeru	kosiraenai
	FORMAL	kosiraemasu	kosiraemaseñ
Imperative	**INFORMAL I**	kosiraero	kosiraeru na
	II	kosiraenasai	kosiraenasaru na
	III	kosiraete kudasai	kosiraenai de kudasai
	FORMAL	okosirae nasaimase	okosirae nasaimasu na
Presumptive	**INFORMAL I**	kosiraeyoo	kosiraemai
	II	kosiraeru daroo	kosiraenai daroo
	FORMAL I	kosiraemasyoo	kosiraemasumai
	II	kosiraeru desyoo	kosiraenai desyoo
Provisional	**INFORMAL**	kosiraereba	kosiraenakereba
	FORMAL	kosiraemaseba	kosiraemaseñ nara
		kosiraemasureba	
Gerund	**INFORMAL I**	kosiraete	kosiraenai de
	II		kosiraenakute
	FORMAL	kosiraemasite	kosiraemaseñ de
Past Ind.	**INFORMAL**	kosiraeta	kosiraenakatta
	FORMAL	kosiraemasita	kosiraemaseñ desita
Past Presump.	**INFORMAL**	kosiraetaroo	kosiraenakattaroo
		kosiraeta daroo	kosiraenakatta daroo
	FORMAL	kosiraemasitaroo	kosiraemaseñ desitaroo
		kosiraeta desyoo	kosiraenakatta desyoo
Conditional	**INFORMAL**	kosiraetara	kosiraenakattara
	FORMAL	kosiraemasitara	kosiraemaseñ desitara
Alternative	**INFORMAL**	kosiraetari	kosiraenakattari
	FORMAL	kosiraemasitari	kosiraemaseñ desitari

INFORMAL AFFIRMATIVE INDICATIVE

Passive		kosiraerareru
Potential		kosiraerareru
Causative		kosiraesaseru
Causative Pass.		kosiraesaserareru

Honorific	**I**	okosirae ni naru
	II	okosirae nasaru
Humble	**I**	okosirae suru
	II	okosirae itasu

TRANSITIVE   *to cross, to pass, to surpass*

		AFFIRMATIVE	NEGATIVE
Indicative	INFORMAL	kosu	kosanai
	FORMAL	kosimasu	kosimaseñ
Imperative	INFORMAL I	kose	kosu na
	II	kosinasai	kosinasaru na
	III	kosite kudasai	kosanai de kudasai
	FORMAL	okosi nasaimase	okosi nasaimasu na
Presumptive	INFORMAL I	kosoo	kosumai
	II	kosu daroo	kosanai daroo
	FORMAL I	kosimasyoo	kosimasumai
	II	kosu desyoo	kosanai desyoo
Provisional	INFORMAL	koseba	kosanakereba
	FORMAL	kosimaseba	kosimaseñ nara
		kosimasureba	
Gerund	INFORMAL I	kosite	kosanai de
	II		kosanakute
	FORMAL	kosimasite	kosimaseñ de
Past Ind.	INFORMAL	kosita	kosanakatta
	FORMAL	kosimasita	kosimaseñ desita
Past Presump.	INFORMAL	kositaroo	kosanakattaroo
		kosita daroo	kosanakatta daroo
	FORMAL	kosimasitaroo	kosimaseñ desitaroo
		kosita desyoo	kosanakatta desyoo
Conditional	INFORMAL	kositara	kosanakattara
	FORMAL	kosimasitara	kosimaseñ desitara
Alternative	INFORMAL	kositari	kosanakattari
	FORMAL	kosimasitari	kosimaseñ desitari

INFORMAL AFFIRMATIVE INDICATIVE

Passive		kosareru
Potential		koseru
Causative		kosaseru
Causative Pass.		kosaserareru
Honorific	I	okosi ni naru
	II	okosi nasaru
Humble	I	
	II	

		AFFIRMATIVE	NEGATIVE
Indicative	**INFORMAL**	kotaeru	kotaenai
	FORMAL	kotaemasu	kotaemaseñ
Imperative	**INFORMAL I**	kotaero	kotaeru na
	II	kotaenasai	kotaenasaru na
	III	kotaete kudasai	kotaenai de kudasai
	FORMAL	okotae nasaimase	okotae nasaimasu na
Presumptive	**INFORMAL I**	kotaeyoo	kotaemai
	II	kotaeru daroo	kotaenai daroo
	FORMAL I	kotaemasyoo	kotaemasumai
	II	kotaeru desyoo	kotaenai desyoo
Provisional	**INFORMAL**	kotaereba	kotaenakereba
	FORMAL	kotaemaseba	kotaemaseñ nara
		kotaemasureba	
Gerund	**INFORMAL I**	kotaete	kotaenai de
	II		kotaenakute
	FORMAL	kotaemasite	kotaemaseñ de
Past Ind.	**INFORMAL**	kotaeta	kotaenakatta
	FORMAL	kotaemasita	kotaemaseñ desita
Past Presump.	**INFORMAL**	kotaetaroo	kotaenakattaroo
		kotaeta daroo	kotaenakatta daroo
	FORMAL	kotaemasitaroo	kotaemaseñ desitaroo
		kotaeta desyoo	kotaenakatta desyoo
Conditional	**INFORMAL**	kotaetara	kotaenakattara
	FORMAL	kotaemasitara	kotaemaseñ desitara
Alternative	**INFORMAL**	kotaetari	kotaenakattari
	FORMAL	kotaemasitari	kotaemaseñ desitari

INFORMAL AFFIRMATIVE INDICATIVE

Passive		kotaerareru
Potential		kotaerareru
Causative		kotaesaseru
Causative Pass.		kotaesaserareru
Honorific	**I**	okotae ni naru
	II	okotae nasaru
Humble	**I**	okotae suru
	II	okotae itasu

		AFFIRMATIVE	NEGATIVE
Indicative	**INFORMAL**	kotonaru	kotonaranai
	FORMAL	kotonarimasu	kotonarimaseñ
Imperative	**INFORMAL I**	kotonare	kotonaru na
	II		
	III	kotonatte kudasai	kotonaranai de kudasai
	FORMAL		
Presumptive	**INFORMAL I**	kotonaroo	kotonarumai
	II	kotonaru daroo	kotonaranai daroo
	FORMAL I	kotonarimasyoo	kotonarimasumai
	II	kotonaru desyoo	kotonaranai desyoo
Provisional	**INFORMAL**	kotonareba	kotonaranakereba
	FORMAL	kotonarimaseba	kotonarimaseñ nara
		kotonarimasureba	
Gerund	**INFORMAL I**	kotonatte	kotonaranai de
	II		kotonaranakute
	FORMAL	kotonarimasite	kotonarimaseñ de
Past Ind.	**INFORMAL**	kotonatta	kotonaranakatta
	FORMAL	kotonarimasita	kotonarimaseñ desita
Past Presump.	**INFORMAL**	kotonattaroo	kotonaranakattaroo
		kotonatta daroo	kotonaranakatta daroo
	FORMAL	kotonarimasitaroo	kotonarimaseñ desitaroo
		kotonatta desyoo	kotonaranakatta desyoo
Conditional	**INFORMAL**	kotonattara	kotonaranakattara
	FORMAL	kotonarimasitara	kotonarimaseñ desitara
Alternative	**INFORMAL**	kotonattari	kotonaranakattari
	FORMAL	kotonarimasitari	kotonarimaseñ desitari

INFORMAL AFFIRMATIVE INDICATIVE

Passive		
Potential		
Causative	kotonaraseru	
Causative Pass.	kotonaraserareru	
Honorific	**I**	
	II	
Humble	**I**	
	II	

		AFFIRMATIVE	NEGATIVE
Indicative	**INFORMAL**	kotowaru	kotowaranai
	FORMAL	kotowarimasu	kotowarimaseñ
Imperative	**INFORMAL I**	kotoware	kotowaru na
	II	kotowarinasai	kotowarinasaru na
	III	kotowatte kudasai	kotowaranai de kudasai
	FORMAL	okotowari nasaimase	okotowari nasaimasu na
Presumptive	**INFORMAL I**	kotowaroo	kotowarumai
	II	kotowaru daroo	kotowaranai daroo
	FORMAL I	kotowarimasyoo	kotowarimasumai
	II	kotowaru desyoo	kotowaranai desyoo
Provisional	**INFORMAL**	kotowareba	kotowaranakereba
	FORMAL	kotowarimaseba	kotowarimaseñ nara
		kotowarimasureba	
Gerund	**INFORMAL I**	kotowatte	kotowaranai de
	II		kotowaranakute
	FORMAL	kotowarimasite	kotowarimaseñ de
Past Ind.	**INFORMAL**	kotowatta	kotowaranakatta
	FORMAL	kotowarimasita	kotowarimaseñ desita
Past Presump.	**INFORMAL**	kotowattaroo	kotowaranakattaroo
		kotowatta daroo	kotowaranakatta daroo
	FORMAL	kotowarimasitaroo	kotowarimaseñ desitaroo
		kotowatta desyoo	kotowaranakatta desyoo
Conditional	**INFORMAL**	kotowattara	kotowaranakattara
	FORMAL	kotowarimasitara	kotowarimaseñ desitara
Alternative	**INFORMAL**	kotowattari	kotowaranakattari
	FORMAL	kotowarimasitari	kotowarimaseñ desitari

INFORMAL AFFIRMATIVE INDICATIVE

Passive		kotowarareru
Potential		kotowareru
Causative		kotowaraseru
Causative Pass.		kotowaraserareru

Honorific	**I**	okotowari ni naru
	II	okotowari nasaru
Humble	**I**	okotowari suru
	II	okotowari itasu

		AFFIRMATIVE	NEGATIVE
Indicative	**INFORMAL**	kowagaru	kowagaranai
	FORMAL	kowagarimasu	kowagarimaseñ
Imperative	**INFORMAL I**	kowagare	kowagaru na
	II	kowagarinasai	kowagarinasaru na
	III	kowagatte kudasai	kowagaranai de kudasai
	FORMAL	okowagari nasaimase	okowagari nasaimasu na
Presumptive	**INFORMAL I**	kowagaroo	kowagarumai
	II	kowagaru daroo	kowagaranai daroo
	FORMAL I	kowagarimasyoo	kowagarimasumai
	II	kowagaru desyoo	kowagaranai desyoo
Provisional	**INFORMAL**	kowagareba	kowagaranakereba
	FORMAL	kowagarimaseba	kowagarimaseñ nara
		kowagarimasureba	
Gerund	**INFORMAL I**	kowagatte	kowagaranai de
	II		kowagaranakute
	FORMAL	kowagarimasite	kowagarimaseñ de
Past Ind.	**INFORMAL**	kowagatta	kowagaranakatta
	FORMAL	kowagarimasita	kowagarimaseñ desita
Past Presump.	**INFORMAL**	kowagattaroo	kowagaranakattaroo
		kowagatta daroo	kowagaranakatta daroo
	FORMAL	kowagarimasitaroo	kowagarimaseñ desitaroo
		kowagatta desyoo	kowagaranakatta desyoo
Conditional	**INFORMAL**	kowagattara	kowagaranakattara
	FORMAL	kowagarimasitara	kowagarimaseñ desitara
Alternative	**INFORMAL**	kowagattari	kowagaranakattari
	FORMAL	kowagarimasitari	kowagarimaseñ desitari

INFORMAL AFFIRMATIVE INDICATIVE

Passive		kowagarareru
Potential		
Causative		kowagaraseru
Causative Pass.		kowagaraserareru
Honorific	**I**	okowagari ni naru
	II	okowagari nasaru
Humble	**I**	
	II	

		AFFIRMATIVE	NEGATIVE
Indicative	**INFORMAL**	kowareru	kowarenai
	FORMAL	kowaremasu	kowaremaseñ
Imperative	**INFORMAL I**	kowarero	kowareru na
	II		
	III		
	FORMAL		
Presumptive	**INFORMAL I**	kowareyoo	kowaremai
	II	kowareru daroo	kowarenai daroo
	FORMAL I	kowaremasyoo	kowaremasumai
	II	kowareru desyoo	kowarenai desyoo
Provisional	**INFORMAL**	kowarereba	kowarenakereba
	FORMAL	kowaremaseba	kowaremaseñ nara
Gerund	**INFORMAL I**	kowarete	kowarenai de
	II		kowarenakute
	FORMAL	kowaremasite	kowaremaseñ de
Past Ind.	**INFORMAL**	kowareta	kowarenakatta
	FORMAL	kowaremasita	kowaremaseñ desita
Past Presump.	**INFORMAL**	kowaretaroo	kowarenakattaroo
		kowareta daroo	kowarenakatta daroo
	FORMAL	kowaremasitaroo	kowaremaseñ desitaroo
		kowareta desyoo	kowarenakatta desyoo
Conditional	**INFORMAL**	kowaretara	kowarenakattara
	FORMAL	kowaremasitara	kowaremaseñ desitara
Alternative	**INFORMAL**	kowaretari	kowarenakattari
	FORMAL	kowaremasitari	kowaremaseñ desitari

INFORMAL AFFIRMATIVE INDICATIVE

Passive	
Potential	kowarerareru
Causative	*
Causative Pass.	*

Honorific	I
	II
Humble	I
	II

*See *kowas.u*, the transitive verb for 'to break.'

TRANSITIVE   *to smash*

		AFFIRMATIVE	NEGATIVE
Indicative	**INFORMAL**	kowasu	kowasanai
	FORMAL	kowasimasu	kowasimaseñ
Imperative	**INFORMAL I**	kowase	kowasu na
	II	kowasinasai	kowasinasaru na
	III	kowasite kudasai	kowasanai de kudasai
	FORMAL	okowasi nasaimase	okowasi nasaimasu na
Presumptive	**INFORMAL I**	kowasoo	kowasumai
	II	kowasu daroo	kowasanai daroo
	FORMAL I	kowasimasyoo	kowasimasumai
	II	kowasu desyoo	kowasanai desyoo
Provisional	**INFORMAL**	kowaseba	kowasanakereba
	FORMAL	kowasimaseba	kowasimaseñ nara
		kowasimasureba	
Gerund	**INFORMAL I**	kowasite	kowasanai de
	II		kowasanakute
	FORMAL	kowasimasite	kowasimaseñ de
Past Ind.	**INFORMAL**	kowasita	kowasanakatta
	FORMAL	kowasimasita	kowasimaseñ desita
Past Presump.	**INFORMAL**	kowasitaroo	kowasanakattaroo
		kowasita daroo	kowasanakatta daroo
	FORMAL	kowasimasitaroo	kowasimaseñ desitaroo
		kowasita desyoo	kowasanakatta desyoo
Conditional	**INFORMAL**	kowasitara	kowasanakattara
	FORMAL	kowasimasitara	kowasimaseñ desitara
Alternative	**INFORMAL**	kowasitari	kowasanakattari
	FORMAL	kowasimasitari	kowasimaseñ desitari

INFORMAL AFFIRMATIVE INDICATIVE

Passive		kowasareru
Potential		kowaseru
Causative		kowasaseru
Causative Pass.		kowasaserareru

Honorific	**I**	okowasi ni naru
	II	okowasi nasaru
Humble	**I**	okowasi suru
	II	okowasi itasu

		AFFIRMATIVE	NEGATIVE
Indicative	**INFORMAL**	kozitukeru	kozitukenai
	FORMAL	kozitukemasu	kozitukemaseñ
Imperative	**INFORMAL I**	kozitukero	kozitukeru na
	II	kozitukenasai	kozitukenasaru na
	III	kozitukete kudasai	kozitukenai de kudasai
	FORMAL	okozituke nasaimase	okozituke nasaimasu na
Presumptive	**INFORMAL I**	kozitukeyoo	kozitukemai
	II	kozitukeru daroo	kozitukenai daroo
	FORMAL I	kozitukemasyoo	kozitukemasumai
	II	kozitukeru desyoo	kozitukenai desyoo
Provisional	**INFORMAL**	kozitukereba	kozitukenakereba
	FORMAL	kozitukemaseba	kozitukemaseñ nara
		kozitukemasureba	
Gerund	**INFORMAL I**	kozitukete	kozitukenai de
	II		kozitukenakute
	FORMAL	kozitukemasite	kozitukemaseñ de
Past Ind.	**INFORMAL**	kozituketa	kozitukenakatta
	FORMAL	kozitukemasita	kozitukemaseñ desita
Past Presump.	**INFORMAL**	kozituketaroo	kozitukenakattaroo
		kozituketa daroo	kozitukenakatta daroo
	FORMAL	kozitukemasitaroo	kozitukemaseñ desitaroo
		kozituketa desyoo	kozitukenakatta desyoo
Conditional	**INFORMAL**	kozituketara	kozitukenakattara
	FORMAL	kozitukemasitara	kozitukemaseñ desitara
Alternative	**INFORMAL**	kozituketari	kozitukenakattari
	FORMAL	kozitukemasitari	kozitukemaseñ desitari

INFORMAL AFFIRMATIVE INDICATIVE

Passive		kozitukerareru
Potential		kozitukerareru
Causative		kozitukesaseru
Causative Pass.		kozitukesaserareru

Honorific	**I**	okozituke ni naru
	II	okozituke nasaru
Humble	**I**	
	II	

		AFFIRMATIVE	NEGATIVE
Indicative	**INFORMAL**	kudaku	kudakanai
	FORMAL	kudakimasu	kudakimaseñ
Imperative	**INFORMAL I**	kudake	kudaku na
	II	kudakinasai	kudakinasaru na
	III	kudaite kudasai	kudakanai de kudasai
	FORMAL	okudaki nasaimase	okudaki nasaimasu na
Presumptive	**INFORMAL I**	kudakoo	kudakumai
	II	kudaku daroo	kudakanai daroo
	FORMAL I	kudakimasyoo	kudakimasumai
	II	kudaku desyoo	kudakanai desyoo
Provisional	**INFORMAL**	kudakeba	kudakanakereba
	FORMAL	kudakimaseba	kudakimaseñ nara
		kudakimasureba	
Gerund	**INFORMAL I**	kudaite	kudakanai de
	II		kudakanakute
	FORMAL	kudakimasite	kudakimaseñ de
Past Ind.	**INFORMAL**	kudaita	kudakanakatta
	FORMAL	kudakimasita	kudakimaseñ desita
Past Presump.	**INFORMAL**	kudaitaroo	kudakanakattaroo
		kudaita daroo	kudakanakatta daroo
	FORMAL	kudakimasitaroo	kudakimaseñ desitaroo
		kudaita desyoo	kudakanakatta desyoo
Conditional	**INFORMAL**	kudaitara	kudakanakattara
	FORMAL	kudakimasitara	kudakimaseñ desitara
Alternative	**INFORMAL**	kudaitari	kudakanakattari
	FORMAL	kudakimasitari	kudakimaseñ desitari

INFORMAL AFFIRMATIVE INDICATIVE

Passive		kudakareru
Potential		kudakeru
Causative		kudakaseru
Causative Pass.		kudakaserareru

Honorific	**I**	okudaki ni naru
	II	okudaki nasaru
Humble	**I**	okudaki suru
	II	okudaki itasu

kudasár.u

to give (to me)*   TRANSITIVE

kudasai

		AFFIRMATIVE	NEGATIVE
Indicative	**INFORMAL**	kudasaru	kudasaranai
	FORMAL	kudasaimasu	kudasaimaseñ
Imperative	**INFORMAL I**	kudasai	kudasaru na
	II		
	III		
	FORMAL	kudasaimase	kudasaimasu na
Presumptive	**INFORMAL I**	kudasaroo	kudasarumai
	II	kudasaru daroo	kudasaranai daroo
	FORMAL I	kudasaimasyoo	kudasaimasumai
	II	kudasaru desyoo	kudasaranai desyoo
Provisional	**INFORMAL**	kudasareba	kudasaranakereba
	FORMAL	kudasaimaseba	kudasaimaseñ nara
		kudasaimasureba	
Gerund	**INFORMAL I**	kudasatte	kudasaranai de
	II		kudasaranakute
	FORMAL	kudasaimasite	kudasaimaseñ de
Past Ind.	**INFORMAL**	kudasatta	kudasaranakatta
	FORMAL	kudasaimasita	kudasaimaseñ desita
Past Presump.	**INFORMAL**	kudasattaroo	kudasaranakattaroo
		kudasatta daroo	kudasaranakatta daroo
	FORMAL	kudasaimasitaroo	kudasaimaseñ desitaroo
		kudasatta desyoo	kudasaranakatta desyoo
Conditional	**INFORMAL**	kudasattara	kudasaranakattara
	FORMAL	kudasaimasitara	kudasaimaseñ desitara
Alternative	**INFORMAL**	kudasattari	kudasaranakattari
	FORMAL	kudasaimasitari	kudasaimaseñ desitari

INFORMAL AFFIRMATIVE INDICATIVE

Passive	
Potential	
Causative	
Causative Pass.	

Honorific	**I**	
	II	
Humble	**I**	
	II	

*Or to a member of my "in group."

256

TRANSITIVE   *to urge, to persuade*

		AFFIRMATIVE	NEGATIVE
Indicative	**INFORMAL**	kudoku	kudokanai
	FORMAL	kudokimasu	kudokimaseñ
Imperative	**INFORMAL I**	kudoke	kudoku na
	II	kudokinasai	kudokinasaru na
	III	kudoite kudasai	kudokanai de kudasai
	FORMAL	okudoki nasaimase	okudoki nasaimasu na
Presumptive	**INFORMAL I**	kudokoo	kudokumai
	II	kudoku daroo	kudokanai daroo
	FORMAL I	kudokimasyoo	kudokimasumai
	II	kudoku desyoo	kudokanai desyoo
Provisional	**INFORMAL**	kudokeba	kudokanakereba
	FORMAL	kudokimaseba	kudokimaseñ nara
		kudokimasureba	
Gerund	**INFORMAL I**	kudoite	kudokanai de
	II		kudokanakute
	FORMAL	kudokimasite	kudokimaseñ de
Past Ind.	**INFORMAL**	kudoita	kudokanakatta
	FORMAL	kudokimasita	kudokimaseñ desita
Past Presump.	**INFORMAL**	kudoitaroo	kudokanakattaroo
		kudoita daroo	kudokanakatta daroo
	FORMAL	kudokimasitaroo	kudokimaseñ desitaroo
		kudoita desyoo	kudokanakatta desyoo
Conditional	**INFORMAL**	kudoitara	kudokanakattara
	FORMAL	kudokimasitara	kudokimaseñ desitara
Alternative	**INFORMAL**	kudoitari	kudokanakattari
	FORMAL	kudokimasitari	kudokimaseñ desitari

INFORMAL AFFIRMATIVE INDICATIVE

Passive		kudokareru
Potential		kudokeru
Causative		kudokaseru
Causative Pass.		kudokaserareru
Honorific	**I**	okudoki ni naru
	II	okudoki nasaru
Humble	**I**	okudoki suru
	II	okudoki itasu

		AFFIRMATIVE	NEGATIVE
Indicative	**INFORMAL**	kuitigau	kuitigawanai
	FORMAL	kuitigaimasu	kuitigaimaseñ
Imperative	**INFORMAL I**	kuitigae	kuitigau na
	II	kuitigainasai	kuitigainasaru na
	III	kuitigatte kudasai	kuitigawanai de kudasai
	FORMAL	okuitigai nasaimase	okuitigai nasaimasu na
Presumptive	**INFORMAL I**	kuitigaoo	kuitigaumai
	II	kuitigau daroo	kuitigawanai daroo
	FORMAL I	kuitigaimasyoo	kuitigaimasumai
	II	kuitigau desyoo	kuitigawanai desyoo
Provisional	**INFORMAL**	kuitigaeba	kuitigawanakereba
	FORMAL	kuitigaimaseba	kuitigaimaseñ nara
		kuitigaimasureba	
Gerund	**INFORMAL I**	kuitigatte	kuitigawanai de
	II		kuitigawanakute
	FORMAL	kuitigaimasite	kuitigaimaseñ de
Past Ind.	**INFORMAL**	kuitigatta	kuitigawanakatta
	FORMAL	kuitigaimasita	kuitigaimaseñ desita
Past Presump.	**INFORMAL**	kuitigattaroo	kuitigawanakattaroo
		kuitigatta daroo	kuitigawanakatta daroo
	FORMAL	kuitigaimasitaroo	kuitigaimaseñ desitaroo
		kuitigatta desyoo	kuitigawanakatta desyoo
Conditional	**INFORMAL**	kuitigattara	kuitigawanakattara
	FORMAL	kuitigaimasitara	kuitigaimaseñ desitara
Alternative	**INFORMAL**	kuitigattari	kuitigawanakattari
	FORMAL	kuitigaimasitari	kuitigaimaseñ desitari

INFORMAL AFFIRMATIVE INDICATIVE

Passive	kuitigawareru
Potential	kuitigaeru
Causative	kuitigawaseru
Causative Pass.	kuitigawaserareru

Honorific	**I**	
	II	
Humble	**I**	
	II	

		AFFIRMATIVE	NEGATIVE
Indicative	**INFORMAL**	kumoru	kumoranai
	FORMAL	kumorimasu	kumorimaseñ
Imperative	**INFORMAL I**	kumore	kumoru na
	II		
	III		
	FORMAL		
Presumptive	**INFORMAL I**	kumoroo	kumorumai
	II	kumoru daroo	kumoranai daroo
	FORMAL I	kumorimasyoo	kumorimasumai
	II	kumoru desyoo	kumoranai desyoo
Provisional	**INFORMAL**	kumoreba	kumoranakereba
	FORMAL	kumorimaseba	kumorimaseñ nara
		kumorimasureba	
Gerund	**INFORMAL I**	kumotte	kumoranai de
	II		kumoranakute
	FORMAL	kumorimasite	kumorimaseñ de
Past Ind.	**INFORMAL**	kumotta	kumoranakatta
	FORMAL	kumorimasita	kumorimaseñ desita
Past Presump.	**INFORMAL**	kumottaroo	kumoranakattaroo
		kumotta daroo	kumoranakatta daroo
	FORMAL	kumorimasitaroo	kumorimaseñ desitaroo
		kumotta desyoo	kumoranakatta desyoo
Conditional	**INFORMAL**	kumottara	kumoranakattara
	FORMAL	kumorimasitara	kumorimaseñ desitara
Alternative	**INFORMAL**	kumottari	kumoranakattari
	FORMAL	kumorimasitari	kumorimaseñ desitari

INFORMAL AFFIRMATIVE INDICATIVE

Passive		kumorareru
Potential		
Causative		kumoraseru
Causative Pass.		kumoraserareru

Honorific	**I**	
	II	
Humble	**I**	
	II	

to put together, to unite   TRANSITIVE

		AFFIRMATIVE	NEGATIVE
Indicative	INFORMAL	kumu	kumanai
	FORMAL	kumimasu	kumimaseñ
Imperative	INFORMAL I	kume	kumu na
	II	kuminasai	kuminasaru na
	III	kuñde kudasai	kumanai de kudasai
	FORMAL	okumi nasaimase	okumi nasaimasu na
Presumptive	INFORMAL I	kumoo	kumumai
	II	kumu daroo	kumanai daroo
	FORMAL I	kumimasyoo	kumimasumai
	II	kumu desyoo	kumanai desyoo
Provisional	INFORMAL	kumeba	kumanakereba
	FORMAL	kumimaseba	kumimaseñ nara
		kumimasureba	
Gerund	INFORMAL I	kuñde	kumanai de
	II		kumanakute
	FORMAL	kumimasite	kumimaseñ de
Past Ind.	INFORMAL	kuñda	kumanakatta
	FORMAL	kumimasita	kumimaseñ desita
Past Presump.	INFORMAL	kuñdaroo	kumanakattaroo
		kuñda daroo	kumanakatta daroo
	FORMAL	kumimasitaroo	kumimaseñ desitaroo
		kuñda desyoo	kumanakatta desyoo
Conditional	INFORMAL	kuñdara	kumanakattara
	FORMAL	kumimasitara	kumimaseñ desitara
Alternative	INFORMAL	kuñdari	kumanakattari
	FORMAL	kumimasitari	kumimaseñ desitari

	INFORMAL AFFIRMATIVE INDICATIVE
Passive	kumareru
Potential	kumeru
Causative	kumaseru
Causative Pass.	kumaserareru

Honorific	I	okumi ni naru
	II	okumi nasaru
Humble	I	okumi suru
	II	okumi itasu

		AFFIRMATIVE	NEGATIVE
Indicative	**INFORMAL**	kuraberu	kurabenai
	FORMAL	kurabemasu	kurabemaseñ
Imperative	**INFORMAL I**	kurabero	kuraberu na
	II	kurabenasai	kurabenasaru na
	III	kurabete kudasai	kurabenai de kudasai
	FORMAL	okurabe nasaimase	okurabe nasaimasu na
Presumptive	**INFORMAL I**	kurabeyoo	kurabemai
	II	kuraberu daroo	kurabenai daroo
	FORMAL I	kurabemasyoo	kurabemasumai
	II	kuraberu desyoo	kurabenai desyoo
Provisional	**INFORMAL**	kurabereba	kurabenakereba
	FORMAL	kurabemaseba	kurabemaseñ nara
		kurabemasureba	
Gerund	**INFORMAL I**	kurabete	kurabenai de
	II		kurabenakute
	FORMAL	kurabemasite	kurabemaseñ de
Past Ind.	**INFORMAL**	kurabeta	kurabenakatta
	FORMAL	kurabemasita	kurabemaseñ desita
Past Presump.	**INFORMAL**	kurabetaroo	kurabenakattaroo
		kurabeta daroo	kurabenakatta daroo
	FORMAL	kurabemasitaroo	kurabemaseñ desitaroo
		kurabeta desyoo	kurabenakatta desyoo
Conditional	**INFORMAL**	kurabetara	kurabenakattara
	FORMAL	kurabemasitara	kurabemaseñ desitara
Alternative	**INFORMAL**	kurabetari	kurabenakattari
	FORMAL	kurabemasitari	kurabemaseñ desitari

INFORMAL AFFIRMATIVE INDICATIVE

Passive	kuraberareru
Potential	kuraberareru
Causative	kurabesaseru
Causative Pass.	kurabesaserareru

Honorific	**I**	okurabe ni naru
	II	okurabe nasaru
Humble	**I**	okurabe suru
	II	okurabe itasu

261

		AFFIRMATIVE	NEGATIVE
Indicative	**INFORMAL**	kuramu	kuramanai
	FORMAL	kuramimasu	kuramimaseñ
Imperative	**INFORMAL I**	kurame	kuramu na
	II		
	III		
	FORMAL		
Presumptive	**INFORMAL I**	kuramoo	kuramumai
	II	kuramu daroo	kuramanai daroo
	FORMAL I	kuramimasyoo	kuramimasumai
	II	kuramu desyoo	kuramanai desyoo
Provisional	**INFORMAL**	kurameba	kuramanakereba
	FORMAL	kuramimaseba	kuramimaseñ nara
		kuramimasureba	
Gerund	**INFORMAL I**	kurañde	kuramanai de
	II		kuramanakute
	FORMAL	kuramimasite	kuramimaseñ de
Past Ind.	**INFORMAL**	kurañda	kuramanakatta
	FORMAL	kuramimasita	kuramimaseñ desita
Past Presump.	**INFORMAL**	kurañdaroo	kuramanakattaroo
		kurañda daroo	kuramanakatta daroo
	FORMAL	kuramimasitaroo	kuramimaseñ desitaroo
		kurañda desyoo	kuramanakatta desyoo
Conditional	**INFORMAL**	kurañdara	kuramanakattara
	FORMAL	kuramimasitara	kuramimaseñ desitara
Alternative	**INFORMAL**	kurañdari	kuramanakattari
	FORMAL	kuramimasitari	kuramimaseñ desitari

		INFORMAL AFFIRMATIVE INDICATIVE
Passive		kuramareru
Potential		
Causative		kuramaseru
Causative Pass.		kuramaserareru

Honorific	**I**
	II
Humble	**I**
	II

		AFFIRMATIVE	NEGATIVE
Indicative	INFORMAL	kurasu	kurasanai
	FORMAL	kurasimasu	kurasimaseñ
Imperative	INFORMAL I	kurase	kurasu na
	II	kurasinasai	kurasinasaru na
	III	kurasite kudasai	kurasanai de kudasai
	FORMAL	okurasi nasaimase	okurasi nasaimasu na
Presumptive	INFORMAL I	kurasoo	kurasumai
	II	kurasu daroo	kurasanai daroo
	FORMAL I	kurasimasyoo	kurasimasumai
	II	kurasu desyoo	kurasanai desyoo
Provisional	INFORMAL	kuraseba	kurasanakereba
	FORMAL	kurasimaseba	kurasimaseñ nara
		kurasimasureba	
Gerund	INFORMAL I	kurasite	kurasanai de
	II		kurasanakute
	FORMAL	kurasimasite	kurasimaseñ de
Past Ind.	INFORMAL	kurasita	kurasanakatta
	FORMAL	kurasimasita	kurasimaseñ desita
Past Presump.	INFORMAL	kurasitaroo	kurasanakattaroo
		kurasita daroo	kurasanakatta daroo
	FORMAL	kurasimasitaroo	kurasimaseñ desitaroo
		kurasita desyoo	kurasanakatta desyoo
Conditional	INFORMAL	kurasitara	kurasanakattara
	FORMAL	kurasimasitara	kurasimaseñ desitara
Alternative	INFORMAL	kurasitari	kurasanakattari
	FORMAL	kurasimasitari	kurasimaseñ desitari

                        INFORMAL AFFIRMATIVE INDICATIVE

Passive	kurasareru
Potential	kuraseru
Causative	kurasaseru
Causative Pass.	kurasaserareru

Honorific	I	okurasi ni naru
	II	okurasi nasaru
Humble	I	
	II	

		AFFIRMATIVE	NEGATIVE
Indicative	**INFORMAL**	kureru	kurenai
	FORMAL	kuremasu	kuremaseñ
Imperative	**INFORMAL I**	kure	kureru na
	II	kurenasai	kurenasaru na
	III		
	FORMAL		
Presumptive	**INFORMAL I**	kureyoo	kuremai
	II	kureru daroo	kurenai daroo
	FORMAL I	kuremasyoo	kuremasumai
	II	kureru desyoo	kurenai desyoo
Provisional	**INFORMAL**	kurereba	kurenakereba
	FORMAL	kuremaseba	kuremaseñ nara
		kuremasureba	
Gerund	**INFORMAL I**	kurete	kurenai de
	II		kurenakute
	FORMAL	kuremasite	kuremaseñ de
Past Ind.	**INFORMAL**	kureta	kurenakatta
	FORMAL	kuremasita	kuremaseñ desita
Past Presump.	**INFORMAL**	kuretaroo	kurenakattaroo
		kureta daroo	kurenakatta daroo
	FORMAL	kuremasitaroo	kuremaseñ desitaroo
		kureta desyoo	kurenakatta desyoo
Conditional	**INFORMAL**	kuretara	kurenakattara
	FORMAL	kuremasitara	kuremaseñ desitara
Alternative	**INFORMAL**	kuretari	kurenakattari
	FORMAL	kuremasitari	kuremaseñ desitari

INFORMAL AFFIRMATIVE INDICATIVE

Passive	kurerareru
Potential	kurerareru
Causative	kuresaseru
Causative Pass.	kuresaserareru

Honorific	**I**	
	II	
Humble	**I**	
	II	

		AFFIRMATIVE	NEGATIVE
Indicative	**INFORMAL**	kureru	kurenai
	FORMAL	kuremasu	kuremaseñ
Imperative	**INFORMAL I**	kurero	kureru na
	II	kurenasai	kurenasaru na
	III	kurete kudasai	kurenai de kudasai
	FORMAL	okure nasaimase	okure nasaimasu na
Presumptive	**INFORMAL I**	kureyoo	kuremai
	II	kureru daroo	kurenai daroo
	FORMAL I	kuremasyoo	kuremasumai
	II	kureru desyoo	kurenai desyoo
Provisional	**INFORMAL**	kurereba	kurenakereba
	FORMAL	kuremaseba	kuremaseñ nara
		kuremasureba	
Gerund	**INFORMAL I**	kurete	kurenai de
	II		kurenakute
	FORMAL	kuremasite	kuremaseñ de
Past Ind.	**INFORMAL**	kureta	kurenakatta
	FORMAL	kuremasita	kuremaseñ desita
Past Presump.	**INFORMAL**	kuretaroo	kurenakattaroo
		kureta daroo	kurenakatta daroo
	FORMAL	kuremasitaroo	kuremaseñ desitaroo
		kureta desyoo	kurenakatta desyoo
Conditional	**INFORMAL**	kuretara	kurenakattara
	FORMAL	kuremasitara	kuremaseñ desitara
Alternative	**INFORMAL**	kuretari	kurenakattari
	FORMAL	kuremasitari	kuremaseñ desitari

		INFORMAL AFFIRMATIVE INDICATIVE
Passive		kurerareru
Potential		kurerareru
Causative		kuresaseru
Causative Pass.		kuresaserareru

Honorific	**I**	
	II	
Humble	**I**	
	II	

kurikaes.u   kurikaesi
to repeat (an action)   TRANSITIVE

		AFFIRMATIVE	NEGATIVE
Indicative	**INFORMAL**	kurikaesu	kurikaesanai
	FORMAL	kurikaesimasu	kurikaesimaseñ
Imperative	**INFORMAL I**	kurikaese	kurikaesu na
	II	kurikaesinasai	kurikaesinasaru na
	III	kurikaesite kudasai	kurikaesanai de kudasai
	FORMAL	okurikaesi nasaimase	okurikaesi nasaimasu na
Presumptive	**INFORMAL I**	kurikaesoo	kurikaesumai
	II	kurikaesu daroo	kurikaesanai daroo
	FORMAL I	kurikaesimasyoo	kurikaesimasumai
	II	kurikaesu desyoo	kurikaesanai desyoo
Provisional	**INFORMAL**	kurikaeseba	kurikaesanakereba
	FORMAL	kurikaesimaseba	kurikaesimaseñ nara
		kurikaesimasureba	
Gerund	**INFORMAL I**	kurikaesite	kurikaesanai de
	II		kurikaesanakute
	FORMAL	kurikaesimasite	kurikaesimaseñ de
Past Ind.	**INFORMAL**	kurikaesita	kurikaesanakatta
	FORMAL	kurikaesimasita	kurikaesimaseñ desita
Past Presump.	**INFORMAL**	kurikaesitaroo	kurikaesanakattaroo
		kurikaesita daroo	kurikaesanakatta daroo
	FORMAL	kurikaesimasitaroo	kurikaesimaseñ desitaroo
		kurikaesita desyoo	kurikaesanakatta desyoo
Conditional	**INFORMAL**	kurikaesitara	kurikaesanakattara
	FORMAL	kurikaesimasitara	kurikaesimaseñ desitara
Alternative	**INFORMAL**	kurikaesitari	kurikaesanakattari
	FORMAL	kurikaesimasitari	kurikaesimaseñ desitari

INFORMAL AFFIRMATIVE INDICATIVE

Passive		kurikaesareru
Potential		kurikaeseru
Causative		kurikaesaseru
Causative Pass.		kurikaesaserareru

Honorific	**I**	okurikaesi ni naru
	II	okurikaesi nasaru
Humble	**I**	
	II	

			AFFIRMATIVE	NEGATIVE
Indicative	**INFORMAL**		kuru	konai
	FORMAL		kimasu	kimaseñ
Imperative	**INFORMAL**	**I**	koi	kuru na
		II	kinasai	kinasaru na
		III	kite kudasai	konai de kudasai
	FORMAL		oide nasaimase	oide nasaimasu na
Presumptive	**INFORMAL**	**I**	koyoo	kurumai
		II	kuru daroo	konai daroo
	FORMAL	**I**	kimasyoo	kimasumai
		II	kuru desyoo	konai desyoo
Provisional	**INFORMAL**		kureba	konakereba
	FORMAL		kimaseba	kimaseñ nara
			kimasureba	
Gerund	**INFORMAL**	**I**	kite	konai de
		II		konakute
	FORMAL		kimasite	kimaseñ de
Past Ind.	**INFORMAL**		kita	konakatta
	FORMAL		kimasita	kimaseñ desita
Past Presump.	**INFORMAL**		kitaroo	konakattaroo
			kita daroo	konakatta daroo
	FORMAL		kimasitaroo	kimaseñ desitaroo
			kita desyoo	konakatta desyoo
Conditional	**INFORMAL**		kitara	konakattara
	FORMAL		kimasitara	kimaseñ desitara
Alternative	**INFORMAL**		kitari	konakattari
	FORMAL		kimasitari	kimaseñ desitari

INFORMAL AFFIRMATIVE INDICATIVE

Passive	korareru	
Potential	korareru	
Causative	kosaseru	
Causative Pass.	kosaserareru	

Honorific	irassyaru	$\begin{cases} \text{oide ni naru (I)} \\ \text{oide nasaru (II)} \end{cases}$
Humble	nairu	

to torment, to persecute   TRANSITIVE

		AFFIRMATIVE	NEGATIVE
Indicative	**INFORMAL**	kurusimeru	kurusimenai
	FORMAL	kurusimemasu	kurusimemaseñ
Imperative	**INFORMAL I**	kurusimero	kurusimeru na
	II	kurusimenasai	kurusimenasaru na
	III	kurusimete kudasai	kurusimenai de kudasai
	FORMAL	okurusime nasaimase	okurusime nasaimasu na
Presumptive	**INFORMAL I**	kurusimeyoo	kurusimemai
	II	kurusimeru daroo	kurusimenai daroo
	FORMAL I	kurusimemasyoo	kurusimemasumai
	II	kurusimeru desyoo	kurusimenai desyoo
Provisional	**INFORMAL**	kurusimereba	kurusimenakereba
	FORMAL	kurusimemaseba	kurusimemaseñ nara
		kurusimemasureba	
Gerund	**INFORMAL I**	kurusimete	kurusimenai de
	II		kurusimenakute
	FORMAL	kurusimemasite	kurusimemaseñ de
Past Ind.	**INFORMAL**	kurusimeta	kurusimenakatta
	FORMAL	kurusimemasita	kurusimemaseñ desita
Past Presump.	**INFORMAL**	kurusimetaroo	kurusimenakattaroo
		kurusimeta daroo	kurusimenakatta daroo
	FORMAL	kurusimemasitaroo	kurusimemaseñ desitaroo
		kurusimeta desyoo	kurusimenakatta desyoo
Conditional	**INFORMAL**	kurusimetara	kurusimenakattara
	FORMAL	kurusimemasitara	kurusimemaseñ desitara
Alternative	**INFORMAL**	kurusimetari	kurusimenakattari
	FORMAL	kurusimemasitari	kurusimemaseñ desitari

INFORMAL AFFIRMATIVE INDICATIVE

Passive		kurusimerareru
Potential		kurusimerareru
Causative		kurusimesaseru
Causative Pass.		kurusimesaserareru

Honorific	**I**	okurusime ni naru
	II	okurusime nasaru
Humble	**I**	okurusime suru
	II	okurusime itasu

		AFFIRMATIVE	NEGATIVE
Indicative	**INFORMAL**	kurusimu	kurusimanai
	FORMAL	kurusimimasu	kurusimimaseñ
Imperative	**INFORMAL I**	kurusime	kurusimu na
	II	kurusiminasai	kurusiminasaru na
	III	kurusiñde kudasai	kurusimanai de kudasai
	FORMAL	okurusimi nasaimase	okurusimi nasaimasu na
Presumptive	**INFORMAL I**	kurusimoo	kurusimumai
	II	kurusimu daroo	kurusimanai daroo
	FORMAL I	kurusimimasyoo	kurusimimasumai
	II	kurusimu desyoo	kurusimanai desyoo
Provisional	**INFORMAL**	kurusimeba	kurusimanakereba
	FORMAL	kurusimimaseba	kurusimimaseñ nara
		kurusimimasureba	
Gerund	**INFORMAL I**	kurusiñde	kurusimanai de
	II		kurusimanakute
	FORMAL	kurusimimasite	kurusimimaseñ de
Past Ind.	**INFORMAL**	kurusiñda	kurusimanakatta
	FORMAL	kurusimimasita	kurusimimaseñ desita
Past Presump.	**INFORMAL**	kurusiñdaroo	kurusimanakattaroo
		kurusiñda daroo	kurusimanakatta daroo
	FORMAL	kurusimimasitaroo	kurusimimaseñ desitaroo
		kurusiñda desyoo	kurusimanakatta desyoo
Conditional	**INFORMAL**	kurusiñdara	kurusimanakattara
	FORMAL	kurusimimasitara	kurusimimaseñ desitara
Alternative	**INFORMAL**	kurusiñdari	kurusimanakattari
	FORMAL	kurusimimasitari	kurusimimaseñ desitari

		INFORMAL AFFIRMATIVE INDICATIVE
Passive		kurusimareru
Potential		kurusimeru
Causative		kurusimaseru
Causative Pass.		kurusimaserareru

Honorific	**I**	okurusimi ni naru
	II	okurusimi nasaru
Humble	**I**	
	II	

to go mad, to get out of order (a machine)

		AFFIRMATIVE	NEGATIVE
Indicative	**INFORMAL**	kuruu	kuruwanai
	FORMAL	kuruimasu	kuruimaseñ
Imperative	**INFORMAL I**	kurue	kuruu na
	II	kuruinasai	kuruinasaru na
	III	kurutte kudasai	kuruwanai de kudasai
	FORMAL	okurui nasaimase	okurui nasaimasu na
Presumptive	**INFORMAL I**	kuruoo	kuruumai
	II	kuruu daroo	kuruwanai daroo
	FORMAL I	kuruimasyoo	kuruimasumai
	II	kuruu desyoo	kuruwanai desyoo
Provisional	**INFORMAL**	kurueba	kuruwanakereba
	FORMAL	kuruimaseba	kuruimaseñ nara
		kuruimasureba	
Gerund	**INFORMAL I**	kurutte	kuruwanai de
	II		kuruwanakute
	FORMAL	kuruimasite	kuruimaseñ de
Past Ind.	**INFORMAL**	kurutta	kuruwanakatta
	FORMAL	kuruimasita	kuruimaseñ desita
Past Presump.	**INFORMAL**	kuruttaroo	kuruwanakattaroo
		kurutta daroo	kuruwanakatta daroo
	FORMAL	kuruimasitaroo	kuruimaseñ desitaroo
		kurutta desyoo	kuruwanakatta desyoo
Conditional	**INFORMAL**	kuruttara	kuruwanakattara
	FORMAL	kuruimasitara	kuruimaseñ desitara
Alternative	**INFORMAL**	kuruttari	kuruwanakattari
	FORMAL	kuruimasitari	kuruimaseñ desitari

		INFORMAL AFFIRMATIVE INDICATIVE
Passive		kuruwareru
Potential		kurueru
Causative		kuruwaseru
Causative Pass.		kuruwaserareru

Honorific	**I**	okurui ni naru
	II	okurui nasaru
Humble	**I**	
	II	

		AFFIRMATIVE	NEGATIVE
Indicative	**INFORMAL**	kusaru	kusaranai
	FORMAL	kusarimasu	kusarimaseñ
Imperative	**INFORMAL I**	kusare	kusaru na
	II	kusarinasai	kusarinasaru na
	III	kusatte kudasai	kusaranai de kudasai
	FORMAL	okusari nasaimase	okusari nasaimasu na
Presumptive	**INFORMAL I**	kusaroo	kusarumai
	II	kusaru daroo	kusaranai daroo
	FORMAL I	kusarimasyoo	kusarimasumai
	II	kusaru desyoo	kusaranai desyoo
Provisional	**INFORMAL**	kusareba	kusaranakereba
	FORMAL	kusarimaseba	kusarimaseñ nara
		kusarimasureba	
Gerund	**INFORMAL I**	kusatte	kusaranai de
	II		kusaranakute
	FORMAL	kusarimasite	kusarimaseñ de
Past Ind.	**INFORMAL**	kusatta	kusaranakatta
	FORMAL	kusarimasita	kusarimaseñ desita
Past Presump.	**INFORMAL**	kusattaroo	kusaranakattaroo
		kusatta daroo	kusaranakatta daroo
	FORMAL	kusarimasitaroo	kusarimaseñ desitaroo
		kusatta desyoo	kusaranakatta desyoo
Conditional	**INFORMAL**	kusattara	kusaranakattara
	FORMAL	kusarimasitara	kusarimaseñ desitara
Alternative	**INFORMAL**	kusattari	kusaranakattari
	FORMAL	kusarimasitari	kusarimaseñ desitari

		INFORMAL AFFIRMATIVE INDICATIVE
Passive		kusarareru
Potential		kusareru
Causative		kusaraseru
Causative Pass.		kusaraserareru
Honorific	**I**	
	II	
Humble	**I**	
	II	

		AFFIRMATIVE	NEGATIVE
Indicative	INFORMAL	kuwadateru	kuwadatenai
	FORMAL	kuwadatemasu	kuwadatemaseñ
Imperative	INFORMAL I	kuwadatero	kuwadateru na
	II	kuwadatenasai	kuwadatenasaru na
	III	kuwadatete kudasai	kuwadatenai de kudasai
	FORMAL	okuwadate nasaimase	okuwadate nasaimasu na
Presumptive	INFORMAL I	kuwadateyoo	kuwadatemai
	II	kuwadateru daroo	kuwadatenai daroo
	FORMAL I	kuwadatemasyoo	kuwadatemasumai
	II	kuwadateru desyoo	kuwadatenai desyoo
Provisional	INFORMAL	kuwadatereba	kuwadatenakereba
	FORMAL	kuwadatemaseba	kuwadatemaseñ nara
		kuwadatemasureba	
Gerund	INFORMAL I	kuwadatete	kuwadatenai de
	II		kuwadatenakute
	FORMAL	kuwadatemasite	kuwadatemaseñ de
Past Ind.	INFORMAL	kuwadateta	kuwadatenakatta
	FORMAL	kuwadatemasita	kuwadatemaseñ desita
Past Presump.	INFORMAL	kuwadatetaroo	kuwadatenakattaroo
		kuwadateta daroo	kuwadatenakatta daroo
	FORMAL	kuwadatemasitaroo	kuwadatemaseñ desitaroo
		kuwadateta desyoo	kuwadatenakatta desyoo
Conditional	INFORMAL	kuwadatetara	kuwadatenakattara
	FORMAL	kuwadatemasitara	kuwadatemaseñ desitara
Alternative	INFORMAL	kuwadatetari	kuwadatenakattari
	FORMAL	kuwadatemasitari	kuwadatemaseñ desitari

INFORMAL AFFIRMATIVE INDICATIVE

Passive	kuwadaterareru
Potential	kuwadaterareru
Causative	kuwadatesaseru
Causative Pass.	kuwadatesaserareru

Honorific	I	okuwadate ni naru
	II	okuwadate nasaru
Humble	I	okuwadate suru
	II	okuwadate itasu

		AFFIRMATIVE	NEGATIVE
Indicative	**INFORMAL**	kuwaeru	kuwaenai
	FORMAL	kuwaemasu	kuwaemaseñ
Imperative	**INFORMAL I**	kuwaero	kuwaeru na
	II	kuwaenasai	kuwaenasaru na
	III	kuwaete kudasai	kuwaenai de kudasai
	FORMAL	okuwae nasaimase	okuwae nasaimasu na
Presumptive	**INFORMAL I**	kuwaeyoo	kuwaemai
	II	kuwaeru daroo	kuwaenai daroo
	FORMAL I	kuwaemasyoo	kuwaemasumai
	II	kuwaeru desyoo	kuwaenai desyoo
Provisional	**INFORMAL**	kuwaereba	kuwaenakereba
	FORMAL	kuwaemaseba	kuwaemaseñ nara
		kuwaemasureba	
Gerund	**INFORMAL I**	kuwaete	kuwaenai de
	II		kuwaenakute
	FORMAL	kuwaemasite	kuwaemaseñ de
Past Ind.	**INFORMAL**	kuwaeta	kuwaenakatta
	FORMAL	kuwaemasita	kuwaemaseñ desita
Past Presump.	**INFORMAL**	kuwaetaroo	kuwaenakattaroo
		kuwaeta daroo	kuwaenakatta daroo
	FORMAL	kuwaemasitaroo	kuwaemaseñ desitaroo
		kuwaeta desyoo	kuwaenakatta desyoo
Conditional	**INFORMAL**	kuwaetara	kuwaenakattara
	FORMAL	kuwaemasitara	kuwaemaseñ desitara
Alternative	**INFORMAL**	kuwaetari	kuwaenakattari
	FORMAL	kuwaemasitari	kuwaemaseñ desitari

		INFORMAL AFFIRMATIVE INDICATIVE
Passive		kuwaerareru
Potential		kuwaerareru
Causative		kuwaesaseru
Causative Pass.		kuwaesaserareru
Honorific	**I**	okuwae ni naru
	II	okuwae nasaru
Humble	**I**	okuwae suru
	II	okuwae itasu

		AFFIRMATIVE	NEGATIVE
Indicative	**INFORMAL**	kuzureru	kuzurenai
	FORMAL	kuzuremasu	kuzuremaseñ
Imperative	**INFORMAL I**	kuzurero	kuzureru na
	II		
	III		
	FORMAL		
Presumptive	**INFORMAL I**	kuzureyoo	kuzuremai
	II	kuzureru daroo	kuzurenai daroo
	FORMAL I	kuzuremasyoo	kuzuremasumai
	II	kuzureru desyoo	kuzurenai desyoo
Provisional	**INFORMAL**	kuzurereba	kuzurenakereba
	FORMAL	kuzuremaseba	kuzuremaseñ nara
		kuzuremasureba	
Gerund	**INFORMAL I**	kuzurete	kuzurenai de
	II		kuzurenakute
	FORMAL	kuzuremasite	kuzuremaseñ de
Past Ind.	**INFORMAL**	kuzureta	kuzurenakatta
	FORMAL	kuzuremasita	kuzuremaseñ desita
Past Presump.	**INFORMAL**	kuzuretaroo	kuzurenakattaroo
		kuzureta daroo	kuzurenakatta daroo
	FORMAL	kuzuremasitaroo	kuzuremaseñ desitaroo
		kuzureta desyoo	kuzurenakatta desyoo
Conditional	**INFORMAL**	kuzuretara	kuzurenakattara
	FORMAL	kuzuremasitara	kuzuremaseñ desitara
Alternative	**INFORMAL**	kuzuretari	kuzurenakattari
	FORMAL	kuzuremasitari	kuzuremaseñ desitari

INFORMAL AFFIRMATIVE INDICATIVE

Passive	kuzurerareru
Potential	
Causative	kuzuresaseru
Causative Pass.	kuzuresaserareru

Honorific	**I**	okuzure ni naru
	II	okuzure nasaru
Humble	**I**	
	II	

			AFFIRMATIVE	NEGATIVE
Indicative	**INFORMAL**		kuzusu	kuzusanai
	FORMAL		kuzusimasu	kuzusimaseñ
Imperative	**INFORMAL**	**I**	kuzuse	kuzusu na
		II	kuzusinasai	kuzusinasaru na
		III	kuzusite kudasai	kuzusanai de kudasai
	FORMAL		okuzusi nasaimase	okuzusi nasaimasu na
Presumptive	**INFORMAL**	**I**	kuzusoo	kuzusumai
		II	kuzusu daroo	kuzusanai daroo
	FORMAL	**I**	kuzusimasyoo	kuzusimasumai
		II	kuzusu desyoo	kuzusanai desyoo
Provisional	**INFORMAL**		kuzuseba	kuzusanakereba
	FORMAL		kuzusimaseba	kuzusimaseñ nara
			kuzusimasureba	
Gerund	**INFORMAL**	**I**	kuzusite	kuzusanai de
		II		kuzusanakute
	FORMAL		kuzusimasite	kuzusimaseñ de
Past Ind.	**INFORMAL**		kuzusita	kuzusanakatta
	FORMAL		kuzusimasita	kuzusimaseñ desita
Past Presump.	**INFORMAL**		kuzusitaroo	kuzusanakattaroo
			kuzusita daroo	kuzusanakatta daroo
	FORMAL		kuzusimasitaroo	kuzusimaseñ desitaroo
			kuzusita desyoo	kuzusanakatta desyoo
Conditional	**INFORMAL**		kuzusitara	kuzusanakattara
	FORMAL		kuzusimasitara	kuzusimaseñ desitara
Alternative	**INFORMAL**		kuzusitari	kuzusanakattari
	FORMAL		kuzusimasitari	kuzusimaseñ desitari

		INFORMAL AFFIRMATIVE INDICATIVE
Passive		kuzusareru
Potential		kuzuseru
Causative		kuzusaseru
Causative Pass.		kuzusaserareru
Honorific	**I**	okuzusi ni naru
	II	okuzusi nasaru
Humble	**I**	okuzusi suru
	II	okuzusi itasu

to turn a corner (transitive) *to bend* (intransitive)

		AFFIRMATIVE	NEGATIVE
Indicative	**INFORMAL**	magaru	magaranai
	FORMAL	magarimasu	magarimaseñ
Imperative	**INFORMAL I**	magare	magaru na
	II	magarinasai	magarinasaru na
	III	magatte kudasai	magaranai de kudasai
	FORMAL	omagari nasaimase	omagari nasaimasu na
Presumptive	**INFORMAL I**	magaroo	magarumai
	II	magaru daroo	magaranai daroo
	FORMAL I	magarimasyoo	magarimasumai
	II	magaru desyoo	magaranai desyoo
Provisional	**INFORMAL**	magareba	magaranakereba
	FORMAL	magarimaseba	magarimaseñ nara
		magarimasureba	
Gerund	**INFORMAL I**	magatte	magaranai de
	II		magaranakute
	FORMAL	magarimasite	magarimaseñ de
Past Ind.	**INFORMAL**	magatta	magaranakatta
	FORMAL	magarimasita	magarimaseñ desita
Past Presump.	**INFORMAL**	magattaroo	magaranakattaroo
		magatta daroo	magaranakatta daroo
	FORMAL	magarimasitaroo	magarimaseñ desitaroo
		magatta desyoo	magaranakatta desyoo
Conditional	**INFORMAL**	magattara	magaranakattara
	FORMAL	magarimasitara	magarimaseñ desitara
Alternative	**INFORMAL**	magattari	magaranakattari
	FORMAL	magarimasitari	magarimaseñ desitari

INFORMAL AFFIRMATIVE INDICATIVE

Passive		
Potential		magareru
Causative		magaraseru
Causative Pass.		magaraserareru

Honorific	**I**	omagari ni naru
	II	omagari nasaru
Humble	**I**	
	II	

276

		AFFIRMATIVE	NEGATIVE
Indicative	**INFORMAL**	mageru	magenai
	FORMAL	magemasu	magemaseñ
Imperative	**INFORMAL I**	magero	mageru na
	II	magenasai	magenasaru na
	III	magete kudasai	magenai de kudasai
	FORMAL	omage nasaimase	omage nasaimasu na
Presumptive	**INFORMAL I**	mageyoo	magemai
	II	mageru daroo	magenai daroo
	FORMAL I	magemasyoo	magemasumai
	II	mageru desyoo	magenai desyoo
Provisional	**INFORMAL**	magereba	magenakereba
	FORMAL	magemaseba	magemaseñ nara
		magemasureba	
Gerund	**INFORMAL I**	magete	magenai de
	II		magenakute
	FORMAL	magemasite	magemaseñ de
Past Ind.	**INFORMAL**	mageta	magenakatta
	FORMAL	magemasita	magemaseñ desita
Past Presump.	**INFORMAL**	magetaroo	magenakattaroo
		mageta daroo	magenakatta daroo
	FORMAL	magemasitaroo	magemaseñ desitaroo
		mageta desyoo	magenakatta desyoo
Conditional	**INFORMAL**	magetara	magenakattara
	FORMAL	magemasitara	magemaseñ desitara
Alternative	**INFORMAL**	magetari	magenakattari
	FORMAL	magemasitari	magemaseñ desitari

INFORMAL AFFIRMATIVE INDICATIVE

Passive		magerareru
Potential		magerareru
Causative		magesaseru
Causative Pass.		magesaserareru
Honorific	**I**	omage ni naru
	II	omage nasaru
Humble	**I**	omage suru
	II	omage itasu

to divert (one's attention), *to equivocate*   TRANSITIVE

			AFFIRMATIVE	NEGATIVE
Indicative	**INFORMAL**		magirasu	magirasanai
	FORMAL		magirasimasu	magirasimaseñ
Imperative	**INFORMAL I**		magirase	magirasu na
		II	magirasinasai	magirasinasaru na
		III	magirasite kudasai	magirasanai de kudasai
	FORMAL		omagirasi nasaimase	omagirasi nasaimasu na
Presumptive	**INFORMAL I**		magirasoo	magirasumai
		II	magirasu daroo	magirasanai daroo
	FORMAL	**I**	magirasimasyoo	magirasimasumai
		II	magirasu desyoo	magirasanai desyoo
Provisional	**INFORMAL**		magiraseba	magirasanakereba
	FORMAL		magirasimaseba	magirasimaseñ nara
			magirasimasureba	
Gerund	**INFORMAL I**		magirasite	magirasanai de
		II		magirasanakute
	FORMAL		magirasimasite	magirasimaseñ de
Past Ind.	**INFORMAL**		magirasita	magirasanakatta
	FORMAL		magirasimasita	magirasimaseñ desita
Past Presump.	**INFORMAL**		magirasitaroo	magirasanakattaroo
			magirasita daroo	magirasanakatta daroo
	FORMAL		magirasimasitaroo	magirasimaseñ desitaroo
			magirasita desyoo	magirasanakatta desyoo
Conditional	**INFORMAL**		magirasitara	magirasanakattara
	FORMAL		magirasimasitara	magirasimaseñ desitara
Alternative	**INFORMAL**		magirasitari	magirasanakattari
	FORMAL		magirasimasitari	magirasimaseñ desitari

		INFORMAL AFFIRMATIVE INDICATIVE
Passive		magirasareru
Potential		magiraseru
Causative		magirasaseru
Causative Pass.		magirasaserareru
Honorific	**I**	omagirasi ni naru
	II	omagirasi nasaru
Humble	**I**	omagirasi suru
	II	omagirasi itasu

		AFFIRMATIVE	NEGATIVE
Indicative	**INFORMAL**	mairu	mairanai
	FORMAL	mairimasu	mairimaseñ
Imperative	**INFORMAL I**	maire	mairu na
	II		
	III		
	FORMAL		
Presumptive	**INFORMAL I**	mairoo	mairumai
	II	mairu daroo	mairanai daroo
	FORMAL I	mairimasyoo	mairimasumai
	II	mairu desyoo	mairanai desyoo
Provisional	**INFORMAL**	maireba	mairanakereba
	FORMAL	mairimaseba	mairimaseñ nara
		mairimasureba	
Gerund	**INFORMAL I**	maitte	mairanai de
	II		mairanakute
	FORMAL	mairimasite	mairimaseñ de
Past Ind.	**INFORMAL**	maitta	mairanakatta
	FORMAL	mairimasita	mairimaseñ desita
Past Presump.	**INFORMAL**	maittaroo	mairanakattaroo
		maitta daroo	mairanakatta daroo
	FORMAL	mairimasitaroo	mairimaseñ desitaroo
		maitta desyoo	mairanakatta desyoo
Conditional	**INFORMAL**	maittara	mairanakattara
	FORMAL	mairimasitara	mairimaseñ desitara
Alternative	**INFORMAL**	maittari	mairanakattari
	FORMAL	mairimasitari	mairimaseñ desitari

INFORMAL AFFIRMATIVE INDICATIVE

Passive		
Potential		
Causative		mairaseru
Causative Pass.		mairaserareru
Honorific	**I**	
	II	
Humble	**I**	
	II	

		AFFIRMATIVE	NEGATIVE
Indicative	**INFORMAL**	makaseru	makasenai
	FORMAL	makasemasu	makasemaseñ
Imperative	**INFORMAL I**	makasero	makaseru na
	II	makasenasai	makasenasaru na
	III	makasete kudasai	makasenai de kudasai
	FORMAL	omakase nasaimase	omakase nasaimasu na
Presumptive	**INFORMAL I**	makaseyoo	makasemai
	II	makaseru daroo	makasenai daroo
	FORMAL I	makasemasyoo	makasemasumai
	II	makaseru desyoo	makasenai desyoo
Provisional	**INFORMAL**	makasereba	makasenakereba
	FORMAL	makasemaseba	makasemaseñ nara
		makasemasureba	
Gerund	**INFORMAL I**	makasete	makasenai de
	II		makasenakute
	FORMAL	makasemasite	makasemaseñ de
Past Ind.	**INFORMAL**	makaseta	makasenakatta
	FORMAL	makasemasita	makasemaseñ desita
Past Presump.	**INFORMAL**	makasetaroo	makasenakattaroo
		makaseta daroo	makasenakatta daroo
	FORMAL	makasemasitaroo	makasemaseñ desitaroo
		makaseta desyoo	makasenakatta desyoo
Conditional	**INFORMAL**	makasetara	makasenakattara
	FORMAL	makasemasitara	makasemaseñ desitara
Alternative	**INFORMAL**	makasetari	makasenakattari
	FORMAL	makasemasitari	makasemaseñ desitari

		INFORMAL AFFIRMATIVE INDICATIVE
Passive		makaserareru
Potential		makaserareru
Causative		makasesaseru
Causative Pass.		makasesaserareru

Honorific	**I**	omakase ni naru
	II	omakase nasaru
Humble	**I**	omakase suru
	II	omakase itasu

		AFFIRMATIVE	NEGATIVE
Indicative	**INFORMAL**	makasu	makasanai
	FORMAL	makasimasu	makasimaseñ
Imperative	**INFORMAL I**	makase	makasu na
	II	makasinasai	makasinasaru na
	III	makasite kudasai	makasanai de kudasai
	FORMAL	omakasi nasaimase	omakasi nasaimasu na
Presumptive	**INFORMAL I**	makasoo	makasumai
	II	makasu daroo	makasanai daroo
	FORMAL I	makasimasyoo	makasimasumai
	II	makasu desyoo	makasanai desyoo
Provisional	**INFORMAL**	makaseba	makasanakereba
	FORMAL	makasimaseba	makasimaseñ nara
		makasimasureba	
Gerund	**INFORMAL I**	makasite	makasanai de
	II		makasanakute
	FORMAL	makasimasite	makasimaseñ de
Past Ind.	**INFORMAL**	makasita	makasanakatta
	FORMAL	makasimasita	makasimaseñ desita
Past Presump.	**INFORMAL**	makasitaroo	makasanakattaroo
		makasita daroo	makasanakatta daroo
	FORMAL	makasimasitaroo	makasimaseñ desitaroo
		makasita desyoo	makasanakatta desyoo
Conditional	**INFORMAL**	makasitara	makasanakattara
	FORMAL	makasimasitara	makasimaseñ desitara
Alternative	**INFORMAL**	makasitari	makasanakattari
	FORMAL	makasimasitari	makasimaseñ desitari

		INFORMAL AFFIRMATIVE INDICATIVE
Passive		makasareru
Potential		makaseru
Causative		
Causative Pass.		
Honorific	**I**	omakasi ni naru
	II	omakasi nasaru
Humble	**I**	omakasi suru
	II	omakasi itasu

to be defeated, to be bested

		AFFIRMATIVE	NEGATIVE
Indicative	**INFORMAL**	makeru	makenai
	FORMAL	makemasu	makemaseñ
Imperative	**INFORMAL I**	makero	makeru na
	II	makenasai	makenasaru na
	III	makete kudasai	makenai de kudasai
	FORMAL	omake nasaimase	omake nasaimasu na
Presumptive	**INFORMAL I**	makeyoo	makemai
	II	makeru daroo	makenai daroo
	FORMAL I	makemasyoo	makemasumai
	II	makeru desyoo	makenai desyoo
Provisional	**INFORMAL**	makereba	makenakereba
	FORMAL	makemaseba	makemaseñ nara
		makemasureba	
Gerund	**INFORMAL I**	makete	makenai de
	II		makenakute
	FORMAL	makemasite	makemaseñ de
Past Ind.	**INFORMAL**	maketa	makenakatta
	FORMAL	makemasita	makemaseñ desita
Past Presump.	**INFORMAL**	maketaroo	makenakattaroo
		maketa daroo	makenakatta daroo
	FORMAL	makemasitaroo	makemaseñ desitaroo
		maketa desyoo	makenakatta desyoo
Conditional	**INFORMAL**	maketara	makenakattara
	FORMAL	makemasitara	makemaseñ desitara
Alternative	**INFORMAL**	maketari	makenakattari
	FORMAL	makemasitari	makemaseñ desitari

		INFORMAL AFFIRMATIVE INDICATIVE
Passive		makerareru
Potential		makerareru
Causative		makesaseru
Causative Pass.		makesaserareru
Honorific	**I**	omake ni naru
	II	omake nasaru
Humble	**I**	omake suru
	II	omake itasu

		AFFIRMATIVE	NEGATIVE
Indicative	**INFORMAL**	mamoru	mamoranai
	FORMAL	mamorimasu	mamorimaseñ
Imperative	**INFORMAL I**	mamore	mamoru na
	II	mamorinasai	mamorinasaru na
	III	mamotte kudasai	mamoranai de kudasai
	FORMAL	omamori nasaimase	omamori nasaimasu na
Presumptive	**INFORMAL I**	mamoroo	mamorumai
	II	mamoru daroo	mamoranai daroo
	FORMAL I	mamorimasyoo	mamorimasumai
	II	mamoru desyoo	mamoranai desyoo
Provisional	**INFORMAL**	mamoreba	mamoranakereba
	FORMAL	mamorimaseba	mamorimaseñ nara
		mamorimasureba	
Gerund	**INFORMAL I**	mamotte	mamoranai de
	II		mamoranakute
	FORMAL	mamorimasite	mamorimaseñ de
Past Ind.	**INFORMAL**	mamotta	mamoranakatta
	FORMAL	mamorimasita	mamorimaseñ desita
Past Presump.	**INFORMAL**	mamottaroo	mamoranakattaroo
		mamotta daroo	mamoranakatta daroo
	FORMAL	mamorimasitaroo	mamorimaseñ desitaroo
		mamotta desyoo	mamoranakatta desyoo
Conditional	**INFORMAL**	mamottara	mamoranakattara
	FORMAL	mamorimasitara	mamorimaseñ desitara
Alternative	**INFORMAL**	mamottari	mamoranakattari
	FORMAL	mamorimasitari	mamorimaseñ desitari

	INFORMAL AFFIRMATIVE INDICATIVE
Passive	mamorareru
Potential	mamoreru
Causative	mamoraseru
Causative Pass.	mamoraserareru

Honorific	**I**	omamori ni naru
	II	omamori nasaru
Humble	**I**	omamori suru
	II	omamori itasu

to learn, to study   TRANSITIVE

		AFFIRMATIVE	NEGATIVE
Indicative	INFORMAL	manabu	manabanai
	FORMAL	manabimasu	manabimaseñ
Imperative	INFORMAL I	manabe	manabu na
	II	manabinasai	manabinasaru na
	III	manañde kudasai	manabanai de kudasai
	FORMAL	omanabi nasaimase	omanabi nasaimasu na
Presumptive	INFORMAL I	manaboo	manabumai
	II	manabu daroo	manabanai daroo
	FORMAL I	manabimasyoo	manabimasumai
	II	manabu desyoo	manabanai desyoo
Provisional	INFORMAL	manabeba	manabanakereba
	FORMAL	manabimaseba	manabimaseñ nara
		manabimasureba	
Gerund	INFORMAL I	manañde	manabanai de
	II		manabanakute
	FORMAL	manabimasite	manabimaseñ de
Past Ind.	INFORMAL	manañda	manabanakatta
	FORMAL	manabimasita	manabimaseñ desita
Past Presump.	INFORMAL	manañdaroo	manabanakattaroo
		manañda daroo	manabanakatta daroo
	FORMAL	manabimasitaroo	manabimaseñ desitaroo
		manañda desyoo	manabanakatta desyoo
Conditional	INFORMAL	manañdara	manabanakattara
	FORMAL	manabimasitara	manabimaseñ desitara
Alternative	INFORMAL	manañdari	manabanakattari
	FORMAL	manabimasitari	manabimaseñ desitari

INFORMAL AFFIRMATIVE INDICATIVE

Passive		manabareru
Potential		manaberu
Causative		manabaseru
Causative Pass.		manabaserareru
Honorific	I	omanabi ni naru
	II	omanabi nasaru
Humble	I	omanabi suru
	II	omanabi itasu

		AFFIRMATIVE	NEGATIVE
Indicative	**INFORMAL**	maneku	manekanai
	FORMAL	manekimasu	manekimaseñ
Imperative	**INFORMAL I**	maneke	maneku na
	II	manekinasai	manekinasaru na
	III	maneite kudasai	manekanai de kudasai
	FORMAL	omaneki nasaimase	omaneki nasaimasu na
Presumptive	**INFORMAL I**	manekoo	manekumai
	II	maneku daroo	manekanai daroo
	FORMAL I	manekimasyoo	manekimasumai
	II	maneku desyoo	manekanai desyoo
Provisional	**INFORMAL**	manekeba	manekanakereba
	FORMAL	manekimaseba	manekimaseñ nara
		manekimasureba	
Gerund	**INFORMAL I**	maneite	manekanai de
	II		manekanakute
	FORMAL	manekimasite	manekimaseñ de
Past Ind.	**INFORMAL**	maneita	manekanakatta
	FORMAL	manekimasita	manekimaseñ desita
Past Presump.	**INFORMAL**	maneitaroo	manekanakattaroo
		maneita daroo	manekanakatta daroo
	FORMAL	manekimasitaroo	manekimaseñ desitaroo
		maneita desyoo	manekanakatta desyoo
Conditional	**INFORMAL**	maneitara	manekanakattara
	FORMAL	manekimasitara	manekimaseñ desitara
Alternative	**INFORMAL**	maneitari	manekanakattari
	FORMAL	manekimasitari	manekimaseñ desitari

INFORMAL AFFIRMATIVE INDICATIVE

Passive		manekareru
Potential		manekeru
Causative		manekaseru
Causative Pass.		manekaserareru
Honorific	**I**	omaneki ni naru
	II	omaneki nasaru
Humble	**I**	omaneki suru
	II	omaneki itasu

to make a mistake, to mistake one thing for another   TRANSITIVE

		AFFIRMATIVE	NEGATIVE
Indicative	**INFORMAL**	matigaeru	matigaenai
	FORMAL	matigaemasu	matigaemaseñ
Imperative	**INFORMAL I**	matigaero	matigaeru na
	II	matigaenasai	matigaenasaru na
	III	matigaete kudasai	matigaenai de kudasai
	FORMAL	omatigae nasaimase	omatigae nasaimasu na
Presumptive	**INFORMAL I**	matigaeyoo	matigaemai
	II	matigaeru daroo	matigaenai daroo
	FORMAL I	matigaemasyoo	matigaemasumai
	II	matigaeru desyoo	matigaenai desyoo
Provisional	**INFORMAL**	matigaereba	matigaenakereba
	FORMAL	matigaemaseba	matigaemaseñ nara
		matigaemasureba	
Gerund	**INFORMAL I**	matigaete	matigaenai de
	II		matigaenakute
	FORMAL	matigaemasite	matigaemaseñ de
Past Ind.	**INFORMAL**	matigaeta	matigaenakatta
	FORMAL	matigaemasita	matigaemaseñ desita
Past Presump.	**INFORMAL**	matigaetaroo	matigaenakattaroo
		matigaeta daroo	matigaenakatta daroo
	FORMAL	matigaemasitaroo	matigaemaseñ desitaroo
		matigaeta desyoo	matigaenakatta desyoo
Conditional	**INFORMAL**	matigaetara	matigaenakattara
	FORMAL	matigaemasitara	matigaemaseñ desitara
Alternative	**INFORMAL**	matigaetari	matigaenakattari
	FORMAL	matigaemasitari	matigaemaseñ desitari

		INFORMAL AFFIRMATIVE INDICATIVE
Passive		matigaerareru
Potential		matigaerareru
Causative		matigaesaseru
Causative Pass.		matigaesaserareru
Honorific	**I**	omatigae ni naru
	II	omatigae nasaru
Humble	**I**	
	II	

		AFFIRMATIVE	NEGATIVE
Indicative	**INFORMAL**	matigau	matigawanai
	FORMAL	matigaimasu	matigaimaseñ
Imperative	**INFORMAL I**		
	II		
	III		
	FORMAL		
Presumptive	**INFORMAL I**	matigaoo	matigaumai
	II	matigau daroo	matigawanai daroo
	FORMAL I	matigaimasyoo	matigaimasumai
	II	matigau desyoo	matigawanai desyoo
Provisional	**INFORMAL**	matigaeba	matigawanakereba
	FORMAL	matigaimaseba	matigaimaseñ nara
		matigaimasureba	
Gerund	**INFORMAL I**	matigatte	matigawanai de
	II		matigawanakute
	FORMAL	matigaimasite	matigaimaseñ de
Past Ind.	**INFORMAL**	matigatta	matigawanakatta
	FORMAL	matigaimasita	matigaimaseñ desita
Past Presump.	**INFORMAL**	matigattaroo	matigawanakattaroo
		matigatta daroo	matigawanakatta daroo
	FORMAL	matigaimasitaroo	matigaimaseñ desitaroo
		matigatta desyoo	matigawanakatta desyoo
Conditional	**INFORMAL**	matigattara	matigawanakattara
	FORMAL	matigaimasitara	matigaimaseñ desitara
Alternative	**INFORMAL**	matigattari	matigawanakattari
	FORMAL	matigaimasitari	matigaimaseñ desitari

	INFORMAL AFFIRMATIVE INDICATIVE
Passive	matigawareru
Potential	matigaeru
Causative	matigawaseru
Causative Pass.	matigawaserareru

Honorific	**I**	
	II	
Humble	**I**	
	II	

to settle (a dispute), *to arrange* (a matter), *to complete*　　TRANSITIVE

		AFFIRMATIVE	NEGATIVE
Indicative	**INFORMAL**	matomeru	matomenai
	FORMAL	matomemasu	matomemaseñ
Imperative	**INFORMAL I**	matomero	matomeru na
	II	matomenasai	matomenasaru na
	III	matomete kudasai	matomenai de kudasai
	FORMAL	omatome nasaimase	omatome nasaimasu na
Presumptive	**INFORMAL I**	matomeyoo	matomemai
	II	matomeru daroo	matomenai daroo
	FORMAL I	matomemasyoo	matomemasumai
	II	matomeru desyoo	matomenai desyoo
Provisional	**INFORMAL**	matomereba	matomenakereba
	FORMAL	matomemaseba	matomemaseñ nara
		matomemasureba	
Gerund	**INFORMAL I**	matomete	matomenai de
	II		matomenakute
	FORMAL	matomemasite	matomemaseñ de
Past Ind.	**INFORMAL**	matometa	matomenakatta
	FORMAL	matomemasita	matomemaseñ desita
Past Presump.	**INFORMAL**	matometaroo	matomenakattaroo
		matometa daroo	matomenakatta daroo
	FORMAL	matomemasitaroo	matomemaseñ desitaroo
		matometa desyoo	matomenakatta desyoo
Conditional	**INFORMAL**	matometara	matomenakattara
	FORMAL	matomemasitara	matomemaseñ desitara
Alternative	**INFORMAL**	matometari	matomenakattari
	FORMAL	matomemasitari	matomemaseñ desitari

INFORMAL AFFIRMATIVE INDICATIVE

Passive		matomerareru
Potential		matomerareru
Causative		matomesaseru
Causative Pass.		matomesaserareru

Honorific	**I**	omatome ni naru
	II	omatome nasaru
Humble	**I**	omatome suru
	II	omatome itasu

		AFFIRMATIVE	NEGATIVE
Indicative	**INFORMAL**	matu	matanai
	FORMAL	matimasu	matimaseñ
Imperative	**INFORMAL I**	mate	matu na
	II	matinasai	matinasaru na
	III	matte kudasai	matanai de kudasai
	FORMAL	omati nasaimase	omati nasaimasu na
Presumptive	**INFORMAL I**	matoo	matumai
	II	matu daroo	matanai daroo
	FORMAL I	matimasyoo	matimasumai
	II	matu desyoo	matanai desyoo
Provisional	**INFORMAL**	mateba	matanakereba
	FORMAL	matimaseba	matimaseñ nara
		matimasureba	
Gerund	**INFORMAL I**	matte	matanai de
	II		matanakute
	FORMAL	matimasite	matimaseñ de
Past Ind.	**INFORMAL**	matta	matanakatta
	FORMAL	matimasita	matimaseñ desita
Past Presump.	**INFORMAL**	mattaroo	matanakattaroo
		matta daroo	matanakatta daroo
	FORMAL	matimasitaroo	matimaseñ desitaroo
		matta desyoo	matanakatta desyoo
Conditional	**INFORMAL**	mattara	matanakattara
	FORMAL	matimasitara	matimaseñ desitara
Alternative	**INFORMAL**	mattari	matanakattari
	FORMAL	matimasitari	matimaseñ desitari

		INFORMAL AFFIRMATIVE INDICATIVE
Passive		matareru
Potential		materu
Causative		mataseru
Causative Pass.		mataserareru
Honorific	**I**	omati ni naru
	II	omati nasaru
Humble	**I**	omati suru
	II	omati itasu

		AFFIRMATIVE	**NEGATIVE**
Indicative	**INFORMAL**	maturu	maturanai
	FORMAL	maturimasu	maturimaseñ
Imperative	**INFORMAL I**	mature	maturu na
	II	maturinasai	maturinasaru na
	III	matutte kudasai	maturanai de kudasai
	FORMAL	omaturi nasaimase	omaturi nasaimasu na
Presumptive	**INFORMAL I**	maturoo	maturumai
	II	maturu daroo	maturanai daroo
	FORMAL I	maturimasyoo	maturimasumai
	II	maturu desyoo	maturanai desyoo
Provisional	**INFORMAL**	matureba	maturanakereba
	FORMAL	maturimaseba	maturimaseñ nara
		maturimasureba	
Gerund	**INFORMAL I**	matutte	maturanai de
	II		maturanakute
	FORMAL	maturimasite	maturimaseñ de
Past Ind.	**INFORMAL**	rnatutta	maturanakatta
	FORMAL	maturimasita	maturimaseñ desita
Past Presump.	**INFORMAL**	matuttaroo	maturanakattaroo
		matutta daroo	maturanakatta daroo
	FORMAL	maturimasitaroo	maturimaseñ desitaroo
		matutta desyoo	maturanakatta desyoo
Conditional	**INFORMAL**	matuttara	maturanakattara
	FORMAL	maturimasitara	maturimaseñ desitara
Alternative	**INFORMAL**	matuttari	maturanakattari
	FORMAL	maturimasitari	maturimaseñ desitari

		INFORMAL AFFIRMATIVE INDICATIVE
Passive		maturareru
Potential		matureru
Causative		maturaseru
Causative Pass.		maturaserareru
Honorific	**I**	omaturi ni naru
	II	omaturi nasaru
Humble	**I**	omaturi suru
	II	omaturi itasu

		AFFIRMATIVE	NEGATIVE
Indicative	**INFORMAL**	mayou	mayowanai
	FORMAL	mayoimasu	mayoimaseñ
Imperative	**INFORMAL I**	mayoe	mayou na
	II	mayoinasai	mayoinasaru na
	III	mayotte kudasai	mayowanai de kudasai
	FORMAL	omayoi nasaimase	omayoi nasaimasu na
Presumptive	**INFORMAL I**	mayooo	mayoumai
	II	mayou daroo	mayowanai daroo
	FORMAL I	mayoimasyoo	mayoimasumai
	II	mayou desyoo	mayowanai desyoo
Provisional	**INFORMAL**	mayoeba	mayowanakereba
	FORMAL	mayoimaseba	mayoimaseñ nara
		mayoimasureba	
Gerund	**INFORMAL I**	mayotte	mayowanai de
	II		mayowanakute
	FORMAL	mayoimasite	mayoimaseñ de
Past Ind.	**INFORMAL**	mayotta	mayowanakatta
	FORMAL	mayoimasita	mayoimaseñ desita
Past Presump.	**INFORMAL**	mayottaroo	mayowanakattaroo
		mayotta daroo	mayowanakatta daroo
	FORMAL	mayoimasitaroo	mayoimaseñ desitaroo
		mayotta desyoo	mayowanakatta desyoo
Conditional	**INFORMAL**	mayottara	mayowanakattara
	FORMAL	mayoimasitara	mayoimaseñ desitara
Alternative	**INFORMAL**	mayottari	mayowanakattari
	FORMAL	mayoimasitari	mayoimaseñ desitari

		INFORMAL AFFIRMATIVE INDICATIVE
Passive		mayowareru
Potential		mayoeru
Causative		mayowaseru
Causative Pass.		mayowaserareru
Honorific	**I**	omayoi ni naru
	II	omayoi nasaru
Humble	**I**	
	II	

		AFFIRMATIVE	**NEGATIVE**
Indicative	**INFORMAL**	mazeru	mazenai
	FORMAL	mazemasu	mazemaseñ
Imperative	**INFORMAL I**	mazero	mazeru na
	II	mazenasai	mazenasaru na
	III	mazete kudasai	mazenai de kudasai
	FORMAL	omaze nasaimase	omaze nasaimasu na
Presumptive	**INFORMAL I**	mazeyoo	mazemai
	II	mazeru daroo	mazenai daroo
	FORMAL I	mazemasyoo	mazemasumai
	II	mazeru desyoo	mazenai desyoo
Provisional	**INFORMAL**	mazereba	mazenakereba
	FORMAL	mazemaseba	mazemaseñ nara
		mazemasureba	
Gerund	**INFORMAL I**	mazete	mazenai de
	II		mazenakute
	FORMAL	mazemasite	mazemaseñ de
Past Ind.	**INFORMAL**	mazeta	mazenakatta
	FORMAL	mazemasita	mazemaseñ desita
Past Presump.	**INFORMAL**	mazetaroo	mazenakattaroo
		mazeta daroo	mazenakatta daroo
	FORMAL	mazemasitaroo	mazemaseñ desitaroo
		mazeta desyoo	mazenakatta desyoo
Conditional	**INFORMAL**	mazetara	mazenakattara
	FORMAL	mazemasitara	mazemaseñ desitara
Alternative	**INFORMAL**	mazetari	mazenakattari
	FORMAL	mazemasitari	mazemaseñ desitari

INFORMAL AFFIRMATIVE INDICATIVE

Passive		mazerareru
Potential		mazerareru
Causative		mazesaseru
Causative Pass.		mazesaserareru

Honorific	**I**	omaze ni naru
	II	omaze nasaru
Humble	**I**	omaze suru
	II	omaze itasu

		AFFIRMATIVE	NEGATIVE
Indicative	**INFORMAL**	maziru	maziranai
	FORMAL	mazirimasu	mazirimaseñ
Imperative	**INFORMAL I**	mazire	maziru na
	II	mazirinasai	mazirinasaru na
	III	mazitte kudasai	maziranai de kudasai
	FORMAL	omaziri nasaimase	omaziri nasaimasu na
Presumptive	**INFORMAL I**	maziroo	mazirumai
	II	maziru daroo	maziranai daroo
	FORMAL I	mazirimasyoo	mazirimasumai
	II	maziru desyoo	maziranai desyoo
Provisional	**INFORMAL**	mazireba	maziranakereba
	FORMAL	mazirimaseba	mazirimaseñ nara
		mazirimasureba	
Gerund	**INFORMAL I**	mazitte	maziranai de
	II		maziranakute
	FORMAL	mazirimasite	mazirimaseñ de
Past Ind.	**INFORMAL**	mazitta	maziranakatta
	FORMAL	mazirimasita	mazirimaseñ desita
Past Presump.	**INFORMAL**	mazittaroo	maziranakattaroo
		mazitta daroo	maziranakatta daroo
	FORMAL	mazirimasitaroo	mazirimaseñ desitaroo
		mazitta desyoo	maziranakatta desyoo
Conditional	**INFORMAL**	mazittara	maziranakattara
	FORMAL	mazirimasitara	mazirimaseñ desitara
Alternative	**INFORMAL**	mazittari	maziranakattari
	FORMAL	mazirimasitari	mazirimaseñ desitari

		INFORMAL AFFIRMATIVE INDICATIVE
Passive		mazirareru
Potential		mazireru
Causative		maziraseru
Causative Pass.		maziraserareru
Honorific	**I**	omaziri ni naru
	II	omaziri nasaru
Humble	**I**	
	II	

		AFFIRMATIVE	NEGATIVE
Indicative	**INFORMAL**	mesiagaru	mesiagaranai
	FORMAL	mesiagarimasu	mesiagarimaseñ
Imperative	**INFORMAL I**	mesiagare	
	II		mesiagarinasaru na
	III	mesiagatte kudasai	mesiagaranai de kudasai
	FORMAL	omesiagari nasaimase	omesiagari nasaimasu na
Presumptive	**INFORMAL I**	mesiagaroo	mesiagarumai
	II	mesiagaru daroo	mesiagaranai daroo
	FORMAL I	mesiagarimasyoo	mesiagarimasumai
	II	mesiagaru desyoo	mesiagaranai desyoo
Provisional	**INFORMAL**	mesiagareba	mesiagaranakereba
	FORMAL	mesiagarimaseba	mesiagarimaseñ nara
		mesiagarimasureba	
Gerund	**INFORMAL I**	mesiagatte	mesiagaranai de
	II		mesiagaranakute
	FORMAL	mesiagarimasite	mesiagarimaseñ de
Past Ind.	**INFORMAL**	mesiagatta	mesiagaranakatta
	FORMAL	mesiagarimasita	mesiagarimaseñ desita
Past Presump.	**INFORMAL**	mesiagattaroo	mesiagaranakattaroo
		mesiagatta daroo	mesiagaranakatta daroo
	FORMAL	mesiagarimasitaroo	mesiagarimaseñ desitaroo
		mesiagatta desyoo	mesiagaranakatta desyoo
Conditional	**INFORMAL**	mesiagattara	mesiagaranakattara
	FORMAL	mesiagarimasitara	mesiagarimaseñ desitara
Alternative	**INFORMAL**	mesiagattari	mesiagaranakattari
	FORMAL	mesiagarimasitari	mesiagarimaseñ desitari

INFORMAL AFFIRMATIVE INDICATIVE

Passive		mesiagarareru
Potential		mesiagareru
Causative		
Causative Pass.		mesiagaraserareru

Honorific	**I**	omesiagari ni naru
	II	omesiagari nasaru
Humble	**I**	
	II	

		AFFIRMATIVE	NEGATIVE
Indicative	**INFORMAL**	mieru	mienai
	FORMAL	miemasu	miemaseñ
Imperative	**INFORMAL I**		
	II		
	III		
	FORMAL		
Presumptive	**INFORMAL I**	mieyoo	miemai
	II	mieru daroo	mienai daroo
	FORMAL I	miemasyoo	miemasumai
	II	mieru desyoo	mienai desyoo
Provisional	**INFORMAL**	miereba	mienakereba
	FORMAL	miemaseba	miemaseñ nara
		miemasureba	
Gerund	**INFORMAL I**	miete	mienai de
	II		mienakute
	FORMAL	miemasite	miemaseñ de
Past Ind.	**INFORMAL**	mieta	mienakatta
	FORMAL	miemasita	miemaseñ desita
Past Presump.	**INFORMAL**	mietaroo	mienakattaroo
		mieta daroo	mienakatta daroo
	FORMAL	miemasitaroo	miemaseñ desitaroo
		mieta desyoo	mienakatta desyoo
Conditional	**INFORMAL**	mietara	mienakattara
	FORMAL	miemasitara	miemaseñ desitara
Alternative	**INFORMAL**	mietari	mienakattari
	FORMAL	miemasitari	miemaseñ desitari

INFORMAL AFFIRMATIVE INDICATIVE

Passive		
Potential		
Causative		
Causative Pass.		

Honorific	**I**	omie ni naru
	II	omie nasaru
Humble	**I**	
	II	

		AFFIRMATIVE	NEGATIVE
Indicative	**INFORMAL**	migaku	migakanai
	FORMAL	migakimasu	migakimaseñ
Imperative	**INFORMAL I**	migake	migaku na
	II	migakinasai	migakinasaru na
	III	migaite kudasai	migakanai de kudasai
	FORMAL	omigaki nasaimase	omigaki nasaimasu na
Presumptive	**INFORMAL I**	migakoo	migakumai
	II	migaku daroo	migakanai daroo
	FORMAL I	migakimasyoo	migakimasumai
	II	migaku desyoo	migakanai desyoo
Provisional	**INFORMAL**	migakeba	migakanakereba
	FORMAL	migakimaseba	migakimaseñ nara
		migakimasureba	
Gerund	**INFORMAL I**	migaite	migakanai de
	II		migakanakute
	FORMAL	migakimasite	migakimaseñ de
Past Ind.	**INFORMAL**	migaita	migakanakatta
	FORMAL	migakimasita	migakimaseñ desita
Past Presump.	**INFORMAL**	migaitaroo	migakanakattaroo
		migaita daroo	migakanakatta daroo
	FORMAL	migakimasitaroo	migakimaseñ desitaroo
		migaita desyoo	migakanakatta desyoo
Conditional	**INFORMAL**	migaitara	migakanakattara
	FORMAL	migakimasitara	migakimaseñ desitara
Alternotive	**INFORMAL**	migaitari	migakanakattari
	FORMAL	migakimasitari	migakimaseñ desitari

	INFORMAL AFFIRMATIVE INDICATIVE
Passive	migakareru
Potential	migakeru
Causative	migakaseru
Causative Pass.	migakaserareru

Honorific	**I**	omigaki ni naru
	II	omigaki nasaru
Humble	**I**	omigaki suru
	II	omigaki itasu

		AFFIRMATIVE	NEGATIVE
Indicative	**INFORMAL**	miharu	miharanai
	FORMAL	miharimasu	miharimaseñ
Imperative	**INFORMAL I**	mihare	miharu na
	II	miharinasai	miharinasaru na
	III	mihatte kudasai	miharanai de kudasai
	FORMAL	omihari nasaimase	omihari nasaimasu na
Presumptive	**INFORMAL I**	miharoo	miharumai
	II	miharu daroo	miharanai daroo
	FORMAL I	miharimasyoo	miharimasumai
	II	miharu desyoo	miharanai desyoo
Provisional	**INFORMAL**	mihareba	miharanakereba
	FORMAL	miharimaseba	miharimaseñ nara
		miharimasureba	
Gerund	**INFORMAL I**	mihatte	miharanai de
	II		miharanakute
	FORMAL	miharimasite	miharimaseñ de
Past Ind.	**INFORMAL**	mihatta	miharanakatta
	FORMAL	miharimasita	miharimaseñ desita
Past Presump.	**INFORMAL**	mihattaroo	miharanakattaroo
		mihatta daroo	miharanakatta daroo
	FORMAL	miharimasitaroo	miharimaseñ desitaroo
		mihatta desyoo	miharanakatta desyoo
Conditional	**INFORMAL**	mihattara	miharanakattara
	FORMAL	miharimasitara	miharimaseñ desitara
Alternative	**INFORMAL**	mihattari	miharanakattari
	FORMAL	miharimasitari	miharimaseñ desitari

	INFORMAL AFFIRMATIVE INDICATIVE
Passive	miharareru
Potential	mihareru
Causative	miharaseru
Causative Pass.	miharaserareru

Honorific	**I**	omihari ni naru
	II	omihari nasaru
Humble	**I**	omihari suru
	II	omihari itasu

to look at again, to reconsider, to discover new merits   TRANSITIVE

		AFFIRMATIVE	NEGATIVE
Indicative	**INFORMAL**	minaosu	minaosanai
	FORMAL	minaosimasu	minaosimaseñ
Imperative	**INFORMAL I**	minaose	minaosu na
	II	minaosinasai	minaosinasaru na
	III	minaosite kudasai	minaosanai de kudasai
	FORMAL	ominaosi nasaimase	ominaosi nasaimasu na
Presumptive	**INFORMAL I**	minaosoo	minaosumai
	II	minaosu daroo	minaosanai daroo
	FORMAL I	minaosimasyoo	minaosimasumai
	II	minaosu desyoo	minaosanai desyoo
Provisional	**INFORMAL**	minaoseba	minaosanakereba
	FORMAL	minaosimaseba	minaosimaseñ nara
		minaosimasureba	
Gerund	**INFORMAL I**	minaosite	minaosanai de
	II		minaosanakute
	FORMAL	minaosimasite	minaosimaseñ de
Past Ind.	**INFORMAL**	minaosita	minaosanakatta
	FORMAL	minaosimasita	minaosimaseñ desita
Past Presump.	**INFORMAL**	minaositaroo	minaosanakattaroo
		minaosita daroo	minaosanakatta daroo
	FORMAL	minaosimasitaroo	minaosimaseñ desitaroo
		minaosita desyoo	minaosanakatta desyoo
Conditional	**INFORMAL**	minaositara	minaosanakattara
	FORMAL	minaosimasitara	minaosimaseñ desitara
Alternative	**INFORMAL**	minaositari	minaosanakattari
	FORMAL	minaosimasitari	minaosimaseñ desitari

INFORMAL AFFIRMATIVE INDICATIVE

Passive		minaosareru
Potential		minaoseru
Causative		minaosaseru
Causative Pass.		minaosaserareru

Honorific	**I**	ominaosi ni naru
	II	ominaosi nasaru
Humble	**I**	ominaosi suru
	II	ominaosi itasu

TRANSITIVE   *to regard as, to look upon as*

		AFFIRMATIVE	NEGATIVE
Indicative	**INFORMAL**	minasu	minasanai
	FORMAL	minasimasu	minasimaseñ
Imperative	**INFORMAL I**	minase	minasu na
	II	minasinasai	minasinasaru na
	III	minasite kudasai	minasanai de kudasai
	FORMAL	ominasi nasaimase	ominasi nasaimasu na
Presumptive	**INFORMAL I**	minasoo	minasumai
	II	minasu daroo	minasanai daroo
	FORMAL I	minasimasyoo	minasimasumai
	II	minasu desyoo	minasanai desyoo
Provisional	**INFORMAL**	minaseba	minasanakereba
	FORMAL	minasimaseba	minasimaseñ nara
		minasimasureba	
Gerund	**INFORMAL I**	minasite	minasanai de
	II		minasanakute
	FORMAL	minasimasite	minasimaseñ de
Past Ind.	**INFORMAL**	minasita	minasanakatta
	FORMAL	minasimasita	minasimaseñ desita
Past Presump.	**INFORMAL**	minasitaroo	minasanakattaroo
		minasita daroo	minasanakatta daroo
	FORMAL	minasimasitaroo	minasimaseñ desitaroo
		minasita desyoo	minasanakatta desyoo
Conditional	**INFORMAL**	minasitara	minasanakattara
	FORMAL	minasimasitara	minasimaseñ desitara
Alternative	**INFORMAL**	minasitari	minasanakattari
	FORMAL	minasimasitari	minasimaseñ desitari

INFORMAL AFFIRMATIVE INDICATIVE

Passive		minasareru
Potential		minaseru
Causative		minasaseru
Causative Pass.		minasaserareru

Honorific	**I**	ominasi ni naru
	II	ominasi nasaru
Humble	**I**	ominasi suru
	II	ominasi itasu

to overlook, to let pass   TRANSITIVE

		AFFIRMATIVE	**NEGATIVE**
Indicative	**INFORMAL**	minogasu	minogasanai
	FORMAL	minogasimasu	minogasimaseñ
Imperative	**INFORMAL I**	minogase	minogasu na
	II	minogasinasai	minogasinasaru na
	III	minogasite kudasai	minogasanai de kudasai
	FORMAL	ominogasi nasaimase	ominogasi nasaimasu na
Presumptive	**INFORMAL I**	minogasoo	minogasumai
	II	minogasu daroo	minogasanai daroo
	FORMAL I	minogasimasyoo	minogasimasumai
	II	minogasu desyoo	minogasanai desyoo
Provisional	**INFORMAL**	minogaseba	minogasanakereba
	FORMAL	minogasimaseba	minogasimaseñ nara
		minogasimasureba	
Gerund	**INFORMAL I**	minogasite	minogasanai de
	II		minogasanakute
	FORMAL	minogasimasite	minogasimaseñ de
Past Ind.	**INFORMAL**	minogasita	minogasanakatta
	FORMAL	minogasimasita	minogasimaseñ desita
Past Presump.	**INFORMAL**	minogasitaroo	minogasanakattaroo
		minogasita daroo	minogasanakatta daroo
	FORMAL	minogasimasitaroo	minogasimaseñ desitaroo
		minogasita desyoo	minogasanakatta desyoo
Conditional	**INFORMAL**	minogasitara	minogasanakattara
	FORMAL	minogasimasitara	minogasimaseñ desitara
Alternative	**INFORMAL**	minogasitari	minogasanakattari
	FORMAL	minogasimasitari	minogasimaseñ desitari

INFORMAL AFFIRMATIVE INDICATIVE

Passive		minogasareru
Potential		minogaseru
Causative		minogasaseru
Causative Pass.		minogasaserareru
Honorific	**I**	ominogasi ni naru
	II	ominogasi nasaru
Humble	**I**	ominogasi suru
	II	ominogasi itasu

		AFFIRMATIVE	NEGATIVE
Indicative	**INFORMAL**	minoru	minoranai
	FORMAL	minorimasu	minorimaseñ
Imperative	**INFORMAL I**	minore	minoru na
	II	minorinasai	minorinasaru na
	III	minotte kudasai	minoranai de kudasai
	FORMAL	ominori nasaimase	ominori nasaimasu na
Presumptive	**INFORMAL I**	minoroo	minorumai
	II	minoru daroo	minoranai daroo
	FORMAL I	minorimasyoo	minorimasumai
	II	minoru desyoo	minoranai desyoo
Provisional	**INFORMAL**	minoreba	minoranakereba
	FORMAL	minorimaseba	minorimaseñ nara
		minorimasureba	
Gerund	**INFORMAL I**	minotte	minoranai de
	II		minoranakute
	FORMAL	minorimasite	minorimaseñ de
Past Ind.	**INFORMAL**	minotta	minoranakatta
	FORMAL	minorimasita	minorimaseñ desita
Past Presump.	**INFORMAL**	minottaroo	minoranakattaroo
		minotta daroo	minoranakatta daroo
	FORMAL	minorimasitaroo	minorimaseñ desitaroo
		minotta desyoo	minoranakatta desyoo
Conditional	**INFORMAL**	minottara	minoranakattara
	FORMAL	minorimasitara	minorimaseñ desitara
Alternative	**INFORMAL**	minottari	minoranakattari
	FORMAL	minorimasitari	minorimaseñ desitari

		INFORMAL AFFIRMATIVE INDICATIVE
Passive		minorareru
Potential		minoreru
Causative		minoraseru
Causative Pass.		minoraserareru
Honorific	**I**	ominori ni naru
	II	ominori nasaru
Humble	**I**	
	II	

to see through, to have an insight into   TRANSITIVE

		AFFIRMATIVE	NEGATIVE
Indicative	**INFORMAL**	minuku	minukanai
	FORMAL	minukimasu	minukimaseñ
Imperative	**INFORMAL I**	minuke	minuku na
	II	minukinasai	minukinasaru na
	III	minuite kudasai	minukanai de kudasai
	FORMAL	ominuki nasaimase	ominuki nasaimasu na
Presumptive	**INFORMAL I**	minukoo	minukumai
	II	minuku daroo	minukanai daroo
	FORMAL I	minukimasyoo	minukimasumai
	II	minuku desyoo	minukanai desyoo
Provisional	**INFORMAL**	minukeba	minukanakereba
	FORMAL	minukimaseba	minukimaseñ nara
		minukimasureba	
Gerund	**INFORMAL I**	minuite	minukanai de
	II		minukanakute
	FORMAL	minukimasite	minukimaseñ de
Past Ind.	**INFORMAL**	minuita	minukanakatta
	FORMAL	minukimasita	minukimaseñ desita
Past Presump.	**INFORMAL**	minuitaroo	minukanakattaroo
		minuita daroo	minukanakatta daroo
	FORMAL	minukimasitaroo	minukimaseñ desitaroo
		minuita desyoo	minukanakatta desyoo
Conditional	**INFORMAL**	minuitara	minukanakattara
	FORMAL	minukimasitara	minukimaseñ desitara
Alternative	**INFORMAL**	minuitari	minukanakattari
	FORMAL	minukimasitari	minukimaseñ desitari

INFORMAL AFFIRMATIVE INDICATIVE

Passive		minukareru
Potential		minukeru
Causative		minukaseru
Causative Pass.		minukaserareru

Honorific	**I**	ominuki ni naru
	II	ominuki nasaru
Humble	**I**	ominuki suru
	II	ominuki itasu

		AFFIRMATIVE	NEGATIVE
Indicative	**INFORMAL**	miru	minai
	FORMAL	mimasu	mimaseñ
Imperative	**INFORMAL I**	miro	miru na
	II	minasai	minasaru na
	III	mite kudasai	minai de kudasai
	FORMAL	gorañ nasaimase	gorañ nasaimasu na
Presumptive	**INFORMAL I**	miyoo	mimai
	II	miru daroo	minai daroo
	FORMAL I	mimasyoo	mimasumai
	II	miru desyoo	minai desyoo
Provisional	**INFORMAL**	mireba	minakereba
	FORMAL	mimaseba	mimaseñ nara
		mimasureba	
Gerund	**INFORMAL I**	mite	minai de
	II		minakute
	FORMAL	mimasite	mimaseñ de
Past Ind.	**INFORMAL**	mita	minakatta
	FORMAL	mimasita	mimaseñ desita
Past Presump.	**INFORMAL**	mitaroo	minakattaroo
		mita daroo	minakatta daroo
	FORMAL	mimasitaroo	mimaseñ desitaroo
		mita desyoo	minakatta desyoo
Conditional	**INFORMAL**	mitara	minakattara
	FORMAL	mimasitara	mimaseñ desitara
Alternative	**INFORMAL**	mitari	minakattari
	FORMAL	mimasitari	mimaseñ desitari

	INFORMAL AFFIRMATIVE INDICATIVE
Passive	mirareru
Potential	mirareru*
Causative	misaseru
Causative Pass.	misaserareru

Honorific	**I**	gorañ ni naru
	II	gorañ nasaru
Humble	**I**	haikeñ suru
	II	haikeñ itasu

*This form means 'can be seen' in the sense that it exists at the time one wants to look at it. 'To be visible' is a separate verb *mieru*.

		AFFIRMATIVE	NEGATIVE
Indicative	**INFORMAL**	miseru	misenai
	FORMAL	misemasu	misemaseñ
Imperative	**INFORMAL I**	misero	miseru na
	II	misenasai	misenasaru na
	III	misete kudasai	misenai de kudasai
	FORMAL	omise nasaimase	omise nasaimasu na
Presumptive	**INFORMAL I**	miseyoo	misemai
	II	miseru daroo	misenai daroo
	FORMAL I	misemasyoo	misemasumai
	II	miseru desyoo	misenai desyoo
Provisional	**INFORMAL**	misereba	misenakereba
	FORMAL	misemaseba	misemaseñ nara
		misemasureba	
Gerund	**INFORMAL I**	misete	misenai de
	II		misenakute
	FORMAL	misemasite	misemaseñ de
Past Ind.	**INFORMAL**	miseta	misenakatta
	FORMAL	misemasita	misemaseñ desita
Past Presump.	**INFORMAL**	misetaroo	misenakattaroo
		miseta daroo	misenakatta daroo
	FORMAL	misemasitaroo	misemaseñ desitaroo
		miseta desyoo	misenakatta desyoo
Conditional	**INFORMAL**	misetara	misenakattara
	FORMAL	misemasitara	misemaseñ desitara
Alternative	**INFORMAL**	misetari	misenakattari
	FORMAL	misemasitari	misemaseñ desitari

INFORMAL AFFIRMATIVE INDICATIVE

Passive		miserareru
Potential		miserareru
Causative		misesaseru
Causative Pass.		misesaserareru

Honorific	**I**	omise ni naru
	II	omise nasaru
Humble		gorañ ni ireru

		AFFIRMATIVE	NEGATIVE
Indicative	**INFORMAL**	mitomeru	mitomenai
	FORMAL	mitomemasu	mitomemaseñ
Imperative	**INFORMAL I**	mitomero	mitomeru na
	II	mitomenasai	mitomenasaru na
	III	mitomete kudasai	mitomenai de kudasai
	FORMAL	omitome nasaimase	omitome nasaimasu na
Presumptive	**INFORMAL I**	mitomeyoo	mitomemai
	II	mitomeru daroo	mitomenai daroo
	FORMAL I	mitomemasyoo	mitomemasumai
	II	mitomeru desyoo	mitomenai desyoo
Provisional	**INFORMAL**	mitomereba	mitomenakereba
	FORMAL	mitomemaseba	mitomemaseñ nara
		mitomemasureba	
Gerund	**INFORMAL I**	mitomete	mitomenai de
	II		mitomenakute
	FORMAL	mitomemasite	mitomemaseñ de
Past Ind.	**INFORMAL**	mitometa	mitomenakatta
	FORMAL	mitomemasita	mitomemaseñ desita
Past Presump.	**INFORMAL**	mitometaroo	mitomenakattaroo
		mitometa daroo	mitomenakatta daroo
	FORMAL	mitomemasitaroo	mitomemaseñ desitaroo
		mitometa desyoo	mitomenakatta desyoo
Conditional	**INFORMAL**	mitometara	mitomenakattara
	FORMAL	mitomemasitara	mitomemaseñ desitara
Alternative	**INFORMAL**	mitometari	mitomenakattari
	FORMAL	mitomemasitari	mitomemaseñ desitari

INFORMAL AFFIRMATIVE INDICATIVE

Passive		mitomerareru
Potential		mitomerareru
Causative		mitomesaseru
Causative Pass.		mitomesaserareru
Honorific	**I**	omitome ni naru
	II	omitome nasaru
Humble	**I**	
	II	

		AFFIRMATIVE	NEGATIVE
Indicative	**INFORMAL**	mitukaru	mitukaranai
	FORMAL	mitukarimasu	mitukarimaseñ
Imperative	**INFORMAL I**		
	II		
	III		
	FORMAL		
Presumptive	**INFORMAL I**	mitukaroo	mitukarumai
	II	mitukaru daroo	mitukaranai daroo
	FORMAL I	mitukarimasyoo	mitukarimasumai
	II	mitukaru desyoo	mitukaranai desyoo
Provisional	**INFORMAL**	mitukareba	mitukaranakereba
	FORMAL	mitukarimaseba	mitukarimaseñ nara
		mitukarimasureba	
Gerund	**INFORMAL I**	mitukatte	mitukaranai de
	II		mitukaranakute
	FORMAL	mitukarimasite	mitukarimaseñ de
Past Ind.	**INFORMAL**	mitukatta	mitukaranakatta
	FORMAL	mitukarimasita	mitukarimaseñ desita
Past Presump.	**INFORMAL**	mitukattaroo	mitukaranakattaroo
		mitukatta daroo	mitukaranakatta daroo
	FORMAL	mitukarimasitaroo	mitukarimaseñ desitaroo
		mitukatta desyoo	mitukaranakatta desyoo
Conditional	**INFORMAL**	mitukattara	mitukaranakattara
	FORMAL	mitukarimasitara	mitukarimaseñ desitara
Alternative	**INFORMAL**	mitukattari	mitukaranakattari
	FORMAL	mitukarimasitari	mitukarimaseñ desitari

INFORMAL AFFIRMATIVE INDICATIVE

Passive		
Potential		
Causative		
Causative Pass.		

Honorific	**I**	
	II	
Humble	**I**	
	II	

		AFFIRMATIVE	NEGATIVE
Indicative	**INFORMAL**	mitukeru	mitukenai
	FORMAL	mitukemasu	mitukemaseñ
Imperative	**INFORMAL I**	mitukero	mitukeru na
	II	mitukenasai	mitukenasaru na
	III	mitukete kudasai	mitukenai de kudasai
	FORMAL	omituke nasaimase	omituke nasaimasu na
Presumptive	**INFORMAL I**	mitukeyoo	mitukemai
	II	mitukeru daroo	mitukenai daroo
	FORMAL I	mitukemasyoo	mitukemasumai
	II	mitukeru desyoo	mitukenai desyoo
Provisional	**INFORMAL**	mitukereba	mitukenakereba
	FORMAL	mitukemaseba	mitukemaseñ nara
		mitukemasureba	
Gerund	**INFORMAL I**	mitukete	mitukenai de
	II		mitukenakute
	FORMAL	mitukemasite	mitukemaseñ de
Past Ind.	**INFORMAL**	mituketa	mitukenakatta
	FORMAL	mitukemasita	mitukemaseñ desita
Past Presump.	**INFORMAL**	mituketaroo	mitukenakattaroo
		mituketa daroo	mitukenakatta daroo
	FORMAL	mitukemasitaroo	mitukemaseñ desitaroo
		mituketa desyoo	mitukenakatta desyoo
Conditional	**INFORMAL**	mituketara	mitukenakattara
	FORMAL	mitukemasitara	mitukemaseñ desitara
Alternative	**INFORMAL**	mituketari	mitukenakattari
	FORMAL	mitukemasitari	mitukemaseñ desitari

INFORMAL AFFIRMATIVE INDICATIVE

Passive		mitukerareru
Potential		mitukerareru
Causative		mitukesaseru
Causative Pass.		mitukesaserareru

Honorific	**I**	omituke ni naru
	II	omituke nasaru
Humble	**I**	
	II	

		AFFIRMATIVE	NEGATIVE
Indicative	**INFORMAL**	modoru	modoranai
	FORMAL	modorimasu	modorimaseñ
Imperative	**INFORMAL I**	modore	modoru na
	II	modorinasai	modorinasaru na
	III	modotte kudasai	modoranai de kudasai
	FORMAL	omodori nasaimase	omodori nasaimasu na
Presumptive	**INFORMAL I**	modoroo	modorumai
	II	modoru daroo	modoranai daroo
	FORMAL I	modorimasyoo	modorimasumai
	II	modoru desyoo	modoranai desyoo
Provisional	**INFORMAL**	modoreba	modoranakereba
	FORMAL	modorimaseba	modorimaseñ nara
		modorimasureba	
Gerund	**INFORMAL I**	modotte	modoranai de
	II		modoranakute
	FORMAL	modorimasite	modorimaseñ de
Past Ind.	**INFORMAL**	modotta	modoranakatta
	FORMAL	modorimasita	modorimaseñ desita
Past Presump.	**INFORMAL**	modottaroo	modoranakattaroo
		modotta daroo	modoranakatta daroo
	FORMAL	modorimasitaroo	modorimaseñ desitaroo
		modotta desyoo	modoranakatta desyoo
Conditional	**INFORMAL**	modottara	modoranakattara
	FORMAL	modorimasitara	modorimaseñ desitara
Alternative	**INFORMAL**	modottari	modoranakattari
	FORMAL	modorimasitari	modorimaseñ desitari

		INFORMAL AFFIRMATIVE INDICATIVE
Passive		modorareru
Potential		modoreru
Causative		modoraseru
Causative Pass.		modoraserareru
Honorific	**I**	omodori ni naru
	II	omodori nasaru
Humble	**I**	omodori suru
	II	omodori itasu

		AFFIRMATIVE	NEGATIVE
Indicative	**INFORMAL**	mookaru	mookaranai
	FORMAL	mookarimasu	mookarimaseñ
Imperative	**INFORMAL I**	mookare	mookaru na
	II		
	III		
	FORMAL		
Presumptive	**INFORMAL I**	mookaroo	mookarumai
	II	mookaru daroo	mookaranai daroo
	FORMAL I	mookarimasyoo	mookarimasumai
	II	mookaru desyoo	mookaranai desyoo
Provisional	**INFORMAL**	mookareba	mookaranakereba
	FORMAL	mookarimaseba	mookarimaseñ nara
		mookarimasureba	
Gerund	**INFORMAL I**	mookatte	mookaranai de
	II		mookaranakute
	FORMAL	mookarimasite	mookarimaseñ de
Past Ind.	**INFORMAL**	mookatta	mookaranakatta
	FORMAL	mookarimasita	mookarimaseñ desita
Past Presump.	**INFORMAL**	mookattaroo	mookaranakattaroo
		mookatta daroo	mookaranakatta daroo
	FORMAL	mookarimasitaroo	mookarimaseñ desitaroo
		mookatta desyoo	mookaranakatta desyoo
Conditional	**INFORMAL**	mookattara	mookaranakattara
	FORMAL	mookarimasitara	mookarimaseñ desitara
Alternative	**INFORMAL**	mookattari	mookaranakattari
	FORMAL	mookarimasitari	mookarimaseñ desitari

INFORMAL AFFIRMATIVE INDICATIVE

Passive		
Potential		
Causative		mookaraseru
Causative Pass.		mookaraserareru
Honorific	**I**	
	II	
Humble	**I**	
	II	

to profit, to make money   TRANSITIVE

		AFFIRMATIVE	NEGATIVE
Indicative	**INFORMAL**	mookeru	mookenai
	FORMAL	mookemasu	mookemaseñ
Imperative	**INFORMAL I**	mookero	mookeru na
	II	mookenasai	mookenasaru na
	III	mookete kudasai	mookenai de kudasai
	FORMAL	omooke nasaimase	omooke nasaimasu na
Presumptive	**INFORMAL I**	mookeyoo	mookemai
	II	mookeru daroo	mookenai daroo
	FORMAL I	mookemasyoo	mookemasumai
	II	mookeru desyoo	mookenai desyoo
Provisional	**INFORMAL**	mookereba	mookenakereba
	FORMAL	mookemaseba	mookemaseñ nara
		mookemasureba	
Gerund	**INFORMAL I**	mookete	mookenai de
	II		mookenakute
	FORMAL	mookemasite	mookemaseñ de
Past Ind.	**INFORMAL**	mooketa	mookenakatta
	FORMAL	mookemasita	mookemaseñ desita
Past Presump.	**INFORMAL**	mooketaroo	mookenakattaroo
		mooketa daroo	mookenakatta daroo
	FORMAL	mookemasitaroo	mookemaseñ desitaroo
		mooketa desyoo	mookenakatta desyoo
Conditional	**INFORMAL**	mooketara	mookenakattara
	FORMAL	mookemasitara	mookemaseñ desitara
Alternative	**INFORMAL**	mooketari	mookenakattari
	FORMAL	mookemasitari	mookemaseñ desitari

		INFORMAL AFFIRMATIVE INDICATIVE
Passive		mookerareru
Potential		mookerareru
Causative		mookesaseru
Causative Pass.		mookesaserareru

Honorific	**I**	omooke ni naru
	II	omooke nasaru
Humble	**I**	
	II	

		AFFIRMATIVE	NEGATIVE
Indicative	**INFORMAL**	morasu	morasanai
	FORMAL	morasimasu	morasimaseñ
Imperative	**INFORMAL I**	morase	morasu na
	II	morasinasai	morasinasaru na
	III	morasite kudasai	morasanai de kudasai
	FORMAL	omorasi nasaimase	omorasi nasaimasu na
Presumptive	**INFORMAL I**	morasoo	morasumai
	II	morasu daroo	morasanai daroo
	FORMAL I	morasimasyoo	morasimasumai
	II	morasu desyoo	morasanai desyoo
Provisional	**INFORMAL**	moraseba	morasanakereba
	FORMAL	morasimaseba	morasimaseñ nara
		morasimasureba	
Gerund	**INFORMAL I**	morasite	morasanai de
	II		morasanakute
	FORMAL	morasimasite	morasimaseñ de
Past Ind.	**INFORMAL**	morasita	morasanakatta
	FORMAL	morasimasita	morasimaseñ desita
Past Presump.	**INFORMAL**	morasitaroo	morasanakattaroo
		morasita daroo	morasanakatta daroo
	FORMAL	morasimasitaroo	morasimaseñ desitaroo
		morasita desyoo	morasanakatta desyoo
Conditional	**INFORMAL**	morasitara	morasanakattara
	FORMAL	morasimasitara	morasimaseñ desitara
Alternative	**INFORMAL**	morasitari	morasanakattari
	FORMAL	morasimasitari	morasimaseñ desitari

		INFORMAL AFFIRMATIVE INDICATIVE
Passive		morasareru
Potential		moraseru
Causative		morasaseru
Causative Pass.		morasaserareru
Honorific	**I**	omorasi ni naru
	II	omorasi nasaru
Humble	**I**	omorasi suru
	II	omorasi itasu

		AFFIRMATIVE	**NEGATIVE**
Indicative	**INFORMAL**	morau	morawanai
	FORMAL	moraimasu	moraimaseñ
Imperative	**INFORMAL I**	morae	morau na
	II	morainasai	morainasaru na
	III	moratte kudasai	morawanai de kudasai
	FORMAL	omorai nasaimase	omorai nasaimasu na
Presumptive	**INFORMAL I**	moraoo	moraumai
	II	morau daroo	morawanai daroo
	FORMAL I	moraimasyoo	moraimasumai
	II	morau desyoo	morawanai desyoo
Provisional	**INFORMAL**	moraeba	morawanakereba
	FORMAL	moraimaseba	moraimaseñ nara
		moraimasureba	
Gerund	**INFORMAL I**	moratte	morawanai de
	II		morawanakute
	FORMAL	moraimasite	moraimaseñ de
Past Ind.	**INFORMAL**	moratta	morawanakatta
	FORMAL	moraimasita	moraimaseñ desita
Past Presump.	**INFORMAL**	morattaroo	morawanakattaroo
		moratta daroo	morawanakatta daroo
	FORMAL	moraimasitaroo	moraimaseñ desitaroo
		moratta desyoo	morawanakatta desyoo
Conditional	**INFORMAL**	morattara	morawanakattara
	FORMAL	moraimasitara	moraimaseñ desitara
Alternative	**INFORMAL**	morattari	morawanakattari
	FORMAL	moraimasitari	moraimaseñ desitari

	INFORMAL AFFIRMATIVE INDICATIVE
Passive	morawareru
Potential	moraeru
Causative	morawaseru
Causative Pass.	morawaserareru

Honorific	**I**	omorai ni naru
	II	omorai nasaru
Humble		itadaku

		AFFIRMATIVE	**NEGATIVE**
Indicative	**INFORMAL**	motarasu	motarasanai
	FORMAL	motarasimasu	motarasimaseñ
Imperative	**INFORMAL I**	motarase	motarasu na
	II	motarasinasai	motarasinasaru na
	III	motarasite kudasai	motarasanai de kudasai
	FORMAL		
Presumptive	**INFORMAL I**	motarasoo	motarasumai
	II	motarasu daroo	motarasanai daroo
	FORMAL I	motarasimasyoo	motarasimasumai
	II	motarasu desyoo	motarasanai desyoo
Provisional	**INFORMAL**	motaraseba	motarasanakereba
	FORMAL	motarasimaseba	motarasimaseñ nara
		motarasimasureba	
Gerund	**INFORMAL I**	motarasite	motarasanai de
	II		motarasanakute
	FORMAL	motarasimasite	motarasimaseñ de
Past Ind.	**INFORMAL**	motarasita	motarasanakatta
	FORMAL	motarasimasita	motarasimaseñ desita
Past Presump.	**INFORMAL**	motarasitaroo	motarasanakattaroo
		motarasita daroo	motarasanakatta daroo
	FORMAL	motarasimasitaroo	motarasimaseñ desitaroo
		motarasita desyoo	motarasanakatta desyoo
Conditional	**INFORMAL**	motarasitara	motarasanakattara
	FORMAL	motarasimasitara	motarasimaseñ desitara
Alternative	**INFORMAL**	motarasitari	motarasanakattari
	FORMAL	motarasimasitari	motarasimaseñ desitari

INFORMAL AFFIRMATIVE INDICATIVE

Passive		motarasareru
Potential		motaraseru
Causative		motarasaseru
Causative Pass.		motarasaserareru

Honorific	**I**	
	II	
Humble	**I**	
	II	

to toy with, to amuse oneself with   TRANSITIVE

			AFFIRMATIVE	NEGATIVE
Indicative	**INFORMAL**		moteasobu	moteasobanai
	FORMAL		moteasobimasu	moteasobimaseñ
Imperative	**INFORMAL I**		moteasobe	moteasobu na
		II	moteasobinasai	moteasobinasaru na
		III	moteasoñde kudasai	moteasobanai de kudasai
	FORMAL		omoteasobi nasaimase	omoteasobi nasaimasu na
Presumptive	**INFORMAL I**		moteasoboo	moteasobumai
		II	moteasobu daroo	moteasobanai daroo
	FORMAL	**I**	moteasobimasyoo	moteasobimasumai
		II	moteasobu desyoo	moteasobanai desyoo
Provisional	**INFORMAL**		moteasobeba	moteasobanakereba
	FORMAL		moteasobimaseba	moteasobimaseñ nara
			moteasobimasureba	
Gerund	**INFORMAL I**		moteasoñde	moteasobanai de
		II		moteasobanakute
	FORMAL		moteasobimasite	moteasobimaseñ de
Past Ind.	**INFORMAL**		moteasoñda	moteasobanakatta
	FORMAL		moteasobimasita	moteasobimaseñ desita
Past Presump.	**INFORMAL**		moteasoñdaroo	moteasobanakattaroo
			moteasoñda daroo	moteasobanakatta daroo
	FORMAL		moteasobimasitaroo	moteasobimaseñ desitaroo
			moteasoñda desyoo	moteasobanakatta desyoo
Conditional	**INFORMAL**		moteasoñdara	moteasobanakattara
	FORMAL		moteasobimasitara	moteasobimaseñ desitara
Alternative	**INFORMAL**		moteasoñdari	moteasobanakattari
	FORMAL		moteasobimasitari	moteasobimaseñ desitari

INFORMAL AFFIRMATIVE INDICATIVE

Passive		moteasobareru
Potential		moteasoberu
Causative		moteasobaseru
Causative Pass.		moteasobaserareru

Honorific	**I**	omoteasobi ni naru
	II	omoteasobi nasaru
Humble	**I**	
	II	

		AFFIRMATIVE	NEGATIVE
Indicative	**INFORMAL**	moteru	motenai
	FORMAL	motemasu	motemaseñ
Imperative	**INFORMAL I**		
	II		
	III		
	FORMAL		
Presumptive	**INFORMAL I**	moteyoo	motemai
	II	moteru daroo	motenai daroo
	FORMAL I	motemasyoo	motemasumai
	II	moteru desyoo	motenai desyoo
Provisional	**INFORMAL**	motereba	motenakereba
	FORMAL	motemaseba	motemaseñ nara
		motemasureba	
Gerund	**INFORMAL I**	motete	motenai de
	II		motenakute
	FORMAL	motemasite	motemaseñ de
Past Ind.	**INFORMAL**	moteta	motenakatta
	FORMAL	motemasita	motemaseñ desita
Past Presump.	**INFORMAL**	motetaroo	motenakattaroo
		moteta daroo	motenakatta daroo
	FORMAL	motemasitaroo	motemaseñ desitaroo
		moteta desyoo	motenakatta desyoo
Conditional	**INFORMAL**	motetara	motenakattara
	FORMAL	motemasitara	motemaseñ desitara
Alternative	**INFORMAL**	motetari	motenakattari
	FORMAL	motemasitari	motemaseñ desitari

	INFORMAL AFFIRMATIVE INDICATIVE
Passive	moterareru
Potential	moterareru
Causative	motesaseru
Causative Pass.	motesaserareru
Honorific **I**	omote ni naru
II	omote nasaru
Humble **I**	
II	

to request, to seek   TRANSITIVE

		AFFIRMATIVE	NEGATIVE
Indicative	**INFORMAL**	motomeru	motomenai
	FORMAL	motomemasu	motomemaseñ
Imperative	**INFORMAL I**	motomero	motomeru na
	II	motomenasai	motomenasaru na
	III	motomete kudasai	motomenai de kudasai
	FORMAL	omotome nasaimase	omotome nasaimasu na
Presumptive	**INFORMAL I**	motomeyoo	motomemai
	II	motomeru daroo	motomenai daroo
	FORMAL I	motomemasyoo	motomemasumai
	II	motomeru desyoo	motomenai desyoo
Provisional	**INFORMAL**	motomereba	motomenakereba
	FORMAL	motomemaseba	motomemaseñ nara
		motomemasureba	
Gerund	**INFORMAL I**	motomete	motomenai de
	II		motomenakute
	FORMAL	motomemasite	motomemaseñ de
Past Ind.	**INFORMAL**	motometa	motomenakatta
	FORMAL	motomemasita	motomemaseñ desita
Past Presump.	**INFORMAL**	motometaroo	motomenakattaroo
		motometa daroo	motomenakatta daroo
	FORMAL	motomemasitaroo	motomemaseñ desitaroo
		motometa desyoo	motomenakatta desyoo
Conditional	**INFORMAL**	motometara	motomenakattara
	FORMAL	motomemasitara	motomemaseñ desitara
Alternative	**INFORMAL**	motometari	motomenakattari
	FORMAL	motomemasitari	motomemaseñ desitari

INFORMAL AFFIRMATIVE INDICATIVE

Passive		motomerareru
Potential		motomerareru
Causative		motomesaseru
Causative Pass.		motomesaserareru

Honorific	**I**	omotome ni naru
	II	omotome nasaru
Humble	**I**	omotome suru
	II	omotome itasu

		AFFIRMATIVE	NEGATIVE
Indicative	**INFORMAL**	motozuku	motozukanai
	FORMAL	motozukimasu	motozukimaseñ
Imperative	**INFORMAL I**	motozuke	motozuku na
	II	motozukinasai	motozukinasaru na
	III	motozuite kudasai	motozukanai de kudasai
	FORMAL		
Presumptive	**INFORMAL I**	motozukoo	motozukumai
	II	motozuku daroo	motozukanai daroo
	FORMAL I	motozukimasyoo	motozukimasumaı
	II	motozuku desyoo	motozukanai desyoo
Provisional	**INFORMAL**	motozukeba	motozukanakereba
	FORMAL	motozukimaseba	motozukimaseñ nara
		motozukimasureba	
Gerund	**INFORMAL I**	motozuite	motozukanai de
	II		motozukanakute
	FORMAL	motozukimasite	motozukimaseñ de
Past Ind.	**INFORMAL**	motozuita	motozukanakatta
	FORMAL	motozukimasita	motozukimaseñ desita
Past Presump.	**INFORMAL**	motozuitaroo	motozukanakattaroo
		motozuita daroo	motozukanakatta daroo
	FORMAL	motozukimasitaroo	motozukimaseñ desitaroo
		motozuita desyoo	motozukanakatta desyoo
Conditional	**INFORMAL**	motozuitara	motozukanakattara
	FORMAL	motozukimasitara	motozukimaseñ desitara
Alternative	**INFORMAL**	motozuitari	motozukanakattari
	FORMAL	motozukimasitari	motozukimaseñ desitari

		INFORMAL AFFIRMATIVE INDICATIVE
Passive		motozukareru
Potential		motozukeru
Causative		motozukaseru
Causative Pass.		motozukaserareru
Honorific	**I**	omotozuki ni naru
	II	omotozuki nasaru
Humble	**I**	
	II	

		AFFIRMATIVE	NEGATIVE
Indicative	**INFORMAL**	motu	motanai
	FORMAL	motimasu	motimaseñ
Imperative	**INFORMAL I**	mote	motu na
	II	motinasai	motinasaru na
	III	motte kudasai	motanai de kudasai
	FORMAL	omoti nasaimase	omoti nasaimasu na
Presumptive	**INFORMAL I**	motoo	motumai
	II	motu daroo	motanai daroo
	FORMAL I	motimasyoo	motimasumai
	II	motu desyoo	motanai desyoo
Provisional	**INFORMAL**	moteba	motanakereba
	FORMAL	motimaseba	motimaseñ nara
		motimasureba	
Gerund	**INFORMAL I**	motte	motanai de
	II		motanakute
	FORMAL	motimasite	motimaseñ de
Past Ind.	**INFORMAL**	motta	motanakatta
	FORMAL	motimasita	motimaseñ desita
Past Presump.	**INFORMAL**	mottaroo	motanakattaroo
		motta daroo	motanakatta daroo
	FORMAL	motimasitaroo	motimaseñ desitaroo
		motta desyoo	motanakatta desyoo
Conditional	**INFORMAL**	mottara	motanakattara
	FORMAL	motimasitara	motimaseñ desitara
Alternative	**INFORMAL**	mottari	motanakattari
	FORMAL	motimasitari	motimaseñ desitari

		INFORMAL AFFIRMATIVE INDICATIVE
Passive		motareru
Potential		moteru
Causative		motaseru
Causative Pass.		motaserareru

Honorific	**I**	omoti ni naru
	II	omoti nasaru
Humble	**I**	omoti suru
	II	omoti itasu

		AFFIRMATIVE	NEGATIVE
Indicative	INFORMAL	mukaeru	mukaenai
	FORMAL	mukaemasu	mukaemaseñ
Imperative	INFORMAL I	mukaero	mukaeru na
	II	mukaenasai	mukaenasaru na
	III	mukaete kudasai	mukaenai de kudasai
	FORMAL	omukae nasaimase	omukae nasaimasu na
Presumptive	INFORMAL I	mukaeyoo	mukaemai
	II	mukaeru daroo	mukaenai daroo
	FORMAL I	mukaemasyoo	mukaemasumai
	II	mukaeru desyoo	mukaenai desyoo
Provisional	INFORMAL	mukaereba	mukaenakereba
	FORMAL	mukaemaseba	mukaemaseñ nara
		mukaemasureba	
Gerund	INFORMAL I	mukaete	mukaenai de
	II		mukaenakute
	FORMAL	mukaemasite	mukaemaseñ de
Past Ind.	INFORMAL	mukaeta	mukaenakatta
	FORMAL	mukaemasita	mukaemaseñ desita
Past Presump.	INFORMAL	mukaetaroo	mukaenakattaroo
		mukaeta daroo	mukaenakatta daroo
	FORMAL	mukaemasitaroo	mukaemaseñ desitaroo
		mukaeta desyoo	mukaenakatta desyoo
Conditional	INFORMAL	mukaetara	mukaenakattara
	FORMAL	mukaemasitara	mukaemaseñ desitara
Alternative	INFORMAL	mukaetari	mukaenakattari
	FORMAL	mukaemasitari	mukaemaseñ desitari

INFORMAL AFFIRMATIVE INDICATIVE

Passive		mukaerareru
Potential		mukaerareru
Causative		mukaesaseru
Causative Pass.		mukaesaserareru
Honorific	I	omukae ni naru
	II	omukae nasaru
Humbl	I	omukae suru
	II	omukae itasu

to face, to head toward, to turn toward

		AFFIRMATIVE	NEGATIVE
Indicative	INFORMAL	mukau	mukawanai
	FORMAL	mukaimasu	mukaimaseñ
Imperative	INFORMAL I	mukae	mukau na
	II	mukainasai	mukainasaru na
	III	mukatte kudasai	mukawanai de kudasai
	FORMAL	omukai nasaimase	omukai nasaimasu na
Presumptive	INFORMAL I	mukaoo	mukaumai
	II	mukau daroo	mukawanai daroo
	FORMAL I	mukaimasyoo	mukaimasumai
	II	mukau desyoo	mukawanai desyoo
Provisional	INFORMAL	mukaeba	mukawanakereba
	FORMAL	mukaimaseba	mukaimaseñ nara
		mukaimasureba	
Gerund	INFORMAL I	mukatte	mukawanai de
	II		mukawanakute
	FORMAL	mukaimasite	mukaimaseñ de
Past Ind.	INFORMAL	mukatta	mukawanakatta
	FORMAL	mukaimasita	mukaimaseñ desita
Past Presump.	INFORMAL	mukattaroo	mukawanakattaroo
		mukatta daroo	mukawanakatta daroo
	FORMAL	mukaimasitaroo	mukaimaseñ desitaroo
		mukatta desyoo	mukawanakatta desyoo
Conditional	INFORMAL	mukattara	mukawanakattara
	FORMAL	mukaimasitara	mukaimaseñ desitara
Alternative	INFORMAL	mukattari	mukawanakattari
	FORMAL	mukaimasitari	mukaimaseñ desitari

		INFORMAL AFFIRMATIVE INDICATIVE
Passive		mukawareru
Potential		mukaeru
Causative		mukawaseru
Causative Pass.		mukawaserareru

Honorific	I	omukai ni naru
	II	omukai nasaru
Humble	I	omukai suru
	II	omukai itasu

TRANSITIVE   *to knot, to make* (a contract)

			AFFIRMATIVE	NEGATIVE
Indicative	**INFORMAL**		musubu	musubanai
	FORMAL		musubimasu	musubimaseñ
Imperative	**INFORMAL I**		musube	musubu na
		II	musubinasai	musubinasaru na
		III	musuñde kudasai	musubanai de kudasai
	FORMAL		omusubi nasaimase	omusubi nasaimasu na
Presumptive	**INFORMAL I**		musuboo	musubumai
		II	musubu daroo	musubanai daroo
	FORMAL	**I**	musubimasyoo	musubimasumai
		II	musubu desyoo	musubanai desyoo
Provisional	**INFORMAL**		musubeba	musubanakereba
	FORMAL		musubimaseba	musubimaseñ nara
			musubimasureba	
Gerund	**INFORMAL I**		musuñde	musubanai de
		II		musubanakute
	FORMAL		musubimasite	musubimaseñ de
Past Ind.	**INFORMAL**		musuñda	musubanakatta
	FORMAL		musubimasita	musubimaseñ desita
Past Presump.	**INFORMAL**		musuñdaroo	musubanakattaroo
			musuñda daroo	musubanakatta daroo
	FORMAL		musubimasitaroo	musubimaseñ desitaroo
			musuñda desyoo	musubanakatta desyoo
Conditional	**INFORMAL**		musuñdara	musubanakattara
	FORMAL		musubimasitara	musubimaseñ desitara
Alternative	**INFORMAL**		musuñdari	musubanakattari
	FORMAL		musubimasitari	musubimaseñ desitara

INFORMAL AFFIRMATIVE INDICATIVE

Passive		musubareru
Potential		musuberu
Causative		musubaseru
Causative Pass.		musubaserareru
Honorific	**I**	omusubi ni naru
	II	omusubi nasaru
Humble	**I**	omusubi suru
	II	omusubi itasu

to watch, to gaze at   TRANSITIVE

		AFFIRMATIVE	NEGATIVE
Indicative	**INFORMAL**	nagameru	nagamenai
	FORMAL	nagamemasu	nagamemaseñ
Imperative	**INFORMAL I**	nagamero	nagameru na
	II	nagamenasai	nagamenasaru na
	III	nagamete kudasai	nagamenai de kudasai
	FORMAL	onagame nasaimase	onagame nasaimasu na
Presumptive	**INFORMAL I**	nagameyoo	nagamemai
	II	nagameru daroo	nagamenai daroo
	FORMAL I	nagamemasyoo	nagamemasumai
	II	nagameru desyoo	nagamenai desyoo
Provisional	**INFORMAL**	nagamereba	nagamenakereba
	FORMAL	nagamemaseba	nagamemaseñ nara
		nagamemasureba	
Gerund	**INFORMAL I**	nagamete	nagamenai de
	II		nagamenakute
	FORMAL	nagamemasite	nagamemaseñ de
Past Ind.	**INFORMAL**	nagameta	nagamenakatta
	FORMAL	nagamemasita	nagamemaseñ desita
Past Presump.	**INFORMAL**	nagametaroo	nagamenakattaroo
		nagameta daroo	nagamenakatta daroo
	FORMAL	nagamemasitaroo	nagamemaseñ desitaroo
		nagameta desyoo	nagamenakatta desyoo
Conditional	**INFORMAL**	nagametara	nagamenakattara
	FORMAL	nagamemasitara	nagamemaseñ desitara
Alternative	**INFORMAL**	nagametari	nagamenakattari
	FORMAL	nagamemasitari	nagamemaseñ desitari

		INFORMAL AFFIRMATIVE INDICATIVE
Passive		nagamerareru
Potential		nagamerareru
Causative		nagamesaseru
Causative Pass.		nagamesaserareru
Honorific	**I**	onagame ni naru
	II	onagame nasaru
Humble	**I**	
	II	

		AFFIRMATIVE	NEGATIVE
Indicative	**INFORMAL**	nagareru	nagarenai
	FORMAL	nagaremasu	nagaremaseñ
Imperative	**INFORMAL I**	nagarero	nagareru na
	II		
	III		
	FORMAL		
Presumptive	**INFORMAL I**	nagareyoo	nagaremai
	II	nagareru daroo	nagarenai daroo
	FORMAL I	nagaremasyoo	nagaremasumai
	II	nagareru desyoo	nagarenai desyoo
Provisional	**INFORMAL**	nagarereba	nagarenakereba
	FORMAL	nagaremaseba	nagaremaseñ nara
		nagaremasureba	
Gerund	**INFORMAL I**	nagarete	nagarenai de
	II		nagarenakute
	FORMAL	nagaremasite	nagaremaseñ de
Past Ind.	**INFORMAL**	nagareta	nagarenakatta
	FORMAL	nagaremasita	nagaremaseñ desita
Past Presump.	**INFORMAL**	nagaretaroo	nagarenakattaroo
		nagareta daroo	nagarenakatta daroo
	FORMAL	nagaremasitaroo	nagaremaseñ desitaroo
		nagareta desyoo	nagarenakatta desyoo
Conditional	**INFORMAL**	nagaretara	nagarenakattara
	FORMAL	nagaremasitara	nagaremaseñ desitara
Alternative	**INFORMAL**	nagaretari	nagarenakattari
	FORMAL	nagaremasitari	nagaremaseñ desitari

		INFORMAL AFFIRMATIVE INDICATIVE
Passive		nagarerareru
Potential		nagarerareru
Causative		nagaresaseru
Causative Pass.		nagaresaserareru
Honorific	**I**	
	II	
Humble	**I**	
	II	

nagás.u

to pour, to let flow   TRANSITIVE

nagasi

		AFFIRMATIVE	NEGATIVE
Indicative	**INFORMAL**	nagasu	nagasanai
	FORMAL	nagasimasu	nagasimaseñ
Imperative	**INFORMAL I**	nagase	nagasu na
	II	nagasinasai	nagasinasaru na
	III	nagasite kudasai	nagasanai de kudasai
	FORMAL	onagasi nasaimase	onagasi nasaimasu na
Presumptive	**INFORMAL I**	nagasoo	nagasumai
	II	nagasu daroo	nagasanai daroo
	FORMAL I	nagasimasyoo	nagasimasumai
	II	nagasu desyoo	nagasanai desyoo
Provisional	**INFORMAL**	nagaseba	nagasanakereba
	FORMAL	nagasimaseba	nagasimaseñ nara
		nagasimasureba	
Gerund	**INFORMAL I**	nagasite	nagasanai de
	II		nagasanakute
	FORMAL	nagasimasite	nagasimaseñ de
Past Ind.	**INFORMAL**	nagasita	nagasanakatta
	FORMAL	nagasimasita	nagasimaseñ desita
Past Presump.	**INFORMAL**	nagasitaroo	nagasanakattaroo
		nagasita daroo	nagasanakatta daroo
	FORMAL	nagasimasitaroo	nagasimaseñ desitaroo
		nagasita desyoo	nagasanakatta desyoo
Conditional	**INFORMAL**	nagasitara	nagasanakattara
	FORMAL	nagasimasitara	nagasimaseñ desitara
Alternative	**INFORMAL**	nagasitari	nagasanakattari
	FORMAL	nagasimasitari	nagasimaseñ desitari

INFORMAL AFFIRMATIVE INDICATIVE

Passive		nagasareru
Potential		nagaseru
Causative		nagasaseru
Causative Pass.		nagasaserareru
Honorific	**I**	onagasi ni naru
	II	onagasi nasaru
Humble	**I**	onagasi suru
	II	onagasi itasu

324

		AFFIRMATIVE	NEGATIVE
Indicative	**INFORMAL**	nageru	nagenai
	FORMAL	nagemasu	nagemaseñ
Imperative	**INFORMAL I**	nagero	nageru na
	II	nagenasai	nagenasaru na
	III	nagete kudasai	nagenai de kudasai
	FORMAL	onage nasaimase	onage nasaimasu na
Presumptive	**INFORMAL I**	nageyoo	nagemai
	II	nageru daroo	nagenai daroo
	FORMAL I	nagemasyoo	nagemasumai
	II	nageru desyoo	nagenai desyoo
Provisional	**INFORMAL**	nagereba	nagenakereba
	FORMAL	nagemaseba	nagemaseñ nara
		nagemasureba	
Gerund	**INFORMAL I**	nagete	nagenai de
	II		nagenakute
	FORMAL	nagemasite	nagemaseñ de
Past Ind.	**INFORMAL**	nageta	nagenakatta
	FORMAL	nagemasita	nagemaseñ desita
Past Presump.	**INFORMAL**	nagetaroo	nagenakattaroo
		nageta daroo	nagenakatta daroo
	FORMAL	nagemasitaroo	nagemaseñ desitaroo
		nageta desyoo	nagenakatta desyoo
Conditional	**INFORMAL**	nagetara	nagenakattara
	FORMAL	nagemasitara	nagemaseñ desitara
Alternative	**INFORMAL**	nagetari	nagenakattari
	FORMAL	nagemasitari	nagemaseñ desitari

INFORMAL AFFIRMATIVE INDICATIVE

Passive		nagerareru
Potential		nagerareru
Causative		nagesaseru
Causative Pass.		nagesaserareru
Honorific	**I**	onage ni naru
	II	onage nasaru
Humble	**I**	onage suru
	II	onage itasu

			AFFIRMATIVE	NEGATIVE
Indicative	**INFORMAL**		naguru	naguranai
	FORMAL		nagurimasu	nagurimaseñ
Imperative	**INFORMAL I**		nagure	naguru na
		II	nagurinasai	nagurinasaru na
		III	nagutte kudasai	naguranai de kudasai
	FORMAL		onaguri nasaimase	onaguri nasaimasu na
Presumptive	**INFORMAL I**		naguroo	nagurumai
		II	naguru daroo	naguranai daroo
	FORMAL	**I**	nagurimasyoo	nagurimasumai
		II	naguru desyoo	naguranai desyoo
Provisional	**INFORMAL**		nagureba	naguranakereba
	FORMAL		nagurimaseba	nagurimaseñ nara
			nagurimasureba	
Gerund	**INFORMAL I**		nagutte	naguranai de
		II		naguranakute
	FORMAL		nagurimasite	nagurimaseñ de
Past Ind.	**INFORMAL**		nagutta	naguranakatta
	FORMAL		nagurimasita	nagurimaseñ desita
Past Presump.	**INFORMAL**		naguttaroo	naguranakattaroo
			nagutta daroo	naguranakatta daroo
	FORMAL		nagurimasitaroo	nagurimaseñ desitaroo
			nagutta desyoo	naguranakatta desyoo
Conditional	**INFORMAL**		naguttara	naguranakattara
	FORMAL		nagurimasitara	nagurimaseñ desitara
Alternative	**INFORMAL**		naguttari	naguranakattari
	FORMAL		nagurimasitari	nagurimaseñ desitari

		INFORMAL AFFIRMATIVE INDICATIVE
Passive		nagurareru
Potential		nagureru
Causative		naguraseru
Causative Pass.		naguraserareru
Honorific	**I**	onaguri ni naru
	II	onaguri nasaru
Humble	**I**	onaguri suru
	II	onaguri itasu

		AFFIRMATIVE	NEGATIVE
Indicative	**INFORMAL**	nagusameru	nagusamenai
	FORMAL	nagusamemasu	nagusamemaseñ
Imperative	**INFORMAL I**	nagusamero	nagusameru na
	II	nagusamenasai	nagusamenasaru na
	III	nagusamete kudasai	nagusamenai de kudasai
	FORMAL	onagusame nasaimase	onagusame nasaimasu na
Presumptive	**INFORMAL I**	nagusameyoo	nagusamemai
	II	nagusameru daroo	nagusamenai daroo
	FORMAL I	nagusamemasyoo	nagusamemasumai
	II	nagusameru desyoo	nagusamenai desyoo
Provisional	**INFORMAL**	nagusamereba	nagusamenakereba
	FORMAL	nagusamemaseba	nagusamemaseñ nara
		nagusamemasureba	
Gerund	**INFORMAL I**	nagusamete	nagusamenai de
	II		nagusamenakute
	FORMAL	nagusamemasite	nagusamemaseñ de
Past Ind.	**INFORMAL**	nagusameta	nagusamenakatta
	FORMAL	nagusamemasita	nagusamemaseñ desita
Past Presump.	**INFORMAL**	nagusametaroo	nagusamenakattaroo
		nagusameta daroo	nagusamenakatta daroo
	FORMAL	nagusamemasitaroo	nagusamemaseñ desitaroo
		nagusameta desyoo	nagusamenakatta desyoo
Conditional	**INFORMAL**	nagusametara	nagusamenakattara
	FORMAL	nagusamemasitara	nagusamemaseñ desitara
Alternative	**INFORMAL**	nagusametari	nagusamenakattari
	FORMAL	nagusamemasitari	nagusamemaseñ desitari

INFORMAL AFFIRMATIVE INDICATIVE

Passive		nagusamerareru
Potential		nagusamerareru
Causative		nagusamesaseru
Causative Pass.		nagusamesaserareru
Honorific	**I**	onagusame ni naru
	II	onagusame nasaru
Humble	**I**	onagusame suru
	II	onagusame itasu

		AFFIRMATIVE	NEGATIVE
Indicative	**INFORMAL**	naku	nakanai
	FORMAL	nakimasu	nakimaseñ
Imperative	**INFORMAL I**	nake	naku na
	II	nakinasai	nakinasaru na
	III	naite kudasai	nakanai de kudasai
	FORMAL	onaki nasaimase	onaki nasaimasu na
Presumptive	**INFORMAL I**	nakoo	nakumai
	II	naku daroo	nakanai daroo
	FORMAL I	nakimasyoo	nakimasumai
	II	naku desyoo	nakanai desyoo
Provisional	**INFORMAL**	nakeba	nakanakereba
	FORMAL	nakimaseba	nakimaseñ nara
		nakimasureba	
Gerund	**INFORMAL I**	naite	nakanai de
	II		nakanakute
	FORMAL	nakimasite	nakimaseñ de
Past Ind.	**INFORMAL**	naita	nakanakatta
	FORMAL	nakimasita	nakimaseñ desita
Past Presump.	**INFORMAL**	naitaroo	nakanakattaroo
		naita daroo	nakanakatta daroo
	FORMAL	nakimasitaroo	nakimaseñ desitaroo
		naita desyoo	nakanakatta desyoo
Conditional	**INFORMAL**	naitara	nakanakattara
	FORMAL	nakimasitara	nakimaseñ desitara
Alternative	**INFORMAL**	naitari	nakanakattari
	FORMAL	nakimasitari	nakimaseñ desitari

		INFORMAL AFFIRMATIVE INDICATIVE
Passive		nakareru
Potential		nakeru
Causative		nakaseru
Causative Pass.		nakaserareru
Honorific	**I**	onaki ni naru
	II	onaki nasaru
Humble	**I**	
	II	

to be missing, to die (polite), *to vanish*

		AFFIRMATIVE	NEGATIVE
Indicative	INFORMAL	nakunaru	nakunaranai
	FORMAL	nakunarimasu	nakunarimaseñ
Imperative	INFORMAL I	nakunare	nakunaru na
	II		
	III		
	FORMAL		
Presumptive	INFORMAL I	nakunaroo	nakunarumai
	II	nakunaru daroo	nakunaranai daroo
	FORMAL I	nakunarimasyoo	nakunarimasumai
	II	nakunaru desyoo	nakunaranai desyoo
Provisional	INFORMAL	nakunareba	nakunaranakereba
	FORMAL	nakunarimaseba	nakunarimaseñ nara
		nakunarimasureba	
Gerund	INFORMAL I	nakunatte	nakunaranai de
	II		nakunaranakute
	FORMAL	nakunarimasite	nakunarimaseñ de
Past Ind.	INFORMAL	nakunatta	nakunaranakatta
	FORMAL	nakunarimasita	nakunarimaseñ desita
Past Presump.	INFORMAL	nakunattaroo	nakunaranakattaroo
		nakunatta daroo	nakunaranakatta daroo
	FORMAL	nakunarimasitaroo	nakunarimaseñ desitaroo
		nakunatta desyoo	nakunaranakatta desyoo
Conditional	INFORMAL	nakunattara	nakunaranakattara
	FORMAL	nakunarimasitara	nakunarimaseñ desitara
Alternative	INFORMAL	nakunattari	nakunaranakattari
	FORMAL	nakunarimasitari	nakunarimaseñ desitari

		INFORMAL AFFIRMATIVE INDICATIVE
Passive		nakunarareru
Potential		nakunareru
Causative		nakunaraseru
Causative Pass.		nakunaraserareru
Honorific	I	onakunari ni naru
	II	onakunari nasaru
Humble	I	
	II	

to lose, to remove, to do away with   TRANSITIVE

			AFFIRMATIVE	NEGATIVE
Indicative	**INFORMAL**		nakusu	nakusanai
	FORMAL		nakusimasu	nakusimaseñ
Imperative	**INFORMAL**	**I**	nakuse	nakusu na
		II	nakusinasai	nakusinasaru na
		III	nakusite kudasai	nakusanai de kudasai
	FORMAL		onakusi nasaimase	onakusi nasaimasu na
Presumptive	**INFORMAL**	**I**	nakusoo	nakusumai
		II	nakusu daroo	nakusanai daroo
	FORMAL	**I**	nakusimasyoo	nakusimasumai
		II	nakusu desyoo	nakusanai desyoo
Provisional	**INFORMAL**		nakuseba	nakusanakereba
	FORMAL		nakusimaseba	nakusimaseñ nara
			nakusimasureba	
Gerund	**INFORMAL**	**I**	nakusite	nakusanai de
		II		nakusanakute
	FORMAL		nakusimasite	nakusimaseñ de
Past Ind.	**INFORMAL**		nakusita	nakusanakatta
	FORMAL		nakusimasita	nakusimaseñ desita
Past Presump.	**INFORMAL**		nakusitaroo	nakusanakattaroo
			nakusita daroo	nakusanakatta daroo
	FORMAL		nakusimasitaroo	nakusimaseñ desitaroo
			nakusita desyoo	nakusanakatta desyoo
Conditional	**INFORMAL**		nakusitara	nakusanakattara
	FORMAL		nakusimasitara	nakusimaseñ desitara
Alternative	**INFORMAL**		nakusitari	nakusanakattari
	FORMAL		nakusimasitari	nakusimaseñ desitari

		INFORMAL AFFIRMATIVE INDICATIVE
Passive		nakusareru
Potential		nakuseru
Causative		nakusaseru
Causative Pass.		nakusaserareru

Honorific	**I**	onakusi ni naru
	II	onakusi nasaru
Humble	**I**	onakusi suru
	II	onakusi itasu

TRANSITIVE   *to be lazy, to neglect one's work*

		AFFIRMATIVE	NEGATIVE
Indicative	**INFORMAL**	namakeru	namakenai
	FORMAL	namakemasu	namakemaseñ
Imperative	**INFORMAL I**	namakero	namakeru na
	II		namakenasaru na
	III		namakenai de kudasai
	FORMAL		onamake nasaimasu na
Presumptive	**INFORMAL I**	namakeyoo	namakemai
	II	namakeru daroo	namakenai daroo
	FORMAL I	namakemasyoo	namakemasumai
	II	namakeru desyoo	namakenai desyoo
Provisional	**INFORMAL**	namakereba	namakenakereba
	FORMAL	namakemaseba	namakemaseñ nara
		namakemasureba	
Gerund	**INFORMAL I**	namakete	namakenai de
	II		namakenakute
	FORMAL	namakemasite	namakemaseñ de
Past Ind.	**INFORMAL**	namaketa	namakenakatta
	FORMAL	namakemasita	namakemaseñ desita
Past Presump.	**INFORMAL**	namaketaroo	namakenakattaroo
		namaketa daroo	namakenakatta daroo
	FORMAL	namakemasitaroo	namakemaseñ desitaroo
		namaketa desyoo	namakenakatta desyoo
Conditional	**INFORMAL**	namaketara	namakenakattara
	FORMAL	namakemasitara	namakemaseñ desitara
Alternative	**INFORMAL**	namaketari	namakenakattari
	FORMAL	namakemasitari	namakemaseñ desitari

		INFORMAL AFFIRMATIVE INDICATIVE
Passive		namakerareru
Potential		namakerareru
Causative		namakesaseru
Causative Pass.		namakesaserareru
Honorific	**I**	onamake ni naru
	II	onamake nasaru
Humble	**I**	
	II	

to lick, to despise, to take advantage of (a person)　　TRANSITIVE

		AFFIRMATIVE	NEGATIVE
Indicative	**INFORMAL**	nameru	namenai
	FORMAL	namemasu	namemaseñ
Imperative	**INFORMAL I**	namero	nameru na
	II	namenasai	namenasaru na
	III	namete kudasai	namenai de kudasai
	FORMAL	oname nasaimase	oname nasaimasu na
Presumptive	**INFORMAL I**	nameyoo	namemai
	II	nameru daroo	namenai daroo
	FORMAL I	namemasyoo	namemasumai
	II	nameru desyoo	namenai desyoo
Provisional	**INFORMAL**	namereba	namenakereba
	FORMAL	namemaseba	namemaseñ nara
		namemasureba	
Gerund	**INFORMAL I**	namete	namenai de
	II		namenakute
	FORMAL	namemasite	namemaseñ de
Past Ind.	**INFORMAL**	nameta	namenakatta
	FORMAL	namemasita	namemaseñ desita
Past Presump.	**INFORMAL**	nametaroo	namenakattaroo
		nameta daroo	namenakatta daroo
	FORMAL	namemasitaroo	namemaseñ desitaroo
		nameta desyoo	namenakatta desyoo
Conditional	**INFORMAL**	nametara	namenakattara
	FORMAL	namemasitara	namemaseñ desitara
Alternative	**INFORMAL**	nametari	namenakattari
	FORMAL	namemasitari	namemaseñ desitari

		INFORMAL AFFIRMATIVE INDICATIVE
Passive		namerareru
Potential		namerareru
Causative		namesaseru
Causative Pass.		namesaserareru
Honorific	**I**	oname ni naru
	II	oname nasaru
Humble	**I**	
	II	

		AFFIRMATIVE	NEGATIVE
Indicative	**INFORMAL**	naoru	naoranai
	FORMAL	naorimasu	naorimaseñ
Imperative	**INFORMAL I**	naore	naoru na
	II	naorinasai	naorinasaru na
	III	naotte kudasai	naoranai de kudasai
	FORMAL	onaori nasaimase	onaori nasaimasu na
Presumptive	**INFORMAL I**	naoroo	naorumai
	II	naoru daroo	naoranai daroo
	FORMAL I	naorimasyoo	naorimasumai
	II	naoru desyoo	naoranai desyoo
Provisional	**INFORMAL**	naoreba	naoranakereba
	FORMAL	naorimaseba	naorimaseñ nara
		naorimasureba	
Gerund	**INFORMAL I**	naotte	naoranai de
	II		naoranakute
	FORMAL	naorimasite	naorimaseñ de
Past Ind.	**INFORMAL**	naotta	naoranakatta
	FORMAL	naorimasita	naorimaseñ desita
Past Presump.	**INFORMAL**	naottaroo	naoranakattaroo
		naotta daroo	naoranakatta daroo
	FORMAL	naorimasitaroo	naorimaseñ desitaroo
		naotta desyoo	naoranakatta desyoo
Conditional	**INFORMAL**	naottara	naoranakattara
	FORMAL	naorimasitara	naorimaseñ desitara
Alternative	**INFORMAL**	naottari	naoranakattari
	FORMAL	naorimasitari	naorimaseñ desitari

INFORMAL AFFIRMATIVE INDICATIVE

Passive		naorareru
Potential		naoreru
Causative		naoraseru
Causative Pass.		

Honorific	**I**	onaori ni naru
	II	onaori nasaru
Humble	**I**	
	II	

to repair, cure   TRANSITIVE

		AFFIRMATIVE	NEGATIVE
Indicative	**INFORMAL**	naosu	naosanai
	FORMAL	naosimasu	naosimaseñ
Imperative	**INFORMAL I**	naose	naosu na
	II	naosinasai	naosinasaru na
	III	naosite kudasai	naosanai de kudasai
	FORMAL	onaosi nasaimase	onaosi nasaimasu na
Presumptive	**INFORMAL I**	naosoo	naosumai
	II	naosu daroo	naosanai daroo
	FORMAL I	naosimasyoo	naosimasumai
	II	naosu desyoo	naosanai desyoo
Provisional	**INFORMAL**	naoseba	naosanakereba
	FORMAL	naosimaseba	naosimaseñ nara
		naosimasureba	
Gerund	**INFORMAL I**	naosite	naosanai de
	II		naosanakute
	FORMAL	naosimasite	naosimaseñ de
Past Ind.	**INFORMAL**	naosita	naosanakatta
	FORMAL	naosimasita	naosimaseñ desita
Past Presump.	**INFORMAL**	naositaroo	naosanakattaroo
		naosita daroo	naosanakatta daroo
	FORMAL	naosimasitaroo	naosimaseñ desitaroo
		naosita desyoo	naosanakatta desyoo
Conditional	**INFORMAL**	naositara	naosanakattara
	FORMAL	naosimasitara	naosimaseñ desitara
Alternative	**INFORMAL**	naositari	naosanakattari
	FORMAL	naosimasitari	naosimaseñ desitari

		INFORMAL AFFIRMATIVE INDICATIVE
Passive		naosareru
Potential		naoseru
Causative		naosaseru
Causative Pass.		naosaserareru
Honorific	**I**	onaosi ni naru
	II	onaosi nasaru
Humble	**I**	onaosi suru
	II	onaosi itasu

		AFFIRMATIVE	NEGATIVE
Indicative	**INFORMAL**	naraberu	narabenai
	FORMAL	narabemasu	narabemaseñ
Imperative	**INFORMAL I**	narabero	naraberu na
	II	narabenasai	narabenasaru na
	III	narabete kudasai	narabenai de kudasai
	FORMAL	onarabe nasaimase	onarabe nasaimasu na
Presumptive	**INFORMAL I**	narabeyoo	narabemai
	II	naraberu daroo	narabenai daroo
	FORMAL I	narabemasyoo	narabemasumai
	II	naraberu desyoo	narabenai desyoo
Provisional	**INFORMAL**	narabereba	narabenakereba
	FORMAL	narabemaseba	narabemaseñ nara
		narabemasureba	
Gerund	**INFORMAL I**	narabete	narabenai de
	II		narabenakute
	FORMAL	narabemasite	narabemaseñ de
Past Ind.	**INFORMAL**	narabeta	narabenakatta
	FORMAL	narabemasita	narabemaseñ desita
Past Presump.	**INFORMAL**	narabetaroo	narabenakattaroo
		narabeta daroo	narabenakatta daroo
	FORMAL	narabemasitaroo	narabemaseñ desitaroo
		narabeta desyoo	narabenakatta desyoo
Conditional	**INFORMAL**	narabetara	narabenakattara
	FORMAL	narabemasitara	narabemaseñ desitara
Alternative	**INFORMAL**	narabetari	narabenakattari
	FORMAL	narabemasitari	narabemaseñ desitari

INFORMAL AFFIRMATIVE INDICATIVE

Passive		naraberareru
Potential		naraberareru
Causative		narabesaseru
Causative Pass.		narabesaserareru
Honorific	**I**	onarabe ni naru
	II	onarabe nasaru
Humble	**I**	onarabe suru
	II	onarabe itasu

		AFFIRMATIVE	NEGATIVE
Indicative	**INFORMAL**	narabu	narabanai
	FORMAL	narabimasu	narabimaseñ
Imperative	**INFORMAL I**	narabe	narabu na
	II	narabinasai	narabinasaru na
	III	narañde kudasai	narabanai de kudasai
	FORMAL	onarabi nasaimase	onarabi nasaimasu na
Presumptive	**INFORMAL I**	naraboo	narabumai
	II	narabu daroo	narabanai daroo
	FORMAL I	narabimasyoo	narabimasumai
	II	narabu desyoo	narabanai desyoo
Provisional	**INFORMAL**	narabeba	narabanakereba
	FORMAL	narabimaseba	narabimaseñ nara
		narabimasureba	
Gerund	**INFORMAL I**	narañde	narabanai de
	II		narabanakute
	FORMAL	narabimasite	narabimaseñ de
Past Ind.	**INFORMAL**	narañda	narabanakatta
	FORMAL	narabimasita	narabimaseñ desita
Past Presump.	**INFORMAL**	narañdaroo	narabanakattaroo
		narañda daroo	narabanakatta daroo
	FORMAL	narabimasitaroo	narabimaseñ desitaroo
		narañda desyoo	narabanakatta desyoo
Conditional	**INFORMAL**	narañdara	narabanakattara
	FORMAL	narabimasitara	narabimaseñ desitara
Alternative	**INFORMAL**	narañdari	narabanakattari
	FORMAL	narabimasitari	narabimaseñ desitari

INFORMAL AFFIRMATIVE INDICATIVE

Passive	narabareru
Potential	naraberu
Causative	narabaseru
Causative Pass.	narabaserareru

Honorific	**I**	onarabi ni naru
	II	onarabi nasaru
Humble	**I**	onarabi suru
	II	onarabi itasu

		AFFIRMATIVE	NEGATIVE
Indicative	INFORMAL	narau	narawanai
	FORMAL	naraimasu	naraimaseñ
Imperative	INFORMAL I	narae	narau na
	II	narainasai	narainasaru na
	III	naratte kudasai	narawanai de kudasai
	FORMAL	onarai nasaimase	onarai nasaimasu na
Presumptive	INFORMAL I	naraoo	naraumai
	II	narau daroo	narawanai daroo
	FORMAL I	naraimasyoo	naraimasumai
	II	narau desyoo	narawanai desyoo
Provisional	INFORMAL	naraeba	narawanakereba
	FORMAL	naraimaseba	naraimaseñ nara
		naraimasureba	
Gerund	INFORMAL I	naratte	narawanai de
	II		narawanakute
	FORMAL	naraimasite	naraimaseñ de
Past Ind.	INFORMAL	naratta	narawanakatta
	FORMAL	naraimasita	naraimaseñ desita
Past Presump.	INFORMAL	narattaroo	narawanakattaroo
		naratta daroo	narawanakatta daroo
	FORMAL	naraimasitaroo	naraimaseñ desitaroo
		naratta desyoo	narawanakatta desyoo
Conditional	INFORMAL	narattara	narawanakattara
	FORMAL	naraimasitara	naraimaseñ desitara
Alternative	INFORMAL	narattari	narawanakattari
	FORMAL	naraimasitari	naraimaseñ desitari

	INFORMAL AFFIRMATIVE INDICATIVE
Passive	narawareru
Potential	naraeru
Causative	narawaseru
Causative Pass.	narawaserareru

Honorific	I	onarai ni naru
	II	onarai nasaru
Humble	I	
	II	

		AFFIRMATIVE	NEGATIVE
Indicative	**INFORMAL**	naru	naranai
	FORMAL	narimasu	narimaseñ
Imperative	**INFORMAL I**	nare	naru na
	II	narinasai	narinasaru na
	III	natte kudasai	naranai de kudasai
	FORMAL	onari nasaimase	onari nasaimasu na
Presumptive	**INFORMAL I**	naroo	narumai
	II	naru daroo	naranai daroo
	FORMAL I	narimasyoo	narimasumai
	II	naru desyoo	naranai desyoo
Provisional	**INFORMAL**	nareba	naranakereba
	FORMAL	narimaseba	narimaseñ nara
		narimasureba	
Gerund	**INFORMAL I**	natte	naranai de
	II		naranakute
	FORMAL	narimasite	narimaseñ de
Past Ind.	**INFORMAL**	natta	naranakatta
	FORMAL	narimasita	narimaseñ desita
Past Presump.	**INFORMAL**	nattaroo	naranakattaroo
		natta daroo	naranakatta daroo
	FORMAL	narimasitaroo	narimaseñ desitaroo
		natta desyoo	naranakatta desyoo
Conditional	**INFORMAL**	nattara	naranakattara
	FORMAL	narimasitara	narimaseñ desitara
Alternative	**INFORMAL**	nattari	naranakattari
	FORMAL	narimasitari	narimaseñ desitari

		INFORMAL AFFIRMATIVE INDICATIVE
Passive		narareru
Potential		nareru
Causative		naraseru
Causative Pass.		naraserareru
Honorific	**I**	onari ni naru
	II	onari nasaru
Humble	**I**	
	II	

		AFFIRMATIVE	NEGATIVE
Indicative	**INFORMAL**	nasaru	nasaranai
	FORMAL	nasaimasu	nasaimaseñ
Imperative	**INFORMAL I**	nasai	nasaru na
	II		
	III	nasatte kudasai	nasaranai de kudasai
	FORMAL	nasaimase	nasaimasu na
Presumptive	**INFORMAL I**	nasaroo	nasarumai
	II	nasaru daroo	nasaranai daroo
	FORMAL I	nasaimasyoo	nasaimasumai
	II	nasaru desyoo	nasaranai desyoo
Provisional	**INFORMAL**	nasareba	nasaranakereba
	FORMAL	nasaimaseba	nasaimaseñ nara
		nasaimasureba	
Gerund	**INFORMAL I**	nasatte	nasaranai de
	II		nasaranakute
	FORMAL	nasaimasite	nasaimaseñ de
Past Ind.	**INFORMAL**	nasatta	nasaranakatta
	FORMAL	nasaimasita	nasaimaseñ desita
Past Presump.	**INFORMAL**	nasattaroo	nasaranakattaroo
		nasatta daroo	nasaranakatta daroo
	FORMAL	nasaimasitaroo	nasaimaseñ desitaroo
		nasatta desyoo	nasaranakatta desyoo
Conditional	**INFORMAL**	nasattara	nasaranakattara
	FORMAL	nasaimasitara	nasaimaseñ desitara
Alternative	**INFORMAL**	nasattari	nasaranakattari
	FORMAL	nasaimasitari	nasaimaseñ desitari

INFORMAL AFFIRMATIVE INDICATIVE

Passive	nasarareru
Potential	nasareru
Causative	
Causative Pass.	

Honorific	I	
	II	
Humble	I	
	II	

		AFFIRMATIVE	NEGATIVE
Indicative	**INFORMAL**	nazimu	nazimanai
	FORMAL	nazimimasu	nazimimaseñ
Imperative	**INFORMAL I**	nazime	nazimu na
	II	naziminasai	naziminasaru na
	III	naziñde kudasai	nazimanai de kudasai
	FORMAL	onazimi nasaimase	onazimi nasaimasu na
Presumptive	**INFORMAL I**	nazimoo	nazimumai
	II	nazimu daroo	nazimanai daroo
	FORMAL I	nazimimasyoo	nazimimasumai
	II	nazimu desyoo	nazimanai desyoo
Provisional	**INFORMAL**	nazimeba	nazimanakereba
	FORMAL	nazimimaseba	nazimimaseñ nara
		nazimimasureba	
Gerund	**INFORMAL I**	naziñde	nazimanai de
	II		nazimanakute
	FORMAL	nazimimasite	nazimimaseñ de
Past Ind.	**INFORMAL**	naziñda	nazimanakatta
	FORMAL	nazimimasita	nazimimaseñ desita
Past Presump.	**INFORMAL**	naziñdaroo	nazimanakattaroo
		naziñda daroo	nazimanakatta daroo
	FORMAL	nazimimasitaroo	nazimimaseñ desitaroo
		naziñda desyoo	nazimanakatta desyoo
Conditional	**INFORMAL**	naziñdara	nazimanakattara
	FORMAL	nazimimasitara	nazimimaseñ desitara
Alternative	**INFORMAL**	naziñdari	nazimanakattari
	FORMAL	nazimimasitari	nazimimaseñ desitari

INFORMAL AFFIRMATIVE INDICATIVE

Passive	nazimareru
Potential	nazimeru
Causative	nazimaseru
Causative Pass.	nazimaserareru

Honorific	**I**	onazimi ni naru
	II	onazimi nasaru
Humble	**I**	onazimi suru
	II	onazimi itasu

			AFFIRMATIVE	NEGATIVE
Indicative	**INFORMAL**		neru	nenai
	FORMAL		nemasu	nemaseñ
Imperative	**INFORMAL**	**I**	nero	neru na
		II	nenasai	nenasaru na
		III	nete kudasai	nenai de kudasai
	FORMAL*		oyasumi nasaimase	oyasumi nasaimasu na
Presumptive	**INFORMAL**	**I**	neyoo	nemai
		II	neru daroo	nenai daroo
	FORMAL	**I**	nemasyoo	nemasumai
		II	neru desyoo	nenai desyoo
Provisional	**INFORMAL**		nereba	nenakereba
	FORMAL		nemaseba	nemaseñ nara
			nemasureba	
Gerund	**INFORMAL**	**I**	nete	nenai de
		II		nenakute
	FORMAL		nemasite	nemaseñ de
Past Ind.	**INFORMAL**		neta	nenakatta
	FORMAL		nemasita	nemaseñ desita
Past Presump.	**INFORMAL**		netaroo	nenakattaroo
			neta daroo	nenakatta daroo
	FORMAL		nemasitaroo	nemaseñ desitaroo
			neta desyoo	nenakatta desyoo
Conditional	**INFORMAL**		netara	nenakattara
	FORMAL		nemasitara	nemaseñ desitara
Alternative	**INFORMAL**		netari	nenakattari
	FORMAL		nemasitari	nemaseñ desitari

		INFORMAL AFFIRMATIVE INDICATIVE
Passive		nerareru
Potential		nerareru
Causative		nesaseru
Causative Pass.		nesaserareru
Honorific*	**I**	oyasumi ni naru
	II	oyasumi nasaru
Humble	**I**	
	II	

*The formal imperative forms and honorific equivalents for *neru* are the same as those of its synonym *yasumu*.

		AFFIRMATIVE	NEGATIVE
Indicative	**INFORMAL**	nigeru	nigenai
	FORMAL	nigemasu	nigemaseñ
Imperative	**INFORMAL I**	nigero	nigeru na
	II	nigenasai	nigenasaru na
	III	nigete kudasai	nigenai de kudasai
	FORMAL	onige nasaimase	onige nasaimasu na
Presumptive	**INFORMAL I**	nigeyoo	nigemai
	II	nigeru daroo	nigenai daroo
	FORMAL I	nigemasyoo	nigemasumai
	II	nigeru desyoo	nigenai desyoo
Provisional	**INFORMAL**	nigereba	nigenakereba
	FORMAL	nigemaseba	nigemaseñ nara
		nigemasureba	
Gerund	**INFORMAL I**	nigete	nigenai de
	II		nigenakute
	FORMAL	nigemasite	nigemaseñ de
Past Ind.	**INFORMAL**	nigeta	nigenakatta
	FORMAL	nigemasita	nigemaseñ desita
Past Presump.	**INFORMAL**	nigetaroo	nigenakattaroo
		nigeta daroo	nigenakatta daroo
	FORMAL	nigemasitaroo	nigemaseñ desitaroo
		nigeta desyoo	nigenakatta desyoo
Conditional	**INFORMAL**	nigetara	nigenakattara
	FORMAL	nigemasitara	nigemaseñ desitara
Alternative	**INFORMAL**	nigetari	nigenakattari
	FORMAL	nigemasitari	nigemaseñ desitari

		INFORMAL AFFIRMATIVE INDICATIVE
Passive		nigerareru
Potential		nigerareru
Causative		nigesaseru
Causative Pass.		nigesaserareru

Honorific	**I**	onige ni naru
	II	onige nasaru
Humble	**I**	
	II	

		AFFIRMATIVE	**NEGATIVE**
Indicative	**INFORMAL**	nigiru	nigiranai
	FORMAL	nigirimasu	nigirimaseñ
Imperative	**INFORMAL I**	nigire	nigiru na
	II	nigirinasai	nigirinasaru na
	III	nigitte kudasai	nigiranai de kudasai
	FORMAL	onigiri nasaimase	onigiri nasaimasu na
Presumptive	**INFORMAL I**	nigiroo	nigirumai
	II	nigiru daroo	nigiranai daroo
	FORMAL I	nigirimasyoo	nigirimasumai
	II	nigiru desyoo	nigiranai desyoo
Provisional	**INFORMAL**	nigireba	nigiranakereba
	FORMAL	nigirimaseba	nigirimaseñ nara
		nigirimasureba	
Gerund	**INFORMAL I**	nigitte	nigiranai de
	II		nigiranakute
	FORMAL	nigirimasite	nigirimaseñ de
Past Ind.	**INFORMAL**	nigitta	nigiranakatta
	FORMAL	nigirimasita	nigirimaseñ desita
Past Presump.	**INFORMAL**	nigittaroo	nigiranakattaroo
		nigitta daroo	nigiranakatta daroo
	FORMAL	nigirimasitaroo	nigirimaseñ desitaroo
		nigitta desyoo	nigiranakatta desyoo
Conditional	**INFORMAL**	nigittara	nigiranakattara
	FORMAL	nigirimasitara	nigirimaseñ desitara
Alternative	**INFORMAL**	nigittari	nigiranakattari
	FORMAL	nigirimasitari	nigirimaseñ desitari

INFORMAL AFFIRMATIVE INDICATIVE

Passive		nigirareru
Potential		nigireru
Causative		nigiraseru
Causative Pass.		nigiraserareru

Honorific	**I**	onigiri ni naru
	II	onigiri nasaru
Humble	**I**	onigiri suru
	II	onigiri itasu

		AFFIRMATIVE	NEGATIVE
Indicative	**INFORMAL**	niramu	niramanai
	FORMAL	niramimasu	niramimaseñ
Imperative	**INFORMAL I**	nirame	niramu na
	II	niraminasai	niraminasaru na
	III	nirañde kudasai	niramanai de kudasai
	FORMAL	onirami nasaimase	onirami nasaimasu na
Presumptive	**INFORMAL I**	niramoo	niramumai
	II	niramu daroo	niramanai daroo
	FORMAL I	niramimasyoo	niramimasumai
	II	niramu desyoo	niramanai desyoo
Provisional	**INFORMAL**	nirameba	niramanakereba
	FORMAL	niramimaseba	niramimaseñ nara
		niramimasureba	
Gerund	**INFORMAL I**	nirañde	niramanai de
	II		niramanakute
	FORMAL	niramimasite	niramimaseñ de
Past Ind.	**INFORMAL**	nirañda	niramanakatta
	FORMAL	niramimasita	niramimaseñ desita
Past Presump.	**INFORMAL**	nirañdaroo	niramanakattaroo
		nirañda daroo	niramanakatta daroo
	FORMAL	niramimasitaroo	niramimaseñ desitaroo
		nirañda desyoo	niramanakatta desyoo
Conditional	**INFORMAL**	nirañdara	niramanakattara
	FORMAL	niramimasitara	niramimaseñ desitara
Alternative	**INFORMAL**	nirañdari	niramanakattari
	FORMAL	niramimasitari	niramimaseñ desitari

		INFORMAL AFFIRMATIVE INDICATIVE
Passive		niramareru
Potential		nirameru
Causative		niramaseru
Causative Pass.		niramaserareru
Honorific	**I**	onirami ni naru
	II	onirami nasaru
Humble	**I**	onirami suru
	II	onirami itasu

		AFFIRMATIVE	NEGATIVE
Indicative	**INFORMAL**	niru	ninai
	FORMAL	nimasu	nimaseñ
Imperative	**INFORMAL I**	niro	niru na
	II	ninasai	ninasaru na
	III	nite kudasai	ninai de kudasai
	FORMAL	oni nasaimase	oni nasaimasu na
Presumptive	**INFORMAL I**	niyoo	nimai
	II	niru daroo	ninai daroo
	FORMAL I	nimasyoo	nimasumai
	II	niru desyoo	ninai desyoo
Provisional	**INFORMAL**	nireba	ninakereba
	FORMAL	nimaseba	nimaseñ nara
		nimasureba	
Gerund	**INFORMAL I**	nite	ninai de
	II		ninakute
	FORMAL	nimasite	nimaseñ de
Past Ind.	**INFORMAL**	nita	ninakatta
	FORMAL	nimasita	nimaseñ desita
Past Presump.	**INFORMAL**	nitaroo	ninakattaroo
		nita daroo	ninakatta daroo
	FORMAL	nimasitaroo	nimaseñ desitaroo
		nita desyoo	ninakatta desyoo
Conditional	**INFORMAL**	nitara	ninakattara
	FORMAL	nimasitara	nimaseñ desitara
Alternative	**INFORMAL**	nitari	ninakattari
	FORMAL	nimasitari	nimaseñ desitari

		INFORMAL AFFIRMATIVE INDICATIVE
Passive		nirareru
Potential		nirareru
Causative		niraseru
Causative Pass.		niraserareru
Honorific	**I**	oni ni naru
	II	oni nasaru
Humble	**I**	
	II	

to postpone, to extend, to lengthen   TRANSITIVE

		AFFIRMATIVE	NEGATIVE
Indicative	**INFORMAL**	nobasu	nobasanai
	FORMAL	nobasimasu	nobasimaseñ
Imperative	**INFORMAL I**	nobase	nobasu na
	II	nobasinasai	nobasinasaru na
	III	nobasite kudasai	nobasanai de kudasai
	FORMAL	onobasi nasaimase	onobasi nasaimasu na
Presumptive	**INFORMAL I**	nobasoo	nobasumai
	II	nobasu daroo	nobasanai daroo
	FORMAL I	nobasimasyoo	nobasimasumai
	II	nobasu desyoo	nobasanai desyoo
Provisional	**INFORMAL**	nobaseba	nobasanakereba
	FORMAL	nobasimaseba	nobasimaseñ nara
		nobasimasureba	
Gerund	**INFORMAL I**	nobasite	nobasanai de
	II		nobasanakute
	FORMAL	nobasimasite	nobasimaseñ de
Past Ind.	**INFORMAL**	nobasita	nobasanakatta
	FORMAL	nobasimasita	nobasimaseñ desita
Past Presump.	**INFORMAL**	nobasitaroo	nobasanakattaroo
		nobasita daroo	nobasanakatta daroo
	FORMAL	nobasimasitaroo	nobasimaseñ desitaroo
		nobasita desyoo	nobasanakatta desyoo
Conditional	**INFORMAL**	nobasitara	nobasanakattara
	FORMAL	nobasimasitara	nobasimaseñ desitara
Alternative	**INFORMAL**	nobasitari	nobasanakattari
	FORMAL	nobasimasitari	nobasimaseñ desitari

		INFORMAL AFFIRMATIVE INDICATIVE
Passive		nobasareru
Potential		nobaseru
Causative		nobasaseru
Causative Pass.		nobasaserareru
Honorific	I	onobasi ni naru
	II	onobasi nasaru
Humble	I	onobasi suru
	II	onobasi itasu

			AFFIRMATIVE	NEGATIVE
Indicative	**INFORMAL**		noboru	noboranai
	FORMAL		noborimasu	noborimaseñ
Imperative	**INFORMAL**	**I**	nobore	noboru na
		II	noborinasai	noborinasaru na
		III	nobotte kudasai	noboranai de kudasai
	FORMAL		onobori nasaimase	onobori nasaimasu na
Presumptive	**INFORMAL**	**I**	noboroo	noborumai
		II	noboru daroo	noboranai daroo
	FORMAL	**I**	noborimasyoo	noborimasumai
		II	noboru desyoo	noboranai desyoo
Provisional	**INFORMAL**		noboreba	noboranakereba
	FORMAL		noborimaseba	noborimaseñ nara
			noborimasureba	
Gerund	**INFORMAL**	**I**	nobotte	noboranai de
		II		noboranakute
	FORMAL		noborimasite	noborimaseñ de
Past Ind.	**INFORMAL**		nobotta	noboranakatta
	FORMAL		noborimasita	noborimaseñ desita
Past Presump.	**INFORMAL**		nobottaroo	noboranakattaroo
			nobotta daroo	noboranakatta daroo
	FORMAL		noborimasitaroo	noborimaseñ desitaroo
			nobotta desyoo	noboranakatta desyoo
Conditional	**INFORMAL**		nobottara	noboranakattara
	FORMAL		noborimasitara	noborimaseñ desitara
Alternative	**INFORMAL**		nobottari	noboranakattari
	FORMAL		noborimasitari	noborimaseñ desitari

		INFORMAL AFFIRMATIVE INDICATIVE
Passive		noborareru
Potential		noboreru
Causative		noboraseru
Causative Pass.		noboraserareru
Honorific	**I**	onobori ni naru
	II	onobori nasaru
Humble	**I**	
	II	

		AFFIRMATIVE	NEGATIVE
Indicative	**INFORMAL**	nokoru	nokoranai
	FORMAL	nokorimasu	nokorimaseñ
Imperative	**INFORMAL I**	nokore	nokoru na
	II	nokorinasai	nokorinasaru na
	III	nokotte kudasai	nokoranaide kudasai
	FORMAL	onokori nasaimase	onokori nasaimasu na
Presumptive	**INFORMAL I**	nokoroo	nokorumai
	II	nokoru daroo	nokoranai daroo
	FORMAL I	nokorimasyoo	nokorimasumai
	II	nokoru desyoo	nokoranai desyoo
Provisional	**INFORMAL**	nokoreba	nokoranakereba
	FORMAL	nokorimaseba	nokorimaseñ nara
		nokorimasureba	
Gerund	**INFORMAL I**	nokotte	nokoranai de
	II		nokoranakute
	FORMAL	nokorimasite	nokorimaseñ de
Past Ind.	**INFORMAL**	nokotta	nokoranakatta
	FORMAL	nokorimasita	nokorimaseñ desita
Past Presump.	**INFORMAL**	nokottaroo	nokoranakattaroo
		nokotta daroo	nokoranakatta daroo
	FORMAL	nokorimasitaroo	nokorimaseñ desitaroo
		nokotta desyoo	nokoranakatta desyoo
Conditional	**INFORMAL**	nokottara	nokoranakattara
	FORMAL	nokorimasitara	nokorimaseñ desitara
Alternative	**INFORMAL**	nokottari	nokoranakattari
	FORMAL	nokorimasitari	nokorimaseñ desitari

		INFORMAL AFFIRMATIVE INDICATIVE
Passive		nokorareru
Potential		nokoreru
Causative		nokoraseru
Causative Pass.		nokoraserareru
Honorific	**I**	onokori ni naru
	II	onokori nasaru
Humble	**I**	
	II	

TRANSITIVE   *to leave behind, to leave unfinished*

		AFFIRMATIVE	**NEGATIVE**
Indicative	**INFORMAL**	nokosu	nokosanai
	FORMAL	nokosimasu	nokosimaseñ
Imperative	**INFORMAL I**	nokose	nokosu na
	II	nokosinasai	nokosinasaru na
	III	nokosite kudasai	nokosanai de kudasai
	FORMAL	onokosi nasaimase	onokosi nasaimasu na
Presumptive	**INFORMAL I**	nokosoo	nokosumai
	II	nokosu daroo	nokosanai daroo
	FORMAL I	nokosimasyoo	nokosimasumai
	II	nokosu desyoo	nokosanai desyoo
Provisional	**INFORMAL**	nokoseba	nokosanakereba
	FORMAL	nokosimaseba	nokosimaseñ nara
		nokosimasureba	
Gerund	**INFORMAL I**	nokosite	nokosanai de
	II		nokosanakute
	FORMAL	nokosimasite	nokosimaseñ de
Past Ind.	**INFORMAL**	nokosita	nokosanakatta
	FORMAL	nokosimasita	nokosimaseñ desita
Past Presump.	**INFORMAL**	nokositaroo	nokosanakattaroo
		nokosita daroo	nokosanakatta daroo
	FORMAL	nokosimasitaroo	nokosimaseñ desitaroo
		nokosita desyoo	nokosanakatta desyoo
Conditional	**INFORMAL**	nokositara	nokosanakattara
	FORMAL	nokosimasitara	nokosimaseñ desitara
Alternative	**INFORMAL**	nokositari	nokosanakattari
	FORMAL	nokosimasitari	nokosimaseñ desitari

	INFORMAL AFFIRMATIVE INDICATIVE
Passive	nokosareru
Potential	nokoseru
Causative	nokosaseru
Causative Pass.	nokosaserareru

Honorific	**I**	onokosi ni naru
	II	onokosi nasaru
Humble	**I**	onokosi suru
	II	onokosi itasu

to drink, to smoke (cigarettes etc.)   TRANSITIVE

			AFFIRMATIVE	NEGATIVE
Indicative	INFORMAL		nomu	nomanai
	FORMAL		nomimasu	nomimaseñ
Imperative	INFORMAL	I	nome	nomu na
		II	nominasai	nominasaru na
		III	noñde kudasai	nomanai de kudasai
	FORMAL		mesiagarimase	mesiagarimasu na
			onomi nasaimase	onomi nasaimasu na
Presumptive	INFORMAL	I	nomoo	nomumai
		II	nomu daroo	nomanai daroo
	FORMAL	I	nomimasyoo	nomimasumai
		II	nomu desyoo	nomanai desyoo
Provisional	INFORMAL		nomeba	nomanakereba
	FORMAL		nomimaseba	nomimaseñ nara
			nomimasureba	
Gerund	INFORMAL	I	noñde	nomanai de
		II		nomanakute
	FORMAL		nomimasite	nomimaseñ de
Past Ind.	INFORMAL		noñda	nomanakatta
	FORMAL		nomimasita	nomimaseñ desita
Past Presump.	INFORMAL		noñdaroo	nomanakattaroo
			noñda daroo	nomanakatta daroo
	FORMAL		nomimasitaroo	nomimaseñ desitaroo
			noñda desyoo	nomanakatta desyoo
Conditional	INFORMAL		noñdara	nomanakattara
	FORMAL		nomimasitara	nomimaseñ desitara
Alternative	INFORMAL		noñdari	nomanakattari
	FORMAL		nomimasitari	nomimaseñ desitari

	INFORMAL AFFIRMATIVE INDICATIVE		
Passive	nomareru		
Potential	nomeru		
Causative	nomaseru		
Causative Pass.	nomaserareru		

Honorific	mesiagaru	I	onomi ni naru
		II	onomi nasaru
Humble	itadaku		

		AFFIRMATIVE	NEGATIVE
Indicative	**INFORMAL**	noru	noranai
	FORMAL	norimasu	norimaseñ
Imperative	**INFORMAL I**	nore	noru na
	II	norinasai	norinasaru na
	III	notte kudasai	noranai de kudasai
	FORMAL	onori nasaimase	onori nasaimasu na
Presumptive	**INFORMAL I**	noroo	norumai
	II	noru daroo	noranai daroo
	FORMAL I	norimasyoo	norimasumai
	II	noru desyoo	noranai desyoo
Provisional	**INFORMAL**	noreba	noranakereba
	FORMAL	norimaseba	norimaseñ nara
		norimasureba	
Gerund	**INFORMAL I**	notte	noranai de
	II		noranakute
	FORMAL	norimasite	norimaseñ de
Past Ind.	**INFORMAL**	notta	noranakatta
	FORMAL	norimasita	norimaseñ desita
Past Presump.	**INFORMAL**	nottaroo	noranakattaroo
		notta daroo	noranakatta daroo
	FORMAL	norimasitaroo	norimaseñ desitaroo
		notta desyoo	noranakatta desyoo
Conditional	**INFORMAL**	nottara	noranakattara
	FORMAL	norimasitara	norimaseñ desitara
Alternative	**INFORMAL**	nottari	noranakattari
	FORMAL	norimasitari	norimaseñ desitari

		INFORMAL AFFIRMATIVE INDICATIVE
Passive		norareru
Potential		noreru
Causative		noraseru
Causative Pass.		noraserareru
Honorific	**I**	onori ni naru
	II	onori nasaru
Humble	**I**	
	II	

to put (on top of), *to put on board*   TRANSITIVE

		AFFIRMATIVE	NEGATIVE
Indicative	**INFORMAL**	noseru	nosenai
	FORMAL	nosemasu	nosemaseñ
Imperative	**INFORMAL I**	nosero	noseru na
	II	nosenasai	nosenasaru na
	III	nosete kudasai	nosenai de kudasai
	FORMAL	onose nasaimase	onose nasaimasu na
Presumptive	**INFORMAL I**	noseyoo	nosemai
	II	noseru daroo	nosenai daroo
	FORMAL I	nosemasyoo	nosemasumai
	II	noseru desyoo	nosenai desyoo
Provisional	**INFORMAL**	nosereba	nosenakereba
	FORMAL	nosemaseba	nosemaseñ nara
		nosemasureba	
Gerund	**INFORMAL I**	nosete	nosenai de
	II		nosenakute
	FORMAL	nosemasite	nosemaseñ de
Past Ind.	**INFORMAL**	noseta	nosenakatta
	FORMAL	nosemasita	nosemaseñ desita
Past Presump.	**INFORMAL**	nosetaroo	nosenakattaroo
		noseta daroo	nosenakatta daroo
	FORMAL	nosemasitaroo	nosemaseñ desitaroo
		noseta desyoo	nosenakatta desyoo
Conditional	**INFORMAL**	nosetara	nosenakattara
	FORMAL	nosemasitara	nosemaseñ desitara
Alternative	**INFORMAL**	nosetari	nosenakattari
	FORMAL	nosemasitari	nosemaseñ desitari

INFORMAL AFFIRMATIVE INDICATIVE

Passive		noserareru
Potential		noserareru
Causative		nosesaseru
Causative Pass.		nosesaserareru

Honorific	**I**	onose ni naru
	II	onose nasaru
Humble	**I**	onose suru
	II	onose itasu

		AFFIRMATIVE	NEGATIVE
Indicative	**INFORMAL**	nureru	nurenai
	FORMAL	nuremasu	nuremaseñ
Imperative	**INFORMAL I**	nurero	nureru na
	II		
	III		
	FORMAL		
Presumptive	**INFORMAL I**	nureyoo	nuremai
	II	nureru daroo	nurenai daroo
	FORMAL I	nuremasyoo	nuremasumai
	II	nureru desyoo	nurenai desyoo
Provisional	**INFORMAL**	nurereba	nurenakereba
	FORMAL	nuremaseba	nuremaseñ nara
		nuremasureba	
Gerund	**INFORMAL I**	nurete	nurenai de
	II		nurenakute
	FORMAL	nuremasite	nuremaseñ de
Past Ind.	**INFORMAL**	nureta	nurenakatta
	FORMAL	nuremasita	nuremaseñ desita
Past Presump.	**INFORMAL**	nuretaroo	nurenakattaroo
		nureta daroo	nurenakatta daroo
	FORMAL	nuremasitaroo	nuremaseñ desitaroo
		nureta desyoo	nurenakatta desyoo
Conditional	**INFORMAL**	nuretara	nurenakattara
	FORMAL	nuremasitara	nuremaseñ desitara
Alternative	**INFORMAL**	nuretari	nurenakattari
	FORMAL	nuremasitari	nuremaseñ desitari

		INFORMAL AFFIRMATIVE INDICATIVE
Passive		nurerareru
Potential		nurerareru
Causative		nuresaseru
Causative Pass.		nuresaserareru
Honorific	**I**	onure ni naru
	II	onure nasaru
Humble	**I**	
	II	

		AFFIRMATIVE	NEGATIVE
Indicative	**INFORMAL**	nuru	nuranai
	FORMAL	nurimasu	nurimaseñ
Imperative	**INFORMAL I**	nure	nuru na
	II	nurinasai	nurinasaru na
	III	nutte kudasai	nuranai de kudasai
	FORMAL	onuri nasaimase	onuri nasaimasu na
Presumptive	**INFORMAL I**	nuroo	nurumai
	II	nuru daroo	nuranai daroo
	FORMAL I	nurimasyoo	nurimasumai
	II	nuru desyoo	nuranai desyoo
Provisional	**INFORMAL**	nureba	nuranakereba
	FORMAL	nurimaseba	nurimaseñ nara
		nurimasureba	
Gerund	**INFORMAL I**	nutte	nuranai de
	II		nuranakute
	FORMAL	nurimasite	nurimaseñ de
Past Ind.	**INFORMAL**	nutta	nuranakatta
	FORMAL	nurimasita	nurimaseñ desita
Past Presump.	**INFORMAL**	nuttaroo	nuranakattaroo
		nutta daroo	nuranakatta daroo
	FORMAL	nurimasitaroo	nurimaseñ desitaroo
		nutta desyoo	nuranakatta desyoo
Conditional	**INFORMAL**	nuttara	nuranakattara
	FORMAL	nurimasitara	nurimaseñ desitara
Alternative	**INFORMAL**	nuttari	nuranakattari
	FORMAL	nurimasitari	nurimaseñ desitari

		INFORMAL AFFIRMATIVE INDICATIVE
Passive		nurareru
Potential		nureru
Causative		nuraseru
Causative Pass.		nuraserareru

Honorific	**I**	onuri ni naru
	II	onuri nasaru
Humble	**I**	onuri suru
	II	onuri itasu

		AFFIRMATIVE	NEGATIVE
Indicative	**INFORMAL**	nusumu	nusumanai
	FORMAL	nusumimasu	nusumimaseñ
Imperative	**INFORMAL I**	nusume	nusumu na
	II	nusuminasai	nusuminasaru na
	III	nusuñde kudasai	nusumanai de kudasai
	FORMAL	onusumi nasaimase	onusumi nasaimasu na
Presumptive	**INFORMAL I**	nusumoo	nusumumai
	II	nusumu daroo	nusumanai daroo
	FORMAL I	nusumimasyoo	nusumimasumai
	II	nusumu desyoo	nusumanai desyoo
Provisional	**INFORMAL**	nusumeba	nusumanakereba
	FORMAL	nusumimaseba	nusumimaseñ nara
		nusumimasureba	
Gerund	**INFORMAL I**	nusuñde	nusumanai de
	II		nusumanakute
	FORMAL	nusumimasite	nusumimaseñ de
Past Ind.	**INFORMAL**	nusuñda	nusumanakatta
	FORMAL	nusumimasita	nusumimaseñ desita
Past Presump.	**INFORMAL**	nusuñdaroo	nusumanakattaroo
		nusuñda daroo	nusumanakatta daroo
	FORMAL	nusumimasitaroo	nusumimaseñ desitaroo
		nusuñda desyoo	nusumanakatta desyoo
Conditional	**INFORMAL**	nusuñdara	nusumanakattara
	FORMAL	nusumimasitara	nusumimaseñ desitara
Alternative	**INFORMAL**	nusuñdari	nusumanakattari
	FORMAL	nusumimasitari	nusumimaseñ desitari

		INFORMAL AFFIRMATIVE INDICATIVE
Passive		nusumareru
Potential		nusumeru
Causative		nusumaseru
Causative Pass.		nusumaserareru
Honorific	**I**	onusumi ni naru
	II	onusumi nasaru
Humble	**I**	
	II	

		AFFIRMATIVE	NEGATIVE
Indicative	**INFORMAL**	oboeru	oboenai
	FORMAL	oboemasu	oboemaseñ
Imperative	**INFORMAL I**	oboero	oboeru na
	II	oboenasai	oboenasaru na
	III	oboete kudasai	oboenai de kudasai
	FORMAL	oboe nasaimase	oboe nasaimasu na
Presumptive	**INFORMAL I**	oboeyoo	oboemai
	II	oboeru daroo	oboenai daroo
	FORMAL I	oboemasyoo	oboemasumai
	II	oboeru desyoo	oboenai desyoo
Provisional	**INFORMAL**	oboereba	oboenakereba
	FORMAL	oboemaseba	oboemaseñ nara
		oboemasureba	
Gerund	**INFORMAL I**	oboete	oboenai de
	II		oboenakute
	FORMAL	oboemasite	oboemaseñ de
Past Ind.	**INFORMAL**	oboeta	oboenakatta
	FORMAL	oboemasita	oboemaseñ desita
Past Presump.	**INFORMAL**	oboetaroo	oboenakattaroo
		oboeta daroo	oboenakatta daroo
	FORMAL	oboemasitaroo	oboemaseñ desitaroo
		oboeta desyoo	oboenakatta desyoo
Conditional	**INFORMAL**	oboetara	oboenakattara
	FORMAL	oboemasitara	oboemaseñ desitara
Alternative	**INFORMAL**	oboetari	oboenakattari
	FORMAL	oboemasitari	oboemaseñ desitari

INFORMAL AFFIRMATIVE INDICATIVE

Passive		oboerareru
Potential		oboerareru
Causative		oboesaseru
Causative Pass.		oboesaserareru
Honorific	**I**	ooboe ni naru
	II	ooboe nasaru
Humble	**I**	
	II	

odoroki   odorók.u

to be surprised

		AFFIRMATIVE	NEGATIVE
Indicative	**INFORMAL**	odoroku	odorokanai
	FORMAL	odorokimasu	odorokimaseñ
Imperative	**INFORMAL I**	odoroke	odoroku na
	II	odorokinasai	odorokinasaru na
	III	odoroite kudasai	odorokanai de kudasai
	FORMAL	oodoroki nasaimase	oodoroki nasaimasu na
Presumptive	**INFORMAL I**	odorokoo	odorokumai
	II	odoroku daroo	odorokanai daroo
	FORMAL I	odorokimasyoo	odorokimasumai
	II	odoroku desyoo	odorokanai desyoo
Provisional	**INFORMAL**	odorokeba	odorokanakereba
	FORMAL	odorokimaseba	odorokimaseñ nara
		odorokimasureba	
Gerund	**INFORMAL I**	odoroite	odorokanai de
	II		odorokanakute
	FORMAL	odorokimasite	odorokimaseñ de
Past Ind.	**INFORMAL**	odoroita	odorokanakatta
	FORMAL	odorokimasita	odorokimaseñ desita
Past Presump.	**INFORMAL**	odoroitaroo	odorokanakattaroo
		odoroita daroo	odorokanakatta daroo
	FORMAL	odorokimasitaroo	odorokimaseñ desitaroo
		odoroita desyoo	odorokanakatta desyoo
Conditional	**INFORMAL**	odoroitara	odorokanakattara
	FORMAL	odorokimasitara	odorokimaseñ desitara
Alternative	**INFORMAL**	odoroitari	odorokanakattari
	FORMAL	odorokimasitari	odorokimaseñ desitari

INFORMAL AFFIRMATIVE INDICATIVE

Passive		odorokareru
Potential		odorokeru
Causative		odorokaseru
Causative Pass.		odorokaserareru

Honorific	**I**	oodoroki ni naru
	II	oodoroki nasaru
Humble	**I**	
	II	

		AFFIRMATIVE	NEGATIVE
Indicative	**INFORMAL**	odoru	odoranai
	FORMAL	odorimasu	odorimaseñ
Imperative	**INFORMAL I**	odore	odoru na
	II	odorinasai	odorinasaru na
	III	odotte kudasai	odoranai de kudasai
	FORMAL	oodori nasaimase	oodori nasaimasu na
Presumptive	**INFORMAL I**	odoroo	odorumai
	II	odoru daroo	odoranai daroo
	FORMAL I	odorimasyoo	odorimasumai
	II	odoru desyoo	odoranai desyoo
Provisional	**INFORMAL**	odoreba	odoranakereba
	FORMAL	odorimaseba	odorimaseñ nara
		odorimasureba	
Gerund	**INFORMAL I**	odotte	odoranai de
	II		odoranakute
	FORMAL	odorimasite	odorimaseñ de
Past Ind.	**INFORMAL**	odotta	odoranakatta
	FORMAL	odorimasita	odorimaseñ desita
Past Presump.	**INFORMAL**	odottaroo	odoranakattaroo
		odotta daroo	odoranakatta daroo
	FORMAL	odorimasitaroo	odorimaseñ desitaroo
		odotta desyoo	odoranakatta desyoo
Conditional	**INFORMAL**	odottara	odoranakattara
	FORMAL	odorimasitara	odorimaseñ desitara
Alternative	**INFORMAL**	odottari	odoranakattari
	FORMAL	odorimasitari	odorimaseñ desitari

		INFORMAL AFFIRMATIVE INDICATIVE
Passive		odorareru
Potential		odoreru
Causative		odoraseru
Causative Pass.		odoraserareru
Honorific	**I**	oodori ni naru
	II	oodori nasaru
Humble	**I**	
	II	

		AFFIRMATIVE	NEGATIVE
Indicative	**INFORMAL**	okiru	okinai
	FORMAL	okimasu	okimaseñ
Imperative	**INFORMAL I**	okiro	okiru na
	II	okinasai	okinasaru na
	III	okite kudasai	okinai de kudasai
	FORMAL	ooki nasaimase	ooki nasaimasu na
Presumptive	**INFORMAL I**	okiyoo	okimai
	II	okiru daroo	okinai daroo
	FORMAL I	okimasyoo	okimasumai
	II	okiru desyoo	okinai desyoo
Provisional	**INFORMAL**	okireba	okinakereba
	FORMAL	okimaseba	okimaseñ nara
		okimasureba	
Gerund	**INFORMAL I**	okite	okinai de
	II		okinakute
	FORMAL	okimasite	okimaseñ de
Past Ind.	**INFORMAL**	okita	okinakatta
	FORMAL	okimasita	okimaseñ desita
Past Presump.	**INFORMAL**	okitaroo	okinakattaroo
		okita daroo	okinakatta daroo
	FORMAL	okimasitaroo	okimaseñ desitaroo
		okita desyoo	okinakatta desyoo
Conditional	**INFORMAL**	okitara	okinakattara
	FORMAL	okimasitara	okimaseñ desitara
Alternative	**INFORMAL**	okitari	okinakattari
	FORMAL	okimasitari	okimaseñ desitari

		INFORMAL AFFIRMATIVE INDICATIVE
Passive		okirareru
Potential		okirareru
Causative		okisaseru
Causative Pass.		okisaserareru
Honorific	**I**	ooki ni naru
	II	ooki nasaru
Humble	**I**	ooki suru
	II	ooki itasu

okós.u
to raise up, to cause to get up   TRANSITIVE

			AFFIRMATIVE	NEGATIVE
Indicative	**INFORMAL**		okosu	okosanai
	FORMAL		okosimasu	okosimaseñ
Imperative	**INFORMAL I**		okose	okosu na
		II	okosinasai	okosinasaru na
		III	okosite kudasai	okosanai de kudasai
	FORMAL		ookosi nasaimase	ookosi nasaimasu na
Presumptive	**INFORMAL I**		okosoo	okosumai
		II	okosu daroo	okosanai daroo
	FORMAL	**I**	okosimasyoo	okosimasumai
		II	okosu daroo	okosanai daroo
Provisional	**INFORMAL**		okoseba	okosanakereba
	FORMAL		okosimaseba	okosimaseñ nara
			okosimasureba	
Gerund	**INFORMAL I**		okosite	okosanai de
		II		okosanakute
	FORMAL		okosimasite	okosimaseñ de
Past Ind.	**INFORMAL**		okosita	okosanakatta
	FORMAL		okosimasita	okosimaseñ desita
Past Presump.	**INFORMAL**		okositaroo	okosanakattaroo
			okosita daroo	okosanakatta daroo
	FORMAL		okosimasitaroo	okosimaseñ desitaroo
			okosita desyoo	okosanakatta desyoo
Conditional	**INFORMAL**		okositara	okosanakattara
	FORMAL		okosimasitara	okosimaseñ desitara
Alternative	**INFORMAL**		okositari	okosanakattari
	FORMAL		okosimasitari	okosimaseñ desitari

INFORMAL AFFIRMATIVE INDICATIVE

Passive		okosareru
Potential		okoseru
Causative		okosaseru
Causative Pass.		okosaserareru

Honorific	**I**	ookosi ni naru
	II	ookosi nasaru
Humble	**I**	ookosi suru
	II	ookosi itasu

		AFFIRMATIVE	NEGATIVE
Indicative	**INFORMAL**	oku	okanai
	FORMAL	okimasu	okimaseñ
Imperative	**INFORMAL I**	oke	oku na
	II	okinasai	okinasaru na
	III	oite kudasai	okanai de kudasai
	FORMAL	ooki nasaimase	ooki nasaimasu na
Presumptive	**INFORMAL I**	okoo	okumai
	II	oku daroo	okanai daroo
	FORMAL I	okimasyoo	okimasumai
	II	oku desyoo	okanai desyoo
Provisional	**INFORMAL**	okeba	okanakereba
	FORMAL	okimaseba	okimaseñ nara
		okimasureba	
Gerund	**INFORMAL I**	oite	okanai de
	II		okanakute
	FORMAL	okimasite	okimaseñ de
Past Ind.	**INFORMAL**	oita	okanakatta
	FORMAL	okimasita	okimaseñ desita
Past Presump.	**INFORMAL**	oitaroo	okanakattaroo
		oita daroo	okanakatta daroo
	FORMAL	okimasitaroo	okimaseñ desitaroo
		oita desyoo	okanakatta desyoo
Conditional	**INFORMAL**	oitara	okanakattara
	FORMAL	okimasitara	okimaseñ desitara
Alternative	**INFORMAL**	oitari	okanakattari
	FORMAL	okimasitari	okimaseñ desitari

INFORMAL AFFIRMATIVE INDICATIVE

Passive		okareru
Potential		okeru
Causative		okaseru
Causative Pass.		okaserareru
Honorific	**I**	ooki ni naru
	II	ooki nasaru
Humble	**I**	ooki suru
	II	ooki itasu

		AFFIRMATIVE	NEGATIVE
Indicative	**INFORMAL**	okureru	okurenai
	FORMAL	okuremasu	okuremaseñ
Imperative	**INFORMAL I**	okurero	okureru na
	II	okurenasai	okurenasaru na
	III	okurete kudasai	okurenai de kudasai
	FORMAL	ookure nasaimase	ookure nasaimasu na
Presumptive	**INFORMAL I**	okureyoo	okuremai
	II	okureru daroo	okurenai daroo
	FORMAL I	okuremasyoo	okuremasumai
	II	okureru desyoo	okurenai desyoo
Provisional	**INFORMAL**	okurereba	okurenakereba
	FORMAL	okuremaseba	okuremaseñ nara
		okuremasureba	
Gerund	**INFORMAL I**	okurete	okurenai de
	II		okurenakute
	FORMAL	okuremasite	okuremaseñ de
Past Ind.	**INFORMAL**	okureta	okurenakatta
	FORMAL	okuremasita	okuremaseñ desita
Past Presump.	**INFORMAL**	okuretaroo	okurenakattaroo
		okureta daroo	okurenakatta daroo
	FORMAL	okuremasitaroo	okuremaseñ desitaroo
		okureta desyoo	okurenakatta desyoo
Conditional	**INFORMAL**	okuretara	okurenakattara
	FORMAL	okuremasitara	okuremaseñ desitara
Alternative	**INFORMAL**	okuretari	okurenakattari
	FORMAL	okuremasitari	okuremaseñ desitari

		INFORMAL AFFIRMATIVE INDICATIVE
Passive		okurerareru
Potential		okurerareru
Causative		okuresaseru
Causative Pass.		okuresaserareru
Honorific	**I**	ookure ni naru
	II	ookure nasaru
Humble	**I**	
	II	

okuri   okur.u

TRANSITIVE   to send (a package), to escort (a person)

		AFFIRMATIVE	NEGATIVE
Indicative	**INFORMAL**	okuru	okuranai
	FORMAL	okurimasu	okurimaseñ
Imperative	**INFORMAL I**	okure	okuru na
	II	okurinasai	okurinasaru na
	III	okutte kudasai	okuranai de kudasai
	FORMAL	ookuri nasaimase	ookuri nasaimasu na
Presumptive	**INFORMAL I**	okuroo	okurumai
	II	okuru daroo	okuranai daroo
	FORMAL I	okurimasyoo	okurimasumai
	II	okuru desyoo	okuranai desyoo
Provisional	**INFORMAL**	okureba	okuranakereba
	FORMAL	okurimaseba	okurimaseñ nara
		okurimasureba	
Gerund	**INFORMAL I**	okutte	okuranai de
	II		okuranakute
	FORMAL	okurimasite	okurimaseñ de
Past Ind.	**INFORMAL**	okutta	okuranakatta
	FORMAL	okurimasita	okurimaseñ desita
Past Presump.	**INFORMAL**	okuttaroo	okuranakattaroo
		okutta daroo	okuranakatta daroo
	FORMAL	okurimasitaroo	okurimaseñ desitaroo
		okutta desyoo	okuranakatta desyoo
Conditional	**INFORMAL**	okuttara	okuranakattara
	FORMAL	okurimasitara	okurimaseñ desitara
Alternative	**INFORMAL**	okuttari	okuranakattari
	FORMAL	okurimasitari	okurimaseñ desitari

		INFORMAL AFFIRMATIVE INDICATIVE
Passive		okurareru
Potential		okureru
Causative		okuraseru
Causative Pass.		okuraserareru
Honorific	**I**	ookuri ni naru
	II	ookuri nasaru
Humble	**I**	ookuri suru
	II	ookuri itasu

		AFFIRMATIVE	**NEGATIVE**
Indicative	**INFORMAL**	omou	omowanai
	FORMAL	omoimasu	omoimaseñ
Imperative	**INFORMAL I**	omoe	omou na
	II	omoinasai	omoi nasaru na
	III	omotte kudasai	omowanai de kudasai
	FORMAL	oomoi nasaimase	oomoi nasaimasu na
Presumptive	**INFORMAL I**	omooo	omoumai
	II	omou daroo	omowanai daroo
	FORMAL I	omoimasyoo	omoimasumai
	II	omou desyoo	omowanai desyoo
Provisional	**INFORMAL**	omoeba	omowanakereba
	FORMAL	omoimaseba	omoimaseñ nara
		omoimasureba	
Gerund	**INFORMAL I**	omotte	omowanai de
	II		omowanakute
	FORMAL	omoimasite	omoimaseñ de
Past Ind.	**INFORMAL**	omotta	omowanakatta
	FORMAL	omoimasita	omoimaseñ desita
Past Presump.	**INFORMAL**	omottaroo	omowanakattaroo
		omotta daroo	omowanakatta daroo
	FORMAL	omoimasitaroo	omoimaseñ desitaroo
		omotta desyoo	omowanakatta desyoo
Conditional	**INFORMAL**	omottara	omowanakattara
	FORMAL	omoimasitara	omoimaseñ desitara
Alternative	**INFORMAL**	omottari	omowanakattari
	FORMAL	omoimasitari	omoimaseñ desitari

		INFORMAL AFFIRMATIVE INDICATIVE		
Passive		omowareru		
Potential		omoeru		
Causative		omowaseru		
Causative Pass.		omowaserareru		
Honorific	**I**	obosimesu	**I**	oomoi ni naru
	II		**II**	oomoi nasaru
Humble	**I**	oomoi suru		
	II	oomoi itasu		

to debark from, to descend from

		AFFIRMATIVE	NEGATIVE
Indicative	**INFORMAL**	oriru	orinai
	FORMAL	orimasu	orimaseñ
Imperative	**INFORMAL I**	oriro	oriru na
	II	orinasai	orinasaru na
	III	orite kudasai	orinai de kudasai
	FORMAL	oori nasaimase	oori nasaimasu na
Presumptive	**INFORMAL I**	oriyoo	orimai
	II	oriru daroo	orinai daroo
	FORMAL I	orimasyoo	orimasumai
	II	oriru desyoo	orinai desyoo
Provisional	**INFORMAL**	orireba	orinakereba
	FORMAL	orimaseba	orimaseñ nara
		orimasureba	
Gerund	**INFORMAL I**	orite	orinai de
	II		orinakute
	FORMAL	orimasite	orimaseñ de
Past Ind.	**INFORMAL**	orita	orinakatta
	FORMAL	orimasita	orimaseñ desita
Past Presump.	**INFORMAL**	oritaroo	orinakattaroo
		orita daroo	orinakatta daroo
	FORMAL	orimasitaroo	orimaseñ desitaroo
		orita desyoo	orinakatta desyoo
Conditional	**INFORMAL**	oritara	orinakattara
	FORMAL	orimasitara	orimaseñ desitara
Alternative	**INFORMAL**	oritari	orinakattari
	FORMAL	orimasitari	orimaseñ desitari

		INFORMAL AFFIRMATIVE INDICATIVE
Passive		orirareru
Potential		orirareru
Causative		orisaseru
Causative Pass.		orisaserareru
Honorific	**I**	oori ni naru
	II	oori nasaru
Humble	**I**	
	II	

to restrain, to control, to catch   TRANSITIVE

		AFFIRMATIVE	NEGATIVE
Indicative	**INFORMAL**	osaeru	osaenai
	FORMAL	osaemasu	osaemaseñ
Imperative	**INFORMAL I**	osaero	osaeru na
	II	osaenasai	osaenasaru na
	III	osaete kudasai	osaenai de kudasai
	FORMAL	oosae nasaimase	oosae nasaimasu na
Presumptive	**INFORMAL I**	osaeyoo	osaemai
	II	osaeru daroo	osaenai daroo
	FORMAL I	osaemasyoo	osaemasumai
	II	osaeru desyoo	osaenai desyoo
Provisional	**INFORMAL**	osaereba	osaenakereba
	FORMAL	osaemaseba	osaemaseñ nara
		osaemasureba	
Gerund	**INFORMAL I**	osaete	osaenai de
	II		osaenakute
	FORMAL	osaemasite	osaemaseñ de
Past Ind.	**INFORMAL**	osaeta	osaenakatta
	FORMAL	osaemasita	osaemaseñ desita
Past Presump.	**INFORMAL**	osaetaroo	osaenakattaroo
		osaeta daroo	osaenakatta daroo
	FORMAL	osaemasitaroo	osaemaseñ desitaroo
		osaeta desyoo	osaenakatta desyoo
Conditional	**INFORMAL**	osaetara	osaenakattara
	FORMAL	osaemasitara	osaemaseñ desitara
Alternative	**INFORMAL**	osaetari	osaenakattari
	FORMAL	osaemasitari	osaemaseñ desitari

		INFORMAL AFFIRMATIVE INDICATIVE
Passive		osaerareru
Potential		osaerareru
Causative		osaesaseru
Causative Pass.		osaesaserareru
Honorific	**I**	oosae ni naru
	II	oosae nasaru
Humble	**I**	oosae suru
	II	oosae itasu

		AFFIRMATIVE	NEGATIVE
Indicative	**INFORMAL**	osieru	osienai
	FORMAL	osiemasu	osiemaseñ
Imperative	**INFORMAL I**	osiero	osieru na
	II	osienasai	osienasaru na
	III	osiete kudasai	osienai de kudasai
	FORMAL	oosie nasaimase	oosie nasaimasu na
Presumptive	**INFORMAL l**	osieyoo	osiemai
	II	osieru daroo	osienai daroo
	FORMAL I	osiemasyoo	osiemasumai
	II	osieru desyoo	osienai desyoo
Provisional	**INFORMAL**	osiereba	osienakereba
	FORMAL	osiemaseba	osiemaseñ nara
		osiemasureba	
Gerund	**INFORMAL I**	osiete	osienai de
	II		osienakute
	FORMAL	osiemasite	osiemaseñ de
Past Ind.	**INFORMAL**	osieta	osienakatta
	FORMAL	osiemasita	osiemaseñ desita
Past Presump.	**INFORMAL**	osietaroo	osienakattaroo
		osieta daroo	osienakatta dàroo
	FORMAL	osiemasitaroo	osiemaseñ desitaroo
		osieta desyoo	osienakatta desyoo
Conditional	**INFORMAL**	osietara	osienakattara
	FORMAL	osiemasitara	osiemaseñ desitara
Alternative	**INFORMAL**	osietari	osienakattari
	FORMAL	osiemasitari	osiemaseñ desitari

INFORMAL AFFIRMATIVE INDICATIVE

Passive		osierareru
Potential		osierareru
Causative		osiesaseru
Causative Pass.		osiesaserareru

Honorific	**I**	oosie ni naru
	II	oosie nasaru
Humble	**I**	oosie suru
	II	oosie itasu

to regret, to begrudge, to be reluctant   TRANSITIVE

		AFFIRMATIVE	NEGATIVE
Indicative	**INFORMAL**	osimu	osimanai
	FORMAL	osimimasu	osimimaseñ
Imperative	**INFORMAL I**	osime	osimu na
	II	osiminasai	osiminasaru na
	III	osiñde kudasai	osimanai de kudasai
	FORMAL	oosimi nasaimase	oosimi nasaimasu na
Presumptive	**INFORMAL I**	osimoo	osimumai
	II	osimu daroo	osimanai daroo
	FORMAL I	osimimasyoo	osimimasumai
	II	osimu desyoo	osimanai desyoo
Provisional	**INFORMAL**	osimeba	osimanakereba
	FORMAL	osimimaseba	osimimaseñ nara
		osimimasureba	
Gerund	**INFORMAL I**	osiñde	osimanai de
	II		osimanakute
	FORMAL	osimimasite	osimimaseñ de
Past Ind.	**INFORMAL**	osiñda	osimanakatta
	FORMAL	osimimasita	osimimaseñ desita
Past Presump.	**INFORMAL**	osiñdaroo	osimanakattaroo
		osiñda daroo	osimanakatta daroo
	FORMAL	osimimasitaroo	osimimaseñ desitaroo
		osiñda desyoo	osimanakatta desyoo
Conditional	**INFORMAL**	osiñdara	osimanakattara
	FORMAL	osimimasitara	osimimaseñ desitara
Alternative	**INFORMAL**	osiñdari	osimanakattari
	FORMAL	osimimasitari	osimimaseñ desitari

INFORMAL AFFIRMATIVE INDICATIVE

Passive		osimareru
Potential		osimeru
Causative		osimaseru
Causative Pass.		osimaserareru

Honorific	**I**	oosimi ni naru
	II	oosimi nasaru
Humble	**I**	oosimi suru
	II	oosimi itasu

		AFFIRMATIVE	NEGATIVE
Indicative	**INFORMAL**	osoreru	osorenai
	FORMAL	osoremasu	osoremaseñ
Imperative	**INFORMAL I**	osorero	osoreru na
	II	osorenasai	osorenasaru na
	III	osorete kudasai	osorenai de kudasai
	FORMAL	oosore nasaimase	oosore nasaimasu na
Presumptive	**INFORMAL I**	osoreyoo	osoremai
	II	osoreru daroo	osorenai daroo
	FORMAL I	osoremasyoo	osoremasumai
	II	osoreru desyoo	osorenai desyoo
Provisional	**INFORMAL**	osorereba	osorenakereba
	FORMAL	osoremaseba	osoremaseñ nara
		osoremasureba	
Gerund	**INFORMAL I**	osorete	osorenai de
	II		osorenakute
	FORMAL	osoremasite	osoremaseñ de
Past Ind.	**INFORMAL**	osoreta	osorenakatta
	FORMAL	osoremasita	osoremaseñ desita
Past Presump.	**INFORMAL**	osoretaroo	osorenakattaroo
		osoreta daroo	osorenakatta daroo
	FORMAL	osoremasitaroo	osoremaseñ desitaroo
		osoreta desyoo	osorenakatta desyoo
Conditional	**INFORMAL**	osoretara	osorenakattara
	FORMAL	osoremasitara	osoremaseñ desitara
Alternative	**INFORMAL**	osoretari	osorenakattari
	FORMAL	osoremasitari	osoremaseñ desitari

INFORMAL AFFIRMATIVE INDICATIVE

Passive		osorerareru
Potential		osorerareru
Causative		osoresaseru
Causative Pass.		osoresaserareru
Honorific	**I**	oosore ni naru
	II	oosore nasaru
Humble	**I**	oosore suru
	II	oosore itasu

to attack, to raid   TRANSITIVE

		AFFIRMATIVE	NEGATIVE
Indicative	**INFORMAL**	osou	osowanai
	FORMAL	osoimasu	osoimaseñ
Imperative	**INFORMAL I**	osoe	osou na
	II	osoinasai	osoinasaru na
	III	osotte kudasai	osowanai de kudasai
	FORMAL	oosoi nasaimase	oosoi nasaimasu na
Presumptive	**INFORMAL I**	osooo	osoumai
	II	osou daroo	osowanai daroo
	FORMAL I	osoimasyoo	osoimasumai
	II	osou desyoo	osowanai desyoo
Provisional	**INFORMAL**	osoeba	osowanakereba
	FORMAL	osoimaseba	osoimaseñ nara
		osoimasureba	
Gerund	**INFORMAL I**	osotte	osowanai de
	II		osowanakute
	FORMAL	osoimasite	osoimaseñ de
Past Ind.	**INFORMAL**	osotta	osowanakatta
	FORMAL	osoimasita	osoimaseñ desita
Past Presump.	**INFORMAL**	osottaroo	osowanakattaroo
		osotta daroo	osowanakatta daroo
	FORMAL	osoimasitaroo	osoimaseñ desitaroo
		osotta desyoo	osowanakatta desyoo
Conditional	**INFORMAL**	osottara	osowanakattara
	FORMAL	osoimasitara	osoimaseñ desitara
Alternative	**INFORMAL**	osottari	osowanakattari
	FORMAL	osoimasitari	osoimaseñ desitari

INFORMAL AFFIRMATIVE INDICATIVE

Passive		osowareru
Potential		osoeru
Causative		osowaseru
Causative Pass.		osowaserareru

Honorific	**I**	oosoi ni naru
	II	oosoi nasaru
Humble	**I**	oosoi suru
	II	oosoi itasu

		AFFIRMATIVE	NEGATIVE
Indicative	**INFORMAL**	ossyaru	ossyaranai
	FORMAL	ossyaimasu	ossyaimaseñ
Imperative	**INFORMAL I**	ossyai	ossyaru na
	II	ossyainasai	ossyainasaru na
	III	ossyatte kudasai	ossyaranai de kudasai
	FORMAL	ossyaimase	ossyaimasu na
Presumptive	**INFORMAL I**	ossyaroo	ossyarumai
	II	ossyaru daroo	ossyaranai daroo
	FORMAL I	ossyaimasyoo	ossyaimasumai
	II	ossyaru desyoo	ossyaranai desyoo
Provisional	**INFORMAL**	ossyareba	ossyaranakereba
	FORMAL	ossyaimaseba	ossyaimaseñ nara
		ossyaimasureba	
Gerund	**INFORMAL I**	ossyatte	ossyaranai de
	II		ossyaranakute
	FORMAL	ossyaimasite	ossyaimaseñ de
Past Ind.	**INFORMAL**	ossyatta	ossyaranakatta
	FORMAL	ossyaimasita	ossyaimaseñ desita
Past Presump.	**INFORMAL**	ossyattaroo	ossyaranakattaroo
		ossyatta daroo	ossyaranakatta daroo
	FORMAL	ossyaimasitaroo	ossyaimaseñ desitaroo
		ossyatta desyoo	ossyaranakatta desyoo
Conditional	**INFORMAL**	ossyattara	ossyaranakattara
	FORMAL	ossyaimasitara	ossyaimaseñ desitara
Alternative	**INFORMAL**	ossyattari	ossyaranakattari
	FORMAL	ossyaimasitari	ossyaimaseñ desitari

INFORMAL AFFIRMATIVE INDICATIVE

Passive	
Potential	ossyareru
Causative	
Causative Pass.	

Honorific	**I**	
	II	
Humble	**I**	
	II	

to push, to press   TRANSITIVE

		AFFIRMATIVE	NEGATIVE
Indicative	**INFORMAL**	osu	osanai
	FORMAL	osimasu	osimaseñ
Imperative	**INFORMAL I**	ose	osu na
	II	osinasai	osinasaru na
	III	osite kudasai	osanai de kudasai
	FORMAL	oosi nasaimase	oosi nasaimasu na
Presumptive	**INFORMAL I**	osoo	osumai
	II	osu daroo	osanai daroo
	FORMAL I	osimasyoo	osimasumai
	II	osu desyoo	osanai desyoo
Provisional	**INFORMAL**	oseba	osanakereba
	FORMAL	osimaseba	osimaseñ nara
		osimasureba	
Gerund	**INFORMAL I**	osite	osanai de
	II		osanakute
	FORMAL	osimasite	osimaseñ de
Past Ind.	**INFORMAL**	osita	osanakatta
	FORMAL	osimasita	osimaseñ desita
Past Presump.	**INFORMAL**	ositaroo	osanakattaroo
		osita daroo	osanakatta daroo
	FORMAL	osimasitaroo	osimaseñ desitaroo
		osita desyoo	osanakatta desyoo
Conditional	**INFORMAL**	ositara	osanakattara
	FORMAL	osimasitara	osimaseñ desitara
Alternative	**INFORMAL**	ositari	osanakattari
	FORMAL	osimasitari	osimaseñ desitari

		INFORMAL AFFIRMATIVE INDICATIVE
Passive		osareru
Potential		oseru
Causative		osaseru
Causative Pass.		osaserareru
Honorific	**I**	oosi ni naru
	II	oosi nasaru
Humble	**I**	oosi suru
	II	oosi itasu

		AFFIRMATIVE	NEGATIVE
Indicative	**INFORMAL**	otiru	otinai
	FORMAL	otimasu	otimaseñ
Imperative	**INFORMAL I**	otiro	otiru na
	II		otinasaru na
	III		otinai de kudasai
	FORMAL		ooti nasaimasu na
Presumptive	**INFORMAL I**	otiyoo	otimai
	II	otiru daroo	otinai daroo
	FORMAL I	otimasyoo	otimasumai
	II	otiru desyoo	otinai desyoo
Provisional	**INFORMAL**	otireba	otinakereba
	FORMAL	otimaseba	otimaseñ nara
		otimasureba	
Gerund	**INFORMAL I**	otite	otinai de
	II		otinakute
	FORMAL	otimasite	otimaseñ de
Past Ind.	**INFORMAL**	otita	otinakatta
	FORMAL	otimasita	otimaseñ desita
Past Presump.	**INFORMAL**	otitaroo	otinakattaroo
		otita daroo	otinakatta daroo
	FORMAL	otimasitaroo	otimaseñ desitaroo
		otita desyoo	otinakatta desyoo
Conditional	**INFORMAL**	otitara	otinakattara
	FORMAL	otimasitara	otimaseñ desitara
Alternative	**INFORMAL**	otitari	otinakattari
	FORMAL	otimasitari	otimaseñ desitari

		INFORMAL AFFIRMATIVE INDICATIVE
Passive		otirareru
Potential		
Causative		otisaseru
Causative Pass.		otisaserareru
Honorific	**I**	ooti ni naru
	II	ooti nasaru
Humble	**I**	
	II	

		AFFIRMATIVE	**NEGATIVE**
Indicative	**INFORMAL**	otoru	otoranai
	FORMAL	otorimasu	otorimaseñ
Imperative	**INFORMAL I**	otore	otoru na
	II	otorinasai	otorinasaru na
	III	ototte kudasai	otoranai de kudasai
	FORMAL	ootori nasaimase	ootori nasaimasu na
Presumptive	**INFORMAL I**	otoroo	otorumai
	II	otoru daroo	otoranai daroo
	FORMAL I	otorimasyoo	otorimasumai
	II	otoru desyoo	otoranai desyoo
Provisional	**INFORMAL**	otoreba	otoranakereba
	FORMAL	otorimaseba	otorimaseñ nara
		otorimasureba	
Gerund	**INFORMAL I**	ototte	otoranai de
	II		otoranakute
	FORMAL	otorimasite	otorimaseñ de
Past Ind.	**INFORMAL**	ototta	otoranakatta
	FORMAL	otorimasita	otorimaseñ desita
Past Presump.	**INFORMAL**	otottaroo	otoranakattaroo
		ototta daroo	otoranakatta daroo
	FORMAL	otorimasitaroo	otorimaseñ desitaroo
		ototta desyoo	otoranakatta desyoo
Conditional	**INFORMAL**	otottara	otoranakattara
	FORMAL	otorimasitara	otorimaseñ desitara
Alternative	**INFORMAL**	otottari	otoranakattari
	FORMAL	otorimasitari	otorimaseñ desitari

		INFORMAL AFFIRMATIVE INDICATIVE
Passive		otorareru
Potential		otoreru
Causative		otoraseru
Causative Pass.		otoraserareru
Honorific	**I**	ootori ni naru
	II	ootori nasaru
Humble	**I**	ootori suru
	II	ootori itasu

		AFFIRMATIVE	NEGATIVE
Indicative	**INFORMAL**	otosu	otosanai
	FORMAL	otosimasu	otosimaseñ
Imperative	**INFORMAL I**	otose	otosu na
	II	otosinasai	otosinasaru na
	III	otosite kudasai	otosanai de kudasai
	FORMAL	ootosi nasaimase	ootosi nasaimasu na
Presumptive	**INFORMAL I**	otosoo	otosumai
	II	otosu daroo	otosanai daroo
	FORMAL I	otosimasyoo	otosimasumai
	II	otosu desyoo	otosanai desyoo
Provisional	**INFORMAL**	otoseba	otosanakereba
	FORMAL	otosimaseba	otosimaseñ nara
		otosimasureba	
Gerund	**INFORMAL I**	otosite	otosanai de
	II		otosanakute
	FORMAL	otosimasite	otosimaseñ de
Past Ind.	**INFORMAL**	otosita	otosanakatta
	FORMAL	otosimasita	otosimaseñ desita
Past Presump.	**INFORMAL**	otositaroo	otosanakattaroo
		otosita daroo	otosanakatta daroo
	FORMAL	otosimasitaroo	otosimaseñ desitaroo
		otosita desyoo	otosanakatta desyoo
Conditional	**INFORMAL**	otositara	otosanakattara
	FORMAL	otosimasitara	otosimaseñ desitara
Alternative	**INFORMAL**	otositari	otosanakattari
	FORMAL	otosimasitari	otosimaseñ desitari

INFORMAL AFFIRMATIVE INDICATIVE

Passive		otosareru
Potential		otoseru
Causative		otosaseru
Causative Pass.		otosaserareru
Honorific	**I**	ootosi ni naru
	II	ootosi nasaru
Humble	**I**	ootosi suru
	II	ootosi itasu

to drive away, to chase, to pursue   TRANSITIVE

			AFFIRMATIVE	NEGATIVE
Indicative	**INFORMAL**		ou	owanai
	FORMAL		oimasu	oimaseñ
Imperative	**INFORMAL**	**I**	oe	ou na
		II	oinasai	oinasaru na
		III	otte kudasai	owanai de kudasai
	FORMAL		ooi nasaimase	ooi nasaimasu na
Presumptive	**INFORMAL**	**I**	ooo	oumai
		II	ou daroo	owanai daroo
	FORMAL	**I**	oimasyoo	oimasumai
		II	ou desyoo	owanai desyoo
Provisional	**INFORMAL**		oeba	owanakereba
	FORMAL		oimaseba	oimaseñ nara
			oimasureba	
Gerund	**INFORMAL**	**I**	otte	owanai de
		II		owanakute
	FORMAL		oimasite	oimaseñ de
Past Ind.	**INFORMAL**		otta	owanakatta
	FORMAL		oimasita	oimaseñ desita
Past Presump.	**INFORMAL**		ottaroo	owanakattaroo
			otta daroo	owanakatta daroo
	FORMAL		oimasitaroo	oimaseñ desitaroo
			otta desyoo	owanakatta desyoo
Conditional	**INFORMAL**		ottara	owanakattara
	FORMAL		oimasitara	oimaseñ desitara
Alternative	**INFORMAL**		ottari	owanakattari
	FORMAL		oimasitari	oimaseñ desitari

		INFORMAL AFFIRMATIVE INDICATIVE
Passive		owareru
Potential		oeru
Causative		owaseru
Causative Pass.		owaserareru

Honorific	**I**	ooi ni naru
	II	ooi nasaru
Humble	**I**	ooi suru
	II	ooi itasu

TRANSITIVE   *to be indebted, to assume responsibility*

		AFFIRMATIVE	NEGATIVE
Indicative	**INFORMAL**	ou	owanai
	FORMAL	oimasu	oimaseñ
Imperative	**INFORMAL I**	oe	ou na
	II	oinasai	oinasaru na
	III	otte kudasai	owanai de kudasai
	FORMAL	ooi nasaimase	ooi nasaimasu na
Presumptive	**INFORMAL I**	ooo	oumai
	II	ou daroo	owanai daroo
	FORMAL I	oimasyoo	oimasumai
	II	ou desyoo	owanai desyoo
Provisional	**INFORMAL**	oeba	owanakereba
	FORMAL	oimaseba	oimaseñ nara
		oimasureba	
Gerund	**INFORMAL I**	otte	owanai de
	II		owanakute
	FORMAL	oimasite	oimaseñ de
Past Ind.	**INFORMAL**	otta	owanakatta
	FORMAL	oimasita	oimaseñ desita
Past Presump.	**INFORMAL**	ottaroo	owanakattaroo
		otta daroo	owanakatta daroo
	FORMAL	oimasitaroo	oimaseñ desitaroo
		otta desyoo	owanakatta desyoo
Conditional	**INFORMAL**	ottara	owanakattara
	FORMAL	oimasitara	oimaseñ desitara
Alternative	**INFORMAL**	ottari	owanakattari
	FORMAL	oimasitari	oimaseñ desitari

		INFORMAL AFFIRMATIVE INDICATIVE
Passive		owareru
Potential		oeru
Causative		owaseru
Causative Pass.		owaserareru

Honorific	**I**	ooi ni naru
	II	ooi nasaru
Humble	**I**	ooi suru
	II	ooi itasu

		AFFIRMATIVE	NEGATIVE
Indicative	**INFORMAL**	owaru	owaranai
	FORMAL	owarimasu	owarimaseñ
Imperative	**INFORMAL I**	oware	owaru na
	II		
	III		
	FORMAL		
Presumptive	**INFORMAL I**	owaroo	owarumai
	II	owaru daroo	owaranai daroo
	EORMAL I	owarimasyoo	owarimasumai
	II	owaru desyoo	owaranai desyoo
Provisional	**INFORMAL**	owareba	owaranakereba
	FORMAL	owarimaseba	owarimaseñ nara
		owarimasureba	
Gerund	**INFORMAL I**	owatte	owaranai de
	II		owaranakute
	FORMAL	owarimasite	owarimaseñ de
Past Ind.	**INFORMAL**	owatta	owaranakatta
	FORMAL	owarimasita	owarimaseñ desita
Past Presump.	**INFORMAL**	owattaroo	owaranakattaroo
		owatta daroo	owaranakatta daroo
	FORMAL	owarimasitaroo	owarimaseñ desitaroo
		owatta desyoo	owaranakatta desyoo
Conditional	**INFORMAL**	owattara	owaranakattara
	FORMAL	owarimasitara	owarimaseñ desitara
Alternative	**INFORMAL**	owattari	owaranakattari
	FORMAL	owarimasitari	owarimaseñ desitari

INFORMAL AFFIRMATIVE INDICATIVE

Passive		
Potential		
Causative	owaraseru	
Causative Pass.	owaraserareru	

Honorific	**I**	
	II	
Humble	**I**	
	II	

		AFFIRMATIVE	NEGATIVE
Indicative	**INFORMAL**	oyobu	oyobanai
	FORMAL	oyobimasu	oyobimaseñ
Imperative	**INFORMAL I**	oyobe	oyobu na
	II		
	III		
	FORMAL		
Presumptive	**INFORMAL I**	oyoboo	oyobumai
	II	oyobu daroo	oyobanai daroo
	FORMAL I	oyobimasyoo	oyobimasumai
	II	oyobu desyoo	oyobanai desyoo
Provisional	**INFORMAL**	oyobeba	oyobanakereba
	FORMAL	oyobimaseba	oyobimaseñ nara
		oyobimasureba	
Gerund	**INFORMAL I**	oyoñde	oyobanai de
	II		oyobanakute
	FORMAL	oyobimasite	oyobimaseñ de
Past Ind.	**INFORMAL**	oyoñda	oyobanakatta
	FORMAL	oyobimasita	oyobimaseñ desita
Past Presump.	**INFORMAL**	oyoñdaroo	oyobanakattaroo
		oyoñda daroo	oyobanakatta daroo
	FORMAL	oyobimasitaroo	oyobimaseñ desitaroo
		oyoñda desyoo	oyobanakatta desyoo
Conditional	**INFORMAL**	oyoñdara	oyobanakattara
	FORMAL	oyobimasitara	oyobimaseñ desitara
Alternative	**INFORMAL**	oyoñdari	oyobanakattari
	FORMAL	oyobimasitari	oyobimaseñ desitari

	INFORMAL AFFIRMATIVE INDICATIVE
Passive	oyobareru
Potential	oyoberu
Causative	oyobaseru
Causative Pass.	oyobaserareru

Honorific	**I**	ooyobi ni naru
	II	ooyobi nasaru
Humble	**I**	
	II	

		AFFIRMATIVE	NEGATIVE
Indicative	**INFORMAL**	oyogu	oyoganai
	FORMAL	oyogimasu	oyogimaseñ
Imperative	**INFORMAL I**	oyoge	oyogu na
	II	oyoginasai	oyoginasaru na
	III	oyoide kudasai	oyoganai de kudasai
	FORMAL	ooyogi nasaimase	ooyogi nasaimasu na
Presumptive	**INFORMAL I**	oyogoo	oyogumai
	II	oyogu daroo	oyoganai daroo
	FORMAL I	oyogimasyoo	oyogimasumai
	II	oyogu desyoo	oyoganai desyoo
Provisional	**INFORMAL**	oyogeba	oyoganakereba
	FORMAL	oyogimaseba	oyogimaseñ nara
		oyogimasureba	
Gerund	**INFORMAL I**	oyoide	oyoganai de
	II		oyoganakute
	FORMAL	oyogimasite	oyogimaseñ de
Past Ind.	**INFORMAL**	oyoida	oyoganakatta
	FORMAL	oyogimasita	oyogimaseñ desita
Past Presump.	**INFORMAL**	oyoidaroo	oyoganakattaroo
		oyoida daroo	oyoganakatta daroo
	FORMAL	oyogimasitaroo	oyogimaseñ desitaroo
		oyoida desyoo	oyoganakatta desyoo
Conditional	**INFORMAL**	oyoidara	oyoganakattara
	FORMAL	oyogimasitara	oyogimaseñ desitara
Alternative	**INFORMAL**	oyoidari	oyoganakattari
	FORMAL	oyogimasitari	oyogimaseñ desitari

		INFORMAL AFFIRMATIVE INDICATIVE
Passive		oyogareru
Potential		oyogeru
Causative		oyogaseru
Causative Pass.		oyogaserareru

Honorific	**I**	ooyogi ni naru
	II	ooyogi nasaru
Humble	**I**	
	II	

		AFFIRMATIVE	NEGATIVE
Indicative	**INFORMAL**	sadameru	sadamenai
	FORMAL	sadamemasu	sadamemaseñ
Imperative	**INFORMAL I**	sadamero	sadameru na
	II	sadamenasai	sadamenasaru na
	III	sadamete kudasai	sadamenai de kudasai
	FORMAL	osadame nasaimase	osadame nasaimasu na
Presumptive	**INFORMAL I**	sadameyoo	sadamemai
	II	sadameru daroo	sadamenai daroo
	FORMAL I	sadamemasyoo	sadamemasumai
	II	sadameru desyoo	sadamenai desyoo
Provisional	**INFORMAL**	sadamereba	sadamenakereba
	FORMAL	sadamemaseba	sadamemaseñ nara
		sadamemasureba	
Gerund	**INFORMAL I**	sadamete	sadamenai de
	II		sadamenakute
	FORMAL	sadamemasite	sadamemaseñ de
Past Ind.	**INFORMAL**	sadameta	sadamenakatta
	FORMAL	sadamamasita	sadamemaseñ desita
Past Presump.	**INFORMAL**	sadametaroo	sadamenakattaroo
		sadameta daroo	sadamenakatta daroo
	FORMAL	sadamemasitaroo	sadamemaseñ desitaroo
		sadameta desyoo	sadamenakatta desyoo
Conditional	**INFORMAL**	sadametara	sadamenakattara
	FORMAL	sadamemasitara	sadamemaseñ desitara
Alternative	**INFORMAL**	sadametari	sadamenakattari
	FORMAL	sadamemasitari	sadamemaseñ desitari

		INFORMAL AFFIRMATIVE INDICATIVE
Passive		sadamerareru
Potential		sadamerareru
Causative		sadamesaseru
Causative Pass.		sadamesaserareru
Honorific	**I**	osadame ni naru
	II	osadame nasaru
Humble	**I**	osadame suru
	II	osadame itasu

		AFFIRMATIVE	NEGATIVE
Indicative	**INFORMAL**	sagasu	sagasanai
	FORMAL	sagasimasu	sagasimaseñ
Imperative	**INFORMAL I**	sagase	sagasu na
	II	sagasinasai	sagasinasaru na
	III	sagasite kudasai	sagasanai de kudasai
	FORMAL	osagasi nasaimase	osagasi nasaimasu na
Presumptive	**INFORMAL I**	sagasoo	sagasumai
	II	sagasu daroo	sagasanai daroo
	FORMAL I	sagasimasyoo	sagasimasumai
	II	sagasu desyoo	sagasanai desyoo
Provisional	**INFORMAL**	sagaseba	sagasanakereba
	FORMAL	sagasimaseba	sagasimaseñ nara
		sagasimasureba	
Gerund	**INFORMAL I**	sagasite	sagasanai de
	II		sagasanakute
	FORMAL	sagasimasite	sagasimaseñ de
Past Ind.	**INFORMAL**	sagasita	sagasanakatta
	FORMAL	sagasimasita	sagasimaseñ desita
Past Presump.	**INFORMAL**	sagasitaroo	sagasanakattaroo
		sagasita daroo	sagasanakatta daroo
	FORMAL	sagasimasitaroo	sagasimaseñ desitaroo
		sagasita desyoo	sagasanakatta desyoo
Conditional	**INFORMAL**	sagasitara	sagasanakattara
	FORMAL	sagasimasitara	sagasimaseñ desitara
Alternative	**INFORMAL**	sagasitari	sagasanakattari
	FORMAL	sagasimasitari	sagasimaseñ desitari

INFORMAL AFFIRMATIVE INDICATIVE

Passive		sagasareru
Potential		sagaseru
Causative		sagasaseru
Causative Pass.		sagasaserareru

Honorific	**I**	osagasi ni naru
	II	osagasi nasaru
Humble	**I**	osagasi suru
	II	osagasi itasu

TRANSITIVE   *to shout, to cry out, to advocate*

		AFFIRMATIVE	NEGATIVE
Indicative	**INFORMAL**	sakebu	sakebanai
	FORMAL	sakebimasu	sakebimaseñ
Imperative	**INFORMAL I**	sakebe	sakebu na
	II	sakebinasai	sakebinasaru **na**
	III	sakeñde kudasai	sakebanai de kudasai
	FORMAL	osakebi nasaimase	osakebi nasaimasu na
Presumptive	**INFORMAL I**	sakeboo	sakebumai
	II	sakebu daroo	sakebanai daroo
	FORMAL I	sakebimasyoo	sakebimasumai
	II	sakebu desyoo	sakebanai desyoo
Provisional	**INFORMAL**	sakebeba	sakebanakereba
	FORMAL	sakebimaseba	sakebimaseñ nara
		sakebimasureba	
Gerund	**INFORMAL I**	sakeñde	sakebanai de
	II		sakebanakute
	FORMAL	sakebimasite	sakebimaseñ de
Past Ind.	**INFORMAL**	sakeñda	sakebanakatta
	FORMAL	sakebimasita	sakebimaseñ desita
Past Presump.	**INFORMAL**	sakeñdaroo	sakebanakattaroo
		sakeñda daroo	sakebanakatta daroo
	FORMAL	sakebimasitaroo	sakebimaseñ desitaroo
		sakeñda desyoo	sakebanakatta desyoo
Conditional	**INFORMAL**	sakeñdara	sakebanakattara
	FORMAL	sakebimasitara	sakebimaseñ desitara
Alternative	**INFORMAL**	sakeñdari	sakebanakattari
	FORMAL	sakebimasitari	sakebimaseñ desitari

INFORMAL AFFIRMATIVE INDICATIVE

Passive		sakebareru
Potential		sakeberu
Causative		sakebaseru
Causative Pass.		sakebaserareru

Honorific	**I**	osakebi ni naru
	II	osakebi nasaru
Humble	**I**	osakebi suru
	II	osakebi itasu

		AFFIRMATIVE	NEGATIVE
Indicative	**INFORMAL**	saku	sakanai
	FORMAL	sakimasu	sakimaseñ
Imperative	**INFORMAL I**	sake	saku na
	II		
	III		
	FORMAL		
Presumptive	**INFORMAL I**	sakoo	sakumai
	II	saku daroo	sakanai daroo
	FORMAL I	sakimasyoo	sakimasumai
	II	saku desyoo	sakanai desyoo
Provisional	**INFORMAL**	sakeba	sakanakereba
	FORMAL	sakimaseba	sakimaseñ nara
		sakimasureba	
Gerund	**INFORMAL I**	saite	sakanai de
	II		sakanakute
	FORMAL	sakimasite	sakimaseñ de
Past Ind.	**INFORMAL**	saita	sakanakatta
	FORMAL	sakimasita	sakimaseñ desita
Past Presump.	**INFORMAL**	saitaroo	sakanakattaroo
		saita daroo	sakanakatta daroo
	FORMAL	sakimasitaroo	sakimaseñ desitaroo
		saita desyoo	sakanakatta desyoo
Conditional	**INFORMAL**	saitara	sakanakattara
	FORMAL	sakimasitara	sakimaseñ desitara
Alternative	**INFORMAL**	saitari	sakanakattari
	FORMAL	sakimasitari	sakimaseñ desitari

INFORMAL AFFIRMATIVE INDICATIVE

Passive		
Potential		sakeru
Causative		sakaseru
Causative Pass.		sakaserareru
Honorific	**I**	
	II	
Humble	**I**	
	II	

		AFFIRMATIVE	NEGATIVE
Indicative	**INFORMAL**	samatageru	samatagenai
	FORMAL	samatagemasu	samatagemaseñ
Imperative	**INFORMAL I**	samatagero	samatageru na
	II	samatagenasai	samatagenasaru na
	III	samatagete kudasai	samatagenai de kudasai
	FORMAL	osamatage nasaimase	osamatage nasaimasu na
Presumptive	**INFORMAL I**	samatageyoo	samatagemai
	II	samatageru daroo	samatagenai daroo
	FORMAL I	samatagemasyoo	samatagemasumai
	II	samatageru desyoo	samatagenai desyoo
Provisional	**INFORMAL**	samatagereba	samatagenakereba
	FORMAL	samatagemaseba	samatagemaseñ nara
		samatagemasureba	
Gerund	**INFORMAL I**	samatagete	samatagenai de
	II		samatagenakute
	FORMAL	samatagemasite	samatagemaseñ de
Past Ind.	**INFORMAL**	samatageta	samatagenakatta
	FORMAL	samatagemasita	samatagemaseñ desita
Past Presump.	**INFORMAL**	samatagetaroo	samatagenakattaroo
		samatageta daroo	samatagenakatta daroo
	FORMAL	samatagemasitaroo	samatagemaseñ desitaroo
		samatageta desyoo	samatagenakatta desyoo
Conditional	**INFORMAL**	samatagetara	samatagenakattara
	FORMAL	samatagemasitara	samatagemaseñ desitara
Alternative	**INFORMAL**	samatagetari	samatagenakattari
	FORMAL	samatagemasitari	samatagemaseñ desitari

INFORMAL AFFIRMATIVE INDICATIVE

Passive		samatagerareru
Potential		samatagerareru
Causativ		samatagesaseru
Causative Pass.		samatagesaserareru

Honorific	**I**	osamatage ni naru
	II	osamatage nasaru
Humble	**I**	osamatage suru
	II	osamatage itasu

		AFFIRMATIVE	NEGATIVE
Indicative	**INFORMAL**	sasou	sasowanai
	FORMAL	sasoimasu	sasoimaseñ
Imperative	**INFORMAL I**	sasoe	sasou na
	II	sasoinasai	sasoinasaru na
	III	sasotte kudasai	sasowanai de kudasai
	FORMAL	osasoi nasaimase	osasoi nasaimasu na
Presumptive	**INFORMAL I**	sasooo	sasoumai
	II	sasou daroo	sasowanai daroo
	FORMAL I	sasoimasyoo	sasoimasumai
	II	sasou desyoo	sasowanai desyoo
Provisional	**INFORMAL**	sasoeba	sasowanakereba
	FORMAL	sasoimaseba	sasoimaseñ nara
		sasoimasureba	
Gerund	**INFORMAL I**	sasotte	sasowanai de
	II		sasowanakute
	FORMAL	sasoimasite	sasoimaseñ de
Past Ind.	**INFORMAL**	sasotta	sasowanakatta
	FORMAL	sasoimasita	sasoimaseñ desita
Past Presump.	**INFORMAL**	sasottaroo	sasowanakattaroo
		sasotta daroo	sasowanakatta daroo
	FORMAL	sasoimasitaroo	sasoimaseñ desitaroo
		sasotta desyoo	sasowanakatta desyoo
Conditional	**INFORMAL**	sasottara	sasowanakattara
	FORMAL	sasoimasitara	sasoimaseñ desitara
Alternative	**INFORMAL**	sasottari	sasowanakattari
	FORMAL	sasoimasitari	sasoimaseñ desitari

INFORMAL AFFIRMATIVE INDICATIVE

Passive		sasowareru
Potential		sasoeru
Causative		sasowaseru
Causative Pass.		sasowaserareru

Honorific	**I**	osasoi ni naru
	II	osasoi nasaru
Humble	**I**	osasoi suru
	II	osasoi itasu

		AFFIRMATIVE	NEGATIVE
Indicative	**INFORMAL**	sawagu	sawaganai
	FORMAL	sawagimasu	sawagimaseñ
Imperative	**INFORMAL I**	sawage	sawagu na
	II	sawaginasai	sawaginasaru na
	III	sawaide kudasai	sawaganai de kudasai
	FORMAL	osawagi nasaimase	osawagi nasaimasu na
Presumptive	**INFORMAL I**	sawagoo	sawagumai
	II	sawagu daroo	sawaganai daroo
	FORMAL I	sawagimasyoo	sawagimasumai
	II	sawagu desyoo	sawaganai desyoo
Provisional	**INFORMAL**	sawageba	sawaganakereba
	FORMAL	sawagimaseba	sawagimaseñ nara
		sawagimasureba	
Gerund	**INFORMAL I**	sawaide	sawaganai de
	II		sawaganakute
	FORMAL	sawagimasite	sawagimaseñ de
Past Ind.	**INFORMAL**	sawaida	sawaganakatta
	FORMAL	sawagimasita	sawagimaseñ desita
Past Presump.	**INFORMAL**	sawaidaroo	sawaganakattaroo
		sawaida daroo	sawaganakatta daroo
	FORMAL	sawagimasitaroo	sawagimaseñ desitaroo
		sawaida desyoo	sawaganakatta desyoo
Conditional	**INFORMAL**	sawaidara	sawaganakattara
	FORMAL	sawagimasitara	sawagimaseñ desitara
Alternative	**INFORMAL**	sawaidari	sawaganakattari
	FORMAL	sawagimasitari	sawagimaseñ desitari

INFORMAL AFFIRMATIVE INDICATIVE

Passive		sawagareru
Potential		sawageru
Causative		sawagaseru
Causative Pass.		sawagaserareru

Honorific	**I**	osawagi ni naru
	II	osawagi nasaru
Humble	**I**	
	II	

to touch or *feel* (with the fingers)

		AFFIRMATIVE	**NEGATIVE**
Indicative	**INFORMAL**	sawaru	sawaranai
	FORMAL	sawarimasu	sawarimaseñ
Imperative	**INFORMAL I**	saware	sawaru na
	II	sawarinasai	sawarinasaru na
	III	sawatte kudasai	sawaranai de kudasai
	FORMAL	osawari nasaimase	osawari nasaimasu na
Presumptive	**INFORMAL I**	sawaroo	sawarumai
	II	sawaru daroo	sawaranai daroo
	FORMAL I	sawarimasyoo	sawarimasumai
	II	sawaru desyoo	sawaranai desyoo
Provisional	**INFORMAL**	sawareba	sawaranakereba
	FORMAL	sawarimaseba	sawarimaseñ nara
		sawarimasureba	
Gerund	**INFORMAL I**	sawatte	sawaranai de
	II		sawaranakute
	FORMAL	sawarimasite	sawarimaseñ de
Past Ind.	**INFORMAL**	sawatta	sawaranakatta
	FORMAL	sawarimasita	sawarimaseñ desita
Past Presump.	**INFORMAL**	sawattaroo	sawaranakattaroo
		sawatta daroo	sawaranakatta daroo
	FORMAL	sawarimasitaroo	sawarimaseñ desitaroo
		sawatta desyoo	sawaranakatta desyoo
Conditional	**INFORMAL**	sawattara	sawaranakattara
	FORMAL	sawarimasitara	sawarimaseñ desitara
Alternative	**INFORMAL**	sawattari	sawaranakattari
	FORMAL	sawarimasitari	sawarimaseñ desitari

INFORMAL AFFIRMATIVE INDICATIVE

Passive	sawarareru
Potential	sawareru
Causative	sawaraseru
Causative Pass.	sawaraserareru

Honorific	**I**	osawari ni naru
	II	osawari nasaru
Humble	**I**	osawari suru
	II	osawari itasu

TRANSITIVE   *to blame, to torment, to urge*

		AFFIRMATIVE	NEGATIVE
Indicative	**INFORMAL**	semeru	semenai
	FORMAL	sememasu	sememaseñ
Imperative	**INFORMAL I**	semero	semeru na
	II	semenasai	semenasaru na
	III	semete kudasai	semenai de kudasai
	FORMAL	oseme nasaimase	oseme nasaimasu na
Presumptive	**INFORMAL I**	semeyoo	sememai
	II	semeru daroo	semenai daroo
	FORMAL I	sememasyoo	sememasumai
	II	semeru desyoo	semenai desyoo
Provisional	**INFORMAL**	semereba	semenakereba
	FORMAL	sememaseba	sememaseñ nara
		sememasureba	
Gerund	**INFORMAL I**	semete	semenai de
	II		semenakute
	FORMAL	sememasite	sememaseñ de
Past Ind.	**INFORMAL**	semeta	semenakatta
	FORMAL	sememasita	sememaseñ desita
Past Presump.	**INFORMAL**	semetaroo	semenakattaroo
		semeta daroo	semenakatta daroo
	FORMAL	sememasitaroo	sememaseñ desitaroo
		semeta desyoo	semenakatta desyoo
Conditional	**INFORMAL**	semetara	semenakattara
	FORMAL	sememasitara	sememaseñ desitara
Alternative	**INFORMAL**	semetari	semenakattari
	FORMAL	sememasitari	sememaseñ desitari

		INFORMAL AFFIRMATIVE INDICATIVE
Passive		semerareru
Potential		semerareru
Causative		semesaseru
Causative Pass.		semesaserareru
Honorific	**I**	oseme ni naru
	II	oseme nasaru
Humble	**I**	oseme suru
	II	oseme itasu

		AFFIRMATIVE	NEGATIVE
Indicative	**INFORMAL**	sibaru	sibaranai
	FORMAL	sibarimasu	sibarimaseñ
Imperative	**INFORMAL I**	sibare	sibaru na
	II	sibarinasai	sibarinasaru na
	III	sibatte kudasai	sibaranai de kudasai
	FORMAL	osibari nasaimase	osibari nasaimasu na
Presumptive	**INFORMAL I**	sibaroo	sibarumai
	II	sibaru daroo	sibaranai daroo
	FORMAL I	sibarimasyoo	sibarimasumai
	II	sibaru desyoo	sibaranai desyoo
Provisional	**INFORMAL**	sibareba	sibaranakereba
	FORMAL	sibarimaseba	sibarimaseñ nara
		sibarimasureba	
Gerund	**INFORMAL I**	sibatte	sibaranai de
	II		sibaranakute
	FORMAL	sibarimasite	sibarimaseñ de
Past Ind.	**INFORMAL**	sibatta	sibaranakatta
	FORMAL	sibarimasita	sibarimaseñ desita
Past Presump.	**INFORMAL**	sibattaroo	sibaranakattaroo
		sibatta daroo	sibaranakatta daroo
	FORMAL	sibarimasitaroo	sibarimaseñ desitaroo
		sibatta desyoo	sibaranakatta desyoo
Conditional	**INFORMAL**	sibattara	sibaranakattara
	FORMAL	sibarimasitara	sibarimaseñ desitara
Alternative	**INFORMAL**	sibattari	sibaranakattari
	FORMAL	sibarimasitari	sibarimaseñ desitari

		INFORMAL AFFIRMATIVE INDICATIVE
Passive		sibarareru
Potential		sibareru
Causative		sibaraseru
Causative Pass.		sibaraserareru

Honorific	**I**	osibari ni naru
	II	osibari nasaru
Humble	**I**	osibari suru
	II	osibari itasu

		AFFIRMATIVE	NEGATIVE
Indicative	**INFORMAL**	sikaru	sikaranai
	FORMAL	sikarimasu	sikarimaseñ
Imperative	**INFORMAL I**	sikare	sikaru na
	II	sikarinasai	sikarinasaru na
	III	sikatte kudasai	sikaranai de kudasai
	FORMAL	osikari nasaimase	osikari nasaimasu na
Presumptive	**INFORMAL I**	sikaroo	sikarumai
	II	sikaru daroo	sikaranai daroo
	FORMAL I	sikarimasyoo	sikarimasumai
	II	sikaru desyoo	sikaranai desyoo
Provisional	**INFORMAL**	sikareba	sikaranakereba
	FORMAL	sikarimaseba	sikarimaseñ nara
		sikarimasureba	
Gerund	**INFORMAL I**	sikatte	sikaranai de
	II		sikaranakute
	FORMAL	sikarimasite	sikarimaseñ de
Past Ind.	**INFORMAL**	sikatta	sikaranakatta
	FORMAL	sikarimasita	sikarimaseñ desita
Past Presump.	**INFORMAL**	sikattaroo	sikaranakattaroo
		sikatta daroo	sikaranakatta daroo
	FORMAL	sikarimasitaroo	sikarimaseñ desitaroo
		sikatta desyoo	sikaranakatta desyoo
Conditional	**INFORMAL**	sikattara	sikaranakattara
	FORMAL	sikarimasitara	sikarimaseñ desitara
Alternative	**INFORMAL**	sikattari	sikaranakattari
	FORMAL	sikarimasitari	sikarimaseñ desitari

INFORMAL AFFIRMATIVE INDICATIVE

Passive		sikarareru
Potential		sikareru
Causative		sikaraseru
Causative Pass.		sikaraserareru
Honorific	**I**	osikari ni naru
	II	osikari nasaru
Humble	**I**	osikari suru
	II	osikari itasu

to spread out flat (as a quilt)   TRANSITIVE

			AFFIRMATIVE	NEGATIVE
Indicative	INFORMAL		siku	sikanai
	FORMAL		sikimasu	sikimaseñ
Imperative	INFORMAL	I	sike	siku na
		II	sikinasai	sikinasaru na
		III	siite kudasai	sikanai de kudasai
	FORMAL		osiki nasaimase	osiki nasaimasu na
Presumptive	INFORMAL	I	sikoo	sikumai
		II	siku daroo	sikanai daroo
	FORMAL	I	sikimasyoo	sikimasumai
		II	siku desyoo	sikanai desyoo
Provisional	INFORMAL		sikeba	sikanakereba
	FORMAL		sikimaseba	sikimaseñ nara
			sikimasureba	
Gerund	INFORMAL	I	siite	sikanai de
		II		sikanakute
	FORMAL		sikimasite	sikimaseñ de
Past Ind.	INFORMAL		siita	sikanakatta
	FORMAL		sikimasita	sikimaseñ desita
Past Presump.	INFORMAL		siitaroo	sikanakattaroo
			siita daroo	sikanakatta daroo
	FORMAL		sikimasitaroo	sikimaseñ desitaroo
			siita desyoo	sikanakatta desyoo
Conditional	INFORMAL		siitara	sikanakattara
	FORMAL		sikimasitara	sikimaseñ desitara
Alternative	INFORMAL		siitari	sikanakattari
	FORMAL		sikimasitari	sikimaseñ desitari

		INFORMAL AFFIRMATIVE INDICATIVE
Passive		sikareru
Potential		sikeru
Causative		sikaseru
Causative Pass.		sikaserareru
Honorific	I	osiki ni naru
	II	osiki nasaru
Humble	I	osiki suru
	II	osiki itasu

		AFFIRMATIVE	NEGATIVE
Indicative	**INFORMAL**	simaru	simaranai
	FORMAL	simarimasu	simarimaseñ
Imperative	**INFORMAL I**	simare	simaru na
	II		
	III		
	FORMAL		
Presumptive	**INFORMAL I**	simaroo	simarumai
	II	simaru daroo	simaranai daroo
	FORMAL I	simarimasyoo	simarimasumai
	II	simaru desyoo	simaranai desyoo
Provisional	**INFORMAL**	simareba	simaranakereba
	FORMAL	simarimaseba	simarimaseñ nara
		simarimasureba	
Gerund	**INFORMAL I**	simatte	simaranai de
	II		simaranakute
	FORMAL	simarimasite	simarimaseñ de
Past Ind.	**INFORMAL**	simatta	simaranakatta
	FORMAL	simarimasita	simarimaseñ desita
Past Presump.	**INFORMAL**	simattaroo	simaranakattaroo
		simatta daroo	simaranakatta daroo
	FORMAL	simarimasitaroo	simarimaseñ desitaroo
		simatta desyoo	simaranakatta desyoo
Conditional	**INFORMAL**	simattara	simaranakattara
	FORMAL	simarimasitara	simarimaseñ desitara
Alternative	**INFORMAL**	simattari	simaranakattari
	FORMAL	simarimasitari	simarimaseñ desitari

INFORMAL AFFIRMATIVE INDICATIVE

Passive		
Potential		
Causative		
Causative Pass.		
Honorific	I	
	II	
Humble	I	
	II	

to put away, to pack away   TRANSITIVE

		AFFIRMATIVE	NEGATIVE
Indicative	**INFORMAL**	simau	simawanai
	FORMAL	simaimasu	simaimaseñ
Imperative	**INFORMAL I**	simae	simau na
	II	simainasai	simainasaru na
	III	simatte kudasai	simawanai de kudasai
	FORMAL	osimai nasaimase	osimai nasaimasu na
Presumptive	**INFORMAL I**	simaoo	simaumai
	II	simau daroo	simawanai daroo
	FORMAL I	simaimasyoo	simaimasumai
	II	simau desyoo	simawanai desyoo
Provisional	**INFORMAL**	simaeba	simawanakereba
	FORMAL	simaimaseba	simaimaseñ nara
		simaimasureba	
Gerund	**INFORMAL I**	simatte	simawanai de
	II		simawanakute
	FORMAL	simaimasite	simaimaseñ de
Past Ind.	**INFORMAL**	simatta	simawanakatta
	FORMAL	simaimasita	simaimaseñ desita
Past Presump.	**INFORMAL**	simattaroo	simawanakattaroo
		simatta daroo	simawanakatta daroo
	FORMAL	simaimasitaroo	simaimaseñ desitaroo
		simatta desyoo	simawanakatta desyoo
Conditional	**INFORMAL**	simattara	simawanakattara
	FORMAL	simaimasitara	simaimaseñ desitara
Alternative	**INFORMAL**	simattari	simawanakattari
	FORMAL	simaimasitari	simaimaseñ desitari

INFORMAL AFFIRMATIVE INDICATIVE

Passive		simawareru
Potential		simaeru
Causative		simawaseru
Causative Pass.		simawaserareru

Honorific	**I**	osimai ni naru
	II	osimai nasaru
Humble	**I**	osimai suru
	II	osimai itasu

		AFFIRMATIVE	NEGATIVE
Indicative	**INFORMAL**	simeru	simenai
	FORMAL	simemasu	simemaseñ
Imperative	**INFORMAL I**	simero	simeru na
	II	simenasai	simenasaru na
	III	simete kudasai	simenai de kudasai
	FORMAL	osime nasaimase	osime nasaimasu na
Presumptive	**INFORMAL I**	simeyoo	simemai
	II	simeru daroo	simenai daroo
	FORMAL I	simemasyoo	simemasumai
	II	simeru desyoo	simenai desyoo
Provisional	**INFORMAL**	simereba	simenakereba
	FORMAL	simemaseba	simemaseñ nara
		simemasureba	
Gerund	**INFORMAL I**	simete	simenai de
	II		simenakute
	FORMAL	simemasite	simemaseñ de
Past Ind.	**INFORMAL**	simeta	simenakatta
	FORMAL	simemasita	simemaseñ desita
Past Presump.	**INFORMAL**	simetaroo	simenakattaroo
		simeta daroo	simenakatta daroo
	FORMAL	simemasitaroo	simemaseñ desitaroo
		simeta desyoo	simenakatta desyoo
Conditional	**INFORMAL**	simetara	simenakattara
	FORMAL	simemasitara	simemaseñ desitara
Alternative	**INFORMAL**	simetari	simenakattari
	FORMAL	simemasitari	simemaseñ desitari

		INFORMAL AFFIRMATIVE INDICATIVE
Passive		simerareru
Potential		simerareru
Causative		simesaseru
Causative Pass.		simesaserareru
Honorific	**I**	osime ni naru
	II	osime nasaru
Humble	**I**	osime suru
	II	osime itasu

to indicate, to point out　　　TRANSITIVE

		AFFIRMATIVE	NEGATIVE
Indicative	**INFORMAL**	simesu	simesanai
	FORMAL	simesimasu	simesimaseñ
Imperative	**INFORMAL I**	simese	simesu na
	II	simesinasai	simesinasaru na
	III	simesite kudasai	simesanai de kudasai
	FORMAL	osimesi nasaimase	osimesi nasaimasu na
Presumptive	**INFORMAL I**	simesoo	simesumai
	II	simesu daroo	simesanai daroo
	FORMAL I	simesimasyoo	simesimasumai
	II	simesu desyoo	simesanai desyoo
Provisional	**INFORMAL**	simeseba	simesanakereba
	FORMAL	simesimaseba	simesimaseñ nara
		simesimasureba	
Gerund	**INFORMAL I**	simesite	simesanai de
	II		simesanakute
	FORMAL	simesimasite	simesimaseñ de
Past Ind.	**INFORMAL**	simesita	simesanakatta
	FORMAL	simesimasita	simesimaseñ desita
Past Presump.	**INFORMAL**	simesitaroo	simesanakattaroo
		simesita daroo	simesanakatta daroo
	FORMAL	simesimasitaroo	simesimaseñ desitaroo
		simesita desyoo	simesanakatta desyoo
Conditional	**INFORMAL**	simesitara	simesanakattara
	FORMAL	simesimasitara	simesimaseñ desitara
Alternative	**INFORMAL**	simesitari	simesanakattari
	FORMAL	simesimasitari	simesimaseñ desitari

INFORMAL AFFIRMATIVE INDICATIVE

Passive		simesareru
Potential		simeseru
Causative		simesaseru
Causative Pass.		simesaserareru
Honorific	**I**	osimesi ni naru
	II	osimesi nasaru
Humble	**I**	osimesi suru
	II	osimesi itasu

		AFFIRMATIVE	NEGATIVE
Indicative	**INFORMAL**	sinu	sinanai
	FORMAL	sinimasu	sinimaseñ
Imperative	**INFORMAL I**	sine	sinu na
	II	sininasai	sininasaru na
	III	siñde kudasai	sinanai de kudasai
	FORMAL		osini nasaimasu na
Presumptive	**INFORMAL I**	sinoo	sinumai
	II	sinu daroo	sinanai daroo
	FORMAL I	sinimasyoo	sinimasumai
	II	sinu desyoo	sinanai desyoo
Provisional	**INFORMAL**	sineba	sinanakereba
	FORMAL	sinimaseba	sinimaseñ nara
		sinimasureba	
Gerund	**INFORMAL I**	siñde	sinanai de
	II		sinanakute
	FORMAL	sinimasite	sinimaseñ de
Past Ind.	**INFORMAL**	siñda	sinanakatta
	FORMAL	sinimasita	sinimaseñ desita
Past Presump.	**INFORMAL**	siñdaroo	sinanakattaroo
		siñda daroo	sinanakatta daroo
	FORMAL	sinimasitaroo	sinimaseñ desitaroo
		siñda desyoo	sinanakatta desyoo
Conditional	**INFORMAL**	siñdara	sinanakattara
	FORMAL	sinimasitara	sinimaseñ desitara
Alternative	**INFORMAL**	siñdari	sinanakattari
	FORMAL	sinimasitari	sinimaseñ desitari

		INFORMAL AFFIRMATIVE INDICATIVE
Passive		sinareru
Potential		sineru
Causative		sinaseru
Causative Pass.		sinaserareru
Honorific	**I**	onakunari ni naru
	II	onakunari nasaru
Humble	**I**	
	II	

		AFFIRMATIVE	**NEGATIVE**
Indicative	**INFORMAL**	siñziru	siñzinai
	FORMAL	siñzimasu	siñzimaseñ
Imperative	**INFORMAL I**	siñziro	siñziru na
	II	siñzinasai	siñzinasaru na
	III	siñzite kudasai	siñzinai de kudasai
	FORMAL	osiñzi nasaimase	osiñzi nasaimasu na
Presumptive	**INFORMAL I**	siñziyoo	siñzimai
	II	siñziru daroo	siñzinai daroo
	FORMAL I	siñzimasyoo	siñzimasumai
	II	siñziru desyoo	siñzinai desyoo
Provisional	**INFORMAL**	siñzireba	siñzinakereba
	FORMAL	siñzimaseba	siñzimaseñ nara
		siñzimasureba	
Gerund	**INFORMAL I**	siñzite	siñzinai de
	II		siñzinakute
	FORMAL	siñzimasite	siñzimaseñ de
Past Ind.	**INFORMAL**	siñzita	siñzinakatta
	FORMAL	siñzimasita	siñzimaseñ desita
Past Presump.	**INFORMAL**	siñzitaroo	siñzinakattaroo
		siñzita daroo	siñzinakatta daroo
	FORMAL	siñzimasitaroo	siñzimaseñ desitaroo
		siñzita desyoo	siñzinakatta desyoo
Conditional	**INFORMAL**	siñzitara	siñzinakattara
	FORMAL	siñzimasitara	siñzimaseñ desitara
Alternative	**INFORMAL**	siñzitari	siñzinakattari
	FORMAL	siñzimasitari	siñzimaseñ desitari

		INFORMAL AFFIRMATIVE INDICATIVE
Passive		siñzirareru
Potential		siñzirareru
Causative		siñzisaseru
Causative Pass.		siñzisaserareru
Honorific	**I**	osiñzi ni naru
	II	osiñzi nasaru
Humble	**I**	osiñzi suru
	II	osiñzi itasu

		AFFIRMATIVE	NEGATIVE
Indicative	**INFORMAL**	siraberu	sirabenai
	FORMAL	sirabemasu	sirabemaseñ
Imperative	**INFORMAL I**	sirabero	siraberu na
	II	sirabenasai	sirabenasaru na
	III	sirabete kudasai	sirabenai de kudasai
	FORMAL	osirabe nasaimase	osirabe nasaimasu na
Presumptive	**INFORMAL I**	sirabeyoo	sirabemai
	II	siraberu daroo	sirabenai daroo
	FORMAL I	sirabemasyoo	sirabemasumai
	II	siraberu desyoo	sirabenai desyoo
Provisional	**INFORMAL**	sirabereba	sirabenakereba
	FORMAL	sirabemaseba	sirabemaseñ nara
		sirabemasureba	
Gerund	**INFORMAL I**	sirabete	sirabenai de
	II		sirabenakute
	FORMAL	sirabemasite	sirabemaseñ de
Past Ind.	**INFORMAL**	sirabeta	sirabenakatta
	FORMAL	sirabemasita	sirabemaseñ desita
Past Presump.	**INFORMAL**	sirabetaroo	sirabenakattaroo
		sirabeta daroo	sirabenakatta daroo
	FORMAL	sirabemasitaroo	sirabemaseñ desitaroo
		sirabeta desyoo	sirabenakatta desyoo
Conditional	**INFORMAL**	sirabetara	sirabenakattara
	FORMAL	sirabemasitara	sirabemaseñ desitara
Alternative	**INFORMAL**	sirabetari	sirabenakattari
	FORMAL	sirabemasitari	sirabemaseñ desitari

INFORMAL AFFIRMATIVE INDICATIVE

Passive		siraberareru
Potential		siraberareru
Causative		sirabesaseru
Causative Pass.		sirabesaserareru
Honorific	**I**	osirabe ni naru
	II	osirabe nasaru
Humble	**I**	osirabe suru
	II	osirabe itasu

		AFFIRMATIVE	**NEGATIVE**
Indicative	**INFORMAL**	siru	siranai
	FORMAL	sirimasu	sirimaseñ
Imperative	**INFORMAL I**	sire	
	II		
	III		
	FORMAL		
Presumptive	**INFORMAL I**	siroo	sirumai
	II	siru daroo	siranai daroo
	FORMAL I	sirimasyoo	sirimasumai
	II	siru desyoo	siranai desyoo
Provisional	**INFORMAL**	sireba	siranakereba
	FORMAL	sirimaseba	sirimaseñ nara
		sirimasureba	
Gerund	**INFORMAL I**	sitte	siranai de
	II		siranakute
	FORMAL	sirimasite	sirimaseñ de
Past Ind.	**INFORMAL**	sitta	siranakatta
	FORMAL	sirimasita	sirimaseñ desita
Past Presump.	**INFORMAL**	sittaroo	siranakattaroo
		sitta daroo	siranakatta daroo
	FORMAL	sirimasitaroo	sirimaseñ desitaroo
		sitta desyoo	siranakatta desyoo
Conditional	**INFORMAL**	sittara	siranakattara
	FORMAL	sirimasitara	sirimaseñ desitara
Alternative	**INFORMAL**	sittari	siranakattari
	FORMAL	sirimasitari	sirimaseñ desitari

	INFORMAL AFFIRMATIVE INDICATIVE
Passive	sirareru
Potential	sireru
Causative	siraseru
Causative Pass.	siraserareru
Honorific	gozoñzi de irassyaru
Humble	zﾝñziru

		AFFIRMATIVE	**NEGATIVE**
Indicative	**INFORMAL**	sitagau	sitagawanai
	FORMAL	sitagaimasu	sitagaimaseñ
Imperative	**INFORMAL I**	sitagae	sitagau na
	II	sitagainasai	sitagainasaru na
	III	sitagatte kudasai	sitagawanai de kudasai
	FORMAL	ositagai nasaimase	ositagai nasaimasu na
Presumptive	**INFORMAL I**	sitagaoo	sitagaumai
	II	sitagau daroo	sitagawanai daroo
	FORMAL I	sitagaimasyoo	sitagaimasumai
	II	sitagau desyoo	sitagawanai desyoo
Provisional	**INFORMAL**	sitagaeba	sitagawanakereba
	FORMAL	sitagaimaseba	sitagaimaseñ nara
		sitagaimasureba	
Gerund	**INFORMAL I**	sitagatte	sitagawanai de
	II		sitagawanakute
	FORMAL	sitagaimasite	sitagaimaseñ de
Past Ind.	**INFORMAL**	sitagatta	sitagawanakatta
	FORMAL	sitagaimasita	sitagaimaseñ desita
Past Presump.	**INFORMAL**	sitagattaroo	sitagawanakattaroo
		sitagatta daroo	sitagawanakatta daroo
	FORMAL	sitagaimasitaroo	sitagaimaseñ desitaroo
		sitagatta desyoo	sitagawanakatta desyoo
Conditional	**INFORMAL**	sitagattara	sitagawanakattara
	FORMAL	sitagaimasitara	sitagaimaseñ desitara
Alternative	**INFORMAL**	sitagattari	sitagawanakattari
	FORMAL	sitagaimasitari	sitagaimaseñ desitari

INFORMAL AFFIRMATIVE INDICATIVE

Passive		sitagawareru
Potential		sitagaeru
Causative		sitagawaseru
Causative Pass.		sitagawaserareru

Honorific	**I**	ositagai ni naru
	II	ositagai nasaru
Humble	**I**	ositagai suru
	II	ositagai itasu

to become intimate with, to get to know

		AFFIRMATIVE	NEGATIVE
Indicative	**INFORMAL**	sitasimu	sitasimanai
	FORMAL	sitasimimasu	sitasimimaseñ
Imperative	**INFORMAL I**	sitasime	sitasimu na
	II	sitasiminasai	sitasiminasaru na
	III	sitasiñde kudasai	sitasimanai de kudasai
	FORMAL	ositasimi nasaimase	ositasimi nasaimasu na
Presumptive	**INFORMAL I**	sitasimoo	sitasimumai
	II	sitasimu daroo	sitasimanai daroo
	FORMAL I	sitasimimasyoo	sitasimimasumai
	II	sitasimu desyoo	sitasimanai desyoo
Provisional	**INFORMAL**	sitasimeba	sitasimanakereba
	FORMAL	sitasimimaseba	sitasimimaseñ nara
		sitasimimasureba	
Gerund	**INFORMAL I**	sitasiñde	sitasimanai de
	II		sitasimanakute
	FORMAL	sitasimimasite	sitasimimaseñ de
Past Ind.	**INFORMAL**	sitasiñda	sitasimanakatta
	FORMAL	sitasimimasita	sitasimimaseñ desita
Past Presump.	**INFORMAL**	sitasiñdaroo	sitasimanakattaroo
		sitasiñda daroo	sitasimanakatta daroo
	FORMAL	sitasimimasitaroo	sitasimimaseñ desitaroo
		sitasiñda desyoo	sitasimanakatta desyoo
Conditional	**INFORMAL**	sitasiñdara	sitasimanakattara
	FORMAL	sitasimimasitara	sitasimimaseñ desitara
Alternative	**INFORMAL**	sitasiñdari	sitasimanakattari
	FORMAL	sitasimimasitari	sitasimimaseñ desitari

		INFORMAL AFFIRMATIVE INDICATIVE
Passive		sitasimareru
Potential		sitasimeru
Causative		sitasimaseru
Causative Pass.		sitasimaserareru

Honorific	**I**	ositasimi ni naru
	II	ositasimi nasaru
Humble	**I**	ositasimi suru
	II	ositasimi itasu

to become quiet, to calm down

		AFFIRMATIVE	NEGATIVE
Indicative	**INFORMAL**	sizumaru	sizumaranai
	FORMAL	sizumarimasu	sizumarimaseñ
Imperative	**INFORMAL I**	sizumare	sizumaru na
	II	sizumarinasai	sizumarinasaru na
	III	sizumatte kudasai	sizumaranai de kudasai
	FORMAL	osizumari nasaimase	osizumari nasaimasu na
Presumptive	**INFORMAL I**	sizumaroo	sizumarumai
	II	sizumaru daroo	sizumaranai daroo
	FORMAL I	sizumarimasyoo	sizumarimasumai
	II	sizumaru desyoo	sizumaranai desyoo
Provisional	**INFORMAL**	sizumareba	sizumaranakereba
	FORMAL	sizumarimaseba	sizumarimaseñ nara
		sizumarimasureba	
Gerund	**INFORMAL I**	sizumatte	sizumaranai de
	II		sizumaranakute
	FORMAL	sizumarimasite	sizumarimaseñ de
Past Ind.	**INFORMAL**	sizumatta	sizumaranakatta
	FORMAL	sizumarimasita	sizumarimaseñ desita
Past Presump.	**INFORMAL**	sizumattaroo	sizumaranakattaroo
		sizumatta daroo	sizumaranakatta daroo
	FORMAL	sizumarimasitaroo	sizumarimaseñ desitaroo
		sizumatta desyoo	sizumaranakatta desyoo
Conditional	**INFORMAL**	sizumattara	sizumaranakattara
	FORMAL	sizumarimasitara	sizumarimaseñ desitara
Alternative	**INFORMAL**	sizumattari	sizumaranakattari
	FORMAL	sizumarimasitari	sizumarimaseñ desitari

INFORMAL AFFIRMATIVE INDICATIVE

Passive		sizumarareru
Potential		sizumareru
Causative		sizumaraseru
Causative Pass.		sizumaraserareru

Honorific	**I**	osizumari ni naru
	II	osizumari nasaru
Humble	**I**	
	II	

		AFFIRMATIVE	NEGATIVE
Indicative	INFORMAL	sizumu	sizumanai
	FORMAL	sizumimasu	sizumimaseñ
Imperative	INFORMAL I	sizume	sizumu na
	II	sizuminasai	sizuminasaru na
	III	sizuñde kudasai	sizumanai de kudasai
	FORMAL	osizumi nasaimase	osizumi nasaimasu na
Presumptive	INFORMAL I	sizumoo	sizumumai
	II	sizumu daroo	sizumanai daroo
	FORMAL I	sizumimasyoo	sizumimasumai
	II	sizumu daroo	sizumanai daroo
Provisional	INFORMAL	sizumeba	sizumanakereba
	FORMAL	sizumimaseba	sizumimaseñ nara
		sizumimasureba	
Gerund	INFORMAL I	sizuñde	sizumanai de
	II		sizumanakute
	FORMAL	sizumimasite	sizumimaseñ de
Past Ind.	INFORMAL	sizuñda	sizumanakatta
	FORMAL	sizumimasita	sizumimaseñ desita
Past Presump.	INFORMAL	sizuñdaroo	sizumanakattaroo
		sizuñda daroo	sizumanakatta daroo
	FORMAL	sizumimasitaroo	sizumimaseñ desitaroo
		sizuñda desyoo	sizumanakatta desyoo
Conditional	INFORMAL	sizuñdara	sizumanakattara
	FORMAL	sizumimasitara	sizumimaseñ desitara
Alternative	INFORMAL	sizuñdari	sizumanakattari
	FORMAL	sizumimasitari	sizumimaseñ desitari

		INFORMAL AFFIRMATIVE INDICATIVE
Passive		sizumareru
Potential		sizumeru
Causative		sizumaseru
Causative Pass.		sizumaserareru

Honorific	I	osizumi ni naru
	II	osizumi nasaru
Humble	I	
	II	

		AFFIRMATIVE	NEGATIVE
Indicative	**INFORMAL**	sodateru	sodatenai
	FORMAL	sodatemasu	sodatemaseñ
Imperative	**INFORMAL I**	sodatero	sodateru na
	II	sodatenasai	sodatenasaru na
	III	sodatete kudasai	sodatenai de kudasai
	FORMAL	osodate nasaimase	osodate nasaimasu na
Presumptive	**INFORMAL I**	sodateyoo	sodatemai
	II	sodateru daroo	sodatenai daroo
	FORMAL I	sodatemasyoo	sodatemasumai
	II	sodateru desyoo	sodatenai desyoo
Provisional	**INFORMAL**	sodatereba	sodatenakereba
	FORMAL	sodatemaseba	sodatemaseñ nara
		sodatemasureba	
Gerund	**INFORMAL I**	sodatete	sodatenai de
	II		sodatenakute
	FORMAL	sodatemasite	sodatemaseñ de
Past Ind.	**INFORMAL**	sodateta	sodatenakatta
	FORMAL	sodatemasita	sodatemaseñ desita
Past Presump.	**INFORMAL**	sodatetaroo	sodatenakattaroo
		sodateta daroo	sodatenakatta daroo
	FORMAL	sodatemasitaroo	sodatemaseñ desitaroo
		sodateta desyoo	sodatenakatta desyoo
Conditional	**INFORMAL**	sodatetara	sodatenakattara
	FORMAL	sodatemasitara	sodatemaseñ desitara
Alternative	**INFORMAL**	sodatetari	sodatenakattari
	FORMAL	sodatemasitari	sodatemaseñ desitari

INFORMAL AFFIRMATIVE INDICATIVE

Passive		sodaterareru
Potential		sodaterareru
Causative		sodatesaseru
Causative Pass.		sodatesaserareru

Honorific	**I**	osodate ni naru
	II	osodate nasaru
Humble	**I**	osodate suru
	II	osodate itasu

		AFFIRMATIVE	NEGATIVE
Indicative	**INFORMAL**	suberu	suberanai
	FORMAL	suberimasu	suberimaseñ
Imperative	**INFORMAL I**	subere	suberu na
	II	suberinasai	suberinasaru na
	III	subette kudasai	suberanai de kudasai
	FORMAL	osuberi nasaimase	osuberi nasaimasu na
Presumptive	**INFORMAL I**	suberoo	suberumai
	II	suberu daroo	suberanai daroo
	FORMAL I	suberimasyoo	suberimasumai
	II	suberu desyoo	suberanai desyoo
Provisional	**INFORMAL**	subereba	suberanakereba
	FORMAL	suberimaseba	suberimaseñ nara
		suberimasureba	
Gerund	**INFORMAL I**	subette	suberanai de
	II		suberanakute
	FORMAL	suberimasite	suberimaseñ de
Past Ind.	**INFORMAL**	subetta	suberanakatta
	FORMAL	suberimasita	suberimaseñ desita
Past Presump.	**INFORMAL**	subettaroo	suberanakattaroo
		subetta daroo	suberanakatta daroo
	FORMAL	suberimasitaroo	suberimaseñ desitaroo
		subetta desyoo	suberanakatta desyoo
Conditional	**INFORMAL**	subettara	suberanakattara
	FORMAL	suberimasitara	suberimaseñ desitara
Alternative	**INFORMAL**	subettari	suberanakattari
	FORMAL	suberimasitari	suberimaseñ desitari

		INFORMAL AFFIRMATIVE INDICATIVE
Passive		suberareru
Potential		subereru
Causative		suberaseru
Causative Pass.		suberaserareru

Honorific	**I**	osuberi ni nara
	II	osuberi nasaru
Humble	**I**	
	II	

			AFFIRMATIVE	NEGATIVE
Indicative	**INFORMAL**		sugiru	suginai
	FORMAL		sugimasu	sugimaseñ
Imperative	**INFORMAL**	**I**	sugiro	sugiru na
		II	suginasai	suginasaru na
		III	sugite kudasai	suginai de kudasai
	FORMAL		osugi nasaimase	osugi nasaimasu na
Presumptive	**INFORMAL**	**I**	sugiyoo	sugimai
		II	sugiru daroo	suginai daroo
	FORMAL	**I**	sugimasyoo	sugimasumai
		II	sugiru desyoo	suginai desyoo
Provisional	**INFORMAL**		sugireba	suginakereba
	FORMAL		sugimaseba	sugimaseñ nara
			sugimasureba	
Gerund	**INFORMAL**	**I**	sugite	suginai de
		II		suginakute
	FORMAL		sugimasite	sugimaseñ de
Past Ind.	**INFORMAL**		sugita	suginakatta
	FORMAL		sugimasita	sugimaseñ desita
Past Presump.	**INFORMAL**		sugitaroo	suginakattaroo
			sugita daroo	suginakatta daroo
	FORMAL		sugimasitaroo	sugimaseñ desitaroo
			sugita desyoo	suginakatta desyoo
Conditional	**INFORMAL**		sugitara	suginakattara
	FORMAL		sugimasitara	sugimaseñ desitara
Alternative	**INFORMAL**		sugitari	suginakattari
	FORMAL		sugimasitari	sugimaseñ desitari

INFORMAL AFFIRMATIVE INDICATIVE

Passive		
Potential		
Causative		
Causative Pass.		

Honorific	**I**	osugi ni naru
	II	osugi nasaru
Humble	**I**	
	II	

to be superior, to surpass, to excel

		AFFIRMATIVE	NEGATIVE
Indicative	**INFORMAL**	sugureru	sugurenai
	FORMAL	suguremasu	suguremaseñ
Imperative	**INFORMAL I**	sugurero	sugureru na
	II	sugurenasai	sugurenasaru na
	III	sugurete kudasai	sugurenai de kudasai
	FORMAL	osugure nasaimase	osugure nasaimasu na
Presumptive	**INFORMAL I**	sugureyoo	suguremai
	II	sugureru daroo	sugurenai daroo
	FORMAL I	suguremasyoo	suguremasumai
	II	sugureru desyoo	sugurenai desyoo
Provisional	**INFORMAL**	sugurereba	sugurenakereba
	FORMAL	suguremaseba	suguremaseñ nara
		suguremasureba	
Gerund	**INFORMAL I**	sugurete	sugurenai de
	II		sugurenakute
	FORMAL	suguremasite	suguremaseñ de
Past Ind.	**INFORMAL**	sugureta	sugurenakatta
	FORMAL	suguremasita	suguremaseñ desita
Past Presump.	**INFORMAL**	suguretaroo	sugurenakattaroo
		sugureta daroo	sugurenakatta daroo
	FORMAL	suguremasitaroo	suguremaseñ desitaroo
		sugureta desyoo	sugurenakatta desyoo
Conditional	**INFORMAL**	suguretara	sugurenakattara
	FORMAL	suguremasitara	suguremaseñ desitara
Alternative	**INFORMAL**	suguretari	sugurenakattari
	FORMAL	suguremasitari	suguremaseñ desitari

INFORMAL AFFIRMATIVE INDICATIVE

Passive		sugurerareru
Potential		sugurerareru
Causative		suguresaseru
Causative Pass.		suguresaserareru

Honorific	**I**	osugure ni naru
	II	osugure nasaru
Humble	**I**	
	II	

		AFFIRMATIVE	NEGATIVE
Indicative	**INFORMAL**	suku	sukanai
	FORMAL	sukimasu	sukimaseñ
Imperative	**INFORMAL I**		
	II		
	III		
	FORMAL		
Presumptive	**INFORMAL I**	sukoo	sukumai
	II	suku daroo	sukanai daroo
	FORMAL I	sukimasyoo	sukimasumai
	II	suku desyoo	sukanai desyoo
Provisional	**INFORMAL**	sukeba	sukanakereba
	FORMAL	sukimaseba	sukimaseñ nara
		sukimasureba	
Gerund	**INFORMAL I**	suite	sukanai de
	II		sukanakute
	FORMAL	sukimasite	sukimaseñ de
Past Ind.	**INFORMAL**	suita	sukanakatta
	FORMAL	sukimasita	sukimaseñ desita
Past Presump.	**INFORMAL**	suitaroo	sukanakattaroo
		suita daroo	sukanakatta daroo
	FORMAL	sukimasitaroo	sukimaseñ desitaroo
		suita desyoo	sukanakatta desyoo
Conditional	**INFORMAL**	suitara	sukanakattara
	FORMAL	sukimasitara	sukimaseñ desitara
Alternative	**INFORMAL**	suitari	sukanakattari
	FORMAL	sukimasitari	sukimaseñ desitari

INFORMAL AFFIRMATIVE INDICATIVE

Passive		
Potential		
Causative		sukaseru
Causative Pass.		sukaserareru
Honorific	**I**	
	II	
Humble	**I**	
	II	

		AFFIRMATIVE	NEGATIVE
Indicative	**INFORMAL**	sukuu	sukuwanai
	FORMAL	sukuimasu	sukuimaseñ
Imperative	**INFORMAL I**	sukue	sukuu na
	II	sukuinasai	sukuinasaru na
	III	sukutte kudasai	sukuwanai de kudasai
	FORMAL	osukui nasaimase	osukui nasaimasu na
Presumptive	**INFORMAL I**	sukuoo	sukuumai
	II	sukuu daroo	sukuwanai daroo
	FORMAL I	sukuimasyoo	sukuimasumai
	II	sukuu desyoo	sukuwanai desyoo
Provisional	**INFORMAL**	sukueba	sukuwanakereba
	FORMAL	sukuimaseba	sukuimaseñ nara
		sukuimasureba	
Gerund	**INFORMAL I**	sukutte	sukuwanai de
	II		sukuwanakute
	FORMAL	sukuimasite	sukuimaseñ de
Past Ind.	**INFORMAL**	sukutta	sukuwanakatta
	FORMAL	sukuimasita	sukuimaseñ desita
Past Presump.	**INFORMAL**	sukuttaroo	sukuwanakattaroo
		sukutta daroo	sukuwanakatta daroo
	FORMAL	sukuimasitaroo	sukuimaseñ desitaroo
		sukutta desyoo	sukuwanakatta desyoo
Conditional	**INFORMAL**	sukuttara	sukuwanakattara
	FORMAL	sukuimasitara	sukuimaseñ desitara
Alternative	**INFORMAL**	sukuttari	sukuwanakattari
	FORMAL	sukuimasitari	sukuimaseñ desitari

		INFORMAL AFFIRMATIVE INDICATIVE
Passive		sukuwareru
Potential		sukueru
Causative		sukuwaseru
Causative Pass.		sukuwaserareru

Honorific	**I**	osukui ni naru
	II	osukui nasaru
Humble	**I**	osukui suru
	II	osukui itasu

		AFFIRMATIVE	NEGATIVE
Indicative	INFORMAL	sumaseru	sumasenai
	FORMAL	sumasemasu	sumasemaseñ
Imperative	INFORMAL I	sumasero	sumaseru na
	II	sumasenasai	sumasenasaru na
	III	sumasete kudasai	sumasenai de kudasai
	FORMAL	osumase nasaimase	osumase nasaimasu na
Presumptive	INFORMAL I	sumaseyoo	sumasemai
	II	sumaseru daroo	sumasenai daroo
	FORMAL I	sumasemasyoo	sumasemasumai
	II	sumaseru desyoo	sumasenai desyoo
Provisional	INFORMAL	sumasereba	sumasenakereba
	FORMAL	sumasemaseba	sumasemaseñ nara
		sumasemasureba	
Gerund	INFORMAL I	sumasete	sumasenai de
	II		sumasenakute
	FORMAL	sumasemasite	sumasemaseñ de
Past Ind.	INFORMAL	sumaseta	sumasenakatta
	FORMAL	sumasemasita	sumasemaseñ desita
Past Presump.	INFORMAL	sumasetaroo	sumasenakattaroo
		sumaseta daroo	sumasenakatta daroo
	FORMAL	sumasemasitaroo	sumasemaseñ desitaroo
		sumaseta desyoo	sumasenakatta desyoo
Conditional	INFORMAL	sumasetara	sumasenakattara
	FORMAL	sumasemasitara	sumasemaseñ desitara
Alternative	INFORMAL	sumasetari	sumasenakattari
	FORMAL	sumasemasitari	sumasemaseñ desitari

		INFORMAL AFFIRMATIVE INDICATIVE
Passive		sumaserareru
Potential		sumaserareru
Causative		
Causative Pass.		
Honorific	I	osumase ni naru
	II	osumase nasaru
Humble		

*This is the causative form of *sum.u* 'to end' and is given to illustrate the full range of inflection found in this type of derived verb.

		AFFIRMATIVE	NEGATIVE
Indicative	**INFORMAL**	sumu	sumanai
	FORMAL	sumimasu	sumimaseñ
Imperative	**INFORMAL I**	sume	sumu na
	II	suminasai	suminasaru na
	III	suñde kudasai	sumanai de kudasai
	FORMAL	osumi nasaimase	osumi nasaimasu na
Presumptive	**INFORMAL I**	sumoo	sumumai
	II	sumu daroo	sumanai daroo
	FORMAL I	sumimasyoo	sumimasumai
	II	sumu desyoo	sumanai desyoo
Provisional	**INFORMAL**	sumeba	sumanakereba
	FORMAL	sumimaseba	sumimaseñ nara
		sumimasureba	
Gerund	**INFORMAL I**	suñde	sumanai de
	II		sumanakute
	FORMAL	sumimasite	sumimaseñ de
Past Ind.	**INFORMAL**	suñda	sumanakatta
	FORMAL	sumimasita	sumimaseñ desita
Past Presump.	**INFORMAL**	suñdaroo	sumanakattaroo
		suñda daroo	sumanakatta daroo
	FORMAL	sumimasitaroo	sumimaseñ desitaroo
		suñda desyoo	sumanakatta desyoo
Conditional	**INFORMAL**	suñdara	sumanakattara
	FORMAL	sumimasitara	sumimaseñ desitara
Alternative	**INFORMAL**	suñdari	sumanakattari
	FORMAL	sumimasitari	sumimaseñ desitari

		INFORMAL AFFIRMATIVE INDICATIVE
Passive		sumareru
Potential		sumeru
Causative		sumaseru
Causative Pass.		sumaserareru

Honorific	**I**	osumi ni naru
	II	osumi nasaru
Humble	**I**	
	II	

		AFFIRMATIVE	NEGATIVE
Indicative	**INFORMAL**	sumu	sumanai
	FORMAL	sumimasu	sumimaseñ
Imperative	**INFORMAL I**	sume	sumu na
	II		
	III		
	FORMAL		
Presumptive	**INFORMAL I**	sumoo	sumumai
	II	sumu daroo	sumanai daroo
	FORMAL I	sumimasyoo	sumimasumai
	II	sumu desyoo	sumanai desyoo
Provisional	**INFORMAL**	sumeba	sumanakereba
	FORMAL	sumimaseba	sumimaseñ nara
		sumimasureba	
Gerund	**INFORMAL I**	suñde	sumanai de
	II		sumanakute
	FORMAL	sumimasite	sumimaseñ de
Past Ind.	**INFORMAL**	suñda	sumanakatta
	FORMAL	sumimasita	sumimaseñ desita
Past Presump.	**INFORMAL**	suñdaroo	sumanakattaroo
		suñda daroo	sumanakatta daroo
	FORMAL	sumimasitaroo	sumimaseñ desitaroo
		suñda desyoo	sumanakatta desyoo
Conditional	**INFORMAL**	suñdara	sumanakattara
	FORMAL	sumimasitara	sumimaseñ desitara
Alternative	**INFORMAL**	suñdari	sumanakattari
	FORMAL	sumimasitari	sumimaseñ desitari

		INFORMAL AFFIRMATIVE INDICATIVE
Passive		sumareru
Potential		sumeru
Causative		sumaseru
Causative Pass.		sumaserareru
Honorific	**I**	osumi ni naru
	II	osumi nasaru
Humble	**I**	
	II	osumi itasu

		AFFIRMATIVE	NEGATIVE
Indicative	**INFORMAL**	suru	sinai
	FORMAL	simasu	simaseñ
Imperative	**INFORMAL I**	siro	suru na
	II	sinasai	sinasaru na
	III	site kudasai	sinai de kudasai
	FORMAL	nasaimase	nasaimasu na
Presumptive	**INFORMAL I**	siyoo	surumai
	II	suru daroo	sinai daroo
	FORMAL I	simasyoo	simasumai
	II	suru desyoo	sinai desyoo
Provisional	**INFORMAL**	sureba	sinakereba
	FORMAL	simaseba	simaseñ nara
		simasureba	
Gerund	**INFORMAL I**	site	sinai de
	II		sinakute
	FORMAL	simasite	simaseñ de
Past Ind.	**INFORMAL**	sita	sinakatta
	FORMAL	simasita	simaseñ desita
Past Presump.	**INFORMAL**	sitaroo	sinakattaroo
		sita daroo	sinakatta daroo
	FORMAL	simasitaroo	simaseñ desitaroo
		sita desyoo	sinakatta desyoo
Conditional	**INFORMAL**	sitara	sinakattara
	FORMAL	simasitara	simaseñ desitara
Alternative	**INFORMAL**	sitari	sinakattari
	FORMAL	simasitari	simaseñ desitari

	INFORMAL AFFIRMATIVE INDICATIVE
Passive	sareru
Potential	dekiru
Causative	saseru
Causative Pass.	saserareru
Honorific	nasaru
Humble	itasu

*This is used to derive verbs from Sino-Japanese nouns. For example, *kekkoñ* ('marriage') plus *su.ru* becomes *kekkoñ-suru* 'to get married.'

TRANSITIVE   *to recommend, to advise*

		AFFIRMATIVE	**NEGATIVE**
Indicative	**INFORMAL**	susumeru	susumenai
	FORMAL	susumemasu	susumemaseñ
Imperative	**INFORMAL I**	susumero	susumeru na
	II	susumenasai	susumenasaru na
	III	susumete kudasai	susumenai de kudasai
	FORMAL	osusume nasaimase	osusume nasaimasu na
Presumptive	**INFORMAL I**	susumeyoo	susumemai
	II	susumeru daroo	susumenai daroo
	FORMAL I	susumemasyoo	susumemasumai
	II	susumeru desyoo	susumenai desyoo
Provisional	**INFORMAL**	susumereba	susumenakereba
	FORMAL	susumemaseba	susumemaseñ nara
		susumemasureba	
Gerund	**INFORMAL I**	susumete	susumenai de
	II		susumenakute
	FORMAL	susumemasite	susumemaseñ de
Past Ind	**INFORMAL**	susumeta	susumenakatta
	FORMAL	susumemasita	susumemaseñ desita
Past Presump.	**INFORMAL**	susumetaroo	susumenakattaroo
		susumeta daroo	susumenakatta daroo
	FORMAL	susumemasitaroo	susumemaseñ desitaroo
		susumeta desyoo	susumenakatta desyoo
Conditional	**INFORMAL**	susumetara	susumenakattara
	FORMAL	susumemasitara	susumemaseñ desitara
Alternative	**INFORMAL**	susumetari	susumenakattari
	FORMAL	susumemasitari	susumemaseñ desitari

INFORMAL AFFIRMATIVE INDICATIVE

Passive		susumerareru
Potential		susumerareru
Causative		susumesaseru
Causative Pass.		susumesaserareru
Honorific	**I**	osusume ni naru
	II	osusume nasaru
Humble	**I**	osusume suru
	II	osusume itasu

		AFFIRMATIVE	NEGATIVE
Indicative	INFORMAL	susumu	susumanai
	FORMAL	susumimasu	susumimaseñ
Imperative	INFORMAL I	susume	susumu na
	II	susuminasai	susuminasaru na
	III	susuñde kudasai	susumanai de kudasai
	FORMAL	osusumi nasaimase	osusumi nasaimasu na
Presumptive	INFORMAL I	susumoo	susumumai
	II	susumu daroo	susumanai daroo
	FORMAL I	susumimasyoo	susumimasumai
	II	susumu desyoo	susumanai desyoo
Provisional	INFORMAL	susumeba	susumanakereba
	FORMAL	susumimaseba	susumimaseñ nara
		susumimasureba	
Gerund	INFORMAL I	susuñde	susumanai de
	II		susumanakute
	FORMAL	susumimasite	susumimaseñ de
Past Ind.	INFORMAL	susuñda	susumanakatta
	FORMAL	susumimasita	susumimaseñ desita
Past Presump.	INFORMAL	susuñdaroo	susumanakattaroo
		susuñda daroo	susumanakatta daroo
	FORMAL	susumimasitaroo	susumimaseñ desitaroo
		susuñda desyoo	susumanakatta desyoo
Conditional	INFORMAL	susuñdara	susumanakattara
	FORMAL	susumimasitara	susumimaseñ desitara
Alternative	INFORMAL	susuñdari	susumanakattari
	FORMAL	susumimasitari	susumimaseñ desitari

INFORMAL AFFIRMATIVE INDICATIVE

Passive		susumareru
Potential		susumeru
Causative		susumaseru
Causative Pass.		susumaserareru
Honorific	I	osusumi ni naru
	II	osusumi nasaru
Humble	I	osusumi suru
	II	osusumi itasu

TRANSITIVE   *to abandon, to throw away*

		AFFIRMATIVE	NEGATIVE
Indicative	INFORMAL	suteru	sutenai
	FORMAL	sutemasu	sutemaseñ
Imperative	INFORMAL I	sutero	suteru na
	II	sutenasai	sutenasaru na
	III	sutete kudasai	sutenai de kudasai
	FORMAL	osute nasaimase	osute nasaimasu na
Presumptive	INFORMAL I	suteyoo	sutemai
	II	suteru daroo	sutenai daroo
	FORMAL I	sutemasyoo	sutemasumai
	II	suteru desyoo	sutenai desyoo
Provisional	INFORMAL	sutereba	sutenakereba
	FORMAL	sutemaseba	sutemaseñ nara
		sutemasureba	
Gerund	INFORMAL I	sutete	sutenai de
	II		sutenakute
	FORMAL	sutemasite	sutemaseñ de
Past Ind.	INFORMAL	suteta	sutenakatta
	FORMAL	sutemasita	sutemaseñ desita
Past Presump.	INFORMAL	sutetaroo	sutenakattaroo
		suteta daroo	sutenakatta daroo
	FORMAL	sutemasitaroo	sutemaseñ desitaroo
		suteta desyoo	sutenakatta desyoo
Conditional	INFORMAL	sutetara	sutenakattara
	FORMAL	sutemasitara	sutemaseñ desitara
Alternative	INFORMAL	sutetari	sutenakattari
	FORMAL	sutemasitari	sutemaseñ desitari

INFORMAL AFFIRMATIVE INDICATIVE

Passive		suterareru
Potential		suterareru
Causative		sutesaseru
Causative Pass.		sutesaserareru
Honorific	I	osute ni naru
	II	osute nasaru
Humble	I	osute suru
	II	osute itasu

		AFFIRMATIVE	NEGATIVE
Indicative	**INFORMAL**	suwaru	suwaranai
	FORMAL	suwarimasu	suwarimaseñ
Imperative	**INFORMAL I**	suware	suwaru na
	II	suwarinasai	suwarinasaru na
	III	suwatte kudasai	suwaranai de kudasai
	FORMAL	osuwari nasaimase	osuwari nasaimasu na
Presumptive	**INFORMAL I**	suwaroo	suwarumai
	II	suwaru daroo	suwaranai daroo
	FORMAL I	suwarimasyoo	suwarimasumai
	II	suwaru desyoo	suwaranai desyoo
Provisional	**INFORMAL**	suwareba	suwaranakereba
	FORMAL	suwarimaseba	suwarimaseñ nara
		suwarimasureba	
Gerund	**INFORMAL I**	suwatte	suwaranai de
	II		suwaranakute
	FORMAL	suwarimasite	suwarimaseñ de
Past Ind.	**INFORMAL**	suwatta	suwaranakatta
	FORMAL	suwarimasita	suwarimaseñ desita
Past Presump.	**INFORMAL**	suwattaroo	suwaranakattaroo
		suwatta daroo	suwaranakatta daroo
	FORMAL	suwarimasitaroo	suwarimaseñ desitaroo
		suwatta desyoo	suwaranakatta desyoo
Conditional	**INFORMAL**	suwattara	suwaranakattara
	FORMAL	suwarimasitara	suwarimaseñ desitara
Alternative	**INFORMAL**	suwattari	suwaranakattari
	FORMAL	suwarimasitari	suwarimaseñ desitari

INFORMAL AFFIRMATIVE INDICATIVE

Passive		suwarareru
Potential		suwareru
Causative		suwaraseru
Causative Pass.		suwaraserareru

Honorific	**I**	osuwari ni naru
	II	osuwari nasaru
Humble	**I**	
	II	

		AFFIRMATIVE	NEGATIVE
Indicative	**INFORMAL**	taberu	tabenai
	FORMAL	tabemasu	tabemaseñ
Imperative	**INFORMAL I**	tabero	taberu na
	II	tabenasai	tabenasaru na
	III	tabete kudasai	tabenai de kudasai
	FORMAL	mesiagarimase	mesiagarimasu na
Presumptive	**INFORMAL I**	tabeyoo	tabemai
	II	taberu daroo	tabenai daroo
	FORMAL I	tabemasyoo	tabemasumai
	II	taberu desyoo	tabenai desyoo
Provisional	**INFORMAL**	tabereba	tabenakereba
	FORMAL	tabemaseba	tabemaseñ nara
		tabemasureba	
Gerund	**INFORMAL I**	tabete	tabenai de
	II		tabenakute
	FORMAL	tabemasite	tabemaseñ de
Past Ind.	**INFORMAL**	tabeta	tabenakatta
	FORMAL	tabemasita	tabemaseñ desita
Past Presump.	**INFORMAL**	tabetaroo	tabenakattaroo
		tabeta daroo	tabenakatta daroo
	FORMAL	tabemasitaroo	tabemaseñ desitaroo
		tabeta desyoo	tabenakatta desyoo
Conditional	**INFORMAL**	tabetara	tabenakattara
	FORMAL	tabemasitara	tabemaseñ desitara
Alternative	**INFORMAL**	tabetari	tabenakattari
	FORMAL	tabemasitari	tabemaseñ desitari

INFORMAL AFFIRMATIVE INDICATIVE

Passive	taberareru
Potential	taberareru
Causative	tabesaseru
Causative Pass.	tabesaserareru
Honorific	mesiagaru
Humble	itadaku

to pursue (a course), *to follow* (a path)   TRANSITIVE

		AFFIRMATIVE	NEGATIVE
Indicative	**INFORMAL**	tadoru	tadoranai
	FORMAL	tadorimasu	tadorimaseñ
Imperative	**INFORMAL I**	tadore	tadoru na
	II	tadorinasai	tadorinasaru na
	III	tadotte kudasai	tadoranai de kudasai
	FORMAL	otadori nasaimase	otadori nasaimasu na
Presumptive	**INFORMAL I**	tadoroo	tadorumai
	II	tadoru daroo	tadoranai daroo
	FORMAL I	tadorimasyoo	tadorimasumai
	II	tadoru desyoo	tadoranai desyoo
Provisional	**INFORMAL**	tadoreba	tadoranakereba
	FORMAL	tadorimaseba	tadorimaseñ nara
		tadorimasureba	
Gerund	**INFORMAL I**	tadotte	tadoranai de
	II		tadoranakute
	FORMAL	tadorimasite	tadorimaseñ de
Past Ind.	**INFORMAL**	tadotta	tadoranakatta
	FORMAL	tadorimasita	tadorimaseñ desita
Past Presump.	**INFORMAL**	tadottaroo	tadoranakattaroo
		tadotta daroo	tadoranakatta daroo
	FORMAL	tadorimasitaroo	tadorimaseñ desitaroo
		tadotta desyoo	tadoranakatta desyoo
Conditional	**INFORMAL**	tadottara	tadoranakattara
	FORMAL	tadorimasitara	tadorimaseñ desitara
Alternative	**INFORMAL**	tadottari	tadoranakattari
	FORMAL	tadorimasitari	tadorimaseñ desitari

INFORMAL AFFIRMATIVE INDICATIVE

Passive		tadorareru
Potential		tadoreru
Causative		tadoraseru
Causative Pass.		tadoraserareru

Honorific	**I**	otadori ni naru
	II	otadori nasaru
Humble	**I**	otadori suru
	II	otadori itasu

		AFFIRMATIVE	NEGATIVE
Indicative	**INFORMAL**	-tagaru	-tagaranai
	FORMAL	-tagarimasu	-tagarimaseñ
Imperative	**INFORMAL I**		
	II		
	III		
	FORMAL		
Presumptive	**INFORMAL I**	-tagaroo	-tagarumai
	II	-tagaru daroo	-tagaranai daɪoʊ
	FORMAL I	-tagarimasyoo	-tagarimasumai
	II	-tagaru desyoo	-tagaranai desyoo
Provisional	**INFORMAL**	-tagareba	-tagaranakereba
	FORMAL	-tagarimaseba	-tagarimaseñ nara
		-tagarimasureba	
Gerund	**INFORMAL I**	-tagatte	-tagaranai de
	II		-tagaranakute
	FORMAL	-tagarimasite	-tagarimaseñ de
Past Ind.	**INFORMAL**	-tagatta	-tagaranakatta
	FORMAL	-tagarimasita	-tagarimaseñ desita
Past Presump.	**INFORMAL**	-tagattaroo	-tagaranakattaroo
		-tagatta daroo	-tagaranakatta daroo
	FORMAL	-tagarimasitaroo	-tagarimaseñ desitaroo
		-tagatta desyoo	-tagaranakatta desyoo
Conditional	**INFORMAL**	-tagattara	-tagaranakattara
	FORMAL	-tagarimasitara	-tagarimaseñ desitara
Alternative	**INFORMAL**	-tagattari	-tagaranakattari
	FORMAL	-tagarimasitari	-tagarimaseñ desitari

INFORMAL AFFIRMATIVE INDICATIVE

Passive	
Potential	
Causative	-tagaraseru
Causative Pass.	-tagaraserareru
Honorific **I**	
II	
Humble **I**	
II	

*-*tagaru* is added to the infinitive of verbs, and like *-masu* does not have any transitive/intransitive bias of its own.

to cultivate the soil   TRANSITIVE

		AFFIRMATIVE	NEGATIVE
Indicative	**INFORMAL**	tagayasu	tagayasanai
	FORMAL	tagayasimasu	tagayasimaseñ
Imperative	**INFORMAL I**	tagayase	tagayasu na
	II	tagayasinasai	tagayasinasaru na
	III	tagayasite kudasai	tagayasanai de kudasai
	FORMAL	otagayasi nasaimase	otagayasi nasaimasu na
Presumptive	**INFORMAL I**	tagayasoo	tagayasumai
	II	tagayasu daroo	tagayasanai daroo
	FORMAL I	tagayasimasyoo	tagayasimasumai
	II	tagayasu desyoo	tagayasanai desyoo
Provisional	**INFORMAL**	tagayaseba	tagayasanakereba
	FORMAL	tagayasimaseba	tagayasimaseñ nara
		tagayasimasureba	
Gerund	**INFORMAL I**	tagayasite	tagayasanai de
	II		tagayasanakute
	FORMAL	tagayasimasite	tagayasimaseñ de
Past Ind.	**INFORMAL**	tagayasita	tagayasanakatta
	FORMAL	tagayasimasita	tagayasimaseñ desita
Past Presump.	**INFORMAL**	tagayasitaroo	tagayasanakattaroo
		tagayasita daroo	tagayasanakatta daroo
	FORMAL	tagayasimasitaroo	tagayasimaseñ desitaroo
		tagayasita desyoo	tagayasanakatta desyoo
Conditional	**INFORMAL**	tagayasitara	tagayasanakattara
	FORMAL	tagayasimasitara	tagayasimaseñ desitara
Alternative	**INFORMAL**	tagayasitari	tagayasanakattari
	FORMAL	tagayasimasitari	tagayasimaseñ desitari

		INFORMAL AFFIRMATIVE INDICATIVE
Passive		tagayasareru
Potential		tagayaseru
Causative		tagayasaseru
Causative Pass.		tagayasaserareru
Honorific	**I**	otagayasi ni naru
	II	otagayasi nasaru
Humble	**I**	otagayasi suru
	II	otagayasi itasu

TRANSITIVE   *to plan, to scheme, to conspire*

		AFFIRMATIVE	NEGATIVE
Indicative	INFORMAL	takuramu	takuramanai
	FORMAL	takuramimasu	takuramimaseñ
Imperative	INFORMAL I	takurame	takuramu na
	II	takuraminasai	takuraminasaru na
	III	takurañde kudasai	takuramanai de kudasai
	FORMAL	otakurami nasaimase	otakurami nasaimasu na
Presumptive	INFORMAL I	takuramoo	takuramumai
	II	takuramu daroo	takuramanai daroo
	FORMAL I	takuramimasyoo	takuramimasumai
	II	takuramu desyoo	takuramanai desyoo
Provisional	INFORMAL	takurameba	takuramanakereba
	FORMAL	takuramimaseba	takuramimaseñ nara
		takuramimasureba	
Gerund	INFORMAL I	takurañde	takuramanai de
	II		takuramanakute
	FORMAL	takuramimasite	takuramimaseñ de
Past Ind.	INFORMAL	takurañda	takuramanakatta
	FORMAL	takuramimasita	takuramimaseñ desita
Past Presump.	INFORMAL	takurañdaroo	takuramanakattaroo
		takurañda daroo	takuramanakatta daroo
	FORMAL	takuramimasitaroo	takuramimaseñ desitaroo
		takurañda desyoo	takuramanakatta desyoo
Conditional	INFORMAL	takurañdara	takuramanakattara
	FORMAL	takuramimasitara	takuramimaseñ desitara
Alternative	INFORMAL	takurañdari	takuramanakattari
	FORMAL	takuramimasitari	takuramimaseñ desitari

		INFORMAL AFFIRMATIVE INDICATIVE
Passive		takuramareru
Potential		takurameru
Causative		takuramaseru
Causative Pass.		takuramaserareru

Honorific	I	otakurami ni naru
	II	otakurami nasaru
Humble	I	
	II	

to save (money etc.), *to store, to lay aside*   TRANSITIVE

		AFFIRMATIVE	NEGATIVE
Indicative	**INFORMAL**	takuwaeru	takuwaenai
	FORMAL	takuwaemasu	takuwaemaseñ
Imperative	**INFORMAL I**	takuwaero	takuwaeru na
	II	takuwaenasai	takuwaenasaru na
	III	takuwaete kudasai	takuwaenai de kudasai
	FORMAL	otakuwae nasaimase	otakuwae nasaimasu na
Presumptive	**INFORMAL I**	takuwaeyoo	takuwaemai
	II	takuwaeru daroo	takuwaenai daroo
	FORMAL I	takuwaemasyoo	takuwaemasumai
	II	takuwaeru desyoo	takuwaenai desyoo
Provisional	**INFORMAL**	takuwaereba	takuwaenakereba
	FORMAL	takuwaemaseba	takuwaemaseñ nara
		takuwaemasureba	
Gerund	**INFORMAL I**	takuwaete	takuwaenai de
	II		takuwaenakute
	FORMAL	takuwaemasite	takuwaemaseñ de
Past Ind.	**INFORMAL**	takuwaeta	takuwaenakatta
	FORMAL	takuwaemasita	takuwaemaseñ desita
Past Presump.	**INFORMAL**	takuwaetaroo	takuwaenakattaroo
		takuwaeta daroo	takuwaenakatta daroo
	FORMAL	takuwaemasitaroo	takuwaemaseñ desitaroo
		takuwaeta desyoo	takuwaenakatta desyoo
Conditional	**INFORMAL**	takuwaetara	takuwaenakattara
	FORMAL	takuwaemasitara	takuwaemaseñ desitara
Alternative	**INFORMAL**	takuwaetari	takuwaenakattari
	FORMAL	takuwaemasitari	takuwaemaseñ desitari

	INFORMAL AFFIRMATIVE INDICATIVE
Passive	takuwaerareru
Potential	takuwaerareru
Causative	takuwaesaseru
Causative Pass.	takuwaesaserareru

Honorific	**I**	otakuwae ni naru
	II	otakuwae nasaru
Humble	**I**	otakuwae suru
	II	otakuwae itasu

TRANSITIVE   *to hesitate, to flinch, to waver*

		AFFIRMATIVE	NEGATIVE
Indicative	**INFORMAL**	tamerau	tamerawanai
	FORMAL	tameraimasu	tameraimaseñ
Imperative	**INFORMAL I**	tamerae	tamerau na
	II	tamerainasai	tamerainasaru na
	III	tameratte kudasai	tamerawanai de kudasai
	FORMAL	otamerai nasaimase	otamerai nasaimasu na
Presumptive	**INFORMAL I**	tameraoo	tameraumai
	II	tamerau daroo	tamerawanai daroo
	FORMAL I	tameraimasyoo	tameraimasumai
	II	tamerau desyoo	tamerawanai desyoo
Provisional	**INFORMAL**	tameraeba	tamerawanakereba
	FORMAL	tameraimaseba	tameraimaseñ nara
		tameraimasureba	
Gerund	**INFORMAL I**	tameratte	tamerawanai de
	II		tamerawanakute
	FORMAL	tameraimasite	tameraimaseñ de
Past Ind.	**INFORMAL**	tameratta	tamerawanakatta
	FORMAL	tameraimasita	tameraimaseñ desita
Past Presump.	**INFORMAL**	tamerattaroo	tamerawanakattaroo
		tameratta daroo	tamerawanakatta daroo
	FORMAL	tameraimasitaroo	tameraimaseñ desitaroo
		tameratta desyoo	tamerawanakatta desyoo
Conditional	**INFORMAL**	tamerattara	tamerawanakattara
	FORMAL	tameraimasitara	tameraimaseñ desitara
Alternative	**INFORMAL**	tamerattari	tamerawanakattari
	FORMAL	tameraimasitari	tameraimaseñ desitari

		INFORMAL AFFIRMATIVE INDICATIVE
Passive		tamerawareru
Potential		tameraeru
Causative		tamerawaseru
Causative Pass.		tamerawaserareru
Honorific	**I**	otamerai ni naru
	II	otamerai nasaru
Humble	**I**	
	II	

to try, to test, to taste   TRANSITIVE

			AFFIRMATIVE	NEGATIVE
Indicative	**INFORMAL**		tamesu	tamesanai
	FORMAL		tamesimasu	tamesimaseñ
Imperative	**INFORMAL**	**I**	tamese	tamesu na
		II	tamesinasai	tamesinasaru na
		III	tamesite kudasai	tamesanai de kudasai
	FORMAL		otamesi nasaimase	otamesi nasaimasu na
Presumptive	**INFORMAL**	**I**	tamesoo	tamesumai
		II	tamesu daroo	tamesanai daroo
	FORMAL	**I**	tamesimasyoo	tamesimasumai
		II	tamesu desyoo	tamesanai desyoo
Provisional	**INFORMAL**		tameseba	tamesanakereba
	FORMAL		tamesimaseba	tamesimaseñ nara
			tamesimasureba	
Gerund	**INFORMAL**	**I**	tamesite	tamesanai de
		II		tamesanakute
	FORMAL		tamesimasite	tamesimaseñ de
Past Ind.	**INFORMAL**		tamesita	tamesanakatta
	FORMAL		tamesimasita	tamesimaseñ desita
Past Presump.	**INFORMAL**		tamesitaroo	tamesanakattaroo
			tamesita daroo	tamesanakatta daroo
	FORMAL		tamesimasitaroo	tamesimaseñ desitaroo
			tamesita desyoo	tamesanakatta desyoo
Conditional	**INFORMAL**		tamesitara	tamesanakattara
	FORMAL		tamesimasitara	tamesimaseñ desitara
Alternative	**INFORMAL**		tamesitari	tamesanakattari
	FORMAL		tamesimasitari	tamesimaseñ desitari

		INFORMAL AFFIRMATIVE INDICATIVE
Passive		tamesareru
Potential		tameseru
Causative		tamesaseru
Causative Pass.		tamesaserareru
Honorific	**I**	otamesi ni naru
	II	otamesi nasaru
Humble	**I**	otamesi suru
	II	otamesi itasu

		AFFIRMATIVE	NEGATIVE
Indicative	**INFORMAL**	tanomu	tanomanai
	FORMAL	tanomimasu	tanomimaseñ
Imperative	**INFORMAL I**	tanome	tanomu na
	II	tanominasai	tanominasaru na
	III	tanoñde kudasai	tanomanai de kudasai
	FORMAL	otanomi nasaimase	otanomi nasaimasu na
Presumptive	**INFORMAL I**	tanomoo	tanomumai
	II	tanomu daroo	tanomanai daroo
	FORMAL I	tanomimasyoo	tanomimasumai
	II	tanomu desyoo	tanomanai desyoo
Provisional	**INFORMAL**	tanomeba	tanomanakereba
	FORMAL	tanomimaseba	tanomimaseñ nara
		tanomimasureba	
Gerund	**INFORMAL I**	tanoñde	tanomanai de
	II		tanomanakute
	FORMAL	tanomimasite	tanomimaseñ de
Past Ind.	**INFORMAL**	tanoñda	tanomanakatta
	FORMAL	tanomimasita	tanomimaseñ desita
Past Presump.	**INFORMAL**	tanoñdaroo	tanomanakattaroo
		tanoñda daroo	tanomanakatta daroo
	FORMAL	tanomimasitaroo	tanomimaseñ desitaroo
		tanoñda desyoo	tamomanakatta desyoo
Conditional	**INFORMAL**	tanoñdara	tanomanakattara
	FORMAL	tanomimasitara	tanomimaseñ desitara
Alternative	**INFORMAL**	tanoñdari	tanomanakattari
	FORMAL	tanomimasitari	tanomimaseñ desitari

		INFORMAL AFFIRMATIVE INDICATIVE
Passive		tanomareru
Potential		tanomeru
Causative		tanomaseru
Causative Pass.		tanomaserareru

Honorific	**I**	otanomi ni naru
	II	otanomi nasaru
Humble	**I**	otanomi suru
	II	otanomi itasu

to enjoy, to take pleasure in   TRANSITIVE

		AFFIRMATIVE	NEGATIVE
Indicative	**INFORMAL**	tanosimu	tanosimanai
	FORMAL	tanosimimasu	tanosimimaseñ
Imperative	**INFORMAL I**	tanosime	tanosimu na
	II	tanosiminasai	tanosiminasaru na
	III	tanosiñde kudasai	tanosimanai de kudasai
	FORMAL	otanosimi nasaimase	otanosimi nasaimasu na
Presumptive	**INFORMAL I**	tanosimoo	tanosimumai
	II	tanosimu daroo	tanosimanai daroo
	FORMAL I	tanosimimasyoo	tanosimimasumai
	II	tanosimu desyoo	tanosimanai desyoo
Provisional	**INFORMAL**	tanosimeba	tanosimanakereba
	FORMAL	tanosimimaseba	tanosimimaseñ de
		tanosimimasureba	
Gerund	**INFORMAL I**	tanosiñde	tanosimanai de
	II		tanosimanakute
	FORMAL	tanosimimasite	tanosimimaseñ de
Past Ind.	**INFORMAL**	tanosiñda	tanosimanakatta
	FORMAL	tanosimimasita	tanosimimaseñ desita
Past Presump.	**INFORMAL**	tanosiñdaroo	tanosimanakattaroo
		tanosiñda daroo	tanosimanakatta daroo
	FORMAL	tanosimimasitaroo	tanosimimaseñ desitaroo
		tanosiñda desyoo	tanosimanakatta desyoo
Conditional	**INFORMAL**	tanosiñdara	tanosimanakattara
	FORMAL	tanosimimasitara	tanosimimaseñ desitara
Alternative	**INFORMAL**	tanosiñdari	tanosimanakattari
	FORMAL	tanosimimasitari	tanosimimaseñ desitari

	INFORMAL AFFIRMATIVE INDICATIVE
Passive	tanosimareru
Potential	tanosimeru
Causative	tanosimaseru
Causative Pass.	tanosimaserareru

Honorific	**I**	otanosimi ni naru
	II	otanosimi nasaru
Humble	**I**	
	II	

to fall over (from a standing position)

		AFFIRMATIVE	NEGATIVE
Indicative	**INFORMAL**	taoreru	taorenai
	FORMAL	taoremasu	taoremaseñ
Imperative	**INFORMAL I**	taorero	taoreru na
	II	taorenasai	taorenasaru na
	III	taorete kudasai	taorenai de kudasai
	FORMAL	otaore nasaimase	otaore nasaimasu na
Presumptive	**INFORMAL I**	taoreyoo	taoremai
	II	taoreru daroo	taorenai daroo
	FORMAL I	taoremasyoo	taoremasumai
	II	taoreru desyoo	taorenai desyoo
Provisional	**INFORMAL**	taorereba	taorenakereba
	FORMAL	taoremaseba	taoremaseñ nara
		taoremasureba	
Gerund	**INFORMAL I**	taorete	taorenai de
	II		taorenakute
	FORMAL	taoremasite	taoremaseñ de
Past Ind.	**INFORMAL**	taoreta	taorenakatta
	FORMAL	taoremasita	taoremaseñ desita
Past Presump.	**INFORMAL**	taoretaroo	taorenakattaroo
		taoreta daroo	taorenakatta daroo
	FORMAL	taoremasitaroo	taoremaseñ desitaroo
		taoreta desyoo	taorenakatta desyoo
Conditional	**INFORMAL**	taoretara	taorenakattara
	FORMAL	taoremasitara	taoremaseñ desitara
Alternative	**INFORMAL**	taoretari	taorenakattari
	FORMAL	taoremasitari	taoremaseñ desitari

INFORMAL AFFIRMATIVE INDICATIVE

Passive		
Potential		
Causative		taoresaseru
Causative Pass.		taoresaserareru
Honorific	**I**	otaore ni naru
	II	otaore nasaru
Humble	**I**	
	II	

		AFFIRMATIVE	NEGATIVE
Indicative	**INFORMAL**	taosu	taosanai
	FORMAL	taosimasu	taosimaseñ
Imperative	**INFORMAL I**	taose	taosu na
	II	taosinasai	taosinasaru na
	III	taosite kudasai	taosanai de kudasai
	FORMAL	otaosi nasaimase	otaosi nasaimasu na
Presumptive	**INFORMAL I**	taosoo	taosumai
	II	taosu daroo	taosanai daroo
	FORMAL I	taosimasyoo	taosimasumai
	II	taosu desyoo	taosanai desyoo
Provisional	**INFORMAL**	taoseba	taosanakereba
	FORMAL	taosimaseba	taosimaseñ nara
		taosimasureba	
Gerund	**INFORMAL I**	taosite	taosanai de
	II		taosanakute
	FORMAL	taosimasite	taosimaseñ de
Past Ind.	**INFORMAL**	taosita	taosanakatta
	FORMAL	taosimasita	taosimaseñ desita
Past Presump.	**INFORMAL**	taositaroo	taosanakattaroo
		taosita daroo	taosanakatta daroo
	FORMAL	taosimasitaroo	taosimaseñ desitaroo
		taosita desyoo	taosanakatta desyoo
Conditional	**INFORMAL**	taositara	taosanakattara
	FORMAL	taosimasitara	taosimaseñ desitara
Alternative	**INFORMAL**	taositari	taosanakattari
	FORMAL	taosimasitari	taosimaseñ desitari

INFORMAL AFFIRMATIVE INDICATIVE

Passive		taosareru
Potential		taoseru
Causative		taosaseru
Causative Pass.		taosaserareru

Honorific	**I**	otaosi ni naru
	II	otaosi nasaru
Humble	**I**	
	II	

		AFFIRMATIVE	NEGATIVE
Indicative	**INFORMAL**	tariru	tarinai
	FORMAL	tarimasu	tarimaseñ
Imperative	**INFORMAL I**		
	II		
	III		
	FORMAL		
Presumptive	**INFORMAL I**	tariyoo	tarimai
	II	tariru daroo	tarinai daroo
	FORMAL I	tarimasyoo	tarimasumai
	II	tariru desyoo	tarinai desyoo
Provisional	**INFORMAL**	tarireba	tarinakereba
	FORMAL	tarimaseba	tarimaseñ nara
		tarimasureba	
Gerund	**INFORMAL I**	tarite	tarinai de
	II		tarinakute
	FORMAL	tarimasite	tarimaseñ de
Past Ind.	**INFORMAL**	tarita	tarinakatta
	FORMAL	tarimasita	tarimaseñ desita
Past Presump.	**INFORMAL**	taritaroo	tarinakattaroo
		tarita daroo	tarinakatta daroo
	FORMAL	tarimasitaroo	tarimaseñ desitaroo
		tarita desyoo	tarinakatta desyoo
Conditional	**INFORMAL**	taritara	tarinakattara
	FORMAL	tarimasitara	tarimaseñ desitara
Alternative	**INFORMAL**	taritari	tarinakattari
	FORMAL	tarimasitari	tarimaseñ desitari

INFORMAL AFFIRMATIVE INDICATIVE

Passive	
Potential	
Causative	
Causative Pass.	

Honorific	**I**	
	II	
Humble	**I**	
	II	

to ascertain, to confirm   TRANSITIVE

		AFFIRMATIVE	NEGATIVE
Indicative	**INFORMAL**	tasikameru	tasikamenai
	FORMAL	tasikamemasu	tasikamemaseñ
Imperative	**INFORMAL I**	tasikamero	tasikameru na
	II	tasikamenasai	tasikamenasaru na
	III	tasikamete kudasai	tasikamenai de kudasai
	FORMAL	otasikame nasaimase	otasikame nasaimasu na
Presumptive	**INFORMAL I**	tasikameyoo	tasikamemai
	II	tasikameru daroo	tasikamenai daroo
	FORMAL I	tasikamemasyoo	tasikamemasumai
	II	tasikameru desyoo	tasikamenai desyoo
Provisional	**INFORMAL**	tasikamereba	tasikamenakereba
	FORMAL	tasikamemaseba	tasikamemaseñ nara
		tasikamemasureba	
Gerund	**INFORMAL I**	tasikamete	tasikamenai de
	II		tasikamenakute
	FORMAL	tasikamemasite	tasikamemaseñ de
Past Ind.	**INFORMAL**	tasikameta	tasikamenakatta
	FORMAL	tasikamemasita	tasikamemaseñ desita
Past Presump.	**INFORMAL**	tasikametaroo	tasikamenakattaroo
		tasikameta daroo	tasikamenakatta daroo
	FORMAL	tasikamemasitaroo	tasikamemaseñ desitaroo
		tasikameta desyoo	tasikamenakatta desyoo
Conditional	**INFORMAL**	tasikametara	tasikamenakattara
	FORMAL	tasikamemasitara	tasikamemaseñ desitara
Alternative	**INFORMAL**	tasikametari	tasikamenakattari
	FORMAL	tasikamemasitari	tasikamemaseñ desitari

INFORMAL AFFIRMATIVE INDICATIVE

Passive		tasikamerareru
Potential		tasikamerareru
Causative		tasikamesaseru
Causative Pass.		tasikamesaserareru

Honorific	**I**	otasikame ni naru
	II	otasikame nasaru
Humble	**I**	otasikame suru
	II	otasikame itasu

		AFFIRMATIVE	NEGATIVE
Indicative	**INFORMAL**	tasukeru	tasukenai
	FORMAL	tasukemasu	tasukemaseñ
Imperative	**INFORMAL I**	tasukero	tasukeru na
	II	tasukenasai	tasukenasaru na
	III	tasukete kudasai	tasukenai de kudasai
	FORMAL	otasuke nasaimase	otasuke nasaimasu na
Presumptive	**INFORMAL I**	tasukeyoo	tasukemai
	II	tasukeru daroo	tasukenai daroo
	FORMAL I	tasukemasyoo	tasukemasumai
	II	tasukeru desyoo	tasukenai desyoo
Provisional	**INFORMAL**	tasukereba	tasukenakereba
	FORMAL	tasukemaseba	tasukemaseñ nara
		tasukemasureba	
Gerund	**INFORMAL I**	tasukete	tasukenai de
	II		tasukenakute
	FORMAL	tasukemasite	tasukemaseñ de
Past Ind.	**INFORMAL**	tasuketa	tasukenakatta
	FORMAL	tasukemasita	tasukemaseñ desita
Past Presump.	**INFORMAL**	tasuketaroo	tasukenakattaroo
		tasuketa daroo	tasukenakatta daroo
	FORMAL	tasukemasitaroo	tasukemaseñ desitaroo
		tasuketa desyoo	tasukenakatta desyoo
Conditional	**INFORMAL**	tasuketara	tasukenakattara
	FORMAL	tasukemasitara	tasukemaseñ desitara
Alternative	**INFORMAL**	tasuketari	tasukenakattari
	FORMAL	tasukemasitari	tasukemaseñ desitari

INFORMAL AFFIRMATIVE INDICATIVE

Passive		tasukerareru
Potential		tasukerareru
Causative		tasukesaseru
Causative Pass.		tasukesaserareru
Honorific	I	otasuke ni naru
	II	otasuke nasaru
Humble	I	otasuke suru
	II	otasuke itasu

433

to fight against, to wage war on, to struggle against   TRANSITIVE

		AFFIRMATIVE	NEGATIVE
Indicative	**INFORMAL**	tatakau	tatakawanai
	FORMAL	tatakaimasu	tatakaimaseñ
Imperative	**INFORMAL I**	tatakae	tatakau na
	II	tatakainasai	tatakainasaru na
	III	tatakatte kudasai	tatakawanai de kudasai
	FORMAL	otatakai nasaimase	otatakai nasaimasu na
Presumptive	**INFORMAL I**	tatakaoo	tatakaumai
	II	tatakau daroo	tatakawanai daroo
	FORMAL I	tatakaimasyoo	tatakaimasumai
	II	tatakau desyoo	tatakawanai desyoo
Provisional	**INFORMAL**	tatakaeba	tatakawanakereba
	FORMAL	tatakaimaseba	tatakaimaseñ nara
		tatakaimasureba	
Gerund	**INFORMAL I**	tatakatte	tatakawanai de
	II		tatakawanakute
	FORMAL	tatakaimasite	tatakaimaseñ de
Past Ind.	**INFORMAL**	tatakatta	tatakawanakatta
	FORMAL	tatakaimasita	tatakaimaseñ desita
Past Presump.	**INFORMAL**	tatakattaroo	tatakawanakattaroo
		tatakatta daroo	tatakawanakatta daroo
	FORMAL	tatakaimasitaroo	tatakaimaseñ desitaroo
		tatakatta desyoo	tatakawanakatta desyoo
Conditional	**INFORMAL**	tatakattara	tatakawanakattara
	FORMAL	tatakaimasitara	tatakaimaseñ desitara
Alternative	**INFORMAL**	tatakattari	tatakawanakattari
	FORMAL	tatakaimasitari	tatakaimaseñ desitari

		INFORMAL AFFIRMATIVE INDICATIVE
Passive		tatakawareru
Potential		tatakaeru
Causative		tatakawaseru
Causative Pass.		tatakawaserareru
Honorific	**I**	otatakai ni naru
	II	otatakai nasaru
Humble	**I**	
	II	

		AFFIRMATIVE	NEGATIVE
Indicative	**INFORMAL**	tataku	tatakanai
	FORMAL	tatakimasu	tatakimaseñ
Imperative	**INFORMAL I**	tatake	tataku na
	II	tatakinasai	tatakinasaru na
	III	tataite kudasai	tatakanai de kudasai
	FORMAL	otataki nasaimase	otataki nasaimasu na
Presumptive	**INFORMAL I**	tatakoo	tatakumai
	II	tataku daroo	tatakanai daroo
	FORMAL I	tatakimasyoo	tatakimasumai
	II	tataku desyoo	tatakanai desyoo
Provisional	**INFORMAL**	tatakeba	tatakanakereba
	FORMAL	tatakimaseba	tatakimaseñ nara
		tatakimasureba	
Gerund	**INFORMAL I**	tataite	tatakanai de
	II		tatakanakute
	FORMAL	tatakimasite	tatakimaseñ de
Past Ind.	**INFORMAL**	tataita	tatakanakatta
	FORMAL	tatakimasita	tatakimaseñ desita
Past Presump.	**INFORMAL**	tataitaroo	tatakanakattaroo
		tataita daroo	tatakanakatta daroo
	FORMAL	tatakimasitaroo	tatakimaseñ desitaroo
		tataita desyoo	tatakanakatta desyoo
Conditional	**INFORMAL**	tataitara	tatakanakattara
	FORMAL	tatakimasitara	tatakimaseñ desitara
Alternative	**INFORMAL**	tataitari	tatakanakattari
	FORMAL	tatakimasitari	tatakimaseñ desitari

	INFORMAL AFFIRMATIVE INDICATIVE
Passive	tatakareru
Potential	tatakeru
Causative	tatakaseru
Causative Pass.	tatakaserareru

Honorific	**I**	otataki ni naru
	II	otataki nasaru
Humble	**I**	otataki suru
	II	otataki itasu

to fold, to close up (one's shop)   TRANSITIVE

		AFFIRMATIVE	NEGATIVE
Indicative	**INFORMAL**	tatamu	tatamanai
	FORMAL	tatamimasu	tatamimaseñ
Imperative	**INFORMAL I**	tatame	tatamu na
	II	tataminasai	tataminasaru na
	III	tatañde kudasai	tatamanai de kudasai
	FORMAL	otatami nasaimase	otatami nasaimasu na
Presumptive	**INFORMAL I**	tatamoo	tatamumai
	II	tatamu daroo	tatamanai daroo
	FORMAL I	tatamimasyoo	tatamimasumai
	II	tatamu desyoo	tatamanai desyoo
Provisional	**INFORMAL**	tatameba	tatamanakereba
	FORMAL	tatamimaseba	tatamimaseñ nara
		tatamimasureba	
Gerund	**INFORMAL I**	tatañde	tatamanai de
	II		tatamanakute
	FORMAL	tatamimasite	tatamimaseñ de
Past Ind.	**INFORMAL**	tatañda	tatamanakatta
	FORMAL	tatamimasita	tatamimaseñ desita
Past Presump.	**INFORMAL**	tatañdaroo	tatamanakattaroo
		tatañda daroo	tatamanakatta daroo
	FORMAL	tatamimasitaroo	tatamimaseñ desitaroo
		tatañda desyoo	tatamanakatta desyoo
Conditional	**INFORMAL**	tatañdara	tatamanakattara
	FORMAL	tatamimasitara	tatamimaseñ desitara
Alternative	**INFORMAL**	tatañdari	tatamanakattari
	FORMAL	tatamimasitari	tatamimaseñ desitari

		INFORMAL AFFIRMATIVE INDICATIVE
Passive		tatamareru
Potential		tatameru
Causative		tatamaseru
Causative Pass.		tatamaserareru
Honorific	**I**	otatami ni naru
	II	otatami nasaru
Humble	**I**	otatami suru
	II	otatami itasu

		AFFIRMATIVE	NEGATIVE
Indicative	**INFORMAL**	tateru	tatenai
	FORMAL	tatemasu	tatemaseñ
Imperative	**INFORMAL I**	tatero	tateru na
	II	tatenasai	tatenasaru na
	III	tatete kudasai	tatenai de kudasai
	FORMAL	otate nasaimase	otate nasaimasu na
Presumptive	**INFORMAL I**	tateyoo	tatemai
	II	tateru daroo	tatenai daroo
	FORMAL I	tatemasyoo	tatemasumai
	II	tateru desyoo	tatenai desyoo
Provisional	**INFORMAL**	tatereba	tatenakereba
	FORMAL	tatemaseba	tatemaseñ nara
		tatemasureba	
Gerund	**INFORMAL I**	tatete	tatenai de
	II		tatenakute
	FORMAL	tatemasite	tatemaseñ de
Past Ind.	**INFORMAL**	tateta	tatenakatta
	FORMAL	tatemasita	tatemaseñ desita
Past Presump.	**INFORMAL**	tatetaroo	tatenakattaroo
		tateta daroo	tatenakatta daroo
	FORMAL	tatemasitaroo	tatemaseñ desitaroo
		tateta desyoo	tatenakatta desyoo
Conditional	**INFORMAL**	tatetara	tatenakattara
	FORMAL	tatemasitara	tatemaseñ desitara
Alternative	**INFORMAL**	tatetari	tatenakattari
	FORMAL	tatemasitari	tatemaseñ desitari

INFORMAL AFFIRMATIVE INDICATIVE

Passive		taterareru
Potential		taterareru
Causative		tatesaseru
Causative Pass.		tatesaserareru
Honorific	**I**	otate ni naru
	II	otate nasaru
Humble	**I**	otate suru
	II	otate itasu

		AFFIRMATIVE	NEGATIVE
Indicative	**INFORMAL**	tatu	tatanai
	FORMAL	tatimasu	tatimaseñ
Imperative	**INFORMAL I**	tate	tatu na
	II	tatinasai	tatinasaru na
	III	tatte kudasai	tatanai de kudasai
	FORMAL	otati nasaimase	otati nasaimasu na
Presumptive	**INFORMAL I**	tatoo	tatumai
	II	tatu daroo	tatanai daroo
	FORMAL I	tatimasyoo	tatimasumai
	II	tatu desyoo	tatanai desyoo
Provisional	**INFORMAL**	tateba	tatanakereba
	FORMAL	tatimaseba	tatimaseñ nara
		tatimasureba	
Gerund	**INFORMAL I**	tatte	tatanai de
	II		tatanakute
	FORMAL	tatimasite	tatimaseñ de
Past Ind.	**INFORMAL**	tatta	tatanakatta
	FORMAL	tatimasita	tatimaseñ desita
Past Presump.	**INFORMAL**	tattaroo	tatanakattaroo
		tatta daroo	tatanakatta daroo
	FORMAL	tatimasitaroo	tatimaseñ desitaroo
		tatta desyoo	tatanakatta desyoo
Conditional	**INFORMAL**	tattara	tatanakattara
	FORMAL	tatimasitara	tatimaseñ desitara
Alternative	**INFORMAL**	tattari	tatanakattari
	FORMAL	tatimasitari	tatimaseñ desitari

INFORMAL AFFIRMATIVE INDICATIVE

Passive		tatareru
Potential		tateru
Causative		tataseru
Causative Pass.		tataserareru
Honorific	**I**	otati ni naru
	II	otati nasaru
Humble	**I**	otati suru
	II	otati itasu

		AFFIRMATIVE	NEGATIVE
Indicative	INFORMAL	tayoru	tayoranai
	FORMAL	tayorimasu	tayorimaseñ
Imperative	INFORMAL I	tayore	tayoru na
	II	tayorinasai	tayorinasaru na
	III	tayotte kudasai	tayoranai de kudasai
	FORMAL	otayori nasaimase	otayori nasaimasu na
Presumptive	INFORMAL I	tayoroo	tayorumai
	II	tayoru daroo	tayoranai daroo
	FORMAL I	tayorimasyoo	tayorimasumai
	II	tayoru desyoo	tayoranai desyoo
Provisional	INFORMAL	tayoreba	tayoranakereba
	FORMAL	tayorimaseba	tayorimaseñ nara
		tayorimasureba	
Gerund	INFORMAL I	tayotte	tayoranai de
	II		tayoranakute
	FORMAL	tayorimasite	tayorimaseñ de
Past Ind.	INFORMAL	tayotta	tayoranakatta
	FORMAL	tayorimasita	tayorimaseñ desita
Past Presump.	INFORMAL	tayottaroo	tayoranakattaroo
		tayotta daroo	tayoranakatta daroo
	FORMAL	tayorimasitaroo	tayorimaseñ desitaroo
		tayotta desyoo	tayoranakatta desyoo
Conditional	INFORMAL	tayottara	tayoranakattara
	FORMAL	tayorimasitara	tayorimaseñ desitara
Alternative	INFORMAL	tayottari	tayoranakattari
	FORMAL	tayorimasitari	tayorimaseñ desitari

		INFORMAL AFFIRMATIVE INDICATIVE
Passive		tayorareru
Potential		tayoreru
Causative		tayoraseru
Causative Pass.		tayoraserareru
Honorific	I	otayori ni naru
	II	otayori nasaru
Humble	I	otayori suru
	II	otayori itasu

to ask (a question), *to search for*   TRANSITIVE

			AFFIRMATIVE	NEGATIVE
Indicative	**INFORMAL**		tazuneru	tazunenai
	FORMAL		tazunemasu	tazunemaseñ
Imperative	**INFORMAL I**		tazunero	tazuneru na
		II	tazunenasai	tazunenasaru na
		III	tazunete kudasai	tazunenai de kudasai
	FORMAL		otazune nasaimase	otazune nasaimasu na
Presumptive	**INFORMAL I**		tazuneyoo	tazunemai
		II	tazuneru daroo	tazunenai daroo
	FORMAL	**I**	tazunemasyoo	tazunemasumai
		II	tazuneru desyoo	tazunenai desyoo
Provisional	**INFORMAL**		tazunereba	tazunenakereba
	FORMAL		tazunemaseba	tazunemaseñ nara
			tazunemasureba	
Gerund	**INFORMAL I**		tazunete	tazunenai de
		II		tazunenakute
	FORMAL		tazunemasite	tazunemaseñ de
Past Ind.	**INFORMAL**		tazuneta	tazunenakatta
	FORMAL		tazunemasita	tazunemaseñ desita
Past Presump.	**INFORMAL**		tazunetaroo	tazunenakattaroo
			tazuneta daroo	tazunenakatta daroo
	FORMAL		tazunemasitaroo	tazunemaseñ desitaroo
			tazuneta desyoo	tazunenakatta desyoo
Conditional	**INFORMAL**		tazunetara	tazunenakattara
	FORMAL		tazunemasitara	tazunemaseñ desitara
Alternative	**INFORMAL**		tazunetari	tazunenakattari
	FORMAL		tazunemasitari	tazunemaseñ desitari

INFORMAL AFFIRMATIVE INDICATIVE

Passive		tazunerareru
Potential		tazunerareru
Causative		tazunesaseru
Causative Pass.		tazunesaserareru

Honorific	**I**	otazune ni naru
	II	otazune nasaru
Humble	**I**	otazune suru
	II	otazune itasu

TRANSITIVE   *to help* (to do work)

		AFFIRMATIVE	NEGATIVE
Indicative	**INFORMAL**	tetudau	tetudawanai
	FORMAL	tetudaimasu	tetudaimaseñ
Imperative	**INFORMAL I**	tetudae	tetudau na
	II	tetudainasai	tetudainasaru na
	III	tetudatte kudasai	tetudawanai de kudasai
	FORMAL	otetudai nasaimase	otetudai nasaimasu na
Presumptive	**INFORMAL I**	tetudaoo	tetudaumai
	II	tetudau daroo	tetudawanai daroo
	FORMAL I	tetudaimasyoo	tetudaimasumai
	II	tetudau desyoo	tetudawanai desyoo
Provisional	**INFORMAL**	tetudaeba	tetudawanakereba
	FORMAL	tetudaimaseba	tetudaimaseñ nara
		tetudaimasureba	
Gerund	**INFORMAL I**	tetudatte	tetudawanai de
	II		tetudawanakute
	FORMAL	tetudaimasite	tetudaimaseñ de
Past Ind.	**INFORMAL**	tetudatta	tetudawanakatta
	FORMAL	tetudaimasita	tetudaimaseñ desita
Past Presump.	**INFORMAL**	tetudattaroo	tetudawanakattaroo
		tetudatta daroo	tetudawanakatta daroo
	FORMAL	tetudaimasitaroo	tetudaimaseñ desitaroo
		tetudatta desyoo	tetudawanakatta desyoo
Conditional	**INFORMAL**	tetudattara	tetudawanakattara
	FORMAL	tetudaimasitara	tetudaimaseñ desitara
Alternative	**INFORMAL**	tetudattari	tetudawanakattari
	FORMAL	tetudaimasitari	tetudaimaseñ desitari

INFORMAL AFFIRMATIVE INDICATIVE

Passive		tetudawareru
Potential		tetudaeru
Causative		tetudawaseru
Causative Pass.		tetudawaserareru

Honorific	**I**	otetudai ni naru
	II	otetudai nasaru
Humble	**I**	otetudai suru
	II	otetudai itasu

		AFFIRMATIVE	NEGATIVE
Indicative	**INFORMAL**	tigau	tigawanai
	FORMAL	tigaimasu	tigaimaseñ
Imperative	**INFORMAL I**		
	II		
	III		
	FORMAL		
Presumptive	**INFORMAL I**	tigaoo	tigaumai
	II	tigau daroo	tigawanai daroo
	FORMAL I	tigaimasyoo	tigaimasumai
	II	tigau desyoo	tigawanai desyoo
Provisional	**INFORMAL**	tigaeba	tigawanakereba
	FORMAL	tigaimaseba	tigaimaseñ nara
		tigaimasureba	
Gerund	**INFORMAL I**	tigatte	tigawanai de
	II		tigawanakute
	FORMAL	tigaimasite	tigaimaseñ de
Past Ind.	**INFORMAL**	tigatta	tigawanakatta
	FORMAL	tigaimasita	tigaimaseñ desita
Past Presump.	**INFORMAL**	tigattaroo	tigawanakattaroo
		tigatta daroo	tigawanakatta daroo
	FORMAL	tigaimasitaroo	tigaimaseñ desitaroo
		tigatta desyoo	tigawanakatta desyoo
Conditional	**INFORMAL**	tigattara	tigawanakattara
	FORMAL	tigaimasitara	tigaimaseñ desitara
Alternative	**INFORMAL**	tigattari	tigawanakattari
	FORMAL	tigaimasitari	tigaimaseñ desitari

INFORMAL AFFIRMATIVE INDICATIVE

Passive		
Potential		tigaeru
Causative		tigawaseru
Causative Pass.		tigawaserareru

Honorific	**I**	
	II	
Humble	**I**	
	II	

TRANSITIVE   *to take an oath, to pledge one's word*

		AFFIRMATIVE	NEGATIVE
Indicative	**INFORMAL**	tikau	tikawanai
	FORMAL	tikaimasu	tikaimaseñ
Imperative	**INFORMAL I**	tikae	tikau na
	II	tikainasai	tikainasaru na
	III	tikatte kudasai	tikawanai de kudasai
	FORMAL	otikai nasaimase	otikai nasaimasu na
Presumptive	**INFORMAL I**	tikaoo	tikaumai
	II	tikau daroo	tikawanai daroo
	FORMAL I	tikaimasyoo	tikaimasumai
	II	tikau desyoo	tikawanai desyoo
Provisional	**INFORMAL**	tikaeba	tikawanakereba
	FORMAL	tikaimaseba	tikaimaseñ nara
		tikaimasureba	
Gerund	**INFORMAL I**	tikatte	tikawanai de
	II		tikawanakute
	FORMAL	tikaimasite	tikaimaseñ de
Past Ind.	**INFORMAL**	tikatta	tikawanakatta
	FORMAL	tikaimasita	tikaimaseñ desita
Past Presump.	**INFORMAL**	tikattaroo	tikawanakattaroo
		tikatta daroo	tikawanakatta daroo
	FORMAL	tikaimasitaroo	tikaimaseñ desitaroo
		tikatta desyoo	tikawanakatta desyoo
Conditional	**INFORMAL**	tikattara	tikawanakattara
	FORMAL	tikaimasitara	tikaimaseñ desitara
Alternative	**INFORMAL**	tikattari	tikawanakattari
	FORMAL	tikaimasitari	tikaimaseñ desitari

		INFORMAL AFFIRMATIVE INDICATIVE
Passive		tikawareru
Potential		tikaeru
Causative		tikawaseru
Causative Pass.		tikawaserareru
Honorific	**I**	otikai ni naru
	II	otikai nasaru
Humble	**I**	otikai suru
	II	otikai itasu

		AFFIRMATIVE	NEGATIVE
Indicative	**INFORMAL**	tikazuku	tikazukanai
	FORMAL	tikazukimasu	tikazukimaseñ
Imperative	**INFORMAL I**	tikazuke	tikazuku na
	II	tikazukinasai	tikazukinasaru na
	III	tikazuite kudasai	tikazukanai de kudasai
	FORMAL	otikazuki nasaimase	otikazuki nasaimasu na
Presumptive	**INFORMAL I**	tikazukoo	tikazukumai
	II	tikazuku daroo	tikazukanai daroo
	FORMAL I	tikazukimasyoo	tikazukimasumai
	II	tikazuku desyoo	tikazukanai desyoo
Provisional	**INFORMAL**	tikazukeba	tikazukanakereba
	FORMAL	tikazukimaseba	tikazukimaseñ nara
		tikazukimasureba	
Gerund	**INFORMAL I**	tikazuite	tikazukanai de
	II		tikazukanakute
	FORMAL	tikazukimasite	tikazukimaseñ de
Past Ind.	**INFORMAL**	tikazuita	tikazukanakatta
	FORMAL	tikazukimasita	tikazukimaseñ desita
Past Presump.	**INFORMAL**	tikazuitaroo	tikazukanakattaroo
		tikazuita daroo	tikazukanakatta daroo
	FORMAL	tikazukimasitaroo	tikazukimaseñ desitaroo
		tikazuita desyoo	tikazukanakatta desyoo
Conditional	**INFORMAL**	tikazuitara	tikazukanakattara
	FORMAL	tikazukimasitara	tikazukimaseñ desitara
Alternative	**INFORMAL**	tikazuitari	tikazukanakattari
	FORMAL	tikazukimasitari	tikazukimaseñ desitari

INFORMAL AFFIRMATIVE INDICATIVE

Passive		tikazukareru
Potential		tikazukeru
Causative		tikazukaseru
Causative Pass.		tikazukaserareru

Honorific	**I**	otikazuki ni naru
	II	otikazuki nasaru
Humble	**I**	otikazuki suru
	II	otikazuki itasu

		AFFIRMATIVE	NEGATIVE
Indicative	**INFORMAL**	tirakaru	tirakaranai
	FORMAL	tirakarimasu	tirakarimaseñ
Imperative	**INFORMAL I**	tirakare	tirakaru na
	II	tirakarinasai	tirakarinasaru na
	III	tirakatte kudasai	tirakaranai de kudasai
	FORMAL	otirakari nasaimase	otirakari nasaimasu na
Presumptive	**INFORMAL I**	tirakaroo	tirakarumai
	II	tirakaru daroo	tirakaranai daroo
	FORMAL I	tirakarimasyoo	tirakarimasumai
	II	tirakaru desyoo	tirakaranai desyoo
Provisional	**INFORMAL**	tirakareba	tirakaranakereba
	FORMAL	tirakarimaseba	tirakarimaseñ nara
		tirakarimasureba	
Gerund	**INFORMAL I**	tirakatte	tirakaranai de
	II		tirakaranakute
	FORMAL	tirakarimasite	tirakarimaseñ de
Past Ind.	**INFORMAL**	tirakatta	tirakaranakatta
	FORMAL	tirakarimasita	tirakarimaseñ desita
Past Presump.	**INFORMAL**	tirakattaroo	tirakaranakattaroo
		tirakatta daroo	tirakaranakatta daroo
	FORMAL	tirakarimasitaroo	tirakarimaseñ desitaroo
		tirakatta desyoo	tirakaranakatta desyoo
Conditional	**INFORMAL**	tirakattara	tirakaranakatta
	FORMAL	tirakarimasitara	tirakarimaseñ desitara
Alternative	**INFORMAL**	tirakattari	tirakaranakattari
	FORMAL	tirakarimasitari	tirakarimaseñ desitari

	INFORMAL AFFIRMATIVE INDICATIVE
Passive	tirakarareru
Potential	tirakareru
Causative	tirakaraseru
Causative Pass.	tirakaraserareru

Honorific	**I**	
	II	
Humble	**I**	
	II	

		AFFIRMATIVE	NEGATIVE
Indicative	**INFORMAL**	tirakasu	tirakasanai
	FORMAL	tirakasimasu	tirakasimaseñ
Imperative	**INFORMAL I**	tirakase	tirakasu na
	II	tirakasinasai	tirakasinasaru na
	III	tirakasite kudasai	tirakasanai de kudasai
	FORMAL	otirakasi nasaimase	otirakasi nasaimasu na
Presumptive	**INFORMAL I**	tirakasoo	tirakasumai
	II	tirakasu daroo	tirakasanai daroo
	FORMAL I	tirakasimasyoo	tirakasimasumai
	II	tirakasu desyoo	tirakasanai desyoo
Provisional	**INFORMAL**	tirakaseba	tirakasanakereba
	FORMAL	tirakasimaseba	tirakasimaseñ nara
		tirakasimasureba	
Gerund	**INFORMAL I**	tirakasite	tirakasanai de
	II		tirakasanakute
	FORMAL	tirakasimasite	tirakasimaseñ de
Past Ind.	**INFORMAL**	tirakasita	tirakasanakatta
	FORMAL	tirakasimasita	tirakasimaseñ desita
Past Presump.	**INFORMAL**	tirakasitaroo	tirakasanakattaroo
		tirakasita daroo	tirakasanakatta daroo
	FORMAL	tirakarimasitaroo	tirakarimaseñ desitaroo
		tirakasita desyoo	tirakasanakatta desyoo
Conditional	**INFORMAL**	tirakasitara	tirakasanakattara
	FORMAL	tirakasimasitara	tirakasimaseñ desitara
Alternative	**INFORMAL**	tirakasitari	tirakasanakattari
	FORMAL	tirakasimasitari	tirakasimaseñ desitari

		INFORMAL AFFIRMATIVE INDICATIVE
Passive		tirakasareru
Potential		tirakaseru
Causative		tirakasaseru
Causative Pass.		tirakasaserareru

Honorific	**I**	otirakasi ni naru
	II	otirakasi nasaru
Humble	**I**	otirakasi suru
	II	otirakasi itasu

		AFFIRMATIVE	NEGATIVE
Indicative	**INFORMAL**	tiru	tiranai
	FORMAL	tirimasu	tirimaseñ
Imperative	**INFORMAL I**	tire	tiru na
	II	tirinasai	tirinasaru na
	III	titte kudasai	tiranai de kudasai
	FORMAL	otiri nasaimase	otiri nasaimasu na
Presumptive	**INFORMAL I**	tiroo	tirumai
	II	tiru daroo	tiranai daroo
	FORMAL I	tirimasyoo	tirimasumai
	II	tiru desyoo	tiranai desyoo
Provisional	**INFORMAL**	tireba	tiranakereba
	FORMAL	tirimaseba	tirimaseñ nara
		tirimasureba	
Gerund	**INFORMAL I**	titte	tiranai de
	II		tiranakute
	FORMAL	tirimasite	tirimaseñ de
Past Ind.	**INFORMAL**	titta	tiranakatta
	FORMAL	tirimasita	tirimaseñ desita
Past Presump.	**INFORMAL**	tittaroo	tiranakattaroo
		titta daroo	tiranakatta daroo
	FORMAL	tirimasitaroo	tirimaseñ desitaroo
		titta desyoo	tiranakatta desyoo
Conditional	**INFORMAL**	tittara	tiranakattara
	FORMAL	tirimasitara	tirimaseñ desitara
Alternative	**INFORMAL**	tittari	tiranakattari
	FORMAL	tirimasitari	tirimaseñ desitari

		INFORMAL AFFIRMATIVE INDICATIVE
Passive		tirareru
Potential		tireru
Causative		tiraseru
Causative Pass.		tiraserareru
Honorific	**I**	otiri ni naru
	II	otiri nasaru
Humble	**I**	
	II	

		AFFIRMATIVE	NEGATIVE
Indicative	**INFORMAL**	tizimeru	tizimenai
	FORMAL	tizimemasu	tizimemaseñ
Imperative	**INFORMAL I**	tizimero	tizimeru na
	II	tizimenasai	tizimenasaru na
	III	tizimete kudasai	tizimenai de kudasai
	FORMAL	otizime nasaimase	otizime nasaimasu na
Presumptive	**INFORMAL I**	tizimeyoo	tizimemai
	II	tizimeru daroo	tizimenai daroo
	FORMAL I	tizimemasyoo	tizimemasumai
	II	tizimeru desyoo	tizimenai desyoo
Provisional	**INFORMAL**	tizimereba	tizimenakereba
	FORMAL	tizimemaseba	tizimemaseñ nara
		tizimemasureba	
Gerund	**INFORMAL I**	tizimete	tizimenai de
	II		tizimenakute
	FORMAL	tizimemasite	tizimemaseñ de
Past Ind.	**INFORMAL**	tizimeta	tizimenakatta
	FORMAL	tizimemasita	tizimemaseñ desita
Past Presump.	**INFORMAL**	tizimetaroo	tizimenakattaroo
		tizimeta daroo	tizimenakatta daroo
	FORMAL	tizimemasitaroo	tizimemaseñ desitaroo
		tizimeta desyoo	tizimenakatta desyoo
Conditional	**INFORMAL**	tizimetara	tizimenakattara
	FORMAL	tizimemasitara	tizimemaseñ desitara
Alternative	**INFORMAL**	tizimetari	tizimenakattari
	FORMAL	tizimemasitari	tizimemaseñ desitari

INFORMAL AFFIRMATIVE INDICATIVE

Passive		tizimerareru
Potential		tizimerareru
Causative		tizimesaseru
Causative Pass.		tizimesaserareru

Honorific	**I**	otizime ni naru
	II	otizime nasaru
Humble	**I**	otizime suru
	II	otizime itasu

		AFFIRMATIVE	NEGATIVE
Indicative	INFORMAL	tizimu	tızimanaı
	FORMAL	tizimimasu	tizimimaseñ
Imperative	INFORMAL I	tizime	tizimu na
	II	tiziminasai	tiziminasaru na
	III	tiziñde kudasai	tizimanai de kudasai
	FORMAL	otizimi nasaimase	otizimi nasaimasu na
Presumptive	INFORMAL I	tizimoo	tizimumai
	II	tizimu daroo	tizimanai daroo
	FORMAL I	tizimimasyoo	tizimimasumai
	II	tizimu desyoo	tizimanai desyoo
Provisional	INFORMAL	tizimeba	tizimanakereba
	FORMAL	tizimimaseba	tizimimaseñ nara
		tizimimasureba	
Gerund	INFORMAL I	tiziñde	tizimanai de
	II		tizimanakute
	FORMAL	tizimimasite	tizimimaseñ de
Past Ind.	INFORMAL	tiziñda	tizimanakatta
	FORMAL	tizimimasita	tizimimaseñ desita
Past Presump.	INFORMAL	tiziñdaroo	tizimanakattaroo
		tiziñda daroo	tizimanakatta daroo
	FORMAL	tizimimasitaroo	tizimimaseñ desitaroo
		tiziñda desyoo	tizimanakatta desyoo
Conditional	INFORMAL	tiziñdara	tizimanakattara
	FORMAL	tizimimasitara	tizimimaseñ desitara
Alternative	INFORMAL	tiziñdari	tizimanakattari
	FORMAL	tizimimasitari	tizimimaseñ desitari

INFORMAL AFFIRMATIVE INDICATIVE

Passive	tizimareru
Potential	tizimeru
Causative	tizimaseru
Causative Pass.	tizimaserareru

Honorific	I	otizimi ni naru
	II	otizimi nasaru
Humble	I	
	II	

449

		AFFIRMATIVE	NEGATIVE
Indicative	**INFORMAL**	tobu	tobanai
	FORMAL	tobimasu	tobimaseñ
Imperative	**INFORMAL I**	tobe	tobu na
	II	tobinasai	tobinasaru na
	III	toñde kudasai	tobanai de kudasai
	FORMAL	otobi nasaimase	otobi nasaimasu na
Presumptive	**INFORMAL I**	toboo	tobumai
	II	tobu daroo	tobanai daroo
	FORMAL I	tobimasyoo	tobimasumai
	II	tobu desyoo	tobanai desyoo
Provisional	**INFORMAL**	tobeba	tobanakereba
	FORMAL	tobimaseba	tobimaseñ nara
		tobimasureba	
Gerund	**INFORMAL I**	toñde	tobanai de
	II		tobanakute
	FORMAL	tobimasite	tobimaseñ de
Past Ind.	**INFORMAL**	toñda	tobanakatta
	FORMAL	tobimasita	tobimaseñ desita
Past Presump.	**INFORMAL**	toñdaroo	tobanakattaroo
		toñda daroo	tobanakatta daroo
	FORMAL	tobimasitaroo	tobimaseñ desitaroo
		toñda desyoo	tobanakatta desyoo
Conditional	**INFORMAL**	toñdara	tobanakattara
	FORMAL	tobimasitara	tobimaseñ desitara
Alternative	**INFORMAL**	toñdari	tobanakattari
	FORMAL	tobimasitari	tobimaseñ desitari

		INFORMAL AFFIRMATIVE INDICATIVE
Passive		tobareru
Potential		toberu
Causative		tobaseru
Causative Pass.		tobaserareru

Honorific	**I**	otobi ni naru
	II	otobi nasaru
Humble	**I**	
	II	

		AFFIRMATIVE	NEGATIVE
Indicative	**INFORMAL**	todokeru	todokenai
	FORMAL	todokemasu	todokemaseñ
Imperative	**INFORMAL I**	todokero	todokeru na
	II	todokenasai	todokenasaru na
	III	todokete kudasai	todokenai de kudasai
	FORMAL	otodoke nasaimase	otodoke nasaimasu na
Presumptive	**INFORMAL I**	todokeyoo	todokemai
	II	todokeru daroo	todokenai daroo
	FORMAL I	todokemasyoo	todokemasumai
	II	todokeru desyoo	todokenai desyoo
Provisional	**INFORMAL**	todokereba	todokenakereba
	FORMAL	todokemaseba	todokemaseñ nara
		todokemasureba	
Gerund	**INFORMAL I**	todokete	todokenai de
	II		todokenakute
	FORMAL	todokemasite	todokemaseñ de
Past Ind.	**INFORMAL**	todoketa	todokenakatta
	FORMAL	todokemasita	todokemaseñ desita
Past Presump.	**INFORMAL**	todoketaroo	todokenakattaroo
		todoketa daroo	todokenakatta daroo
	FORMAL	todokemasitaroo	todokemaseñ desitaroo
		todoketa desyoo	todokenakatta desyoo
Conditional	**INFORMAL**	todoketara	todokenakattara
	FORMAL	todokemasitara	todokemaseñ desitara
Alternative	**INFORMAL**	todoketari	todokenakattari
	FORMAL	todokemasitari	todokemaseñ desitari

		INFORMAL AFFIRMATIVE INDICATIVE
Passive		todokerareru
Potential		todokerareru
Causative		todokesaseru
Causative Pass.		todokesaserareru
Honorific	**I**	otodoke ni naru
	II	otodoke nasaru
Humble	**I**	otodoke suru
	II	otodoke itasu

		AFFIRMATIVE	NEGATIVE
Indicative	**INFORMAL**	todoku	todokanai
	FORMAL	todokimasu	todokimaseñ
Imperative	**INFORMAL I**	todoke	todoku na
	II	todokinasai	todokinasaru na
	III	todoite kudasai	todokanai de kudasai
	FORMAL	otodoki nasaimase	otodoki nasaimasu na
Presumptive	**INFORMAL I**	todokoo	todokumai
	II	todoku daroo	todokanai daroo
	FORMAL I	todokimasyoo	todokimasumai
	II	todoku desyoo	todokanai desyoo
Provisional	**INFORMAL**	todokeba	todokanakereba
	FORMAL	todokimaseba	todokimaseñ nara
		todokimasureba	
Gerund	**INFORMAL I**	todoite	todokanai de
	II		todokanakute
	FORMAL	todokimasite	todokimaseñ de
Past Ind.	**INFORMAL**	todoita	todokanakatta
	FORMAL	todokimasita	todokimaseñ desita
Past Presump.	**INFORMAL**	todoitaroo	todokanakattaroo
		todoita daroo	todokanakatta daroo
	FORMAL	todokimasitaroo	todokimaseñ desitaroo
		todoita desyoo	todokanakatta desyoo
Conditional	**INFORMAL**	todoitara	todokanakattara
	FORMAL	todokimasitara	todokimaseñ desitara
Alternative	**INFORMAL**	todoitari	todokanakattari
	FORMAL	todokimasitari	todokimaseñ desitari

INFORMAL AFFIRMATIVE INDICATIVE

Passive		
Potential		todokeru
Causative		todokaseru
Causative Pass.		todokaserareru
Honorific	**I**	
	II	
Humble	**I**	
	II	

		AFFIRMATIVE	NEGATIVE
Indicative	**INFORMAL**	tokeru	tokenai
	FORMAL	tokemasu	tokemaseñ
Imperative	**INFORMAL I**	tokero	tokeru na
	II		
	III		
	FORMAL		
Presumptive	**INFORMAL I**	tokeyoo	tokemai
	II	tokeru daroo	tokenai daroo
	FORMAL I	tokemasyoo	tokemasumai
	II	tokeru desyoo	tokenai desyoo
Provisional	**INFORMAL**	tokereba	tokenakereba
	FORMAL	tokemaseba	tokemaseñ nara
		tokemasureba	
Gerund	**INFORMAL I**	tokete	tokenai de
	II		tokenakute
	FORMAL	tokemasite	tokemaseñ de
Past Ind.	**INFORMAL**	toketa	tokenakatta
	FORMAL	tokemasita	tokemaseñ desita
Past Presump.	**INFORMAL**	toketaroo	tokenakattaroo
		toketa daroo	tokenakatta daroo
	FORMAL	tokemasitaroo	tokemaseñ desitaroo
		toketa desyoo	tokenakatta desyoo
Conditional	**INFORMAL**	toketara	tokenakattara
	FORMAL	tokemasitara	tokemaseñ desitara
Alternative	**INFORMAL**	toketari	tokenakattari
	FORMAL	tokemasitari	tokemaseñ desitari

INFORMAL AFFIRMATIVE INDICATIVE

Passive	
Potential	
Causative	
Causative Pass.	

Honorific	**I**	
	II	
Humble	**I**	
	II	

		AFFIRMATIVE	NEGATIVE
Indicative	**INFORMAL**	tomaru	tomaranai
	FORMAL	tomarimasu	tomarimaseñ
Imperative	**INFORMAL I**	tomare	tomaru na
	II	tomarinasai	tomarinasaru na
	III	tomatte kudasai	tomaranai de kudasai
	FORMAL	otomari nasaimase	otomari nasaimasu na
Presumptive	**INFORMAL I**	tomaroo	tomarumai
	II	tomaru daroo	tomaranai daroo
	FORMAL I	tomarimasyoo	tomarimasumai
	II	tomaru desyoo	tomaranai desyoo
Provisional	**INFORMAL**	tomareba	tomaranakereba
	FORMAL	tomarimaseba	tomarimaseñ nara
		tomarimasureba	
Gerund	**INFORMAL I**	tomatte	tomaranai de
	II		tomaranakute
	FORMAL	tomarimasite	tomarimaseñ de
Past Ind.	**INFORMAL**	tomatta	tomaranakatta
	FORMAL	tomarimasita	tomarimaseñ desita
Past Presump.	**INFORMAL**	tomattaroo	tomaranakattaroo
		tomatta daroo	tomaranakatta daroo
	FORMAL	tomarimasitaroo	tomarimaseñ desitaroo
		tomatta desyoo	tomaranakatta desyoo
Conditional	**INFORMAL**	tomattara	tomaranakattara
	FORMAL	tomarimasitara	tomarimaseñ desitara
Alternative	**INFORMAL**	tomattari	tomaranakattari
	FORMAL	tomarimasitari	tomarimaseñ desitari

INFORMAL AFFIRMATIVE INDICATIVE

Passive	tomarareru
Potential	tomareru
Causative	tomaraseru
Causative Pass.	tomaraserareru

Honorific	**I**	otomari ni naru
	II	otomari nasaru
Humble	**I**	otomari suru
	II	otomari itasu

		AFFIRMATIVE	NEGATIVE
Indicative	**INFORMAL**	tomeru	tomenai
	FORMAL	tomemasu	tomemaseñ
Imperative	**INFORMAL I**	tomero	tomeru na
	II	tomenasai	tomenasaru na
	III	tomete kudasai	tomenai de kudasai
	FORMAL	otome nasaimase	otome nasaimasu na
Presumptive	**INFORMAL I**	tomeyoo	tomemai
	II	tomeru daroo	tomenai daroo
	FORMAL I	tomemasyoo	tomemasumai
	II	tomeru desyoo	tomenai desyoo
Provisional	**INFORMAL**	tomereba	tomenakereba
	FORMAL	tomemaseba	tomemaseñ nara
		tomemasureba	
Gerund	**INFORMAL I**	tomete	tomenai de
	II		tomenakute
	FORMAL	tomemasite	tomemaseñ de
Past Ind.	**INFORMAL**	tometa	tomenakatta
	FORMAL	tomemasita	tomemaseñ desita
Past Presump.	**INFORMAL**	tometaroo	tomenakattaroo
		tometa daroo	tomenakatta daroo
	FORMAL	tomemasitaroo	tomemaseñ desitaroo
		tometa desyoo	tomenakatta desyoo
Conditional	**INFORMAL**	tometara	tomenakattara
	FORMAL	tomemasitara	tomemaseñ desitara
Alternative	**INFORMAL**	tometari	tomenakattari
	FORMAL	tomemasitari	tomemaseñ desitari

INFORMAL AFFIRMATIVE INDICATIVE

Passive		tomerareru
Potential		tomerareru
Causative		tomesaseru
Causative Pass.		tomesaserareru
Honorific	**I**	otome ni naru
	II	otome nasaru
Humble	**I**	otome suru
	II	otome itasu

			AFFIRMATIVE	NEGATIVE
Indicative	**INFORMAL**		tooru	tooranai
	FORMAL		toorimasu	toorimaseñ
Imperative	**INFORMAL**	**I**	toore	tooru na
		II	toorinasai	toorinasaru na
		III	tootte kudasai	tooranai de kudasai
	FORMAL		otoori nasaimase	otoori nasaimasu na
Presumptive	**INFORMAL**	**I**	tooroo	toorumai
		II	tooru daroo	tooranai daroo
	FORMAL	**I**	toorimasyoo	toorimasumai
		II	tooru desyoo	tooranai desyoo
Provisional	**INFORMAL**		tooreba	tooranakereba
	FORMAL		toorimaseba	toorimaseñ nara
			toorimasureba	
Gerund	**INFORMAL**	**I**	tootte	tooranai de
		II		tooranakute
	FORMAL		toorimasite	toorimaseñ de
Past Ind.	**INFORMAL**		tootta	tooranakatta
	FORMAL		toorimasita	toorimaseñ desita
Past Presump.	**INFORMAL**		toottaroo	tooranakattaroo
			tootta daroo	tooranakatta daroo
	FORMAL		toorimasitaroo	toorimaseñ desitaroo
			tootta desyoo	tooranakatta desyoo
Conditional	**INFORMAL**		toottara	tooranakattara
	FORMAL		toorimasitara	toorimaseñ desitara
Alternative	**INFORMAL**		toottari	tooranakattari
	FORMAL		toorimasitari	toorimaseñ desitari

	INFORMAL AFFIRMATIVE INDICATIVE
Passive	toorareru
Potential	tooreru
Causative	tooraseru
Causative Pass.	tooraserareru

Honorific	**I**	otoori ni naru
	II	otoori nasaru
Humble	**I**	
	II	

		AFFIRMATIVE	NEGATIVE
Indicative	**INFORMAL**	torikaesu	torikaesanai
	FORMAL	torikaesimasu	torikaesimaseñ
Imperative	**INFORMAL I**	torikaese	torikaesu na
	II	torikaesinasai	torikaesinasaru na
	III	torikaesite kudasai	torikaesanai de kudasai
	FORMAL	otorikaesi nasaimase	otorikaesi nasaimasu na
Presumptive	**INFORMAL I**	torikaesoo	torikaesumai
	II	torikaesu daroo	torikaesanai daroo
	FORMAL I	torikaesimasyoo	torikaesimasumaı
	II	torikaesu desyoo	torikaesanai desyoo
Provisional	**INFORMAL**	torikaeseba	torikaesanakereba
	FORMAL	torikaesimaseba	torikaesimaseñ nara
		torikaesimasureba	
Gerund	**INFORMAL I**	torikaesite	torikaesanai de
	II		torikaesanakute
	FORMAL	torikaesimasite	torikaesimaseñ de
Past Ind.	**INFORMAL**	torikaesita	torikaesanakatta
	FORMAL	torikaesimasita	torikaesimaseñ desita
Past Presump.	**INFORMAL**	torikaesitaroo	torikaesanakattaroo
		torikaesita daroo	torikaesanakatta daroo
	FORMAL	torikaesimasitaroo	torikaesimaseñ desitaroo
		torikaesita desyoo	torikaesanakatta desyoo
Conditional	**INFORMAL**	torikaesitara	torikaesanakattara
	FORMAL	torikaesimasitara	torikaesimaseñ desitara
Alternative	**INFORMAL**	torikaesitari	torikaesanakattari
	FORMAL	torikaesimasitari	torikaesimaseñ desitari

		INFORMAL AFFIRMATIVE INDICATIVE
Passive		torikaesareru
Potential		torikaeseru
Causative		torikaesaseru
Causative Pass.		torikaesaserareru
Honorific	**I**	otorikaesi ni naru
	II	otorikaesi nasaru
Humble	**I**	otorikaesi suru
	II	otorikaesi itasu

		AFFIRMATIVE	NEGATIVE
Indicative	**INFORMAL**	toru	toranai
	FORMAL	torimasu	torimaseñ
Imperative	**INFORMAL I**	tore	toru na
	II	torinasai	torinasaru na
	III	totte kudasai	toranai de kudasai
	FORMAL	otori nasaimase	otori nasaimasu na
Presumptive	**INFORMAL I**	toroo	torumai
	II	toru daroo	toranai daroo
	FORMAL I	torimasyoo	torimasumai
	II	toru desyoo	toranai desyoo
Provisional	**INFORMAL**	toreba	toranakereba
	FORMAL	torimaseba	torimaseñ nara
		torimasureba	
Gerund	**INFORMAL I**	totte	toranai de
	II		toranakute
	FORMAL	torimasite	torimaseñ de
Past Ind.	**INFORMAL**	totta	toranakatta
	FORMAL	torimasita	torimaseñ desita
Past Presump.	**INFORMAL**	tottaroo	toranakattaroo
		totta daroo	toranakatta daroo
	FORMAL	torimasitaroo	torimaseñ desitaroo
		totta desyoo	toranakatta desyoo
Conditional	**INFORMAL**	tottara	toranakattara
	FORMAL	torimasitara	torimaseñ desitara
Alternative	**INFORMAL**	tottari	toranakattari
	FORMAL	torimasitari	torimaseñ desitari

	INFORMAL AFFIRMATIVE INDICATIVE
Passive	torareru
Potential	toreru
Causative	toraseru
Causative Pass.	toraserareru

Honorific	**I**	otori ni naru
	II	otori nasaru
Humble	**I**	otori suru
	II	otori itasu

TRANSITIVE   *to prepare, to arrange, to adjust*

		AFFIRMATIVE	**NEGATIVE**
Indicative	**INFORMAL**	totonoeru	totonoenai
	FORMAL	totonoemasu	totonoemaseñ
Imperative	**INFORMAL I**	totonoero	totonoeru na
	II	totonoenasai	totonoenasaru na
	III	totonoete kudasai	totonoenai de kudasai
	FORMAL	ototonoe nasaimase	ototonoe nasaimasu na
Presumptive	**INFORMAL I**	totonoeyoo	totonoemai
	II	totonoeru daroo	totonoenai daroo
	FORMAL I	totonoemasyoo	totonoemasumai
	II	totonoeru desyoo	totonoenai desyoo
Provisional	**INFORMAL**	totonoereba	totonoenakereba
	FORMAL	totonoemaseba	totonoemaseñ nara
		totonoemasureba	
Gerund	**INFORMAL I**	totonoete	totonoenai de
	II		totonoenakute
	FORMAL	totonoemasite	totonoemaseñ de
Past Ind.	**INFORMAL**	totonoeta	totonoenakatta
	FORMAL	totonoemasita	totonoemaseñ desita
Past Presump.	**INFORMAL**	totonoetaroo	totonoenakattaroo
		totonoeta daroo	totonoenakatta daroo
	FORMAL	totonoemasitaroo	totonoemaseñ desitaroo
		totonoeta desyoo	totonoenakatta desyoo
Conditional	**INFORMAL**	totonoetara	totonoenakattara
	FORMAL	totonoemasitara	totonoemaseñ desitara
Alternative	**INFORMAL**	totonoetari	totonoenakattari
	FORMAL	totonoemasitari	totonoemaseñ desitari

		INFORMAL AFFIRMATIVE INDICATIVE
Passive		totonoerareru
Potential		totonoerareru
Causative		totonoesaseru
Causative Pass.		totonoesaserareru
Honorific	**I**	ototonoe ni naru
	II	ototonoe nasaru
Humble	**I**	ototonoe suru
	II	ototonoe itasu

to catch, to seize   TRANSITIVE

		AFFIRMATIVE	NEGATIVE
Indicative	**INFORMAL**	tukamaeru	tukamaenai
	FORMAL	tukamaemasu	tukamaemaseñ
Imperative	**INFORMAL I**	tukamaero	tukamaeru na
	II	tukamaenasai	tukamaenasaru na
	III	tukamaete kudasai	tukamaenai de kudasai
	FORMAL	otukamae nasaimase	otukamae nasaimasu na
Presumptive	**INFORMAL I**	tukamaeyoo	tukamaemai
	II	tukamaeru daroo	tukamaenai daroo
	FORMAL I	tukamaemasyoo	tukamaemasumai
	II	tukamaeru desyoo	tukamaenai desyoo
Provisional	**INFORMAL**	tukamaereba	tukamaenakereba
	FORMAL	tukamaemaseba	tukamaemaseñ nara
		tukamaemasureba	
Gerund	**INFORMAL I**	tukamaete	tukamaenai de
	II		tukamaenakute
	FORMAL	tukamaemasite	tukamaemaseñ de
Past Ind.	**INFORMAL**	tukamaeta	tukamaenakatta
	FORMAL	tukamaemasita	tukamaemaseñ desita
Past Presump.	**INFORMAL**	tukamaetaroo	tukamaenakattaroo
		tukamaeta daroo	tukamaenakatta daroo
	FORMAL	tukamaemasitaroo	tukamaemaseñ desitaroo
		tukamaeta desyoo	tukamaenakatta desyoo
Conditional	**INFORMAL**	tukamaetara	tukamaenakattara
	FORMAL	tukamaemasitara	tukamaemaseñ desitara
Alternative	**INFORMAL**	tukamaetari	tukamaenakattari
	FORMAL	tukamaemasitari	tukamaemaseñ desitari

		INFORMAL AFFIRMATIVE INDICATIVE
Passive		tukamaerareru
Potential		tukamaerareru
Causative		tukamaesaseru
Causative Pass.		tukamaesaserareru

Honorific	**I**	otukamae ni naru
	II	otukamae nasaru
Humble	**I**	
	II	

		AFFIRMATIVE	**NEGATIVE**
Indicative	**INFORMAL**	tukareru	tukarenai
	FORMAL	tukaremasu	tukaremaseñ
Imperative	**INFORMAL I**		
	II		
	III		
	FORMAL		
Presumptive	**INFORMAL I**	tukareyoo	tukaremai
	II	tukareru daroo	tukarenai daroo
	FORMAL I	tukaremasyoo	tukaremasumai
	II	tukareru desyoo	tukarenai desyoo
Provisional	**INFORMAL**	tukarereba	tukarenakereba
	FORMAL	tukaremaseba	tukaremaseñ nara
		tukaremasureba	
Gerund	**INFORMAL I**	tukarete	tukarenai de
	II		tukarenakute
	FORMAL	tukaremasite	tukaremaseñ de
Past Ind.	**INFORMAL**	tukareta	tukarenakatta
	FORMAL	tukaremasita	tukaremaseñ desita
Past Presump.	**INFORMAL**	tukaretaroo	tukarenakattaroo
		tukareta daroo	tukarenakatta daroo
	FORMAL	tukaremasitaroo	tukaremaseñ desitaroo
		tukareta desyoo	tukarenakatta desyoo
Conditional	**INFORMAL**	tukaretara	tukarenakattara
	FORMAL	tukaremasitara	tukaremaseñ desitara
Alternative	**INFORMAL**	tukaretari	tukarenakattari
	FORMAL	tukaremasitari	tukaremaseñ desitari

INFORMAL AFFIRMATIVE INDICATIVE

Passive		
Potential		
Causative		tukaresaseru
Causative Pass.		tukaresaserareru
Honorific	**I**	otukare ni naru
	II	otukare nasaru
Humble	**I**	otukare suru
	II	otukare itasu

		AFFIRMATIVE	NEGATIVE
Indicative	**INFORMAL**	tukau	tukawanai
	FORMAL	tukaimasu	tukaimaseñ
Imperative	**INFORMAL I**	tukae	tukau na
	II	tukainasai	tukainasaru na
	III	tukatte kudasai	tukawanai de kudasai
	FORMAL	otukai nasaimase	otukai nasaimasu na
Presumptive	**INFORMAL I**	tukaoo	tukaumai
	II	tukau daroo	tukawanai daroo
	FORMAL I	tukaimasyoo	tukaimasumai
	II	tukau desyoo	tukawanai desyoo
Provisional	**INFORMAL**	tukaeba	tukawanakereba
	FORMAL	tukaimaseba	tukaimaseñ nara
		tukaimasureba	
Gerund	**INFORMAL I**	tukatte	tukawanai de
	II		tukawanakute
	FORMAL	tukaimasite	tukaimaseñ de
Past Ind.	**INFORMAL**	tukatta	tukawanakatta
	FORMAL	tukaimasita	tukaimaseñ desita
Past Presump.	**INFORMAL**	tukattaroo	tukawanakattaroo
		tukatta daroo	tukawanakatta daroo
	FORMAL	tukaimasitaroo	tukaimaseñ desitaroo
		tukatta desyoo	tukawanakatta desyoo
Conditional	**INFORMAL**	tukattara	tukawanakattara
	FORMAL	tukaimasitara	tukaimaseñ desitara
Alternative	**INFORMAL**	tukattari	tukawanakattari
	FORMAL	tukaimasitari	tukaimaseñ desitari

INFORMAL AFFIRMATIVE INDICATIVE

Passive		tukawareru
Potential		tukaeru
Causative		tukawaseru
Causative Pass.		tukawaserareru

Honorific	**I**	otukai ni naru
	II	otukai nasaru
Humble	**I**	otukai suru
	II	otukai itasu

TRANSITIVE   *to attach, to add to, to stick on*

		AFFIRMATIVE	NEGATIVE
Indicative	**INFORMAL**	tukeru	tukenai
	FORMAL	tukemasu	tukemaseñ
Imperative	**INFORMAL I**	tukero	tukeru na
	II	tukenasai	tukenasaru na
	III	tukete kudasai	tukenai de kudasai
	FORMAL	otuke nasaimase	otuke nasaimasu na
Presumptive	**INFORMAL I**	tukeyoo	tukemai
	II	tukeru daroo	tukenai daroo
	FORMAL I	tukemasyoo	tukemasumai
	II	tukeru desyoo	tukenai desyoc
Provisional	**INFORMAL**	tukereba	tukenakereba
	FORMAL	tukemaseba	tukemaseñ nara
		tukemasureba	
Gerund	**INFORMAL I**	tukete	tukenai de
	II		tukenakute
	FORMAL	tukemasite	tukemaseñ de
Past Ind.	**INFORMAL**	tuketa	tukenakatta
	FORMAL	tukemasita	tukemaseñ desita
Past Presump.	**INFORMAL**	tuketaroo	tukenakattaroo
		tuketa daroo	tukenakatta daroo
	FORMAL	tukemasitaroo	tukemaseñ desitaroo
		tuketa desyoo	tukenakatta desyoo
Conditional	**INFORMAL**	tuketara	tukenakattara
	FORMAL	tukemasitara	tukemaseñ desitara
Alternative	**INFORMAL**	tuketari	tukenakattari
	FORMAL	tukemasitari	tukemaseñ desitari

		INFORMAL AFFIRMATIVE INDICATIVE
Passive		tukerareru
Potential		tukerareru
Causative		tukesaseru
Causative Pass.		tukesaserareru
Honorific	**I**	otuke ni naru
	II	otuke nasaru
Humble	**I**	otuke suru
	II	otuke itasu

		AFFIRMATIVE	NEGATIVE
Indicative	**INFORMAL**	tukiau	tukiawanai
	FORMAL	tukiaimasu	tukiaimaseñ
Imperative	**INFORMAL I**	tukiae	tukiau na
	II	tukiainasai	tukiainasaru na
	III	tukiatte kudasai	tukiawanai de kudasai
	FORMAL	otukiai nasaimase	otukiai nasaimasu na
Presumptive	**INFORMAL I**	tukiaoo	tukiaumai
	II	tukiau daroo	tukiawanai daroo
	FORMAL I	tukiaimasyoo	tukiaimasumai
	II	tukiau desyoo	tukiawanai desyoo
Provisional	**INFORMAL**	tukiaeba	tukiawanakereba
	FORMAL	tukiaimaseba	tukiaimaseñ nara
		tukiaimasureba	
Gerund	**INFORMAL I**	tukiatte	tukiawanai de
	II		tukiawanakute
	FORMAL	tukiaimasite	tukiaimaseñ de
Past Ind.	**INFORMAL**	tukiatta	tukiawanakatta
	FORMAL	tukiaimasita	tukiaimaseñ desita
Past Presump.	**INFORMAL**	tukiattaroo	tukiawanakattaroo
		tukiatta daroo	tukiawanakatta daroo
	FORMAL	tukiaimasitaroo	tukiaimaseñ desitaroo
		tukiatta desyoo	tukiawanakatta desyoo
Conditional	**INFORMAL**	tukiattara	tukiawanakattara
	FORMAL	tukiaimasitara	tukiaimaseñ desitara
Alternative	**INFORMAL**	tukiattari	tukiawanakattari
	FORMAL	tukiaimasitari	tukiaimaseñ desitari

INFORMAL AFFIRMATIVE INDICATIVE

Passive		
Potential		tukiaeru
Causative		tukiawaseru
Causative Pass.		tukiawaserareru

Honorific	**I**	otukiai ni naru
	II	otukiai nasaru
Humble	**I**	otukiai suru
	II	otukiai itasu

		AFFIRMATIVE	NEGATIVE
Indicative	**INFORMAL**	tuku	tukanai
	FORMAL	tukimasu	tukimaseñ
Imperative	**INFORMAL I**	tuke	tuku na
	II		
	III		
	FORMAL		
Presumptive	**INFORMAL I**	tukoo	tukumai
	II	tuku daroo	tukanai daroo
	FORMAL I	tukimasyoo	tukimasumai
	II	tuku desyoo	tukanai desyoo
Provisional	**INFORMAL**	tukeba	tukanakereba
	FORMAL	tukimaseba	tukimaseñ nara
		tukimasureba	
Gerund	**INFORMAL I**	tuite	tukanai de
	II		tukanakute
	FORMAL	tukimasite	tukimaseñ de
Past Ind.	**INFORMAL**	tuita	tukanakatta
	FORMAL	tukimasita	tukimaseñ desita
Past Presump.	**INFORMAL**	tuitaroo	tukanakattaroo
		tuita daroo	tukanakatta daroo
	FORMAL	tukimasitaroo	tukimaseñ desitaroo
		tuita desyoo	tukanakatta desyoo
Conditional	**INFORMAL**	tuitara	tukanakattara
	FORMAL	tukimasitara	tukimaseñ desitara
Alternative	**INFORMAL**	tuitari	tukanakattari
	FORMAL	tukimasitari	tukimaseñ desitari

INFORMAL AFFIRMATIVE INDICATIVE

Passive		
Potential		tukeru
Causative		tsukaseru
Causative Pass.		tsukaserareru
Honorific	**I**	otuki ni naru
	II	otuki nasaru
Humble	**I**	
	II	

		AFFIRMATIVE	NEGATIVE
Indicative	**INFORMAL**	tukuru	tukuranai
	FORMAL	tukurimasu	tukurimaseñ
Imperative	**INFORMAL I**	tukure	tukuru na
	II	tukurinasai	tukurinasaru na
	III	tukutte kudasai	tukuranai de kudasai
	FORMAL	otukuri nasaimase	otukuri nasaimasu na
Presumptive	**INFORMAL I**	tukuroo	tukurumai
	II	tukuru daroo	tukuranai daroo
	FORMAL I	tukurimasyoo	tukurimasumai
	II	tukuru desyoo	tukuranai desyoo
Provisional	**INFORMAL**	tukureba	tukuranakereba
	FORMAL	tukurimaseba	tukurimaseñ nara
		tukurimasureba	
Gerund	**INFORMAL I**	tukutte	tukuranai de
	II		tukuranakute
	FORMAL	tukurimasite	tukurimaseñ de
Past Ind.	**INFORMAL**	**tukutta**	tukuranakatta
	FORMAL	tukurimasita	tukurimaseñ desita
Past Presump.	**INFORMAL**	tukuttaroo	tukuranakattaroo
		tukutta daroo	tukuranakatta daroo
	FORMAL	tukurimasitaroo	tukurimaseñ desitaroo
		tukutta desyoo	tukuranakatta desyoo
Conditional	**INFORMAL**	tukuttara	tukuranakattara
	FORMAL	tukurimasitara	tukurimaseñ desitara
Alternative	**INFORMAL**	tukuttari	tukuranakattari
	FORMAL	tukurimasitari	tukurimaseñ desitari

INFORMAL AFFIRMATIVE INDICATIVE

Passive		tukurareru
Potential		tukureru
Causative		tukuraseru
Causative Pass.		tukuraserareru

Honorific	**I**	otukuri ni naru
	II	otukuri nasaru
Humble	**I**	otukuri suru
	II	otukuri itasu

TRANSITIVE   *to use up, to exhaust, to do one's best*

			AFFIRMATIVE	NEGATIVE
Indicative	**INFORMAL**		tukusu	tukusanai
	FORMAL		tukusimasu	tukusimaseñ
Imperative	**INFORMAL**	**I**	tukuse	tukusu na
		II	tukusinasai	tukusinasaru na
		III	tukusite kudasai	tukusanai de kudasai
	FORMAL		otukusi nasaimase	otukusi nasaimasu na
Presumptive	**INFORMAL**	**I**	tukusoo	tukusumai
		II	tukusu daroo	tukusanai daroo
	FORMAL	**I**	tukusimasyoo	tukusimasumai
		II	tukusu desyoo	tukusanai desyoo
Provisional	**INFORMAL**		tukuseba	tukusanakereba
	FORMAL		tukusimaseba	tukusimaseñ nara
			tukusimasureba	
Gerund	**INFORMAL**	**I**	tukusite	tukusanai de
		II		tukusanakute
	FORMAL		tukusimasite	tukusimaseñ de
Past Ind.	**INFORMAL**		tukusita	tukusanakatta
	FORMAL		tukusimasita	tukusimaseñ desita
Past Presump.	**INFORMAL**		tukusitaroo	tukusanakattaroo
			tukusita daroo	tukusanakatta daroo
	FORMAL		tukusimasitaroo	tukusimaseñ desitaroo
			tukusita desyoo	tukusanakatta desyoo
Conditional	**INFORMAL**		tukusitara	tukasanakattara
	FORMAL		tukusimasitara	tukusimaseñ desitara
Alternative	**INFORMAL**		tukusitari	tukusanakattari
	FORMAL		tukusimasitari	tukusimaseñ desitari

	INFORMAL AFFIRMATIVE INDICATIVE
Passive	tukusareru
Potential	tukuseru
Causative	tukusaseru
Causative Pass.	tukusaserareru

Honorific	**I**	otukusi ni naru
	II	otukusi nasaru
Humble	**I**	otukusi suru
	II	otukusi itasu

		AFFIRMATIVE	NEGATIVE
Indicative	**INFORMAL**	tumoru	tumoranai
	FORMAL	tumorimasu	tumorimaseñ
Imperative	**INFORMAL I**	tumore	tumoru na
	II		
	III		
	FORMAL		
Presumptive	**INFORMAL I**	tumoroo	tumorumai
	II	tumoru daroo	tumoranai daroo
	FORMAL I	tumorimasyoo	tumorimasumai
	II	tumoru desyoo	tumoranai desyoo
Provisional	**INFORMAL**	tumoreba	tumoranakereba
	FORMAL	tumorimaseba	tumorimaseñ nara
		tumorimasureba	
Gerund	**INFORMAL I**	tumotte	tumoranai de
	II		tumoranakute
	FORMAL	tumorimasite	tumorimaseñ de
Past Ind.	**INFORMAL**	tumotta	tumoranakatta
	FORMAL	tumorimasita	tumorimaseñ desita
Past Presump.	**INFORMAL**	tumottaroo	tumoranakattaroo
		tumotta daroo	tumoranakatta daroo
	FORMAL	tumorimasitaroo	tumorimaseñ desitaroo
		tumotta desyoo	tumoranakatta desyoo
Conditional	**INFORMAL**	tumottara	tumoranakattara
	FORMAL	tumorimasitara	tumorimaseñ desitara
Alternative	**INFORMAL**	tumottari	tumoranakattari
	FORMAL	tumorimasitari	tumorimaseñ desitari

INFORMAL AFFIRMATIVE INDICATIVE

Passive		
Potential		
Causative		
Causative Pass.		
Honorific	**I**	
	II	
Humble	**I**	
	II	

		AFFIRMATIVE	NEGATIVE
Indicative	**INFORMAL**	tunagu	tunaganai
	FORMAL	tunagimasu	tunagimaseñ
Imperative	**INFORMAL I**	tunage	tunagu na
	II	tunaginasai	tunaginasaru na
	III	tunaide kudasai	tunaganai de kudasai
	FORMAL	otunagi nasaimase	otunagi nasaimasu na
Presumptive	**INFORMAL I**	tunagoo	tunagumai
	II	tunagu daroo	tunaganai daroo
	FORMAL I	tunagimasyoo	tunagimasumai
	II	tunagu desyoo	tunaganai desyoo
Provisional	**INFORMAL**	tunageba	tunaganakereba
	FORMAL	tunagimaseba	tunagimaseñ nara
		tunagimasureba	
Gerund	**INFORMAL I**	tunaide	tunaganai de
	II		tunaganakute
	FORMAL	tunagimasite	tunagimaseñ de
Past Ind.	**INFORMAL**	tunaida	tunaganakatta
	FORMAL	tunagimasita	tunagimaseñ desita
Past Presump.	**INFORMAL**	tunaidaroo	tunaganakattaroo
		tunaida daroo	tunaganakatta daroo
	FORMAL	tunagimasitaroo	tunagimaseñ desitaroo
		tunaida desyoo	tunaganakatta desyoo
Conditional	**INFORMAL**	tunaidara	tunaganakattara
	FORMAL	tunagimasitara	tunagimaseñ desitara
Alternative	**INFORMAL**	tunaidari	tunaganakattari
	FORMAL	tunagimasitari	tunagimaseñ desitari

		INFORMAL AFFIRMATIVE INDICATIVE
Passive		tunagareru
Potential		tunageru
Causative		tunagaseru
Causative Pass.		tunagaserareru
Honorific	**I**	otunagi ni naru
	II	otunagi nasaru
Humble	**I**	otunagi suru
	II	otunagi itasu

		AFFIRMATIVE	NEGATIVE
Indicative	**INFORMAL**	tutaeru	tutaenai
	FORMAL	tutaemasu	tutaemaseñ
Imperative	**INFORMAL I**	tutaero	tutaeru na
	II	tutaenasai	tutaenasaru na
	III	tutaete kudasai	tutaenai de kudasai
	FORMAL	otutae nasaimase	otutae nasaimasu na
Presumptive	**INFORMAL I**	tutaeyoo	tutaemai
	II	tutaeru daroo	tutaenai daroo
	FORMAL I	tutaemasyoo	tutaemasumai
	II	tutaeru desyoo	tutaenai desyoo
Provisional	**INFORMAL**	tutaereba	tutaenakereba
	FORMAL	tutaemaseba	tutaemaseñ nara
		tutaemasureba	
Gerund	**INFORMAL I**	tutaete	tutaenai de
	II		tutaenakute
	FORMAL	tutaemasite	tutaemaseñ de
Past Ind.	**INFORMAL**	tutaeta	tutaenakatta
	FORMAL	tutaemasita	tutaemaseñ desita
Past Presump.	**INFORMAL**	tutaetaroo	tutaenakattaroo
		tutaeta daroo	tutaenakatta daroo
	FORMAL	tutaemasitaroo	tutaemaseñ desitaroo
		tutaeta desyoo	tutaenakatta desyoo
Conditional	**INFORMAL**	tutaetara	tutaenakattara
	FORMAL	tutaemasitara	tutaemaseñ desitara
Alternative	**INFORMAL**	tutaetari	tutaenakattari
	FORMAL	tutaemasitari	tutaemaseñ desitari

INFORMAL AFFIRMATIVE INDICATIVE

Passive		tutaerareru
Potential		tutaerareru
Causative		tutaesaseru
Causative Pass.		tutaesaserareru
Honorific	**I**	otutae ni naru
	II	otutae nasaru
Humble	**I**	otutae suru
	II	otutae itasu

		AFFIRMATIVE	NEGATIVE
Indicative	**INFORMAL**	tutomeru	tutomenai
	FORMAL	tutomemasu	tutomemaseñ
Imperative	**INFORMAL I**	tutomero	tutomeru na
	II	tutomenasai	tutomenasaru na
	III	tutomete kudasai	tutomenai de kudasai
	FORMAL	otutome nasaimase	otutome nasaimasu na
Presumptive	**INFORMAL I**	tutomeyoo	tutomemai
	II	tutomeru daroo	tutomenai daroo
	FORMAL I	tutomemasyoo	tutomemasumai
	II	tutomeru desyoo	tutomenai desyoo
Provisional	**INFORMAL**	tutomereba	tutomenakereba
	FORMAL	tutomemaseba	tutomemaseñ nara
		tutomemasureba	
Gerund	**INFORMAL I**	tutomete	tutomenai de
	II		tutomenakute
	FORMAL	tutomemasite	tutomemaseñ de
Past Ind.	**INFORMAL**	tutometa	tutomenakatta
	FORMAL	tutomemasita	tutomemaseñ desita
Past Presump.	**INFORMAL**	tutometaroo	tutomenakattaroo
		tutometa daroo	tutomenakatta daroo
	FORMAL	tutomemasitaroo	tutomemaseñ desitaroo
		tutometa desyoo	tutomenakatta desyoo
Conditional	**INFORMAL**	tutometara	tutomenakattara
	FORMAL	tutomemasitara	tutomemaseñ desitara
Alternative	**INFORMAL**	tutometari	tutomenakattari
	FORMAL	tutomemasitari	tutomemaseñ desitari

		INFORMAL AFFIRMATIVE INDICATIVE
Passive		tutomerareru
Potential		tutomerareru
Causative		tutomesaseru
Causative Pass.		tutomesaserareru
Honorific	**I**	otutome ni naru
	II	otutome nasaru
Humble	**I**	otutome suru
	II	otutome itasu

		AFFIRMATIVE	NEGATIVE
Indicative	**INFORMAL**	tutumu	tutumanai
	FORMAL	tutumimasu	tutumimaseñ
Imperative	**INFORMAL I**	tutume	tutumu na
	II	tutuminasai	tutuminasaru na
	III	tutuñde kudasai	tutumanai de kudasai
	FORMAL	otutumi nasaimase	otutumi nasaimasu na
Presumptive	**INFORMAL I**	tutumɔo	tutumumai
	II	tutumu daroo	tutumanai daroo
	FORMAL I	tutumimasyoo	tutumimasumai
	II	tutumu desyoo	tutumanai desyoo
Provisional	**INFORMAL**	tutumeba	tutumanakereba
	FORMAL	tutumimaseba	tutumimaseñ nara
		tutumimasureba	
Gerund	**INFORMAL I**	tutuñde	tutumanai de
	II		tutumanakute
	FORMAL	tutumimasite	tutumimaseñ de
Past Ind.	**INFORMAL**	tutuñda	tutumanakatta
	FORMAL	tutumimasita	tutumimaseñ desita
Past Presump.	**INFORMAL**	tutuñdaroo	tutumanakattaroo
		tutuñda daroo	tutumanakatta daroo
	FORMAL	tutumimasitaroo	tutumimaseñ desitaroo
		tutuñda desyoo	tutumanakatta desyoo
Conditional	**INFORMAL**	tutuñdara	tutumanakattara
	FORMAL	tutumimasitara	tutumimaseñ desitara
Alternative	**INFORMAL**	tutuñdari	tutumanakattari
	FORMAL	tutumimasitari	tutumimaseñ desitari

		INFORMAL AFFIRMATIVE INDICATIVE
Passive		tutumareru
Potential		tutumeru
Causative		tutumaseru
Causative Pass.		tutumaserareru

Honorific	**I**	otutumi ni naru
	II	otutumi nasaru
Humble	**I**	otutumi suru
	II	otutumi itasu

TRANSITIVE   *to make oneself understood, to transmit*

		AFFIRMATIVE	NEGATIVE
Indicative	**INFORMAL**	tuuziru	tuuzinai
	FORMAL	tuuzimasu	tuuzimaseñ
Imperative	**INFORMAL I**	tuuziro	tuuziru na
	II	tuuzinasai	tuuzinasaru na
	III	tuuzite kudasai	tuuzinai de kudasai
	FORMAL	otuuzi nasaimase	otuuzi nasaimasu na
Presumptive	**INFORMAL I**	tuuziyoo	tuuzimai
	II	tuuziru daroo	tuuzinai daroo
	FORMAL I	tuuzimasyoo	tuuzimasumai
	II	tuuziru desyoo	tuuzinai desyoo
Provisional	**INFORMAL**	tuuzireba	tuuzinakereba
	FORMAL	tuuzimaseba	tuuzimaseñ nara
		tuuzimasureba	
Gerund	**INFORMAL I**	tuuzite	tuuzinai de
	II		tuuzinakute
	FORMAL	tuuzimasite	tuuzimaseñ de
Past Ind.	**INFORMAL**	tuuzita	tuuzinakatta
	FORMAL	tuuzimasita	tuuzimaseñ desita
Past Presump.	**INFORMAL**	tuuzitaroo	tuuzinakattaroo
		tuuzita daroo	tuuzinakatta daroo
	FORMAL	tuuzimasitaroo	tuuzimaseñ desitaroo
		tuuzita desyoo	tuuzinakatta desyoo
Conditional	**INFORMAL**	tuuzitara	tuuzinakattara
	FORMAL	tuuzimasitara	tuuzimaseñ desitara
Alternative	**INFORMAL**	tuuzitari	tuuzinakattari
	FORMAL	tuuzimasitari	tuuzimaseñ desitari

		INFORMAL AFFIRMATIVE INDICATIVE
Passive		tuuzirareru
Potential		tuuzirareru
Causative		tuuzisaseru
Causative Pass.		tuuzisaserareru
Honorific	**I**	otuuzi ni **naru**
	II	otuuzi nasaru
Humble	**I**	
	II	

		AFFIRMATIVE	NEGATIVE
Indicative	**INFORMAL**	tuzukeru	tuzukenai
	FORMAL	tuzukemasu	tuzukemaseñ
Imperative	**INFORMAL I**	tuzukero	tuzukeru na
	II	tuzukenasai	tuzukenasaru na
	III	tuzukete kudasai	tuzukenai de kudasai
	FORMAL	otuzuke nasaimase	otuzuke nasaimasu na
Presumptive	**INFORMAL I**	tuzukeyoo	tuzukemai
	II	tuzukeru daroo	tuzukenai daroo
	FORMAL I	tuzukemasyoo	tuzukemasumai
	II	tuzukeru desyoo	tuzukenai desyoo
Provisional	**INFORMAL**	tuzukereba	tuzukenakereba
	FORMAL	tuzukemaseba	tuzukemaseñ nara
		tuzukemasureba	
Gerund	**INFORMAL I**	tuzukete	tuzukenai de
	II		tuzukenakute
	FORMAL	tuzukemasite	tuzukemaseñ de
Past Ind.	**INFORMAL**	tuzuketa	tuzukenakatta
	FORMAL	tuzukemasita	tuzukemaseñ desita
Past Presump.	**INFORMAL**	tuzuketaroo	tuzukenakattaroo
		tuzuketa daroo	tuzukenakatta daroo
	FORMAL	tuzukemasitaroo	tuzukemaseñ desitaroo
		tuzuketa desyoo	tuzukenakatta desyoo
Conditional	**INFORMAL**	tuzuketara	tuzukenakattara
	FORMAL	tuzukemasitara	tuzukemaseñ desitara
Alternative	**INFORMAL**	tuzuketari	tuzukenakattari
	FORMAL	tuzukemasitari	tuzukemaseñ desitari

		INFORMAL AFFIRMATIVE INDICATIVE
Passive		tuzukerareru
Potential		tuzukerareru
Causative		tuzukesaseru
Causative Pass.		tuzukesaserareru

Honorific	**I**	otuzuke ni naru
	II	otuzuke nasaru
Humble	**I**	otuzuke suru
	II	otuzuke itasu

TRANSITIVE   *to pay attention*

		AFFIRMATIVE	**NEGATIVE**
Indicative	**INFORMAL**	tyuui suru	tyuui sinai
	FORMAL	tyuui simasu	tyuui simaseñ
Imperative	**INFORMAL I**	tyuui siro	tyuui suru na
	II	tyuui sinasai	tyuui sinasaru na
	III	tyuui site kudasai	tyuui sinai de kudasaı
	FORMAL	gotyuui nasaimase	gotyuui nasaimasu na
Presumptive	**INFORMAL I**	tyuui siyoo	tyuui surumai
	II	tyuui suru daroo	tyuui sinai daroo
	FORMAL I	tyuui simasyoo	tyuui simasumai
	II	tyuui suru desyoo	tyuui sinai desyoo
Provisional	**INFORMAL**	tyuui sureba	tyuui sinakereba
	FORMAL	tyuui simaseba	tyuui simaseñ nara
		tyuui simasureba	
Gerund	**INFORMAL I**	tyuui site	tyuui sinai de
	II		tyuui sinakute
	FORMAL	tyuui simasite	tyuui simaseñ de
Past Ind.	**INFORMAL**	tyuui sita	tyuui sinakatta
	FORMAL	tyuui simasita	tyuui simaseñ desita
Past Presump.	**INFORMAL**	tyuui sitaroo	tyuui sinakattaroo
		tyuui sita daroo	tyuui sinakatta daroo
	FORMAL	tyuui simasitaroo	tyuui simaseñ desitaroo
		tyuui sita desyoo	tyuui sinakatta desyoo
Conditional	**INFORMAL**	tyuui sitara	tyuui sinakattara
	FORMAL	tyuui simasitara	tyuui simaseñ desitara
Alternative	**INFORMAL**	tyuui sitari	tyuui sinakattari
	FORMAL	tyuui simasitari	tyuui simaseñ desitari

INFORMAL AFFIRMATIVE INDICATIVE

Passive		tyuui sareru
Potential		tyuui dekiru
Causative		tyuui saseru
Causative Pass.		tyuui saserareru

Honorific	**I**	gotyuui ni naru
	II	gotyuui nasaru
Humble	**I**	gotyuui suru
	II	gotyuui itasu

to order (something from a firm etc.)   TRANSITIVE

		AFFIRMATIVE	NEGATIVE
Indicative	**INFORMAL**	tyuumoñ suru	tyuumoñ sinai
	FORMAL	tyuumoñ simasu	tyuumoñ simaseñ
Imperative	**INFORMAL I**	tyuumoñ siro	tyuumoñ suru na
	II	tyuumoñ sinasai	tyuumoñ sinasaru na
	III	tyuumoñ site kudasai	tyuumoñ sinai de kudasai
	FORMAL	gotyuumoñ nasaimase	gotyuumoñ nasaimasu na
Presumptive	**INFORMAL I**	tyuumoñ siyoo	tyuumoñ surumai
	II	tyuumoñ suru daroo	tyummoñ sinai daroo
	FORMAL I	tyuumoñ simasyoo	tyuumoñ simasumai
	II	tyuumoñ suru desyoo	tyuumoñ sinai desyoo
Provisional	**INFORMAL**	tyuumoñ sureba	tyuumoñ sinakereba
	FORMAL	tyuumoñ simaseba	tyuumoñ simaseñ nara
		tyuumoñ simasureba	
Gerund	**INFORMAL I**	tyuumoñ site	tyuumoñ sinai de
	II		tyuumoñ sinakute
	FORMAL	tyuumoñ simasite	tyummoñ simaseñ de
Past Ind.	**INFORMAL**	tyuumoñ sita	tyuumoñ sinakatta
	FORMAL	tyuumoñ simasita	tyummoñ simaseñ desita
Past Presump.	**INFORMAL**	tyuumoñ sitaroo	tyuumoñ sinakattaroo
		tyuumoñ sita daroo	tyuumoñ sinakatta daroo
	FORMAL	tyuumoñ simasitaroo	tyuumoñ simaseñ desitaroo
		tyuumoñ sita desyoo	tyuumoñ sinakatta desyoo
Conditional	**INFORMAL**	tyuumoñ sitara	tyuumoñ sinakattara
	FORMAL	tyuumoñ simasitara	tyuumoñ simaseñ desitara
Alternative	**INFORMAL**	tyuumoñ sitari	tyuumoñ sinakattari
	FORMAL	tyuumoñ simasitari	tyuumoñ simaseñ desitari

INFORMAL AFFIRMATIVE INDICATIVE

Passive		tyuumoñ sareru
Potential		tyuumoñ dekiru
Causative		tyuumoñ saseru
Causative Pass.		tyuumoñ saserareru
Honorific	**I**	gotyuumoñ ni naru
	II	gotyuumoñ nasaru
Humble	**I**	gotyuumoñ suru
	II	gotyuumoñ itasu

		AFFIRMATIVE	NEGATIVE
Indicative	**INFORMAL**	ueru	uenai
	FORMAL	uemasu	uemaseñ
Imperative	**INFORMAL I**	uero	ueru na
	II	uenasai	uenasaru na
	III	uete kudasai	uenai de kudasai
	FORMAL	oue nasaimase	oue nasaimasu na
Presumptive	**INFORMAL I**	ueyoo	uemai
	II	ueru daroo	uenai daroo
	FORMAL I	uemasyoo	uemasumai
	II	ueru desyoo	uenai desyoo
Provisional	**INFORMAL**	uereba	uenakereba
	FORMAL	uemaseba	uemaseñ nara
		uemasureba	
Gerund	**INFORMAL I**	uete	uenai de
	II		uenakute
	FORMAL	uemasite	uemaseñ de
Past Ind.	**INFORMAL**	ueta	uenakatta
	FORMAL	uemasita	uemaseñ desita
Past Presump.	**INFORMAL**	uetaroo	uenakattaroo
		ueta daroo	uenakatta daroo
	FORMAL	uemasitaroo	uemaseñ desitaroo
		ueta desyoo	uenakatta desyoo
Conditional	**INFORMAL**	uetara	uenakattara
	FORMAL	uemasitara	uemaseñ desitara
Alternative	**INFORMAL**	uetari	uenakattari
	FORMAL	uemasitari	uemaseñ desitari

		INFORMAL AFFIRMATIVE INDICATIVE
Passive		uerareru
Potential		uerareru
Causative		uesaseru
Causative Pass.		uesaserareru
Honorific	**I**	oue ni naru
	II	oue nasaru
Humble	**I**	oue suru
	II	oue itasu

			AFFIRMATIVE	NEGATIVE
Indicative	**INFORMAL**		ugoku	ugokanai
	FORMAL		ugokimasu	ugokimaseñ
Imperative	**INFORMAL**	**I**	ugoke	ugoku na
		II	ugokinasai	ugokinasaru na
		III	ugoite kudasai	ugokanai de kudasai
	FORMAL		ougoki nasaimase	ougoki nasaimasu na
Presumptive	**INFORMAL**	**I**	ugokoo	ugokumai
		II	ugoku daroo	ugokanai daroo
	FORMAL	**I**	ugokimasyoo	ugokimasumai
		II	ugoku desyoo	ugokanai desyoo
Provisional	**INFORMAL**		ugokeba	ugokanakereba
	FORMAL		ugokimaseba	ugokimaseñ nara
			ugokimasureba	
Gerund	**INFORMAL**	**I**	ugoite	ugokanai de
		II		ugokanakute
	FORMAL		ugokimasite	ugokimaseñ de
Past Ind.	**INFORMAL**		ugoita	ugokanakatta
	FORMAL		ugokimasita	ugokimaseñ desita
Past Presump.	**INFORMAL**		ugoitaroo	ugokanakattaroo
			ugoita daroo	ugokanakatta daroo
	FORMAL		ugokimasitaroo	ugokimaseñ desitaroo
			ugoita desyoo	ugokanakatta desyoo
Conditional	**INFORMAL**		ugoitara	ugokanakattara
	FORMAL		ugokimasitara	ugokimaseñ desitara
Alternative	**INFORMAL**		ugoitari	ugokanakattari
	FORMAL		ugokimasitari	ugokimaseñ desitari

		INFORMAL AFFIRMATIVE INDICATIVE
Passive		ugokareru
Potential		ugokeru
Causative		ugokaseru
Causative Pass.		ugokaserareru
Honorific	**I**	ougoki ni naru
	II	ougoki nasaru
Humble	**I**	
	II	

		AFFIRMATIVE	NEGATIVE
Indicative	**INFORMAL**	ukabu	ukabanai
	FORMAL	ukabimasu	ukabimaseñ
Imperative	**INFORMAL I**	ukabe	ukabu na
	II		
	III		
	FORMAL		
Presumptive	**INFORMAL I**	ukaboo	ukabumai
	II	ukabu daroo	ukabanai daroo
	FORMAL I	ukabimasyoo	ukabimasumai
	II	ukabu desyoo	ukabanai desyoo
Provisional	**INFORMAL**	ukabeba	ukabanakereba
	FORMAL	ukabimaseba	ukabimaseñ nara
		ukabimasureba	
Gerund	**INFORMAL I**	ukañde	ukabanai de
	II		ukabanakute
	FORMAL	ukabimasite	ukabimaseñ de
Past Ind.	**INFORMAL**	ukañda	ukabanakatta
	FORMAL	ukabimasita	ukabimaseñ desita
Past Presump.	**INFORMAL**	ukañdaroo	ukabanakattaroo
		ukañda daroo	ukabanakatta daroo
	FORMAL	ukabimasitaroo	ukabimaseñ desitaroo
		ukañda desyoo	ukabanakatta desyoo
Conditional	**INFORMAL**	ukañdara	ukabanakattara
	FORMAL	ukabimasitara	ukabimaseñ desitara
Alternative	**INFORMAL**	ukañdari	ukabanakattari
	FORMAL	ukabimasitari	ukabimaseñ desitari

	INFORMAL AFFIRMATIVE INDICATIVE
Passive	ukabareru
Potential	ukaberu
Causative	ukabaseru
Causative Pass.	ukabaserareru

Honorific	**I**	oukabi ni naru
	II	oukabi nasaru
Humble	**I**	
	II	

to visit, to inquire, to hear (news etc.)   TRANSITIVE

		AFFIRMATIVE	NEGATIVE
Indicative	**INFORMAL**	ukagau	ukagawanai
	FORMAL	ukagaimasu	ukagaimaseñ
Imperative	**INFORMAL I**	ukagae	ukagau na
	II	ukagainasai	ukagainasaru na
	III	ukagatte kudasai	ukagawanai de kudasai
	FORMAL	oukagai nasaimase	oukagai nasaimasu na
Presumptive	**INFORMAL I**	ukagaoo	ukagaumai
	II	ukagau daroo	ukagawanai daroo
	FORMAL I	ukagaimasyoo	ukagaimasumai
	II	ukagau desyoo	ukagawanai desyoo
Provisional	**INFORMAL**	ukagaeba	ukagawanakereba
	FORMAL	ukagaimaseba	ukagaimaseñ nara
		ukagaimasureba	
Gerund	**INFORMAL I**	ukagatte	ukagawanai de
	II		ukagawanakute
	FORMAL	ukagaimasite	ukagaimaseñ de
Past Ind.	**INFORMAL**	ukagatta	ukagawanakatta
	FORMAL	ukagaimasita	ukagaimaseñ desita
Past Presump.	**INFORMAL**	ukagattaroo	ukagawanakattaroo
		ukagatta daroo	ukagawanakatta daroo
	FORMAL	ukagaimasitaroo	ukagaimaseñ desitaroo
		ukagatta desyoo	ukagawanakatta desyoo
Conditional	**INFORMAL**	ukagattara	ukagawanakattara
	FORMAL	ukagaimasitara	ukagaimaseñ desitara
Alternative	**INFORMAL**	ukagattari	ukagawanakattari
	FORMAL	ukagaimasitari	ukagaimaseñ desitari

INFORMAL AFFIRMATIVE INDICATIVE

Passive		
Potential		ukagaeru
Causative		ukagawaseru
Causative Pass.		ukagawaserareru
Honorific	**I**	oukagai ni naru
	II	oukagai nasaru
Humble	**I**	oukagai suru
	II	oukagai itasu

		AFFIRMATIVE	NEGATIVE
Indicative	**INFORMAL**	uketoru	uketoranai
	FORMAL	uketorimasu	uketorimaseñ
Imperative	**INFORMAL I**	uketore	uketoru na
	II	uketorinasai	uketorinasaru na
	III	uketotte kudasai	uketoranai de kudasai
	FORMAL	ouketori nasaimase	ouketori nasaimasu na
Presumptive	**INFORMAL I**	uketoroo	uketorumai
	II	uketoru daroo	uketoranai daroo
	FORMAL I	uketorimasyoo	uketorimasumai
	II	uketoru desyoo	uketoranai desyoo
Provisional	**INFORMAL**	uketoreba	uketoranakereba
	FORMAL	uketorimaseba	uketorimaseñ nara
		uketorimasureba	
Gerund	**INFORMAL I**	uketotte	uketoranai de
	II		uketoranakute
	FORMAL	uketorimasite	uketorimaseñ de
Past Ind.	**INFORMAL**	uketotta	uketoranakatta
	FORMAL	uketorimasita	uketorimaseñ desita
Past Presump.	**INFORMAL**	uketottaroo	uketoranakattaroo
		uketotta daroo	uketoranakatta daroo
	FORMAL	uketorimasitaroo	uketorimaseñ desitaroo
		uketotta desyoo	uketoranakatta desyoo
Conditional	**INFORMAL**	uketottara	uketoranakattara
	FORMAL	uketorimasitara	uketorimaseñ desitara
Alternative	**INFORMAL**	uketottari	uketoranakattari
	FORMAL	uketorimasitari	uketorimaseñ desitari

INFORMAL AFFIRMATIVE INDICATIVE

Passive		uketorareru
Potential		uketoreru
Causative		uketoraseru
Causative Pass.		uketoraserareru

Honorific	**I**	ouketori ni naru
	II	ouketori nasaru
Humble	**I**	ouketori suru
	II	ouketori itasu

		AFFIRMATIVE	NEGATIVE
Indicative	**INFORMAL**	umareru	umarenai
	FORMAL	umaremasu	umaremaseñ
Imperative	**INFORMAL I**	umarero	umareru na
	II		
	III		
	FORMAL		
Presumptive	**INFORMAL I**	umareyoo	umaremai
	II	umareru daroo	umarenai daroo
	FORMAL I	umaremasyoo	umaremasumai
	II	umareru desyoo	umarenai desyoo
Provisional	**INFORMAL**	umarereba	umarenakereba
	FORMAL	umaremaseba	umaremaseñ nara
		umaremasureba	
Gerund	**INFORMAL I**	umarete	umarenai de
	II		umarenakute
	FORMAL	umaremasite	umaremaseñ de
Past Ind.	**INFORMAL**	umareta	umarenakatta
	FORMAL	umaremasita	umaremaseñ desita
Past Presump.	**INFORMAL**	umaretaroo	umarenakattaroo
		umareta daroo	umarenakatta daroo
	FORMAL	umaremasitaroo	umaremaseñ desitaroo
		umareta desyoo	umarenakatta desyoo
Conditional	**INFORMAL**	umaretara	umarenakattara
	FORMAL	umaremasitara	umaremaseñ desitara
Alternative	**INFORMAL**	umaretari	umarenakattari
	FORMAL	umaremasitari	umaremaseñ desitari

INFORMAL AFFIRMATIVE INDICATIVE

Passive		
Potential		
Causative		umaresaseru
Causative Pass.		umaresaserareru

Honorific	**I**	oumare ni naru
	II	oumare nasaru
Humble	**I**	
	II	

*This corresponds to the passive derived form of *um.u* 'to give birth.'

		AFFIRMATIVE	NEGATIVE
Indicative	**INFORMAL**	uramu	uramanaı
	FORMAL	uramimasu	uramimaseñ
Imperative	**INFORMAL I**	urame	uramu na
	II	uraminasai	uraminasaru na
	III	urañde kudasai	uramanai de kudasai
	FORMAL	ourami nasaimase	ourami nasaimasu na
Presumptive	**INFORMAL I**	uramoo	uramumai
	II	uramu daroo	uramanai daroo
	FORMAL I	uramimasyoo	uramimasumai
	II	uramu desyoo	uramanai desyoo
Provisional	**INFORMAL**	urameba	uramanakereba
	FORMAL	uramimaseba	uramimaseñ nara
		uramimasureba	
Gerund	**INFORMAL I**	urañde	uramanai de
	II		uramanakute
	FORMAL	uramimasite	uramimaseñ de
Past Ind.	**INFORMAL**	urañda	uramanakatta
	FORMAL	uramimasita	uramimaseñ desita
Past Presump.	**INFORMAL**	urañdaroo	uramanakattaroo
		urañda daroo	uramanakatta daroo
	FORMAL	uramimasitaroo	uramimaseñ desitaroo
		urañda desyoo	uramanakatta desyoo
Conditional	**INFORMAL**	urañdara	uramanakattara
	FORMAL	uramimasitara	uramimaseñ desitara
Alternative	**INFORMAL**	urañdari	uramanakattari
	FORMAL	uramimasitari	uramimaseñ desitari

INFORMAL AFFIRMATIVE INDICATIVE

Passive		uramareru
Potential		urameru
Causative		uramaseru
Causative Pass.		uramaserareru

Honorific	**I**	ourami ni naru
	II	ourami nasaru
Humble	**I**	ourami suru
	II	ourami itasu

		AFFIRMATIVE	NEGATIVE
Indicative	**INFORMAL**	uru	uranai
	FORMAL	urimasu	urimaseñ
Imperative	**INFORMAL I**	ure	uru na
	II	urinasai	urinasaru na
	III	utte kudasai	uranai de kudasai
	FORMAL	ouri nasaimase	ouri nasaimasu na
Presumptive	**INFORMAL I**	uroo	urumai
	II	uru daroo	uranai daroo
	FORMAL I	urimasyoo	urimasumai
	II	uru desyoo	uranai desyoo
Provisional	**INFORMAL**	ureba	uranakereba
	FORMAL	urimaseba	urimaseñ nara
		urimasureba	
Gerund	**INFORMAL I**	utte	uranai de
	II		uranakute
	FORMAL	urimasite	urimaseñ de
Past Ind.	**INFORMAL**	utta	uranakatta
	FORMAL	urimasita	urimaseñ desita
Past Presump.	**INFORMAL**	uttaroo	uranakattaroo
		utta daroo	uranakatta daroo
	FORMAL	urimasitaroo	urimaseñ desitaroo
		utta desyoo	uranakatta desyoo
Conditional	**INFORMAL**	uttara	uranakattara
	FORMAL	urimasitara	urimaseñ desitara
Alternative	**INFORMAL**	uttari	uranakattari
	FORMAL	urimasitari	urimaseñ desitari

		INFORMAL AFFIRMATIVE INDICATIVE
Passive		urareru
Potential		ureru
Causative		uraseru
Causative Pass.		uraserareru
Honorific	**I**	ouri ni naru
	II	ouri nasaru
Humble	**I**	ouri suru
	II	ouri itasu

		AFFIRMATIVE	NEGATIVE
Indicative	**INFORMAL**	utau	utawanai
	FORMAL	utaimasu	utaimaseñ
Imperative	**INFORMAL I**	utae	utau na
	II	utainasai	utainasaru na
	III	utatte kudasai	utawanai de kudasai
	FORMAL	outai nasaimase	outai nasaimasu na
Presumptive	**INFORMAL I**	utaoo	utaumai
	II	utau daroo	utawanai daroo
	FORMAL **I**	utaimasyoo	utaimasumai
	II	utau desyoo	utawanai desyoo
Provisional	**INFORMAL**	utaeba	utawanakereba
	FORMAL	utaimaseba	utaimaseñ nara
		utaimasureba	
Gerund	**INFORMAL I**	utatte	utawanai de
	II		utawanakute
	FORMAL	utaimasite	utaimaseñ de
Past Ind.	**INFORMAL**	utatta	utawanakatta
	FORMAL	utaimasita	utaimaseñ desita
Past Presump.	**INFORMAL**	utattaroo	utawanakattaroo
		utatta daroo	utawanakatta daroo
	FORMAL	utaimasitaroo	utaimaseñ desitaroo
		utatta desyoo	utawanakatta desyoo
Conditional	**INFORMAL**	utattara	utawanakattara
	FORMAL	utaimasitara	utaimaseñ desitara
Alternative	**INFORMAL**	utattari	utawanakattari
	FORMAL	utaimasitari	utaimaseñ desitari

		INFORMAL AFFIRMATIVE INDICATIVE
Passive		utawareru
Potential		utaeru
Causative		utawaseru
Causative Pass.		utawaserareru

Honorific	**I**	outai ni naru
	II	outai nasaru
Humble	**I**	outai suru
	II	outai itasu

		AFFIRMATIVE	NEGATIVE
Indicative	**INFORMAL**	utu	utanai
	FORMAL	utimasu	utimaseñ
Imperative	**INFORMAL I**	ute	utu na
	II	utinasai	utinasaru na
	III	utte kudasai	utanai de kudasai
	FORMAL	outi nasaimase	outi nasaimasu na
Presumptive	**INFORMAL I**	utoo	utumai
	II	utu daroo	utanai daroo
	FORMAL I	utimasyoo	utimasumai
	II	utu desyoo	utanai desyoo
Provisional	**INFORMAL**	uteba	utanakereba
	FORMAL	utimaseba	utimaseñ nara
		utimasureba	
Gerund	**INFORMAL I**	utte	utanai de
	II		utanakute
	FORMAL	utimasite	utimaseñ de
Past Ind.	**INFORMAL**	utta	utanakatta
	FORMAL	utimasita	utimaseñ desita
Past Presump.	**INFORMAL**	uttaroo	utanakattaroo
		utta daroo	utanakatta daroo
	FORMAL	utimasitaroo	utimaseñ desitaroo
		utta desyoo	utanakatta desyoo
Conditional	**INFORMAL**	uttara	utanakattara
	FORMAL	utimasitara	utimaseñ desitara
Alternative	**INFORMAL**	uttari	utanakattari
	FORMAL	utimasitari	utimaseñ desitari

		INFORMAL AFFIRMATIVE INDICATIVE
Passive		utareru
Potential		uteru
Causative		utaseru
Causative Pass.		utaserareru
Honorific	**I**	outi ni naru
	II	outi nasaru
Humble	**I**	outi suru
	II	outi itasu

		AFFIRMATIVE	NEGATIVE
Indicative	**INFORMAL**	wakaru	wakaranai
	FORMAL	wakarimasu	wakarimaseñ
Imperative	**INFORMAL I**	wakare	
	II		
	III	wakatte kudasai	
	FORMAL		
Presumptive	**INFORMAL I**	wakaroo	wakarumai
	II	wakaru daroo	wakaranai daroo
	FORMAL I	wakarimasyoo	wakarimasumai
	II	wakaru desyoo	wakaranai desyoo
Provisional	**INFORMAL**	wakareba	wakaranakereba
	FORMAL	wakarimaseba	wakarimaseñ nara
		wakarimasureba	
Gerund	**INFORMAL I**	wakatte	wakaranai de
	II		wakaranakute
	FORMAL	wakarimasite	wakarimaseñ de
Past Ind.	**INFORMAL**	wakatta	wakaranakatta
	FORMAL	wakarimasita	wakarimaseñ desita
Past Presump.	**INFORMAL**	wakattaroo	wakaranakattaroo
		wakatta daroo	wakararakatta daroo
	FORMAL	wakarimasitaroo	wakarimaseñ desitaroo
		wakatta desyoo	wakaranakatta desyoo
Conditional	**INFORMAL**	wakattara	wakaranakattara
	FORMAL	wakarimasitara	wakarimaseñ desitara
Alternative	**INFORMAL**	wakattari	wakaranakattari
	FORMAL	wakarimasitari	wakarimaseñ desitari

INFORMAL AFFIRMATIVE INDICATIVE

Passive		
Potential		
Causative		wakaraseru
Causative Pass.		wakaraserareru

Honorific	**I**	owakari ni naru
	II	owakari nasaru
Humble	**I**	
	II	

487

		AFFIRMATIVE	NEGATIVE
Indicative	INFORMAL	warau	warawanai
	FORMAL	waraimasu	waraimaseñ
Imperative	INFORMAL I	warae	warau na
	II	warainasai	warainasaru na
	III	waratte kudasai	warawanai de kudasai
	FORMAL	owarai nasaimase	owarai nasaimasu na
Presumptive	INFORMAL I	waraoo	waraumai
	II	warau daroo	warawanai daroo
	FORMAL I	waraimasyoo	waraimasumai
	II	warau desyoo	warawanai desyoo
Provisional	INFORMAL	waraeba	warawanakereba
	FORMAL	waraimaseba	waraimaseñ nara
		waraimasureba	
Gerund	INFORMAL I	waratte	warawanai de
	II		warawanakute
	FORMAL	waraimasite	waraimaseñ de
Past Ind.	INFORMAL	waratta	warawanakatta
	FORMAL	waraimasita	waraimaseñ desita
Past Presump.	INFORMAL	warattaroo	warawanakattaroo
		waratta daroo	warawanakatta daroo
	FORMAL	waraimasitaroo	waraimaseñ desitaroo
		waratta desyoo	warawanakatta desyoo
Conditional	INFORMAL	warattara	warawanakattara
	FORMAL	waraimasitara	waraimaseñ desitara
Alternative	INFORMAL	warattari	warawanakattari
	FORMAL	waraimasitari	waraimaseñ desitari

		INFORMAL AFFIRMATIVE INDICATIVE
Passive		warawareru
Potential		waraeru
Causative		warawaseru
Causative Pass.		warawaserareru
Honorific	I	owarai ni naru
	II	owarai nasaru
Humble	I	
	II	

		AFFIRMATIVE	NEGATIVE
Indicative	**INFORMAL**	wasureru	wasurenai
	FORMAL	wasuremasu	wasuremaseñ
Imperative	**INFORMAL I**	wasurero	wasureru na
	II	wasurenasai	wasurenasaru na
	III	wasurete kudasai	wasurenai de kudasai
	FORMAL	owasure nasaimase	owasure nasaimasu na
Presumptive	**INFORMAL I**	wasureyoo	wasuremai
	II	wasureru daroo	wasurenai daroo
	FORMAL I	wasuremasyoo	wasuremasumai
	II	wasureru desyoo	wasurenai desyoo
Provisional	**INFORMAL**	wasurereba	wasurenakereba
	FORMAL	wasuremaseba	wasuremaseñ nara
		wasuremasureba	
Gerund	**INFORMAL I**	wasurete	wasurenai de
	II		wasurenakute
	FORMAL	wasuremasite	wasuremaseñ de
Past Ind.	**INFORMAL**	wasureta	wasurenakatta
	FORMAL	wasuremasita	wasuremaseñ desita
Past Presump.	**INFORMAL**	wasuretaroo	wasurenakattaroo
		wasureta daroo	wasurenakatta daroo
	FORMAL	wasuremasitaroo	wasuremaseñ desitaroo
		wasureta desyoo	wasurenakatta desyoo
Conditional	**INFORMAL**	wasuretara	wasurenakattara
	FORMAL	wasuremasitara	wasuremaseñ desitara
Alternative	**INFORMAL**	wasuretari	wasurenakattari
	FORMAL	wasuremasitari	wasuremaseñ desitari

INFORMAL AFFIRMATIVE INDICATIVE

Passive	wasurerareru
Potential	wasurerareru
Causative	wasuresaseru
Causative Pass.	wasuresaserareru

Honorific	**I**	owasure ni naru
	II	owasure nasaru
Humble	**I**	owasure suru
	II	owasure itasu

		AFFIRMATIVE	NEGATIVE
Indicative	INFORMAL	yaku	yakanaı
	FORMAL	yakimasu	yakimaseñ
Imperative	INFORMAL I	yake	yaku na
	II	yakinasai	yakinasaru na
	III	yaite kudasai	yakanai de kudasai
	FORMAL	oyaki nasaimase	oyaki nasaimasu na
Presumptive	INFORMAL I	yakoo	yakumai
	II	yaku daroo	yakanai daroo
	FORMAL I	yakimasyoo	yakimasumai
	II	yaku desyoo	yakanai desyoo
Provisional	INFORMAL	yakeba	yakanakereba
	FORMAL	yakimaseba	yakimaseñ nara
		yakimasureba	
Gerund	INFORMAL I	yaite	yakanai de
	II		yakanakute
	FORMAL	yakimasite	yakimaseñ de
Past Ind.	INFORMAL	yaita	yakanakatta
	FORMAL	yakimasita	yakimaseñ desita
Past Presump.	INFORMAL	yaitaroo	yakanakattaroo
		yaita daroo	yakanakatta daroo
	FORMAL	yakimasitaroo	yakimaseñ desitaroo
		yaita desyoo	yakanakatta desyoo
Conditional	INFORMAL	yaitara	yakanakattara
	FORMAL	yakimasitara	yakimaseñ desitara
Alternative	INFORMAL	yaitari	yakanakattari
	FORMAL	yakimasitari	yakimaseñ desitari

		INFORMAL AFFIRMATIVE INDICATIVE
Passive		yakareru
Potential		yakeru
Causative		yakaseru
Causative Pass.		yakaserareru
Honorific	I	oyaki ni naru
	II	oyaki nasaru
Humble	I	oyaki suru
	II	oyaki itasu

TRANSITIVE   *to stop, to give up* (doing something)

		AFFIRMATIVE	NEGATIVE
Indicative	**INFORMAL**	yameru	yamenai
	FORMAL	yamemasu	yamemaseñ
Imperative	**INFORMAL I**	yamero	yameru na
	II	yamenasai	yamenasaru na
	III	yamete kudasai	yamenai de kudasai
	FORMAL	oyame nasaimase	oyame nasaimasu na
Presumptive	**INFORMAL I**	yameyoo	yamemai
	II	yameru daroo	yamenai daɪoo
	FORMAL I	yamemasyoo	yamemasumai
	II	yameru desyoo	yamenai desyoo
Provisional	**INFORMAL**	yamereba	yamenakereba
	FORMAL	yamemaseba	yamemaseñ nara
		yamemasureba	
Gerund	**INFORMAL I**	yamete	yamenai de
	II		yamenakuṭ
	FORMAL	yamemasite	yamemaseñ de
Past Ind.	**INFORMAL**	yameta	yamenakatta
	FORMAL	yamemasiʔa	yamemaseñ desita
Past Presump.	**INFORMAL**	yametaroo	yamenakattaroo
		yameta daroo	yamenakatta ḷaroo
	FORMAL	yamemasitaroo	yamemaseñ desitaroo
		yameta des·oo	yamenakatta desyoo
Conditional	**INFORMAL**	yametara	yamenakattara
	FORMAL	yamemasitara	yamemaseñ desitara
Alternative	**INFORMAL**	yametari	yamenakattari
	FORMAL	yamemasitari	yamemaseñ desitari

INFORMAL AFFIRMATIVE INDICATIVE

Passive		yamerareru
Potential		yamerareru
Causative		yamesaseru
Causative Pass.		yamesaserareru
Honorific	**I**	oyame ni naru
	II	oyame nasaru
Humble	**I**	oyame suru
	II	oyame itasu

		AFFIRMATIVE	NEGATIVE
Indicative	**INFORMAL**	yaru	yaranai
	FORMAL	yarimasu	yarimaseñ
Imperative	**INFORMAL I**	yare	yaru na
	II	yarinasai	yarinasaru na
	III	yatte kudasai	yaranai de kudasai
	FORMAL	oyari nasaimase	oyari nasaimasu na
Presumptive	**INFORMAL I**	yaroo	yarumai
	II	yaru daroo	yaranai daroo
	FORMAL I	yarimasyoo	yarimasumai
	II	yaru desyoo	yaranai desyoo
Provisional	**INFORMAL**	yareba	yaranakereba
	FORMAL	yarimaseba	yarimaseñ nara
		yarimasureba	
Gerund	**INFORMAL I**	yatte	yaranai de
	II		yaranakute
	FORMAL	yarimasite	yarimaseñ de
Past Ind.	**INFORMAL**	yatta	yaranakatta
	FORMAL	yarimasita	yarimaseñ desita
Past Presump.	**INFORMAL**	yattaroo	yaranakattaroo
		yatta daroo	yaranakatta daroo
	FORMAL	yarimasitaroo	yarimaseñ desitaroo
		yatta desyoo	yaranakatta desyoo
Conditional	**INFORMAL**	yattara	yaranakattara
	FORMAL	yarimasitara	yarimaseñ desitara
Alternative	**INFORMAL**	yattari	yaranakattari
	FORMAL	yarimasitari	yarimaseñ desitari

		INFORMAL AFFIRMATIVE INDICATIVE
Passive		yarareru
Potential		yareru
Causative		yaraseru
Causative Pass.		yaraserareru
Honorific	**I**	oyari ni naru
	II	oyari nasaru
Humble	**I**	
	II	

		AFFIRMATIVE	NEGATIVE
Indicative	**INFORMAL**	yaseru	yasenai
	FORMAL	yasemasu	yasemaseñ
Imperative	**INFORMAL I**	yasero	yaseru na
	II	yasenasai	yasenasaru na
	III	yasete kudasai	yasenai de kudasai
	FORMAL	oyase nasaimase	oyase nasaimasu na
Presumptive	**INFORMAL I**	yaseyoo	yasemai
	II	yaseru daroo	yasenai daroo
	FORMAL I	yasemasyoo	yasemasumai
	II	yaseru desyoo	yasenai desyoo
Provisional	**INFORMAL**	yasereba	yasenakereba
	FORMAL	yasemaseba	yasemaseñ nara
		yasemasureba	
Gerund	**INFORMAL I**	yasete	yasenai de
	II		yasenakute
	FORMAL	yasemasite	yasemaseñ de
Past Ind.	**INFORMAL**	yaseta	yasenakatta
	FORMAL	yasemasita	yasemaseñ desita
Past Presump.	**INFORMAL**	yasetaroo	yasenakattaroo
		yaseta daroo	yasenakatta daroo
	FORMAL	yasemasitaroo	yasemaseñ desitaroo
		yaseta desyoo	yasenakatta desyoo
Conditional	**INFORMAL**	yasetara	yasenakattara
	FORMAL	yasemasitara	yasemaseñ desitara
Alternative	**INFORMAL**	yasetari	yasenakattari
	FORMAL	yasemasitari	yasemaseñ desitari

		INFORMAL AFFIRMATIVE INDICATIVE
Passive		yaserareru
Potential		yaserareru
Causative		yasesaseru
Causative Pass.		yasesaserareru
Honorific	**I**	oyase ni naru
	II	oyase nasaru
Humble	**I**	
	II	

		AFFIRMATIVE	NEGATIVE
Indicative	INFORMAL	yasumu	yasumanai
	FORMAL	yasumimasu	yasumimaseñ
Imperative	INFORMAL I	yasume	yasumu na
	II	yasuminasai	yasuminasaru na
	III	yasuñde kudasai	yasumanai de kudasai
	FORMAL	oyasumi nasaimase	oyasumi nasaimasu na
Presumptive	INFORMAL I	yasumoo	yasumumai
	II	yasumu daroo	yasumanai daroo
	FORMAL I	yasumimasyoo	yasumimasumai
	II	yasumu desyoo	yasumanai desyoo
Provisional	INFORMAL	yasumeba	yasumanakereba
	FORMAL	yasumimaseba	yasumimaseñ nara
		yasumimasureba	
Gerund	INFORMAL I	yasuñde	yasumanai de
	II		yasumanakute
	FORMAL	yasumimasite	yasumimaseñ de
Past Ind.	INFORMAL	yasuñda	yasumanakatta
	FORMAL	yasumimasita	yasumimaseñ desita
Past Presump.	INFORMAL	yasuñdaroo	yasumanakattaroo
		yasuñda daroo	yasumanakatta daroo
	FORMAL	yasumimasitaroo	yasumimaseñ desitaroo
		yasuñda desyoo	yasumanakatta desyoo
Conditional	INFORMAL	yasuñdarə	yasumanakattara
	FORMAL	yasumimasitara	yasumimaseñ desitara
Alternative	INFORMAL	yasuñdari	yasumimasitari
	FORMAL	yasumimasitari	yasumimaseñ desitari

		INFORMAL AFFIRMATIVE INDICATIVE
Passive		yasumareru
Potential		yasumeru
Causative		yasumaseru
Causative Pass.		yasumaserareru
Honorific	I	oyasumi ni naru
	II	oyasumi nasaru
Humble	I	
	II	

TRANSITIVE   *to hire, to employ*

		AFFIRMATIVE	NEGATIVE
Indicative	**INFORMAL**	yatou	yatowanai
	FORMAL	yatoimasu	yatoimaseñ
Imperative	**INFORMAL I**	yatoe	yatou na
	II	yatoinasai	yatoinasaru na
	III	yatotte kudasai	yatowanai de kudasai
	FORMAL	oyatoi nasaimase	oyatoi nasaimasu na
Presumptive	**INFORMAL I**	yatooo	yatoumai
	II	yatou daroo	yatowanai daroo
	FORMAL I	yatoimasyoo	yatoimasumai
	II	yatou desyoo	yatowanai desyoo
Provisional	**INFORMAL**	yatoeba	yatowanakereba
	FORMAL	yatoimaseba	yatoimaseñ nara
		yatoimasureba	
Gerund	**INFORMAL I**	yatotte	yatowanai de
	II		yatowanakute
	FORMAL	yatoimasite	yatoimaseñ de
Past Ind.	**INFORMAL**	yatotta	yatowanakatta
	FORMAL	yatomasita	yatoimaseñ desita
Past Presump.	**INFORMAL**	yatottaroo	yatowanakattaroo
		yatotta daroo	yatowanakatta daroo
	FORMAL	yatoimasitaroo	yatoimaseñ desitaroo
		yatotta desyoo	yatowanakatta desyoo
Conditional	**INFORMAL**	yatottara	yatowanakattara
	FORMAL	yatoimasitara	yatoimaseñ desitara
Alternative	**INFORMAL**	yatottari	yatowanakattari
	FORMAL	yatoimasitari	yatoimaseñ desitari

INFORMAL AFFIRMATIVE INDICATIVE

Passive		yatowareru
Potential		yatoeru
Causative		yatowaseru
Causative Pass.		yatowaserareru

Honorific	**I**	oyatoi ni naru
	II	oyatoi nasaru
Humble	**I**	oyatoi suru
	II	oyatoi itasu

495

		AFFIRMATIVE	**NEGATIVE**
Indicative	**INFORMAL**	yobu	yobanai
	FORMAL	yobimasu	yobimaseñ
Imperative	**INFORMAL I**	yobe	yobu na
	II	yobinasai	yobinasaru na
	III	yoñde kudasai	yobanai de kudasai
	FORMAL	oyobi nasaimase	oyobi nasaimasu na
Presumptive	**INFORMAL I**	yoboo	yobumai
	II	yobu daroo	yobanai daroo
	FORMAL I	yobimasyoo	yobimasumai
	II	yobu desyoo	yobanai desyoo
Provisional	**INFORMAL**	yobeba	yobanakereba
	FORMAL	yobimaseba	yobimaseñ nara
		yobimasureba	
Gerund	**INFORMAL I**	yoñde	yobanai de
	II		yobanakute
	FORMAL	yobimasite	yobimaseñ de
Past Ind.	**INFORMAL**	yoñda	yobanakatta
	FORMAL	yobimasita	yobimaseñ desita
Past Presump.	**INFORMAL**	yoñdaroo	yobanakattaroo
		yoñda daroo	yobanakatta daroo
	FORMAL	yobimasitaroo	yobimaseñ desitaroo
		yoñda desyoo	yobanakatta desyoo
Conditional	**INFORMAL**	yoñdara	yobanakattara
	FORMAL	yobimasitara	yobimaseñ desitara
Alternative	**INFORMAL**	yoñdari	yobanakattari
	FORMAL	yobimasitari	yobimaseñ desitari

		INFORMAL AFFIRMATIVE INDICATIVE
Passive		yobareru
Potential		yoberu
Causative		yobaseru
Causative Pass.		yobaserareru
Honorific	**I**	oyobi ni naru
	II	oyobi nasaru
Humble	**I**	oyobi suru
	II	oyobi itasu

		AFFIRMATIVE	NEGATIVE
Indicative	**INFORMAL**	yomu	yomanai
	FORMAL	yomimasu	yomimaseñ
Imperative	**INFORMAL I**	yome	yomu na
	II	yominasai	yominasaru na
	III	yoñde kudasai	yomanai de kudasai
	FORMAL	oyomi nasaimase	oyomi nasaimasu na
Presumptive	**INFORMAL I**	yomoo	yomumai
	II	yomu daroo	yomanai daroo
	FORMAL I	yomimasyoo	yomimasumai
	II	yomu desyoo	yomanai desyoo
Provisional	**INFORMAL**	yomeba	yomanakereba
	FORMAL	yomimaseba	yomimaseñ nara
		yomimasureba	
Gerund	**INFORMAL I**	yoñde	yomanai de
	II		yomanakute
	FORMAL	yomimasite	yomimaseñ de
Past Ind.	**INFORMAL**	yoñda	yomanakatta
	FORMAL	yomimasita	yomimaseñ desita
Past Presump.	**INFORMAL**	yoñdaroo	yomanakattaroo
		yoñda daroo	yomanakatta daroo
	FORMAL	yomimasitaroo	yomimaseñ desitaroo
		yoñda desyoo	yomanakatta desyoo
Conditional	**INFORMAL**	yoñdara	yomanakattara
	FORMAL	yomimasitara	yomimaseñ desitara
Alternative	**INFORMAL**	yoñdari	yomanakattari
	FORMAL	yomimasitari	yomimaseñ desitari

		INFORMAL AFFIRMATIVE INDICATIVE
Passive		yomareru
Potential		yomeru
Causative		yomaseru
Causative Pass.		yomaserareru

Honorific	**I**	oyomi ni naru
	II	oyomi nasaru
Humble	**I**	oyomi suru
	II	oyomi itasu

		AFFIRMATIVE	NEGATIVE
Indicative	**INFORMAL**	yorokobu	yorokobanai
	FORMAL	yorokobimasu	yorokobimaseñ
Imperative	**INFORMAL I**	yorokobe	yorokobu na
	II	yorokobinasai	yorokobinasaru na
	III	yorokoñde kudasai	yorokobanai de kudasai
	FORMAL	oyorokobi nasaimase	oyorokobi nasaimasu na
Presumptive	**INFORMAL I**	yorokoboo	yorokobumai
	II	yorokobu daroo	yorokobanai daroo
	FORMAL I	yorokobimasyoo	yorokobimasumai
	II	yorokobu desyoo	yorokobanai desyoo
Provisional	**INFORMAL**	yorokobeba	yorokobanakereba
	FORMAL	yorokobimaseba	yorokobimaseñ nara
		yorokobimasureba	
Gerund	**INFORMAL I**	yorokoñde	yorokobanai de
	II		yorokobanakute
	FORMAL	yorokobimasite	yorokobimaseñ de
Past Ind.	**INFORMAL**	yorokoñda	yorokobanakatta
	FORMAL	yorokobimasita	yorokobimaseñ desita
Past Presump.	**INFORMAL**	yorokoñdaroo	yorokobanakattaroo
		yorokoñda daroo	yorokobanakatta daroo
	FORMAL	yorokobimasitaroo	yorokobimaseñ desitaroo
		yorokoñda desyoo	yorokobanakatta desyoo
Conditional	**INFORMAL**	yorokoñdara	yorokobanakattara
	FORMAL	yorokobimasitara	yorokobimaseñ desitara
Alternative	**INFORMAL**	yorokoñdari	yorokobanakattari
	FORMAL	yorokobimasitari	yorokobimaseñ desitari

		INFORMAL AFFIRMATIVE INDICATIVE
Passive		yorokobareru
Potential		yorokoberu
Causative		yorokobaseru
Causative Pass.		yorokobaserareru

Honorific	**I**	oyorokobi ni naru
	II	oyorokobi nasaru
Humble	**I**	oyorokobi suru
	II	oyorokobi itasu

			AFFIRMATIVE	NEGATIVE
Indicative	**INFORMAL**		yoru	yoranai
	FORMAL		yorimasu	yorimaseñ
Imperative	**INFORMAL**	**I**	yore	yoru na
		II	yorinasai	yorinasaru na
		III	yotte kudasai	yoranai de kudasai
	FORMAL		oyori nasaimase	oyori nasaimasu na
Presumptive	**INFORMAL**	**I**	yoroo	yorumai
		II	yoru daroo	yoranai daroo
	FORMAL	**I**	yorimasyoo	yorimasumai
		II	yoru desyoo	yoranai desyoo
Provisional	**INFORMAL**		yoreba	yoranakereba
	FORMAL		yorimaseba	yorimaseñ nara
			yorimasureba	
Gerund	**INFORMAL**	**I**	yotte	yoranai de
		II		yoranakute
	FORMAL		yorimasita	yorimaseñ de
Past Ind.	**INFORMAL**		yotta	yoranakatta
	FORMAL		yorimasita	yorimaseñ desita
Past Presump.	**INFORMAL**		yottaroo	yoranakattaroo
			yotta daroo	yoranakatta daroo
	FORMAL		yorimasitaroo	yorimaseñ desitaroo
			yotta desyoo	yoranakatta desyoo
Conditional	**INFORMAL**		yottara	yoranakattara
	FORMAL		yorimasitara	yorimaseñ desitara
Alternative	**INFORMAL**		yottari	yoranakattari
	FORMAL		yorimasitari	yorimaseñ desitari

		INFORMAL AFFIRMATIVE INDICATIVE
Passive		yorareru
Potential		yoreru
Causative		yoraseru
Causative Pass.		yoraserareru
Honorific	**I**	oyori ni naru
	II	oyori nasaru
Humble	**I**	oyori suru
	II	oyori itasu

		AFFIRMATIVE	NEGATIVE
Indicative	**INFORMAL**	you	yowanai
	FORMAL	yoimasu	yoimaseñ
Imperative	**INFORMAL I**	yoe	you na
	II	yoinasai	yoinasaru na
	III	yotte kudasai	yowanai de kudasai
	FORMAL	oyoi nasaimase	oyoi nasaimasu na
Presumptive	**INFORMAL I**	yooo	youmai
	II	you daroo	yowanai daroo
	FORMAL I	yoimasyoo	yoimasumai
	II	you desyoo	yowanai desyoo
Provisional	**INFORMAL**	yoeba	yowanakereba
	FORMAL	yoimaseba	yoimaseñ nara
		yoimasureba	
Gerund	**INFORMAL I**	yotte	yowanai de
	II		yowanakute
	FORMAL	yoimasite	yoimaseñ de
Past Ind.	**INFORMAL**	yotta	yowanakatta
	FORMAL	yoimasita	yoimaseñ desita
Past Presump.	**INFORMAL**	yottaroo	yowanakattaroo
		yotta daroo	yowanakatta daroo
	FORMAL	yoimasitaroo	yoimaseñ desitaroo
		yotta desyoo	yowanakatta desyoo
Conditional	**INFORMAL**	yottara	yowanakattara
	FORMAL	yoimasitara	yoimaseñ desitara
Alternative	**INFORMAL**	yottari	yowanakattari
	FORMAL	yoimasitari	yoimaseñ desitarı

INFORMAL AFFIRMATIVE INDICATIVE

Passive		yowareru
Potential		yoeru
Causative		yowaseru
Causative Pass.		yowaserareru
Honorific	**I**	oyoi ni naru
	II	oyoi nasarʋ
Humble	**I**	
	II	

		AFFIRMATIVE	NEGATIVE
Indicative	**INFORMAL**	yurusu	yurusanai
	FORMAL	yurusimasu	yurusimaseñ
Imperative	**INFORMAL I**	yuruse	yurusu na
	II	yurusinasai	yurusinasaru na
	III	yurusite kudasai	yurusanai de kudasai
	FORMAL	oyurusi nasaimase	oyurusi nasaimasu na
Presumptive	**INFORMAL I**	yurusoo	yurusumai
	II	yurusu daroo	yurusanai daroo
	FORMAL I	yurusimasyoo	yurusimasumai
	II	yurusu desyoo	yurusanai desyoo
Provisional	**INFORMAL**	yuruseba	yurusanakereba
	FORMAL	yurusimaseba	yurusimaseñ nara
		yurusimasureba	
Gerund	**INFORMAL I**	yurusite	yurusanai de
	II		yurusanakute
	FORMAL	yurusimasite	yurusimaseñ de
Past Ind.	**INFORMAL**	yurusita	yurusanakatta
	FORMAL	yurusimasita	yurusimaseñ desita
Past Presump.	**INFORMAL**	yurusitaroo	yurusanakattaroo
		yurusita daroo	yurusanakatta daroo
	FORMAL	yurusimasitaroo	yurusimaseñ desitaroo
		yurusita desyoo	yurusanakatta desyoo
Conditional	**INFORMAL**	yurusitara	yurusanakattara
	FORMAL	yurusimasitara	yurusimaseñ desitara
Alternative	**INFORMAL**	yurusitari	yurusanakattari
	FORMAL	yurusimasitari	yurusimaseñ desitari

INFORMAL AFFIRMATIVE INDICATIVE

Passive	yurusareru
Potential	yuruseru
Causative	yurusaseru
Causative Pass.	yurusaserareru

Honorific	**I**	oyurusi ni naru
	II	oyurusi nasaru
Humble	**I**	oyurusi suru
	II	oyurusi itasu

VERBS OF GIVING AND RECEIVING

In Japanese many verbs of giving and receiving have an intrinsic 'directionality which helps to identify the person performing the act of giving. This is a big help to English-speaking students, because Japanese often omits explicit reference to the subject of a sentence.

The four verbs for giving which occur most often in spoken Japanese are *ageru*, *yaru*, *kudasaru*, and *kureru*.

Ageru means 'I (you, he, she, or they) give TO SOMEONE OTHER THAN THE SPEAKER.' Thus *Okane o agemasita.* could mean 'I gave you money,' 'You gave him money,' or 'She gave them money,' but it could not mean 'You (he, she, or they) gave me money.' *Ageru* also has an intrinsic element of politeness to the receiver of the gift, so it is used to describe giving to equals or superiors, or to anyone to whom the speaker wishes to express politeness or respect.

Examples:

Señsei ni agete mo ii desu. 'You may give it to the teacher.'
Moo sukosi agemasyoo ka. 'Shall I give you a little more?'
Okaasañ ni agete kudasai. 'Please give it to your mother.'

Yaru too means 'give TO SOMEONE OTHER THAN THE SPEAKER,' but it differs greatly in that it lacks the politeness of *ageru*. Thus it is used to describe giving to an inferior. It is sometimes used for giving to an equal when speaking very plainly and informally, but since such judgments are extremely difficult for students, and since using *yaru* at the wrong time could offend the person one is speaking to or about, they are advised to use *yaru* only when talking about giving things to plants and animals. This is a safe usage, and one which is common in Japan.

Examples:

Imooto ni okasi o takusañ yarimasita. 'I gave a lot of candy to my little sister.' *Sañzi ni inu ni esa o yatta.* 'She fed the dog at three o'clock.' *Taroo wa mada hana ni mizu o yarimaseñ.* 'Taroo has not watered the flowers yet.'

Kudasaru means 'giving BY SOMEONE OTHER THAN THE SPEAKER,' and is usually used to describe giving to the speaker or to a member of the speaker's in-group such as a family member. *Kudasaru* forms a pair with *ageru*, but whereas *ageru* shows politeness to the recipient of the gift *kudasaru* shows politeness to the giver. It implies that the giver's position is superior to that of the speaker, or that the speaker is showing respect to the giver in order to be polite, as would commonly be done when the giver is present.

Examples:

Akai no o kudasai. 'Please give me the red one.' *Señsei ga kudasatta hoñ desu.* 'It's the book the teacher gave me.' *Hiroko ni mo kudasatta no?* 'You mean you gave some to (my child) Hiroko too?'

Kureru also means 'giving BY SOMEONE OTHER THAN THE SPEAKER' but it implies that the giver is equal or inferior to the receiver, so it is not used when one desires to show politeness or respect to the giver. It is often used when the giver is an institution rather than a person. It is also often used when describing a gift to the speaker by a person of roughly equivalent status who is not present. Though it is sometimes used to mean 'someone (other than the speaker) gives to you,' this usage is best avoided by students because it could give offense if used to the wrong person.

Examples:

Tomodati ga kudamono o kuremasita. 'My friend gave me some fruit.' *Unteñsyu wa oturi mo kurenai de itte simatta.* 'The driver went off without giving me my change.' '*Kodomotati ga hañkati o kureta.* 'The kids gave me some handkerchiefs.'

The two common verbs for receiving are *itadaku* and *morau*. *Itadaku* means 'something is received by me or by a member of my in-group such as a close relative.' It is a humble verb which shows deference to the giver by placing the receiver in an inferior position. Therefore, it would not be used for 'you receive' unless the receiver is an inferior member of the speaker's in-group. A mother might say to her small child *Maa señsei ni itadaita no?* 'Did you receive it from your teacher?' when the teacher is present in order to show respect to the teacher.

Examples:

Okusañ ni kippu o itadaita no de, sibai o mite kimasita. 'We received tickets from your wife, so we went to the play.' *Tomita señsei kara itadaita syasiñ wa doko desu ka.* 'Where is the photo that you received from Professor Tomita?' *Oheñzi o itadaite añsiñ itasimasita.* 'I was relieved to receive your reply '

Morau lacks the directionality of the verbs discussed above. It can mean 'I, you, he, she, or they receive.' Since it has the standard honorific forms of *omorai ni naru* and *omorai nasaru*, it can be used to express deferrence or politeness to the receiver. Its humble form is *itadaku*.
Examples:
Tomodati kara iroiro na mono o moraimasita. 'I (you, he, she, they) received all sorts of things from friends.' *Zuibuñ ii tokei o omorai ni narimasita nee.* 'My, you certainly got a nice watch.' *Tanakasañ ni moratta no wa dore desyoo ka.* 'Which is the one that we got from Mr. Tanaka?' *Mada moraimaseñ ka?* 'Haven't you received it yet?' *Miñna nani ka ii mono o morau desyoo.* 'Probably everyone will get something good.'

A thorough grasp of these verbs is required because, in addition to describing the giving and receiving of objects, they are also widely employed in describing actions done for another person's benefit. In this construction the informal gerund of the verb which describes the action is used immediately before the appropriate form of the verb of giving or receiving. We have already encountered this construction in the imperative III in which the gerund is used before the informal imperative form of *kudasaru* to make a polite request. The same directionality applies as did in the giving and receiving of objects. That is, just as *Riñgo o ageta.* means 'Someone gave an apple to someone other than the speaker,' *Riñgo o katte ageta.* means 'Someone bought an apple for someone other than the speaker.' and so on.
Examples:
Kodomodati ni kurisumasu torii o katte yatta. 'We bought a Christmas tree for the children.' *Kanai ga itumo boku no suki na mono o tukutte kureru.* 'My wife always cooks things that I like for me.' *Moo sukosi matte kudasaimaseñ ka.* 'Would you please wait a bit longer for me.' *Okaasama ni oisii okasi o motte kite itadakimasita.* 'Your mother brought delicious cake for us.' (Literally 'We received the bringing of delicious cake by your mother.') *Dare mo osiete kuremaseñ desita.* 'Nobody told me.' *Sono hana*

wa dare ni okutte moraimasita ka. 'Who sent you the flowers?' (Literally 'As for those flowers, by whom did you receive the sending?'). *Misete agemasyoo ka.** 'Shall I show it to you.'* *Señsei ga nañkai mo setumei site kudasaimasita.* 'The teacher explained it to me any number of times.'

A gerund plus *morau* or *itadaku* is also used when one person has another do something for them.

Examples:

Otetudaisañ ni señtakumono o tatañde moraimasita. 'She had the maid fold the laundry.' *Nikuyasañ ni tori no ii tokoro o totte oite moratta.* 'I had the butcher save the good part of the chicken for me.' *Señsei ni setumei site itadakimasita.* 'I had the teacher explain it for me.' *Biiru o todokete moraeru desyoo.* 'You can probably have the beer delivered.'

We should also mention that a gerund plus *moraitai* or *itadakitai* constitutes an indirect request meaning 'I want to have something done by someone.' With *itadakitai* it usually means 'I want to have something done by you.'

Examples:

Dare ka ni tana o tukutte moraitai desu. 'I would like to have someone build me a shelf.' *Isya ni mite moraitai.* 'I want to have the doctor take a look at it.' *Sañzi ni irasite itadakitai desu.* 'I want to have you come at three o'clock.' *Ookiku site moraitai ñ desu.* 'I want to have them enlarge it.'

---

* Since this use of *ageru* implies the doing of a favor, it would not be used to a superior or to someone to whom special politeness or deference was intended. Instead, one would use the humble form of the verb describing the action. Thus, a clerk in a department store would not use this *ageru* construction when addressing a customer, but would say *Omise simasyoo ka.* or *Omise itasimasyoo ka.* for 'I shall show it to you?'

This index includes all of the verbs found in the foregoing tables. Transitive verbs are followed by T.

INDEX OF VERBS BY GERUND

In the early stages of learning Japanese, students often have trouble in identifying a verb on the basis of its informal affirmative gerund. The following index should be of some help in this respect. It lists alphabetically all the informal affirmative gerunds found in the text and gives the citation form of the verb or verbs which correspond to each gerund.

The sound changes which occur when forming the gerund also take place when any suffix beginning with -t is added to the verb stem. Therefore, this index will also help in identifying a verb by its (informal affirmative) past indicative, conditional, or alternative forms. For example: the gerund of a verb whose past indicative is *todoketa* will be *todokete*; that of a verb whose past indicative is *totta* will be *totte*. Consulting our list of gerunds we find that these belong to *todokeru* (p. 451) and *toru* (p. 458), and if we consult the tables for these verbs we will find that, indeed, their past indicative forms are *todeketa* and *totta* respectively.

A

agatte	**agaru**
agete	**ageru**
aite	**aku**
akasite	**akasu**
akete	**akeru**
akiramete	**akirameru**
akite	**akiru**
anadotte	**anadoru**
aññai site	**aññai suru**
añsiñ site	**añsiñ suru**
arasite	**arasu**
arasotte	**arasou**
aratamatte	**aratamaru**
aratamete	**aratameru**
aratte	**arau**
arawarete	**arawareru**
arawasite	**arawasu**
aruite	**aruku**
asoñde	**asobu**
atatamatte	**atatamaru**
atatamete	**atatameru**
atatte	**ataru**
atte	**aru, au**
atumatte	**atumaru**
atumete	**atumeru**
awatete	**awateru**
ayamatte	**ayamaru**
ayasiñde	**ayasimu**
ayatutte	**ayaturu**
azukatte	**azukaru**
azukete	**azukeru**

B

beñkyoo site	**beñkyoo suru**
bikkuri site	**bikkuri suru**
butukatte	**butukaru**
butukete	**butukeru**

D

daihyoo site	**daihyoo suru**
daite	**daku**
damasite	**damasu**
damatte	**damaru**
dasite	**dasu**
deatte	**deau**
dekite	**dekiru**
dete	**deru**

E

eñryo site	**eñryo suru**
erañde	**erabu**
ete	**eru**

G

gakkari site	**gakkari suru**
gañbatte	**gañbaru**

H

hagemasite **hagemasu**
hageñde **hagemu**
haite **haku**
haitte **hairu**
hakatte **hakaru**
hakkeñ site **hakkeñ suru**
hanarete **hanareru**
hanasite **hanasu**
hanete **haneru**
hañtai site **hañtai suru**
haratte **harau**
harete **hareru**
hasañde **hasamu**
hasitte **hasiru**
hataraite **hataraku**
hatumei site **hatumei suru**
hayatte **hayaru**
hazimatte **hazimaru**
hazimete **hazimeru**
hazurete **hazureru**
hazusite **hazusu**
hete **heru (to decrease)**
hette **heru (to pass through)**
heturatte **heturau**
hiite **hiku**
hikatte **hikaru**
hikiukete **hikiukeru**
hinete **hineru**
hiraite **hiraku**
hiromatte **hiromaru**
hiromete **hiromeru**
hirotte **hirou**
hisomete **hisomeru**
hisoñde **hisomu**
hiyakasite **hiyakasu**
hiyasite **hiyasu**
hizamazuite **hizamazuku**
hodoite **hodoku**
hodokete **hodekeru**
homete **homeru**
honomekasite **honomekasu**
hoomutte **hoomuru**
horete **horeru**
horobite **horobiru**

horobosite **horobosu**
hosigatte **hosigaru**
hosite **hosu**
hotte **horu**
huete **hueru**
huite **huku**
hukamatte **hukamaru**
hukamete **hukameru**
hukumete **hukumeru**
huñde **humu**
hurete **hureru**
hurikaette **hurikaeru**
hurimawasite **hurimawasu**
huruete **hurueru**
husagatte **husagaru**
husaide **husagu**
huseide **husegu**
husete **huseru (to lay something down)**
husette **huseru (to lie down)**
hutotte **hutoru**
hutte **huru**
huyasite **huyasu**
huzakete **huzakeru**

I

ibatte **ibaru**
idoñde **idomu**
iiarawasite **iiarawasu**
iiawasete **iiaswaseru**
iidasite **iidasu**
iihurasite **iihurasu**
iikaesite **iikaesu**
iinaosite **iinaosu**
iinukete **iinukeru**
iisugite **iisugiru**
iitukete **iitukeru**
iitukurotte **iitukurou**
iitukusite **iitukusu**
iiyotte **iiyoru**
ikite **ikiru**
imasimete **imasimeru**
inaotte **inaoru**
inotte **inoru**
irasite **irassyaru**

irassyatte **irassyaru**
irete **ireru**
isoide **isogu**
itadaite **itadaku**
itañde **itamu**
itasite **itasu**
ite **iru (to exist)**
itte **iku, iru (to be necessary), iu**
ituwatte **ituwaru**
iwatte **iwau**
iyagatte **iyagaru**
iyasiñde **iyasimu**
izimete **izimeru**
izitte **iziru**

K

kabatte **kabu**
kabutte **kaburu**
kaesite **kaesu**
kaete **kaeru (to change)**
kaette **kaeru (to return)**
kagayaite **kagayaku**
kagitte **kagiru**
kaite **kaku**
kakaete **kakaeru**
kakagete **kakageru**
kakatte **kakaru**
kakawatte **kakawaru**
kakete **kakeru**
kakoñde **kakomu**
kakurete **kakureru**
kakusite **kakusu**
kamaete **kamaeru**
kamatte **kamau**
kanaete **kanaeru**
kañde **kamu**
kanasiñde **kanasimu**
kanatte **kanau**
kañgaete **kañgaeru**
kañzite **kañziru**
karakatte **karakau**
karete **kareru**
karite **kariru**
kasanatte **kasanaru**

kasanete **kasaneru**
kaseide **kasegu**
kasite **kasu**
kasuñde **kasumu**
katamatte **katamaru**
katamete **katameru**
katamuite **katamuku**
katazukete **katazukeru**
katte **katu, kau**
katuide **katugu**
kawaigatte **kawaigaru**
kawaite **kawaku**
kawakasite **kawakasu**
kawatte **kawaru**
kayotte **kayou**
kazatte **kazaru**
kazitte **kaziru**
kazoete **kazoeru**
kegasite **kegasu**
kesite **kesu**
kidotte **kidoru**
kiete **kieru**
kiite **kiku**
kikaete **kikaeru**
kikoete **kikoeru**
kimatte **kimaru**
kimete **kimeru**
kiñzite **kiñziru**
kisotte **kisou**
kite **kiru (to wear), kuru**
kitte **kiru (to cut)**
kiwamatte **kiwamaru**
kizuite **kizuku**

kizukatte **kizukau**
kizutukete **kuzutukeru**
kobañde **kobamu**
koborete **koboreru**
kobosite **kobosu**
kodawatte **kodawaru**
koete **koeru**
kogete **kogeru**
koide **kogu**
kokıtukatte **kokitukau**
kokoroete **kokoroeru**
kokoromite **kokoromiru**

kokorozasite **kokorozasu**
komatte **komaru**
koñde **komu**
konoñde **konomu**
kootte **kooru**
koraete **koraeru**
korasimete **korasimeru**
korasite **korasu**
koroñde **korobu**
korosite **korosu**
kosikakete **kosikakeru**
kosiraete **kosiraeru**
kosite **kosu**
kotaete **kotaeru**
kotonatte **kotonaru**
kotowatte **kotowaru**
kowagatte **kowagaru**
kowarete **kowareru**
kowasite **kowasu**
kozitukete **kozitukeru**
kudaite **kudaku**
kudasatte **kudasaru**
kudoite **kudoku**
kuitigatte **kuitigau**
kumotte **kumoru**
kuñde **kumu**
kurabete **kuraberu**
kurañde **kuramu**
kurasite **kurasu**
kurete **kureru**
kurikaesite **kurikaesu**
kurusimete **kurusimeru**
kurusiñde **kurusimu**
kurutte **kuruu**
kusatte **kusaru**
kuwadatete **kuwadateru**
kuwaete **kuwaeru**
kuzurete **kuzureru**
kuzusite **kuzusu**

M

magatte **magaru**
magete **mageru**

magirasite **magirasu**
maitte **mairu**
makasete **makaseru**
makasite **makasu**
makete **makeru**
mamotte **mamoru**
manañde **manabu**
maneite **maneku**
matigaete **matigaeru**
matigatte **matigau**
matomete **matomeru**
matte **matu**
matutte **maturu**
mayotte **mayou**
mazete **mazeru**
mazitte **maziru**
mesiagatte **mesiagaru**
miete **mieru**
migaite **migaku**
mihatte **miharu**
minaosite **minaosu**
minasite **minasu**
minogasite **minogasu**
minotte **minoru**
minuite **minuku**
misete **miseru**
mite **miru**
mitomete **mitomeru**
mitukatte **mitukaru**
mitukete **mitukeru**
modotte **modoru**
mookatte **mookaru**
mookete **mookeru**
morasite **morasu**
moratte **morau**
motarasite **motarasu**
moteasoñde **moteasobu**
motete **moteru**
motomete **motomeru**
motozuite **motozuku**
motte **motu**
mukaete **mukaeru**
mukatte **mukau**
musuñde **musubu**

N

nagamete **nagameru**
nagarete **nagareru**
nagasite **nagasu**
nagete **nageru**
nagusamete **nagusameru**
nagutte **naguru**
naite **naku**
nakunatte **nakunaru**
nakusite **nakusu**
namakete **namakeru**
namete **nameru**
naosite **naosu**
naotte **naoru**
narabete **naraberu**
narañde **narabu**
narattc **narau**
nasatte **nasaru**
natte **naru**
naziñde **nazimu**
nete **neru**
nigete **nigeru**
nigitte **nigiru**
nirañde **niramu**
nite **niru**
nobasite **nobasu**
nobotte **noboru**
nokosite **nokosu**
nokotte **nokoru**
noñde **nomu**
nosete **noseru**
notte **noru**
nurete **nureru**
nusuñde **nusumu**
nutte **nuru**

O

oboete **oboeru**
odoroite **odoroku**
odotte **odoru**
oite **oku**

okite **okiru**
okosite **okosu**
okurete **okureru**
okutte **okuru**
omotte **omou**
orite **oriru**
osaete **osaeru**
osiete **osieru**
osiñde **osimu**
osite **osu**
osorete **osoreru**
osotte **osou**
ossyatte **ossyaru**
otite **otiru**
otosite **otosu**
ototte **otoru**
otte **ou**
owatte **owaru**
oyoide **oyogu**
oyoñde **oyobu**

S

sadamete **sadameru**
sagasite **sagasu**
saite **saku**
sakeñde **sakebu**
samatagete **samatageru**
sasotte **sasou**
sawaide **sawagu**
sawatte **sawaru**
semete **semeru**
sibatte **sibaru**
siite **siku**
sikatte **sikaru**
simatte **simaru, simau**
simesite **simesu**
simete **simeru**
siñde **sinu**
siñzite **siñziru**
sirabete **siraberu**
sitagatte **sitagau**
sıtasiñde **sitasimu**

site **suru**
sitte **siru**
sizumatte **sizumaru**
sizuñde **sizumu**
sodatete **sodateru**
subette **suberu**
sugite **sugiru**
sugurete **sugureru**
suite **suku**
sukutte **sukuu**
sumasete **sumaseru**
suñde **sumu**
susumete **susumeru**
susuñde **susumu**
sutete **suteru**
suwatte **suwaru**

T

tabete **taberu**
tadotte **tadoru**
-tagatte **-tagaru**
tagayasite **tagayasu**
takurānde **takuramu**
takuwaete **takuwaeru**
tameratte **tamerau**
tamesite **tamesu**
tanoñde **tanomu**
tanosiñde **tanosimu**
taorete **taoreru**
taosite **taosu**
tarite **tariru**
tasikamete **tasikameru**
tasukete **tasukeru**
tataite **tataku**
tatakatte **tatakau**
tatañde **tatamu**
tatete **tateru**
tatte **tatu**
tayotte **tayoru**
tazunete **tazuneru**
tetudatte **tetudau**
tigatte **tigau**
tikatte **tikau**
tikazuite **tikazuku**

tirakasite **tirakasu**
tirakatte **tirakaru**
titte **tiru**
tizimete **tizimeru**
tiziñde **tizimu**
todoite **todoku**
todokete **todokeru**
tokete **tokeru**
tomatte **tomaru**
tomete **tomeru**
toñde **tobu**
tootte **tooru**
torikaesite **torikaesu**
totonoete **totonoeru**
totte **toru**
tuite **tuku**
tukamaete **tukamaeru**
tukarete **tukareru**
tukatte **tukau**
tukete **tukeru**
tukiatte **tukiau**
tukusite **tukusu**
tukutte **tukuru**
tumotte **tumoru**
tunaide **tunagu**
tutaete **tutaeru**
tutomete **tutomeru**
tutuñde **tutumu**
tuuzite **tuuziru**
tuzukete **tuzukeru**
tyuui site **tyuui suru**
tyuumoñ site **tyuumoñ suru**

U

uete **ueru**
ugoite **ugoku**
ukagatte **ukagau**
ukañde **ukabu**
uketotte **uketoru**
umarete **umareru**
urañde **uramu**
utatte **utau**
utte **uru, utu**

W

wakatte **wakaru**
waratte **warau**
wasurete **wasureru**

Y

yaite **yaku**
yamete **yameru**
yasete **yaseru**
yasuñde **yasumu**
yatotte **yatou**
yatte **yaru**
yoñde **yobu, yomu**
yorokoñde **yorokobu**
yotte **yoru, you**
yurusite **yurusu**